Programming and Designing with the 68000 Family

Including the 68000, the 68010/12, the 68020, and the 68030

TIBET MIMAR
Compression Labs, Inc.

Prentice Hall
Englewood Cliffs, New Jersey 07632

Library of Congress Cataloging-in-Publication Data
Mimar, Tibet,
Programming and designing with the 68000 family : including 68000.
68010/12, 68020, and 68030 / by Tibet Mimar.
p. cm.
Includes bibliographical references and index.
ISBN 0-13-731 498-1
1. Motorola 68000 series microprocessors—Programming.
2. Computer architecture. I. Title.
QA76.8.M6895M56 1990
004.165—dc20 90–36115
CIP

To my son, Tuvan

Editorial/production supervision and
interior design: Fred Dahl and Rose Kerman
Cover design: Karen Salzbach
Pre-press buyer: Patrice Fraccio
Manufacturing buyer: Margret Rizzi
Acquisitions editor: Tom McElwee

Printed in the United States of America
10 9 8 7 6 5 4 3 2 1

ISBN 0-13-731498-1

Prentice-Hall International (UK) Limited, *London*
Prentice-Hall of Australia Pty. Limited, *Sydney*
Prentice-Hall Canada Inc., *Toronto*
Prentice-Hall Hispanoamericana, S.A., *Mexico*
Prentice-Hall of India Private Limited, *New Delhi*
Prentice-Hall of Japan, Inc., *Tokyo*
Simon & Schuster Asia Pte. Ltd., *Singapore*
Editora Prentice-Hall do Brasil, Ltda., *Rio de Janeiro*

Contents

Chapter 2
68000 FAMILY OVERVIEW, 32

Chapter 3
PROGRAMMING THE 68000 MICROPROCESSOR, 46

Chapter 4
68000 EXCEPTION PROCESSING, 160

Chapter 8
HARDWARE DESIGN WITH THE 68000 AND 68010, 360

Preface

The purpose of this book is to provide a complete and in-depth coverage of both hardware and software aspects of designing with the popular 68000 family of processors. The information presented here is intended to be equally helpful to a student learning the subject, as well as to a practicing engineer involved in the hardware design or programming with the 68000 family.

The processors covered are the 68000, 68008, 68010, 68012, 68020, and an introduction to the 68030. The book is organized into three sections. The first section (Chapters 1 and 2) introduces the 68000 architecture and gives an overview and comprehensive comparison of the 68000 family of processors. The family support such as the peripheral chips designed for the 68000 are also discussed here. The second section (Chapters 3 through 7) discusses the assembly language programming. The third section (Chapters 8 through 9) discusses the hardware design using a 68000 family processor. The hardware submodules (such as RAM memory and peripheral controllers) and the interfaces to the processor that are necessary to design a microcomputer or controller are discussed in this section.

This book is intended to contain all necessary information in order to program and design with the 68000 family with the exception of some references necessary to the Motorola's 68000 family user manuals. As such, it includes a vast amount of information on the family, with numerous illustrations about the architecture, concepts, and the operation of instructions. In the software section, many useful code fragments are included. The instructions are covered in functional groups, emphasizing their practical applications and areas of special attention such as any shortcomings. In the hardware design section, the operation of each interface signal group and their critical signal timing are examined. Possible design approaches, trade-offs, and potential pitfalls are discussed. Many design examples are given, including circuit schematics, timing diagrams, and PLD code listings. The emphasis here is on practical, workable, and reliable circuit design methods which are typically used in the industry applications.

Relevant computer science topics and other necessary background material are also discussed in detail throughout this book in conjunction with their 68000 family applications. These include the following:

Software Related

- Subroutine Usage and Parameter Passing Techniques
- Macros
- Program Looping Structures and Jump Tables
- Use of Look-up Tables
- Multiprocessor Systems
- Instruction Timing Calculations
- Virtual Memory Concept and Techniques
- Review of Floating-point Notation and IEEE P754 Standard
- Coprocessors Floating-point and Virtual Memory Management

Hardware Related

- Designing with Programmable Logic Devices (PLDs)
- Circuit Hazards to Watch such as Glitches, Metastability, Bus Contention, and so on
- Overview of Semiconductor Memory Devices (SRAM, NVRAM, EPROM, DRAM, DPRAM, and so on)
- SRAM Memory Design
- Intricacies and Operation of DRAMs
- NVRAM Memory Design
- EPROM Memory Design
- Dual-port Memory Design

Many end-of-chapter references and exercises are also provided in order to further review the discussed topics and to reinforce concepts. The exercises are divided into categories and follow the presentation sequence.

Acknowledgments

I like to express my thanks to the fine folks at Motorola for providing me with various material and support during the preparation of this book. Several figures in this book are reproduced from Motorola application notes and user manuals. Their permission to reprint these items is gratefully acknowledged.

I acknowledge with pleasure my debt to Prof. Richard Haskell who has reviewed the text in detail. His feedback has been extremely helpful in making many corrections and improvements. Also, his graduate student C. Srinivas has tested most of the program examples.

I am also grateful to Paul Lum from Hewlett-Packard for his inputs. Paul, who has taught several courses on this topic, reviewed the work in different stages of the production process and gave valuable feedback for improvements and corrections.

I would also like to thank those at Prentice Hall and Inkwell Publishing Services for their help and guidance through the many stages in the production of this book. To Jim Fegen, who helped during the initial phase of the book; the acquisitions editor, Tom McElwee, for his support and encouragement; and the production editor, Rose Kernan, for her great efforts in making it all happen, my special thanks.

Tibet Mimar

1

68000 Architecture Overview

The purpose of this chapter is to introduce the reader to the architecture of the 68000 microprocessor. We will begin by outlining the basic features of the 68000. Once the reader is familiar with the 68000 architecture, studying details of programming and design will be simpler. Furthermore, since the later members of the 68000 family of microprocessors have a lot in common, it will be easier to emphasize enhancements and differences between them. Most of the features introduced in this chapter will be covered in later chapters in more depth.

1.1 REGISTER SET

The 68000 register set consists of sixteen 32-bit registers, a 23-bit *program counter* (PC), and a 16-bit *Status Register* (SR). The sixteen registers are divided into two categories of eight address registers (referred to as A0-A7), and eight data registers (D0-D7). The register set of the 68000 is illustrated in Figure 1-1.

The data registers are primarily used for data manipulation or they may be used only as index registers in memory addressing. The *Address Registers*, as the name implies, are used in addressing memory in various addressing modes. One of the address registers has a use dictated by the 68000 architecture: A7 is used as a stack pointer. Actually, there are two A7 stack pointers, only one of which is active at any time, as shown in Figure 1-1.

The 68000 can operate in two different modes—the *supervisor mode* and the *user mode*. The supervisor mode is the privileged mode intended for operating systems and the user mode is the mode under which application programs are

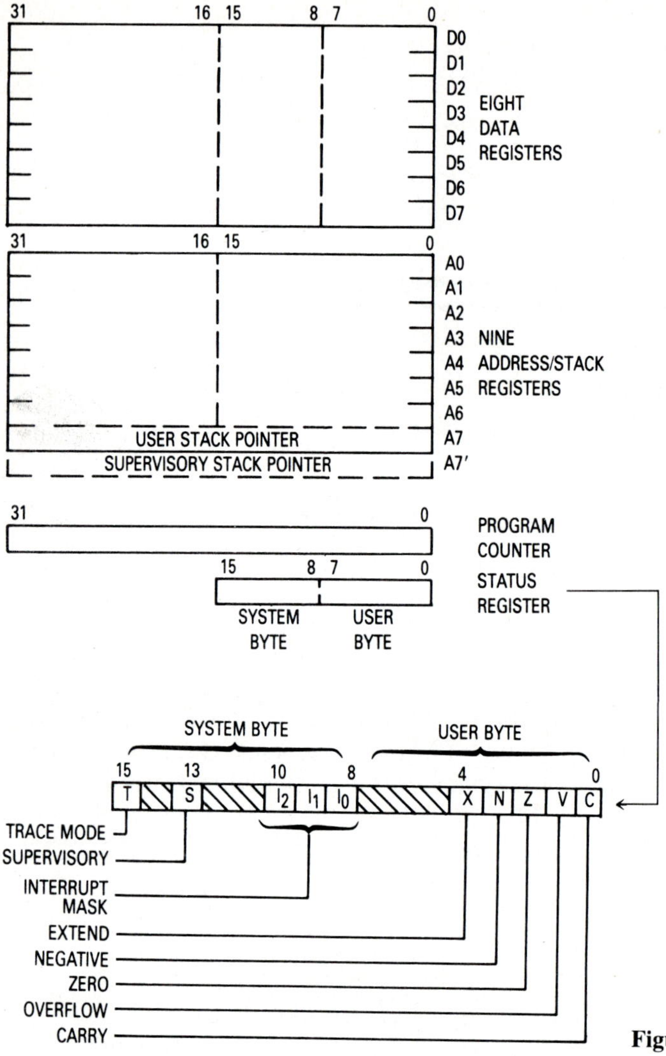

Figure 1-1 68000 Register Set.

typically run. Separate stack pointers are used in each mode. These two pointers are usually distinguished explicitly by *User Stack Pointer* (USP) and *Supervisor Stack Pointer* (SSP) in assembly language, or implicitly by using A7 or SP. The supervisor/user mode is determined by the S-bit of the status register.

The 16-bit *Status Register* (SR) consists of system byte and *Condition Code Register* (CCR) as shown in Figure 1-1. The CCR, as with other microprocessors, carries information about the results of arithmetic and logical operations. The system byte has S-bit to determine supervisor/user mode, T-bit for tracing program flow during software debugging, and interrupt mask bits I2-I0. Instructions modifying the status byte are privileged instructions, and therefore, can only be executed in supervisor mode without generating a fault condition.

When one of the bits of status register is one, it indicates the corresponding condition or status is true. For example, T = 1; V = 0; and Z = 1 indicates that the trace mode is active, there is no overflow condition, and the zero condition is true. The interrupt mask bits I2-I0 indicate the interrupt mask level (the purpose of which is to mask all external interrupts with priorities less than or equal to I2-I0). The mask bits I2-I0 determine one of the eight mask levels where I2 is the most significant bit. For example, if I2-I0 is 011, only interrupts with priority levels four through seven are recognized by the 68000.

Example 1-1

Explain the mode and status of condition codes for SR = 2208_{16}.

Solution The system byte indicates a supervisor mode, the trace is off, and the interrupt mask level is four. The CCR indicates that only a negative condition is true.

1.2 INSTRUCTION SET

The 68000 has 56 basic instruction types. The instruction set summary of the 68000 is given in Figure 1-2. Operations on five data types are supported by the instruction set. These data types are as follows:

1. Bytes (8-bits);
2. Words (16-bits);
3. Long-words (32-bits);
4. Bits; and
5. Binary-coded decimal (BCD) digits (4-bits).

Most of the 68000 data-handling instructions can work on bytes, words, or long words. The selection is made by following the instruction mnemonic with a period and either a "B", "W", or "L" for byte, word, and long-word operations, respectively. If no size is specified, the assembler will usually assume a word operation. The general format of a 68000 instruction in assembly language is given by

```
mnemonic[.size] [source],[destination]
```

where source and destination are also referred to as *operands*. An operand is an entity on which operations are performed. An operand may also be an argument, a result, a parameter, or an indication of the location of the next instructions. *Mnemonic* is the term used for instruction abbreviations such as MOVE, ADD, TST, and so on.

Mnemonic	Description
ABCD	Add Decimal with Extend
ADD	Add
AND	Logical AND
ASL	Arithmetic Shift Left
ASR	Arithmetic Shift Right
B<*cc*>	Branch Conditionally
BCHG	Bit Test and Change
BCLR	Bit Test and Clear
BRA	Branch Always
BSET	Bit Test and Set
BSR	Branch to Subroutine
BTST	Bit Test
CHK	Check Register Against Bounds
CLR	Clear Operand
CMP	Compare
DB<*cc*>	Decrement and Branch Conditionally
DIVS	Signed Divide
DIVU	Unsigned Divide
EOR	Exclusive OR
EXG	Exchange Registers
EXT	Sign Extend
JMP	Jump
JSR	Jump to Subroutine
LEA	Load Effective Address
LINK	Link Stack
LSL	Logical Shift Left
LSR	Logical Shift Right

Figure 1-2 68000 Instruction Set Summary. (Courtesy of Motorola.)

Not all instructions have two operands; some have only one, and some has none. Examples are the following:

```
ADD.L    D1,D2          (Two operands)
MOVE.B   #15,-1(A0)     (Two operands)
ADD      D1,D2          (Size assumed to be "W")
BNE      LOOP4          (Only one operand)
RTS                     (No operands)
```

The 68000 has no dedicated or special instructions for data transfer between the 68000 and peripheral devices. All devices including *Input/Output* (I/O) interface peripherals are mapped into the address space of the 68000. In other words, each I/O port occupies an address range in the memory map of the 68000. This is referred to as *memory-mapped I/O*.

Mnemonic	Description
MOVE	Move Source to Destination
MULS	Signed Multiply
MULU	Unsigned Multiply
NBCD	Negate Decimal with Extend
NEG	Negate
NOP	No Operation
NOT	One's Complement
OR	Logical OR
PEA	Push Effective Address
RESET	Reset External Devices
ROL	Rotate Left without Extend
ROR	Rotate Right without Extend
ROXL	Rotate Left with Extend
ROXR	Rotate Right with Extend
RTD	Return and Deallocate
RTE	Return from Exception
RTR	Return and Restore
RTS	Return from Subroutine
SBCD	Subtract Decimal with Extend
S<*cc*>	Set Conditional
STOP	Stop
SUB	Subtract
SWAP	Swap Data Register Halves
TAS	Test and Set Operand
TRAP	Trap
TRAPV	Trap on Overflow
TST	Test

Figure 1-2 (*Continued*)

1.3 SIGNAL LINES AND BUS OPERATION

The 68000 is available in four different package types:

1. The 64-pin dual-in-line-plastic package;
2. The 68-pin dual-in-line-ceramic package;
3. The 68-pin grid array;
4. The 68-pin quad pack version.

The 68000 uses 60 signal lines for signal input and output. The input and output signal lines of 68000 can be functionally organized into the groups shown in Figure

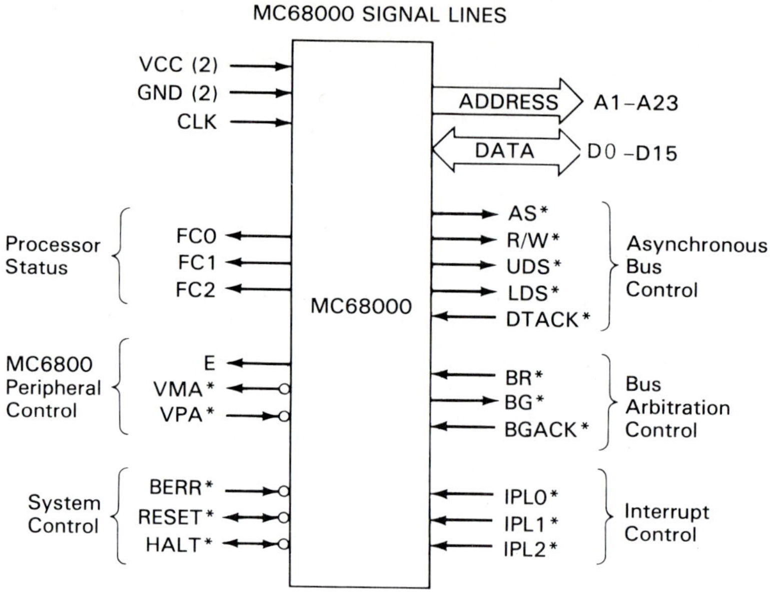

Figure 1-3 Input and output signal lines of 68000. (Courtesy of Motorola.)

1-3. Next, we will describe the operation of each of these signal groups and bus interface of the 68000 to external memory and peripherals.

In describing the signal lines and their operation throughout the rest of this book, we will adopt the following notation used by Motorola: The term *assert* or *assertion* will be used to indicate that a signal is active or true, independent of whether that level is represented by a high or low voltage. The term *negate* or *negation* is used to indicate that a signal is inactive or false. The purpose of this is to avoid confusion when dealing with a mixture of *active-low* and *active-high* signals. The active-low signals are usually shown with either a bar over the signal name or with an asterisk following it. We will use the asterisk (*) where possible during the rest of this book for consistency. The reader should keep in mind that the overbar and the asterisk are interchangeable. For example, AS* (Address Strobe) is an active-low signal (i.e., it is low (logic-0 level voltage) when asserted).

Sometimes the *bubble* notation used in conjunction with active-low signals. The bubble is an abbreviated form of inverter. It is convenient usually to think of it in terms of active-high signals. It is usually assumed that all the signals within the body of a device are active-high and that any active-low signals are indicated by the bubble notation and/or asterisk in their signal name. This is illustrated in Figure 1-4. We are also going to use "L" and "H" to refer to logic-0 and logic-1 voltage levels on signal lines, respectively. This should clarify any confusion that saying a signal is true ("1") may cause.

<signal-name>* : Indicates active-low signal

(device) : Also indicates active-low signal

L (low) : Signal is low (i.e., TTL logic-0 level = 0-0.8 V)
H(high) : Signal is high (i.e., TTL logic-1 level = 2-5 V)

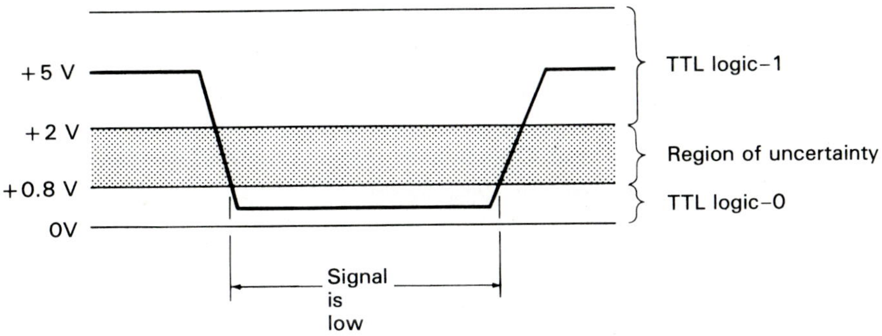

Example: SIGNAL1* is asserted ⟶ SIGNAL1 is low.
SIGNAL1* is negated ⟶ SIGNAL1 is high.
SIGNAL2 is asserted ⟶ SIGNAL2 is high.
SIGNAL2 is negated ⟶ SIGNAL2 is low.

Figure 1-4 Signal Conventions Used in This Book.

1.3.1 Address and Data Bus

The 68000 features a non-multiplexed address and data bus (i.e., separate signal lines are used for each). Multiplexing is not used because it would penalize the system in both throughput speed and increased system parts count. The *unidirectional* 23-bit address bus (A23-A01) can address a memory space of 8,388,608 words. A23 is the *Most Significant Bit* (MSB), and A01 is the *Least Significant Bit* (LSB) of word addresses. The *bi-directional* data bus is 16-bits wide (D15-D0), and can be used to transfer 16-bit words, or just the upper or lower byte of a 16-bit word. Thus, the total address space of the 68000 processor in bytes is 16,777,216 bytes, or 16 Megabytes in short. This is, coincidentally, the same address space as the IBM 370 mainframe computer!

The 68000 has no separate address space for peripheral devices. The control between the 68000 and a peripheral controller is achieved by having the 68000 write to certain reserved words of memory addresses. These reserved words are called *control words*. The *memory-mapped input/output* concept used by the 68000 simplifies the control and I/O interface to peripheral devices. (There are no special signal lines or instructions designated only for communication with peripheral devices.)

The 68000's address space is not paged or segmented, therefore, any memory location of 16 Mbytes can be accessed directly. This is referred to as *linear addressing* of memory space.

1.3.2 Processor Status

The function code outputs (FC0-FC2) indicate the 68000's mode during each bus cycle. These 3-bit outputs inform the memory and peripheral chips that the state of the 68000 is user or supervisor and whether the current bus cycle is for program or data access or is an interrupt acknowledge cycle. Table 1-1 lists the function code assignments.

1.3.3 Bus Control and Operation

The bus control signal lines supply all the necessary control during all data transfer operations between the 68000 and the memory and between the 68000 and other peripheral devices. In the 68000 literature, any single bus operation is referred to as a *bus cycle*.

The following signals control the data bus operation:

Address Strobe (AS*) — This signal, when asserted, indicates that there is a valid address on the address bus (A23-A01).

Read/Write (R/W*) — This signal defines the data bus transfer as a read or write cycle. When the R/W* line is high, it indicates a read cycle. When the R/W* line is low, it indicates a write cycle. During a read cycle, the 68000 receives data from memory or a peripheral device. During a write cycle, the 68000 writes data to a memory location or to a control word of peripheral devices.

TABLE 1-1 FUNCTION CODE ASSIGNMENTS

Function Code			
FC2	FC1	FC0	Reference Type
L	L	L	Unassigned
L	L	H	User Data
L	H	L	User Program
L	H	H	Unassigned
H	L	L	Unassigned
H	L	H	Supervisor Data
H	H	L	Supervisor Program
H	H	H	Interrupt Acknowledge

Upper-Data Strobe (UDS*)	This signal is asserted during a read or write cycle when the data is to be transferred on the high-byte of the data bus (i.e., D15-D8).
Lower-Data Strobe (LDS*)	This signal is asserted during a read or write cycle when data is to be transferred on the low-byte of the data bus (i.e., D7-D0).
DTACK*	Data-Transfer ACKnowledge. This handshake signal is generated by a memory controller or a peripheral device to indicate that a data transfer is complete.

A 68000-based microcomputer will typically have memory and one or more peripheral controllers as part of its bus interface as shown in Figure 1-5. *Memory* which consists of RAM and ROM, is used for program and data storage. ROM is *read-only memory* which is considered non-volatile which means that its information content is retained during a power loss. RAM, on the other hand, is *read/write memory* and it is considered volatile.

The read cycle is used to read instructions from memory or to read data from memory or peripherals. The following steps take place during a read cycle:

1. The 68000 sets R/W* signal to read and places a valid function code and address in order to select a particular memory location or a control word of a peripheral controller on the bus.
2. The 68000 asserts the address strobe (AS*) to indicate a valid address and function code values to the memory and peripherals.
3. Simultaneously, the 68000 asserts one or both of the data strobes (LDS* and/or UDS*) to indicate the selected byte or word read cycle, respectively.

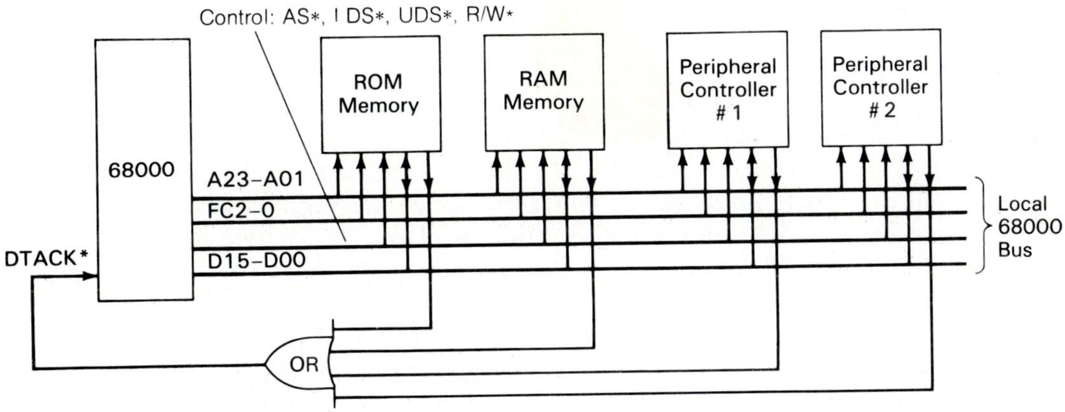

Figure 1-5 Block Diagram of Simplified 68000 Bus Interface.

4. Each device decodes the address to see if it is being selected. If so, the selected memory or peripheral will access the selected location and place the data on the bus. All non-selected devices will not affect the data bus because their tri-state outputs will be disabled (referred to as *Hi-Z*) condition.
5. The selected device asserts DTACK* to signal the 68000 that the data is ready to read.
6. The 68000 reads the data and terminates bus cycle (i.e., negates the address and data strobes).
7. Thereafter, the selected device removes data from the data bus and negates DTACK*.

During a write cycle, the 68000 writes data to the RAM memory or the peripherals. It could be a simple data write or pushing of values onto the stack. Or, it could be a write to a control word of the peripheral controller in order to change its setup or to send data to the peripheral. Similar to the read cycle, the sequence of events during a normal write cycle is the same regardless of the destination of data. The following summarizes the steps of operation during a write cycle:

1. The 68000 places a valid function code and address on the bus.
2. The 68000 asserts the address strobe and R/W*.
3. Each device decodes the address on the bus to see if it is being selected.
4. Simultaneously with step (3), the 68000 places valid data on the bus (byte or word) and then asserts the corresponding data strobes to indicate whether low, high, or both bytes are to be written.
5. The selected device writes the data byte(s) and asserts DTACK* to signal the 68000 that the write operation is complete.
6. The 68000 negates data and address strobes, removes the data from the bus, and sets R/W* to read in anticipation of a read cycle next.

From the programmer's point of view, all the 68000 addresses are byte addresses. In other words, the memory is viewed as a string of bytes. For example, the contents of an address register points to a byte address. The reader can note that, as we stated earlier, external address bus A23-A01 determines only the word address. Therefore, LDS* and UDS* signals are used as an extension of the address bus. A word transfer operation, read or write cycle, is simple: The 68000 asserts both data strobes to transfer both upper and lower data bytes simultaneously. During byte transfers only the corresponding data strobe is asserted. The data-strobe control of the data bus is illustrated in Table 1-2.

The question that should be raised next is how the internal A0 address bit is mapped to LDS* and UDS* during byte transfer operations. It could have been done in two different ways: For A0 = 0, the processor could use the upper byte

TABLE 1-2 DATA STROBE CONTROL OF DATA BUS

UDS*	LDS*	R/W*	D8–D15	D0–D7
High	High	—	No valid data	No valid data
Low	Low	High	Valid data bits 8–15	Valid data bits 0–7
High	Low	High	No valid data	Valid data bits 0–7
Low	High	High	Valid data bits 8–15	No valid data
Low	Low	Low	Valid data bits 8–15	Valid data bits 0–7
High	Low	Low	Valid data bits 0–7*	0–7
Low	High	Low	Valid data bits 8–15	8–15*

* These conditions are a result of current implementation and may not appear on future devices.

or lower byte, and vice versa for A0 = 1. This determines the *memory organization* of a processor. The designers of 68000 have chosen to do the memory organization as follows:

$$A0 = 0 \rightarrow UDS* = L \text{ and } LDS* = H \text{ (Upper-byte used)}$$

and for $$A0 = 1 \rightarrow UDS* = H \text{ and } LDS* = L \text{ (Lower-byte used)}$$

The memory organization of the 68000 is illustrated in Figure 1-6. Note that the 68000 allows word addresses only at word boundaries (i.e., at even addresses), otherwise, an address error is generated internally. Furthermore, it is important to note that the word at $3000 consists of high-byte at $3000 and low-byte at $3001.

The next example will illustrate the operation of bus operation, but first, let us give an incomplete description of the MOVE instruction which we will use in this example. The MOVE instruction has several variations and possible data addressing modes. The ones we will use next are the following:

```
MOVE.X   #<data>,<address>
MOVE.X   <address>,Dn
```

where X = B, W, or L for byte, word, and long-word transfers. The < > indicates the substitution of a desired value which can be usually given in hex, decimal, or octal. Motorola notation requires $ preceding the indication hex value and uses % preceding the binary notation. The omission of $ or % usually defaults to a decimal number base (which is what we will assume throughout the rest of this

Word Address	Upper-Byte 15 … 8	Lower-Byte 7 … 0	{BIT #
\$0	BYTE 000000_{16}	BYTE 000001_{16}	{ WORD #0
\$2	000002_{16}	000003_{16}	{ WORD #1
	⋮	⋮	⋮
\$3000	3000_{16}	3001_{16}	
	⋮	⋮	
\$FFFFFE	BYTE $FFFFFE_{16}$	BYTE $FFFFFF_{16}$	

Figure 1-6 Memory Organization of 68000.

book). The particular notation may vary from assembler to assembler, so the reader should refer to the user's manual of the particular system being used. Some assemblers, for example, allow lower case mnemonics and operand specification.

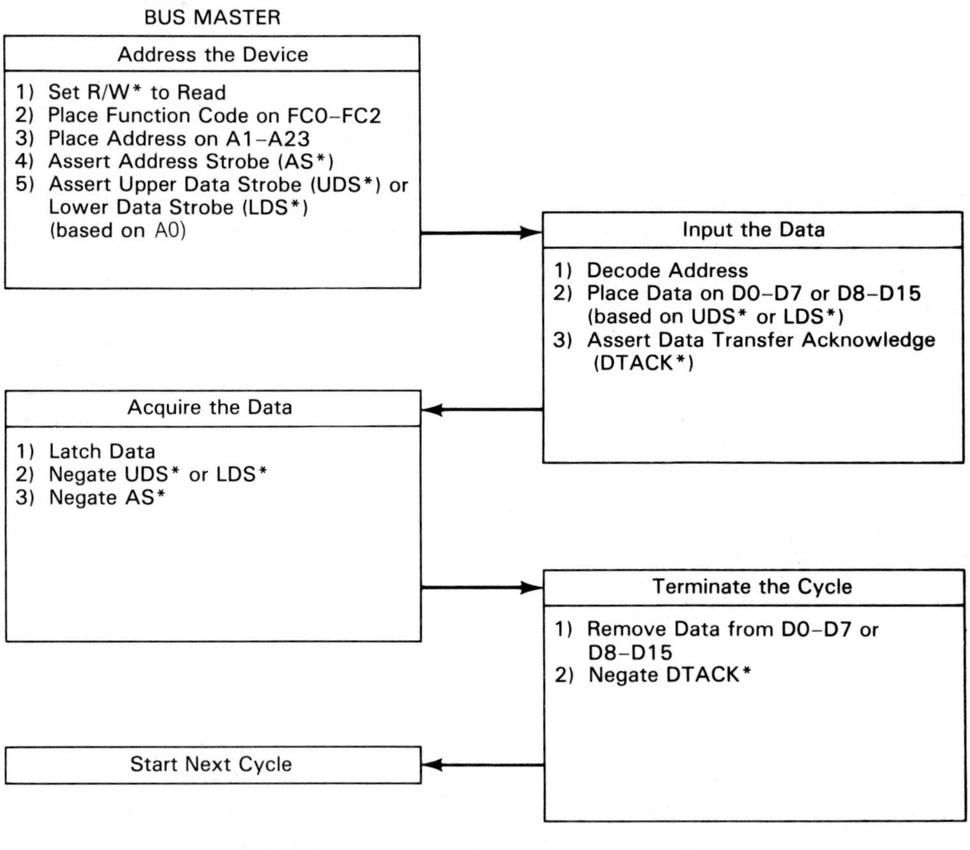

Figure 1-7-a Byte and Read Cycle Flowchart. (Courtesy of Motorola.)

The first MOVE instruction above moves the given data that is part of the instruction to the contents of the memory location specified. The second one moves the contents of specified memory location into a given data register. For example,

```
MOVE.W #$4F,$3000
```

moves 00 into memory location 3000_{16}, and $4F_{16}$ into memory location 3001_{16}.

Example 1-2

Specify the address and data bus signals, and bus control signals LDS*, UDS*, and R/W* during the execution of the following bus cycles:

```
a. MOVE.B   #09,$13FF
b. MOVE.B   $3000,D0
c. MOVE.W   #19,$13FF
d. MOVE.W   #19,$13FE
e. MOVE.W   $3000,D0
```

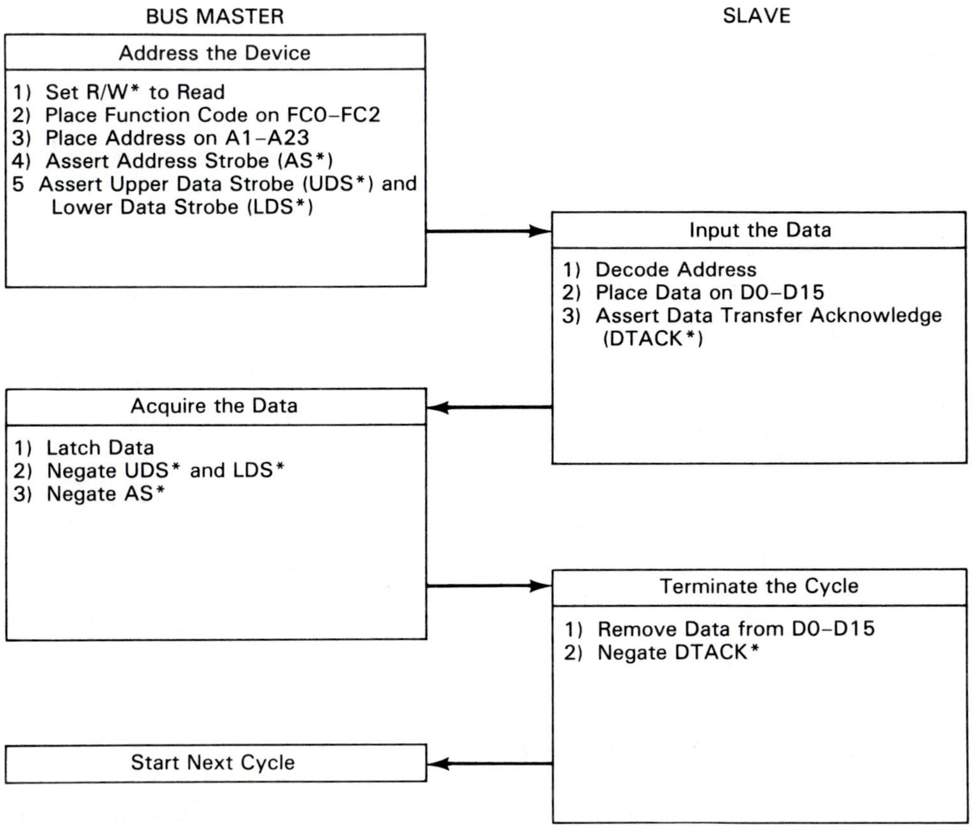

Figure 1-7-b Word Read Cycle Flowchart. (Courtesy of Motorola.)

Assume that the contents of the memory location $3000 is $0F and the contents of $3001 is $94.

Solution The following table gives the required signal states:

Part	A23-A01	D15-D08	D07-D00	LDS*	UDS*	R/W*
a	$13FE	$XX	09	L	H	L
b	$3000	$XX	$0F	H	L	H
c	(Address Error Generated)					
d	$13FE	00	$13	L	L	L
e	$3000	$0F	$94	L	L	H

Note: "XX" indicates no valid data or don't care.

The organization of memory might seem backwards because low-byte has a higher address than the high-byte, especially to the reader familiar with PDP-11 and some other computers which use the opposite organization. It is important to remember the following:

1. Word address is always an even address;
2. Low-byte address is always an odd address; and
3. High-byte address is always an even address.

The normal sequence of operations during a read cycle and write cycle is summarized in flowcharts given in Figure 1-7 and 1-8, respectively.

1.3.4 Interrupt Request Lines

The signal lines IPL0-2* indicate the binary-encoded priority of requested interrupt. The priority level of request is given by:

IPL2*	IPL1*	IPL0*	Priority
L	L	L	7
L	L	H	6
L	H	L	5
L	H	H	4
H	L	L	3
H	L	H	2
H	H	L	1
H	H	H	0

where level zero corresponds to a no-interrupt request.

1.3.5 Clock Signal and Bus States

The clock signal is a continuous TTL-compatible signal. All 68000's internal operations are synchronous to this clock. An internal operation takes place during each high and low portion of clock cycle initiated by clock edges. For example,

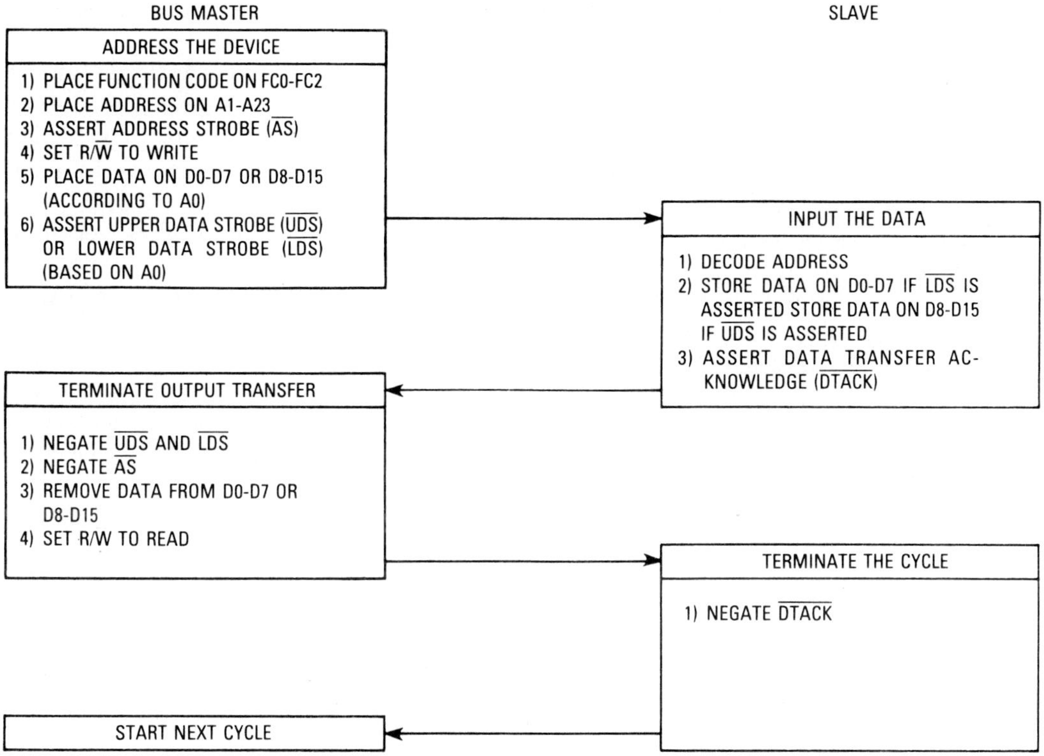

Figure 1-8-a Byte Write Cycle Flowchart. (Courtesy of Motorola.)

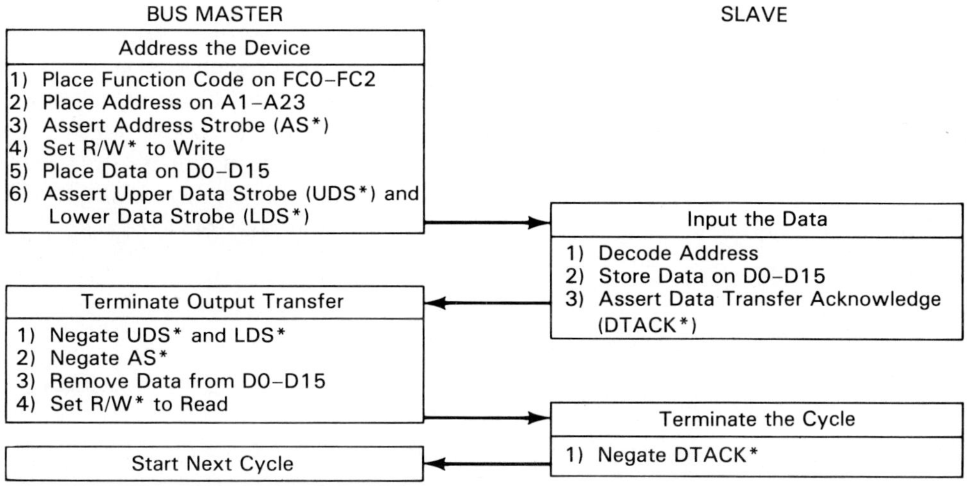

Figure 1-8-b Word Write Cycle Flowchart. (Courtesy of Motorola.)

a read or write bus cycle normally takes four clock periods which consists of eight states as shown in Figure 1-9. If DTACK* is received before the falling edge of state S4, then the bus cycle terminates in eight states. Otherwise, the length of the bus cycle is increased in increments of a clock period until DTACK* is received. These extra clock periods are usually referred to as *wait-cycles*. Each wait-cycle consists of two *wait-states*. Figure 1-10 illustrates bus cycles with and without wait-states.

There is usually a lot of confusion about wait-states and wait-cycles. In performance specifications, one may come across something like "the memory has one wait-state." Actually, it refers to wait-cycles because wait-states always occur in pairs. Although it is possible to dynamically stretch the 68000 clock to have only one wait-state, this is seldom done.

The 68000 bus control is referred to as *asynchronous* because DTACK* and other signal inputs do not need to be synchronous to 68000's clock. The 68000 is actually quasi-synchronous in the sense that all received external signals are first synchronized to clock internally.

The 68000 is available in various clock speeds from 4 to 16 MHz. The bus cycle is as small as 240 nano-seconds for a 16 MHz 68000 with no wait-cycles.

1.3.6 Bus Arbitration

Bus arbitration logic of the 68000 simplifies the transfer of the bus control between the 68000 and other possible bus master type devices. *Bus master*, at any given time, is the device driving address lines, control lines such as address and data strobes, and so forth to control data transfer operations. The bus arbitration is typically used in conjunction with *Direct Memory Access* (DMA) controller. The purpose of the DMA controller is to transfer data at very high data rates which are unattainable with a processor under software control. Another processor, possibly another 68000, can also be a secondary bus master. However, this is rarely useful because the system would like to be I/O bound (while one is transferring data, the other one has to wait for any data transfers).

The following signal lines control the operation of bus arbitration:

Bus Request (BR*)	This input indicates to the 68000 that another device is requesting to become bus master.

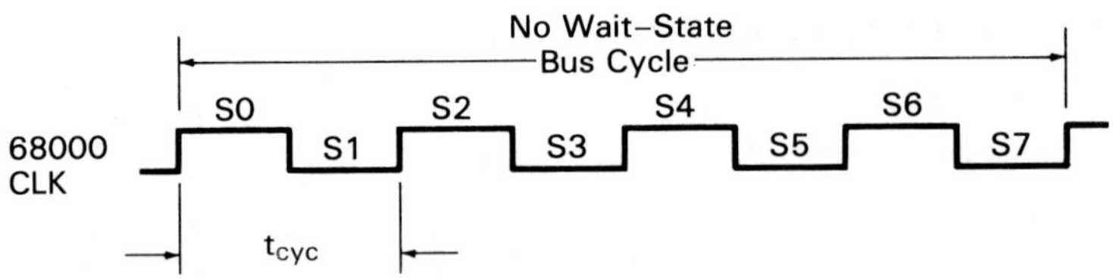

Figure 1-9 68000 Internal States during Bus Cycle. (Courtesy of Motorola.)

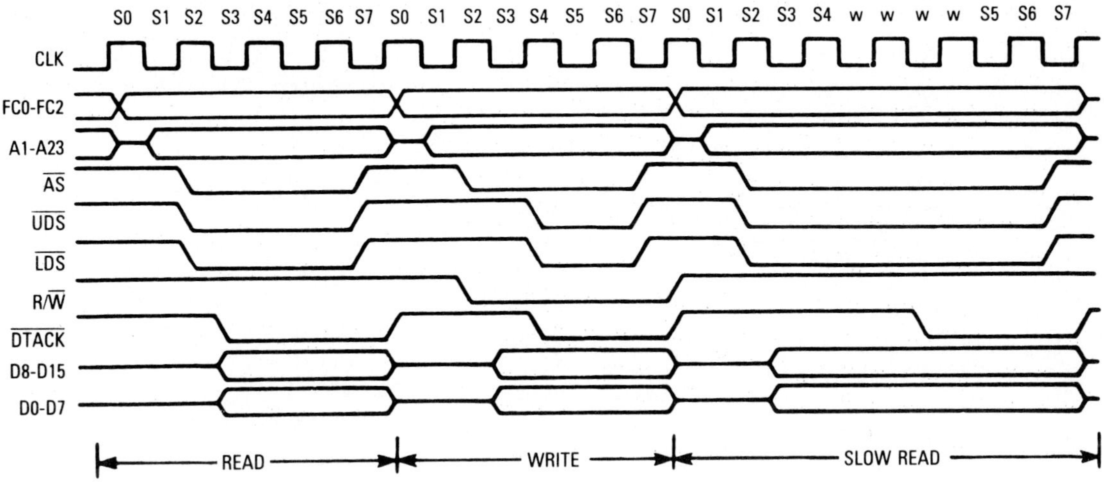

Figure 1-10 Bus Cycle with and without Wait-States. (Courtesy of Motorola.)

Bus Grant (BG*) — This output indicates to all other potential bus master devices that the 68000 will release the bus at the end of the current bus cycle.

Bus Grant Acknowledge (BGACK*) — This input indicates to the 68000 that some other device has become the bus master.

While the 68000 is not driving the bus, it monitors the BGACK* line. When BGACK* is negated, assuming that there is no other device other than the 68000 waiting to be bus master, the 68000 resumes where it had left processing. The flowchart in Figure 1-11 illustrates the bus arbitration of the 68000.

1.3.7 6800 Peripheral Control

The 68000 provides three control signals for direct interface to 8-bit 6800 peripherals. These control signals are described next.

Valid Peripheral Address (VPA*) — During a bus cycle, an addressed device returns VPA* (i.e., asserts VPA*) instead of DTACK* to indicate it is a 6800-type peripheral.

Enable (E) — This signal corresponds to E or phase 2 signal in existing M6800 systems. Enable is a free-running clock generated from the 68000 clock with a duty cycle

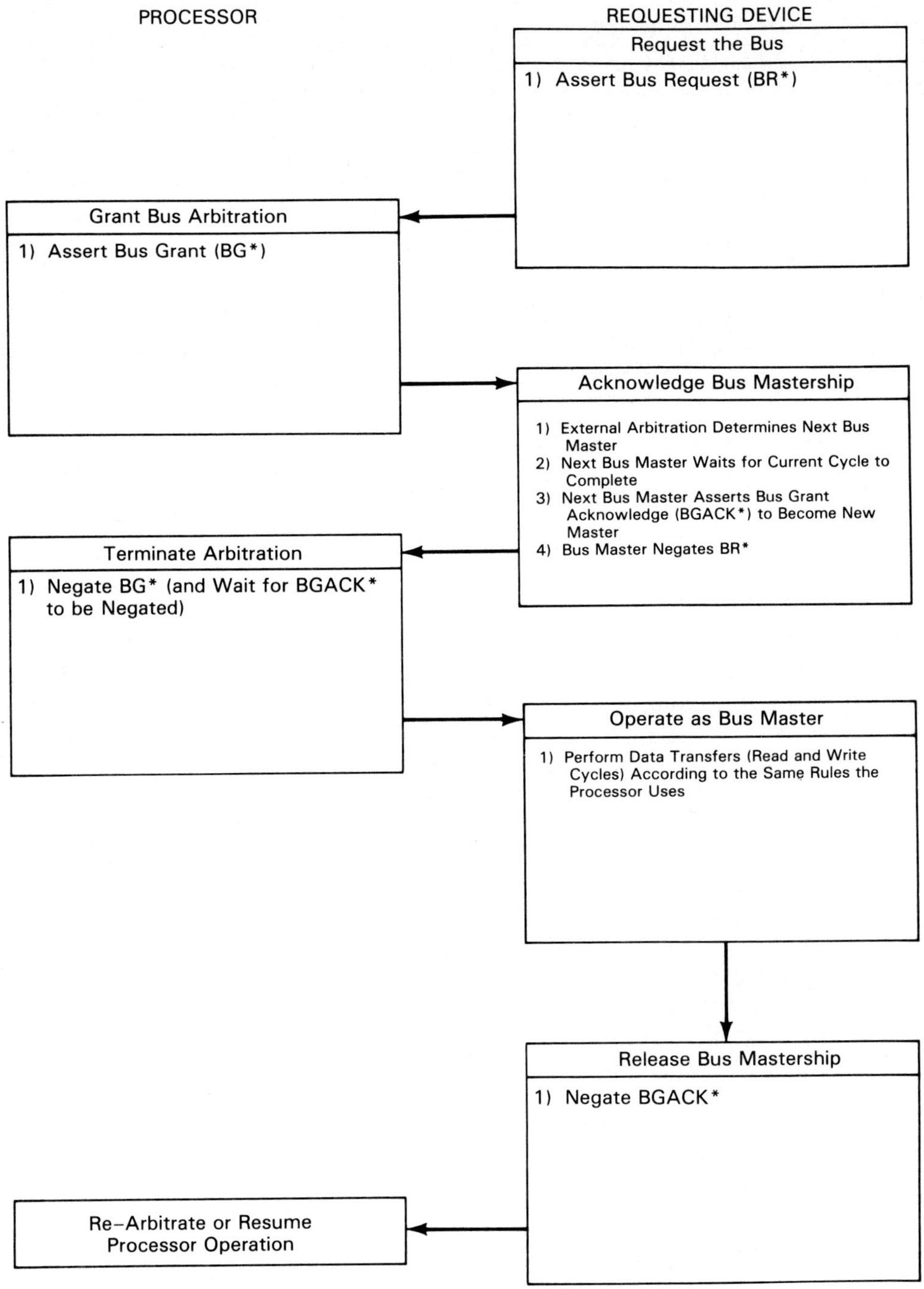

Figure 1-11 Bus Arbitration Flowchart. (Courtesy of Motorola.)

	of low for six input clocks, and high for four input clock periods.
Valid Memory Address (VMA*)	This output signal is used with the M6800 peripheral when the valid address is on the address bus. This signal also acts as a acknowledgment of M6800-type peripheral.

When the 68000 receives a VPA* asserted during a bus cycle, it responds by synchronizing the data transfer to the Enable (E) signal. The 68000 asserts wait-states automatically into the bus cycle to synchronize with Enable, and then asserts VMA* signal. Since E is free-running, it is possible to have a few or many wait-states inserted. The idea behind the 60/40 percent duty cycle for E clock is that in successive M6800-type bus cycles, the wait-states for later ones are minimized after synchronization during the first cycle. Figure 1-12 illustrates the best and worst-case timing in interfacing to M6800 peripherals. The best case is when the VPA* is recognized as being asserted on the falling edge of a 68000 clock, three clock cycles before the E signal goes high. If the VPA* is recognized any later with respect to the E signal, the 68000 will wait till the next cycle of E before asserting VMA*.

During a read cycle, M6800 peripheral will place the valid data before the falling edge of the E signal. At the falling edge of E, the 68000 reads the data and terminates the cycle as in a normal cycle by negating strobes and putting the address bus in high-impedance state. The peripheral is expected to remove the VPA* one clock cycle after the address strobe is negated.

The flowchart given in Figure 1-13 summarizes the interface with M6800 peripherals. Reader familiar with the M6800 can note that VMA* is active-low as opposed to being active-high in the M6800 VMA. This change allows the 68000 to put its buses in the high-impedance state on DMA-type requests without inadvertently selecting a M6800 peripheral.

1.3.8 System Control

Three control signals are used to facilitate various system control functions, where RESET* and HALT* are bi-directional signal lines and BERR* (bus error) is input only. The following describes the relation between these signals in implementing system control.

68000 reset operation. The reset of the 68000, at power-up time or after a system failure, is done by asserting both RESET* and HALT* lines for a minimum of 100 milliseconds at power-up after Vcc is stabilized. Other times, HALT* and RESET* need to be asserted for 10 clock cycles in order to reset the 68000.

Bus error condition. We mentioned earlier that the 68000 will wait indefinitely till it receives DTACK* or VPA* from the addressed device. Then,

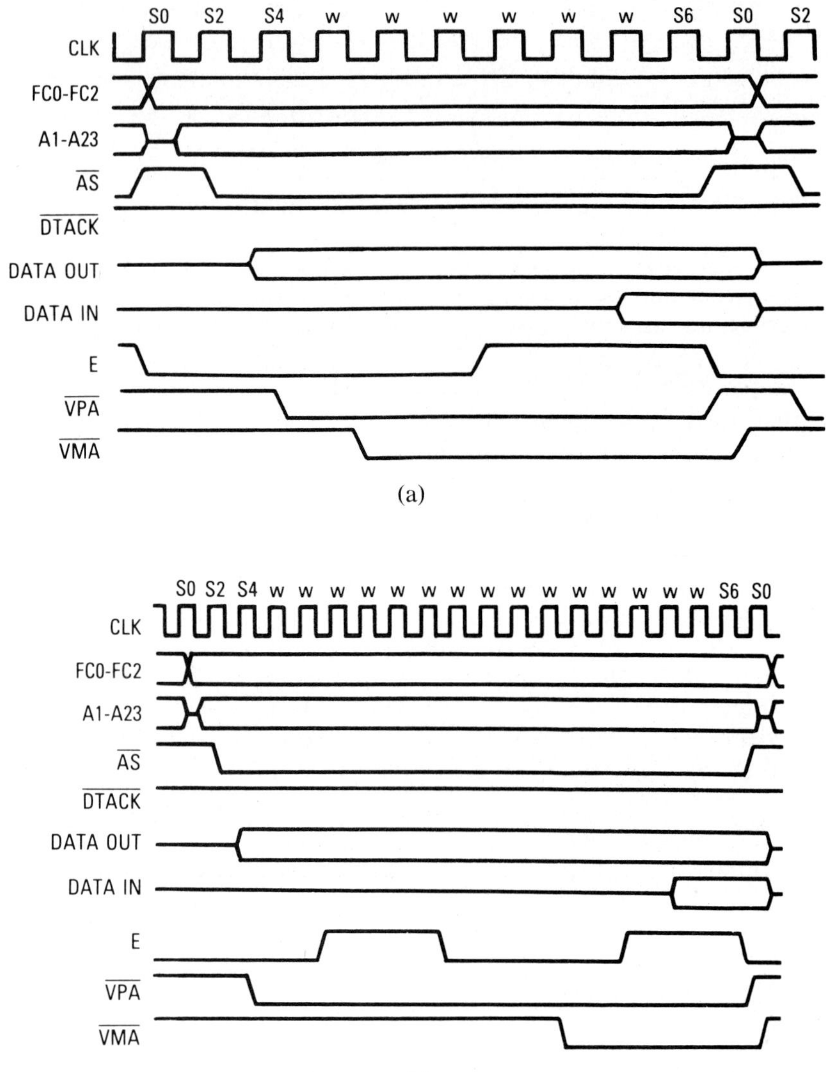

(a)

(b)

Figure 1-12 68000 to 6800 Timing. (a) Best Case. (b) Worst Case. (Courtesy of Motorola.)

what happens if due to a hardware problem the device does not respond? Or maybe due to a programming error, unpopulated memory space is addressed so that no device responds. Either of these conditions would cause system "lock-up" and requires system reset operation unless hardware design provides for handling of these type of errors with a bus cycle.

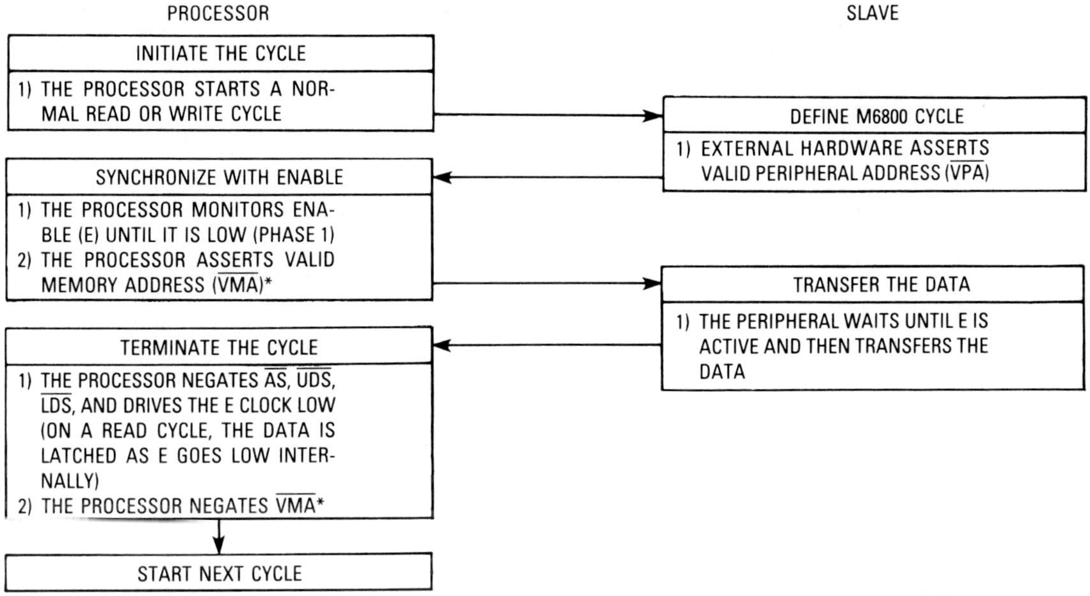

*For MC68008-based systems, $\overline{VMA}$ is supplied by external circuitry.

Figure 1-13 M6800 Interfacing Flowchart. (Courtesy of Motorola.)

A very simple solution is to provide a time-out on any bus cycle. In other words, if a bus cycle is not completed within a predefined period of time, then the bus error (BERR*) input signal is asserted to indicate a problem with the current bus cycle. A time-out circuit, usually a simple counter, monitors address strobe as shown in Figure 1-14. Upon receiving the BERR* signal asserted, in

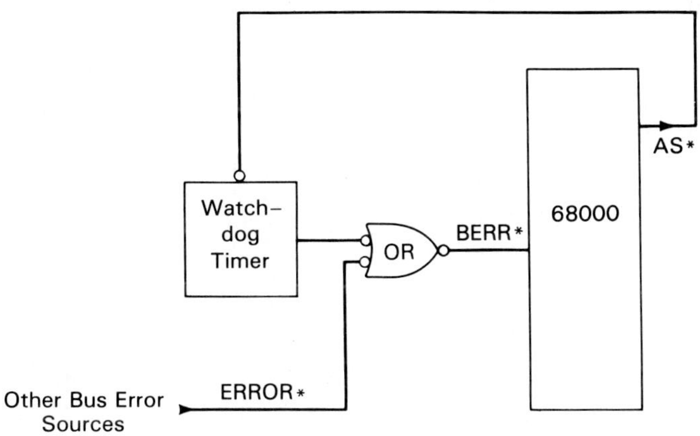

Figure 1-14 Bus Error (BERR) Input Connection.

TABLE 1-3 SUMMARY OF THE 68000 SIGNALS

Signal Name	Mnemonic	Input/Output	Active State	Hi-Z	
				On HALT*	On BGACK*
Address Bus	A1–A23	Output	High	Yes	Yes
Data Bus	D0–D15	Input/Output	High	Yes	Yes
Address Strobe	AS*	Output	Low	No	Yes
Read/Write	R/W*	Output	Read-High Write-Low	No	Yes
Upper and Lower Data Strobes	UDS*, LDS*	Output	Low	No	Yes
Data Transfer Acknowledge	DTACK*	Input	Low	No	No
Bus Request	BR*	Input	Low	No	No
Bus Grant	BG*	Output	Low	No	No
Bus Grant Acknowledge	BGACK*	Input	Low	No	No
Interrupt Priority Level	IPL0*, IPL1*, IPL2*	Input	Low	No	No
Bus Error	BERR*	Input	Low	No	No
Reset	RESET*	Input/Output	Low	No[1]	No[1]
Halt	HALT*	Input/Output	Low	No[1]	No[1]
Enable	E	Output	High	No	No
Valid Memory Address	VMA*	Output	Low	No	Yes
Valid Peripheral Address	VPA*	Input	Low	No	No
Function Code Output	FC0, FC1, FC2	Output	High	No[2]	Yes
Clock	CLK	Input	High	No	No
Power Input	V_{CC}	Input	—	—	—
Ground	GND	Input	—	—	—

[1] Open drain.

[2] Function codes are placed in high-impedance state during HALT for R9M, T6E, and BF4 mask sets.

lieu of or in conjunction with the DTACK* signal, the 68000 terminates current the bus cycle and transfers control to a routine for handling the bus error condition.

Other sources of BERR* input are typically due to parity check error in accessing a memory and illegal access request as determined by the memory management unit external to the 68000. Also, bus error input is used conjunction with HALT* input to re-run a bus cycle as we will explain next.

Bus cycle re-run. During a bus-error condition, if both BERR* and HALT* are asserted then the 68000 terminates the current cycle and repeats it again. The 68000 will keep re-running a particular bus cycle as long as the external hardware requests it.

Bus cycle single stepping. When HALT* is asserted by a external device, it will cause the processor to stop at the completion of the current bus cycle. During the halted-state, all output lines of the 68000 are in the high-impedance state as with other microprocessors. When HALT* is negated, the 68000 will start the next bus cycle.

Peripheral reset operation. The 68000 has a special instruction to reset all peripherals connected to it: when a RESET instruction is executed, the 68000 asserts the RESET* signal line for 124 clock periods. This has no effect on the internal state of the 68000.

Double bus fault condition. When a bus error occurs, the 68000 will first attempt to save several words of information onto a stack about its internal state including the address which caused the bus error. This information is saved so that it can later be used by the bus error handling routine. However, if another bus error occurs while saving these values, the 68000 will halt and assert the HALT* signal to indicate it ceased processing.

In general, any second bus error condition happening before the execution of the next instruction during a bus error or reset operation will cause a double bus-fault condition. Only a 68000 reset operation can restart the 68000 in this case.

68000 Signal Line Summary

Table 1-3 gives a summary of the 68000 signal lines discussed in the previous paragraphs.

1.4 EXCEPTION PROCESSING

There are several conditions that could change the normal running sequence of a program. These conditions can be due to detected errors, such as divide by zero, or external conditions such as interrupts. These conditions are collectively referred to as *exceptions*, and handling of these exceptions are usually referred to as *exception handling* or *exception processing*. When the occurrence of an exception results in the automatic transfer of program control to a special routine for handling that exception, this program transfer is called a *trap*. The trap and exception are sometimes used as synonyms.

The 68000 architecture supports an extensive list of exception processing for both internally and externally generated exceptions. The above definition of exception and trap has to be loosened in order for the 68000 to include the TRAP instruction (which when executed generates an exception unconditionally). Therefore, the TRAP instruction is sometimes referred to as a *software interrupt* instruction.

The external exceptions are generated due to following conditions:

1. Bus errors;
2. 68000 reset operation; and
3. Interrupt requests.

Internally generated exceptions are detected errors during the instruction execution, instruction exceptions such as TRAP, and trace condition that occur when the T bit is set. The detected errors are listed below:

Privilege Violation	This exception is generated when trying to execute a privileged instruction in the user mode.
Illegal Instruction	This exception is generated when trying to execute an unknown/unimplemented instruction.
Zero Divide	This exception is generated when a divide instruction attempts to divide by zero.
Address Error	This exception is generated when a bus cycle attempts to transfer a word from an odd address.

The instruction exceptions are caused by TRAP, TRAPV, and CHK instructions. The TRAP instruction is usually used for *operating system* (OS) calls from application programs. The TRAPV instruction causes an exception only if there is an overflow condition. The CHK instruction checks the bounds of a register and generates an exception if the given bounds are exceeded.

1.5 EXECUTION AND CONTROL UNIT

The 68000 execution unit consists of register files and arithmetic units connected in a dual-bus architecture as shown in Figure 1-15. Each section is either isolated or connected to the next one using bi-directional bus switches. This allows data transfers between the three sections (e.g., between address and data registers) or

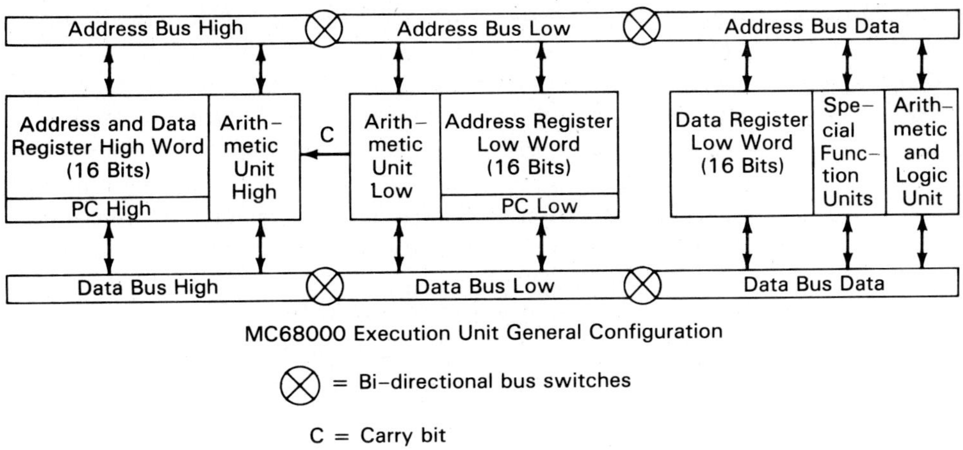

Figure 1-15 The 68000 Execution Unit.

simultaneous calculations on address and data words. Note that only the low-order 16-bits of data registers has immediate access to 16-bit ALU and special function units, whereas the other sections use a limited function arithmetic unit. A special function unit is used for bit manipulation and other special functions not supported by the ALU.

The 68000 control unit uses a two-level micro-programmed control structure as shown in Figure 1-16. The instruction decoder decodes each 68000 instruction (also called *macro-instruction* in this context) and sends the starting address to micro-instruction store. Each macro-instruction has been divided into a sequence of elementary tasks which are stored in the *micro-instruction* store.

The control unit of the 68000 uses a next instruction pre-fetch mechanism

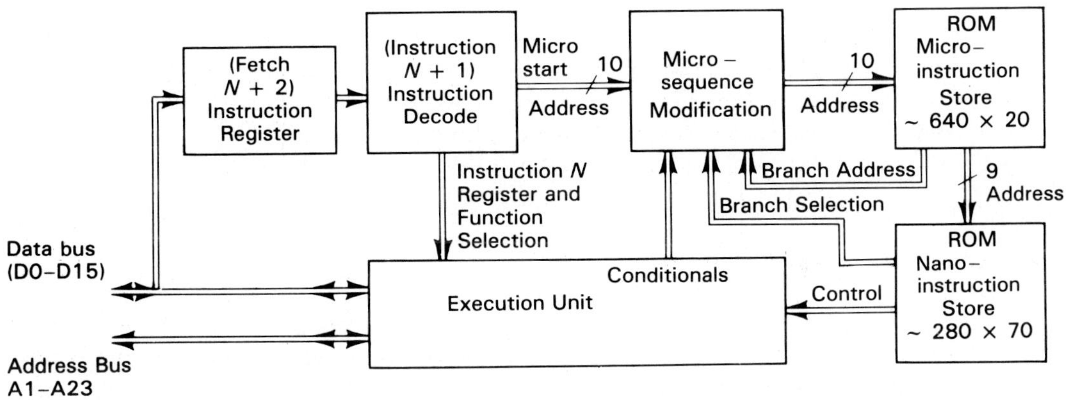

Figure 1-16 The 68000 Control Unit Structure.

to speed up program execution. This mechanism effectively overlaps the instruction fetch, decode, and execution as follows:

1. When the execution of instruction #N starts, instruction #$(N + 1)$ and the word following have already been fetched. Instruction #$(N + 1)$ is in the instruction decoder as shown in Figure 1-17.
2. In case of multi-word instructions, a fetch is made to the instruction stream for next data as each word of the instruction is used internally.
3. If the instruction is a single-word instruction causing a branch, the second word following it is not used. It is impossible to avoid this superfluous fetch because this word is fetched by the preceding instruction.
4. In case of an interrupt or trace exception, both pre-fetched words are not used.
5. The program counter (PC) usually points to the last word fetched from the instruction stream.

The 68000 execution unit has about 170 control points that need to be selected (as "1" or "0") by the control unit. Coding each field of control, such as register selection, the 68000 control bits are reduced to approximately 70 bits. Since the 68000 uses a fixed-instruction format, such functions as register selection or ALU function can be extracted directly from known positions in an instruction-by-instruction decoder. Furthermore, the register and ALU function stays the same during the execution of the instruction. Therefore, this information can be routed directly to the execution unit bypassing the control store and thus simplifying the control structure.

Each required control word is stored in *nano-store*, sometimes called *nano-instructions* because they are called by micro-instructions. The implementation of the 68000 requires about 280 nano-instructions or nano-words in short. This is much less than the total possible 2^{70} nano-words. Therefore, only nine bits are required to address any nano-word.

The *micro-instruction* store area stores pointers (i.e., addresses) to nano-instructions and also the address of next micro-instruction to execute, sometimes as a conditional branch. The following gives the details of operation of the control unit at the micro- and nano-instruction level:

1. Each micro-instruction *points* to only one nano-instruction, not a sequence of nano-instructions.
2. The conditional branching of micro-instructions is provided by nano-instructions.
3. Nano-store contains a randomly ordered set of unduplicated control words.
4. Each nano-store control word is used by approximately two micro-instructions.

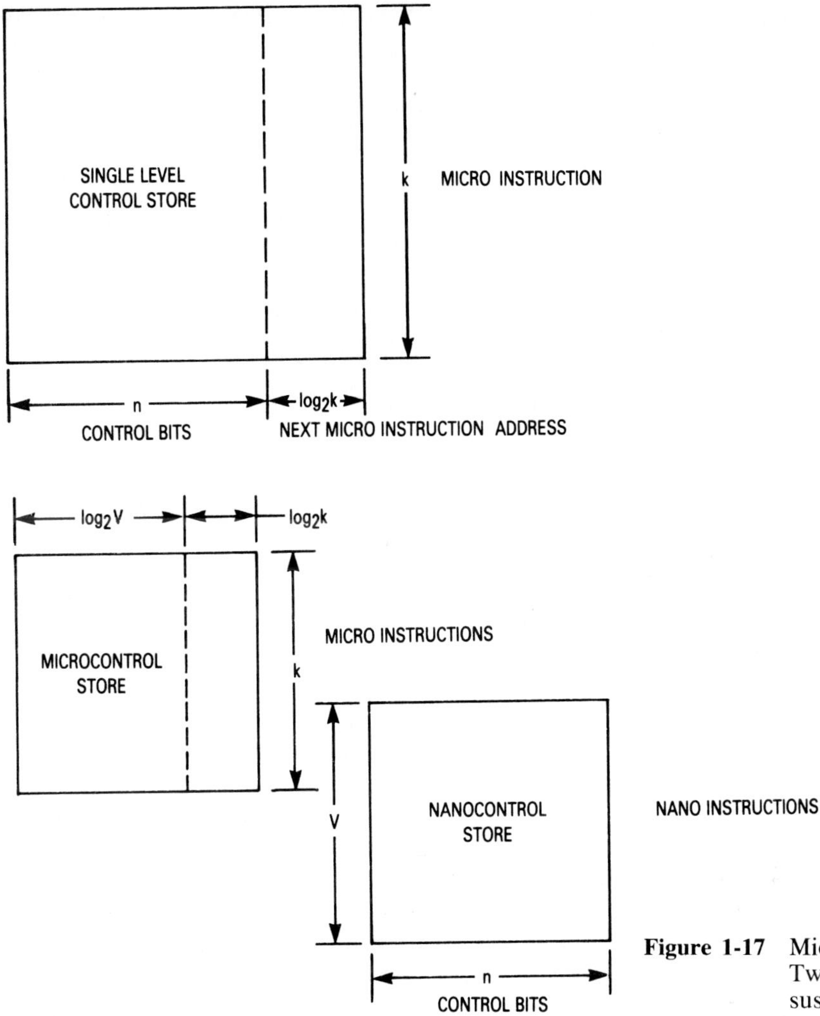

Figure 1-17 Microprogram Size of Two-level Store versus One Level.

The main purpose behind using the two-level control store was to reduce the micro-program memory size. The micro-nano implementation reduces micro-program ROM size to approximately 32 Kbits as illustrated in Figure 1-17.

1.6 DESIGN PHILOSOPHY BEHIND THE 68000

In 1977, a new project was started at Motorola to develop a new family of microprocessors which implement a consistent, extensible, and high-performance computer architecture. This project was internally known as Motorola's Advanced Computer System on Silicon, or MACSS in short. The MACSS design team had four basic objectives which we will describe next.

Performance

The objective that took top priority was to develop a microprocessor with an approximate order of magnitude better performance than its 8-bit predecessor, the 6800 family. Features such as instruction pre-fetch, non-multiplexed address and data buses, and separate units for address and data arithmetic were provided to meet this goal. On the more subtle side, other features such as 15 general purpose registers and a large linear address space also support this goal. The large number of on-board registers enables the programmer to keep necessary variables in these registers thus saving time-consuming memory accesses. Because of the 68000's 16 Mbyte linear address space, the programmer can concentrate on accessing any memory location directly. In contrast, with a paged or segmented architecture, such as in Intel's 80286, a programmer has to pay special attention to what page or segment is being currently accessed. This not only requires special attention in programming but, more importantly, results in a slower program because of overhead to verify correct page/segment in a running program using large data sizes. A good example is drawing a circle or filling a boundary with the processor in a high-resolution graphics system.

Breaking with the Past for Programmers

The early 8-bit microprocessors were basically designed to replace logic circuits. Their software aspects such as the support of high-level languages and the ease of programmability were not given much consideration. Designer's of the MACSS team wanted to make the 68000 architecture consistent with respect to hardware and software. In view of the new architecture and features for software aspects, software compatibility with the 6800 was not provided. One of the ways MACSS team made the 68000 instruction set consistent is by allowing the 68000 to perform all operations on all registers, on all data types, and in all addressing modes. This is called *orthogonality*. As the reader will realize later, 68000 is certainly not 100 percent orthogonal due to practical limitations: there are a few exceptions to the above. However, for the most part, it is very consistent, and this makes the programmer's job easier because they do not have to memorize a long list of exceptions to the instruction set.

The 68000 is certainly a processor designed to make the programmer's job easier: It provides special instructions in support of structured modular programming and high-level programming. It incorporates features in order to detect the occurrence of programming errors or bugs. The most frequently used instruction in any program, the MOVE instruction, is optimized so that it is the most flexible instruction of the 68000. It can be used in more than 1,000 different ways! Table 1-4 highlights the software aspects of 68000.

TABLE 1-4 SOFTWARE HIGHLIGHTS OF THE 68000 ARCHITECTURE

Objective	Supporting Feature(s)
Ease of programmability	15 general purpose registers. Nearly orthogonal instruction set.
High-level language support	MOVEM, PEA, LEA, LINK, UNLK, TRAP instructions.
Operating system support	User/supervisor modes. TRAP instruction.
Software testability	Exceptions on various errors. Instruction trace mode. Double bus fault detection.

An Eye for the Future

One of the important objectives of MACSS team was to design an architecture that would extend well into 1990s with future siblings of the 68000 family, all software compatible with the 68000 in the user mode. In anticipation of future needs and enhancements, various measures are taken for planned expansion. Unused opcodes are reserved for future expansion of the instruction set. Compatibility of other possible enhancements are carefully examined. The upward compatibility of user software requires that the basic architecture stays the same including the programming model (i.e., register set) and instruction set in running the user's application programs. New instructions could be added without disturbing this forward-compatibility requirement. Even though the design team set out to design a 16-bit microprocessor, all internal registers are made 32-bits wide to provide for a easy migration path to 32-bit processors of the family.

Interface Compatibility with 8-Bit 6800 Peripherals

Although 6800 peripherals are hardly used for new designs today because of the wide variety of 68000 peripherals available, this was not the case when 68000 was first introduced in 1979. For 68000's initial success in the marketplace it was essential to provide for interface compatibility to 6800 peripherals.

FURTHER READING

Microprocessor Evolution

1. Garetz, Mark. "Evolution of the Microprocessor (An Informal History)." *Byte Magazine*, September 1985, p. 209–215.
2. Russo, Paul M. "VLSI Impact on Microprocessor Evolution, Usage, and System Design." *IEEE Transactions on Electron Devices*, August 1980, Vol. ED-27, No. 8, p. 1332–1341.

68000 Architecture

3. Mothersole, David S. *The M68000—The Evolution of a True 32-Bit Architecture*, p. 1–15, __________.
4. Hartman, Brad. "16-Bit 68000 Microprocessor Camps on 32-Bit Frontier." *Electronics*, October 11, 1979, p. 118–125.
5. Stritter, Edward and Gunter, Tom. "A Microprocessor Architecture for a Changing World: The Motorola 68000." *IEEE Computer*, February 1979, p. 43–52.
6. "An Architectural Contrast: The M68000 Microprocessor Family and the 8086/iAPX 286." *Motorola Application Note: BR147*, November 1983.

68000 Design Philosophy and Implementation

7. Starnes, Thomas W. "Design Philosophy Behind Motorola's MC68000." *Motorola Application Note: AR208*, May 1985. Originally published in *Byte* magazine in three parts in issues of April, May, and June 1983.
8. Stritter, Skip and Tredennick, Nick. "Microprogrammed Implementation of a Single Chip Microprocessor." *ACM SIGMICRO Newsletter* 9(4), 1978, Proc. 11th Annual Microprogramming Workshop, p. 8–15.
9. Bryce, Heather. "Microprogramming Makes the 68000 a Processor Ready for the Future." *Electronic Design* 22, October 25, 1979, p. 98–99.
10. Tredennick, Nick. *Implementation Decisions for the MC68000 Microprocessor*, p. 30–35, 1980, IEEE (CH1463-9/80).
11. Nash, James and Spak, Mike. "Hardware and Software Tools for the Development of a Micro-Programmed Microprocessor." *ACM SIGMICRO Newsletter* 10(4), 1979, Proc. 12th Annual Microprogramming Workshop, p. 73–83.

EXERCISES

1. How many general purpose registers does 68000 have? What is the purpose behind the two modes of operation (supervisor/user)? Please explain.

2. Explain the mode and status of condition codes for SR = $604. Can the instruction `MOVE.W #$2000,SR` be executed properly in this mode?

3. What are the data types supported by the 68000 instruction set?

4. Select the features supported by the 68000 architecture:

Separate I/O address space/memory-mapped I/O.
Linear addressing/paged addressing/segmented addressing.
Multiplexed I/O signal lines/separate I/O signal lines.
Synchronous bus protocol/asynchronous bus protocol.
Random-logic control unit/microprogrammed control unit.

5. What is the purpose of function code signal lines?

6. Specify the address and data bus signals, and bus control signals LDS*, UDS*, and R/W* during the execution of following instructions (Assume the contents of location $A001 is $9F):

   a. `MOVE.B #00,D4`

   b. `MOVE.W #00,D4`

   c. `MOVE.W #00,$A001`

   d. `MOVE.B $A001,D0`

   e. `MOVE.W #1234,9000`

7. What is the interrupt priority of request when IPL2* = L, IPL1* = L, and IPL0* = H?

8. What happens if DTACK* is not received during a bus cycle? What is a good way of handling this situation?

9. Explain the multi-functional usage of BERR* and HALT* signal lines.

2

68000 Family Overview

The purpose of this chapter is to introduce the 68000 family of processors and family support. In Chapter 1 we studied the architecture of the first member of the 68000 family. Here, we will cover what other members of the 68000 family are, their enhanced features, and the common features of 68000 family of processors. The family support such as peripheral chips will also be outlined here. This discussion is intended to give the reader the "big picture" about the 68000 family before we delve into the details of programming and designing with it in later chapters.

2.1 THE 68000 FAMILY OF PROCESSORS

Since the 68000's introduction in 1979, things have come a long way. Now, there is a whole family of 68000 processors (see Figure 2-1) which are very popular in the marketplace. Currently, the six members of the 68000 family are the following in chronological order of introduction:

1. The 68000 with 16-bit data bus;
2. The low-cost 8-bit data bus version, the 68008;
3. The enhanced version 68010 with virtual memory support;
4. The 68012, an extended address bus version of the 68010;
5. The full 32-bit microprocessor 68020; and
6. The 68030 which is basically the 68020 with enhanced performance and a built-in memory management unit.

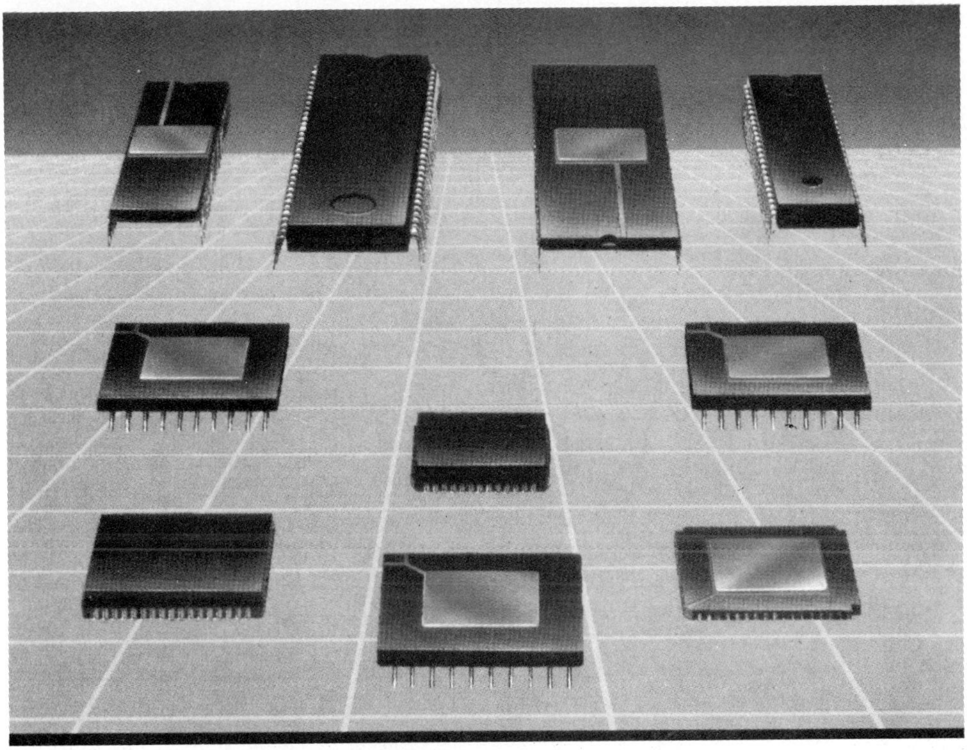

Figure 2-1 Picture of the 68000 Family.

The genealogy of the 68000 family is illustrated in Figure 2-2. Motorola seems to be staying ahead of its competition introducing faster and enhanced newer members of the family while maintaining the basic architecture and software upgradability depicted before the introduction of the first 68000.

Aside from its ease of programmability, another reason for Motorola's success has been due to its number of second sources. As some of the readers might have noted earlier, we have left out the prefixes in the MC68000. The reason for this is that different manufacturers second-sourcing the 68000 family of processors and peripherals use their own prefixes. For example, Hitachi's 68000 is called HD68000. Table 2-1 lists the manufacturers of the 68000 family along with their prefixes. We will continue omitting the prefixes throughout the rest of this book.

The 68000's success is also due to its close ties to the currently popular Unix operating system because the 68000 architecture is particularly well suited to Unix implementation. The 68000's large linear address space simplifies programmer's task in writing assembly-language programs and compilers. The management of address space for large data structures commonly encountered in Unix applications programs becomes a relatively simple task. Also, recursive programs which are heavy stack users can be accommodated without any problem, whereas this

TABLE 2-1 MANUFACTURER'S OF THE 68000 FAMILY

Manufacturer	Processor[1]	Clock Speed
Motorola	MC68⟨HC⟩000⟨*pt*⟩8	8 MHz
	MC68000⟨*pt*⟩10	10 MHz
	MC68000⟨*pt*⟩12	12.5 MHz
	MC68000⟨*pt*⟩16	16 MHz
	MC68008⟨*pt*⟩8	8 MHz
	MC68008⟨*pt*⟩10	10 MHz
	MC68008⟨*pt*⟩12	12.5 MHz
	MC68010/12⟨*pt*⟩8	8 MHz
	MC68010/12⟨*pt*⟩10	10 MHz
	MC68010/12⟨*pt*⟩12	12.5 MHz
	MC68020⟨*pt*⟩16	12.5 MHz
	MC68020⟨*pt*⟩20	16.67 MHz
	MC68020⟨*pt*⟩25	20 MHz
	MC68020⟨*pt*⟩33	25 MHz
	MC68020⟨*pt*⟩33	33 MHz
	MC68030⟨*pt*⟩20	20 MHz
	MC68030⟨*pt*⟩25	25 MHz
Thompson/Mostek	MK68000⟨*pt*⟩8	8 MHz
	MK68000⟨*pt*⟩10	10 MHz
	MK68000⟨*pt*⟩12	12.5 MHz
	MK68000⟨*pt*⟩16	16 MHz
Hitachi	HD68000⟨*pt*⟩6	6 MHz
	HD68⟨HC⟩000⟨*pt*⟩8	8 MHz
	HD68000⟨*pt*⟩10	10 MHz
	HD68000⟨*pt*⟩12	12.5 MHz
Signetics/Philipps	SG68000⟨*pt*⟩8	8 MHz
	SG68000⟨*pt*⟩10	10 MHz
	SG68000⟨*pt*⟩12	12.5 MHz

[1] ⟨*pt*⟩ indicates package type.
[2] ⟨HC⟩ indicates a low-power CMOS version.

might not be the case for a processor such as Intel's 80286 with a 64 Kbytes stack limit. Furthermore, 68000's dual-state structure (supervisor/user) fits well with Unix's kernel and user modes. Because of the above reasons, almost all of the Unix systems using microprocessors employ one of the 68000 family of processors.

The 68000 family has also made in-roads into the personal computer market which has been dominated by Intel's iAPX-86 series microprocessors. The first personal computer using the 68000 was Apple's Macintosh in February 1984, later followed by Commodore's Amiga and Atari's ST series. The price of the 68000 went down considerably from about \$150 to less than \$10. In the meantime, it was opening new application areas such as in robotics, intelligent peripheral controllers, or as an automobile engine controllers (as one of the large car manufacturers will be using soon). On the other end of the spectrum, the 68020/68030

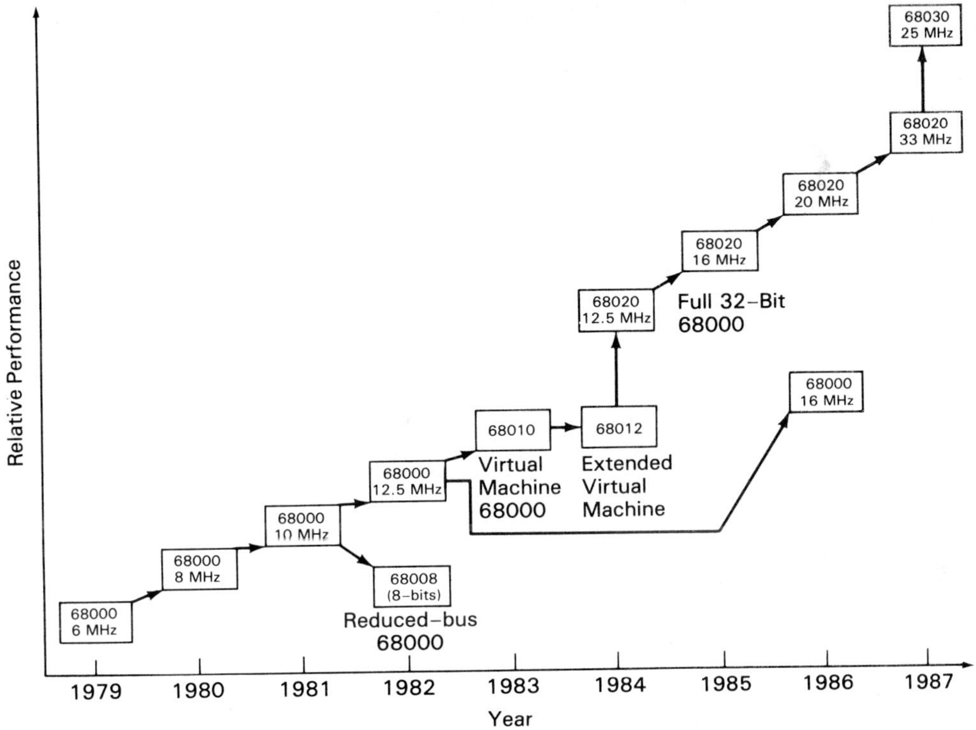

Figure 2-2 The genealogy of the 68000 family.

dominate applications in high-end engineering workstation and Unix microcomputer market at the time of this writing.

The important feature of the 68000 family is the upward software compatibility between its members. *All* members have the same user-programming model as shown in Figure 2-3. The user-programming model consists of lists of registers accessible in the user mode of operation. Each processor supplements the user-programming model with additional registers in the supervisor mode depending upon a particular member. In addition to the same user-programming model, the software upgradability requires that the instruction set, data addressing modes, and data types supported are upwardly compatible from one family member to another. This guarantees that each new member of family is a proper superset.

Due to the internal architecture of the processors, the family can be grouped in four classes:

1. The 68000/68008 architecture;
2. The 68010/68012 architecture;
3. The 68020 architecture; and
4. The 68030 architecture.

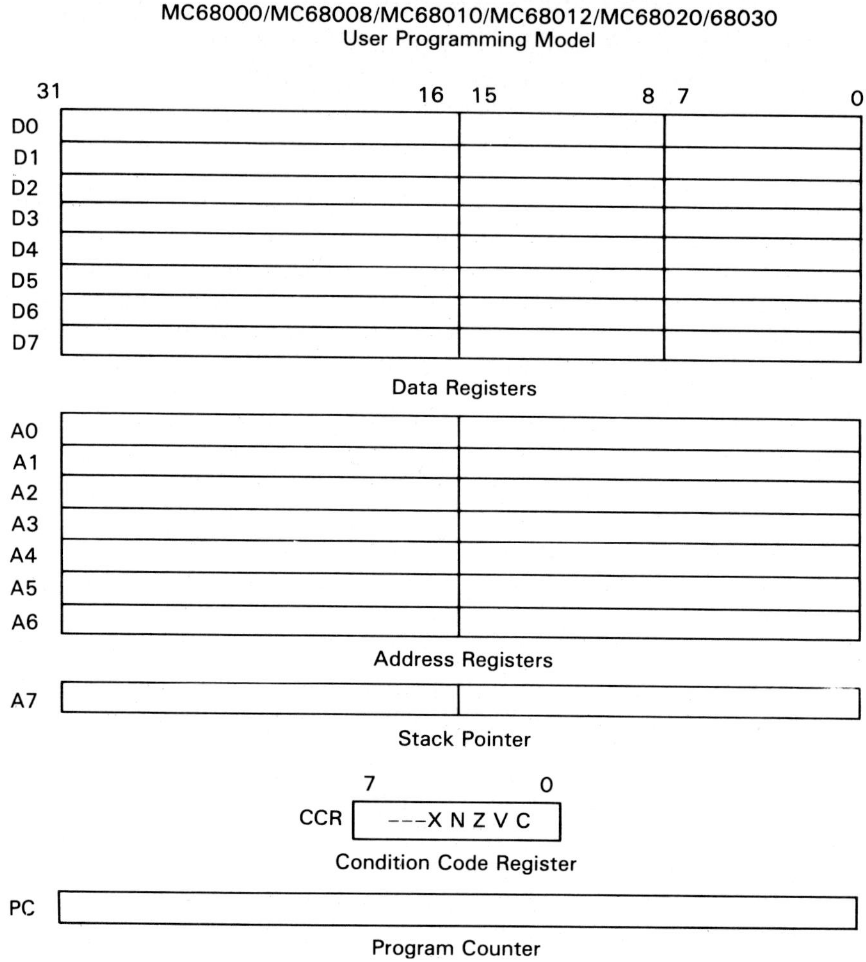

Figure 2-3 User-level Programming Model of the 68000 Family. (Courtesy of Motorola.)

Any user-level (i.e., application) programs written for the 68000/68008 will run unchanged[1] on any of the other processors, and any similarly codes written for the 68010/68012 will execute unchanged on the 68020/68030. The major difference between processors is supplementary supervisor registers and what information is stored on the stack during exception processing. Therefore, supervisor-level programs might not be 100% upwardly compatible depending on the program.

The 68000 family also provides a high degree of compatibility at the bus

[1] There is only one exception to this: MOVE from SR instruction which allows a user-level program to view system byte is made privileged starting with the 68010.

interface level. For example, the 68000, the 68010, and the 68012 are pin-to-pin 100% upward compatible. Furthermore, the 68020/68030 can be substituted for the 68000/68010/68012 using a small adapter board with minimal logic in order to increase the performance of an old design.

Next, we will give an overview of each processor.

The 68000

The 68000, also referred to as 68K in short, is generally known as a 0.7 MIPS (Mega-Instructions Per Second) machine at 8 MHz. This means that it executes an average of 700,000 instructions per second. The 68000 is the first member of family introduced in 1979 with a 4 MHz clock speed which is rarely used now.

We have already covered the architectural overview of the 68K in Chapter 1, so let us proceed to the other members of the family.

The 68008

The 68008 is identical to the 68000 except its bus interface is a subset of the 68000's. It features an 8-bit data bus and 20-bit address bus for a total address space of 1 Mbyte. Therefore, the 68008 has to make twice as many bus accesses in order to read instructions or to transfer word and long word data, resulting in lower performance with respect to the 68000.

The purpose of the 68008 is that all the memory and data buffers are halved, thus reducing cost. Furthermore, the chip resides in a smaller 48-pin package. This is illustrated in Figure 2-4. As far as peripherals are concerned, the 68008 is compatible with both the 68000 and the 6800 peripherals.

The 68010/68012

The major enhancement incorporated into the 68010 is its support of virtual memory/virtual machine concepts. In a nutshell, virtual memory refers to the use of secondary storage such as disk media when it is not practical to populate the entire addressing range of the processor with fast random-access memory (RAM/ROM). We will postpone detailed discussion of virtual memory/machine techniques to Chapter 5.

The second important enhancement of the 68010 is the loop mode of operation. This mode allows two-instruction looping program sequences to be latched in the processors's instruction pipeline thus preventing instruction fetches each time through the loop. The second instruction of the sequence has to be *Decrement-and-Branch-Conditionally* (DB⟨*cc*⟩) which uses one of the data registers as a loop counter. Furthermore, the branch displacement has to be -4 in order to qualify for the loop mode of operation as shown in Figure 2-5. The 68010 places the three-word instruction sequence in its instruction pipeline (one word in the instruction decoder, two words in pre-fetch queue) and suppresses all further

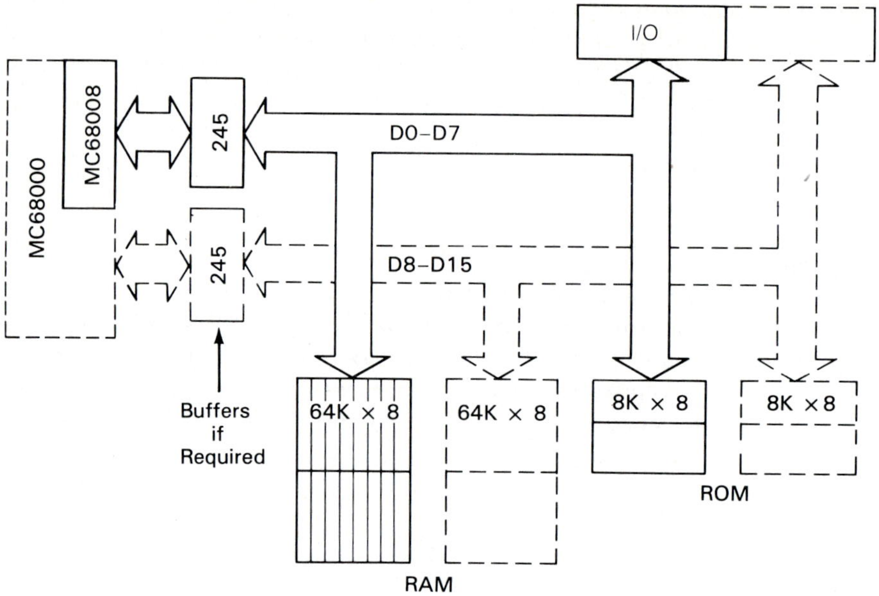

Figure 2-4 The 68008 Reduced Cost System. (Courtesy of Motorola.)

instruction fetches. Only operand reads and writes are performed till the loop-exit condition is met. The loop mode is useful in moving blocks of data and in handling character strings. The instructions in the internal pipeline can be accessed in two clock cycles as opposed to four clock cycles for no-wait-state accessing of the external memory. Therefore, during loop mode operation, 50% performance improvement over the 68000 is possible.

The 68012 features are extended address space of one gigabytes with two non-contiguous 500 Mbytes of memory spaces. The only other difference to the 68010 is that it offers an additional signal line (RMC*) in order to indicate indivisible read-modify-write bus cycle at hardware level.

The 68020

This is the first processor in the family with full 32-bit implementation: it has a separate 32-bit data bus and 32-bit address bus which can address a memory space

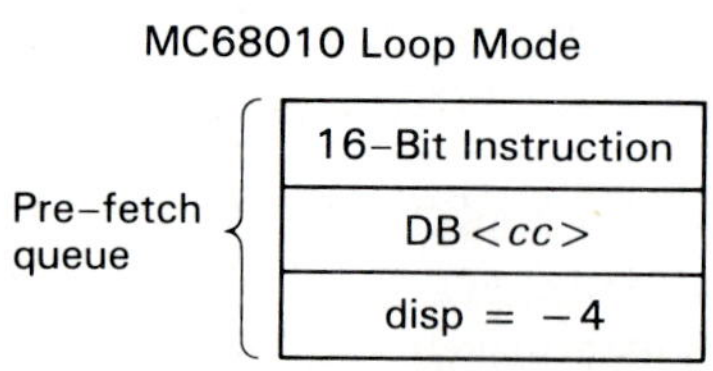

Figure 2-5 The 68010/68012 Two-instruction Sequence for the Loop Mode.

of four gigabytes (4,294,967,296) linearly. The 68020 includes all the features of the 68000/10/12 with significant additional enhancements.[2]

The 68020 takes the loop-mode operation of the 68010/12 one step further by providing an *instruction cache*[3] which consists of 128 word entries. During an instruction fetch, the 68020 first checks whether the instruction is already in the cache. If so, the instruction is read from an on-board cache. This is referred to as a *cache hit*. If the instruction is not found in the cache, it is fetched from the external memory (a *cache miss*). An instruction is searched in cache using address tags as we will describe in detail in Chapter 6.

Another new feature of the 68020 is its inherent *coprocessor* support where a coprocessor can be a floating-point processor (the MC68881 peripheral chip), a *memory management unit* (MMU) such as the MC68851 used in multitasking/multiuser applications, or any other user-defined function. The idea behind coprocessor interface is to enhance the capabilities and performance of the 68020 for a specific application. The 68020 provides dedicated coprocessor instructions in order to use coprocessors capabilities while maintaining interaction between the 68020 and the coprocessor transparent to the programmer.

The 68020 supports two new data types—unpacked BCD and bit fields. Additional instructions (PACK, UNPK) packs the low 4-bits of each of the two given bytes into a single byte, or vice versa. A new category of instructions operate on variable length bit fields, such as bit field extraction/insertion with any offset and field width within 32-bits.

Aside from additional instructions for system control (cache, and so on), coprocessor interface, and additional data types, the 68020 also provides additional addressing modes which is a superset of the double-indirect addressing modes of the LSI-11 processor from DEC. Motorola refers to this new addressing mode as *memory indirect*.

From a hardware perspective, one of the convenient features of the 68020 is its *dynamic bus sizing*. In other words, the 68020 adjusts its bus size to match the addressed device on every bus cycle. If the addressed device, let's say, has an 8-bit port size. It signals this to the 68020 by encoding the two data-transfer-acknowledge signals (DSACK0/1*) at the end of the current bus cycle. If the 68020 is trying to transfer 32-bits, then it responds by making three more sequential bus cycles.

The 68020's bus interface has also been improved in that a bus cycle without wait-states completes in three clock cycles instead of four for earlier processors of the family. There are other relatively less important enhancements which we will describe in Chapter 6.

[2] According to Motorola, the 68020 contains approximately 200,000 transistors and entailed 60 man-years of design effort.

[3] A buffer type of high-speed memory that is filled at medium speed from the main memory and can be accessed by the processor at relatively high speed. Typically, used to read instructions or operands from the main memory.

TABLE 2-2 THE 68000 FAMILY COMPARISON

Feature	68000	68008	68010	68012	68020	68030
Bus Interface						
Addressing Range	16 Mbytes	1 Mbyte	16 Mbytes	2 Gbytes	4 Gbytes	4 Gbytes
Databus Width	16 bits	8 bits	16 bits	16 bits	32 bits	32 bits
No-wait Bus Cycle (In clock periods)	4	4	4	4	3	3[1] 2[2] 1[3]
Dynamic Bus Sizing?	No	No	No	No	Yes	Yes
Bus Protocol				Asynchronous or synchronous handshake		
Instruction Set						
Addressing Modes		Same				Yes
New Instructions?		None		Yes		Yes
User Programming Model				Same		
Virtual Memory/Machine Support?	No	No	Yes	Yes	Yes	Yes
On-chip Cache Memory						
Instruction Cache?	No	No	No	No	Yes	Yes
Data Cache?	No	No	No	No	No	Yes
Technology	HMOS/HCMOS	HMOS/HCMOS	HMOS/HCMOS	HMOS/HCMOS	HCMOS	HCMOS
Maximum Clock Speed	16.67 MHz	12.5 MHz	12.5 MHz	12.5 MHz	33 MHz	25 MHz
Bus Arbitration				Same		

[1] Asynchronous interface.

[2] Synchronous interface using STERM* signal.

[3] Burst Mode.

The 68030

The 68000 family has been criticized for not having a built-in memory-management unit (MMU) in applications such as engineering workstations or microcomputers using multitasking/multiuser operating systems. Actually, this was not really an architectural deficiency of Motorola. Their policy has been to leave the choice of MMU to the system designer. One problem, though, was that using Motorola's earlier MMU (MC68451) resulted in significantly lowered system performance, and thus, some designers resorted to custom MMUs. The latest MMU from Motorola (namely, the MC68851) eliminated the speed problem and is quite versatile (it can be connected to the 68020 as a coprocessor). However, system designers looking to design high-performance systems still have to trade off cost and performance goals while deciding how much data cache to provide. While the performance of processors are continuously increasing, it is becoming harder and harder for the memory chips to keep up with the processor without any wait-states. Improvement in the memory front has been largely in memory sizes per chip.

The 68030 is the Motorola's answer to the previously discussed issues. It incorporates an on-chip '68851 MMU along with separate data and instruction caches. Its instruction set is the same as the 68020's plus a subset of a '68851 instruction set. The 68030 maintains 68020's coprocessor interface for floating-point coprocessors. Furthermore, it has the same bus interface and dynamic bus sizing as the 68020.

There is an important additional advantage to the 68030 other than reducing cost and simplifying the task of the system designer. Having an on-chip separate instruction and data caches, the MMU allows the intelligent controller of the 68030 to overlap the operations of CPU, caches, MMU, and the external bus controller. The 68030 also incorporates other features to handle caches significantly increasing the hit rates. All of the these factors approximately doubles the average execution rate in comparison to the 68020 plus '68851 MMU at the same clock rate.

Summary

Table 2-2 gives a summary of the 68000 family comparison.

2.2 68000 FAMILY SUPPORT

The 68000 family support can be divided into three categories:

1. Peripheral chip support;
2. Software support; and
3. Hardware/software development system support.

TABLE 2-3 THE 68000 FAMILY PERIPHERAL SUPPORT CHIPS

Function	Peripheral Chip	Manufacturer(s)
Coprocessors	68681 Floating-point Coprocessor	Motorola
	68682 Floating-point Coprocessor (Enhanced version of 68681)	Motorola
Memory Management	68451 MMU	Motorola
	68851 Paged MMU	Motorola
	68905 BMAC	Signetics
DMA Controllers	68430 Single-channel DMA	Signetics
	68440 Dual DMA Channels	Motorola
	68442 Expanded Dual DMA	Motorola
	68450 Single-Channel DMA	Hitachi, Motorola
Data Communications	68562 DUSCC (sync/async)	Signetics
	68564 SIO (Serial I/O)	Thomson/Mostek
	68605 X.25 Protocol Controller	Motorola
	68652 Multi-protocol Controller	Motorola
	68681 DUART	Signetics, Motorola
	68661 EPCI (sync/async)	Signetics, Motorola
General Purpose I/O	68302 Multi-Protocal Processor[1]	Motorola
	68230 Parallel Interface/Timer	Motorola, Thomson
	68901 Multi-function Peripheral	Motorola, Thomson
Network Control	68824 Token Bus Controller	Motorola
	68184 Broadband Interface Cont.	Motorola
	68194 Carrierband Modem	Motorola
System Interface	68153 Bus Interrupt Module	Motorola
	68154 Interrupt Generator	Signetics
	68155 Interrupt Handler	Signetics
	68171 VMS Bus Serial Interface	Signetics
	68172 VME Bus Controller	Signetics
	68173 VMS Bus Controller	Signetics
	68174 VME Bus Arbiter	Signetics
	68452 Bus Arbitration Module	Motorola
Disk Controller	68454 Multiple Disk Controller	Signetics
	63463 Hard Disk Controller (HDC)	Hitachi

[1] 68000 Core + Timers + DMA + Serial Ports + BTO + RISC Controller.

Since its introduction, the 68000 family support has matured such that we cannot give a comprehensive coverage within the modest scope of this chapter. The interested reader is referred to *The Source*,[4] a comprehensive listing of software tools and programs for the 68000 family.

Table 2-3 lists the peripheral support chips specifically designed for the 68000 family. The 6800 peripherals, as we stated earlier can also be used, but is rarely used for new designs because of the wide variety and availability of 68000 peripherals which provide easier and faster interface.

[4] Motorola Publication #:BR506. It lists application programs and operating system software for the 68000 family including the 68020.

Development System Support and Emulators

A microprocessor development system provides a complete environment and tools for both hardware and software development of a microprocessor-based system. It includes editor, compiler(s), assembler, linker, along with debugging and testing tools. It also includes an in-circuit emulator, usually as an option. Let us look at an emulator more closely.

When using an *in-circuit emulator* (ICE), the actual microprocessor of target system is replaced by a multipinned header plug connected with a cable to the emulator pod which contains the same microprocessor. The emulator pod allows buffering, monitoring, and control of all microprocessor signals without disturbing the target circuitry. The pod connects to the emulator that contains the supervisory control logic, resources such as memory that could be mapped into a target system.

Alternative to an integrated development system is the stand-alone ICE which is connected to a computer system that has these software development tools. The ready-to-run object code could be down-loaded into the emulator over a link such as the RS-232 or the fast SCSI interface and debugged using the utilities of emulator. Such an ICE provides flexibility because it could be linked to a variety of computers and is thus called a *satellite emulator*. A leading manufacturer of such emulators is the Applied Microsystems illustrated in Figure 2-6 connected to a Sun workstation.

The ICE are sometimes considered as a basic hardware debugging tool. This perception is certainly true, but is inaccurate because an ICE also provides significant software development support. The following gives an overview of advantages an ICE may provide:

1. Let us assume that we are working on a project that involves hardware and software development of a module containing a 68020 microprocessor. Typically, hardware and software development progress somewhat in parallel. Suppose that the memory circuit, for some reason, is not yet functional but we have software ready to debug and test. Using an ICE, such as Applied Microsystems', we can map the emulation memory to appear as if we have target memory functional. Certain memory map regions may be designated as read-only. This simple substitution of target memory with emulator memory allows software development to continue concurrently with hardware debugging. When target memory is functional, the emulator mapping is typically changed to use target memory again, and without bugs, software should work the same.
2. The ICE provides an easy and convenient way of updating system software that would eventually reside in a read-only memory (ROM). Instead of continuously programming and replacing PROMs, the emulator memory may be used.

Figure 2-6 Applied Microsystems' Satellite Emulator. (Courtesy of Applied Microsystems.)

3. The ICE allows user to read and manipulate the registers of microprocessor and memory locations of target system.
4. The ICE typically provides event monitoring capabilities. The simplest example of this is a breakpoint. When ICE detects a certain address value on address lines, it may be setup to halt thus allowing the user to examine memory and CPU registers. Or, the emulator may simply capture the status of selected signal lines of the CPU and continue execution. A more complexed trigger mechanism may be devised. For example, an intermittent error may be traced by halting when address lines are within a certain range, when the data bus has a certain value, and when other signal lines are in a certain state.
5. A trace of program execution flow (e.g., the last 1,024 assembly statements

that are executed) can be displayed in raw or disassembled format. The ICE typically captures all current activity on all signal lines of the CPU and saves it in a buffer area. This could be very useul in software debugging. For example, programmer may even examine when a given interrupt request is asserted and when it is acknowledged.

6. When a software bug is found, in order to be able to fix it quickly and test again, the ICE usually provides a single-line assembler.
7. The ICE allows single-stepping of programs for debugging.
8. Other features such as memory testing allows testing of the target memory for the hardware designer. Another useful feature sometimes provided is keeping a histogram of execution activity. This shows the spread of execution times over a selected address range so that the time-critical code can be optimized where it matters most.

FURTHER READING

1. *M68000 Family Technology Seminar*, Seminar notes printed by Motorola, BR247, 1984.
2. Zorpette, Glenn. "Microprocessors." *IEEE Spectrum*, January 1985, p. 53–55.
3. Farrell, James J. "The Advancing Technology of Motorola's Microprocessors and Microcomputers." *IEEE Micro*, October 1984, p. 55–63.
4. Beims, Robert. *The M68000 Family Architecture Gets the Power of a 32-Bit Bus*, p. 1–11,__________.
5. "The M68000 Family." *Motorola Application Note: BR176*, Rev 2.
6. "68000 Machines." *Byte Magazine*, A collection of six articles, September 1986, p. 161–217.

3

Programming the 68000 Microprocessor

In this chapter we will discuss the details of assembly-language programming of the 68000. All of the material we cover here will be directly applicable to later members of the 68000 family. This is due to the upward compatibility of the 68000 family software.

The 68000 assembly language is a symbolic language defined by Motorola to code 68000 source programs and is used to avoid coding directly into object-code. The assembler, a program itself, translates a program expressed in assembly language to the object-code which consists of executable binary machine codes. We will hereafter use the Motorola's 68000 assembly notation. Although some of the independent software vendor's assembly notation and syntax might differ from Motorola's, the differences are usually easy to grasp.

Figure 3-1 shows the source-code of a typical subroutine as entered by the programmer and Figure 3-2 gives the corresponding listing-output of the assembler. This subroutine uses a small look-up table to convert a digit of hex data to ASCII representation. The details of this program will be clarified during the rest of this chapter. You may want to come back to it later.

For now, let's just focus on the assembly-listing format. The first column from the left indicates the line number of the source-code. The second column gives the relative address of locations of each instruction. These addresses are relative since this subroutine will be linked with a calling program, and so forth, possibly relocating its final addresses in memory. The third column consists of the object-code of the assembler. The rest of the file is replicated from the source-program with the exception of the symbol table appended at the end of the file. The symbol table summarizes the relative addresses of symbols or their values.

```
* SUBROUTINE XTOASCII
*
* PURPOSE: This subroutine converts a hex digit
*          to ASCII representation.
*
* SAMPLE CALLING SEQUENCE:
*
*                   MOVE.W  <ea>,-(SP)      Hex digit.
*                   JSR     XTOASCII
*                   LEA     2(SP),SP        Deallocate stack.
*
* OUTPUT: The ASCII character is given in the low
*         byte of D0 register.
*
EXAMPLE3.1 IDNT     1,0
         SECTION  0
         XDEF     XTOASCII
HEX      SET      +8                        Offset to input parameter.
*
XTOASCII MOVE.L   A0,-(SP)                  Save used registers.
         LEA      CHTABLE,A0                A0 → CHTABLE
         MOVE.W   HEX(SP),D0                Get parameter.
         MOVE.B   0(A0,D0.W),D0             Look-up ASCII code.
         MOVEA.L  (SP)+,A0                  Restore A0.
         RTS
CHTABLE  DC.B     '0123456789ABCDEF'        ASCII Table.
         END
```

Figure 3-1 A Typical 68000 Program.

3.1 PROGRAM DEVELOPMENT WITH THE 68000

Program development consists of analysis of requirements, software design, coding and documentation, followed by debugging and testing. The mechanics of program development, that is, the edit-assemble-link process are illustrated in Figure 3-3. These steps are usually iterated many times.

The assembler output is usually not in a format that can be executed directly. The linkage editor, or simply linker, combines several separately assembled parts of a program creating an executable *load-module*. The load-module is not simply concatenated object-code files. It also includes what is called a *loader-information block* at the beginning. The purpose of this header is to indicate to a particular operating system, where to load the object-code, its starting address, and so forth.

As good programming practice, a large program is usually divided into different parts called *modules*. A module is a logically self-contained and discrete part of a complete program. Each module is assembled independently and later linked together. The advantage of modular programming is that different modules

```
Motorola M68000 ASM Version  1.80 SYST:  1.        .XTOASCII.SA 07/17/87 12:56:49

  1                           * SUBROUTINE XTOASCII
  2                           *
  3                           * PURPOSE: This subroutine converts a hex digit
  4                           *          to ASCII representation.
  5                           *
  6                           * SAMPLE CALLING SEQUENCE:
  7                           *
  8                           *                    MOVE.W <ea>,-(SP)    Hex digit.
  9                           *                    JSR    XTOASCII
 10                           *                    LEA    2(SP),SP     Deallocate stack.
 11                           *
 12                           * OUTPUT: The ASCII character is given in the low
 13                           *         byte of D0 register.
 14                           *
 15                           EXAMPLE3.1  IDNT    1,0
 16          00000000                   SECTION 0
 17                                     XDEF    XTOASCII
 18          00000008         HEX       SET     +8                  Offset to input parameter.
 19                           *
 20 0 00000000 2F08           XTOASCII  MOVE.L  A0,-(SP)            Save used registers.
 21 0 00000002 41F900000012             LEA     CHTABLE,A0          A0 → CHTABLE
 22 0 00000008 302FFFF8                 MOVE.W  HEX(SP),D0          Get parameter.
 23 0 0000000C 10300000                 MOVE.B  0(A0,D0.W),D0       Look-up ASCII code.
 24 0 00000010 205F                     MOVEA.L (SP)+,A0             Restore A0.
 25 0 00000012 4E75                     RTS
 26 0 00000014 303132333435   CHTABLE   DC.B    '0123456789ABCDEF'   ASCII Table.
 27                                     END

****** TOTAL ERRORS     0--
****** TOTAL WARNINGS   0--

    Motorola M68000 ASM Version  1. 80 SYST:  1.     .XTOASCII. SA 07/17/87 13:01:53
    SYMBOL TABLE LISTING
    SYMBOL NAME     SECT   VALUE     CROSS-REF (LINENUMBERS)

    CHTABLE            0   00000014  -26    -21
    HEX                    00000008  -18     22
    XTOASCII   XDEF    0   00000000  -20    -17
```

Figure 3.2 Listing Output of Assembler

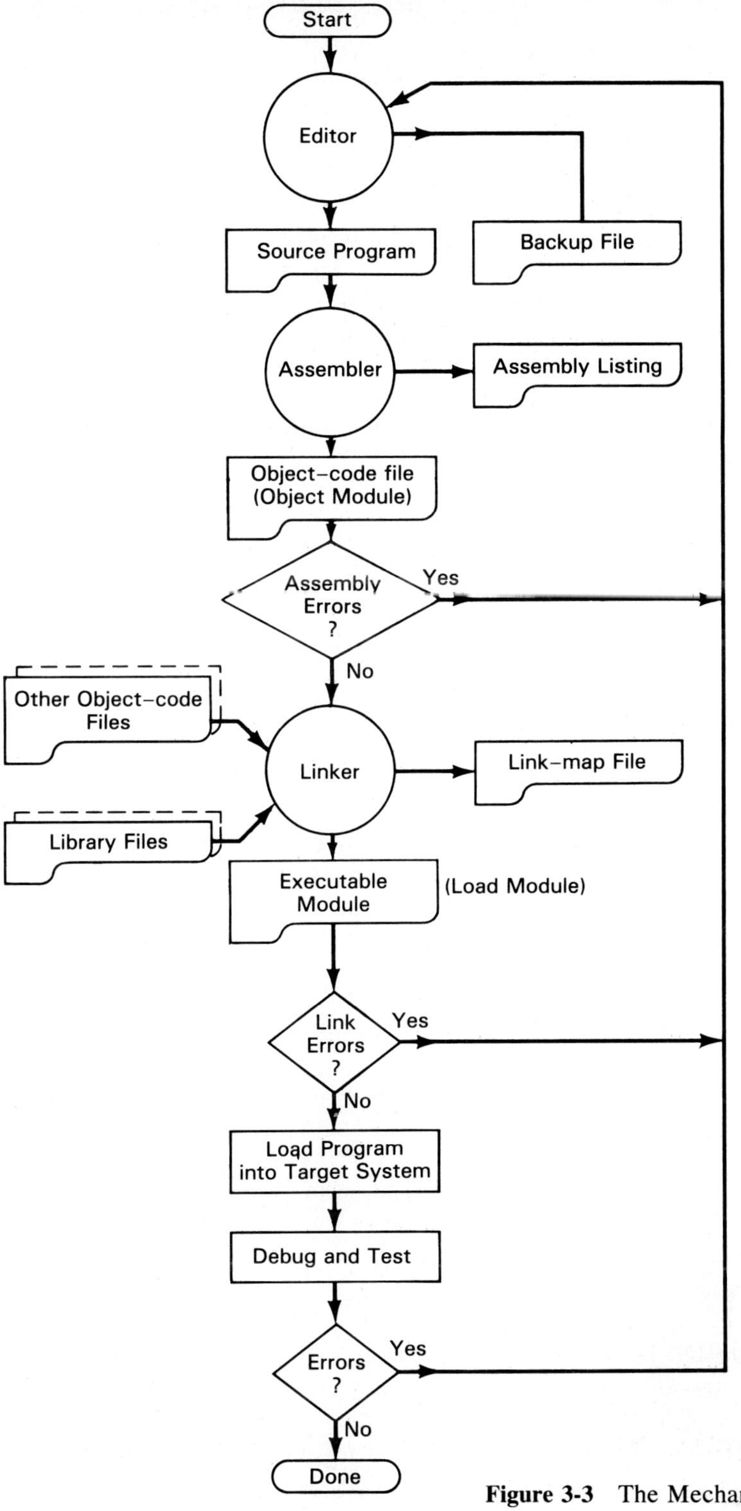

Figure 3-3 The Mechanics of Program Development.

can be designed, coded, and assembled by different programmers at the same time so as to divide a complex task into workable-size subtasks. Also, changing a part of a large program does not require assembling the whole thing.

An important criteria in decomposing a large program into various modules is the principle of *information hiding*. This requires that a module hide all unnecessary information from all others. Modules must exhibit independence in the form of high cohesion and low coupling[1]. The benefit of such a modular organization is the ease of maintenance.

Several modules are "bound" together by the linker while resolving any inter-module references between them. The linker can also extract any required object-modules from a given library file. In addition to the load-module, a link-map file is created indicating the beginning address of each object-module and global symbols after relocation.

3.1.1 Assembly Format

Assembly language source programs consist of a logical sequence of statements. Each statement occupies a line of text and may have as many as four fields of the following form

```
           ┌ <instruction mnemonic> ┐
[<label>]  │           or           │  [<Operands, if any>]  [<Comments>]
           └ <directive mnemonic>   ┘
```

where `[ ]` indicates an optional field that is not always required. These four fields are separated by at least one space or a tab character. One special case is when there is an asterisk (*) in the first column. This indicates the whole line is a comment, and will be ignored by the assembler except for listing purposes. If the first character of a statement is not an asterisk, then it either contains an assembler directive or a 68000 instruction.

The *assembler directive*, as the name implies, directs and controls the assembly process. The directive statements are also referred to as *pseudo-opcodes* since they do not generate any executable code. For example, the ORG (origin) directive

```
ORG   $2000   Load Following Program Lines at $2000.
```

indicates where the following instructions are to be located in memory. We will discuss directives in the next section.

Label field. The *label field* consists of a string of alphanumeric characters that make up a meaningful signal name. It either starts in the first column and terminates with a blank character (space or tab), or it starts in any column and terminates with a colon (:). There are three different usages of the label field:

1. It is used optionally to assign a symbol name to a location in a program. The label symbol is, in this case, assigned the address of the first byte of instruction or data it is associated with. (Example: CHTABLE in Figure 3-2).
2. It is used to assign the value of an expression or a constant to a symbol using the EQU (equate) or SET directive.
3. It is used to define the name of a macro.

The next example will illustrate these three items.

Example 3-1

```
        .
        .
LOOPCNT EQU     500             Assign the value 500 to LOOPCNT
                                symbol.
        .
        .
        .
BACK    CMPI.W #LOOPCNT,D0      BACK is assigned the beginning
*       .                       address of CMPI instruction.
        .
        .
PRINT   MACRO                   PRINT is the name of a macro.
        .
        .
        .
```

The Motorola assembler restricts the labels to a maximum of 30 characters where the first one must be alphabetic (A through Z). Since only the first eight characters are shown on the symbol table, it is recommended that they be unique.

With one exception, a symbol cannot occur in more than one label field (i.e., it cannot have a multiple definition). Otherwise, each reference to that symbol causes an assembly error. The exception is the SET directive which allows a symbol to be redefined by another SET directive.

Comment field. This field allows comments after an instruction or assembler directive. It is optionally inserted to clarify the purpose of an individual or group of statements. Even though comments are ignored by the assembler, they highly benefit the programmer who is debugging, maintaining, or upgrading a portion of program code. While it may not be useful to comment every line, they are very useful for all instructions whose purpose is not clear. A comment should briefly describe the *purpose* behind an instruction, and not just reiterate its operation. For example:

```
BTST   #7,STAT1   Test bit-7 of status register
```

Or

```
BTST   #7,STAT1   Is printer ready?
```

where the first comment is bad because it does not convey any new information. The second one is good since it briefly describes the purpose.

Use of constants and expressions. We have seen earlier that constants with different number bases may be used. For example,

```
MOVE.W   #-2,D0
```

and

```
MOVE.W   #$FFFE,D0
```

are exactly the same since `$FFFE` is equal to -2_{10} in two's complement format. Constants that are made up of ASCII strings may also be specified. For example, 'A' is the same as $41, and 'AB01' evaluates as $40413031.

An assembly statement can also specify an expression, which is a combination of symbols, constants, algebraic operators, and parentheses. All expressions are evaluated at assembly time. The assembly syntax for constants and expressions are shown in Table 3-1.

The assembler uses 32-bit precision to evaluate an expression and any operators of the same precedence are evaluated in left-to-right order.

TABLE 3-1 ASSEMBLER SYMBOLS FOR CONSTANTS AND EXPRESSIONS

Type	Syntax	Interpretation
Constant	$<number>	Hexadecimal number
	<number>	Decimal number
	%<number>	Binary number
	@<number>	Octal number
	'<string>'	ASCII string of characters
Operator	( )	Parentheses used for grouping
	-	Unary minus
	>>	Binary right shift with zero-fill
	<<	Binary left shift with zero-fill
	&	Binary AND
	!	Binary OR
	*	Multiplication
	/	Division
	+	Addition
	-	Subtraction

Note: Some assemblers default to hexadecimal when there is no identifier, and require & for decimal.

Example 3-2

Let symbol TABLE correspond to the address of the first element of an array of 16-bit numbers. To move the third element to D0, we can simply write

```
MOVE.W  TABLE+(3-1)*2,D0   Get the third element.
```

where multiplying by two is necessary because of two byte addresses per word. We can alternatively write

```
MOVE.W  TABLE+4,D0   Get the third element.
```

However, this is not as readable as the first one.

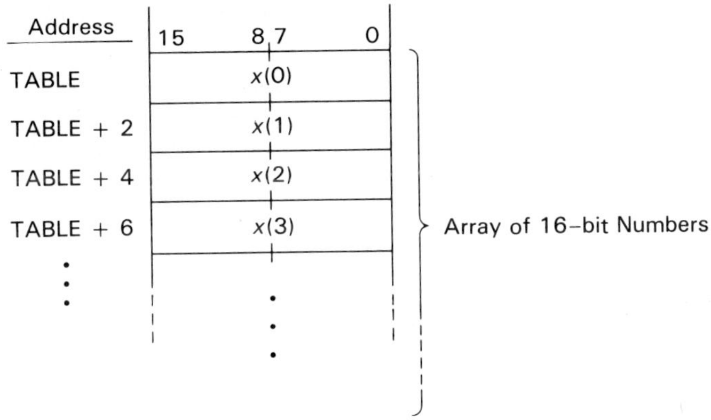

3.1.2 Assembly Directives

The assembly directives serves three purposes. First, they provide information to control the assembly process. Second, they provide a way for the definition of data-words and storage allocation. Third, they provide various listing-control commands to obtain a desired listing format.

Table 3-2 gives an overview of these directives. A detailed discussion of each of these is beyond the scope of this chapter. We will discuss some important ones here and defer the discussion of macros to the end of this chapter. We hope to intrigue the reader enough here to refer to the assembler manual of the system at hand.

Assembly control. The syntax of these directives are given by

```
           ORG       <expression>            [<comment>]
[<name>]   SECTION   <number>                [<comment>]
           END       [<start-address>]       [<comment>]
           INCLUDE   <file-specification>    [<comment>]
```

TABLE 3-2 OVERVIEW OF MOTOROLA'S 68000 ASSEMBLY DIRECTIVES

Directive Type	Directive	Function
Assembly Control	ORG SECTION INCLUDE END	Sets location counter to an absolute origin Indicates relocatable program section Includes another file in assembly Indicates end of source file
Symbol Definition	EQU SET	Assigns a permanent value to a symbol name Assigns a temporary value to a symbol name
Data-storage Control	DC DS	Define constant(s) Allocate storage
Linkage-editor Control	IDNT XDEF XREF	Identification of a relocatable module External symbol definition External symbol reference
Macro Definition	MACRO ENDM MEXIT	Begin macro definition End macro definition Skips to end of macro generation
Listing Control	PAGE LIST NOLIST SPC TTL LLEN	Skips to new page in listing Enable the listing Disable the listing Insert n blank lines into listing Creates a listing header Sets line-length of listing

The ORG directive changes the location counter[1] to the value specified by the expression. This also indicates that the following statements are to be located at these absolute addresses that are not to be relocated by the linker. The SECTION directive, on the other hand, indicates the following statement labels will be marked relative and assigned relative locations. The Motorola assembler allows 16 relocatable sections with section numbers 0 through 15. Each time a SECTION directive is encountered by the assembler, it causes the location counter to be restored to the address following the last location used in that section or to zero if used the first time. To create a common area, a section may be given a name.

The END directive indicates the end of a source module. Any subsequent statements are ignored by the assembler.

The INCLUDE directive instructs the assembler to include the specified file in the assembly process at the location of this directive, just as if it is part of the module being assembled. When used under a Unix operating system, the file specification is lower/upper case sensitive. The main advantage of the INCLUDE directive is to have global data structures defined in a separate file which is later "included" in each module accessing it. This eliminates any discrepancies that

[1] The location counter has the same value as the PC in this context.

may result in a big project from multiple definitions, as well as making it easier to make changes later.

Symbol definition. The syntax of EQU and SET are

```
<label>  EQU  <expression>  [<comment>]
<label>  SET  <expression>  [<comment>]
```

where both statements require a label as shown above.

Example 3-3

Define the addresses of a peripheral whose memory map is shown below.

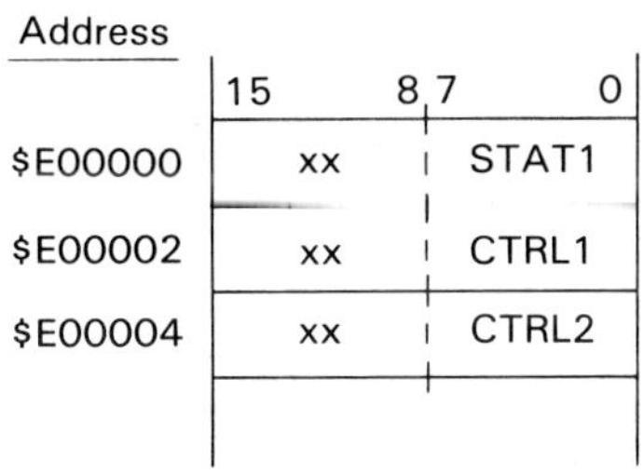

xx: Not Used.

```
PERIPHERAL  EQU  $E00000+1     Base address of peripheral.
STAT1       EQU  PERIPHERAL    Status register.
CTRL1       EQU  PERIPHERAL+2  Control register #1.
CTRL2       EQU  PERIPHERAL+4  Control register #2.
```

We defined the addresses in a relative fashion even though we could have also used absolute addresses. The above relative form makes it more readable and easier to change.

Data storage control. The syntax of DC and DS directives are

```
[<label>]  DC.<s>  <operand>[,<operand>,...]  [<comment>]
[<label>]  DS.<s>  <operand>                  [<comment>]
```

where size is B (byte), W (word), or L (long-word) just like the operand size specification of instructions as illustrated in Figure 3-4. The DS directive is used to reserve the memory location of a specified size which is not initialized. Its operand specifies the number of locations allocated.

The DC directive initializes one or more memory locations. The operand

```
Motorola M68000 ASM Version  1. 80 SYST:    1.     .DCDS   .SA 07/17/87 13:38:13
   1             00004000            ORG     $4000
   2   00004000 40                   DC.B    64
   3   00004002 0040                 DC.W    64
   4   00004004 0064                 DC.W    $64
   5   00004006 9F                   DC.B    %10011111
   6   00004007 41                   DC.B    'A'
   7   00004008 4100                 DC.W    'A'
   8   0000400A 41000000             DC.L    'A'
   9   0000400E 546869732069         DC.B    'This is a message.',0
  10   00004021 40000A41             DC.B    $40,0,%1010,'A'
  11   00004025 00000008     T1      DS.B    8                    Reserve 8 bytes.
  12   0000402E 00000080     T2      DS.W    64                   Reserve 64 words.
  13   000040AE 00000040             DS.L    16                   Reserve 16 long-words.
  14   000040EE 0000C081             DS.B    2*T2+T1              Reserve 2*T2 + T1 bytes.
  15   0001016F 81                   DC.B    2*T2+T1              Initialize to 2*T2+T1.
****** ERROR    251--
  16   00010170 C081                 DC.W    2*T2+T1              No error this time.
  17                                 END

****** TOTAL ERRORS     1--   15
****** TOTAL WARNINGS   0--   15
```

Figure 3-4 Examples of DC and DS Directives.

field may contain a constant or an expression. The ASCII messages are usually stored using the DC.B since they require only one byte per character.

Linkage-editor control. The syntax of these directives are

```
<module-name> IDNT <version>,<revision>          [<description>]
              XDEF <symbol>[,<symbol>...]        [<comment>]
              XREF [<section>:]<symbol>[,...]    [<comment>]
```

Every relocatable object module must contain an IDNT directive to identify it at link time. The directive pair XDEF and XREF are used for any inter-module reference of symbols. The XDEF directive gives the list of symbols defined in the current module and referenced elsewhere. The corresponding directive XREF specifies a list of symbols referenced in the current module but defined in another one.

3.2 PROGRAMMER'S MODEL

The programmer's model of 68000 registers is divided into two parts:

1. The user-programmer's model which consists of the registers that are accessible in user mode.
2. The supervisor programmer's model supplementary registers as shown in Figure 3-5.

In the supervisor mode, all registers are available to the programmer. The curious reader might wonder why the register set is divided into address and data registers instead of one set of registers for both address and data manipulations such as in the LSI-11 processor. The main reason is due to the 68000's architecture. The address and data registers have separate arithmetic units (see Figure 1-18) so that operations on address and data can proceed simultaneously thus resulting in higher throughput. Secondly, it takes only three bits to decode a register, and the operation mode implies whether to use an address or a data register.

Next, we will look at the different registers of the programmer's model in detail.

Data registers. The eight data registers (D0-D7) are generally used to manipulate data. The data can be byte, word, or long-word size where the byte and word data is limited to low-order bits as indicated by the dashed lines in Figure 3-5.

When a data register is used with a byte or word-size code (i.e., `.B` or `.W`), only the used portion of data register is affected; the remaining high-order bits

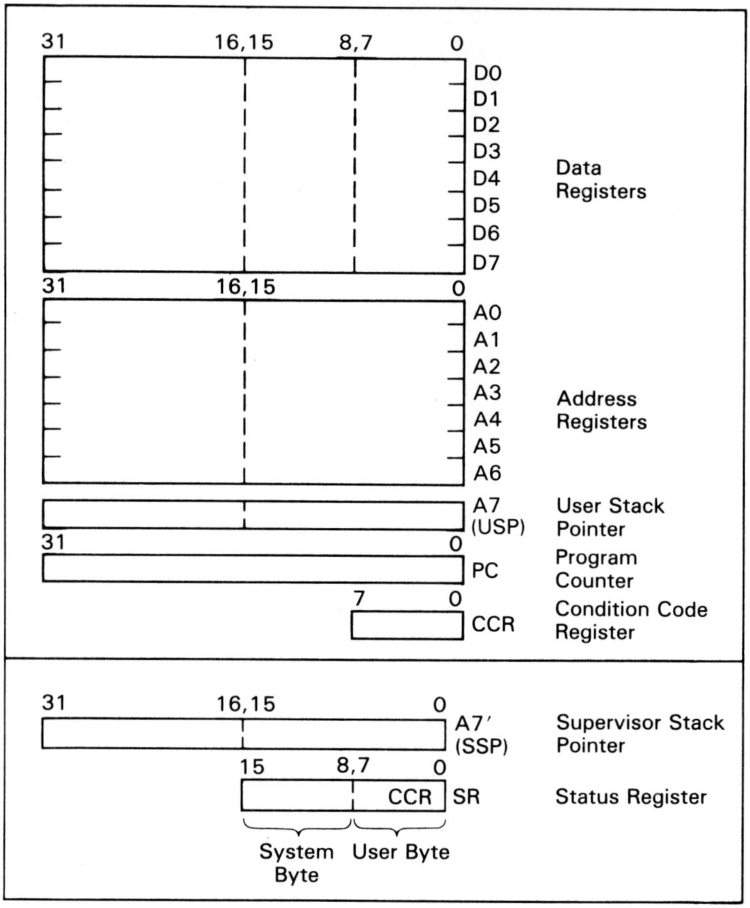

Figure 3-5 The 68000 Programmer's Model.

are unchanged. For example, assume

```
D0 = $34FE9054
```

initially. Then, the execution of the instruction

```
MOVE.W #1234,D0
```

will result with D0 = $34FE1234. The same also applies to a byte-size operation where the bits [31:8] remain unchanged.

The data registers D0-D7 are general purpose in that they have no dedicated uses for certain instructions. In other words, the registers D0-D7 offer complete symmetry, and thus, leave the choice up to the programmer.

The possible numeric range for a data register depends upon whether its contents are interpreted as a signed or an unsigned number, and also on the data-size selected. For example, the unsigned long-word data in a register can be in the range 0 through $2^{32} - 1$, whereas the signed representation with a two's complement form allows a range of -2^{31} through $2^{31} - 1$. The data register numeric ranges are illustrated in Figure 3-6, where note that the position of sign-bit for signed numbers depends on the data-size used.

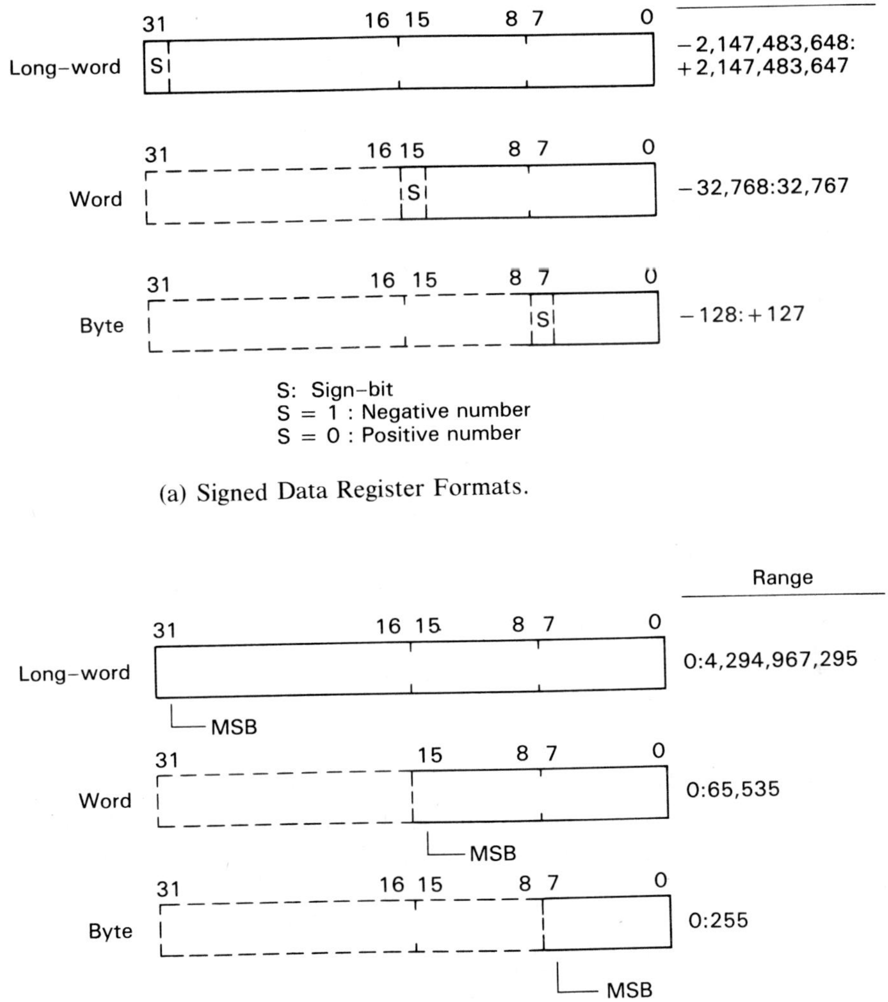

(a) Signed Data Register Formats.

(b) Unsigned Data Register Formats.

Figure 3-6 Data Register Formats for Unsigned and Signed Numbers.

Example 3-4

The instruction ADD.<s> Dn,Dm adds the contents of two data registers and stores the contents in D*m*, where the data-size of the operation is given by ⟨*s*⟩ = B, W, or L (byte, word, or long-word). In other words, D*n* + D*m* → D*m*. Let us assume ADD.W D0,D3 here. Then, addition will be done with 16-bit precision and only the low-word of D3 will be changed. The following describes the values before and after the execution of the ADD instruction.

Instruction: ADD.W D0,D3

	Before		After
D0	4037 A049	D0	4037 A049
D3	FFF0 2001	D3	FFF9 C04A

If the contents of D0 and D3 are interpreted as two's complement signed numbers, then we have

$$\begin{array}{rl} & A049_{16}\ (-24{,}503_{10}) \\ + & 2001_{16}\ (+\ 8{,}193_{10}) \\ \hline & C04A_{16}\ (-16{,}310_{10}). \end{array}$$

And if the contents are interpreted as unsigned numbers, then we have

$$\begin{array}{rl} & A049_{16}\ (41{,}033_{10}) \\ + & 2001_{16}\ (\ 8{,}193_{10}) \\ \hline & C04A_{16}\ (49{,}226_{10}). \end{array}$$

Note that the binary result is the same regardless of the interpretation.

One important conclusion from the above example is that the 68000 is not aware whether the numbers it is processing are unsigned or signed. This is not unique to 68000 and applies to most other microprocessors. The data registers can also be used as an index register as we will later see in addressing modes.

Address registers. The 68000 has seven general purpose address registers (A0-A6) which are used to hold and manipulate memory addresses or as index registers. A7 is dedicated as a stack pointer which we will discuss separately in the following discussion.

Only word and long-word address sizes are supported by 68000 architecture as shown by dashed lines in Figure 3-5. Furthermore, when a word size address is loaded into an address register, it is sign-extended to 32 bits as shown in Figure 3-7. The reason for this is that all address register arithmetic is done with 32-bit precision and, even though the physical address has to positive, a relative address offset can be negative.

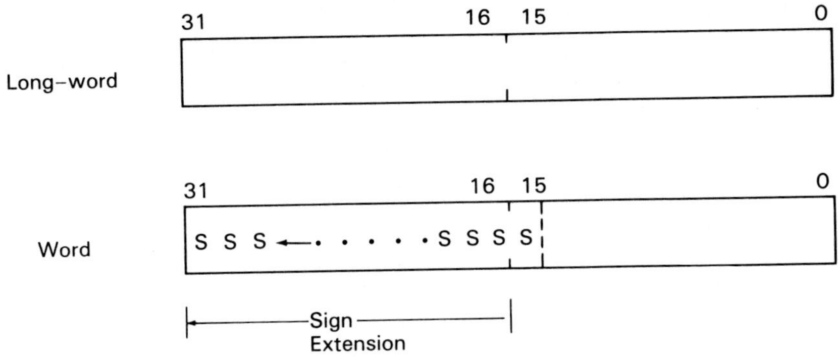

Figure 3-7 Address Register Format.

Example 3-5

Instruction	A0 After Move is Executed
`MOVE.W #$8F00,A0`	FFFF 8F00
`MOVE.L #$8F00,A0`	0000 8F00
`MOVE.L #$12348F00,A0`	1234 8F00

Stack pointers. The 68000 has a stack architecture similar to other microprocessors wherein any portion of the external memory is generally used as a stack to store and retrieve contents of registers, the program counter, and exception related information. The 68000 actually maintains two stacks: the *user-mode stack* (USP) and the *supervisor-mode stack* (SSP), each with a separate stack pointer. Only one stack pointer is active at any given time, as we stated in Chapter 1, referred implicitly as SP. However, in the supervisor-mode, both stack pointer values can be changed.

The two stack pointers are also referred to as A7 and A7′ because the active stack pointer can be manipulated as any other register by the programmer. But the 68000 architecture permits only word and long-word data sizes during stack operations in order to keep stack aligned on word boundaries. Table 3-3 gives an overview of stack usage by implicitly the 68000 or by the programmer.

The two basic stack operations on a stack are called *push and pop* (or pull). The *push* operation inserts a new data item on the top of stack and *pop* pulls the top item off the stack in a last-in/first-out (LIFO) order. In 68000 architecture, the stack grows toward lower memory and the stack pointer always points to the top item of stack. Therefore, for a push operation, the stack pointer (USP or SSP) is first decremented by the size of the item to be pushed (word or long-word). Next, the new entry is stored on the stack as illustrated in Figure 3-8. The pop,

TABLE 3-3 68000 STACK USAGE

Type	Purpose	Stack Usage
Implicitly by 68000	Subroutine call	PC
	Exceptions	At minimum PC and SR
Specified by programmer	Saving registers	68000 registers
	Space for local subroutine variables	As required
	Passing subroutine parameters and return values	As required

on the other hand, first removes the top entry then increments the stack pointer by the proper amount (2 or 4 bytes).

```
Stack Push Operation: MOVE.<s>  <operand>,-(SP)
Stack Pull Operation: MOVE.<s>  (SP),<operand>
```

where ⟨*s*⟩ is B, W, or L.

Example: `MOVE.W  D0,-(SP)`

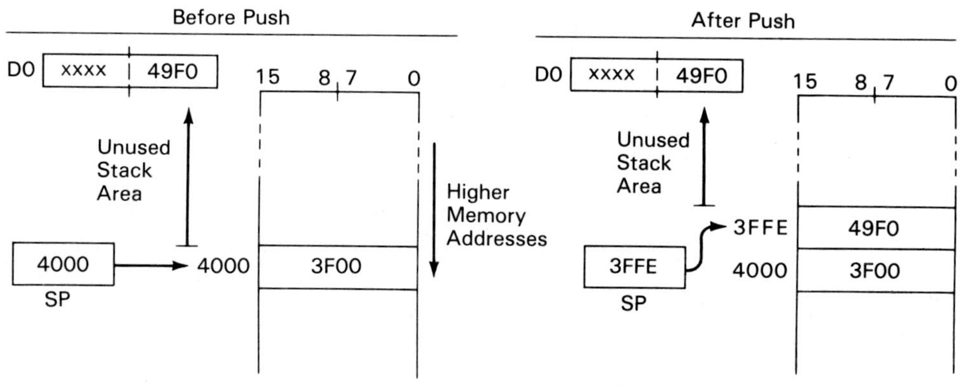

Figure 3-8 68000 Stack Operation.

Program counter (PC). The program counter register is used to control the sequence of instruction execution. As each instruction is executed, the program counter is incremented to point to the next instruction. Since the instruction length may vary from one to five words, the 68000 will increment the PC by the proper offset for each particular instruction. The following conditions affect the normal incrementing of the PC:

1. Unconditional branch and jump instruction change the contents of the PC unconditionally.
2. Conditional branch instructions affect the contents of the PC register only if a tested condition is valid. Otherwise, program execution continues with the next instruction.
3. Subroutine-call instructions and return-from-subroutine instructions also affect the PC register.

The above conditions constitute a program flow as defined by the programmer. There is also another set of conditions, namely exceptions that change the normal program flow, and thus, the PC register.

Because of the 68000's 24-bit address space, the upper 8 bits of the PC register is not used. Furthermore, since instructions always start on a word boundary, the least significant bit of PC is always zero.

Status register (SR). The status register consists of system byte and user byte (CCR). The system byte can only be modified in the supervisor mode whereas the user byte is accessible in both supervisor and user modes. The unused bits of SR will always read as zero.

The control bits of system byte are described below:

T (Trace)	In trace mode, that is when T = 1, a trace exception occurs at the end of each instruction. This mode is to facilitate instruction single-stepping during program debugging.
S (Supervisor)	The 68000 is in supervisor-mode when the S-bit is set to one, and when S = 0, the 68000 is in user mode. As an exception processing starts, the S-bit is set to supervisor mode by the 68000 after the contents of SR is saved on the stack.
I2,I1,I0	Defines the current interrupt mask level. This allows 68000 to ignore certain interrupts with priority level equal or below this mask level.

The user byte, also called the *condition code register* (CCR), carries information about the results of arithmetic and logical operations, or data manipulation (e.g., MOVE). Operations on addresses, on the other hand, does not affect any of the condition codes. The following defines the bits of CCR:

X (Extend)	This bit is set the same as the carry bit (C-bit) only by

instructions that can be used to facilitate multiprecision arithmetic. Otherwise, it is unaffected, therefore, allowing other instructions between multiprecision operations without having to save the C-bit.

N (Negative) This bit is set if the sign-bit of result is one. In two's complement signed format, when sign-bit is one, it indicates negative number.

Z (Zero) This bit is set if the result of a data operation is zero.

V (Overflow) This bit, when set, indicates arithmetic overflow in two's complement signed format. Overflow indicates that operation yields an incorrect result in signed format because number of bits is not sufficient to properly represent the result.

C (Carry) This bit, when set, indicates a carry out of the most significant bit of a data operation. In a subtraction operation, it is also set if a borrow is generated.

Not all 68000 instructions affect condition codes in the same manner. Whereas the arithmetic addition instruction (ADD) affects all the condition codes, the MOVE instruction only sets the N- and Z-bits conditionally, while it clears the N- and V-bit unconditionally. The programmer has to refer to Motorola's User's Manual to see how a particular instruction affects condition codes.

It is important to remember that the 68000 does not know whether it is manipulating signed or unsigned numbers. As we saw earlier, the bit-level result is the same regardless of the interpretation of the operands. Therefore, it generates condition codes for both interpretations. Using signed numbers, The codes N, V, and Z are important and the C-bit is irrelevant. Conversely, for unsigned numbers, the N and V codes are irrelevant and the C-bit is important. Next example illustrates the meaning of condition codes.

Example 3-6

The arithmetic addition instruction given in form

```
ADD.W  D0,D3
```

affects the CCR as follows:

X Set the same as the C-bit.

N Set if the result is negative. Cleared otherwise.

Z Set if the result is zero. Cleared otherwise.

V Set if an overflow is generated. Cleared otherwise.

C Set if a carry is generated. Cleared otherwise.

The condition code computations for this instruction is given by

$$\left.\begin{aligned} X &= C \\ N &= R_m \\ Z &= \overline{R}_m \wedge \overline{R}_{m-1} \wedge \ldots \overline{R0} \end{aligned}\right\} \text{General case}$$

and

$$\left.\begin{aligned} V &= (S_m \wedge D_m \wedge R_m) \vee (\overline{S}_m \wedge \overline{D}_m \wedge R_m) \\ C &= (S_m \wedge D_m) \vee (\overline{R}_m \wedge D_m) \vee (S_m \wedge \overline{R}_m) \end{aligned}\right\} \text{ADD specific computation}$$

from User's Manual where

R_m = Most significant bit of resultant operand

S_m = Most significant bit of source operand

D_m = Most significant bit of destination operand

and

$\wedge$: Logical AND-operation

$\vee$: Logical OR-operation.

Let us assume the contents of D0 and D3 are given initially as shown below before the execution of ADD. Then,

	Before	After
D0	xxxx 69 3F	xxxx 69 3F
D3	xxxx A1 00	xxxx 0A 3F
CCR	0 0 0 0 0 1 0 0	0 0 0 1 0 0 0 1
	(X N Z V C = last five bits)	(X N Z V C = last five bits)

where "x" indicates "don't care." The reader should verify the above results.

3.3 DATA ORGANIZATION IN MEMORY

In the previous section, we discussed how data and addresses are handled with the 68000's on-board registers. It is also necessary to understand how various data types supported by the 68000 are organized in memory. The different data types are:

Bit data;
Byte data;
Word data;
Long-word data or address; and
Binary-coded decimal (BCD) data.

From the programmer's viewpoint, the linear memory space consists of a string of byte addresses $000000 through $FFFFFF or 16 Mbytes. The 68000 always accesses memory as either a 8-bit byte or 16-bit word entity because of its bus structure. Bit manipulation in external memory is limited to byte size data due to the 68000 architecture (see Figure 3-9-a). Word data in external memory is limited to even-byte addresses where the high (most significant) byte of the word is stored at even-byte address as shown in Figure 3-9-b.

The long-word (32 bits) data or address stored in memory are organized such that the high-order (most-significant) word is stored at the specified long-word address, and the low-order word is stored in the following word address as shown in Figure 3-9-c. The long-word accesses to memory will take two bus cycles, but this is transparent to the programmer.

The above might be confusing, although it is consistent, due to the high-order byte/word is always stored at the lower address than low-order the byte/word.

The BCD digits are also limited to byte-size in memory with *most-significant digit* (MSD) in the high-order nibble of a byte as shown in Figure 3-9-d

Example 3-7

Let us examine the contents of memory after the following instructions are executed:

```
MOVE.B   #$12,$3000
MOVE.W   #$1234,$4000
MOVE.L   #$12345678,$5000
```

The memory contents is shown in Figure 3-10 where unaffected bytes are shown as "xx".

3.4 OPERAND ADDRESSING MODES

In general, a processor instruction requires an operand or operands to be referenced. An operand can be a data or address to be manipulated and typically resides in a register or in the external memory. Several addressing modes are used to provide a variety of ways that an operand may be accessed where an operand address might be too long to be efficiently included as part of an instruction or when it is not possible or even necessary to assign an explicit address. The actual operand address that is obtained at the time of instruction execution is referred to as the *effective address* (EA) of the operand.

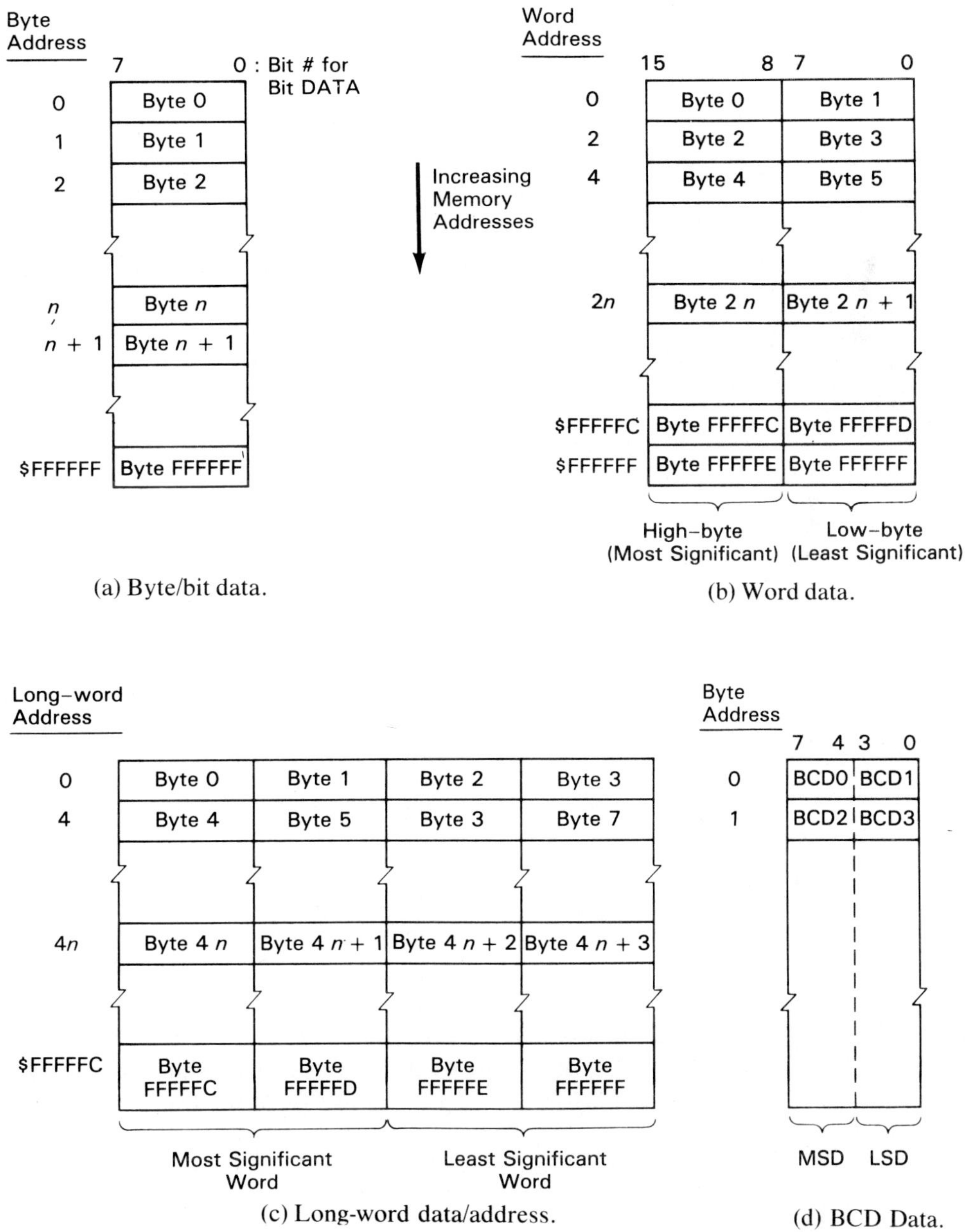

Figure 3-9 Data Organization in Memory.

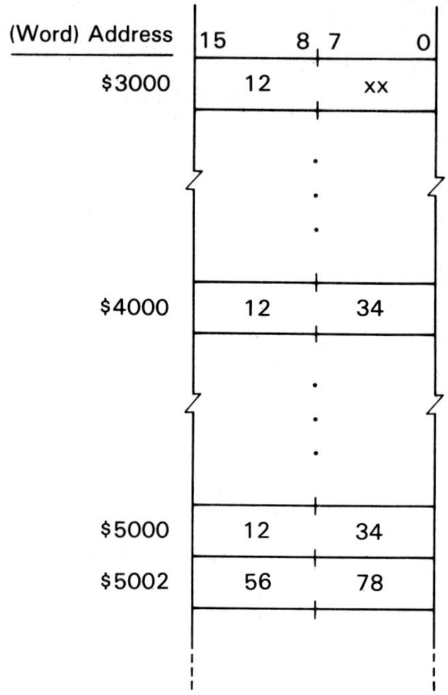

Figure 3-10 Illustration of Memory Organization.

The 68000 provides 14 addressing modes which we will describe next. To illustrate the use of the various addressing modes clearly, we will use a form of addition (ADD) instruction given by

```
ADD.<s>   <ea>,Dn
```

where <ea>: Specifies the effective address of operand using one of the applicable addressing modes.

<s>: B (byte), W (word), or L (long-word).

Dn: Is one of the data registers (D0-D7).

We have chosen the ADD instruction in the above form because it allows all fourteen addressing modes to be used. With each addressing mode, we will also cover the corresponding assembly syntax of EA.

3.4.1 Register Direct Addressing

The data is in the specified register for this addressing mode. This mode provides faster instruction execution because there is no need to access external memory to retrieve an operand. There are two addressing modes in this category: data-register direct addressing and address-register direct addressing. The first uses a

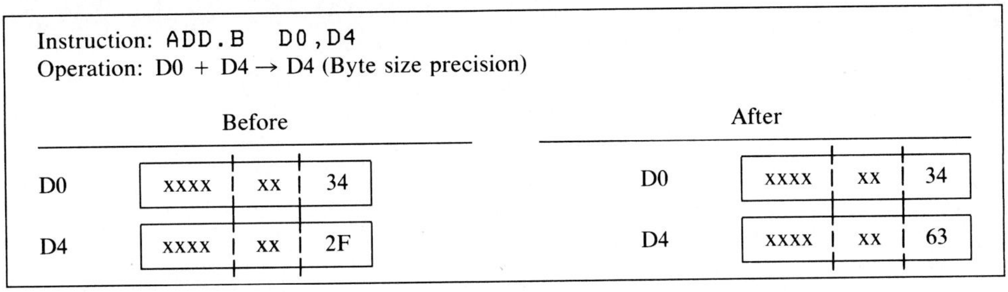

Figure 3-11 Illustration of Data-register Direct Addressing.

data register to contain the operand with assembly syntax

```
Dn
```

where n = 0-7 (data register number) as illustrated in Figure 3-11.

In the address-register direct addressing mode, the operand, an address, or an index is given by the contents of an address register. As we stated earlier, the data sizes involving an address register are restricted to word and long-word. The EA syntax of this addressing mode is

```
An
```

where n = 0-7 (address register number) as illustrated in Figure 3-12.

3.4.2 Absolute Data Addressing

In this addressing category, the effective address of the operand is specified explicitly as part of the instruction. The absolute-short address mode specifies only the low-order 16 bits of the address which is sign-extended before it is used. The absolute-long address mode, on the other hand, specifies the full 32-bits address (only low-order 24 bits are used for the 68000). The absolute-short address mode is faster than the long form because of a shorter instruction word, but the ad-

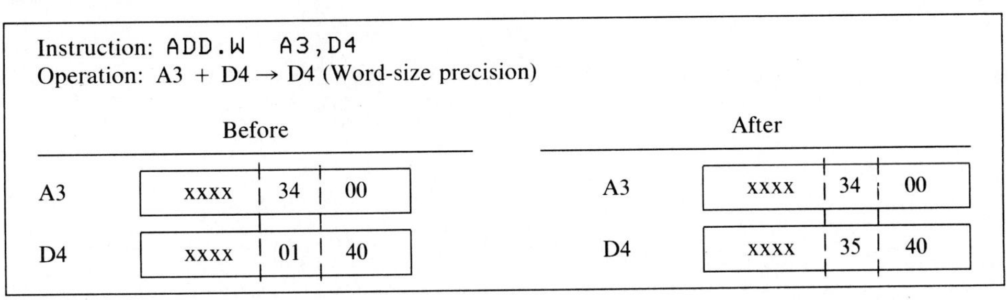

Figure 3-12 Illustration of Address-register Direct Addressing.

dressable memory space is limited to the 32 Kbytes on both ends of the total address space as shown in Figure 3-13.

The EA syntax of this absolute addressing mode is

<label>

or

<address>

as illustrated in Figure 3-14. The first form, <label>, generates absolute addressing mode only if it is in a section of program that follows the ORG directive. Otherwise, assembler will use PC-relative addressing to replace the label.

The short or long form of absolute addressing is determined by the assembler as appropriate, unless one of the modes are explicitly specified. To force the long form, we can use

(<label>).L

or

(<address>).L

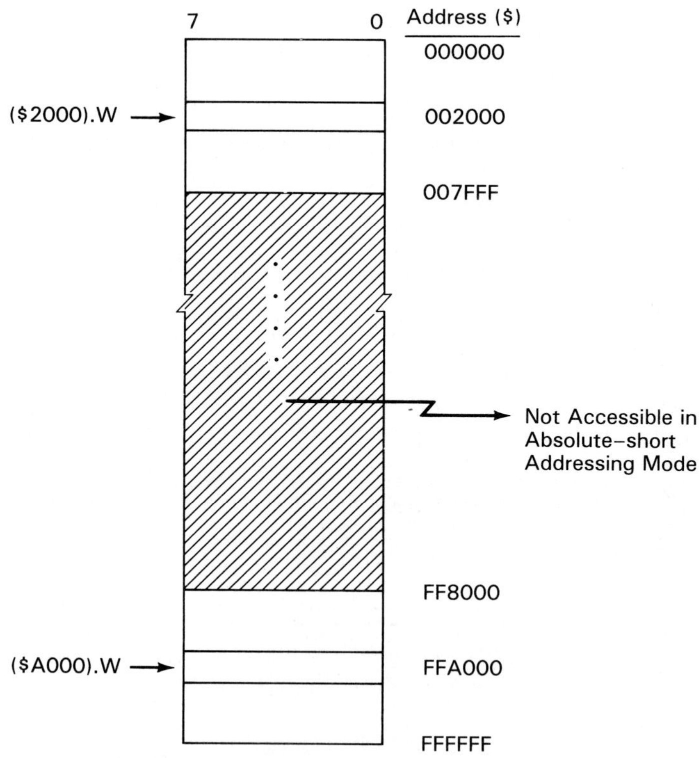

Figure 3-13 Absolute-short Addressing Range.

and similarly, the short form can be specified by

```
(<label>).W
```

or

```
(<address>).W
```

which may generate an assembly-error message if the address does not fit in word-size.

Example 3-8

This example illustrates four different ways an operand with an absolute address can be accessed.

```
        ORG       $1000
TX1     SET       $2000
TX2     SET       $A000
        .
        .
        .
        MOVE.W    TX1,D0
        .
        .
        .
        MOVE.W    (TX2).L,D0
        .
        .
        .
        MOVE.W    (TX1).W,D0
        .
        .
        .
        MOVE.W    $A000,D0
```

3.4.3 Immediate Data Addressing

In this addressing mode, the operand value is given as part of the instruction as shown in Figure 3-15. The EA syntax is

```
#<data>
```

where # signifies the immediate mode and data is any allowed constant or an expression evaluated at assembly time. One common mistake for beginning programmers is to confuse the following two statements:

```
MOVE.L    COUNT,D0
MOVE.L    #COUNT,D0
```

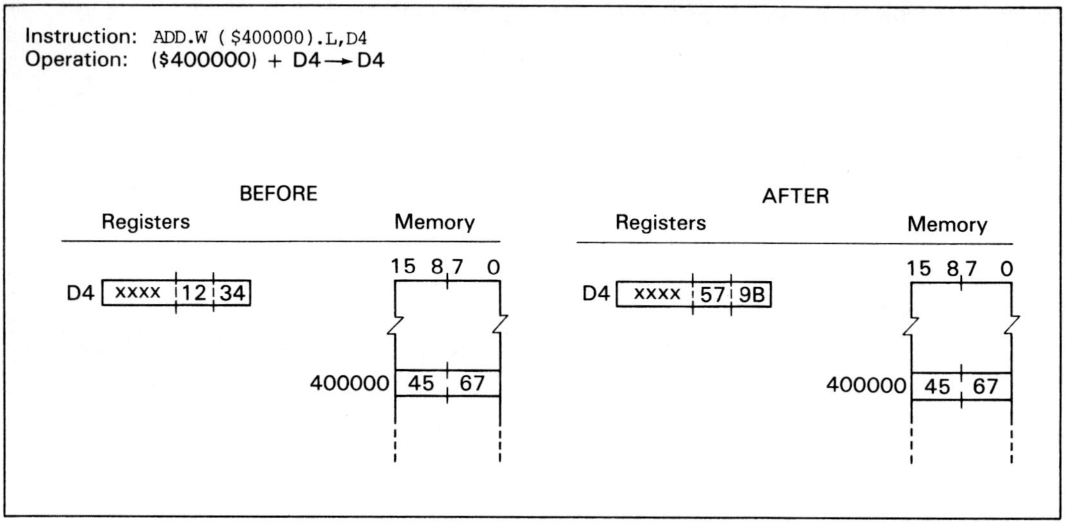

Figure 3-14 Illustration of Absolute Addressing Mode.

where the first statement moves the long-word operand at address COUNT and the second statement moves the *address* of COUNT to D0.

Example 3-9

```
* PROGRAM SECTION
CR       EQU       $0D          Carriage Return

         MOVE.B    #CR,D0       Immediate data = $0D
         .
         .
         .
         MOVE.W    #512,D1      Immediate data = 512 (Decimal)
         .
         .
         .
         MOVEA.L   #XP1+4,A0    Get address of XP2.
         MOVEA.L   #XP2,A0      Same as previous statement
*
* DATA SECTION
XP1      DS.L      1            Pointer XP1 (address).
XP2      DS.L      1            Pointer XP2.
         .
         .
         .
```

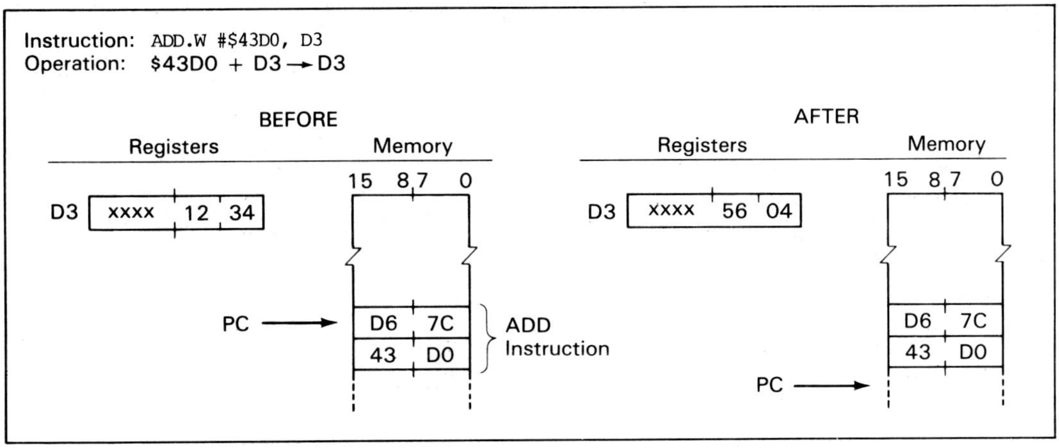

Figure 3-15 Illustration of Immediate Addressing Mode.

3.4.4 Register Indirect Addressing Modes

This addressing category is an expanded form of indexed addressing used by some other microprocessors. The effective address is formed by modifying the contents of an address register. In its simplest mode, the contents of an address register is the effective address as we shall see next.

Address register indirect addressing. In this addressing mode, the operand is located in external memory with address given in an address register. The address register, in this case, is said to be pointing to operand in memory. The EA syntax is

```
(An)
```

where parenthesis signifies the address register indirection, and `n` is the address register number. The parentheses are the equivalent of "the contents of", thus

$$EA = (An)$$

means effective address is given by the contents of A*n*. The clear understanding of distinction between `An` and `(An)` is important. This addressing mode is illustrated in Figure 3-16.

Address register indirect addressing with post-increment. This addressing mode is the same as address register indirect except the selected address register contents is incremented by the operand size of operation as shown in

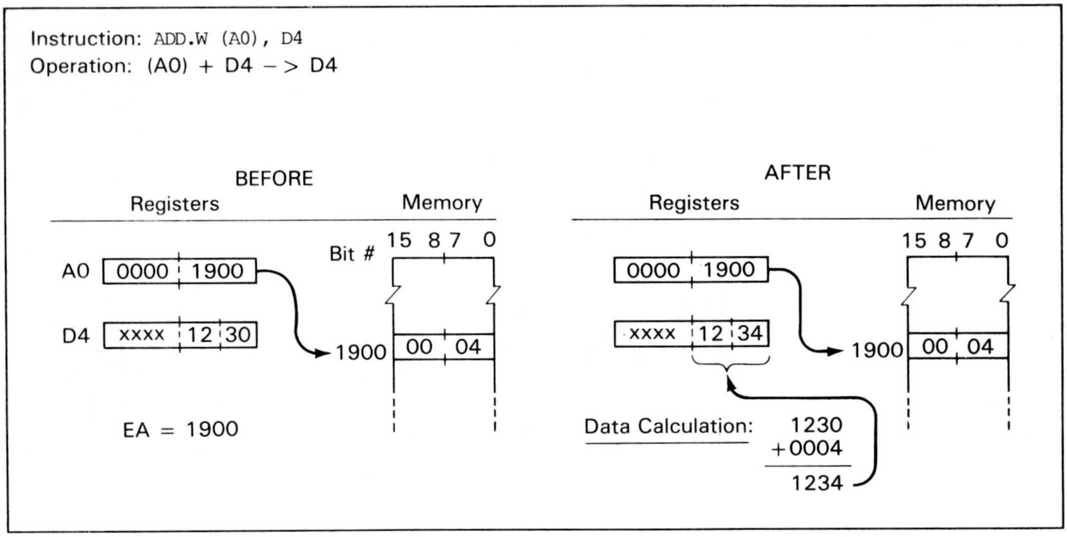

Figuer 3-16 Illustration of Address Register Indirect Addressing.

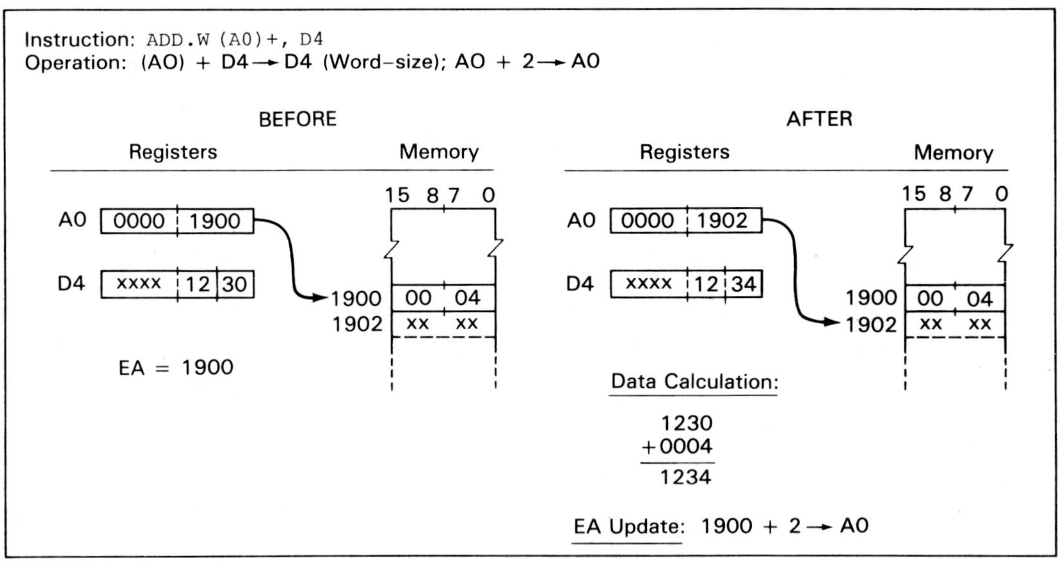

Figure 3-17 Address Register Indirect With Post-increment.

Figure 3-17. The register increment depends on the operand size so that it points to the next possible operand. This addressing mode is useful when working on a block of contiguous data in memory such as a data table or character string.

As shown in Table 3-4, when A7 (USP or SSP) is selected in this addressing mode in conjunction with byte operand, the address register is still incremented by two in order to maintain word alignment for stack operations.

The EA syntax is

```
(An)+
```

where n is the address number as usual, and + indicates post-incrementing.

Address register indirect with pre-decrement. This addressing mode is similar to the previous one except the specified address register is pre-decremented by the operand size before the operand is referenced, as shown in Figure 3-18. Again, if A7 (USP or SSP) is used with byte size, it is decremented by two rather than one to keep the 68000 stack aligned on word boundaries.

The EA syntax is

```
-(An)
```

where - indicates pre-decrement. Therefore, the effective address is given by

$$EA = An - N$$

where N is 1, 2, or 4, depending on selected data size.

Example 3-10

In addition to user- and supervisor-mode stacks, other stack structures can be easily implemented using one of the address registers A0 through A6 with post-increment and pre-decrement addressing modes. For example, to implement a user stack that grows toward higher memory addresses using A5, we need

```
MOVE.W   <operand>,(A5)+     Stack Push
MOVE.W   -(A5),<operand>     Stack Pull
```

where A5 points to the first available empty position on top of the stack. With user-

TABLE 3-4 ADDRESS REGISTER POST-INCREMENT

Operand Size	Address Register (An)	An Update
Byte	A0–A6	$An + 1 \rightarrow An$
Byte	A7 (USP or SSP)	$An + 2 \rightarrow An$
Word	A0–A7	$An + 2 \rightarrow An$
Long-word	A0–A7	$An + 4 \rightarrow An$

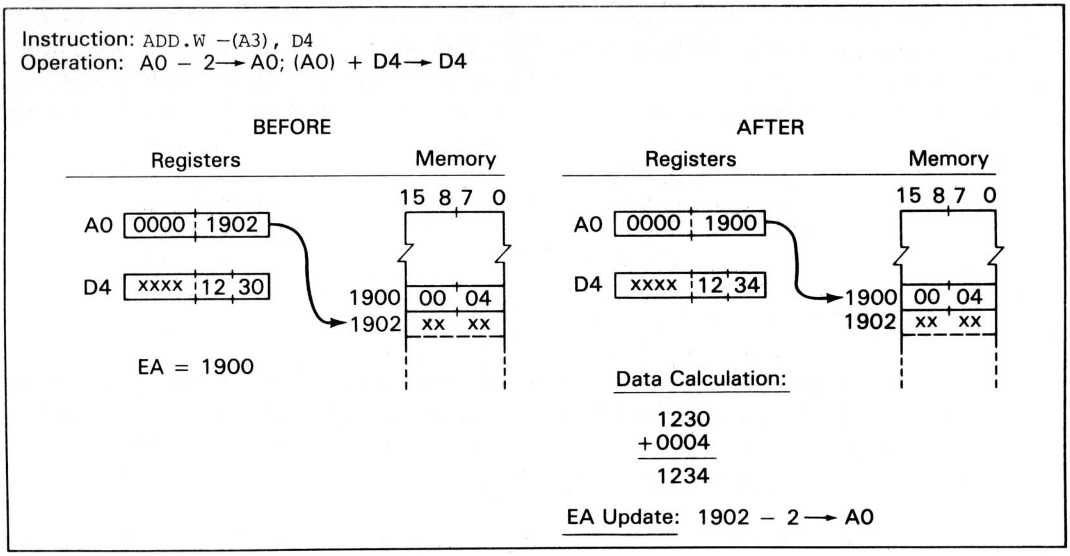

Figure 3-18 Address Register Indirect with Pre-decrement.

defined stocks, care must be exercised so that stack does not get misaligned when dealing with byte data.

Example 3-11

The use of post-increment or pre-decrement register-indirect addressing modes makes implementation of a queue data structure simpler. Whereas stack structure processes the elements of a linear list in last-in/first-out (LIFO) basis, the elements of a queue are processed on a first-in/first-out (FIFO) basis, reminiscent of first-come/first-serve at a service station. The queue structure requires two address registers to point to the beginning and to the end of a list. Insertion of a new element is performed at the rear and elements are dequeued from the front of the list. To implement a queue which grows toward higher memory addresses requires the following:

Queue operation: `MOVE.<s> <operand>,(An)+`
Dequeue operation: `MOVE.<s> (Am)+,<operand>`

For example

```
MOVE.W    D0,(A0)]        Insert new element.
MOVE.W    (A1)],D0        Dequeue an element.
```

where `An` points to the empty position at the front of the queue and `Am` points to the occupied location at the tail of the queue. Alternatively, we can use the pre-decrement addressing mode, making the queue grow toward lower memory addresses. However, this would not be preferable, because pre-decrement takes longer to execute, as we are going to see later. One commonly used approach to queue implementation is the *circular queue* illustrated in Figure 3-19. This technique wraps around addresses as flowcharted in Figure 3-20. There are several schemes to decide when a circular queue is full or empty. One that makes verification simple is given by

Queue empty condition: $Am = An$

Queue full condition: $(Am + \langle s \rangle = An)$ OR

$(Am = \text{QEND})$ AND $(An = \text{QBEGIN})$

where $\langle s \rangle$ is the size of an element in bytes.

Address register indirect with displacement. The effective address in this mode is the sum of the address in an address register and a 16-bit signed displacement value. Since the contents of the address register is 32-bits wide, it is necessary to sign-extend the displacement value before summation. In other words, the effective address is

$$\text{EA} = (An) + \text{d16}_{32}$$

where d16 is 16-bit displacement value and $\langle\ \rangle_{32}$ indicates sign-extension to 32 bits. Therefore, this addressing mode gives a ∓32 Kbytes of possible offset from the address pointed by A*n*. The assembly syntax of EA is

```
d16(An)
```

or

```
(d16,An)
```

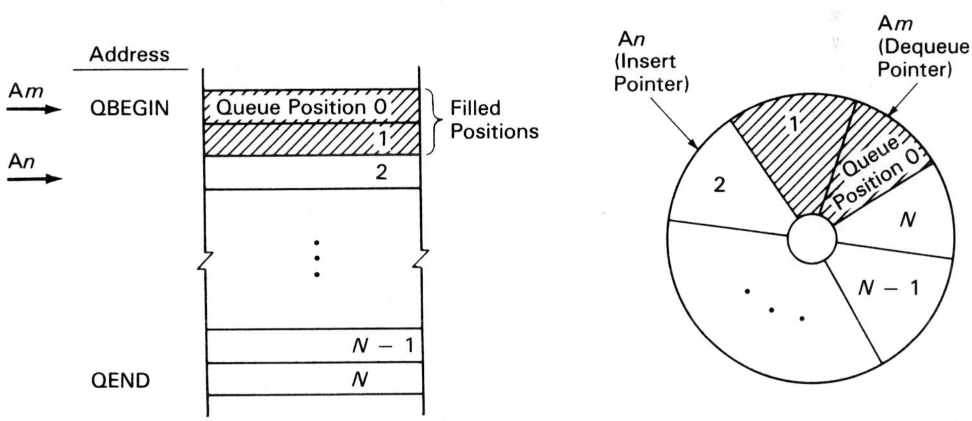

(a) Memory Organization. (b) Logical Organization.

Figure 3-19 Circular Queue.

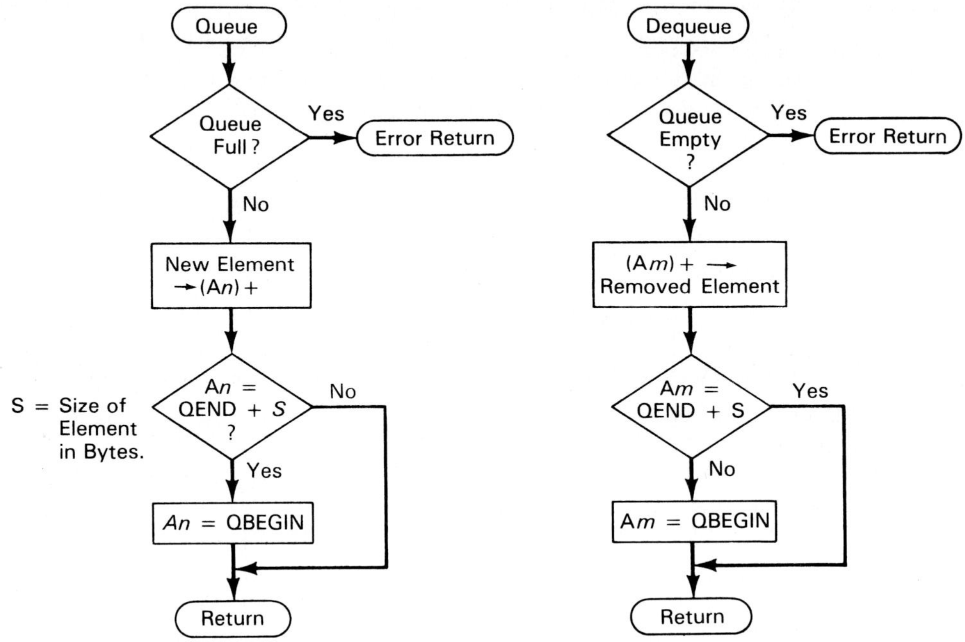

Figure 3-20 Flowchart of Queue and Dequeue Operations.

The displacement d16 is a constant since it is part of the instruction. It can be a simple constant or an expression evaluated at assembly time. For example, the instruction

```
ADD.W    -16(A2),D1
```

adds the contents of the address specified by register A2 minus 16_{10} to the contents of D1 as illustrated in Figure 3-21. The main application of this addressing mode is to reference a particular element of an array or list as the next two examples will illustrate.

Example 3-12

Suppose we want to reference a moving window of elements of one-dimensional array of elements, as the window moves from the beginning to the end of the array. This is useful in implementing moving average or digital filtering algorithms. Let our window size be five elements, and that each element has word-size. Figure 3-22 illustrates how we can reference the elements of the window, where A*m* points to the first element of current window position. As A*m* is incremented, the window moves as required.

Example 3-13

Let a record consist of three fields as shown in Figure 3-23. We can point to the base of the record with an address register, and then use a displacement to refer to

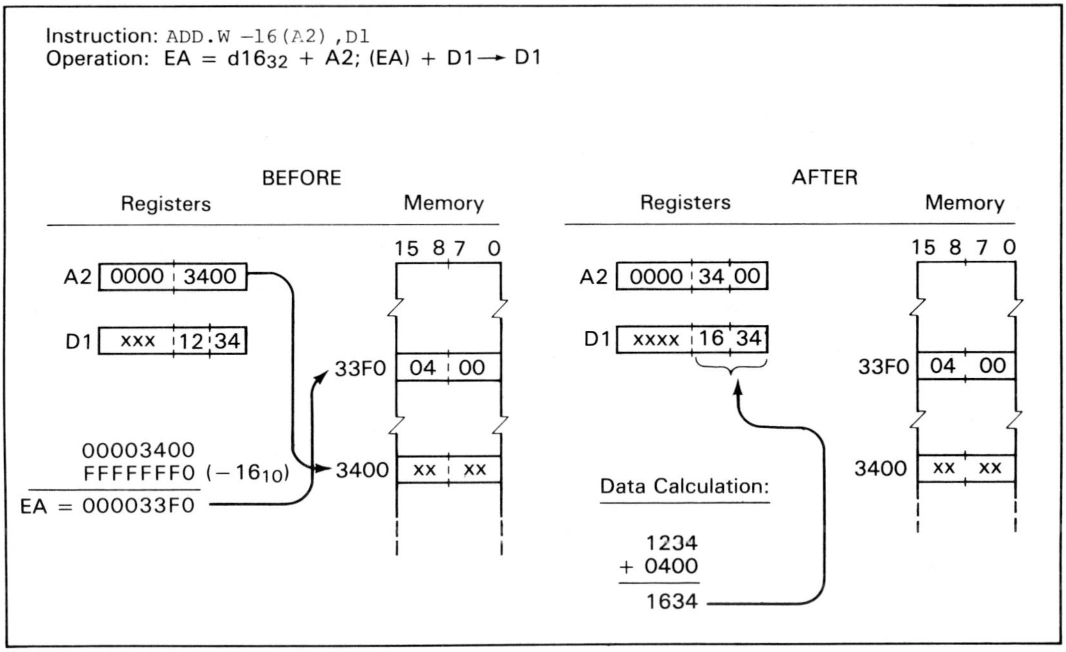

Figure 3-21 Address Register Indirect with Displacement.

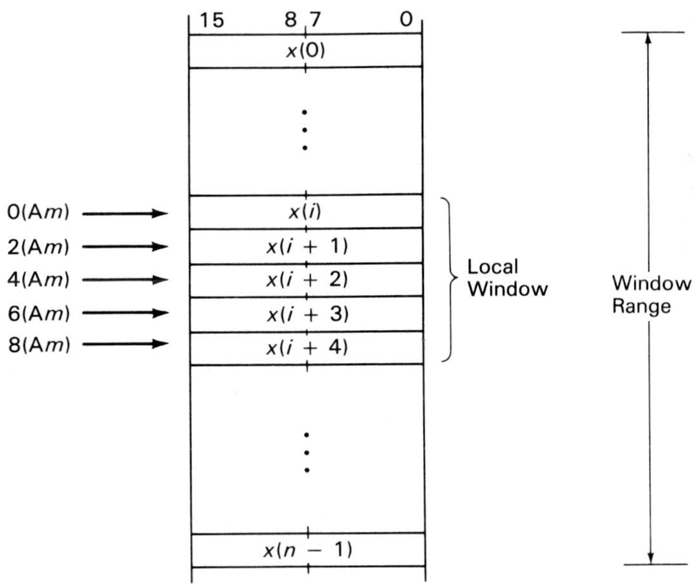

Figure 3-22 Referencing a Local Window of an Array.

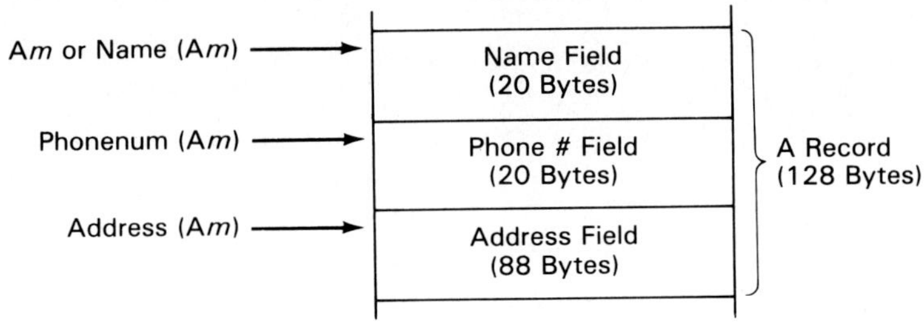

Figure 3-23 Referencing Fields of a Record.

a particular field of that record. Defining offsets with a EQU or SET directive makes the program more readable. For this example, we need:

```
NAME        EQU    0
PHONENUM    EQU    20
ADDRESS     EQU    PHONENUM+20
```

Address register indirect with index. In this addressing mode, EA is calculated as the sum of a base address in an address register, a displacement value, and the contents of an index register such as

$$EA = (An) + (Xm) + d8_{32}$$

where

- A*n*: Base address in one of the address registers (A0-A7),
- X*m*: An address or a data register where either low-word or entire register can be used as index value.
- $d8_{32}$: 8-bit signed displacement value that is sign-extended to 32 bits.

The assembly syntax of EA is given by

```
d8(An,Xm.W)
```

or

```
(d8,An,Xm.W)
```

for word-size index, and

```
d8(An,Xm.L)
```

or

```
(d8,An,Xm.L)
```

for long-word size index. When index size is not specified, it defaults to word size. Figure 3-24 illustrates this addressing mode.

This addressing mode is very useful for accessing elements of an array, since it combines an index register as well as a constant displacement. To address an one-dimensional array, we would have A*n* pointing to the beginning of array, and X*m* would contain the offset. For example, to reference `X(i)`, where elements of `X(i)` has long-word size, we could write the following statements:

```
*         D0[15:0] contains index i.
*         A0 points to the beginning of X.
*
          LSL.W      #2,D0              Offset= 4 * index.
          MOVE.L      0(A0,D0.W),D1     X(i) → D1.
          .
          .
          .
```

A data register is usually used as index because it could be manipulated, such as shifting left by two.

Graphics, image processing, and scientific applications often require manipulating two-dimensional (2-D) arrays. A 2-D array of size $M \times N$ is usually

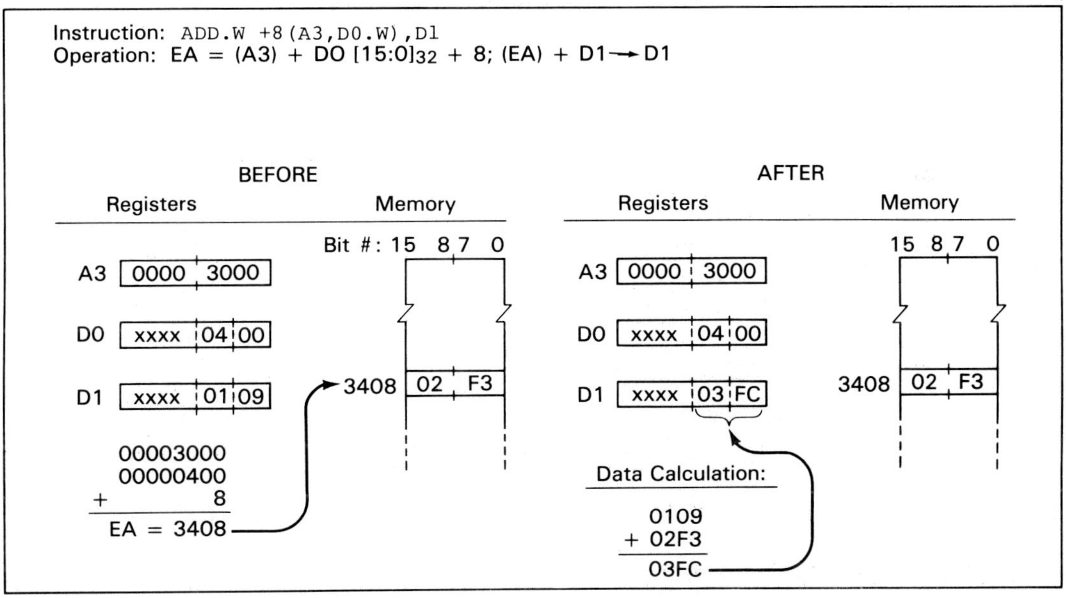

Figure 3-24 Address Register Indirect with Index.

stored in row-sequential format given by

```
X(0,0), X(0,1), X(0,2),...,X(0,M-1)
X(1,0), X(1,1), X(1,2),...,X(1,M-1)
X(2,0), X(1,1), X(1,2),...,X(1,M-1)
.
.
.
X(N-1,0), X(N-1,1), X(N-1,2),...,X(N-1,M-1)
```

Then, to access element X(*i* , *j*), the effective address is

$$EA = \text{Base Address} + i * M * \text{size} + j * \text{size}$$

where size is the size of element X(*i* , *j*) in bytes. We would use the constant displacement as the base address, use A*n* to point to a row and the index X*m* to have the offset value within a row. But, since displacement is limited to 8 bits, this is not possible[2]. Instead we have to use A*n* to point to the base address of the array, use zero as displacement, and a data register that contains the offset in bytes from the base address. This address calculation might be too time-consuming for some applications. An alternative approach is to store an array of *N* pointers, containing the beginning address of each row, as illustrated in Figure 3-25. If A*n* has the base address of pointer array *xp*, then to access element X(*i* , *j*), we could write the following statements:

```
*       Initially, assume the following register contents:
*       D0[15:0] has index i.
*       D1[15:0] has index j.
*       A0 → xp(0)
*       Size of X(i,j) is word.
*
        LSL.W     #2,D0
        MOVE.L    0(A0,D0.W),A1      A1= Row-i address.
        LSL.W     #1,D1              Offset to element-j.
        ADDA.L    D1,A1              A1 = Address of X(i,j).
```

Perhaps the most suited application of this addressing mode is in accessing an array of records. Register A*n* can point to the base of the array, D*m* will have the offset value of *k*th record, and the displacement value d8 will contain the constant offset to a particular field of a record, as illustrated in Figure 3-26. For

[2] We will later see that 68020 relieves this restriction.

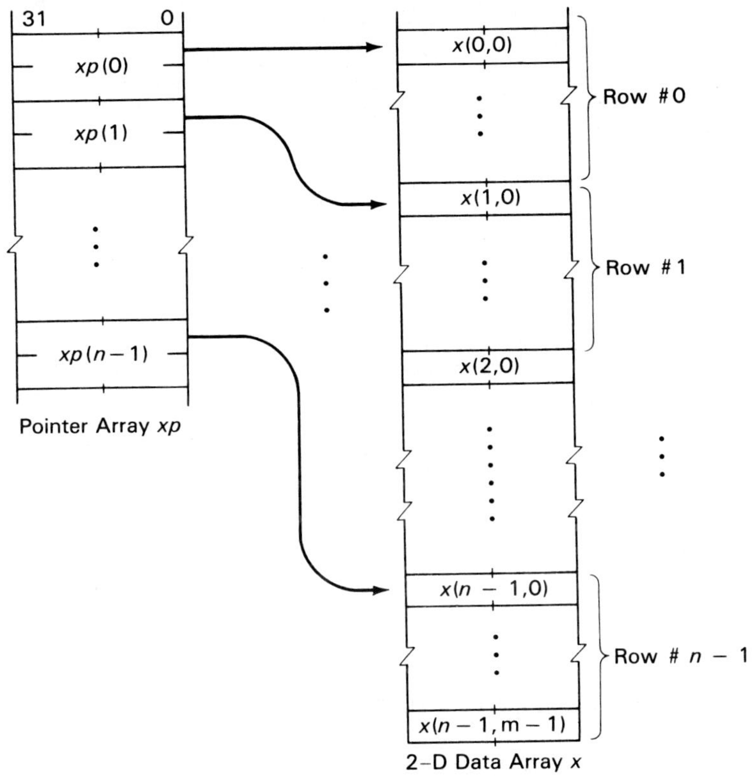

Figure 3-25 Accessing a 2-D Array with an Array of Pointers.

example, if each record occupies 128 bytes, as given in an earlier example, the effective address of a field can be calculated simply by

```
*       D0[15:0] = Record index i.
*       A0 = Base address of array.
*
        LSL.W   #7,D0                  D0 = Offset to record-i.
        MOVE.B PHONENUM(A0,D0.W),D1    D1 = First byte of phone
*                                           number field.
            .
            .
```

In summary, the shortcomings of this powerful addressing mode are the limited size of displacement d8, and the lack of an automatic scaling factor for index register X*m*.

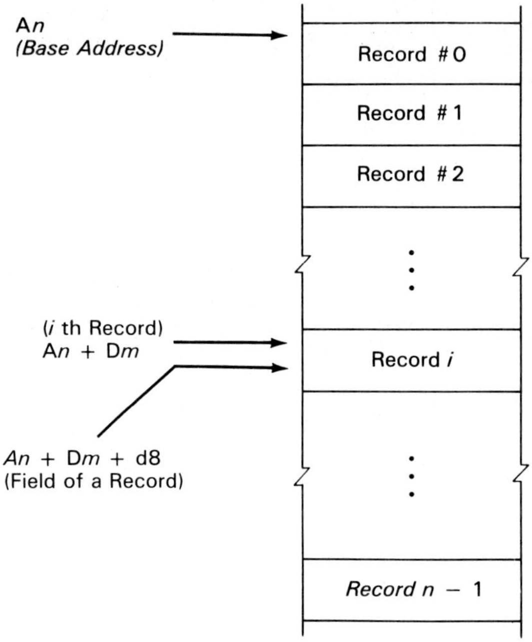

Figure 3-26 Accessing an Array of Records.

3.4.5 Program Counter Relative Modes

It is sometimes desirable to have a program code that can be placed anywhere in the memory map. By making memory references relative to the program counter, we can have a program that can be loaded or mapped at any available memory locations without any changes, and even relocate during its execution. This is referred to as *position-independent code*. For example, to reference a program variable we can use absolute addressing, such as $40000 as we saw earlier. Or, alternatively, we can give the relative position of the operand with respect to the instruction that is referencing it, for example, +2000 bytes from current PC. Of course, control and status registers of a particular system still have to be addressed using absolute addressing.

The position-independent code should not be confused with relocatable code. The first can be moved any time, even during its execution. The later, once loaded must stay in the same position, since its addresses are modified as required at link or load time.

The motivations behind position-independent code include the following:

1. It requires no modification of relative addresses during linking with other program modules, or at load time.
2. Such a program can be loaded in ROM memory, and used at different address locations in different configurations of a product or different products.

3. It is sometimes required to have multiple copies of a program, such as an editor, available to many users simultaneously. It is not known a priori where a program will be loaded.

The PC-relative addressing modes are used mainly for program jumps, and to read constant operands embedded within a program. This is due to the 68000 architecture which restricts this addressing category to read access of an operand only. This is basically to prevent programmers from writing self-modifying code (an undesirable practice) and encouraging the separation of program and data areas. This restriction also protects a program from inadvertently changing itself.

For example, suppose we have the following assembly statements:

```
              SECTION    0
*          PROGRAM SECTION
*
              .
              .
              MOVE.W     TABLE+4,D0
              .
              .
              JMP        CASE2
              .
              .
TABLE         DC.W       $4718,$3486,$AF04,$0099
              .
              .
CASE2         .
              .
```

where the addressing of `TABLE+4` and `CASE2` will be using a program-counter relative with displacement since they are preceded by the `SECTION` directive.

Program counter with displacement. This addressing mode is very similar to address-indirect with displacement except that PC is used as the base address, such as the address of the operand is given with respect to the PC value with a 16-bit signed displacement.

The EA syntax is

```
d16(PC)
```

or

```
(d16,PC)
```

The EA is calculated as

$$EA = (PC_{d16}) + d16_{32}$$

where PC_{d16}: The PC value used is the second word of the instruction which is the address of the constant d16,

$d16_{32}$: Is the 16-bit signed displacement which is sign-extended to 32 bits,

as illustrated in Figure 3-27.

Program counter with index. This addressing mode is very similar to its address-indirect with index counterpart. The effective address of operand is specified relative to PC value as

$$EA = (PC) + (Xn)_{32} + d8_{32}$$

where PC: The PC value used is the address of instruction plus two.

Xn: Is an address or data register used as index register with word or long-word size. The index value is sign-extended to 32 bits before addition.

d8: Is the 8-bit signed displacement value which is sign-extended to 32 bits before addition.

The assembly syntax of EA is given by

```
d8(PC,Xn.W)
```

or

```
(d8,PC,Xn.W)
```

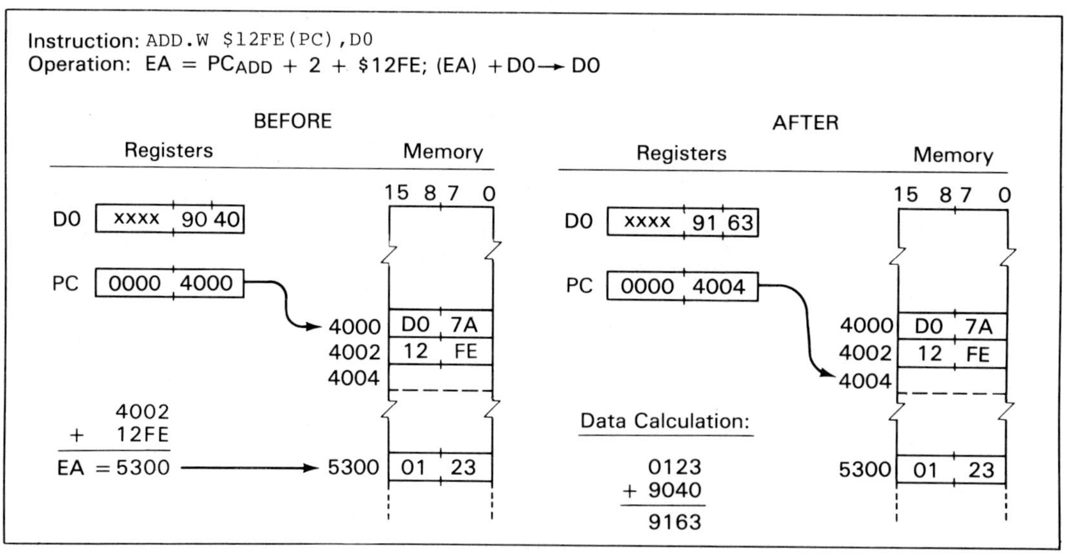

Figure 3-27 Program Counter Relative with Displacement.

for word-size index, and

```
d8(PC,Xn.L)
```

or

```
(d8,PC,Xn.L)
```

for long-word size index. Figure 3-28 illustrates this addressing mode. When the index size is not specified, it defaults to word size.

Addressing mode summary. Table 3-5 summarizes the addressing modes of the 68000. Based on their functionality, we can also categorize the addressing modes in terms of four addressing groups:

- Data — If the addressing mode can be used to refer to data operands, it is considered a data addressing mode. This group includes all except address-register direct.
- Memory — If the addressing mode can be used to refer to an operand in memory, it is considered a memory addressing mode. This group includes all except A*n* and D*n*, the register-direct addressing modes.
- Alterable — If the addressing mode can be used to refer to an alterable (i.e., writable) operand, it is considered an alterable addressing mode. This group includes all except PC-relative addressing modes.

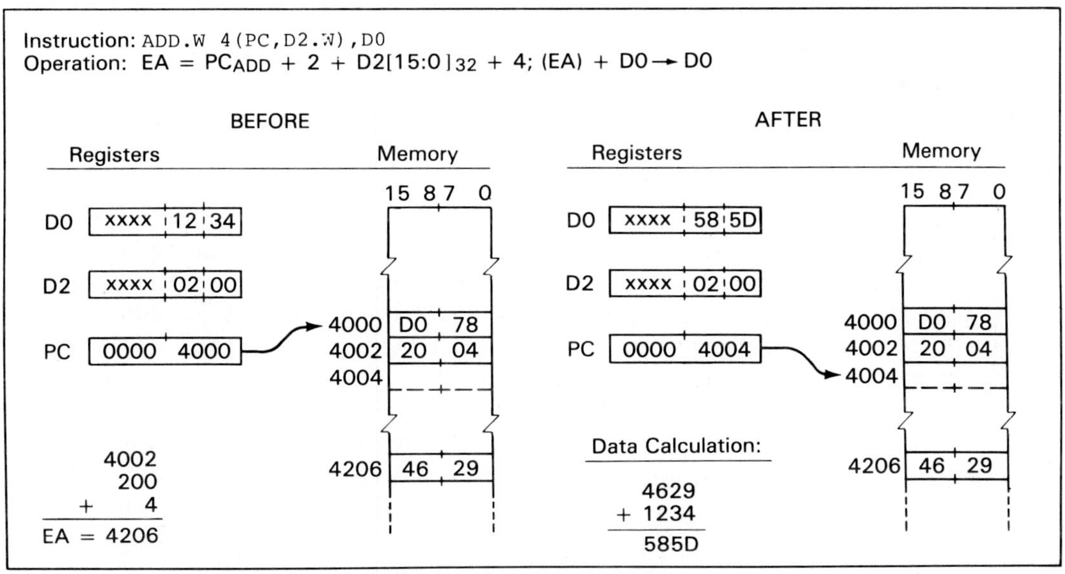

Figure 3-28 Program Counter Relative with Index.

TABLE 3-5 SUMMARY OF ADDRESSING MODES

Addressing Category/Mode	EA Syntax	EA Calculation; Operation
Register Direct Addressing		
Data Register Direct	Dn	EA = Dn
Address Register Direct	An	EA = An
Absolute Data Addressing[1]		(EA is part of instruction)
Absolute Short	(<label>)	(EA is one word)
Absolute Long	<label>	(EA is two words)
Immediate Data Addressing	#<value>	Operand part of instruction
Register Indirect Addressing		
Register Indirect	(An)	EA = (An)
Postincrement Register Indirect	(An)+	EA = (An); An + size → An
Predecrement Register Indirect	-(An)	An - size → An; EA = (An)
Register Indirect With Offset	d16(An) (d16,An)	EA = (An) + $d16_{32}$
Indexed Register Indirect with Offset[2]	d16(An,Xm.S) or (d16,An,Xm.S)	EA = (An) + $d16_{32}$ + Xn_{32}
Program Counter Relative Addressing		
Relative With Offset	d16(PC) (d16,PC)	EA = (PC) + $d16_{32}$
Relative With Index and Offset[2]	d16(PC,Xm.S) or (d16,PC,Xm.S)	EA = (PC) + $d16_{32}$ + Xm_{32}

[1] Gives the most commonly used syntax. For other variations refer to text.

[2] Two possible assembly syntaxes given; S is size of index ("W" or "L").

Control — If an addressing mode can be used to refer to a memory operand without an associated size, it is considered a control addressing mode. This group is a subset of memory addressing group, and is used by program flow control instructions to specify relative branch or jump address.

What is the use for the above-grouping of addressing modes? We will use these addressing groups to specify the allowed addressing modes of an instruction without having to list each one. Some instructions use a more restrictive combination of these addressing groups. For example, alterable-memory addressing modes refers to addressing modes that are both alterable and memory addresses.

The above classification does not indicate whether a memory reference is for program or for data. The program references are used to read instructions from program memory, and data references are used for reading or writing data operands in memory. For example, the *jump* (JMP) *instruction* can use the address-register indirect mode to specify the jump address. On the other hand, the same addressing mode can be used to read or write a memory operand. As we discussed in Chapter 1, during any bus cycle, the 68000 indicates the reference classification (program or data) and processor status (supervisor, user, or interrupt acknowledge).

Table 3-6 summarizes the addressing modes including addressing groups and reference classification.

3.5 INSTRUCTION SET

Most 68000 instructions can operate on more than one data size, in which case the operand size need to be specified or a default size of word is assumed. The data-size selection is made by appending the instruction mnemonic with a period followed by B (byte), W (word), or L (long-word) which we illustrated earlier. The data-size code is not permitted, however, for some instructions that can work with only one data size. It is a good practice to specify data size explicitly, when possible, to make a program more readable and easier to debug.

As noted earlier, the 68000 instruction set has one, two, or no-operand instructions. An operand is specified by its effective address as shown in Table 3-7. We have discussed the assembly syntax of different effective-address modes in the previous section.

The majority of the 68000 instructions require two operands where the first

TABLE 3-6 ADDRESSING MODES GROUPING AND CLASSIFICATION

Addressing Category/mode	Address Grouping[1] D	M	C	A	Address Space
Register Direct Addressing					
Data Register Direct	x	-	-	x	-
Address Register Direct	-	-	-	x	-
Absolute Data Addressing[1]					
Absolute Short	x	x	x	x	Data (Prog.[2])
Absolute Long	x	x	x	x	Data (Prog.[2])
Immediate Data Addressing	x	x	-	-	Program
Register Indirect Addressing					
Register Indirect	x	x	x	x	Data (Prog.[2])
Postincrement Register Indirect	x	x	-	x	Data
Predecrement Register Indirect	x	x	-	x	Data
Register Indirect With Offset	x	x	-	x	Data (Prog.[2])
Indexed Register Indirect with Offset	x	x	x	x	Data (Prog.[2])
Program Counter Relative Addressing					
Relative With Offset	x	x	x	-	Program
Relative With Index and Offset[2]	x	x	x	-	Program

[1] D (Data), M (Memory), C (Control), A (Alterable).

[2] For JMP and JSR instructions, it is classified as program reference.

TABLE 3-7 ASSEMBLY FORMAT OF INSTRUCTIONS

(Explicit) Operand(s)	Assembly Format[1]	Example
None	OPR	RTS
Single[2,3]	OPR <EA$_{DEST}$>	JMP 2(A0)
Double[2,4]	OPR <EA$_{SRC}$>,<EA$_{DEST}$>	SUB.W $200(A1),D1

[1] OPR is any valid instruction name plus data-size code, if any.

[2] ⟨EA$_{SRC}$⟩: effective address of source-operand.
⟨EA$_{DEST}$⟩: effective address of destination-operand.

[3] Also called single-address instruction.

[4] Also called double-address instruction.

operand is called the *source-operand* and second operand is called the *destination-operand*. The contents of the source operand is never modified by any of the two-operand instructions. The destination operand, the other hand, is where the resultant value is stored, if any, overwriting the operand value. Not all instructions affect the destination-operand contents. For example, the compare instruction (CMP) compares the source and destination operands and sets the condition codes of CCR accordingly, i.e. the destination operand is not affected.

It is important to note that the order of double-operand operation is given by

$$\langle d\text{-}operand\rangle \left\{ \begin{array}{c} - \\ * \\ / \\ \leftarrow \\ \leftrightarrow \\ \vdots \\ \langle etc.\rangle \end{array} \right\} \langle s\text{-}operand\rangle$$

where

d-operand: Destination-operand
s-operand: Source-operand
+: Binary addition
-: Subtract or Compare operation
*: Multiply operation
/: Divide operation
←: Move operation
↔: Exchange operation.

For example, `MOVE.W  D0,D1` moves D0 to D1. This order of operation is consistent among the 68000 instructions[3] and are important to remember for op-

[3] The System V/68 assembler of Motorola is different than the usual convention, in that the opposite of above order is used for CMP instruction. This is to follow the convention of the Unix operating system.

erations such as subtract or divide that are not symmetrical. For example, the subtract instruction given by

```
SUB.<s> <EA_SRC>,<EA_DEST>
```

performs the operation

$$\langle\text{d-operand}\rangle - \langle\text{s-operand}\rangle \rightarrow \langle\text{d-operand}\rangle.$$

Similarly, the compare instruction given by

```
CMP.<s> <EA_SRC>,<EA_DEST>
```

performs the operation

$$\langle\text{d-operand}\rangle - \langle\text{s-operand}\rangle$$

where the result of comparison is given by the condition codes of CCR.

In Table 3-7, we saw the assembly instruction formats where an operand is explicitly referenced. Some instructions, however, also make an implicit reference to certain 68000 registers and/or the system stack for the operand(s). For example, the *return from subroutine* (RTS) instruction, which has no explicit operands, but references the active stack pointer (USP or SSP) to fetch subroutine return address stored on the stack. Only two 68000 instructions have no explicit or implicit operands, namely RESET and NOP (*no operation*). RESET is used to reset peripheral device controllers. Otherwise, the effect of these two instructions is to simply increment the PC register by two.

Certain 68000 instructions allow variations in their basic instruction types, as shown in Table 3-8. Some of these variations are recognized by a single letter appended to the instruction mnemonic. The variations A, Q, I, and X are used by more than one instruction consistently, and are described below:

A (Address): Specifies manipulation of an address value. This variation requires the destination operand to be an address register. Remember two important points about address manipulations: First, data-sizes are limited to word and long-word; second, the address manipulations do not affect condition codes.

Q (Quick): This variation is referred to as quick and requires an immediate operand in a certain small size range, whereby it can be contained as part of the instruction's operation word. Therefore, this variation executes faster than the general format which uses one or two extension words appended to the operation word to specify the immediate operand.

TABLE 3-8 VARIATIONS OF INSTRUCTION TYPES

Instruction Type	Variation	Description
ADD	ADD	Add
	ADDA	Add Address
	ADDQ	Add Quick
	ADDI	Add Immediate
	ADDX	Add Extended
AND	AND	Logical AND
	ANDI	AND Immediate
	ANDI to CCR	AND Immediate to CCR
	ANDI to SR	AND Immediate to SR
CMP	CMP	Compare
	CMPA	Compare Address
	CMPI	Compare Immediate
	CMPM	Compare Memory
EOR	EOR	Exclusive OR
	EORI	Exclusive OR Immediate
	EORI to CCR	EOR Immediate to CCR
	EORI to SR	EOR Immediate to SR
MOVE	MOVE	Move
	MOVEA	Move Address
	MOVEQ	Move Quick
	MOVEM	Move Multiple Registers
	MOVEP	Move Peripheral Data
	MOVE from SR	Move from SR Register
	MOVE to SR	Move to SR Register
	MOVE from CCR	Move from CCR Register
	MOVE to CCR	Move to CCR Register
	MOVE USP	Move User Stack Pointer
NEG	NEG	Negate
	NEGX	Negate with Extend
OR	OR	Logical OR
	ORI	Logical OR Immediate
	ORI to CCR	OR Immediate to CCR
	ORI to SR	OR Immediate to SR
SUB	SUB	Subtract
	SUBA	Subtract Address
	SUBI	Subtract Immediate
	SUBQ	Subtract Quick
	SUBX	Subtract with Extend

I (Immediate): This variation indicates that the source-operand is given by an immediate value within the operation size specified.

X (Extended): This variation is used for arithmetic operations requiring greater than 32-bits precision. Instructions with this variation uses the X-bit of CCR to implement extended precision as we will discuss later.

The 68000 instruction code (i.e., the object code) in program memory is at least one word and up to five words in length as shown in Figure 3-29. The first word of the instruction, called the *operation word*, specifies the operation to be performed, operands, and mode selection, if any. The operand specification is done as part of the operation word and, where necessary, extension words further specify the instruction and operands. The addressing modes that require one or two extension words are listed in Table 3-9. The instructions that can use a group of addressing modes to specify an operand use the general effective-address specification. This 6-bit EA field consists of a 3-bit address-mode and a 3-bit register definition as given in Table 3-10.

Example 3-14

The instruction coding of the MOVE instruction is shown in Figure 3-30. The following illustrates the coding of various addressing modes and operand sizes.

TABLE 3-9 LIST OF ADDRESSING MODES THAT REQUIRE EXTENSION WORD(S)

Addressing Category/Mode	Extension Word(s)
Absolute Data Addressing Absolute Short Absolute Long	 One word containing 16-bit address Two words containing 32-bit address
Immediate Data Addressing	One or two words of immediate value.
Register Indirect Addressing Register Indirect With Offset Indexed Register Indirect with Offset	 One word containing displacement value. One word extension with format: 15: D/A; 14–12: Reg. #; 11: W/L; 10 9 8: 0 0 0; 7–0: Displacement D/A = 0 (Data Register Index) = 1 (Address Register Index) Reg. # = Register Number (0–7) W/L = 0 for word-size Index = 1 for long-word size Index.
Program Counter Relative Addressing Relative With Offset Relative With Index and Offset	 One word containing displacement value. Same as indexed register-indirect with offset.

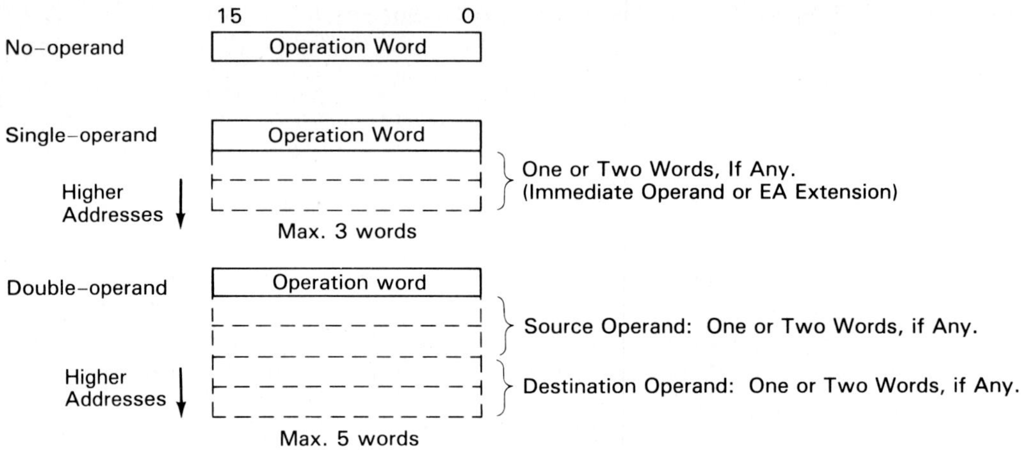

Figure 3-29 Object Code Format of Instructions.

Instruction	Object Code
MOVE.B D1,(A1)	12 81
MOVE.B (A0)+,D0	10 18
MOVEA.L -6(A5),A0	20 6D
	FF FA
MOVE.B CTL_REG,D6	1C 39 (CTL_REG= $F00004)
	00 F0
	00 04
MOVE.W D1,-(SP)	3F 01
MOVE.W #800-1,D1	32 3C
	03 1F

To get a better perspective of the 68000 instruction set, we can classify instructions based on the operation type, resulting in the following categories:

1. Data and Address Movement Instructions;
2. Integer Arithmetic Instructions;
3. Program Control Instructions;
4. Logical Operation Instructions;
5. Shift and Rotate Instructions;
6. Bit Manipulation Instructions;
7. BCD Arithmetic Instructions;
8. System Control Instructions; and
9. Multiprocessor Instructions.

TABLE 3-10 EFFECTIVE-ADDRESS ENCODING

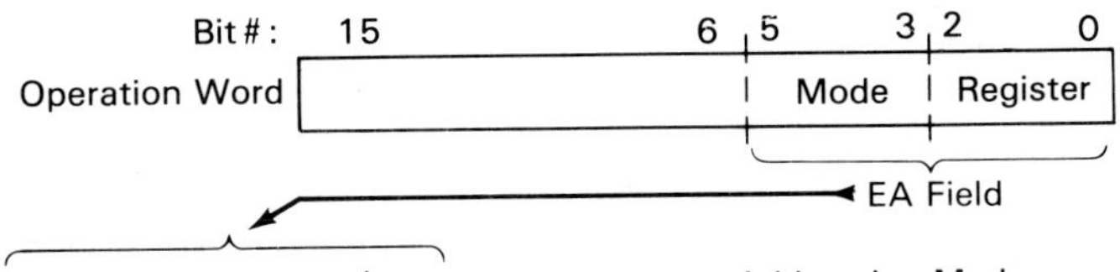

Mode	Register[1]	Addressing Mode
000	Register Number	Data Register Direct
001	Register Number	Address Register Direct
010	Register Number	Address Register Indirect
011	Register Number	Address Register Indirect With Postincrement
100	Register Number	Address Register Indirect With Predecrement
101	Register Number	Address Register Indirect With Displacement
110	Register Number	Address Register Indirect With Index
111	000	Absolute Short
111	001	Absolute Long
111	010	Program Counter With Displacement
111	011	Program Counter With Index
111	100	Immediate

Next, we will discuss each of these instruction groups. The reader should refer to the 68000 programmer's manual[4] for detailed description of an instruction. Figure 3-31 illustrates the format used in programmer's manual for the ADD instruction. Note that the assembler syntax does not indicate whether an operand-size specification (B, W, or L) is necessary explicitly, as we have been doing. We would write the following instead:

Assembly Syntax:

```
ADD.<s>   <ea>,Dn
ADD.<s>   Dn,<amea>
```

The allowed sizes are given by the attributes. If there is only one attribute, then no size specification needs to be appended (for example, the BTST instruction).

3.5.1 Data and Address Movement Instructions

The basic means of address and data transfer is accomplished by a group of instructions given in this group as shown in Table 3-11. These instructions allow transfers of byte, word, and long-word operands from memory to memory, memory to register, register to memory, and register to register. The address transfers are limited to word and long-word sizes to be consistent with the programming model of the 68000. Let us take a closer look at these movement operations.

Based on instruction-frequency statistics, one in every five assembly instructions is, on the average, an operand transfer instruction. Therefore, the

[4] Appendix B, 68000 Programmer's Reference Manual, Fifth Ed., Rev. 6.

Instruction Format:

15	14	13	12	11	10	9	8	7	6	5	4	3	2	1	0
0	0	SIZE		DESTINATION						SOURCE					
				REGISTER			MODE			MODE			REGISTER		

Instruction Fields:

Size field — Specifies the size of the operand to be moved:
- 01 — Byte operation
- 11 — Word operation
- 10 — Long operation

Destination Effective Address field — Specifies the destination location. Only data alterable addressing modes are allowed as shown:

Addressing Mode	Mode	Register
Dn	000	reg. number:Dn
An	—	—
(An)	010	reg. number:An
(An) +	011	reg. number:An
− (An)	100	reg. number:An
(d_{16},An)	101	reg. number:An
(d_8,An,Xn)	110	reg. number:An

Addressing Mode	Mode	Register
(xxx).W	111	000
(xxx).L	111	001
#⟨data⟩	—	—
(d_{16},PC)	—	—
(d_8,PC,Xn)	—	—

Source Effective Address field — Specifies the source operand. All addressing modes are allowed as shown:

Addressing Mode	Mode	Register
Dn	000	reg. number:Dn
An*	001	reg. number:An
(An)	010	reg. number:An
(An)+	011	reg. number:An
−(An)	100	reg. number:An
(d_{16},An)	101	reg. number:An
(d_8,An,Xn)	110	reg. number:An

Addressing Mode	Mode	Register
(xxx).W	111	000
(xxx).L	111	001
#⟨data⟩	111	100
(d_{16},PC)	111	010
(d_8,PC,Xn)	111	011

*For byte size operation, address register direct is not allowed.

Notes:

1. Most assemblers use MOVEA when the destination is an address register.
2. MOVEQ can be used to move an immediate 8-bit value to a data register.

Figure 3-30 Instruction Coding of MOVE Instruction.

ADD — Add — ADD

Operation: Source + Destination ➧ Destination

Assembler Syntax:
ADD ⟨ea⟩,Dn
ADD Dn,⟨ea⟩

Attributes: Size = (Byte, Word, Long)

Description: Adds the source operand to the destination operand using binary addition, and stores the result in the destination location. The size of the operation may be specified as byte, word, or long. The mode of the instruction indicates which operand is the source and which is the destination as well as the operand size.

Condition Codes:

X	N	Z	V	C
*	*	*	*	*

X Set the same as the carry bit.
N Set if the result is negative. Cleared otherwise.
Z Set if the result is zero. Cleared otherwise.
V Set if an overflow is generated. Cleared otherwise.
C Set if a carry is generated. Cleared otherwise.

Instruction Format:

15	14	13	12	11	10	9	8	7	6	5	4	3	2	1	0
1	1	0	1	REGISTER			OP-MODE			EFFECTIVE ADDRESS					
										MODE			REGISTER		

Instruction Fields:

Register field — Specifies any of the eight data registers.

Op-Mode field —

Byte	Word	Long	Operation
000	001	010	⟨ea⟩+⟨Dn⟩ → ⟨n⟩
100	101	110	⟨Dn⟩+⟨ea⟩ → ⟨ea⟩

Effective Address Field — Determines addressing mode:

a. If the location specified is a source operand, all addressing modes are allowed as shown:

Addressing Mode	Mode	Register
Dn	000	reg. number:Dn
An*	001	reg. number:An
(An)	010	reg. number:An
(An)+	011	reg. number:An
−(An)	100	reg. number:An
(d_{16},An)	101	reg. number:An
(d_8,An,Xn)	110	reg. number:An

Addressing Mode	Mode	Register
(xxx).W	111	000
(xxx).L	111	001
#⟨data⟩	111	100
(d_{16},PC)	111	010
(d_8,PC,Xn)	111	011

*Word and Long only.

Figure 3-31 ADD Instruction as Shown in the Programmer's Manual.

b. If the location specified is a destination operand, only memory alterable addressing modes are allowed as shown:

Addressing Mode	Mode	Register
Dn	—	—
An	—	—
(An)	010	reg. number:An
(An)+	011	reg. number:An
−(An)	100	reg. number:An
(d_{16},An)	101	reg. number:An
(d_8,An,Xn)	110	reg. number:An

Addressing Mode	Mode	Register
(xxx).W	111	000
(xxx).L	111	001
#⟨data⟩	—	—
(d_{16},PC)	—	—
(d_8,PC,Xn)	—	—

Notes:

1. The Dn mode is used when the destination is a data register; the destination ⟨ea⟩ mode is invalid for a data register.
2. ADDA is used when the destination is an address register. ADDI and ADDQ are used when the source is immediate data. Most assemblers automatically make this distinction.

Figure 3-31 *Continued*

TABLE 3-11 DATA AND ADDRESS MOVEMENT INSTRUCTIONS

Instruction	Syntax	Size	Operation
EXG	`EXG Rn,Rm`	(L)	Rn ↔ Rm
LEA	`LEA <cea>,An`	(L)	⟨cea⟩ → An
LINK	`LINK An,#<d16>`	-	SP-4 → SP; An → (SP); SP → An; SP + d16 → SP
MOVE MOVEA	`MOVE.<s> <ea>,<daea>` `MOVEA.<s> ,ea>,An`	W,L W,L	Source → Destination Source → Destination(long-word)
MOVEM	`MOVEM.<s> <list>,<caea>` `MOVEM.<s> <cea>,<list>`	W,L W,L	Listed Registers → Destination Source → Listed Registers
MOVEP	`MOVEP.<s> Dn,d16(Am)` `MOVEP.<s> d16(Am),Dn`	W,L W,L	Dn → (Byte-wide Peripheral.) (Byte-wide Peripheral) → Dn
MOVEQ	`MOVEQ #<d8>,Dn`	—	8-bit Data → Dn (sign-extended)
PEA	`PEA <cea>`	(L)	SP-4 → SP; ⟨cea⟩ → (SP)
UNLK	`UNLK An`	—	An → SP; (SP) → An; SP + 4 → SP

[1] `<s>` is operand size (B, W, L).

[2] `d16`: 16-bit constant.

[3] `d8`: 8-bit constant.

[4] `<daea>`: data-alterable addressing modes;
`<ea>`: All addressing modes;
`<cea>`: Control addressing modes;
`<caea>`: Control-alterable addressing modes.

[5] `Rn`: Address or data register.

designers of the 68000 made the MOVE instruction the most flexible instruction of the set. The MOVE and MOVEA combination supports all addressing modes we discussed for both source and destination operands, where the destination operand is restricted to any of the alterable addressing modes due to the 68000 architecture. The difference between MOVE and MOVEA is that MOVE does not support address register as destination, but MOVEA allows only an address register as destination. In other words, MOVE is intended for data, and MOVEA is intended for address movement. Most assemblers automatically make this distinction, so using MOVE for both cases will usually assemble without any error messages.

The rest of this group are not used as frequently as MOVE and MOVEA, but are quite useful, especially in writing compact-code or when execution time is important. These instructions are described below.

EXG (Exchange) instruction. This instruction exchanges the contents of two registers and, thus, is equivalent to three MOVE operations. The exchange is always a long (32-bit) operation, so no size-code needs to be specified with the instruction mnemonic. The exchange works in three modes:

1. Exchange two data registers, i.e., EXG D*n*, D*m*;
2. Exchange two address registers, i.e., EXG A*n*, A*m*;
3. Exchange a data and an address register, i.e., EXG D*n*, A*m*.

It is not uncommon for beginners to try to use this instruction to exchange two memory locations. Just remember: EXG works only with registers.

LEA (Load Effective Address). This instruction loads the effective address of the source operand into the specified address register. The assembly syntax is

```
LEA <cae>,An
```

where `<cae>` is the control addressing modes and only long-word size is allowed. If you do not remember what control addressing modes are refer to Table 3-6. It is important to note that the address of the operand, and not the operand contents are loaded into an address register. It might be confusing at first how this instruction is useful. Actually, LEA has two important applications. First, LEA can help save effective-address calculation when an operand or sequence of operands in consecutive memory locations need to be referenced many times in a program. For example, each time we reference an operand with effective address given by `(d8,A0,D3.W)`, the 68000 has to calculate

$$EA = d8_{32} + A0 + D3_{32}$$

whereas if we use

```
LEA (d8,A0,D3.W),A1
```

then we can use EA = (A1), or EA = (A1)+ for consecutive operands, in all subsequent operand references, resulting in faster execution time.[5]

The second and more important application of the LEA instruction is in implementing position-independent program modules. For example, let us say that we want to read the address of a buffer into an address register. We can write

```
MOVEA.L    #DBUFFER,A0
```

but then DBUFFER address is evaluated at assembly time, and thus, this instruction is not position-independent. If the reason for loading A0 is to move data into the buffer, we cannot use the PC-relative addressing modes either. As we stated

[5] Using LEA as such will save up to 6 processor clock cycles for each operand access.

earlier, PC-relative addressing cannot be used to alter an operand. What can we do? We must use the LEA instruction such as

```
LEA    DBUFFER,A0
```

which calculates the address of DBUFFER at execution time. It uses a PC-relative addressing mode d16(PC) in a relocatable section (such as, after a SECTION directive). The only requirement is that DBUFFER be within ∓ 32 Kbytes of the LEA instruction.

This instruction also allows the indirect addressing mode for the sake of consistency, although this form is of limited use. (What does `LEA (An),Am` do?)

Example 3-15

Figure 3-32 illustrates the operation of the LEA instruction.

Example 3-16

The program shown in Figure 3-33 is the listing of a position-independent subroutine that moves a block of data.

LINK and UNLK (Link and Un-Link) instructions. LINK and UNLK are typically used to respectively allocate and deallocate a stack area for local and temporary variables of a subroutine. We will defer detailed discussion of this instruction pair until Section 3.7.

MOVEM (Move Multiple Registers) instruction. This instruction transfers selected address and data registers to or from consecutive memory locations. It is typically used to save or restore a list of registers. The assembly syntax to save registers is

```
MOVEM.<s>   <register-list>,   <ea>
```

where `<ea>` is only control-alterable addressing modes or the pre-decrement addressing mode. The allowed data sizes are only word and long-word. The register-list syntax depends on the particular assembler, but commonly a slash (/) is used

Instruction		Before	A0 After
`LEA $A(A0),A0`	A0	00E0 0000	00E0 000A
`LEA (A0),A0`	A0	00E0 0000	00E0 0000
`LEA $2AE(PC),A0`	PC	0040 2240	0040 24EE

Figure 3-32 Example of LEA Instructions.

```
* SUBROUTINE BLKCOPY
*
* Purpose: This subroutine copies a block of word-size data from a
*          specified address to buffer DBUFFER.
*
* Inputs:  D0[15:0] = Number of words to move.
*          A0[31:0] = Beginning address of source.
*
         SECTION    0                Program Section.
*
BLKCOPY  MOVEM.L    D0/A0-A1,-(SP)   Save used registers.
         LEA        DBUFFER,A1       Calculate buffer address.
*
BLKLOOP  MOVE.W     (A0)+,(A1)+      Move a word.
         SUBQ.W     #1,D0            -Count.
         BNE        BLKLOOP          Loop until D0=0.
*
         MOVEM.L    (SP)+,D0/A0-A1   Restore used registers.
         RTS
*
         SECTION    1                Data Section
DBUFFER  DS.W       512
         END
```

Figure 3-33 A Position-independent Subroutine Example.

to separate individual names and dash (-) is used to specify a range, such as D0-D6/A1-A3/A5.

Similarly, the assembly syntax to restore registers from memory is

```
MOVEM.<s> <ea>, <register-list>
```

where <ea> is only the control-alterable addressing modes or the post-increment addressing mode, and only word and long-word data sizes are allowed. When word-size is used to restore registers, each word is sign-extended to 32 bits, including data registers. There is no apparent reason to sign-extend data-register values, so this is probably due to the way it is implemented.

There are three basic ways to use the MOVEM instruction as illustrated in Table 3-12. Note that the register-list is saved or restored in a predetermined way regardless of the order given in register-list. The operation word of MOVEM has the extension word following which defines the register-list. A register is transferred if the bit corresponding to that register is set in the extension word. The next example will clarify the use of the MOVEM instruction.

TABLE 3-12 MOVEM INSTRUCTION'S THREE FORMS OF PROGRAMMING

Assembly Format	Description
`MOVEM.<s> <register-list>,-(An)`	The order of saving registers is from A7 to A0, then from D7 to D0.
`MOVEM.<s> (An)+,<Register-list>`	The order of restoring is from D0 to D7, then from A0 to A7.
`MOVEM.<s> <Register-list>,<ea>` `MOVEM.<s> <ea>,<Register-list>`	The ⟨ea⟩ is limited to control-alterable addressing modes. The order is from D0 to D7, then from A0 to A7, for both cases.

Example 3-17

The following is used to save and restore registers D0-D7 and A0-A6 on the active system stack as illustrated in Figure 3-34. Long-word size is used to save all 32-bits.

```
   .
   MOVEM.L   D0-D7/A0-A6,-(A7)   Save Registers
   .
   .
   .
   MOVEM.L   (A7)+,D0-D7/A0-A6   Restore Registers
```

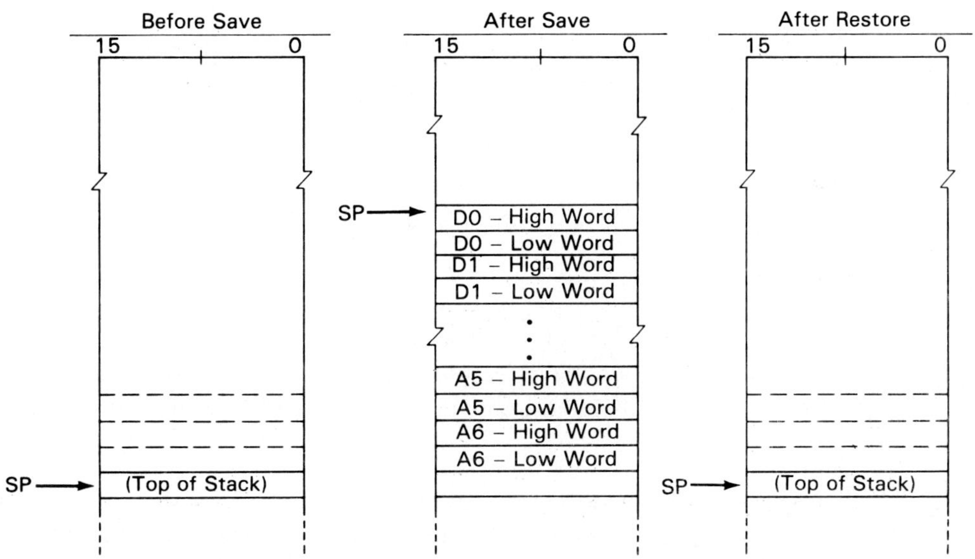

Figure 3-34 Illustration of saving/restoring registers with MOVEM.

It is important to note that we have same set of registers for both the save and restore operations, and the order in the register-list does not matter.

MOVEP (Move Peripheral Data) instruction. The majority of 68000 peripherals, including new ones, feature 8-bit data buses for control and data transfers. The 8-bit peripheral data lines are connected to either the high-byte or the low-byte of the 16-bit 68000 data bus, and thus, use alternate byte addresses in the 68000's address space. Therefore, the word and long-word transfers to and from these peripherals would not be straightforward using the MOVE instruction. As usual, Motorola designers wanted to make it convenient for the software engineer by providing the MOVEP instruction, which is intended to work with 8-bit peripherals on a 16-bit data bus. MOVEP transfers data between a data register and alternate bytes of memory, starting at the location specified and incrementing by two. Only address-indirect with displacement and data register direct addressing modes are permitted. The assembly syntax is

```
MOVEP.<s> Dn,(d16,Am)
```

or

```
MOVEP.<s> (d16,Am),Dn
```

where `<s>`: is word or long-word.
`d16`: is the 16-bit signed displacement.

The high-order byte of the data register is transferred first and the low-order byte is transferred last as shown in Figure 3-35. If the effective address specified is even, all the transfers are made on the high-order half of the data bus; if it is odd, all the transfers are made on the low-order half of the bus.

MOVEQ (Move Quick) instruction. This is the quick variation of MOVE instruction with assembly syntax

```
MOVEQ  #<data>,Dn
```

where the immediate data is limited to 8 bits so it can be specified as part of the operation word. The immediate data is sign-extended to 32 bits before transferring to the data register.

PEA (Push Effective Address) instruction. This instruction is very similar to the LEA instruction except it pushes the long-word effective-address value onto the active system stack. It is typically used to pass the address of a parameter to a subroutine which we will discuss in detail in Section 3.7.

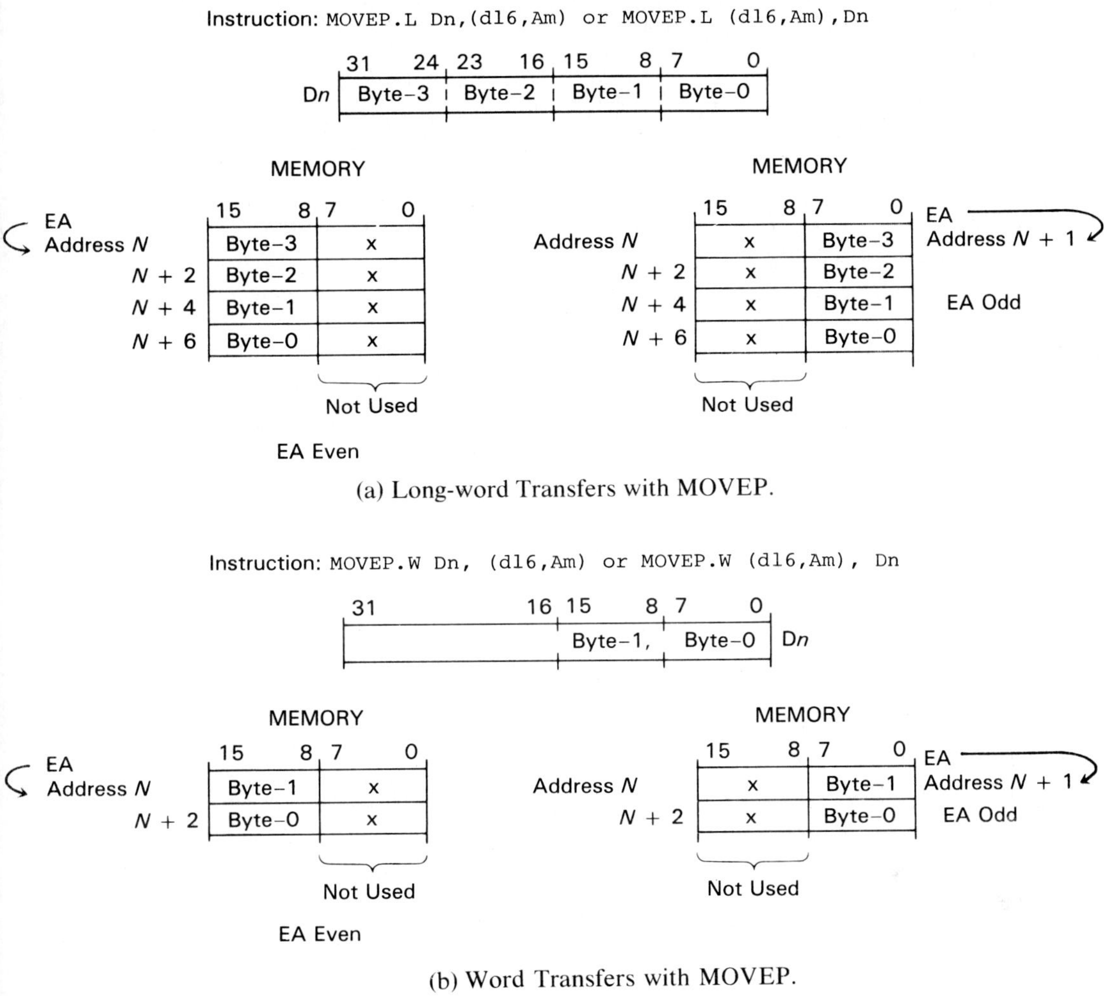

(a) Long-word Transfers with MOVEP.

(b) Word Transfers with MOVEP.

Figure 3-35 MOVEP Instruction.

3.5.2 Integer Arithmetic Operations

The arithmetic consists of the basic operations of addition, subtraction, multiply and divide as well as arithmetic compare, clear and negate, as shown in Table 3-13. All data sizes are supported for data operands, except for multiply and divide, and address operations are limited to legal sizes of word and long-word.

ADD and SUB instructions and their -A,I,Q variations. The add (ADD) and subtract (SUB) instructions perform binary arithmetic, and therefore, can

TABLE 3-13 INTEGER ARITHMETIC OPERATIONS

Instruction	Syntax	Size	Operation
ADD	ADD.<s> Dn,<amea> ADD.<s> <ea>,Dn ADDA.<s> <ea>,An	B,W,L B,W,L W,L	Source + destination → destination
ADDI ADDQ	ADDI.<s> #<data>,<daea> ADDQ.<s> #<1-8>,<aea>	B,W,L B,W,L	Data + destination → destination
ADDX	ADDX.<s> Dn,Dm ADDX.<s> -(An),-(Am)	B,W,L B,W,L	Source + destination + X → destination.
CLR	CLR.<s> <daea>	B,W,L	0 → destination.
CMP CMPA	CMP.<s> <ea>,Dn CMPA.<s> <ea>,An	B,W,L W,L	Destination − source
CMPI	CMPI.<s> #<data>,<daea>	B,W,L	Destination − data
CMPM	CMPM.<s> (An)+,(Am)+	B,W,L	Destination − source
DIVS DIVU	DIVS <dea>,Dn DIVU <dea>,Dn	— —	*Dn*[31:0] / source[15:0] → *Dn* (Remainder: D[31:16]; Quotient: D[15:0]) DIVS: Signed; DIVU: Unsigned
EXT	EXT.<s> Dn	W,L	Sign extend Dn.
MULS MULU	MULS <ea>,Dn MULU <ea>,Dn	— —	Source * *Dn* → *Dn* (W * W → L) Same but unsigned version.
NEG	NEG.<s> <daea>	B,W,L	0 − destination → destination
NEGX	NEGX.<s> <daea>	B,W,L	0 − destination − X → destination
SUB SUBA	SUB.<s> <ea>,Dn SUB.<s> Dn,<amea> SUBA.<s> <ea>,An	B,W,L B,W,L W,L	Destination − source → destination
SUBI SUBQ	SUBI.<s> #<data>,<daea> SUBQ.<s> #<1-8>,<daea>	B,W,L B,W,L	Destination − data → destination
SUBX	SUBX.<s> Dn,Dm SUBX.<s> -(An),-(Am)	B,W,L B,W,L	Destination − source − X → destination
TST	TST.<s> <daea>	B,W,L	Destination tested, affecting CCR

[1] <s>: operand size (B, W, L).

[2] <daea>: data-alterable addressing modes.
<ea>: all addressing modes.
<cea>: control addressing modes.
<daea>: data-alterable addressing modes.
<amea>: alterable-memory addressing modes.

operate on both unsigned and two's complement signed numbers. The condition codes are affected, except for the A-variation (e.g., ADDA), for both signed and unsigned interpretation of the result.

The 68000 has no increment-by-one, or decrement-by-one instructions. Instead, it provides the more general add-quick (ADDQ) and subtract-quick (SUBQ) instructions which can add or subtract an immediate number in the range 1 to 8.

Example 3-18

The subroutine shown in Figure 3-36 adds an array of word-size integers. It assumes that D0 contains the number of unsigned integers, and A0 points to the starting location of array. The result is given in register D1 as 32 bits. Note that we had to use a temporary register D2, since we want a 32-bit addition, but using ADD.L (A0)+,D1 would increment the pointer by four.

Division Instructions—DIVS and DIVU. The 68000 has separate instructions to divide signed and unsigned numbers. The signed-divide assembly syntax is

```
DIVS  <dea>,Dn
```

```
* SUBROUTINE ADDNUMS
*
* Purpose: This subroutine sums an array of 16-bit unsigned integers.
*
* Inputs: D0[15:0] = Number of integers to add.
*         A0[31:0] = Beginning address of integers.
*
* Output: The result of addition is given in D1[31:0].
*
          SECTION    0
ADDNUMS   MOVEM.L    D0/D2/A0,-(SP)     Save used registers.
          CLR.L      D1
          CLR.L      D2
          MOVE.W     (A0)+,D1           D1[31:0] = First number.
          SUBQ.W     #1,D0              -Count.
*
ADDLOOP   MOVE.W     (A0)+,D2           Get a number.
          ADD.L      D2,D1              32-bit addition.
          SUBQ.W     #1,D0              -Count.
          BNE        ADDLOOP            Loop until D0=0.
*
          MOVEM.L    (SP)+,A0/D0/D2     Restore used registers.
          RTS
          END
```

Figure 3-36 ADDNUMS Program for Example 3-18.

and similarly for unsigned divide

```
DIVU   <dea>,Dn
```

where, for both cases, the destination-operand is the 32-bit dividend and the source-operand is a 16-bit divisor specified by one of the data addressing modes. The resultant 16-bit quotient is given in the low-order word of data register where it could be easily accessed, and the remainder is in the high-order word of data register, i.e.,

```
Dn[31:0] / (dea)[15:0] → Dn[31:16]  : Remainder
                          Dn[15:0]   : Quotient
```

The sign of the quotient depends on the dividend and divisor's sign, whereas the sign of the remainder is always the same as the sign of the dividend.

Two special conditions might arise in execution of DIVS and DIVU. If the divisor is zero, this causes a trap to the divide-by-zero exception routine of the operating system or supervisor program. It is usually a good practice to verify and handle the divisor-is-zero condition as part of the program. The second special condition is overflow which occurs when the quotient size is larger than could be accommodated in 16 bits (i.e. [-32, 767, 32768] for DIVS and [0, 65, 536] for DIVU). The overflow condition sets the V-flag of condition codes, and the destination-operand contents remain unaffected in order to make it easy to recover from this error condition.

Example 3-19

Figure 3-37 illustrates the divide instructions. The first part shows the unsigned division

$$4294966896/3 = 1431655632$$

in decimal. D0, in this case, remains unchanged because of the overflow condition, i.e. the quotient is larger than $FFFF_{16}$. The second part shows the two's complement interpretation of the same division. In decimal, this is

$$-400/3 = 133 \text{ (quotient) and the remainder is } -1.$$

Instruction		Before		After	
DIVU #3,D0	D0	FFFF FE70	D0	FFFF FE70	V = 1
DIVS #3,D0	D0	FFFF FE70	D0	FFFF FF7B	V = 0

Figure 3-37 Example of DIVx Instructions.

Multiply Instructions—MULU and MULS. Similar to division instructions, two separate instructions are available: *signed-multiply* (MULS) and *unsigned multiply* (MULU). The assembly syntax is

```
MULS  <ea>,Dn
```

and

```
MULU  <ea>,Dn
```

where, for both cases, two 16-bit operands (multiplier and multiplicand) are multiplied to generate a 32-bit result stored in the destination-operand (data register). This is illustrated in Figure 3-38. Of course, it is assumed that source and destination are both signed or unsigned, to get meaningful results. There are no conditions which can cause overflow, so both V- and C-flags are cleared.

EXT (Extend) instruction. The extend instruction is used for signed arithmetic where the operands have different sizes. For example, when adding or multiplying two-signed numbers where one operand size is a word, and the other one is a byte, it is first necessary to sign-extend the byte-operand to a word.

The assembly syntax is

```
EXT.W Dn
```

which sign-extends low-byte of D*n* into word, and

```
EXT.L Dn
```

which sign-extends the low-order word of D*n* into a long-word. Therefore, sign-extending a byte to a long-word will require two EXT instructions, the first extending a byte into a word, and second extending a word into a long-word.

Instruction	Before		After		
MULU #3,D0	D0	0000 FE70 (D0[15:0] = 65136_{10})	D0	0002 FB50 (DO[31:0] = 195408)	V,C = 0
MULS #3,D0	D0	0000 FE70 (D0[15:0] = -400_{10})	D0	FFFF FB50 (D0[31:0] = −1200)	V,C = 0

Figure 3-38 Example of MULx Instructions.

Example 3-20

Assume we wish to add two-signed numbers: one given in the low-byte of D0 and the second given in D1 with word-size. Then, we need the following instruction sequence:

```
EXT.W     D0          Extend D0 to word-size
ADD.W     D0,D1       Add. Result in D1[15:0].
```

	Before		After EXT.W		After ADD.W	
(-2_{10})	XXXX | XX | FE	D0	XXXX | FF | FE	D0	XXXX | FF | FE	D0 (-2_{10})
	XXXX | 00 | 31	D1	XXXX | 00 | 31	D1	XXXX | 00 | 2F	D1 $(+47_{10})$

CLR (Clear) instruction. The clear instruction is simple: it zeroes the contents of destination operand. The assembly syntax is

```
CLR.<s> <daea>
```

where data-alterable addressing modes and all data sizes are allowed. Two things about CLR should be noted. First, an address register cannot be cleared. Second, CLR reads the memory operand before writing zeros into it for no apparent reason. An address register is most efficiently cleared by the instruction

```
SUBA.<s>   An,An
```

and we recommend using

```
MOVE.<s>   #0,<amea>
```

instead of CLR for memory operands.

Compare instructions—CMP, CMPM, CMPA, CMPI, TST. The four compare instructions are very much like a subtract operation, except the result of subtraction is not saved, as we mentioned earlier. Only the condition codes are affected.

These compare instructions cover all possible uses as shown in Table 3-13. The *compare memory* (CMPM) is useful, for example, in comparing two strings of data in memory. The *compare address* (CMPA) is useful for checking that an address register is within some given bounds. But, how is this possible? We noted earlier that address manipulations do not affect condition codes. The only exception to this rule is the CMPA instruction.

TST is a special form of compare instruction in that it compares an operand with zero (i.e., it is equivalent to CMPI.⟨s⟩ #0,⟨ea⟩).

NEG (Negate) instruction. The negate instruction calculates the negative of a given destination operand. This is the same as calculating the two's complement of destination. The assembly syntax is

```
NEG.<s>    <daea>
```

where only data-alterable addressing modes and all data sizes are allowed.

Note that an overflow condition will arise when negating the most negative number of a given data size. For example, D0 = 80_{16} will cause overflow condition when negated, setting the V-flag.

Extended arithmetic operations—ADDX, SUBX, NEGX. The 68000 arithmetic instructions can operate on operands with up to 32-bits of precision. Although this is usually enough, some applications might require more precision (e.g., 48-bit addition operation). The extended (X) variation of arithmetic instructions, ADDX, SUBX, and NEGX are provided to extend precision beyond 32-bits in increments of byte, word, or long-word sizes. The implemention of extended data-size operations requires multiple arithmetic instructions, each working on a portion of the operand, with carries and borrows between intermediate results handled properly. Such extended arithmetic operations beyond what is directly available by a CPU architecture is called *multiprecision arithmetic*.

As shown in Table 3-13, the extended instructions use the X-bit of the condition codes for carry or borrow between different portions of an operand. For example, to perform a 64-bit addition (double-precision) of two operands, we can use the following steps:

1. Perform addition on the least-significant 32-bit portion of two operands. Since there is no carry or borrow into this portion, we can use the ADD instruction for this step. Any carry generated by this step is stored in both the C- and X-flags. On the other hand, any overflow (V) or N-flag generated by this step has no significance and thus should be ignored.
2. Perform the addition on the most-significant 32-bit portion of the two operands adding in the carry bit, if any, contained in the X-flag from step 1. The ADDX instruction is used for this step. An overflow recorded in this step (i.e., V or C), and the N-flag when adding signed numbers, carries significance. How about the Z-flag? Does it indicate whether the entire 64-bits are zero or not?

The Z-flag is affected differently for extended operations. It is cleared when ADDX, SUBX, or NEGX generates a non-zero result, and otherwise, it is *unchanged*. Therefore, if we set Z = 1 before using one of the extended instructions (ADDX, SUBX, NEGX), it will remain set, unless any of the intermediate results is nonzero, in which case it is cleared to indicate a nonzero result. It seems that the Motorola designers have given serious consideration to the programmer's point of view.

Most of the other microprocessors offer similar instructions but use the C-bit instead (such as, add-with-carry). We noted earlier that the X-bit is set the same as the C-bit by most operations. However, the X-bit is not affected by data-movement or compare instructions, thereby allowing such instructions to be used in between the extended instructions without having to save the C-bit.

The assembly syntax for extended instructions are

```
ADDX.<s>   Dn,Dm
ADDX.<s>   -(An),-(Am)
SUBX.<s>   Dn,Dm
SUBX.<s>   -(An),(Am)
```

and

```
NEGX.<s>   <daea>
```

where all data sizes are allowed and ⟨daea⟩ is all data-alterable addressing modes. Since data registers can hold a maximum of 32-bits, rather than shuffling multiple register values, it is more convenient to store multiprecision operands in memory. To provide for this memory-to-memory mode, the pre-decrement addressing mode was chosen to be consistent with the 68000's data-organization in memory. In other words, the most significant portion of a multiprecision operand resides at a lower address than the least significant part as the next example will illustrate.

Example 3-21

Assume we wish to add two 48-bit operands in memory with address pointers initialized as shown in Figure 3-39 (Why?). The operation is given by

```
  0094FA23A98C
  00A043FACB46
  ------------
  0135441E7402
```

We can perform the above addition using the following instructions:

```
MOVE     #4,CCR        Clear X and set Z-flag.
ADDX.L  -(A0),-(A1)  Add low-order 32 bits.
ADDX.W  -(A0),-(A1)  Add high-order 16 bits.
```

Example 3-22

The program shown in Figure 3-40 multiplies two unsigned 32-bit numbers to generate a 64-bit product[6]. Since MULU multiplies two 16-bit unsigned numbers, we used it

[6] Adapted from Motorola.

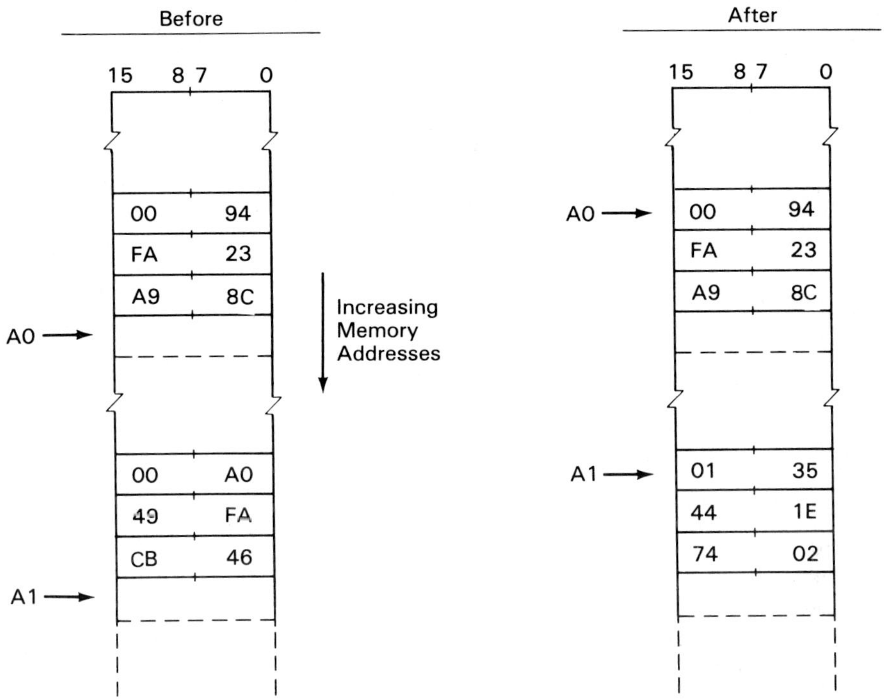

Figure 3-39 Addition of two 48-bit operands given in Example 3-21.

four times to calculate the partial products as shown in Figure 3-41. These 32-bit partial products are then added with proper displacement using the ADDX and ADD instructions.

3.5.3 Program Control Instructions

The instructions in a program are normally executed starting with the first one and continuing on to the last instruction. This normal sequence of instruction-to-next-instruction flow can be altered using instructions that control the flow of the program. Such program control instructions may be used to jump or branch forward or backward over a group of instructions, and continue execution with another group of instructions. The branching can be performed unconditionally, or conditionally based on the contents of the condition code register, to implement program loops or constructs such as if-then-else.

All instructions in this group control program flow with the exception of conditional S⟨*cc*⟩, and no instructions in this group affect any of the condition codes. We will next examine each of the program control instructions.

NOP (No Operation) instruction. This instruction does nothing other than taking execution time and incrementing the PC value by 2 so that execution

```
* SUBROUTINE MULU32
*
* Purpose: This subroutine multiplies two unsigned 32-bit numbers to generate
*          a 64-bit result.
*
* Inputs:  D0[31:0] : Multiplier.
*          D1[31:0] : Multiplicand.
* Outputs: Upon return from subroutine D0[31:0] has the upper 32-bits of result,
*          and the lower 32-bits is in D1[31:0].
*
          SECTION    0
MULU32    MOVEM.L    D3-D5,-(SP)     Save used registers.
          MOVE.L     D1,D3           Prepare for partial-products.
          MOVE.L     D1,D4
          SWAP       D4
          MOVE.L     D0,D5
          SWAP       D5
          MULU       D0,D1           D1= First line of partial products.
          MULU       D4,D0           D0= Second line of partial products.
          MULU       D5,D3           D3= Third line of partial products.
          MULU       D5,D4           D4= Fourth line of partial products.
          SWAP       D1
          CLR.L      D5
          ADD.W      D0,D1           Add partial-products.
          ADDX.L     D5,D4
          ADD.W      D3,D1
          ADDX.L     D5,D4
          SWAP       D1
          CLR.W      D0
          CLR.W      D3
          SWAP       D0
          SWAP       D3
          ADD.L      D3,D0
          ADD.L      D4,D0
          MOVEM.L    (SP)+,D3-D5     Restore used registers.
          RTS
          END
```

Figure 3-40 32 × 32-bit Unsigned Multiply Subroutine.

```
33334444₁₆ * 11112222₁₆ = 369D4C3A86419081₁₆
                        =  2222 * 4444 +
                          (2222 * 3333) * 2^16 +
                          (4444 * 1111) * 2^16 +
                          (3333 * 1111) * 2^32


             91A 1908
        6D3 92C6
        98D 0C84
    369 C963
    +
    369 D4C3 A864 1908
```

Figure 3-41 Illustration of 32 × 32 Multiply of Subroutine MULU32.

continues with the following instruction. Then, why do we need the NOP? The answer is it comes handy in implementing time delays, and during debugging to overwrite an undesired instruction.

BRA (Branch) instruction. The BRA instruction transfers control to another area of program memory by specifying a displacement relative to itself. The program execution continues at the location given by

$$\text{New PC Address} = PC_{BRA} + 2 + \langle\text{displacement}\rangle_{32}$$

where

PC_{BRA}: Is the address of the branch instruction's operation word.

$\langle\text{displacement}\rangle_{32}$: Is an 8- or 16-bit signed number which is sign-extended to 32 bits before addition.

Note that the displacement value has to take into account that the PC is already pointing to the word following the BRA instruction's operation word when execution of BRA starts. Therefore, for an 8-bit displacement, the range is −126 to +128 bytes with respect to the beginning of BRA instruction. Similarly, for a 16-bit displacement, the range is −32,766 to +32,768 bytes. Remember that the program counter can only branch or jump to an even (word) address, otherwise an address error will occur.

The BRA instruction is not conditional (i.e., the branch is taken regardless of the setting of the condition codes). The object code of BRA takes either one or two words depending on the size of the displacement as illustrated in Figure 3-42.

Instruction Format:

15	14	13	12	11	10	9	8	7	6	5	4	3	2	1	0
0	1	1	0	0	0	0	0	8-bit Displacement							
16-bit Displacement if 8-bit Displacement = $00															

Figure 3-42 BRA Object Code Format.

The assembly syntax of BRA instruction is

```
BRA[.S]   <displacement>
```

or more commonly as

```
BRA[.S]   <label>
```

where [.S] indicates optional displacement size specification (short or long).[7] In the first form, the displacement is given by a constant in hex, decimal, and so on. Using the second form, as most programmers do, assembler automatically calculates the necessary displacement. If the optional size specification is omitted then the assembler automatically chooses the long form. Alternatively, short form can be explicitly selected by using BRA.S form.

Example 3-23

The first branch illustrates the typical use of BRA. The second one shows an infinite loop that can only be interrupted by exception processing.

Label	Instruction	Program Flow
	.	
BACK5	.	
	.	
	.	
	.	
	BRA BACK5	
	.	
	.	
	BRA.S $FE	
	.	
	.	

JMP (Jump) instruction. The jump instruction offers a more flexible transfer of program control than is available with the BRA instruction. The control

[7] Some assemblers uses `.B` and `.W` instead.

may be transferred anywhere within the 16 Mbytes addressing range of the 68000. The assembly syntax of JMP is

```
JMP    <cae>
```

and performs the operation

$$\text{New PC Address} = \langle \text{cae} \rangle$$

where ⟨cae⟩ is the control-addressing modes as we defined earlier, given by

```
         ┌ (An)          ┐
         │ (d16,An)      │
         │ (d16,An,Xn)   │
<cae> =  │ (xxx).W       │
         │ (xxx).L       │
         │ (d16,PC)      │
         └ (d16,PC,Xn)   ┘
```

Note that when ⟨cae⟩ = (d16,PC), the jump instruction is equivalent to the long-form of the BRA instruction. The two most common usage of JMP are

```
JMP    <label>
```

and

```
JMP    (An)
```

where the second form transfers program execution to the address pointed to by one of the address registers[8], and the first form is resolved using one of the control addressing modes. The address of a label can be given either as absolute value (i.e., absolute short or long addressing modes) or as a relative value (such as, PC-relative addressing mode without index) if within the range. The assembler will choose the relative value within a relocatable program section (i.e., after a SECTION directive) otherwise any addressing mode will work and the selection will depend on the assembler.

The operation of the register indirect form shown above is simple. It transfers the contents of A*n* to the PC register. The notation, though, might be confusing. The instruction MOVEA.L (A0),A1 transfers the contents of location pointed by A0 to A1. Similarly, we might think JMP (A0) loads PC with the contents of location pointed by A0. This is *not* the case. Although this seems like an inconsistency, this can be clarified by remembering that a operand is specified by its effective-address. The JMP instruction *jumps* to the effective address of operand, whereas the MOVE instruction *moves* the actual operand.

One typical application of JMP (A*n*) is implementing an *N*-way conditional

[8] More on the application of this form in Chapter 6.

branch depending on an index value. This requires the addresses of routines to be stored in a table, and hence is often referred to as a *jump-table*. For example, the program shown in Figure 3-43 illustrates a jump-table using D0 as an index with value 0 through $N - 1$.

B⟨cc⟩ (Branch Conditionally) instruction. The B⟨*cc*⟩ instruction transfers control conditionally to another area of program memory. If the selected condition is true, then the branch is taken and execution continues with the next instruction. The general form of the conditional branch instruction is

```
B<cc>[.S]  <label>
```

where ⟨*cc*⟩ suffix of instruction mnemonic specifies one of the conditions given in Table 3-14. The branch displacement is a signed 8- or 16-bit number to implement forward or backward branches very similar to the BRA instruction. The 8-bit short-form can be explicitly selected by appending `.S` to the instruction mnemonic, or if this optional branch-size is omitted, then assembler will choose the long or short form automatically.

Figure 3-44 illustrates the operation of the B⟨*cc*⟩ instruction. Actually, the BRA instruction can be considered a special case of B⟨*cc*⟩ where the condition is always true. When a selected condition is false, B⟨*cc*⟩ performs like a NOP instruction.

Since the assembly language does not have any constructs such as if-then-else, the processor assumes that the condition codes have been set properly before the conditional branch instruction. Some of the conditions are simple: Only the

```
* JUMP TABLE EXAMPLE
*
          LSL.W      #2,D0            Calculate table offset.
          LEA        JMPTBL,A0        Table address → A0.
          MOVEA.L    0(A0,D0.W),A0    Look-up address of routine.
          JMP        (A0)             Jump to that routine.
           .
           .
           .
* JUMP TABLE
JMPTBL    DS.L       ROUTINE1         Index D0=0
          DS.L       ROUTINE2         Index D0=1
          DS.L       ROUTINE3         Index D0=2
           .
           .
           .
          DS.L       ROUTINEN         Index D0= N-1.
```

Figure 3-43 Jump-Table Program

TABLE 3-14 B⟨*cc*⟩ Conditional Tests

⟨*cc*⟩ =	Condition	Test	Signed/Unsigned
CC (HS)	Carry Clear (Higher or Same)	$\overline{C}$	Unsigned
CS (LO)	Carry Set (LOwer)	C	Unsigned
EQ	EQual	Z	Both
GE	Greater or Equal	$(N \cdot V) + (\overline{N} \cdot \overline{V})$	Signed
GT	Greater Than	$(N \cdot V \cdot \overline{Z}) + (\overline{N} \cdot \overline{V} \cdot \overline{Z})$	Signed
HI	HIgher than	$\overline{C} \cdot \overline{Z}$	Unsigned
LE	Less or Equal	$Z + (N \cdot \overline{V}) + (\overline{N} \cdot V)$	Signed
LS	Lower or Same	$C + Z$	Unsigned
LT	Less Than	$(N \cdot \overline{V}) + (\overline{N} \cdot V)$	Signed
MI	Minus	N	Signed
NE	Not Equal	$\overline{Z}$	Both
PL	Plus	$\overline{N}$	Signed
VC	Overflow Clear	$\overline{V}$	Signed
VS	Overflow Set	V	Signed

state of one condition code is tested. On the other hand, some of the other conditions involve Boolean logic of multiple condition codes. As we noted earlier, the relevant condition codes for unsigned numbers are {C, Z}, whereas the codes {N, V, Z} are relevant for two's complement signed numbers. Therefore, there are two sets of condition mnemonics, one for signed numbers, and another for unsigned numbers. For example, signed GT (greater than) and unsigned HI (higher

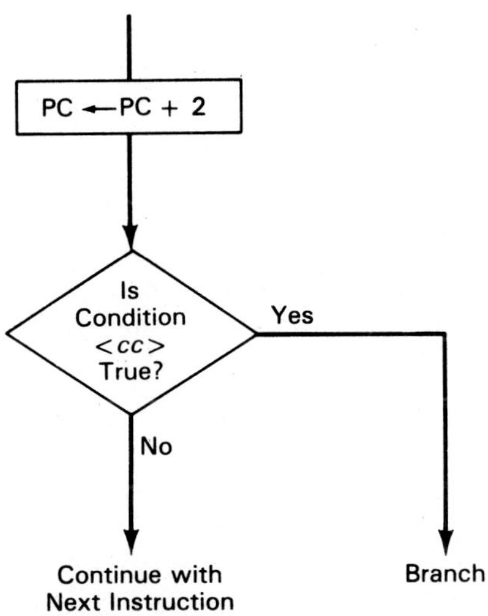

Figure 3-44 Operation of the B⟨*cc*⟩ Instruction.

than). The selection of correct condition mnemonic is important as the next example will illustrate.

Example 3-24

Assume we wish to change program flow based on the comparison of two word-size operands where

```
EA of operand #1 : (A2)
EA of operand #2 : D0
```

When (A2) < D0 we want to skip some instructions. The way we would program this depends on whether both operands are signed or unsigned, as shown below:

Signed-operands

```
        .
        .
        .
        CMP.W   (A2),D0
        BGT     NEXT
        .
        .
        .
NEXT    .
        .
        .
```

Unsigned Operands

```
        .
        .
        .
        CMP.W   (A2),D0
        BHI     NEXT
        .
        .
        .
NEXT    .
        .
        .
```

Flowchart

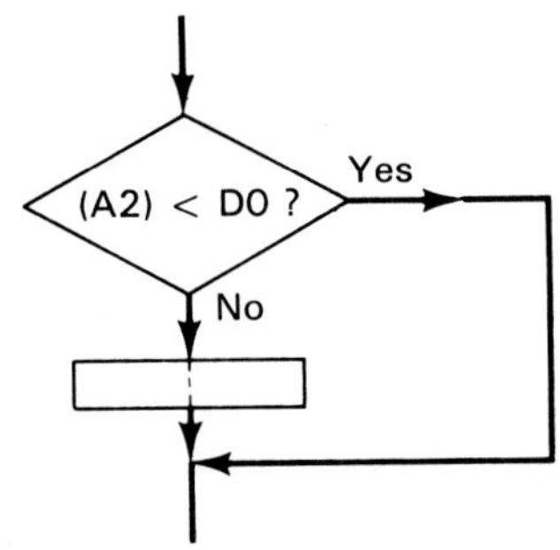

What happens when one operand is signed, and the other one unsigned?

Example 3-25.

Program shown in Figure 3-45 compares two strings.

DB⟨cc⟩ (Test Condition, Decrement-and-branch Conditionally) instruction. This instruction is a looping primitive to implement the various type of program loops. The assembly syntax is

```
DB<cc>  Dn,<label>
```

where

`<cc>`: Is the suffix selecting one of the conditions listed in Table 3-15.

`Dn`: Is one of the data registers functioning as the loop counter.

`<label>`: Is the 16-bit signed displacement value.

The DB⟨*cc*⟩ instruction first tests the condition ⟨*cc*⟩ to determine if the termination condition for the loop has been met, and if so, no operation is performed.

```
* SUBROUTINE STRCMP
*
* Purpose: This subroutine compares to check if two strings are the
           same.
*
* Inputs:  A0 → String 1
*          A1 → String 2
*
* Output:  Upon return D0=1 if strings are equal, otherwise D0=0.
*
* Description: It is assumed that a string is terminated by a null
*              character $0 (="\0").
*
         SECTION  0
STRCMP   MOVEM.L  A0-A1,-(SP)     Save used registers.
         CLR.L    D0              Initialize D0 as "not equal".
*
STRLOOP  TST.B    (A0)             End of string 1?
         BEQ      STROUT
         CMPM.B   (A0)+,(A1)+      Compare a character.
         BEQ      STRLOOP            If equal: continue testing.
         BRA      STRRET             else: return (not equal).
*
STROUT   TST.B    (A1)            Also end of string 2?
         BNE      STRRET             No, return (not equal).
         MOVEQ    #1,D0              Yes, strings are equal.
*
STRRET   MOVEM.L  (SP)+,A0-A1        Restore used registers.
         RTS
         END
```

Figure 3-45 STRCMP Subroutine of Example 3-25.

If the termination condition is not true, then the low-order 16 bits of selected data register is decremented by one. If Dn[15:0] is equal to -1, this indicates the loop iteration count is exhausted and execution continues with the next instruction. If Dn[15:0] is not -1, then the branch is taken so that program execution continues at ⟨label⟩ such as:

$$\text{New PC Address} = PC_{DB\langle cc \rangle} + 2 + \langle \text{displacement} \rangle_{32}$$

where $PC_{DB\langle cc \rangle}$: Is the address of first word of the DB⟨cc⟩ instruction;

$\langle \text{displacement} \rangle_{32}$: Is the 16-bit displacement given by ⟨label⟩ which is sign-extended to 32-bits before summation.

As with the BRA and B⟨*cc*⟩ instructions, in calculating the required displacement, the offset of two shown above comes into affect because the PC is already pointing to the extension word of DB⟨*cc*⟩ when its execution starts. The operation of DB⟨*cc*⟩ is illustrated in Figure 3-46. Note that the DB⟨*cc*⟩ instruction replaces three other instructions as shown below:

```
        ┌B<cc>     <next>  ┐
        │SUBQ.W    #1,Dn   │  =  DB<cc> Dn,<label>
        │BPL       <label> │
<next>  └...               ┘
```

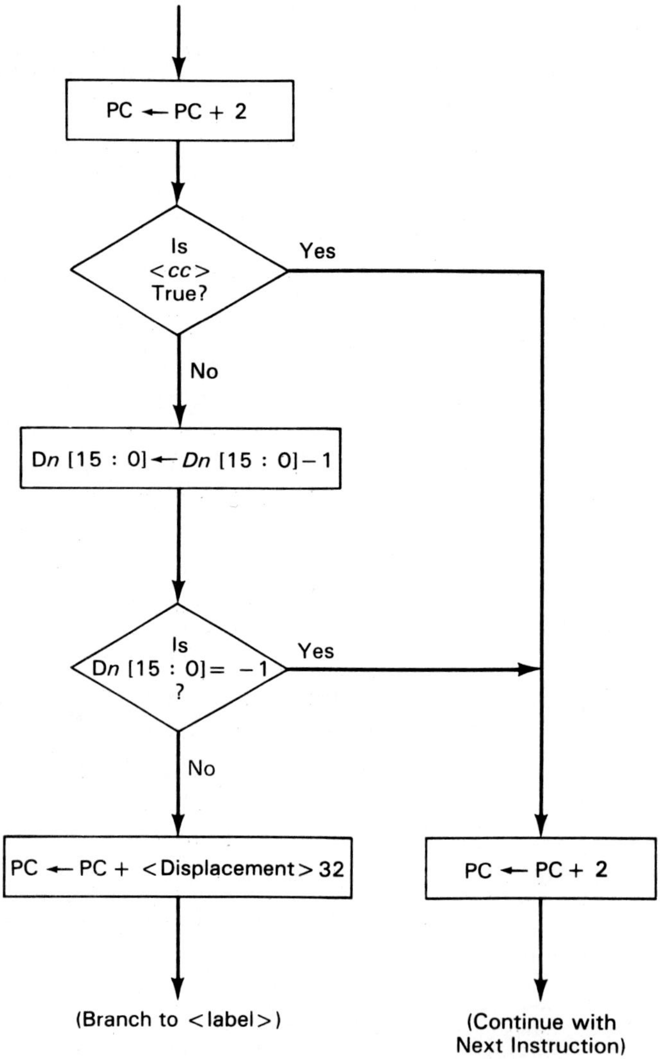

Figure 3-46 Operation of DB⟨*cc*⟩ D*n*,⟨label⟩ Instruction.

Thus, DB⟨*cc*⟩ will execute faster and occupy two less words in program memory.

Initially, this instruction might seem confusing. Some of this is due to differences between DB⟨*cc*⟩ and B⟨*cc*⟩ as listed below:

1. The DB⟨*cc*⟩ handles the condition the opposite way to B⟨*cc*⟩ instruction i.e., when executing DB⟨*cc*⟩, the branch is not taken if the condition is true.
2. The DB⟨*cc*⟩ always has a 16-bit signed displacement whereas B⟨*cc*⟩ has both short and long forms of signed displacement.
3. The DB⟨*cc*⟩ supports two more conditions than B⟨*cc*⟩, namely T (True) and F (False), as shown in Table 3-15. The DBT form is of limited practical use: it never branches, and is equivalent to a long NOP instruction.

Using the DB⟨*cc*⟩, we can program the two basic looping structures conveniently: *do-while* and *do-until*. These two structures are fundamentally different in two ways. First, the do-until form tests the loop termination condition(s) after each execution of loop-processing section. Therefore, even when termination condition(s) is not true, the processing section is executed once. Second, the do-until loop terminates when the termination condition(s) is true, whereas the do-while terminates the loop when the condition is false. The DB⟨*cc*⟩ programming of these two loop structures is illustrated in Figure 3-47. Note that do-until uses an index count of one less than the maximum loop iteration count. This is because the loop terminates when count equals −1 and not 0.

TABLE 3-15 DB⟨*cc*⟩ AND S⟨*cc*⟩ INSTRUCTION CONDITIONAL TESTS

⟨*cc*⟩ =	Condition	Test	Signed/Unsigned
CC (HS)	Carry Clear (Higher or Same)	$\overline{C}$	Unsigned
CS (LO)	Carry Set (LOwer)	C	Unsigned
EQ	EQual	Z	Both
F	False	0	Both
GE	Greater or Equal	$(N \cdot V) + (\overline{N} \cdot \overline{V})$	Signed
GT	Greater Than	$(N \cdot V \cdot \overline{Z}) + (\overline{N} \cdot \overline{V} \cdot \overline{Z})$	Signed
HI	HIgher than	$\overline{C} \cdot \overline{Z}$	Unsigned
LE	Less or Equal	$Z + (N \cdot \overline{V}) + (\overline{N} \cdot V)$	Signed
LS	Lower or Same	$C + Z$	Unsigned
LT	Less Than	$(N \cdot \overline{V}) + (\overline{N} \cdot V)$	Signed
MI	Minus	N	Signed
NE	Not Equal	$\overline{Z}$	Both
PL	Plus	$\overline{N}$	Signed
T	True	1	Both
VC	Overflow Clear	$\overline{V}$	Signed
VS	Overflow Set	V	Signed

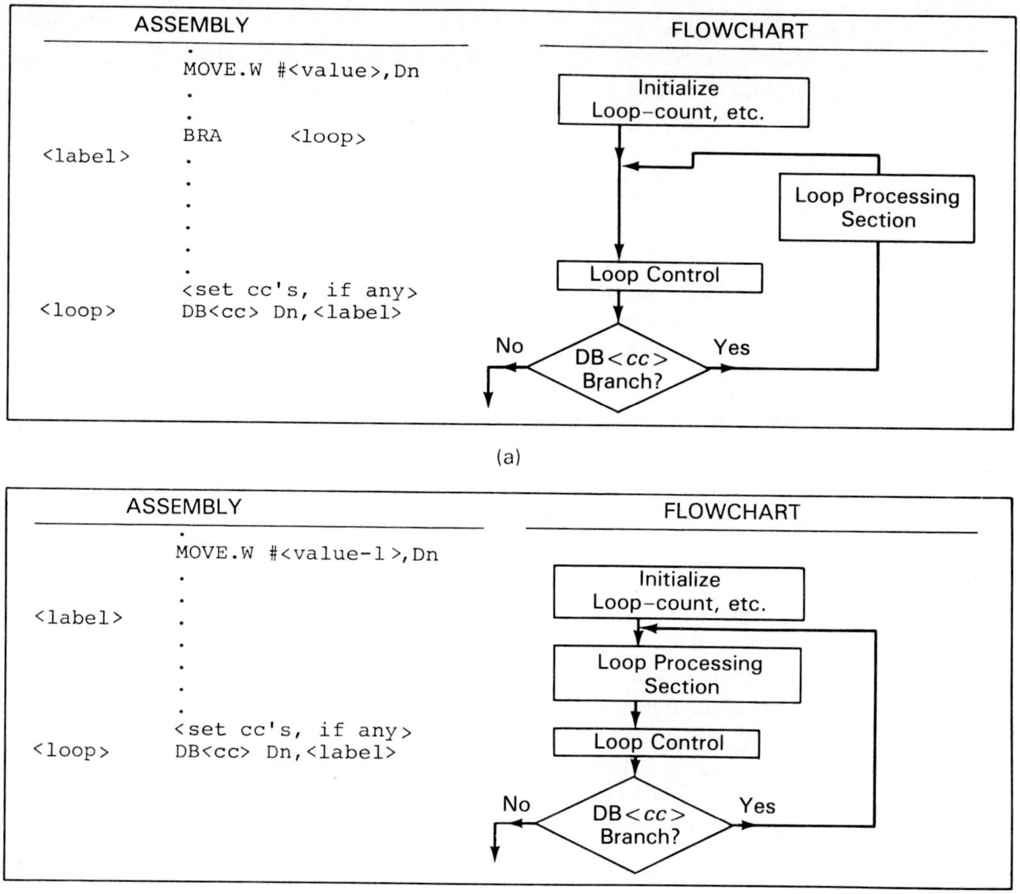

Figure 3-47 (a) Do-While and (b) Do-Until Looping Structures.

Not all program loops use both the termination conditions of DB⟨*cc*⟩. The following lists the typical uses of the DB⟨*cc*⟩ instruction:

1. To loop a section of program *N*-times, we can use:

```
        MOVE.W  #N-1,Dn
<back>  .
        .
        .
        DBF     Dn,<back>
```

   where the maximum iteration count is 65,535.
2. When waiting for a condition to be true, we can use the loop-count as a

time-out so that the program does not get stuck if the condition never becomes true. Detecting time-out, we can handle the error condition.

```
        MOVE.W   #-1,Dn      Maximum Loop Count
<back>  .
        .
        .
        DB<cc>  Dn,<back>
        CMP.W   #-1,Dn       Test termination condition.
        BEQ     <error>
```

3. While searching for a condition to become true, we can use the Dn as an index register. For example, in a character string while searching for a blank character, we can use Dn to find the length of the string. Since Dn counts down instead of up, we can use

```
<back>  MOVE.W   #-1,Dn
        .
        .
        .
        DB<cc>   Dn,<back>
        NOT.W    Dn
        .
```

Example 3-26

Program shown in Figure 3-48 finds the length of a string. The DB⟨*cc*⟩ instruction is used to check the end of string while also counting the string length. Does this subroutine work when the string length is zero? How many instructions would this take if we did not use the DB⟨*cc*⟩?

S⟨cc⟩ (Set According to Condition) instruction. This instruction tests the specified condition and sets the destination operand to all one's if the condition is true or to all zero's if the condition is false, as illustrated in Figure 3-49. The assembly syntax is

```
S<cc>  <daea>
```

where <cc>: Is one of the conditions listed in Table 3-15.
<daea>: Is the data-alterable addressing modes.

The destination operand is limited to byte size. This instruction is used to flag certain application-specific conditions.

Subroutine-control instructions—JSR, BSR, RTS, and RTR. This group of instructions handle subroutine calls and returns as illustrated in Table

```
* SUBROUTINE STRLNGTH
*
* Purpose:   This subroutine finds the length of a string that is
*            terminated by a null character ($00).
*
* Input:     A0 → String.
*
* Output:    D0 equal to string length excluding the null character.
*
* Description: It is assumed that the string ends with a null
*              character ($00).
*
            SECTION     0
STRLNGTH    MOVE.L      A0,-(SP)          Save A0.
*
            MOVE.W      #-1,D0
STRLOOP     TST.B       (A0)+             End of string?
            DBEQ        D0,STRLOOP        If not, continue searching.
*
            NOT.W       D0                D0 = string length.
            MOVE.L      (SP)+,A0          Restore A0.
            RTS
            END
```

Figure 3-48 Subroutine STRLNGTH Illustrating DBEQ.

3-16. The *subroutine-call instructions, jump to subroutine* (JSR) and *branch to subroutine* (BSR) are close relatives of JMP and BRA, respectively, in the way they handle branching. The difference is that both JSR and BSR saves the address of the next instruction on the active system stack as return addresses. The JSR

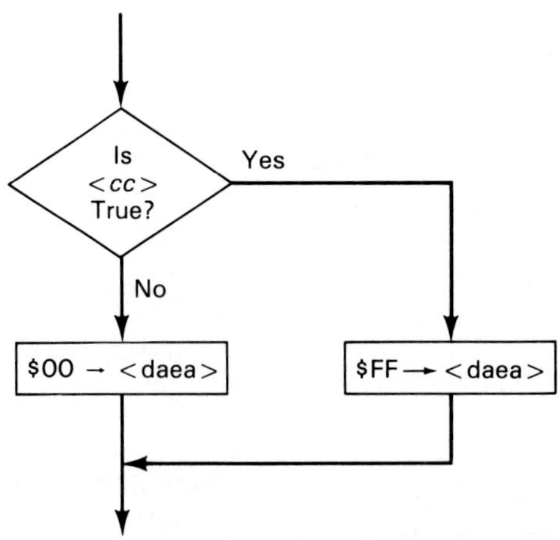

Figure 3-49 Operation of S⟨cc⟩ Instruction.

TABLE 3-16 SUBROUTINE CONTROL INSTRUCTIONS

Assembly Syntax	Operation Sequence	Description
BSR[.S] <label>	1. SP − 4 → SP 2. PC → (SP) 3. PC + ⟨displacement⟩$_{32}$ → PC	After JSR or BSR: Address | 15 8 7 0 SP → n | PC-Return-High $n + 2$ | PC-Return-Low
JSR <cea>[1]	1. SP − 4 → SP 2. PC → (SP) 3. ⟨cea⟩ → PC	
RTS	1. (SP) → PC 2. SP + 4 → SP	
RTR	1. (SP) → CCR 2. SP + 2 → SP 3. (SP) → PC 4. SP + 4 → SP	RTR pulls CCR before pulling PC-return address into PC.

[1] ⟨cea⟩ is the control addressing modes.

and BSR are functionally equivalent, but JSR is more flexible because of the possible branching range and addressing modes.

The return instructions *return from subroutine* (RTS) and *return-and-restore condition codes* (RTR) pull the return address of calling instruction from the top of stack into PC, and thus, continuing program execution with the instruction following the subroutine-call instruction. Sometimes it is necessary to save and restore the CCR so that condition codes remain unaffected by instructions within the subroutine. Although, this can be done as part of a calling program, it is more convenient to do this as part of a subroutine when necessary. The RTR instruction provides an easy way to restore condition codes from the top of the stack before returning to the calling program, assuming that the CCR is saved at the beginning of the subroutine as illustrated in Figure 3-50.

3.5.4 Logical Operations

This group of instructions provides four basic logical operations: AND, OR, EOR, and NOT. These instructions perform bit-wise Boolean operations on operands. All data-sizes are allowed and, except for NOT, all have immediate variations as shown in Table 3-17. The exclusive-OR (EOR) is more limited than AND or OR, since source-operand has to be given in a data register unless immediate data is used. The NOT instruction performs a one's complement operation in a data register or a memory operand.

Example 3-27

Do the following operations on the specified bit-field without affecting the other bits of the operand.

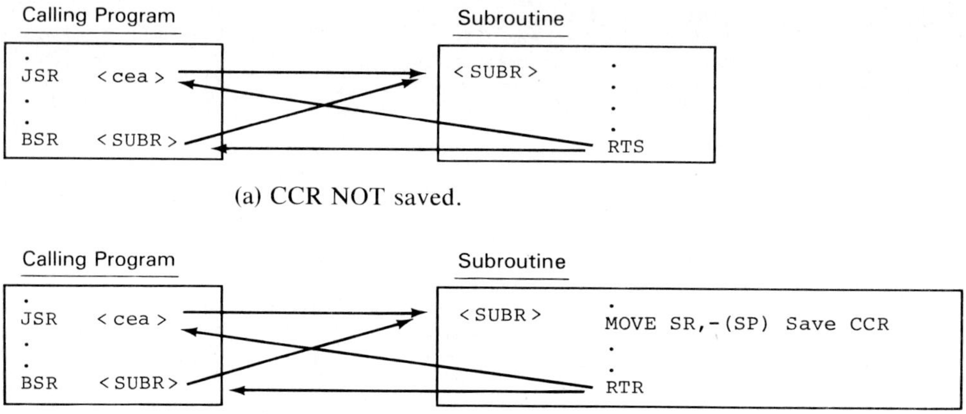

(a) CCR NOT saved.

(b) CCR saved.

Figure 3-50 Subroutine Calls and Returns.

1. Clear bits 4 to 6 of memory location $4001: ANDI.B #$8F,$4001
2. Invert bits 4 to 6 of memory location $4001: EORI.B #$70,4001
3. Set bits 4 to 6 of memory location $4001 to one: ORI.B #$70,$4001

3.5.5 Shift and Rotate Operations

This group of instructions (illustrated in Table 3-18) perform arithmetic and logical shifts as well as circular rotates of operands. The *arithmetic-shift instructions* (ASL and ASR) are used in shifting two's complement signed numbers, preserving the sign-bit during right-shifts, and reporting any sign changes via the V-flag during left shifts. The *logical-shift instructions* (LSL and LSR) are used in shifting unsigned numbers, left or right. The rotate-instructions (ROR and ROL) set up a circular path for bits to follow. The bit shifted out of one end of the operand is shifted into the other end of the operand. With the *extended-rotate instructions* (ROXL and ROXR), the bit shifted out of one end of the operand is stored into the X-flag, and the previous X-flag is shifted into the opposite end. Also included in this group is the SWAP instruction which exchanges the 16-bit halves of a register.

All shift and rotate operations can be performed on either registers or memory. The shifts or rotates of a memory operand is limited to word size operands and a shift-count of one.

The shift-count is either specified as an immediate value in the range one to eight, or by the low-order 6 bits of another data register D*n* (other bits are ignored). The immediate values of 1 to 7 represent shifts of 1 to 7, and an immediate value of 0 specifies a shift count of 8. In the latter case, the possible shift-count is 0-63, where, for zero, no shifts occur but condition codes are affected. As with

TABLE 3-17 LOGICAL OPERATIONS

Instruction	Syntax	Size	Description
AND	AND.<s> <dea>,Dn AND.<s> Dn,<amea>	B,W,L B,W,L	(dea) AND D*n* → D*n* D*n* AND (amea) → (amea)
ANDI	ANDI.<s> #<data>,<daea>	B,W,L	Immediate data AND (daea) → (daea)
EOR[1]	EOR.<s> Dn,<daea>	B,W,L	D*n* EOR (daea) → (daea)
EORI	EORI.<s> #<data>,<daea>	B,W,L	Immediate data EOR (daea) → (daea)
NOT	NOT.<s> <daea>	B,W,L	Takes one's complement of (daea)
OR	OR.<s> <dea>,Dn OR.<s> Dn,<amea>	B,W,L B,W,L	(dea) OR D*n* → D*n* D*n* OR (amea) → (amea)
ORI	ORI.<s> #<data>,<daea>	B,W,L	Immediate data AND (daea) → (daea)

[1] Exclusive-OR operation.

TABLE 3-18 SHIFT AND ROTATE OPERATIONS

Instruction	Syntax	Size	Description
ASL	ASL.<s> Dn,Dm ASL.<s> #<data>,Dm ASL <maea>	B,W,L B,W,L W	[X&C] ← [←Destination] ←0
ASR	ASR.<s> Dn,Dm ASR.<s> #<data>,Dm ASR <maea>	B,W,L B,W,L W	[Destination→] → [X&C]
LSL	LSL.<s> Dn,Dm LSL.<s> #<data>,Dm LSL <maea>	B,W,L B,W,L W	[X&C] ← [←Destination] ← 0
LSR	LSR.<s> Dn,Dm LSR.<s> #<data>,Dm LSR <maea>	B,W,L B,W,L W	0 → [Destination →] → [X&C]
ROL	ROL.<s> Dn,Dm ROL.<s> #<data>,Dm ROL <maea>	B,W,L B,W,L W	[C] ← [←Destination] ← (rotated back around)
ROR	ROR.<s> Dn,Dm ROR.<s> #<data>,Dm ROR <maea>	B,W,L B,W,L W	→ [Destination →] → [C] (rotated back around)
ROXL	ROXL.<s> Dn,Dm ROXL.<s> #<data>,Dm ROXL <maea>	B,W,L B,W,L W	[C] ← [←Destination] ← [X] (rotated back around)
ROXR	ROXR.<s> Dn,Dm ROXR.<s> #<data>,Dm ROXR <maea>	B,W,L B,W,L W	[X] → [Destination→] → [C] (rotated back around)
SWAP	SWAP Dn	L	$Dn[31:16] \leftrightarrow Dn[15:0]$.

arithmetic and data movement operations, shift and rotate affect only the portion of the destination register specified by the data size code.

The execution time of a shift or rotate instruction is proportional to the shift count. Since a shift or rotate is performed one bit at a time (each bit taking 2 clock cycles of the 68000), it is good practice to minimize the shift-count for faster execution.

Unfortunately, SWAP does not support exchanging bytes of a register. One way to implement this is by using `ROR.W #8,Dn`

Example 3-28

Extract the bit field D0[15:12] and store it in D1[3:0], so that D1[7:4] is zero and the original D0 is not affected.

```
MOVE.W  D0,D1
ROL.L   #4,D1   Shift/Rotate in the shorter direction
SWAP    D1
ANDI.B  #0F,D1
```

Example 3-29

The program shown in Figure 3-51 finds the number of bits that are one ("1") in D0[15:0]. The LSL is used to shift D0[15:0] left by one bit, and then the C-bit is checked to see if D0[15] was zero or not.

3.5.6 Bit Manipulation Instructions

The bit-manipulation instructions operate on an individual bit of an operand as described below:

BTST (Bit Test)	Tests the state of a bit.
BSET (Bit Test and Set)	Tests the state of a bit, then sets it to logic "1".
BCLR (Bit Test and Clear)	Tests the state of a bit, then clears it to logic "0".
BCHG (Bit Test and Change)	Tests the state of a bit, then inverts that bit.

```
* SUBROUTINE BITCNT
*
* Purpose: The subroutine counts the bits that are "1" in
           register D0[15:0].
*
* Inputs: D0[15:0] where "1"s will be counted.
*
* Outputs: D1 = Number "1" bit count.
*
           SECTION    0
BITCNT     MOVEM.W    D0/D2,-(SP)     Save used registers.
*
           MOVE.W     #16-1,D2        D2= Loop count -1.
           MOVE.W     #0,D1           Initialize bit-count to zero.
*
BITLOOP    LSL.W      #1,D0           D0[15] → C-bit.
           BCC.S      BITNEXT         Bit = 0?
           ADDQ.W     #1,D1              No: +Bit count.
BITNEXT    DBF        D2,BITLOOP      Loop until all 16-bits are
                                      tested.
*
           MOVEM.W    (SP)+,D0/D2     Restore used registers.
           RTS
           END
```

Figure 3-51 Bit-count Program of Example 3-29.

The state of the bit tested is indicated by the Z-bit of condition codes as follows:

$$\text{Bit tested} = 0, \text{ then } Z = 1$$

$$\text{Bit tested} = 1, \text{ then } Z = 0$$

which is consistent with the definition of Z-bit. None of the other condition codes are affected by the bit-manipulation instructions.

All bit manipulation operations can be performed on either memory or register operands. The register operands are limited to long-word data size. The bit number in this case is specified by an immediate value or by a data register. If the bit number is not in the range [0-31], then the number will be treated as modulo 32.

The memory operands are limited to byte data-size, where the source-operand is the bit-number in the range [0-7]. Numbers outside this range are treated as modulo 8 to calculate the bit number. Note that BTST does not alter the operand, therefore all data-addressing modes except immediate are allowed.

The bit manipulation instructions are summarized in Table 3-19.

3.5.7 Binary-coded Decimal (BCD) Instructions

This group of instructions perform addition, subtraction, and negation of binary-coded decimal (BCD) operands. The three BCD-arithmetic instructions are de-

TABLE 3-19 BIT MANIPULATION INSTRUCTIONS

Instruction	Syntax	Size	Description
BCHG	BCHG #<data>,Dn BCHG Dm,Dn BCHG Dm,<daea> BCHG #<data>,<daea>	L L B B	Test and invert a specified bit.
BCLR	BCLR #<data>,Dn BCLR Dm,Dn BCLR Dm,<daea> BCLR #<data>,<daea>	L L B B	Test and clear a specified bit.
BSET	BSET #<data>,Dn BSET Dm,Dn BSET Dm,<daea> BSET #<data>,<daea>	L L B B	Test and set a sepcified bit.
BTST	BTST #<data>,Dn BTST Dm,Dn BTST Dm,<dea> BTST #<data>,<dea>	L L B B	Test a specified bit.

[1] Data = 0–31 is the bit number.

[2] Dm(mod 32) = 0–31 is the bit number.

fined in Table 3-20 where each instruction can operate only on byte-size data containing two decimal digits. Addition and subtraction are done as decimal operations, also including the X-bit so that carry or borrows between bytes in multiprecision decimal arithmetic can be handled.

Although the BCD instructions can work with operands in data registers, this is usually of limited use since these instructions can only work on byte-size data. Higher bytes of a register are not conveniently accessible and, furthermore, the rotate instruction between multiple BCD instructions will affect the intermediate Z-flag. Hence, it is recommended that BCD operands longer than two digits be stored as multiple bytes in memory, in the 68000's usual high-to-low order so as to make use of the pre-decrement addressing mode of BCD instructions.

The *negate-decimal* (NEGX) *instruction* performs the ten's complement of an operand when X = 0, and nine's complement when X = 1.

The condition codes are affected as follows by the BCD instructions:

X (Extend):	Set same as Carry bit.
N (Negate):	Undefined.
Z (Zero):	Cleared if (intermediate) result is non-zero; unchanged otherwise.
V (Overflow):	Undefined.
C (Carry):	Set if a decimal carry or borrow is generated; cleared otherwise.

Similar to extended binary-arithmetic operations, it is necessary to set Z = 1, and X = 0 before the first BCD operation. Then, upon completion of a multiple-precision operation, the Z-bit will carry valid information. If the overall result is zero, the Z-bit remains set, and if there is a decimal overflow both X- and C-bits are set. However, unlike binary operations, the N- and V-bits do not carry any meaningful information.

The BCD values do not carry any sign information. Then, how do we handle

TABLE 3-20 BCD ARITHMETIC INSTRUCTIONS

Instruction	Syntax	Size	Operation
ABCD	`ABCD Dn,Dm` `ABCD -(An),-(Am)`	B B	$Dn_{10} + Dm_{10} + X \rightarrow Dm$ $(An - 1)_{10} + (Am - 1)_{10} + X \rightarrow (Am - 1)$
NBCD	`NBCD <daea>`	B	$0 - (daea)_{10} - X \rightarrow (daea)$
SBCD	`SBCD Dn,Dm` `SBCD -(An),-(Am)`	B B	$Dn_{10} - Dm_{10} - X \rightarrow Dm$ $(An - 1)_{10} - (Am - 1)_{10} - X \rightarrow (Am - 1)$

signed BCD numbers? If a carry bit is set during subtraction, this indicates a negative result. Since there is no inherent sign-bit of BCD numbers, sign-information has to be stored separately (for example, by using an extra byte), depending upon the application.

Example 3-30

Assume A0 and A1 points to the MSD of the source and destination operands, respectively, where both operands have 8-BCD digits (i.e., 4 bytes). Give the instruction sequence to add these two operands.

```
ADDQ.L  #4,A0           Prepare A0 & A1 for pre-decrement.
ADDQ.L  #4,A1
MOVE    #4,CCR          X=0, Z=1.
ABCD    -(A0),-(A1)     Add in LSD-to MSD order.
ABCD    -(A0),-(A1)
ABCD    -(A0),-(A1)
ABCD    -(A0),-(A1)
```

Operation:

```
   49833469 (BCD)
 + 02579444 (BCD)
 ---------------
   52412913
```

3.5.8 System Control Instructions

This group of instructions consists of privileged instructions that can be only executed in the supervisor mode, trap-generating instructions, and instructions that modify the CCR (as illustrated in Table 3-21). All the system control instructions have fixed data sizes, and mostly are special variations of regular instructions such as MOVE, ADDI, etc. The two priviledged instructions we have not seen so far are *return from exception* (RTE) and STOP. The RTE instruction is used to return from an exception-handling routine, and is the last instruction of any exception routine. The STOP instruction loads the PC with the address of next instruction and the SR is loaded with the immediate value given, before stopping the processor. For example,

```
STOP   #$2000
```

loads the SR with $2000 and then stops the processor. Only an exception condition such as external interrupt will take the 68000 out of the stopped state. Meanwhile, no indication is given to peripherals regarding the stopped state of the 68000.

The trap-generating instructions are typically used for error-handling and operating system calls which we will cover in more detail in Chapter 4.

TABLE 3-21 SYSTEM CONTROL INSTRUCTIONS

Instruction Syntax	Size	Operation
Privileged		
ANDI #<data>,SR	W	Immediate data AND SR → SR.
EORI #<data>,SR	W	Immediate data EOR SR → SR.
MOVE <dea>,SR	W	Operand → SR.
MOVE USP,An	L	USP → A*n*.
MOVE An,USP	L	An → USP.
ORI #<data>,SR	W	Immediate data OR SR → SR.
RESET	—	Assert RESET* for 124 clocks.
RTE	—	(SP) → SR; SP + 2 → SP; (SP) → PC; SP + 4 → SP.
STOP #<data>	W	Immediate data → SR; Stop.
Trap Generating		
CHK <dea>,Dn	W	If D*n* < 0 or D*n* > (dea), then CHK exception.
TRAP #<data>	—	TRAP exception #(data = 1 − 16)
TRAPV	—	If V = 1 then TRAPV exception.
Condition Code Register		
ANDI #<data>,CCR	B	Immediate data AND CCR → CCR.
EORI #<data>,CCR	B	Immediate data EOR CCR → CCR.
MOVE <dea>,CCR	B(W)[1]	Operand → CCR.
MOVE CCR,<daea>	W[2]	CCR → Operand.
ORI #<data>,CCR	B	Immediate data OR CCR → CCR.
Other (68000/68008 Only)		
MOVE SR,<daea>	W	SR → Operand.

[1] Is a word operation, but only CCR is affected. The upper-byte is ignored.

[2] Is a word operation, but only low-byte contains CCR. The upper-byte is all zeros.

3.5.9 Multiprocessor Instructions

The 68000 has only one instruction, namely test and set (TAS), to support multiprocessor operations. The TAS instruction first tests the destination operand, and then sets bit 7 of the operand to one unconditional bit. The N- and Z-flags reflect the state of operand before setting the bit 7. The assembly syntax is

```
TAS  <daea>
```

where ⟨daea⟩ is the data-alterable addressing modes, and the operand size is limited to a byte. So far, it sounds like just another bit-manipulation instruction. What is unique about TAS to classify it as a multiprocessor control instruction?

The test and set operation of TAS is indivisible (i.e., it is performed in *one* bus cycle which we earlier referred to as a read-modify-write bus cycle). The typical application of TAS is to provide synchronization of processes and resource allocation when two or more processors have access to shared resources. In a multiprocessor system, there are usually dedicated program and data memory to each processor, as well as several shared resources as shown in Figure 3-52.

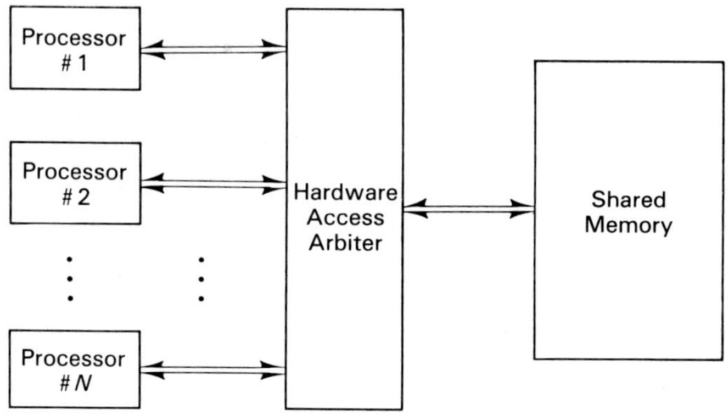

(a) Logical Organization of Shared Memory.

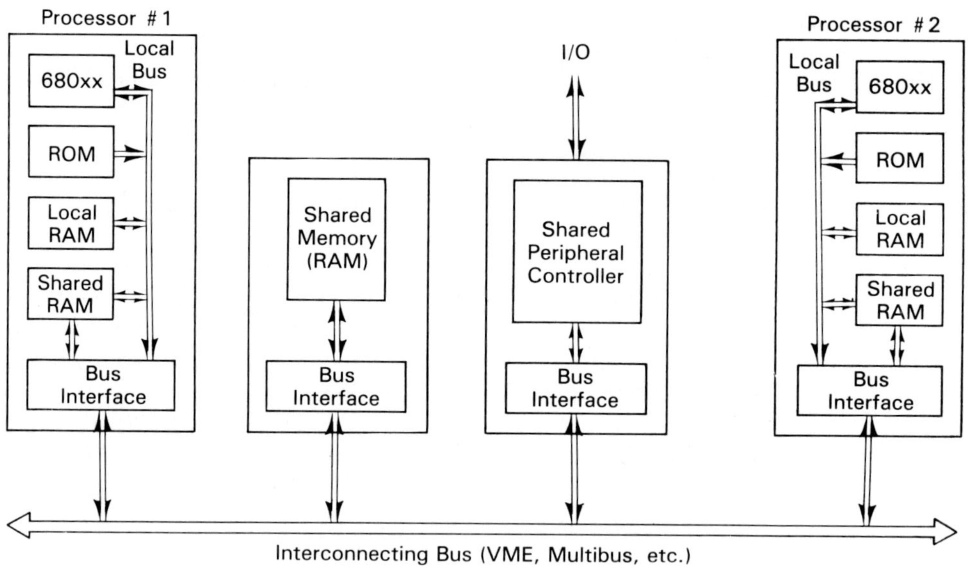

(b) A Possible Physical Configuration.

Figure 3-52 A Multiprocessor System.

Among possible shared resources are memory for inter-processor communication, disk controller, printer interface, and so on.

For example, let us say that two processors are trying to communicate using a shared memory. We need a flag to indicate that a certain portion of memory is being used by one, so that the other one does not try to write at the same time to the same memory locations. Because there is only one bus, and memory itself is single-ported, the accesses from processors are arbitrated in the hardware for each bus cycle. This arbitration is transparent to a processor other than the possible wait-cycles while another processor finishes its access. Hence, a mechanism is needed to synchronize multiple processors that may try to access the shared memory simultaneously.

Such a flag to control access to a shared and critical resource is called a *semaphore*[9] reminiscent of mechanical arms on railroad crossings. Again, the important feature of TAS is that it performs an indivisible operation in one bus cycle, therefore, no other processor can access the semaphore while one processor is testing and setting it. The following example will illustrate a problem scenario when TAS is not used.

Example 3-31

Assume two processors are attempting to access and modify the same data file on a shared resource such as secondary storage. Each processor will test a semaphore called *DLOCK* residing in shared memory to see if it is currently being used and, if not, allocate it to itself. The first scheme, shown in Figure 3-53-a, uses the BSET instruction. Although this approach will work most of the time, it is bound to fail intermittently when both processors try to access DLOCK almost at the same time. In such a case, both processors will find that the data file is free and both will allocate it to themselves with erroneous consequences. The second scheme, shown in Figure 3-53-b, will work with no problems.

A semaphore might also be used with a single-processor system where several tasks are run in an interleaved fashion. This is referred to as *multitasking* or *concurrent programming*. In such systems, timer-interrupts are typically used to switch tasks that the processor is running. The TAS instruction can be used to handle resource allocation between tasks. However, TAS is not the only possible instruction in this case. The instructions *BCLR*, *BCHG*, and *BSET* can also be used as well, since they all perform a test-and-set type of operation in a single instruction (but not in a single bus cycle). In other words, no other task can alter a semaphore while another one is examining and setting it because no exceptions (except bus/address error and reset) can interrupt the operation of a *single* instruction.

[9] Semaphore is a special data type initially introduced by Dijkstra in 1965. The definition of semaphore is not limited to multi-processor systems.

Processor A			Processor B		
PROCA	BSET	#7,DLOCK	PROCB	BSET	#7,DLOCK
	BNE	PROCA		BNE	PROCB
	.			.	
	.			.	
	.			.	
	MOVE.B	#0,DLOCK		MOVE.B	#0,DLOCK

(a) Intermittently Erroneous Resource Allocation.

Processor A			Processor B		
PROCA	TAS	DLOCK	PROCB	TAS	DLOCK
	BNE	PROCA		BNE	PROCB
	.			.	
	.			.	
	.			.	
	MOVE.B	#0,DLOCK		MOVE.B	#0,DLOCK
	.			.	

(b) Correct Resource Allocation.

Figure 3-53 Resource Allocation in a Multiprocessor System.

3.6 INSTRUCTION TIMING

So far we have not addressed how long a 68000 instruction takes to execute. In general, the time to execute an instruction depends on the particular instruction and its operand-addressing modes. During the execution of an instruction, one or two words of the following instruction is prefetched to keep the two-word instruction-queue full. The execution of an instruction involves necessary effective-address calculation, fetching and/or writing operands, and performing the desired operation. As we stated in Chapter 1, the 68000 has two 16-bit *arithmetic units* (AU) and one *arithmetic-and-logic unit* (ALU). Usually, the two arithmetic units perform 32-bit effective-address calculation, while concurrently, the ALU performs data operations. Most of the 16-bit ALU operations such as addition and logical operations are performed in one clock cycle. The ALU operation is overlapped with the prefetch of the next instruction word, and thus, is hidden for most instructions. However, not all instructions can completely overlap data operations with the prefetch. For example, the multiply operation (MULU or MULS) is performed iteratively, taking many clock cycles.

For example, let us consider the following sequence of instructions after a reset operation[10]:

[10] Adapted from *Hitachi 68000 User Manual #U155*.

```
START NOP                    The first instruction after reset.
      BRA.S NEXT
      ADD.W D0,D1
NEXT  SUB.W VARX(A0),D0      VARX is the offset.
      CMP.W D0,D1
      NOP
      .
      .
      .
```

Table 3-22 illustrates the execution of these instructions. Note, for example, that the subtraction operation is performed concurrently with the prefetch of next instruction NOP.

The instruction timings in the Motorola's User's Manual are given in terms of processor clock cycles, and assume no wait-cycles. The format used is

```
# of Processor Clocks (# of Read Cycles / # of Write Cycles)
```

where the number of bus read and write cycles are shown in parentheses. As we saw earlier, a bus cycle (read or write) without any wait cycles will take four clock cycles. The number of clock cycles to execute an instruction is equal to or greater than the time shown for the required bus cycles in parentheses.

Example 3-32

The time to execute

```
MOVE.W (An)+,Dn
```

using a 10 MHz 68000 and assuming no wait-cycles is given as

8(2,0)

Then, the execution time is 0.8 microseconds. This means that it requires two read bus cycles and no write bus cycles. One of the reads is to prefetch next instruction, and the other one for reading in the data operand.

We mentioned earlier that the prefetch mechanism of the 68000 is used for instructions. There is one exception to this. During the execution of the MOVEM instruction, the data-stream is also prefetched to improve performance.

When programming a time-critical section of code for best execution time, keep the following guidelines in mind:

1. Concentrate on optimizing code within the most inner loop of the critical section. Saving a few clock cycles here will probably produce a noticeable difference.
2. Avoid using MULx and DIVx if possible. For example, to calculate 3*X, we can shift left by one and then add X.

TABLE 3-22 ILLUSTRATION OF INSTRUCTION PREFETCH AND EXECUTION

Microroutine	I/O Activity		AU/ALU Activity
	Operation	Operand	
Reset	Read	SSP-High	
	Read	SSP-low	
	Read	PC-high	
	Read	PC-low	
	Read	NOP	
	Read	BRA	
NOP	Read	ADD	
BRA	Read	SUB	PC = PC + d16 (AUs)
	Read	VARX	
SUB	Read	CMP	VARX + A0 (AUs)
	Read	VARX(A0)	
	Read	NOP	D0 − VARX(A0) → D0 (ALU)

3. Avoid long shifts. When shifting, shift in the direction that minimizes the shift-count.
4. Minimize accesses to memory by having the frequently used data and pointers in registers.
5. Access and manipulate large data structures in a way that reduces the effective-address calculations.
6. Explore using an alternate approach or algorithm.

In practice, it is possible and likely to have different wait-cycles, if any, for program and data memory. In this case, program and data bus cycles have to be separated for accurate calculation. Also, some instruction timings given in User's Manual specify that the EA calculation timing has to be added separately depending upon the addressing mode chosen.

Example 3-33

Calculate the time to execute ADD.L d16(A*n*),D*n* for 12.5 MHz 68000 and no wait-cycles.

ADDA	6(1,0)	
EA Calculation	12(3/0)	
Total	18(4/0)	→ 1.44 microseconds

3.7 SUBROUTINE USAGE AND PARAMETER PASSING

Here we will discuss programming techniques regarding subroutine usage and parameter passing. Considering that any program consists of a main routine and several subroutines, this is an important topic.

A subroutine should, in general, not change the contents of any address or data registers unless the register is used to return a result to the calling program. There are two main reasons for this. First, it makes writing a program easier since it eliminates any concern about a register being changed when a subroutine is called. The called subroutine might call another subroutine, and so on, but this will not affect the registers as seen by a calling program at any level of nested subroutines. Secondly, this is necessary to write reentrant subroutines, which we will discuss later in this section. As we have been using in the previous examples, the MOVEM instruction is typically used for saving any used address or data registers at the beginning of a subroutine, and restoring them at the end, as shown below:

```
SUBRX MOVEM.L Dm-Dn/Ai-Aj,-(SP)    Save used registers.
        .
        .
        .
      MOVEM.L (SP)+,Dm-Dn/Ai-Aj    Restore used registers.
      RTS
```

To illustrate the various parameter passing techniques, let us consider a subroutine of the form

```
ADDNUMS (N,IARRAY,V)
```

the purpose of which is to add N numbers of the array IARRAY(0:$N - 1$), and the 32-bit result is given by parameter V. The IARRAY parameter would be passed by using the beginning address of the array (i.e., address of IARRAY(0)). The parameter N can be specified either by its actual value, or by its address. The former is called *passed-by-value*, and the latter is called *passed-by-reference*, which is familiar terminology used often by high-level languages. Summarizing, we have

Input Parameters:	N:	16-bit value indicating the number of elements to be added. Can be passed by address or value.
	IARRAY:	Starting address of array.
Output parameters:	V:	32-bit result. Passed by address, indicating where we want the result stored, or passed by value.

There are basically three approaches to pass parameters to a subroutine:

1. Pass parameters in address or data registers.
2. Place parameters in-line, immediately after the JSR or BSR instruction.
3. Transfer parameters on the stack, pushed before the JSR or BSR instruction.

The first approach is the simplest (we used it in Example 3-18). Parameters can be passed in any register, but usually address values are passed in address registers, and data values are passed in data registers limiting the maximum number of parameters to 15. This approach is fast since it requires little overhead in passing parameters, but it lacks generality because of the limited number of registers.

The second approach, the in-line coding of parameters, requires that the parameters be placed following the call to the subroutine, as shown in Figure 3-54. The advantage of this is that return address pushed onto stack points to the first parameter. Therefore, it requires the subroutine to alter the return address to skip over the parameter area. The in-line coding approach has the disadvantage that parameters that are passed by value are fixed at assembly time, as part of the program code, and thus cannot be changed dynamically during program ex-

```
*           PROGRAM SECTION
*
N           EQU         512                 Array size is 512 words.
            .
            .
            .
            JSR         ADDNUMS
            DC.W        N                   N passed by value.
            DC.L        IARRAY              Starting address of IARRAY.
            DC.L        V                   V passed by address.
            .
            .
            .
ADDNUMS     MOVEM.L     D0-D1/A0-A2,-(SP)   Save used registers.
            MOVEA.L     (SP),A2             Get return address.
            MOVE.W      (A2)+,D0            D0 = N (First parameter).
            MOVEA.L     (A2)+,A0            A0 → IARRAY (Second
*                                                   parameter).
            MOVEA.L     (A2)+,A1            A1 → Result (Third
*                                                   parameter).
            MOVEA.L     A2,(SP)             Fix return address.
            .
            .
            .
*           DATA SECTION
IARRAY      DS.W        N
V           DS.L        1
            .
            .
            .
            END
```

Figure 3-54 In-line Coding Example to Pass Parameters.

ecution. This is because the program section is usually stored in read-only memory, or is write-protected. Even if this were not the case, it would not be good programming practice to modify a program section during execution, since this would then be considered self-modifying code. To eliminate this limitation, we can pass *N* by address.

The third approach, passing parameters on the stack, is the most general one. In the subroutine, the parameters can be accessed with fixed offsets from the stack pointer as illustrated in Figure 3-55. The contents of the stack after the subroutine call is shown in Figure 3-56. Upon return from the subroutine, the parameter area must be deallocated, usually with a LEA or ADDQ instruction.

The choice of a particular approach depends on the application. Once chosen, it is usually best to use one approach consistently throughout the program. Simple programs can use the first approach. For large programs, we recommend passing parameters on stack. This approach is widely used by compilers, and thus is necessary to interface to high-level language programs. We may, for instance, do most of our programming in C language and call assembly language subroutines for time-critical sections of the program. C programs usually pass parameters in reverse order and the value returned is in data register D0 or D7. Hence, it uses a combination of two approaches. For example, the C call given by

```
int a,b,result
int *c
.
.
.
result= subrx (a,b,c)
.
.
.
```

generates the following assembly code:

```
MOVE.L  C(A6),-(SP)      Parameter c.
MOVE.W  B(A6),-(SP)      Parameter b.
MOVE.W  A(A6),-(SP)      Parameter a.
JSR     SUBRX
LEA     8(SP),SP         Deallocate stack.
MOVE.W  D0,RESULT(A6)    Store result from subroutine.
```

where variables {*a*, *b*, *c*, result} are stored on the system stack, and are accessed using fixed negative offsets from pointer A6. The offset values are equated to symbol names using the SET directive by the compiler.

In addition to parameters, another design issue regarding subroutines is the use of local variables. So far, in our examples we have been using the address and data registers for these. This, again, lacks generality. Compilers commonly

```
*         PROGRAM SECTION
*
N         EQU          512                   Array size is 512 words.
          .
          .
          .
          MOVE.W       #N,-(SP)              Parameter N (passed by
*                                            value).
          PEA          IARRAY                Parameter IARRAY (passed
*                                            by address).
          SUBQ.L       #4,SP                 Return area for V (passed
*                                            by value).
          JSR          ADDNUMS
          .
          .
          .
*         ADDNUMS SUBROUTINE
*         Local parameter declarations:
*
NUM       SET          32
ARRAY     SET          28
RESULT    SET          24
*
*         Main Body of ADDNUMS:
*
ADDNUMS   MOVEM.L      D0-D1/A0-A2,-(SP)     Save used registers.
          MOVE.W       NUM(SP),D0            D0= parameter N.
          MOVEA.L      ARRAY(SP),20          A0= Parameter IARRAY.
          .
          .
          .
          MOVE.L       D1,RESULT(SP)         Store result in D1 to output
*                                            area.
          MOVEM.L      (SP)+,D0-D1/A0-A2     Restore used registers.
          RTS
*
*
*         DATA SECTION
IARRAY    DS.W         N
          .
          .
          .
          END
```

Figure 3-55 Program Illustrating Passing Parameters on Stack.

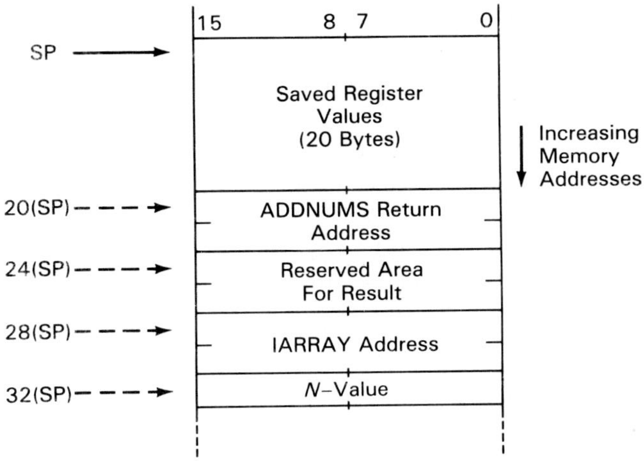

Figure 3-56 Stack After Subroutine Call of Figure 3-55.

use the stack to store local variables. These variables are active during the execution of a subroutine and are deallocated before returning from the subroutine. The 68000 provides the LINK and UNLK instruction pair for this purpose[11], as described in Table 3-23. The LINK instruction, used at the beginning of a subroutine, allocates stack area and sets up an address register to point to the beginning of this area. The UNLK reverses the operation of LINK and deallocates the local variable area, as illustrated in Figure 3-57. The general form of a subroutine body is then shown in Figure 3-58.

An area of stack containing a block of data is called a *stack frame*. The stack frame of a subroutine may include parameters, saved register values, and local variables, if any, as illustrated in Figure 3-59. The address register pointing to local variable area is usually referred to as *frame-pointer* (FP). The register A6 is typically used as the frame-pointer. It is important to note the following:

1. The displacement value of LINK must be a negative and even number (why?).
2. Register A*k* does not need to be included in the MOVEM list, since it is saved by LINK.
3. The local variables can be accessed using negative offsets from frame-pointer A*k*. Just as in parameter passing, the use of SET directive is recommended for better readability.
4. The passed parameters may be accessed using positive offsets from SP or frame-pointer A*k*. It is easier to use A*k* (Why?).

[11] Another application for LINK and UNLK is in implementing linked lists.

TABLE 3-23 LINK AND UNLK INSTRUCTIONS

Instruction	Syntax	Operation
LINK	`LINK Ak,#<d16>`	1. SP − 4 → SP 2. A*k* → (SP) 3. SP → A*k*; SP + d16 → SP
UNLK	`UNLK Ak`	1. A*k* → SP 2. (SP) → A*k* 3. SP + 2 → SP

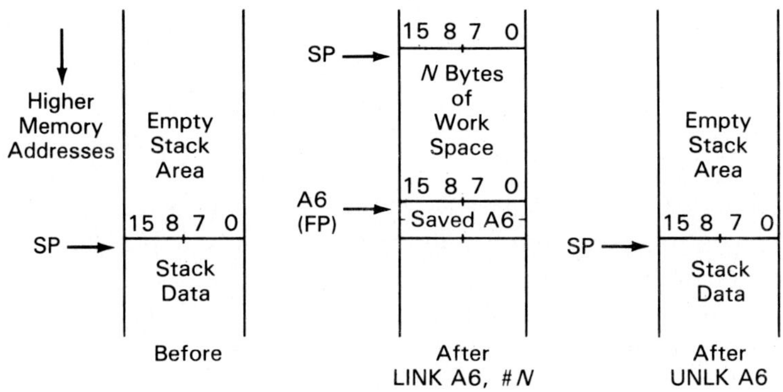

Figure 3-57 Illustration of LINK and UNLK Instructions.

```
SUBRX   LINK       Ak,#-<s>            Allocate <s> bytes for local
*                                      variables.
        MOVEM.L    Dm-Dn/Ai-Aj,-(SP)   Save used registers.
        .
        .
        .
        MOVEM.L    (SP)+,Dm-Dn/Ai-Aj   Restore used registers.
        UNLK       Ak                  Deallocate local variable area.
        RTS
```

Figure 3-58 Structure of a Subroutine using LINK and UNLK.

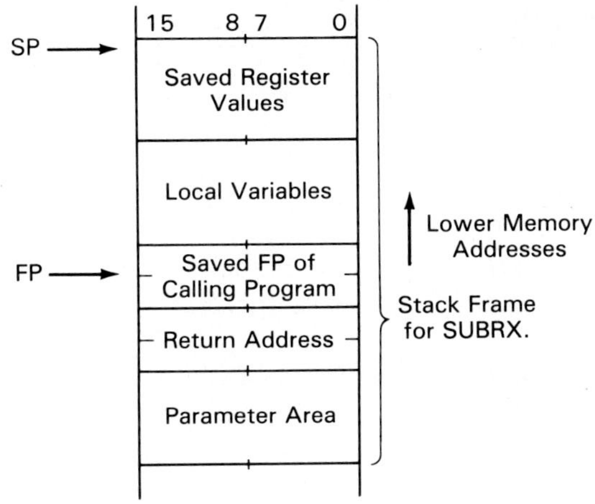

Figure 3-59 Stack Frame of Subroutine Shown in Figure 3-58.

Reentrancy. In a multitasking/multiuser environment, a single copy of a subroutine may be shared by more than one task (see Figure 3-60). A subroutine may be called by task A, interrupted before its execution is complete, called by task B, and then re-entered again at the point of interruption of task A. Such a subroutine is called *reentrant*, and differs from ordinary subroutines in that it could be called again before its current execution is complete, without any adverse effects. The requirements that are necessary and sufficient to make a subroutine reentrant are the following:

1. Any parameters or local variables stored in memory must be restricted to the stack frame of the subroutine.
2. Registers may be used for parameters and local variables. But, all used address and data registers must be saved at the beginning of the subroutine, and restored at the end.

The above guarantees that each invocation of a subroutine will create a separate stack frame, thereby maintaining data integrity of previous calls that are

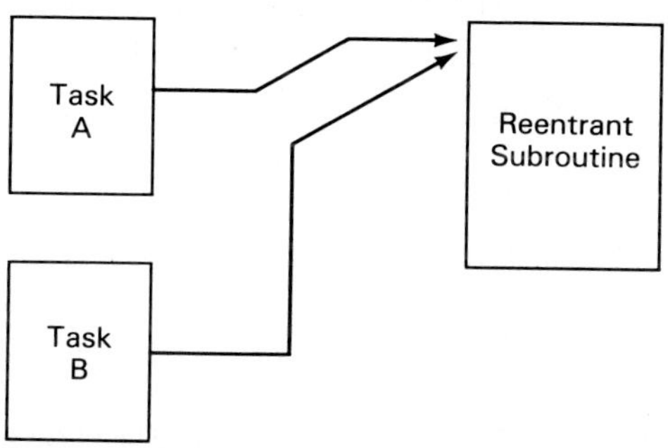

Figure 3-60 Sharing of a Reentrant Subroutine.

not completed. One of the applications of reentrancy is when a subroutine calls itself. This is called *self-reentrancy* or *recursion*. The classic example of this is the factorial subroutine that recursively calls itself.

3.8 MACROS

Another important tool in assembly language is the use of macros. On encountering a macro instruction, the assembler replaces it with the predefined sequence of instructions, substituting any arguments in the places marked in the macro definition. The syntax of a macro definition is assembler dependent[12]. Figure 3-61 illustrates the syntax used by the Motorola assembler.

Macros, unlike subroutines, are expanded each time they are used, so they do not save any memory. The advantage of macros is that they make programming easier, they are faster than a subroutine since there is no calling overhead and they make a program more readable as the next example will illustrate.

Example 3-34

Suppose we call a subroutine many times, passing parameters to it via the stack as shown in Figure 3-62-a. If we define the macro ADDNUMSM given by:

```
ADDNUMSM MACRO
*
*        Calling Format:
*
*        ADDNUMSM <N>,<IARRAY>,<V>
*
         MOVE.W     \1,-(SP)     Push N.
         PEA        \2           Push address of IARRAY.
         SUBQ.L     #4,SP        Reserve area for V.
         JSR        ADDNUMS
         MOVE.L     0(SP),\3     Get result V.
         LEA        10(SP),SP    Deallocate parameters.
         ENDM
```

Then, we can invoke all calls to ADDNUMS subroutine with the macro, as shown in Figure 3-62-b.

3.9 USE OF LOOK-UP TABLES

Microprocessor programs often require the calculation of a function. This could simply be a code conversion, calculating the square-root of a number, and so on. In such cases, the use of *look-up tables* (LUTs) provide a good trade-off between

[12] Assembler with macro processing capability is called macro assembler.

```
<macro-name>      MACRO
                  .
                  .
                  .
                  ENDM

Argument Definitions: \1 : Replaced by first argument(of invocation).
                      \2 : Replaced by second argument.
                      .
                      .
                      \9 : Replaced by 9th argument.
                      .
                      .
                      \0 : Replaced by operand size qualifier of
                           macro name.

Labels Within a Macro: \@<label> where \@ generates a new label for
                       each invocation, guaranteeing label uniqueness.

                  MACRO INVOCATION

[<label>]   <macro-name>[.<qualifier>]   <argument #1>,<argument #2>,...

     Qualifier is B, W, or L, replacing \0 within macro definition.
```

Figure 3-61 Illustration of Motorola Syntax for Macros.

execution speed and program memory size. A univariate function of the form

$$y = f(x)$$

can be precalculated for each possible x value and stored in a table. The time to look up a value from the table is much less than calculating it. Of course, for very simple functions like $y = 2 * x$, it would not be advantageous to use a look-up table.

For example, if y has word size, then to look up a value, we need the following instructions:

```
* Input : D0 = x value between 0 and N-1, inclusive.
* Output: D1 = y value.
        LEA         TABLE,A0          Get LUT starting address. (8 cycles)
        LSL.W       #1,D0             Scale index value. (8 cycles)
        MOVE.W      0(A0,D0.W),D1     Table look-up (14 cycles)
        .
        .
        .
```

where the size of TABLE is N words. The total time required for look-up operation is only 30 clock cycles.

```
MOVE.W      #512,-(SP)
PEA         BUFFERA
SUBQ.W      #4,SP
JSR         ADDNUMS
MOVE.W      0(SP),D0
LEA         10(SP),SP
.
.
.
MOVE.W      N,-(SP)
PEA         BUFFERB
SUBQ.W      #4,SP
JSR         ADDNUMS
MOVE.W      0(SP),D1
LEA         10(SP),SP
.
.
.
MOVE.W      6(SP),-(SP)
PEA         ARRAYX
SUBQ.W      #4,SP
JSR         ADDNUMS
MOVE.W      0(SP),(A0)
LEA         10(SP),SP
```

(a) Various Subroutine calls to ADDUMS

```
ADDNUMSM    #512,BUFFERA,D0
.
.
.
ADDNUMS     N,BUFFERB,D1
.
.
.
ADDNUMS     6(SP),ARRAYX,(A0)
```

(b) Macro version of subroutine calls.

Figure 3-62 Illustration of Macros for Example 3-34.

We have already seen two examples using LUTs: the hex-to-ASCII routine (Figure 3-1) and the jump tables where the entries are not data but routine addresses. In general, the applications of LUT include the following:

1. Scaling (e.g., $y = a * x + b$).
2. Trigonometric functions (sine, cosine, and so on).
3. Square root, logarithm.

```
* SUBROUTINE SINE
*
* Purpose: This subroutine calculates the sine of an integer angle
*          between 0 and 359 degrees.
*
* Input: Angle passed by value on the stack.
* Output: Returned in D0[15:0].
*
* Calling Sample: MOVE.W   D0,-(SP)    D0 has angle (0-359 degrees).
*                 JSR      SINE
*                 <D0 has the sine value.>
*
* Description: The order of error is O(2^-15).
*
* Main Body of SINE:
*
            SECTION     0
ANGLE       SET         +8
*
SINE        MOVEM.L     A0,-(SP)          Save A0.
*
            MOVE.W      ANGLE(SP),D0      Get angle.
            LEA         SINELUT,A0        Get LUT starting address.
            LSL.W       #1,D0             Scale index value.
            MOVE.W      0(A0,D0.W),D0     Table look-up.
*
            MOVEM.L     (SP)+,A0          Restore A0.
            RTS
*
*           SINE TABLE  (HEX)             DEGREE SINE(DECIMAL)
SINELUT     DC.W        0000                0        0
            DC.W        023C                1        0.0174524
            DC.W        0477                2        0.0348995
            DC.W        06B2                3        0.0523360
            .                               .        .
            .                               .        .
            .                               .        .
            DC.W        7FFF                90       1.0
            DC.W        7FFB                91       0.9998477
            .                               .        .
            .                               .        .
            .                               .        .
            DC.W        8000                270     -1.0
            DC.W        8005                271     -0.9998477
            .                               .        .
            .                               .        .
            DC.W        FD74                359     -0.0174524
*
            END
```

Figure 3-63 Calculating Sine of an Angle Using a LUT.

4. Inverse ($1/x$).
5. Code conversions.

Example 3-35

Program shown in Figure 3-63 calculates the sine of all integer angles between 0 and 359 degrees. Instead of calculating the sine using the series expansion given by

$$\sin(x) = x - x^3/3! + x^5/5! - x^7/7! \ldots$$

We can store these sine values in a LUT of 360 words. Each word of the LUT will have the two's complement format scaled down by 2^{-15}. Thus the range of sine values stored is approximately between -1 and 1.

FURTHER READING

Program Development

1. An excellent discussion of program modularity and development is given by Pressman in his book titled *Software Engineering: A Practitioner's Approach*, published by McGraw-Hill in 1982.

EXERCISES

Program Development

1. What is the purpose of a linkage editor?
2. What are the two files an assembler usually generates? What files does a linkage editor generate?
3. Discuss how a large program can be partitioned into various modules.

Assembly Format and Directives

4. Indicate if the following statements are valid. If not, please indicate the reason.
   a. `DC.W %1101`
   b. `DC.B '123456789A',0,$FF,'\0'`
   c. `VARX SET $4000`
      `DC.W $3A000,VARX`
   d. `DC.L 2*$A000`
   e. `DS.B 400,$FF`
5. What is the difference between the ORG and SECTION directives?
6. What is the difference between the EQU and SET directives?

Programming Model

7. Specify the contents of affected address/data registers after executing the following instructions (indicate any parts of register that is not affected with "x"'s):
   a. `MOVE.B #00,D3`
   b. `MOVE.W #$49FF,D0`
   c. `MOVEA.W #$3FFE,A2`
8. How do the following instructions affect the condition codes? Please specify the value of CCR, assuming initially CCR = $00.
   a. `MOVE.W #$A249,D4`
   b. `MOVEA.W D2,A3`
   c. `SUB.L D0,D1` (Assume D0 = $64A27 and D1 = $AF002039 initially.)
9. a. Does the 68000 system stack(s) grow toward higher or lower memory addresses?
   b. What data sizes are allowed for stack operations?
   c. Explain the operation of PUSH and POP for USP and SSP.
   d. Can we change the value of USP in supervisor mode?
10. What are the two limitations on the values of the PC?
11. List the differences between the address and data registers of a 68000.

Data Organization In Memory

12. Display the contents of affected memory locations after executing the following instructions.
    a. `MOVE.W D0,$1000` (D0 = $1234 initially)
    b. `MOVE.L #$1234,$1000`

Operand Addressing Modes

13. In addressing mode register indirect with index and offset, answer the following questions: a) What is the size of the offset? b) What are the allowed sizes for the index register?
14. What is the effective address for source and destination operands of the following instructions? Assume A0 = $2000, A1 = $900000, and D0 = $12FA40 initially.
    a. `MOVE.B (A1),D0`
    b. `MOVE.W (A0),(A1)`
    c. `MOVE.W (A0)+,-(A1)`
    d. `ADD.L $34(A1,D0.W),D1`
    e. `LEA 20(PC)` (Assume address of LEA instruction is $4000)
15. Sometimes the operand addressing architecture of the 68000 is said to have $1\frac{1}{2}$ addressing structure because most of the instructions require one of the operands to be in an address or data register. Give a list of the 68000 instructions that support memory operands for both source and destination.

16. What instruction groups of the 68000 do not affect the CCR? Are there any exceptions in these groups?

Instruction Set

17. Specify the byte address of memory locations affected by executing each of the following instructions (Assume A3 = $4000):
    a. `CLR.L (A3)`
    b. `MOVEM.L D0-D3,(A3)`
    c. `MOVEM.L D0-D3,-(A3)`
18. Point out what is wrong with each of the following instructions. Please be specific.
    a. `ADD.W (A2)+,(A3)+`
    b. `MOVE.W #20,$3401`
    c. `SWAP.B D3`
    d. `EXG (A4),D0`
    e. `EXT.L D0`
    f. `LSL.W #4,(A0)`
    g. `JMP A1`
    h. `BSET #8,$40(A2)`
    i. `MOVE.B D0,A6`
    j. `BCHG #0,$F0(PC)`
    k. `MOVE.W $200(PC,D2.L),D4`
    l. `JMP ERR` (where ERR = $1203)
    m. `MOVEQ #$140,D4`
    n. `EOR.B (A3),D0`
    o. `JSR A0`
    p. `STOP`
19. What is the difference between the ADDI and ADDQ instructions?
20. What is the only operand size allowed for logical and shift instructions?
21. What is the only CCR bit that compare instructions do not affect? Why?
22. List the three conditions under which the processor starts execution after a STOP instruction.
23. What is the difference, if any, between the following instruction pairs. Please explain.
    a.
    ```
    MOVE.W   $1000,D3
    MOVE.W   #$1000,D3
    ```
    b.
    ```
    MOVEA.L  #TABLE,A0
    LEA      TABLE,A0
    ```
    c.
    ```
    TAS      SEMAPH
    BSET     #7,SEMAPH
    ```
    d.
    ```
    MOVE.L   (A2),D0
    MOVE.L   A2,D0
    ```

e.
```
MOVE.L   (A2),D0
MOVE.L   0(A2),D0
```
f.
```
BRA      <label>
JMP      <label>
```
g.
```
BSR      <label>
JSR      <label>
```
h.
```
MOVE.W   ($E000).W,D0
MOVE.W   ($E000).L,D0
```

24. What is the difference between the RTR and RTS instructions?
25. Let D0 be 00A02000 initially. Indicate the contents of D0 after executing the following instructions.
    a. `DIVU #9,D0?`
    b. `DIVS #9,D0?`
    c. `MULU #9,D0?`
    d. `MULS #-9,D0?`
26. Find a problem, if any, with the following subroutines:

a.
```
SUBR MOVEM.L D0-D7/A0-A6,-(SP)    Save Registers
     .
     .
     .
     MOVEM.L (SP)+,A0-A7/D0-D7    Restore Registers
     RTS
```
b.
```
SUBR MOVEM.L A0-A6/D0-D7,-(SP)    Save Registers
     MOVE    SR,-(SP)             Save CCR.
     .
     .
     .
     MOVEM.L (SP)+,A0-A6/D0-D7    Restore Registers
     RTR
```

27. Write a program to compute $X^2 + Y^2$ where X = D0[15:0] and Y = D1[15:0]. If there is any possibility for overflow in computation, detect the error condition and branch to an error-handling routine.
28. Compute $(X1 + 2 * X2 + 4 * X3 + 2 * X4 + X5)$ where $X1$ through $X5$ has byte size data stored in consecutively increasing memory locations and $X1$ is pointed to by A0. Give the result in one of the data registers in word-size.
29. Write a subroutine that calculates 32 × 32 signed multiplication of two register operands. (Hint: Use or modify subroutine MULU32 of Example 3-22.)
30. Modify the subroutine of Figure 3-1 to implement a ASCII to hex code conversion.
31. Change subroutine BLKCOPY of Example 3-16 by using DB⟨*cc*⟩ for looping.
32. What is a practical application of JSR (A*n*).
33. Program a IF $(X > Y)$ THEN . . . ELSE . . . type construct when X is signed and has word size, and Y is unsigned with byte size. Assume X and Y are address labels of the operands.

34. Specify the instructions to perform the following extended operations. Do all condition codes carry significance at the end of the operation?

a. 128-bit addition.

b. 128-bit negation.

35. Specify the number of iterations of the following loop:

```
        MOVE.L   #90000,D0
BACK    .
         .
         .
         DBF    D0,BACK
```

Instruction Timing

36. What are the two instructions of the 68000 with the longest execution time?

37. Write a loop using the DB⟨*cc*⟩ instruction that generates 1 millisecond delay. Assume no wait-cycles.

38. How much execution speed can be gained by changing the processor and its clock from 8 MHz to 12.5 MHz for the following instructions? Please specify percentage improvement assuming no wait-cycles for both speeds.

a. `MOVE.W (A1)+,D0 (I/O Intensive)`

b. `ROR.L  #4,D0     (Computation Intensive)`

39. Repeat Exercise 38 but assume 2 wait-cycles at 12.5 MHz for data-memory accesses only, and otherwise no wait cycles for program fetches.

40. Suppose the last instruction of a program is BRA, which is stored in the last word of RAM or ROM memory. If the next location is unoccupied (i.e., no DTACK* returned), would this present any problem? Please explain.

Subroutine Usage and Parameter Passing

41. a. Does the order of LINK and MOVEM instructions matter for a reentrant subroutine? Please explain.

b. Change the program of Figure 3-55 to use LINK A6,#0 and UNLK A6. Access passed parameters using offsets with respect to A6.

42. If the 68000 did not have a LINK instruction, write the instructions that would be necessary to replace LINK A6,#-$A.

43. Make the following changes to the BITCNT subroutine in Figure 3-51:

1. Operand is a long-word passed-by-value on the stack; and

2. Result is returned in D0.

44. Write the program for the following subroutine:

```
* SUBROUTINE STRCOPY
*
* Purpose: This subroutine copies a string from a
*          given source to a destination.
*
* Inputs: (passed on stack) Pointer to source
*         and destination.
* Output: None.
*
* Description: Assume string is terminated by
*              a null character.
```

45. Write a subroutine to find the maximum value of an array. Make necessary assumptions.

Macros

46. Write a macro that generates a N-millisecond delay of the form

```
DELAY <N>
```

Assume N is less than 64K. Make sure that any registers used by this routine are restored at the end.

47. Write a macro of the form MUL9 ⟨D*n*⟩ that multiplies a data register by nine. Use shift and add to implement multiplication. Again, restore all used registers.

Programming with LUTs

48. Change the subroutine SINE in Figure 3-63 to calculate the square root of an integer between 0 and 255.

49. **a.** Assuming a very time-critical section of program, write a macro of the form, BITCNT ⟨D*n*⟩, that accesses a 64 Kbyte LUT to count the number bits that are one in D*n*[15:0].

b. Compare the clock cycles of above approach with the subroutine BITCNT of example 3-51. Discuss whether the time difference justifies the use of 64 Kbytes of memory.

4

68000 Exception Processing

As we introduced in Chapter 1, Motorola refers to the wide variety of conditions that can change the program flow during execution of a program as *exceptions*. These exceptions can be due to external events such as an interrupt from a peripheral or can be due to run-time errors detected by the 68000. For example, a divide-by-zero condition detected during a DIVS or DIVU instruction causes an exception. The internal and external exceptions are summarized in Table 4-1. We will discuss each of these in detail in this chapter.

When an exception condition is recognized, the program flow is diverted from the current program to an exception handler. The general sequence of events before automatically invoking the service routine is done in the following identifiable steps by the 68000:

1. A temporary copy of the status register is made internally.
2. The S-bit is set and the T-bit of SR is cleared. The trace mode is disabled during exception processing or it will cause an endless series of exceptions (why?).
3. If the exception is due to an interrupt, the mask level of SR (I2-I0) is changed to the priority level of the acknowledged interrupt. This is to lock out the other possible incoming interrupts of lower or the same priority until the current interrupt is serviced.
4. The address of the exception handler is determined. We will discuss the details of this in the next section.
5. The current processor context is saved on the stack. All exceptions, except

TABLE 4-1 OVERVIEW OF INTERNAL AND EXTERNAL EXCEPTIONS

Source	Exception Type	Cause
External	Reset	Power-up or system reset (RESET* and HALT* asserted)
	Bus Error	BERR* input asserted
	Interrupts	Interrupt from peripherals
Internal	Instruction Traps	TRAP, TRAPV, CHK, DIVS, DIVU may cause exception
	Privilege Violation	Attempting to execute privileged instructions in the user-mode.
	Illegal/Unimplemented Instruction	Invalid instruction bit patterns
	Trace	Trace mode enabled (T = 1)
	Address Error	Attempting word access at an odd address.

reset, pushes the current program counter and saved copy of the status register on stack. The bus and address error exceptions saves additional information such as fault address to indicate the source of the error.

6. The program counter is loaded with the address from step 4 and the instruction execution continues with the first instruction of the exception handler.

The above sequence is illustrated in Figure 4-1. It is important to note that all exception processing is done in the privileged-supervisor mode. To change from supervisor mode to user mode, we can execute one of the following instructions:

```
ANDI   #<value>,SR
EORI   #<value>,SR
MOVE   #<value>, SR
```

or using

```
RTE
```

indirectly. Once in the user mode, the only way we can have a transition back to the supervisor state is by an exception as illustrated in Figure 4-2.

The exception handler will take appropriate action, then either resume the execution of the interrupted program or terminate and transfer control to the operating system in case of a program error. Since an exception condition can happen asynchronously anywhere in a program, an exception handler should save and restore the registers it uses. This is typically accomplished with a MOVEM instruction as shown in Figure 4-3. The handler is usually terminated with a RTE instruction which restores previously stored PC and SR from the supervisor stack.

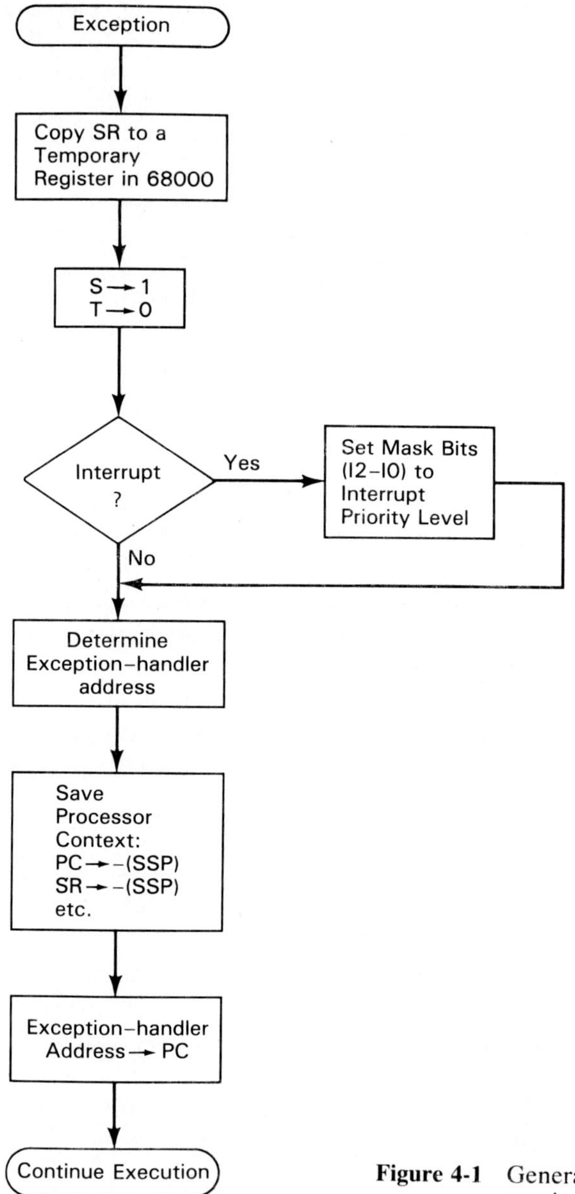

Figure 4-1 General Exception-processing Sequence.

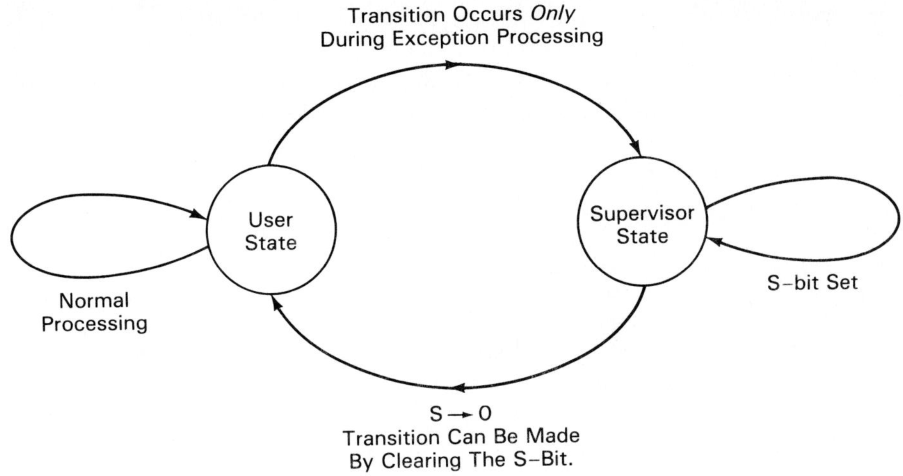

Figure 4-2 Transition Between User and Supervisor Modes.

In the following sections we will discuss how the exception-handler address is determined, exception grouping and priorities, exception stack frames, and details of each exception.

4.1 EXCEPTION VECTOR TABLE

So far we have not described how the 68000 determines the address of an exception handler. The 68000 family architecture uses a general scheme which allows a separate handler routine for each exception type and for each interrupt. The first 1024 bytes (i.e., address range \$0 through \$3FF) are reserved to hold the address of the exception-handler routines. Each handler address is contained in a long-

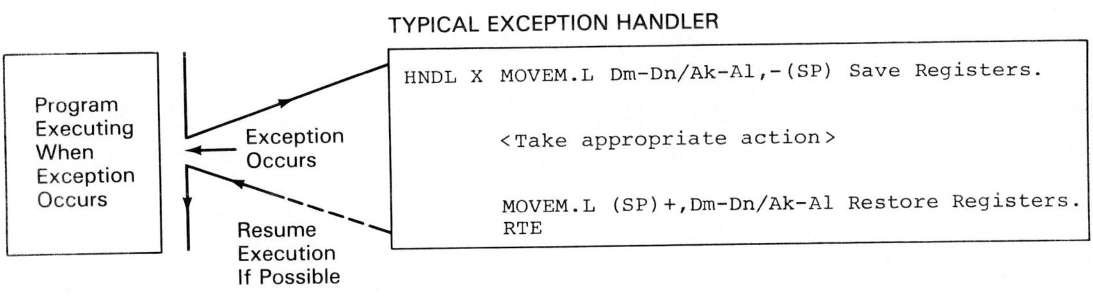

Figure 4-3 Program Flow During Exception Handling.

word slot referred to as an *exception vector*. The 68000 has 256 exception vectors, shown in Table 4-2, which are labeled with vector numbers 0 through 255. The exception vector address is just the vector number multiplied by four.

Some of the vector numbers are generated internally by the microcode of the 68000. Others, such as user-vectored interrupts use a vector number received from the interrupting peripheral. The second column of Table 4-2 indicates the

TABLE 4-2 EXCEPTION VECTOR ASSIGNMENTS

Vector #	Source of Vector #	Address (Hex)	Assignment
0 (1)	Internal	0 4	Reset: Initial SSP Reset: Initial PC
2	Internal	8	Bus Error
3	Internal	C	Address Error
4	Internal	10	Illegal Instruction
5	Internal	14	Zero Divide
6	Internal	18	CHK Instruction
7	Internal	1C	TRAPV Instruction
8	Internal	20	Privilege Violation
9	Internal	24	Trace
10	Internal	28	Line 1010 Emulator
11	Internal	2C	Line 1111 Emulator
12–14		30–38	(Unassigned, Reserved)
15	External	3C	Uninitialized Interrupt Vector
16–23		40–5C	(Unassigned, Reserved)
24	Internal	60	Spurious Interrupt
25	Internal	64	Level 1 Interrupt Autovector
26	Internal	68	Level 2 Interrupt Autovector
27	Internal	6C	Level 3 Interrupt Autovector
28	Internal	70	Level 4 Interrupt Autovector
29	Internal	74	Level 5 Interrupt Autovector
30	Internal	78	Level 6 Interrupt Autovector
31	Internal	7C	Level 7 Interrupt Autovector
32–47	Internal	80–BC	Trap Instruction Vectors (16)
48–63		C0–FF	(Unassigned, Reserved)
64–255	External	100–3FC	User Interrupt Vectors (192)

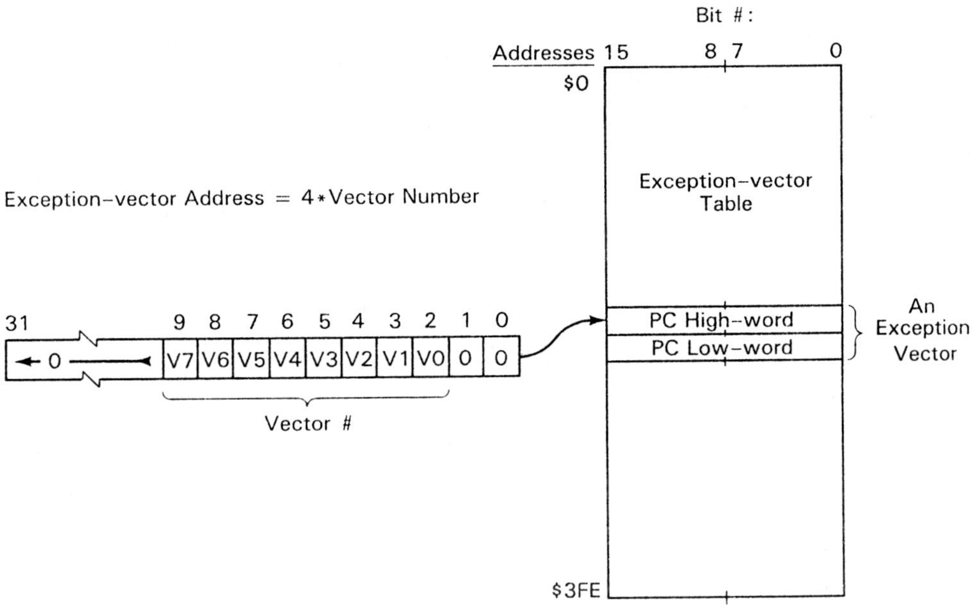

Figure 4-4 Exception Vector Table and its Address Calculation.

source of the vector number for each exception. After obtaining the vector number, internally or externally, the 68000 forms the exception vector address by left-shifting the the 8-bit vector number two bit positions and zero filling the high-order bits as illustrated in Figure 4-4. For example, when the BERR* input of the 68000 is asserted it generates vector number two internally which translates to $8 address in memory for the exception-vector address. The long-word at $8 contains the bus-error handler address.

The reset exception is a special case in that it consists of two exception vectors. The first one contains the initial stack pointer (SSP) and the second one has the initial program counter value. Hence, vector number one is not really used. Also, the reset vector is in the supervisor program space whereas all other vectors reside in the supervisor data space.

4.2 EXCEPTION GROUPING AND PRIORITIES

The exceptions can be grouped according to their characteristics and priorities (see Table 4-3). The group 0 exceptions are reset, bus error and address error. These exceptions will cause exception processing to start within two clock cycles. For example, a bus error, while fetching the source operand, stops the execution of the instruction in midstream and commences bus-error exception processing.

TABLE 4-3 EXCEPTION GROUPING AND PRIORITIES

Group	Exception	Processing
0	Reset Address Error Bus Error	Exception Processing Begins Within Two Clock Cycles
1	Trace Interrupt Illegal Privilege	Exception Processing Begins Before The Next Instruction
2	TRAP, TRAPV, CHK Zero Divide	Exception Processing Is Started By Normal Instruction Execution

↑ Increasing Priority

The processing of group 1 exceptions begin at the end of the current instruction. For example, an interrupt pending during a MOVEM instruction will wait till the end of the instruction execution (i.e., several bus cycles) before its processing begins. Exception processing of group 3 instructions may start as part of normal instruction execution. For example, TRAPV (trap on overflow) forces an exception if the V-bit of SR is set.

How does the 68000 handle multiple exception conditions? Which exception takes precedence in such a case? Table 4-3 lists the exception types in decreasing order of priority. Group zero has the highest priority and group 2 has the lowest priority. Within group 0, reset has the highest priority followed by address error and then bus error. Similarly, group 1 exceptions are also listed in decreasing order of priority, where trace has the highest priority. All group 3 exceptions have the same priority since there can be only one exception from this group at any time.

This priority relation determines which exception is taken first. This does not mean, however, that the handler of an exception with the higher priority will execute first, as the next two examples will illustrate.

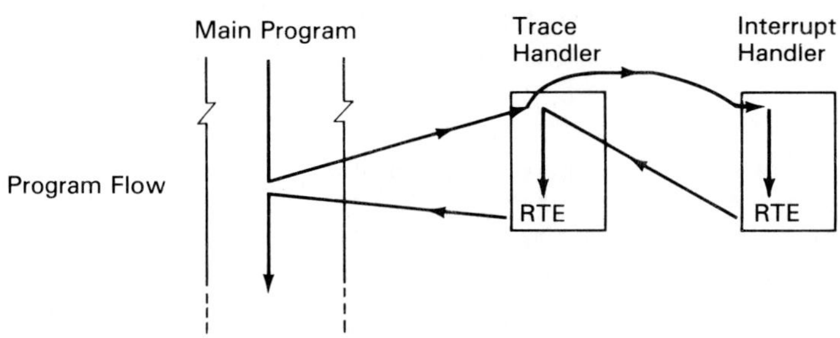

Figure 4-5 Concurrent Interrupt and Trace Exceptions.

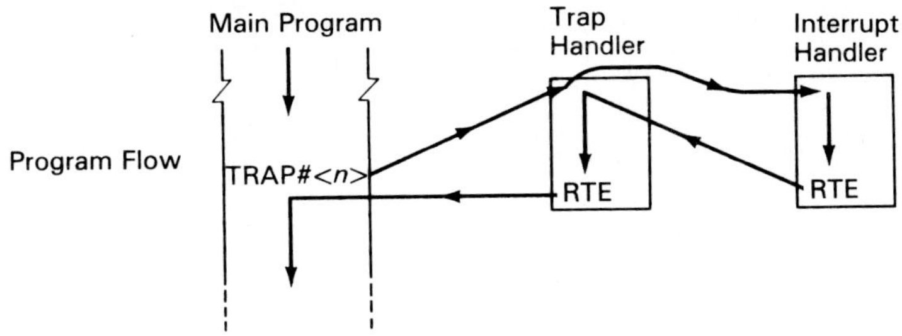

Figure 4-6 Concurrent Trap and Interrupt Exceptions.

Example 4-1

Let us say that an interrupt occurs while the trace mode is enabled. What is the order of exception processing? Since the trace exception has a higher priority, it is processed first. By processing, we mean the exception processing sequence of setting the S-bit and so on and not executing the handler. Before the first instruction of the trace handler is executed, the interrupt exception is also processed and the instruction execution finally starts at the beginning of the interrupt handler routine. This is due to the fact that the trace exception handler cannot block the pending interrupt. Upon return from the interrupt handler, the trace exception handler is executed as illustrated in Figure 4-5.

Example 4-2

What happens if an interrupt is pending when executing a TRAP instruction? A TRAP instruction forces an exception unconditionally and as part of instruction execution. Thus, the trap exception is taken first even though the interrupt has higher priority as shown in Figure 4-6.

4.3 EXCEPTION STACK FRAMES

We mentioned earlier that exception processing saves the current CPU context on the supervisor stack. The context information is stored in a format called the *exception stack frame*. The 68000 has two different stack frames. Group 2 and 3

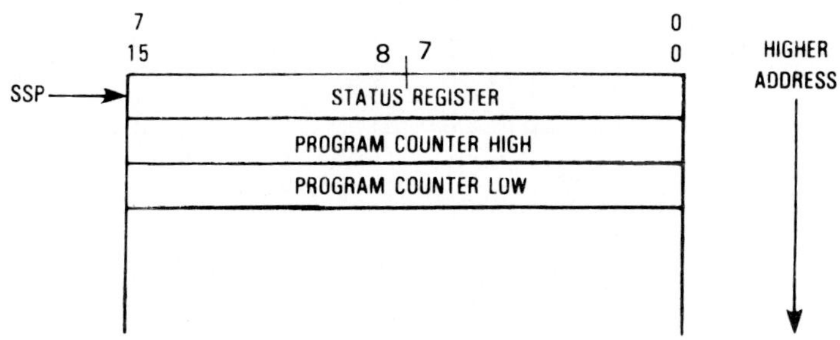

Figure 4-7 Group 2 and 3 Exception Stack Frames.

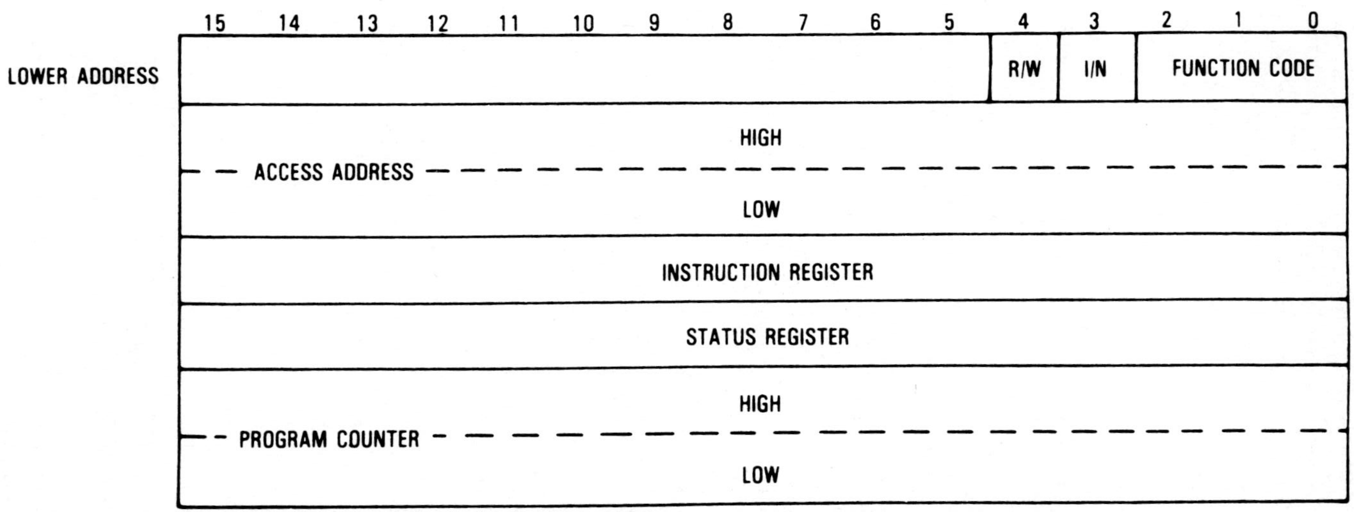

R/W (Read/Write): Write = 0, Read = 1. I/N (Instruction/Not): Instruction = 0, Not = 1

Figure 4-8 Bus- or Address-error Exception Stack Frames.

exceptions save only current PC and SR using the stack frame shown in Figure 4-7. The SR is saved as part of the most volatile context. This is enough to continue execution from where the exception occurred since group 2 and 3 exceptions always occur on instruction boundaries and the saved PC value always points to the next instruction to be executed. The RTE instruction at the end of the handler will restore the context for group 2 and 3 exceptions with the operation given by

1. (SSP) → SR
2. SSP + 2 → SSP
3. (SSP) → PC (long word)
4. SSP + 4 → SSP

which will undo the changes to the S- and T-bits, if any, and also restore the interrupt mask and condition codes.

The privilege violations and illegal/unimplemented-instruction exceptions are detected when they are the next instruction to be executed. The exception processing starts at the end of the current instruction. This is due to the prefetch mechanism of the 68000 which overlaps the execution of the current instruction with the prefetch and decoding of the next instruction. Therefore, the saved PC value points to the instruction that caused such an exception and not to the instruction following it.

The group 1 exceptions, except reset, use a stack frame containing additional information about the error as shown in Figure 4-8. Because of these additional words, RTE cannot be used directly to return from these exceptions. The instruction register has the first word of the instruction that was being executed when a bus or address error occurred. The access address contains the faulted address. A status word indicates whether the error occurred during a read or write cycle; during instruction or operand access; and the function codes of faulted bus cycle. The saved program counter value might not point to the next instruction due to the prefetch mechanism and the fact that the processor may not be on an instruction boundary when the exception processing takes place.

4.4 EXTERNAL EXCEPTIONS

4.4.1 Reset

The reset operation, by asserting RESET* and HALT* inputs to the 68000, will cause a reset exception. This exception is used at power-up time and to recover from any fatal system failure that caused a double bus-fault condition. The reset differs from all other exceptions for the following reasons:

1. The reset has two exception vectors. The first is the initial SSP value and the second is the initial PC value.
2. The reset exception does not save any processor context since no assumptions can be made about the processor's state before the reset operation.
3. The reset exception vectors has to be stored in nonvolatile (ROM) memory.

The detailed processing sequence during the reset exception is illustrated in Figure 4-9. If a bus error occurs during the fetching of either the initial PC or SSP, the 68000 decides the system is not usable and halts any further processing. This is also considered a double bus-fault condition even though only one bus error occurred.

Whereas other exception vectors can be stored in volatile (RAM with no battery backup) or nonvolatile memory, this is not the case for reset. This is because the 68000 will load the initial SSP and PC during its first four bus cycles. The other exception vectors can be initialized later by software if they reside in the read/write memory. The implication of this is that the ROM memory has to reside starting at $0 address, the first 1 Kbytes of which will contain exception vectors. However, such an implementation is not flexible because it does not permit changing the exception-handler address directly. During a certain part of the program, it might be desirable to use a different handler for certain exceptions. We can design the address decoding hardware to enable the ROM located anywhere in the memory map during the first four bus cycles after the reset operation. These two approaches are illustrated in Figure 4-10. We will discuss the hardware implementation of these in Chapter 8.

Example 4-3

The file XVEC.ASM shown in Figure 4-11 initializes the exception-vector table that is stored in ROM. This file cannot be assembled by itself since the exception-handler addresses are not defined. Also unknown here is the *RAM address* (RAMADDR) used for the initial stack pointer. Let us say that all system addresses including RAMADDR are defined in another file called SYSADDR.ASM. We can assemble the exception-handler routines using XVEC.ASM and SYSADDR.ASM as include files (see Figure 4-12) which can later be linked with other modules of the program.

We assume in this example that only the user vector #64 and the auto vector #3 are used by the system hardware. All other interrupts, if they occur erroneously for some reason, are handled by the generic spurious interrupt handler. It is good practice to initialize all exception vectors. This way, if an unexpected exception occurs, the handler will display an error message rather than crashing the system or terminating the program without any warning.

Example 4-4

If the exception vectors (except reset) are stored in RAM, the beginning of the program code in ROM can be as follows:

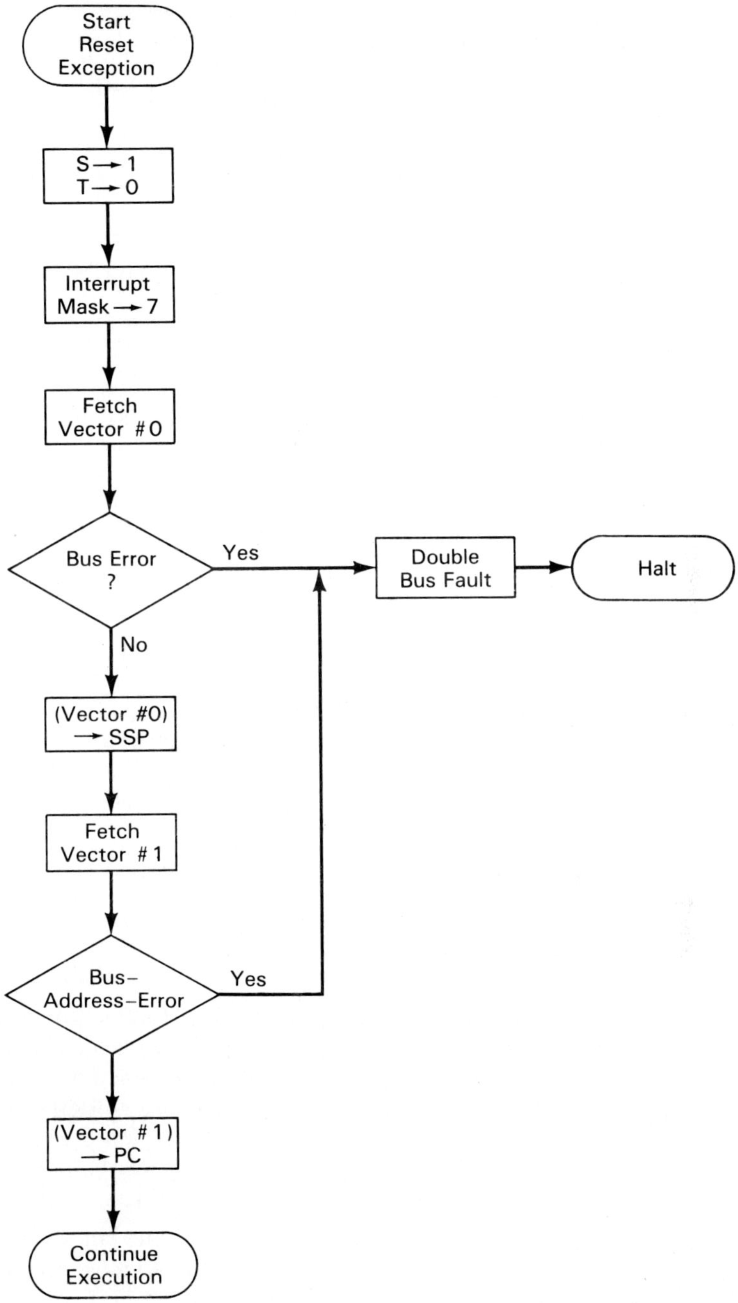

Figure 4-9 Reset Exception Processing Sequence.

```
        ORG   ROMADDR            Beginning of ROM Address.
        DC.L  RAMADDR + 40000    Initial SSP.
        DC.L  INITPC             Initial PC.
 INITPC JSR   INITXVEC           Initialize other exception vectors.
```

where the INITXVEC subroutine can be as follows:

```
* SUBROUTINE INITXVEC
*
* Purpose: This subroutine initializes the exception vectors
*          stored in RAM.
*
* Sample Call: JSR INITXVEC
*
INITXVEC MOVEA.L #8,A0                Initialize all vectors to spu-
*                                     rious.
ILOOP    MOVEA.L #SPURIOUS,(A0)
         ADDQ.L  #4,A0
         CMPA.L  #4*256,A0
         BNE     ILOOP
*
         MOVE.L  #BUSERR,2*4          Initialize Bus-Error Handler.
         MOVE.L  #ADRERR,3*4          Initialize Address-Error Handler.
*        <Initilize other
*        used exceptions>
*        RTS                          Return
```

The handler addresses SPURIOUS, BUSERR, ADDERR, and so on are defined by the exception-handling routines.

4.4.2 Bus Error

The bus error is the most common exception that happens due to some error condition. The most typical example is attempting to access part of the unoccupied address space. In such a case, no DTACK* is returned and a bus time-out occurs causing an external watch-dog timer to assert the BERR* signal (see Figure 1-15).

We mentioned earlier that the bus-error exception occurs when the BERR* input is asserted. There are two cases in which BERR* is asserted but does not cause a bus-error exception. The first one is the bus-cycle rerun where both BERR* and HALT* are asserted. During a bus-cycle rerun, the bus-error exception does not occur because the intention is to repeat the current bus cycle after possibly fixing the error by external hardware. The second case is when BERR* asserted at the end of an interrupt acknowledge bus cycle. This will cause a spurious-interrupt exception, which will be discussed in the next section.

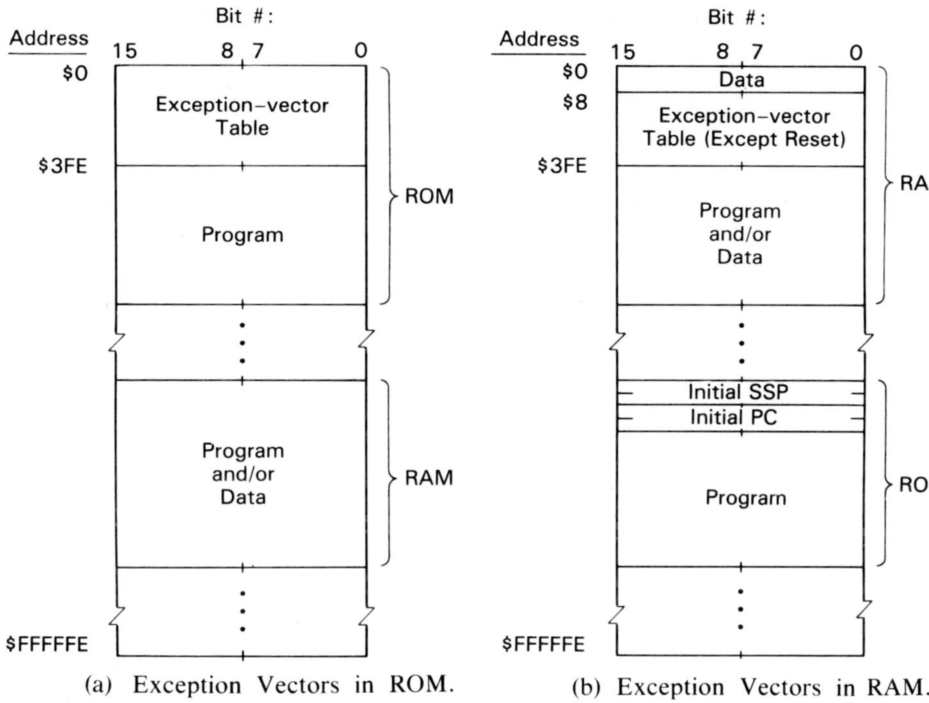

Figure 4-10 Two Different Mappings for Reset-exception Vectors.

The detailed processing sequence of a bus-error exception is illustrated in Figure 4-13. A double bus-fault condition occurs if an address error or another bus error happens before fetching the first instruction of the bus-error handler. The 68000 halts all further processing after a double bus fault until a reset operation. There are two commonly encountered reasons for a double bus fault to occur. The first is when the SSP is corrupted by the program or due to a bad SSP vector. The second is when the memory where the stack resides is not accessible due to a hardware error.

Additional information is stored on the supervisor stack during the bus-error exception since the 68000 is not necessarily on an instruction boundary when it happens. The bus-error exception can begin in one of the following bus cycles during an instruction execution:

1. Accessing the source operand.
2. Accessing the destination operand.
3. Prefetch of extension words or next instruction.

The bus-error handler can find the address of the first word of instruction

```
* EXCEPTION VECTOR ASSIGNMENTS
*
* PURPOSE: This file initializes the exception vector table.
*
*
        ORG     $0
        DC.L    RAMADDR + 400000        39K Bytes allowed for stack.
        DC.L    INITPC                  Initial PC address.
        DC.L    BUSERR                  Bus-Error Handler.
        DC.L    ADRERR                  Address-Error Handler.
        DC.L    XINST                   Illegal Instruction Handler.
        DC.L    ZDIV                    Zero Divide Handler.
        DC.L    CHK                     CHK Instruction Handler.
        DC.L    OVRFLW                  TRAPV Handler.
        DC.L    PVIOL                   Privilege-Violation Handler.
        DC.L    TRACE                   Trace Handler.
        ORG     $3C
        DC.L    SPURIOUS                Uninitialized Interrupt.
        ORG     $60
        DC.L    SPURIOUS                Spurious Interrupt.
        DC.L    SPURIOUS                Level 1 Autovector.
        DC.L    SPURIOUS                Level 2 Autovector.
        DC.L    AUTO3                   Level 3 Autovector.
        DC.L    SPURIOUS                Level 4 Autovector.
        DC.L    SPURIOUS                Level 5 Autovector.
        DC.L    SPURIOUS                Level 6 Autovector.
        DC.L    SPURIOUS                Level 7 Autovector.
        DC.L    TRAP0                   Trap 0 Handler.
        DC.L    NOTUSED                 Trap 1 Handler.
*       <The rest of Trap handlers>
        ORG     $64
        DC.L    USER1                   User 1 Interrupt Handler.
        DC.L    SPURIOUS                User 2 Interrupt Handler.
*       <The rest of user-vectored interrupt handlers>
*
        END
```

Figure 4-11 XVEC.ASM File for Example 4-3.

```
* EXCEPTION HANDLER MODULE
*
* Purpose: This file contains all exception handler routines.
*
*
        INCLUDE  SYSADDR.ASM
        INCLUDE  XVEC.ASM
*
         <Insert routines BUSERR, ADERR, XINST, etc. here>
*
          END
```

Figure 4-12 Exception Handler Module for Example 4-3.

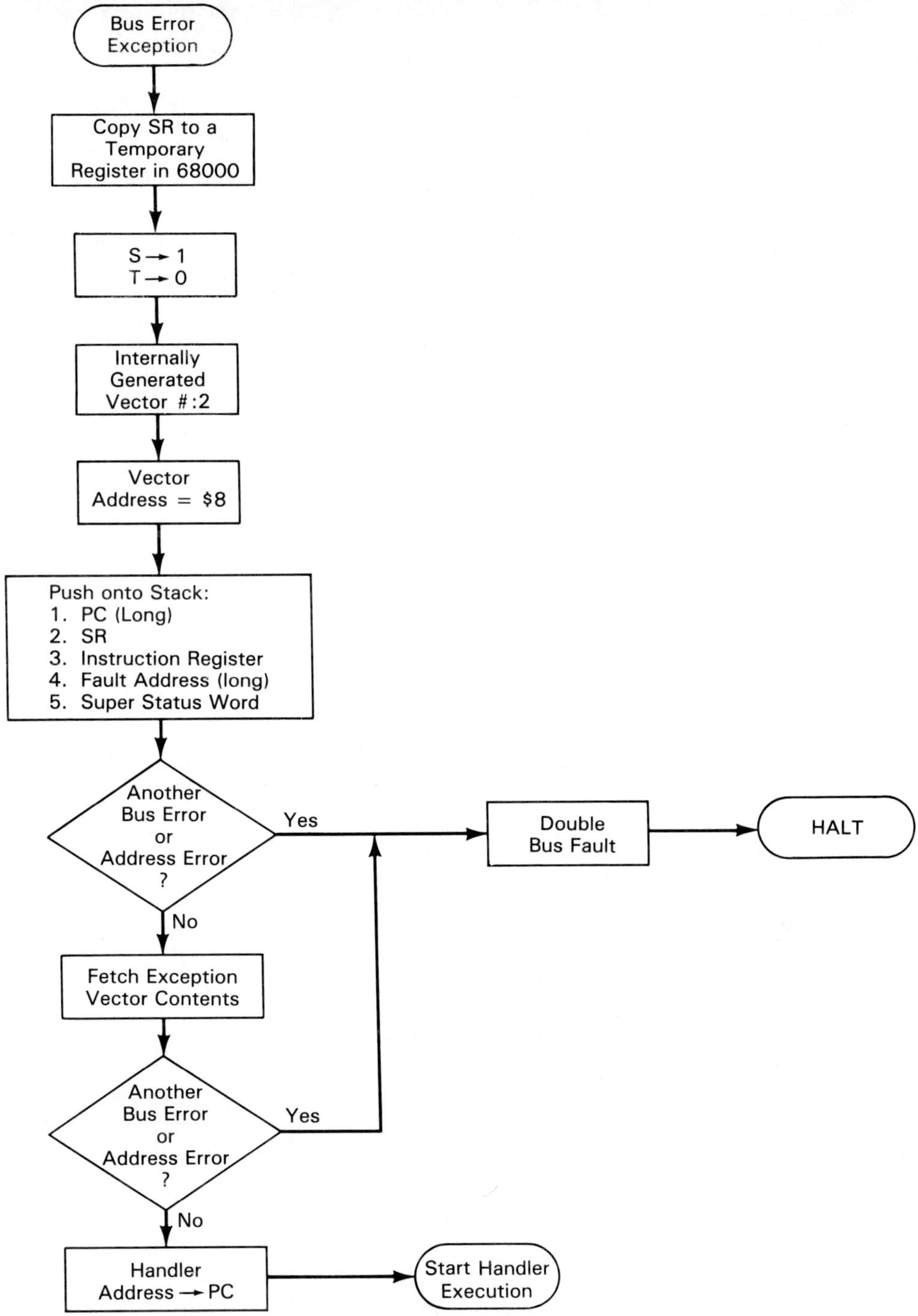

Figure 4-13 Bus-error Exception Processing Sequence.

```
* SUBROUTINE MEMSIZE
*
* Purpose: This subroutine finds the size of RAM memory.
*
* Sample Call: JSR  MEMSIZE
*
* Description: Only A0 is affected and upon return will contain the
*              size of RAM memory in bytes. Assume that the base address
*              of RAM is $0. We will start testing the existence of memory
*              10000, allowing for vector table, stack area, and diagnostic
*              program area.
            RORG
BERR        EQU      8                Bus-Error Exception Vector Address.
STADDR      EQU      $10000           Test Start Address.
*
MEMSIZE     MOVEM.L  A1-A4/D0,-(SP)   Save used registers except A0.
            LEA      MEXIT,A1         A1 → Exit address of MEMSIZE.
            LEA      BERR,A3          Save old Bus-Error Handler Address.
            MOVEA.L  (A3),A3
            LEA      MBERR,A4         Point to new handler.
            MOVE.L   A4,BERR
            LEA.L    STADDR,A0        A0 → Beginning of test area.
*
MLOOP       MOVE.B   #00,(A0)         Store $00 and verify.
            CMPI.B   #00,(A0)+
            BNE      MEXIT
            MOVE.B   #$FF,(A0)        Store $FF and verify.
            CMPI.B   #$FF,(A0)+
            BNE      MEXIT
            ADDQ.L   #1,A0            Increment pointer
            BRA      MLOOP
*
MEXIT       MOVE.L   A3,BERR          Restore Bus-error exception vector.
            MOVEM.L  (SP)+,A1-A4/D0   Restore registers.
            RTS                       Return
*
*
MBERR       MOVE.W   8(SP),D0         Get saved SR (for system byte).
            LEA      14(SP),SP        Deallocate bus-error stack frame.
            MOVE.L   A1,-(SP)         Return Address.
            MOVE.W   D0,-(SP)         SR
            RTE                       Return
*
            END
```

Figure 4-14 Use of Bus Error Example to Find Memory Size.

during which the bus error occurred by searching back from the stored PC value. If the current instruction is a branch, jump, or return instruction, the PC points to the first word of the current instruction. Otherwise, the saved PC value is between the beginning of the current instruction and the next instruction.

It is the responsibility of the handler to diagnose the source of the error and recover, if possible. Typically, such an error is not recoverable and the handler does the following:

1. Display an error message indicating a bus error has happened including the fault address, the PC value, and so on.
2. Deallocate error information from the stack.
3. Replace the return address and the saved SR value on stack so that the control is returned to the operating system upon executing an RTE instruction.

The bus-error exception is also used for purposes other than error detection. For example, it can be used to find the system configuration as the next example will illustrate.

Example 4-5

The subroutine shown in Figure 4-14 finds the size of the read/write (RAM) memory in a system. Let us assume that this subroutine resides in the ROM memory and is executed immediately after power-up. This is because it will overwrite the contents of the RAM. The stack area of the RAM needs to be excluded since it will be used by the bus error and other exceptions. Also, we assume that the exception vectors (except reset) are stored in RAM as shown in Figure 4-10-b. This is not a rigorous memory test routine. It merely finds the size by storing $0 and $FF patterns and verifying the contents. This is necessary in addition to checking the bus-error condition because some systems use an address decoder that returns DTACK* for the maximum possible memory range even though some of it might not be occupied. Such unoccupied areas will read as $FF and will not verify when we write $0 into those locations.

4.4.3 Interrupts

The 68000 family provides a prioritized interrupt structure with seven priority levels. An interrupt request is made to the 68000 by encoding its 3-bit priority level on IPL2*-IPL0* signal inputs. IPL stands for interrupt priority level. As we saw in Chapter 1, IPL2*-IPL0* = (HHH) means no interrupt request is pending and (LLL) means level seven, the highest priority interrupt request. If the encoded request level is equal to or less than the value of the interrupt mask (I2-I0 of the SR), the 68000 will simply ignore the request, continuing normal processing. If, however, the request has a higher priority level than the mask level, the 68000 will initiate exception processing at the end of the current instruction.

The interrupt encoding of the 68000 is shown in Table 4-4. Interrupts with

TABLE 4-4 INTERRUPT ENCODING OF THE 68000 FAMILY

Priority	IPL2–IPL0* Control Lines	Requested Interrupt Level	SR Interrupt Mask (I2–I0)	Recognized Interrupt Level
Highest	LLL	7	111	7
↑	LLH	6	110	7
	LHL	5	101	6–7
	LHH	4	100	5–7
	HLL	3	011	4–7
	HLH	2	010	3–7
	HHL	1	001	2–7
Lowest	HHH	None	000	1–7

a priority level seven are treated differently than the rest of the interrupts in that they cannot be masked even if the mask level is set to seven. Hence, it is usually referred to as a *nonmaskable interrupt* (NMI). The practical application of a NMI is in situations where an interrupt needs to be serviced urgently, such as in a power-failure condition to save vital system data before the system becomes inoperational.

What is the difference between a level six and a level seven interrupt masks? Examining Table 4-4, we find that only interrupt request level seven is recognized in either case. The difference is due to the NMI characteristic of level seven. The interrupt levels one through six are level-sensitive, whereas the level seven is edge-triggered. The interrupt level is sampled for two clock cycles by the 68000. A level sensitive interrupt is detected by the 68000 when the same level is sampled twice. The edge-triggered NMI is detected when a transition to level seven from a lower level is detected.

The 68000 supports both user- and auto-vectored interrupts. In a user-vectored interrupt, the interrupting peripheral provides the vector number during the interrupt-acknowledge bus cycle. There are 192 vectors ($40-$FF shown in Table 4-2) allocated for user interrupts. In an auto-vectored interrupt, the 68000 generates the vector number internally, depending upon the priority level. The auto-vectored interrupts use vector numbers 25 through 31 corresponding to interrupt levels one to seven, respectively. For example, if the priority level of an auto-vectored interrupt is four, then auto-vector four is used. The purpose of auto-vectored interrupts is to support peripherals which cannot supply a vector number. The 68000 uses auto-vectoring if the peripheral asserts VPA* instead of DTACK* during an interrupt acknowledge bus cycle.

There is always the unlikely possibility that no device responds by asserting DTACK* or VPA* during an interrupt acknowledge. This may be due to a glitch in the system or it may happen if the interrupter negates the request just before it is acknowledged. In such a case, a bus time-out will occur, assuming there is a watch-dog timer, causing BERR* to be asserted. The 68000 then generates vector number 24 internally, referencing the spurious interrupt handler.

The exception processing sequence during an interrupt acknowledge is illustrated in Figure 4-15. Note that the exception vector is fetched from the low-order byte of the data bus (D0-D7). During an interrupt acknowledge, the priority level is driven onto A3-A1 of the address bus, while A23-A4 are kept high. This is to indicate to the external devices what priority level is currently being acknowledged. Assuming there is only one interrupter per priority level, the peripheral with the matching interrupt level will respond with an interrupt vector and DTACK*, or with VPA*. The function codes (FC2-FC0) are set to (HHH) to indicate that the current bus cycle is for an interrupt acknowledge.

If we actually observe the bus-cycle activity for interrupt exception processing, we would notice that it is somewhat different from that implied by Figure 4-15. The bus-cycle activity after the last bus cycle of the instruction during which the interrupt was recognized is as follows:

1. Push PC low-word.
2. Interrupt acknowledge bus cycle.
3. Save SR at (SSP − 4).
4. Push PC high-word.
5. Read high-word of exception vector.
6. Read low-word of exception vector.

In addition to spurious interrupts, there are two other possibilities for error in processing interrupts. First, what happens if the interrupt vector of a peripheral was not initialized due to some programming oversight? Upon reset, most of the 68000 peripherals initialize their vector register to $0F which corresponds to the uninitialized-interrupt vector of the 68000 (see Table 4-2). Second, the interrupt vector might be incorrect. It might not even correspond to one of the 192 vectors. The 68000 does not internally verify that a user-vectored interrupt corresponds to one of the 192 user vectors or uninitialized vector is $0F! For example, it is possible to trap to the zero-divide handler if the vector number happens to be five. It is also possible to crash the system if the user-interrupt vector corresponds to the bus or address error because the handler assumes there is additional error information, when only the PC and SR are saved on the stack.

The block diagram of a peripheral requesting interrupt is shown in Figure 4-16. The priority-encoder logic codes the highest priority interrupt request and presents it to the 68000. For example, if one peripheral asserts IRQ3*, and another one requests using IRQ1*, priority three will be coded (i.e., IPL2*-IPL0* = (HLL). A 68000 peripheral, such as the '68681 DUART has multiple conditions which may cause an interrupt. Each such condition will set a bit IR*k* in the interrupt-request register. An interrupt is requested to the 68000 if the corresponding enable bit IE*k* was set by 68000 software. All possible interrupts are ORed and connected to the selected priority line IRQ*n**. Some 68000 peripherals use the same vector register for each interrupt condition, while some others use more than one.

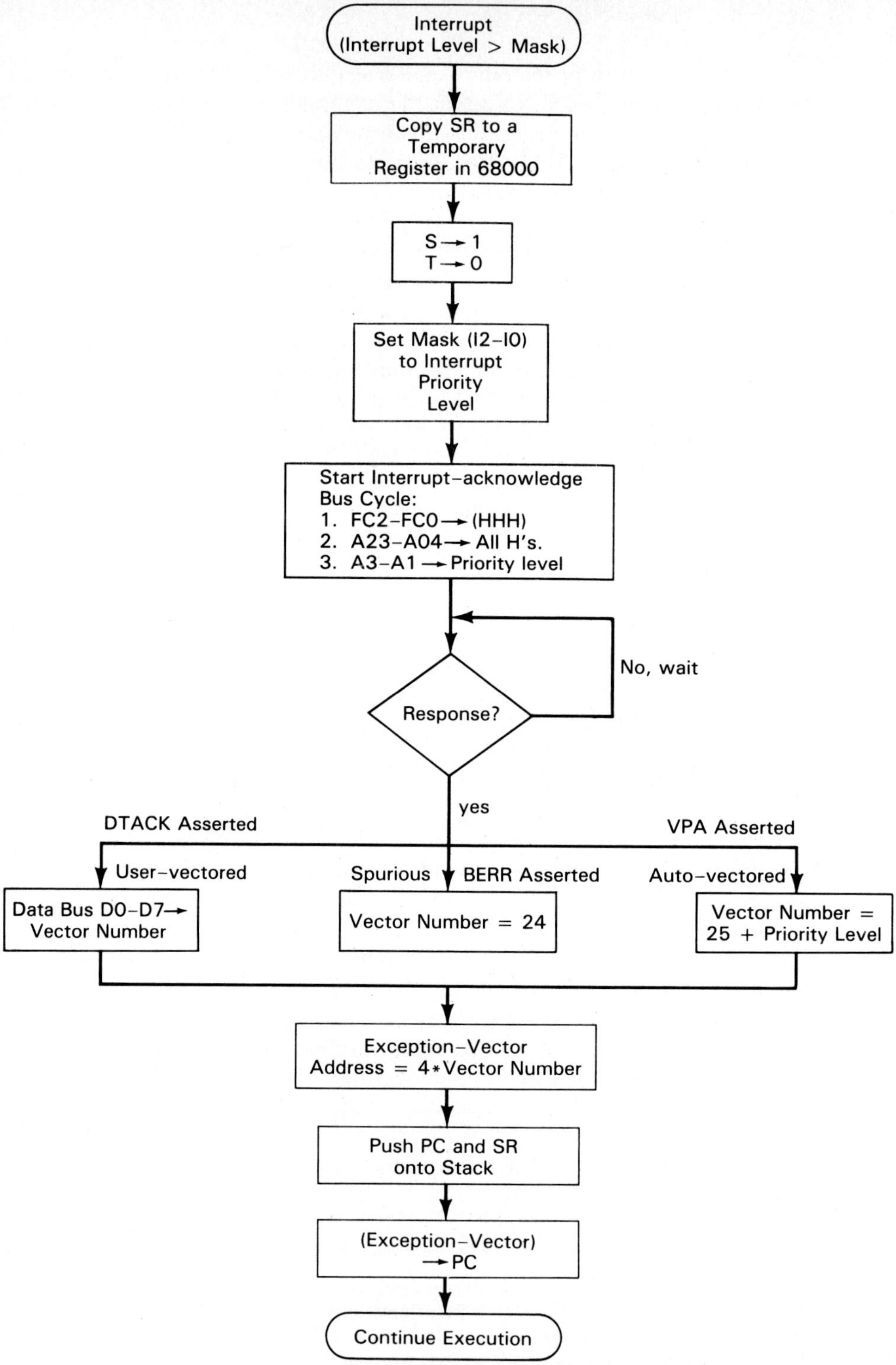

Figure 4-15 Interrupt Processing Flowchart.

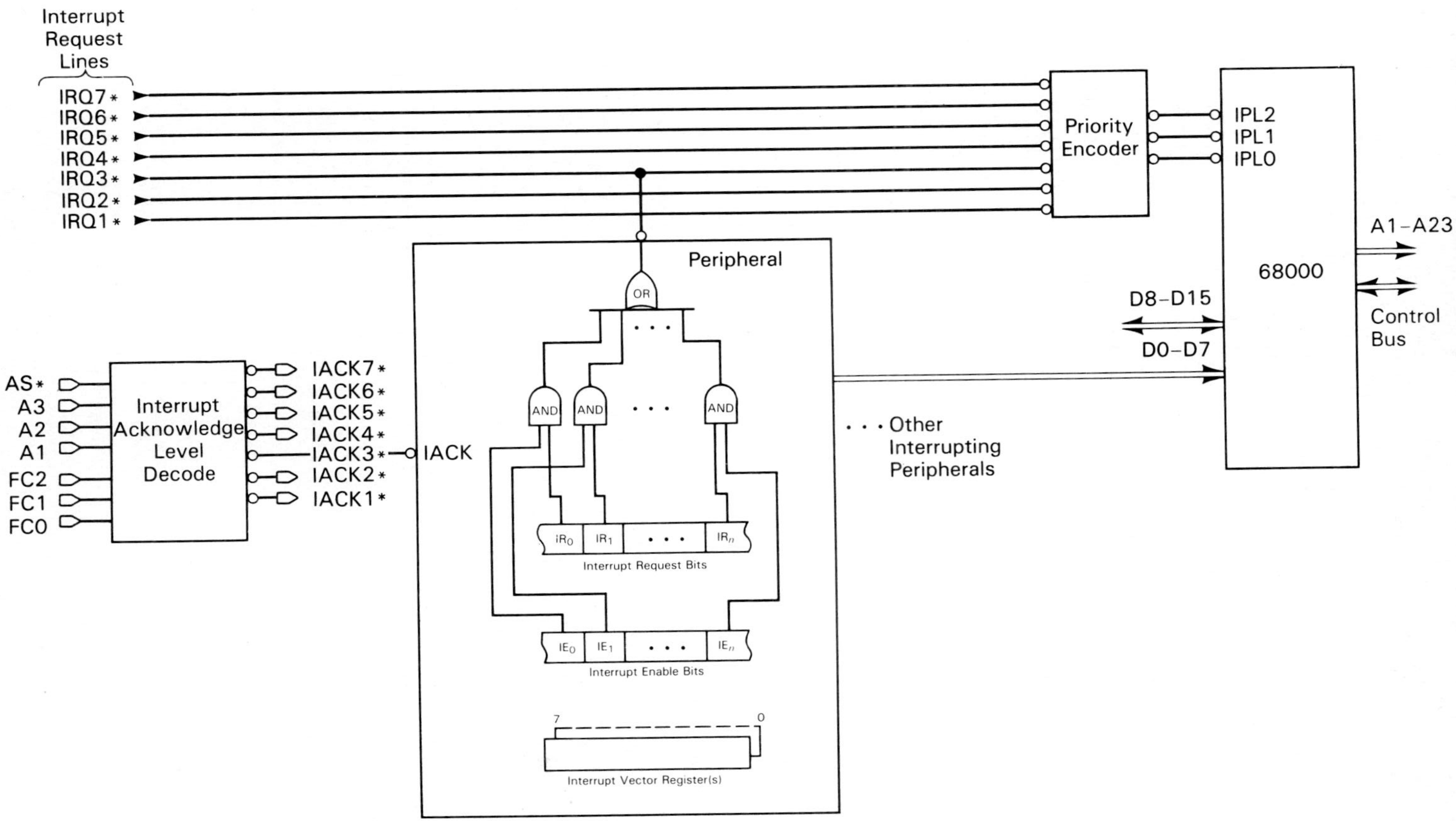

Figure 4-16 Illustration of Interrupt Requests from Peripherals.

The software can selectively enable certain interrupt conditions. For example, the transmitter-buffer-ready condition of the '68681 DUART is irrelevant if no character is to be sent and, thus, is disabled. The software can choose to disable all interrupts from a peripheral, and instead can keep reading the interrupt-request register until a certain condition is true. This method of I/O is called *polled I/O*. The interrupt, however, provides a mechanism by which a peripheral can quickly request the attention of the processor. The I/O transfer using interrupts is called *interrupt-driven I/O*.

We previously made the assumption that only one request line is connected to each priority level. Such an assumption is valid for most practical purposes, limiting the number of peripherals to seven. We will discuss in Chapter 8 how this number can be expanded. The interrupt-acknowledge level-decode logic decodes the priority level that is being acknowledged, and asserting the corresponding interrupt-acknowledge line IACK*n**. This, in turn, enables the vector register of peripheral onto the data bus and the peripheral then returns DTACK*.

Table 4-5 lists the typical 68000 peripherals that may request interrupts. High-data-rate or time-critical devices are usually associated with high-priority interrupt requests. We mentioned earlier that an interrupt service routine blocks any pending interrupts of lower or the same priority, unless it lowers the mask level in software. Therefore, it is recommended that the higher the priority level of an interrupt, the shorter it should be so that any lower-priority interrupts can also be served as quickly as possible.

Example 4-6

Let us consider the following case. Channel A of the '68681 DUART is connected to another computer from which we are going to transfer data to the 68000 system at a 9600 baud rate. Let us assume that there are ten bits per character including start, stop, and parity bits. The input to the '68681 has a 3-byte receiver FIFO buffer that acts like a circular queue. The serial-input data is first assembled in an input

TABLE 4-5 TYPICAL INTERRUPTING 68000 PERIPHERALS

Peripheral Type	Can Request Interrupt When
Serial I/O (e.g., '68681 DUART, '68661 EPCI)	1. A character is received. 2. Transmitter buffer is empty. 3. Channel "Break" Condition. 4. Error condition.
DMA	1. Channel operation complete. 2. Error Condition.
Real-time Clock or Timer	1. A time-out occurs, once or periodically. 2. Time-of-day alarm occurs
Parallel I/O (e.g., '68230)	1. Output buffer is empty. 2. Data received.

shift buffer which is later transferred to the FIFO if there is an empty position. Thus the data input is quadruply buffered (see datasheet), so we must read at least one input before the fifth character is transmitted. This means

$$4*10/9600 = 4.16 \text{ milliseconds}$$

before we loose any data. Therefore, any higher priority interrupt-service routine plus any other overhead must be less than the above figure. If this is not possible, the DUART can be programmed to automatically negate a channel-ready signal to pause the transmission when the buffer is full.

So far we have assumed that an interrupt request is somehow negated before the end of the service routine. Otherwise, after RTE, the control will be transferred back again to the interrupt handler. There are two ways that an interrupt request may be negated:

1. The interrupt service routine clears the interrupt as part of the exception handling. The interrupt condition is negated by accessing a certain peripheral register. For example, reading the input data register of the '68681 DUART will automatically clear the associated interrupt request bit.
2. The interrupt can be cleared by hardware during the interrupt-acknowledge cycle. This method is used if there is only one interrupt condition for a given peripheral.

The former approach is used by most peripherals. Software has to decide which interrupt request(s) to clear when there are multiple interrupt conditions. The latter is usually used by application-specific peripherals. Since there is only one interrupt condition, it can be cleared when the corresponding IACKn* is asserted.

Example 4-7

This example illustrates reading a line of data from a console using a '68681 DUART. (See Figure 4-17.) The user program may call this routine via a TRAP instruction where the trap handler sets up the following parameters before calling the LINERD subroutine:

A0 = Buffer starting address

A1 = Address of return status byte

The CHNA_INT is the interrupt handling routine for channel A, and we assume here that the DUART control registers and exception vector are initialized as required. For correct execution, the interrupt vector register of the DUART must have the vector number that contains the address of CHNA_INT. (See Figure 4-18.)

Upon return from LINERD, the status byte will indicate any errors. In our routine, we only check to make sure that the line length is less than 255 characters.

```
* LINERD SUBROUTINE
*
* Purpose: This subroutine reads a line of data from channel A of a
*          DUART.
*
* Sample Calling: BUFFER      DS.B     255            Line Buffer.
*                 ERRSTAT     DS.B     1              Status Byte.
*                             LEA      BUFFER,A0
*                             LEA      ERRSTAT,A1
*                             JSR      LINERD
*
* Description: Upon return, A0 will point to the last character (CR if
*              no errors) received.
*
* Error Handling: (A1) = $00   : No errors.
*                 (A1) = $01   : Overrun, max. line length is exceeded.
*
            RORG
CR          EQU      $0D              Carriage Return.
MAXCNT      EQU      255              Maximum line length.
DUART       EQU      $E00000          Address of DUART.
RBA         EQU      DUART + $6       Read-Buffer A Data Register.
SRA         EQU      DUART + $2       Status Register A (Read-only).
IMR         EQU      DUART + $A       Interrupt Mask Register.
ISR         EQU      IMR              Interrupt Status Register.
*
LINERD      MOVE.B   #00,(A1)         Initialize as no errors.
            CLR.B    DONEFLAG         Will be set by CHNA_INT when done.
            CLR.W    BYTECNT          Initialize BYTECNT.
            MOVE.L   A0,BUFFADDR      Initialize BUFFADDR.
*
            BSET     #1,IMR           Enable Channel A Interrupts.
*
WAIT        TST.B    DONEFLAG         Wait for DONEFLAG set.
            BEQ      WAIT
*
            RTS                       Return.
```

Figure 4-17 Example Subroutine to Read a Line of Data.

An actual routine should also check for other error conditions from the DUART status register such as a frame error and so forth.

When carriage-return is detected, DONEFLAG is set and interrupts are disabled by the interrupt service routine. Then, the LINERD gets out of the busy-wait loop and control is returned to the trap handler.

```
*
* INTERRUPT SERVICE ROUTINE
*
CHNA_INT    MOVEM.L  A0-A1/D0,-(SP)    Save used registers.
*
            BTST     #1,ISR            Is interrupt due to data received?
            BNE      CHA_DATA
            <Check and handle other interrupt conditions here.>
            BRA      EXIT
*
CHA_DATA    LEA      BUFFADDR,A0
            MOVE.W   BYTECNT,D0        Verify BYTECNT <= MAXCNT.
            CMPI.W   #MAXCNT,D0
            BLS      NEXTCH
            MOVE.B   #$01,(A1)         Set status byte to overrun.
            BRA      END_CHNA
*
NEXTCH      BTST     #1,ISR            Verify data present.
            BEQ      OUT_CHNA
            MOVE.B   RBA,(A0)+         Read & clear interrupt.
            ADDQ.W   #1,BYTECNT        Increment BYTECNT.
            CMPI.B   #CR,-1(A0)        CR ?
            BNE      NEXTCH
*
END_CHNA    BCLR     #1,IMR            Disable Interrupts.
            ST       DONEFLAG          Done.
            BRA      OUT_CHNA
*
OUT_CHNA    MOVE.L   A0,BUFFADDR       Update BUFFADDR.
*
EXIT        MOVEM.L  (SP)+,A0-A1/D0    Restore used registers.
            RTS
*
* DATA SECTION: (This section needs to reside in RAM memory)
*
DONEFLAG    DS.B     1                 =$FF when a line is read.
BUFFADDR    DS.L     1                 Current end of buffer address.
BYTECNT     DS.W     1                 Byte count.
*
            END
```

Figure 4-18 Example Interrupt Service Routine to Read a Line of Data.

4.5 INTERNAL EXCEPTIONS

4.5.1 Instruction Traps

The 68000 instructions that can cause exceptions are CHK, TRAPV, DIVS, DIVU, and TRAP. Of these, TRAP instruction will always force an exception; the others may or may not depending upon some condition. The divide instructions DIVS and DIVU cause a zero-divide exception when the divisor is found to be zero, thereby trapping to vector number five.

The TRAPV (trap on overflow) will cause an exception with vector number seven if the overflow (V) bit of the CCR is set to one. It is typically inserted after an arithmetic operation. For example,

```
ADD.W   (A0),D4
TRAPV
ASL.W   #1,D4
TRAPV
```

Note that TRAPV has no operands.

The CHK instruction checks the bounds of a destination operand, and is intended for checking the subscripts of an array for out-of-bounds condition. The assembly syntax is

```
CHK   <dea>,Dn
```

where the source-operand defines the upper bound, and the lower bound is taken as zero. The CHK exception is generated if D*n*[15:0] $<$ 0, or if D*n*[15:0] $>$ ⟨dea⟩. In comparison operation, the upper bound is treated as a two's complement number which limits the maximum possible range to [0-32,767]. For example,

```
CHK     #512,D0                Verify that offset is within range.
MOVE.W D2,0(A1,D0.W)           Access array.
```

where, let's say, A1 is the base address of an array of 256 words and D0 is the offset (in bytes) to a particular element. Both TRAPV and CHK provide a uniform way of handling such errors, making it especially convenient for compiler programmers.

Trap instruction. The TRAP instruction provides a powerful programming tool to make service calls to the operating system. For application programs running in the user mode, TRAP provides a convenient transition to the supervisor-mode utility programs. The application program need not know the address of the system routine that is being called. When RTE is executed at the end of the TRAP-handler, control is returned back to the application program pulling the saved SR from stack thus causing the processor to switch back to the user mode.

The TRAP instruction causes an unconditional exception to one of the sixteen trap vectors with an assembly syntax given by

```
TRAP    #<trap-number>
```

where *trap-number* is 0-15 corresponding to vector numbers 32 through 47, respectively.

The typical usage of TRAP is to perform various I/O operations, or to transfer control back to the operating system at the completion of an application program. Sixteen TRAP vectors are somewhat extravagant because most operating systems use only one or two. The required parameters are passed in the 68000 registers and/or immediately follow the TRAP instruction. For example, the VMEbug monitor by Motorola provides the routines listed in Table 4-6 to the user. These routines can be called with the following format:

```
<Set-up necessary registers>
TRAP    #15
DC.W    $000n    (n = 0-15 which defines the function)
```

TABLE 4-6 VMEbug ROUTINES AVAILABLE TO THE USER VIA TRAP #15 [1]

Function (n)	Port	Description
0	None	Display registers and go to VMEbug.
1	CONSOLE[1]	Input line. Parameters: Both A5 and A6 point to the beginning of the input buffer. Exit conditions: A5 is unchanged; A6 points to the end plus 1.
2	CONSOLE[1]	Output line (with CR and LF). Parameters: A5 points to the beginning of string and A6 point to the end plus 1.
3	HOST[2]	Read line (no echo). Parameters same as function 1.
4	HOST[2]	Output line (with CR, LF). Parameters same as function 2.
5	PRINTER[4]	Read line (no echo). Parameters same as function 1.
6	CONSOLE[1]	Output line (no CR, LF). Parameters same as function 2.
7	HOST[2]	Output line (no CR, LF). Parameters same as function 2.
8	PRINTER[4]	Output line (no CR, LF). Parameters same as function 2.
9	HOST[3]	Read line (no echo). Parameters same as function 1.
A	HOST[3]	Output line (with CR, LF). Parameters same as function 2.
B	HOST[3]	Output line (no CR, LF). Parameters same as function 2.
C	PRINTER[5]	Output line (with CR, LF). Parameters same as function 2.
D	PRINTER[5]	Output line (no CR, LF). Parameters same as function 2.

[1–5] Indicates actual port number used.

The TRAP-15 handler has to modify the return-PC to skip over the function definition. Another approach is to point to the parameter block with an address register before the TRAP instruction. The operating system can return the status indicating the success or failure of a requested operation in a data register.

Example 4-8

The following prints the message "Hello World. . ." using console output.

```
*
* Example 4-8
* Uses VMEbug user-I/O via TRAP #15.
*
        ORG     $4000
START   MOVE.L  #START,SP         Initialize SP.
        MOVE.L  #MSG,A5           A5 → Beginning of message
        MOVE.L  #MSGE,A6          A6 → End of message.
        TRAP    #15               Call I/O Routines.
        DC.W    $2                Function #.
        TRAP    #15               Stop Here and Display Reg.
        DC.W    0
*
MSG     DC.B    'Hello World...'  Message.
MSGE
        END
```

4.5.2 Privilege-violation Exception

If a program running in the user mode attempts to execute a privileged instruction, this will cause a privilege-violation exception. These privileged instructions are:

```
RESET
RTE
STOP #<value>
ANDI #<value>,SR
EORI #<value>,SR
ORI  #<value>,SR
MOVE USP,An
MOVE An,USP
```

RTE cannot be used directly after a privilege-violation exception since the PC points to the instruction that caused the exception. However, this is not inconvenient since this exception usually indicates a fatal error in the user program which cannot be continued.

4.5.3 Trace Exception

When the T-bit of the SR is set to one, a trace exception is forced after each instruction is executed. The main purpose of this is to assist in program development and debugging. The trace handler can capture the contents of registers and store them away, which can later be displayed and analyzed by the programmer. The disadvantage of this approach is that the program executes much slower due to the trace-handler overhead. Also, the amount of collected data might overwhelm the programmer. Another application of trace exception is to single-step programs. When the user enters a single-step command, the operating system will perform the following:

1. Restore the user's address and data register contents from a table stored in memory.
2. Set the T-bit in the saved value of the user's status register and push it onto the stack.
3. Push the saved PC of the user's program onto the stack.
4. Execute RTE.

After executing one instruction, the control will trap to a trace handler. It is possible, however, that the trace exception will not occur if the instruction is not executed due to privilege violation, illegal/unimplemented instructions, or if the instruction is aborted due to a group 1 exception.

4.5.4 Address Error

This exception is very similar to a bus error and shares the same stack frame, it is detected internally. It could happen, typically due to programming errors, by attempting an instruction fetch or an access of a word operand at an odd address. For example:

```
MOVE.L #$E00003,A0
MOVE.W (A0),D0       Address-error
```

or

```
MOVE.L #$4001,A0
JMP    (A0)          Address-error
```

will cause an address-error exception. Just like a bus error, this exception may break the execution of an instruction in midstream. Thus, the saved PC value points in the vicinity of the offending instruction, the same as a bus-error exception.

The exception processing sequence is exactly the same as the bus error (see Figure 4-13). If another bus or address error happens before the first instruction of the address-error handler is fetched, a double bus-fault condition will occur halting the processor.

4.5.5 Illegal and Unimplemented Instructions

When the operation word of an instruction does not correspond to any of the bit patterns of a valid 68000 instruction, an exception occurs. The instruction-word patterns $AXXX or $FXXX (X: don't care) are called *unimplemented instructions* since they are reserved for additional instructions in later members of the family. These two patterns are also referred to as line-A and line-F opcodes in Motorola literature, and traps to separate exception vectors (see Table 4-2). Other invalid operation-word patterns are called *illegal instructions*, which consists of the following:

1. The word patterns $4AFA, $4AFB, and $4AFC.
2. Illegal effective-address, operation-size, or operation-mode specifications for a given instruction. For example, selecting a byte size with a MOVEA instruction.

The bit patterns $4AFA and $4AFB are reserved for Motorola, whereas the pattern $4AFC can be used by system programmers by using the instruction ILLEGAL with no operands. For example, it could be used to put breakpoint in a program by replacing the instruction where the breakpoint is desired with ILLEGAL. The exception handler can then replace the saved instruction so that the program may be continued.

Of course, an assembler will not generate an invalid object code. Any programming errors from using a wrong addressing mode and the like will be flagged by an assembler-error message. It is still possible though, for a 68000 to encounter an invalid code because of programming errors such as "jumping" to a wrong address, or, explicitly, by using the ILLEGAL instruction. In addition to detecting errors, unused instruction patterns can be used to emulate new or application-specific instructions. For example, line-A opcode pattern can be used to emulate a floating point instructions as part of the exception handler. The disadvantage of such an approach is that the overhead associated with the exception processing and decoding of the user-specific instructions in software. The use of macros might be a better alternative[2].

FURTHER READING

1. Motorola, *VMEbug User Manual, MVMEBUG/D2, Second Edition*, December, 1982.
2. Harris, S., Johnson, Tom. "Application Note AR233 by Motorola: Software Links Math Chip to 68000-family Microprocessors," *EDN*, January 23, 1986.

EXERCISES

Exception Processing

1. Which stack, user or supervisor, is affected by exception processing? Please explain.

2. Suppose the SR is $2004 before an interrupt exception with priority 4. What is the contents of the SR at the beginning of the interrupt service routine?

3. If the program is to resume where it left off after an exception, why is it necessary to save the used address and data registers at the beginning of an exception handler and restore them at the end?

4. What is an exception vector? What is the exception vector number that must be provided by a peripheral for the user-vector #2.

5. How does the 68000 determine the address of an exception-handling routine for the following:
a) Address error.
b) User-vectored interrupts.
c) Spurious interrupt.

6. How can the 68000 change from the user mode to supervisor mode?

Exception Grouping and Priorities

7. Indicate when the exception processing for the following conditions will start:
a) Interrupt.
b) TRAP.
c) Bus error.

8. Suppose an interrupt is pending when an instruction is executing and when attempting to fetch the source operand if an address error occurs. Which exception is taken first? Which handler is executed first?

9. Can the execution of the TAS instruction be interrupted by the following exceptions?
a) Interrupts.
b) Address error.
c) Bus error.

10. Suppose an interrupt is pending when executing a DIVU instruction where the divisor happens to be zero. Which exception is taken first? Which handler is executed first?

Exception Stack Frames

11. What is a stack frame? What are the different exception stack frames used by the 68000?

12. Indicate where the saved PC value points for the following exceptions:
a) Interrupts.
b) TRAP instruction.
c) Privilege violation.
d) Bus error.
e) Trace.
f) Illegal instruction.
g) Address error.

13. What is the purpose of saving the instruction word for bus- and address-error exceptions?

Reset Exception

14. What happens if the initial PC value of exception vector 1 contains an odd address?

15. What is the contents of the system byte of SR after a reset exception?

16. Suppose the exception vectors, except reset, are stored in RAM memory. Describe how a user program can change the exception vectors to make a transition to the supervisor mode and take over the operating system. Is this possible if the first 1K bytes of memory can only be accessed in the supervisor mode?

Bus-error Exception

17. What is a double bus-fault-condition? List the possible conditions that will cause a double bus fault.

18. Which of the following conditions will cause a bus-error exception?
a) BERR* and HALT* are asserted at the same time to rerun a bus cycle.
b) BERR* is asserted by a watch-dog timer during a read or write bus cycle.
c) BERR* is asserted during an interrupt-acknowledge bus cycle by a watch-dog timer.

Interrupts

19. How does a peripheral request auto-vectoring?

20. What happens if no peripheral responds during an interrupt acknowledge cycle? What are the possible reasons for this?

21. What is the difference between level six and level seven interrupts?

22. When does an uninitalized-interrupt exception occur?

23. What happens, if during a user-vectored interrupt, the peripheral transfers vector number eight?

24. Let us say that we do not want to allow any interrupts except level seven during a critical portion of your program:

a) Write a sequence of instructions to increase the mask level to seven without changing the rest of SR. Save the old mask level in a register or on the stack.

b) Write a sequence of instructions to restore the old mask level.

25. List the following for the devices listed below (see datasheets):

a) Interrupt conditions.

b) One or more interrupt-vector registers.

c) How each interrupt condition is cleared.

1. '68681 DUART

2. '68230 PI/T

3. '68450 DMA

26. Improve the interrupt-service routine given in Example 4-7 by checking other channel A error conditions detected by the '68681 DUART (refer to datasheet).

27. Change the interrupt routine given in Example 4-7 to use a circular buffer with three pointers:

```
DS.L   1    Write pointer.
DS.L   1    Read pointer.
DS.L   1    Pointer to beginning of current line.
```

Other Exceptions

28. What happens when the 68000 encounters the instruction word $F000?

29. What is the purpose of the ILLEGAL instruction?

30. Can an RTE instruction be executed immediately after a privilege violation?

31. What is the main application of the TRAP instruction?

32. Write a small routine to read a line of data from the console and print it using port 5 with CR and LF included.

5

68010 and 68012 Architecture and Programming

This chapter will focus on the 68010 and the 68012 which are basically improved versions of the 68000. The bus interface and user-programming model of these new siblings stay the same as the 68000. From a programming point of view, the only difference between the 68010 and the 68012 is the range of the address space where the 68012, using additional address lines, expands the available address space to 2 gigabytes. We will refer to the 68010 and the 68012 pair as the 6801X during the rest of our discussion.

The most important enhancement with respect to the 68000 is the support of virtual memory and virtual machine operation. The performance is also increased because of the improvements in the microcode of some of the instructions and the new loop mode of operation to speed up two-instruction program loops.

5.1 PROGRAMMING MODEL

The user-mode registers stay the same as the 68000, whereas three new control registers are added to the supervisor-mode supplementary registers as shown in Figure 5-1. The additional resources in the supervisor mode are a *Vector Base Register* (VBR) and two alternate function code registers. The VBR is used to locate the exception vector table anywhere in the address space. The alternate source and destination function code registers, SFC and DFC, are used only by the new instruction MOVES as we shall discuss in the next section.

The main reason behind the VBR is the ability to support multiple exception vector tables. In calculating the exception vector address, the vector offset is

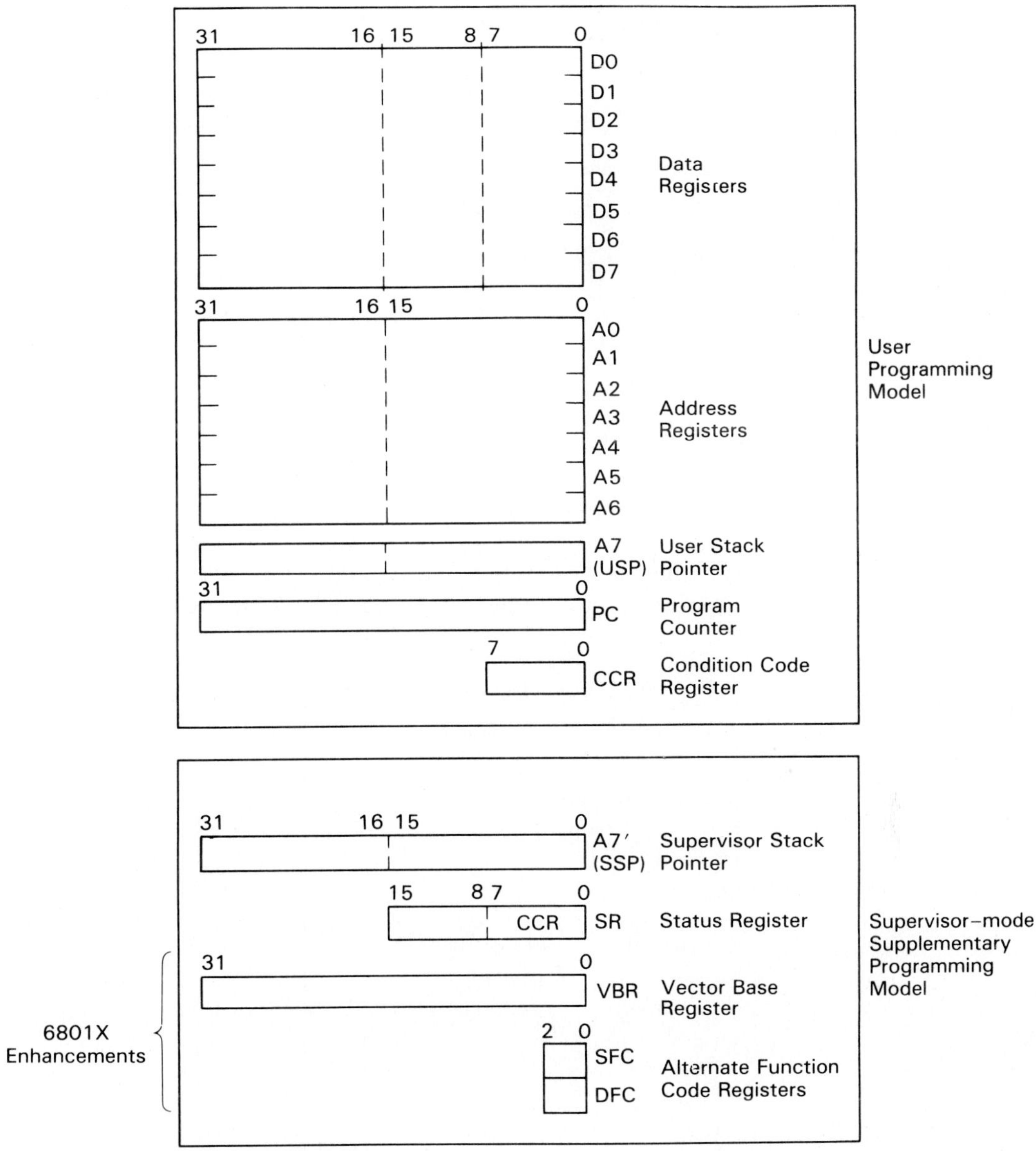

Figure 5-1 6801X Programmer's Model.

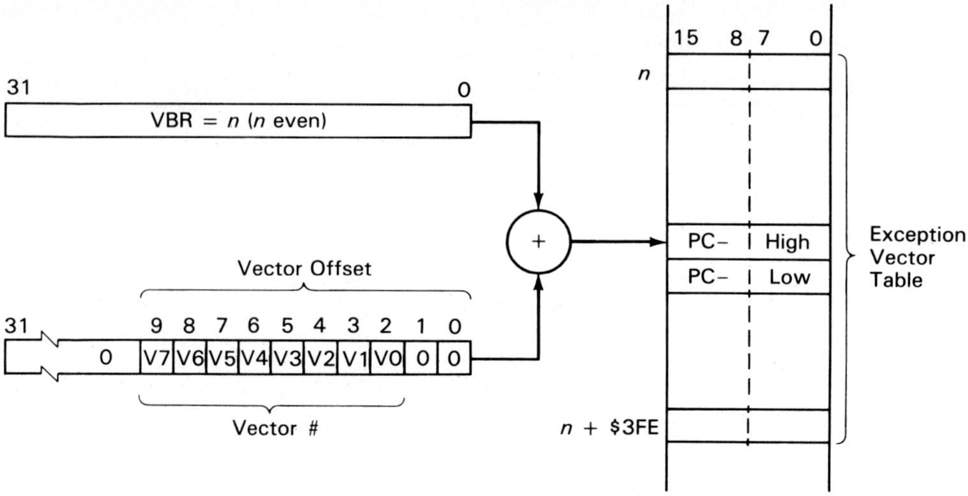

Figure 5-2 Exception Vector Address Calculation.

added to the 32-bit VBR generating a 32-bit result limited by the physical address space as illustrated in Figure 5-2. For example, if VBR = $2000 and a bus error occurs (vector: #2), then the exception vector address is $2008. The VBR is cleared to zero on power-up or external reset, thus emulating the 68000's excep-

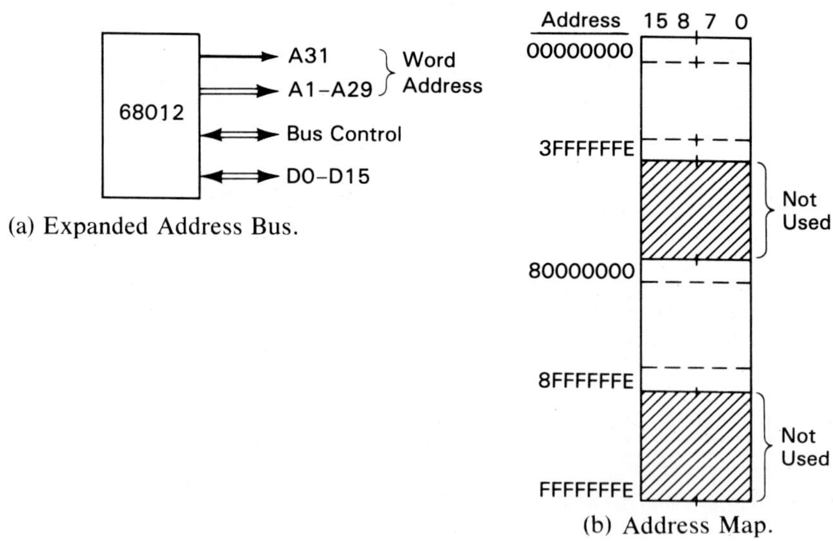

Figure 5-3 Expanded Address Space of the 68012.

tion processing until a non-zero offset is loaded. Note that this offset has to have an even value, otherwise it will cause an address error (why?).

The 68010 provides a 16-Megabyte address space, the same as the 68000. The 68012, on the other hand, expands the available address space to two gigabytes. This space is divided into two non-contiguous sections, as shown in Figure 5-3. The non-contiguousness of the address space is merely due to packaging considerations as there was difficulty bonding address line A30 to an external pin of the package. The 68012 was initially developed for a particular customer by Motorola and is used generally for applications such as image processing or databases requiring large address spaces.

5.2 INSTRUCTION SET ENHANCEMENTS

The instruction set enhancements include the addition of some new instructions and improvements to some of the existing ones. The improved instructions (see Table 5-1) are transparent to the programmer with the exception of MOVE from SR, which is changed to be privileged on the 6801X. Thus, the 68000 program reading SR in the user mode will cause a violation error. As we shall see in Section 5.5, this change was done to support virtual machine operation. The RTE instruction is expanded to support virtual memory operation. Also, some of the instructions feature improved microcode by decreasing their execution time. Most notable are the multiply and divide instructions. As mentioned earlier, the 68000's CLR instruction reads the destination operand before writing zeros into it. This was due to its implementation where CLR shares the read-modify-write microcode with the TAS instruction. This superfluous read is eliminated in the 6801X.

The new instructions of the 6801X are given in Table 5-2. Next, we will discuss each of these instructions.

TABLE 5-1 IMPROVED INSTRUCTIONS OF THE 68000

Improvement	Instruction(s)	Description
Virtual Machine Support	MOVE from SR, RTE	To be discussed in 5.5.
Improved Execution Time	CLR	Superfluous read of operand is eliminated.
	MULU, MULS, DIVU, DIVS	Significant improvement in execution time.
	Immediate (I) variation of instructions	Small improvement in execution time.
Virtual Memory Support	RTE	To be discussed in 5.4.

TABLE 5-2 NEW INSTRUCTIONS OF THE 6801X

Instruction	Syntax	Privileged?
MOVE from CCR	MOVE CCR,<daea>	No

MOVEC	MOVEC Rc,Rn
	or
	MOVEC Rn,Rc
	
	where R*c* = VBR, DFC, SFC, or USP
	and R*n* = A*n* or D*n*.
		Yes

MOVES	MOVES.<s> Rn,<amea> or MOVES.<s> <ea>,Rn where s = B, W, or L.	Yes
RTD	RTD #<d16>	No
BKPT	BKPT #<0-7>	No

Move from CCR instruction. This instruction replaces the MOVE from SR instruction. It is used to read the CCR in the user mode and complements the MOVE to CCR instruction. Even though the operation size of this instruction is word, only the low-order byte has the condition code information with the upper byte reading as all zeros.

MOVEC (move control register) instruction. With the addition of new registers to the supervisor mode, Motorola added a new instruction, MOVEC, to transfer data to and from these control registers. The advantage of this is that, for the later members of the family, the MOVEC instruction is expanded to cover the additional new control registers instead of adding a new instruction for each control register as was done earlier (e.g., MOVE USP).

Since it controls access to the supervisor-mode registers, MOVEC is a privileged instruction. The transfer is always 32 bits. The condition codes are not affected and note that no immediate addressing mode is allowed. For example, to set VBR to $20000, we can write:

```
MOVE.L  #$20000,D0
MOVEC   D0,VBR
```

CPU space cycles and MOVES (move address space) instruction. Similar to the 68000, the new members of the 68000 family (starting with the 68010), have five different address spaces:

1. Supervisor program space.
2. Supervisor data space.

3. User program space.
4. User data space.
5. CPU space.

The type of address space is indicated on each bus cycle by the function code outputs. The address space type should not be confused with the addressing range. The address space type indicated by function codes can be thought of as additional address lines. The reader might note that the only difference to the 68000 in the above is the designation of *CPU space* as opposed to an interrupt acknowledge. Motorola designers realized that they need to incorporate other special bus cycles such as breakpoints, coprocessors, and so forth in later members of the family. So the CPU space includes the interrupt acknowledge, where the function codes defined in Table 5-3 with expanded coverage for FC2-FC0 = (HHH).

Only address lines A16-A19 are used to determine sixteen different types of space cycles as shown in Figure 5-4. The 6801X only features two different CPU-space types: Interrupt acknowledge ($F) and breakpoint cycle ($0) used in conjunction with the BKPT instruction.

What does all this have to do with the MOVES instruction? Since the CPU sets the function codes automatically depending on the bus cycle performed, it is difficult, if not impossible, depending on the system design, to cross these address-space boundaries. For example, let us say that the application program is trying to pass a parameter to the operating system, typical in a system call. The application program is in the user mode and the operating system (OS) is running in the supervisor mode, of course. Let us further assume that address of the parameter (i.e., a pointer) is passed. Then, the OS will use this address, but this time the address space used will be the supervisor data. Such an access might not be permitted directly (i.e., without changing some setup or without causing access-fault condition), such as in a virtual memory system as we will discuss later.

The MOVES removes any obstacles in transferring data between different

TABLE 5-3 6801X BUS-CYCLE CLASSIFICATION

Function Code FC2	FC1	FC0	Reference Type
L	L	L	Unassigned, reserved
L	L	H	User data
L	H	L	User program
L	H	H	Unassigned, reserved[1]
H	L	L	Unassigned, reserved
H	L	H	Supervisor data
H	H	L	Supervisor program
H	H	H	CPU space

[1] Reserved for User Definition.

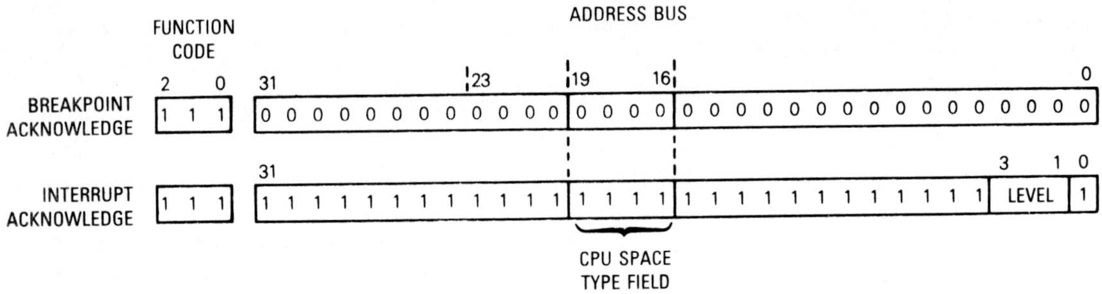

Figure 5-4 6801X CPU-space Encoding.

address spaces by using the function codes specified by the *Source Function Code* (SFC) or the *Destination Function Code* (DFC) register instead of the type of bus cycle used. The assembly syntax is

```
MOVES.<s>   Rn,<amea>
```

which uses the DFC register to set function codes in the bus cycle writing the destination operand and

```
MOVE.<s>   <caea>,Rn
```

which uses the SFC register to set function codes in the bus cycle reading the source operand. All sizes are allowed.

It is important to remember that the control registers SFC and DFC affect only the function codes when executing the MOVES instruction. In the current implementation, having the same A*n* for both source and destination should be avoided since it produces incorrect results.

Example 5-1

Suppose the OS wants to read a word-size parameter value pointed to by A0 from the user-address space. Then, we can write

```
USERFC  EQU        $01
        MOVE.W     #USERFC,D0
        MOVEC      D0,SFC           SFC = %001
        MOVES.W    (A0),D0          Get parameter
```

RTD (return and reallocate) instruction. This instruction intends to make returns from subroutines easier by automatically deallocating the stack area used for parameters. The assembly syntax is

```
RTD   #<d16>
```

where d16 is a 16-bit two's complement value. The operation performed is given by

1. (SP) → PC
2. SP + 4 + $\langle d16 \rangle_{32}$ → SP

as illustrated in Figure 5-5 where $\langle\ \rangle_{32}$ indicates a sign-extension to 32 bits prior to addition. The RTD instruction makes the calling program easier to read since the adjustment of SP following the subroutine call is no longer necessary. The main disadvantage, however, is that the offset value is constant and fixed at assembly time. This limits the usage of the RTD to subroutines with a fixed number of parameters. It would have been more convenient if an address or data register were allowed to contain the offset value.

Even though the offset value is allowed to be negative, the reader should realize that specifying a negative offset is not of any practical value and will cause hours of unnecessary debugging.

Example 5-2

Let us assume that a subroutine requires two parameters to be passed on stack as follows:

Parameter #1: Passed by reference.

Parameter #2: Passed by value and its size is word.

The following gives a program to do this on a 68000 and a 6801X.

```
*       68000 Case:

        PEA       parm1           Parameter #1.
        MOVE.W    parm2,-(SP)     Parameter #2.
        JSR       subrt           Call subrt.
        LEA       6(SP),SP        Deallocate Stack.
        .
        .
        .
subrt   .
        .
        RTS                       Return

*       6801X Case:
        PEA       parm1           Parameter #1.
        MOVE.W    parm2,-(SP)     Parameter #2.
        JSR       subrt           Call subrt.
        .
        .
        .
subrt   .
        .
        RTD       #6              Return and deallocate stack.
```

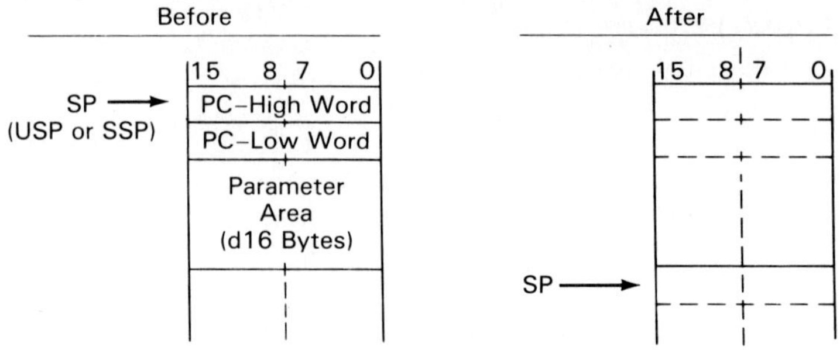

Figure 5-5 Illustration of `RTD #<d16>`.

BKPT (breakpoint) instruction. Execution of this instruction will cause an illegal instruction exception. It is different from other illegal instruction patterns in that it causes a CPU-space cycle, called the *breakpoint bus cycle*, to be executed before saving the exception information on the stack. The main application of this is to indicate a program breakpoint to the external hardware such as debug monitors and real-time hardware emulators. Thus, it is mainly used for program debugging applications.

The assembly syntax of BKPT is

```
BKPT #<0-7>
```

corresponding to the illegal operation word patterns #4848-$484F, encoding eight software breakpoints. The exception handler can examine the stack to figure out the breakpoint number.

5.3 LOOP MODE OF OPERATION

One of the important enhancements of the 6801X is the two-instruction loop mode of operation. An instruction sequence such as

```
back   CMPM.W   (Am)+,(An)+
       DB<cc>   Dk,back
```

is recognized by the 6801X control unit whereby it automatically alters its normal execution activity to take advantage of the fact that the two instructions are already in its prefetch queue as shown in Figure 5-6. By circulating the instructions in the internal queue via the local data bus, all further instruction fetches are suppressed until a loop-exit condition occurs. The only external references made during loop-mode operation are operand transfers. The result is an approximate 50% reduction in execution time.

The loop-mode operation is transparent to the programmer, with the following three conditions required to enter the loop mode:

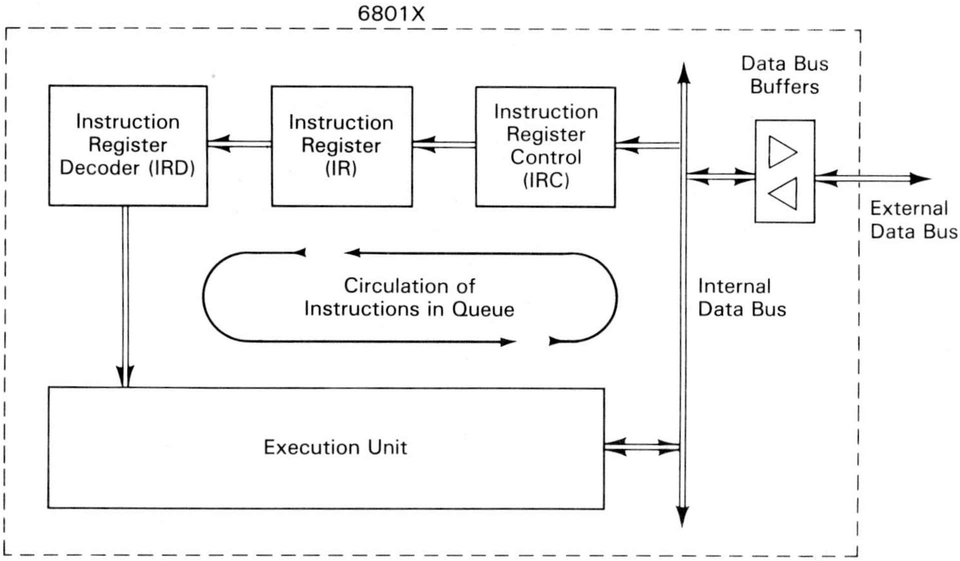

Figure 5-6 Internal Circulation of Instruction Queue.

1. The first instruction of the loop is limited to certain one-word instructions with only certain addressing modes allowed for loop-mode operation as displayed in Table 5-4.
2. The DB⟨*cc*⟩ instruction must be executed with both branch conditions as true and with branch displacement equal to −4.
3. The trace bit (T) is not set.

The first time such a loop is executed, both the loopable instruction and the DB⟨*cc*⟩ are executed normally, after which the loop mode is entered if the above conditions are met. Once in the loop mode, the 6801X executes a different microinstruction routine which executes both instructions as an integral part.

The loop mode is terminated when a loop-exit condition of DB⟨*cc*⟩ becomes true or when an exception occurs. Interrupts are acknowledged only after the execution of DB⟨*cc*⟩, not after the execution of the looped instruction since the two run as a composite instruction in the loop mode.

The main limitation of the loop-mode operation is, of course, that it is limited to the two-instruction looping sequences. It uses the current architecture of the 6801X without much additional overhead and, thus, it is like a "poor man's instruction cache."

The main design goal behind the loop mode was to speed up the basic operations of moving blocks of data and handling character strings, which is exactly what it does, as the next two examples will illustrate.

TABLE 5-4 6801X LOOPABLE INSTRUCTIONS

Loopable Instructions	
Op Codes	Applicable Addressing Modes
MOVE [BWL]	(Ay) to (Ax) (Ay) to (Ax)+ (Ay) to −(Ax) (Ay)+ to (Ax) (Ay)+ to (Ax)+ (Ay)+ to −(Ax) −(Ay) to (Ax) −(Ay) to (Ax)+ −(Ay) to −(Ax) Ry to (Ax) Ry to (Ax)+
ADD [BWL] AND [BWL] CMP [BWL] OR [BWL] SUB [BWL]	(Ay) to Dx (Ay)+ to Dx −(Ay) to Dx
ADDA [WL] CMPA [WL] SUBA [WL]	(Ay) to Ax −(Ay) to Ax (Ay)+ to Ax
ADD [BWL] AND [BWL] EOR [BWL] OR [BWL] SUB [BWL]	Dx to (Ay) Dx to (Ay)+ Dx to −(Ay)
ABCD [B] ADDX [BWL] SBCD [B] SUBX [BWL]	−(Ay) to −Ax
CMP [BWL]	(Ay)+ to (Ax)+
CLR [BWL] NEG [BWL] NEGX [BWL] NOT [BWL] NOT [BWL] TST [BWL] NBCD [B]	(Ay) (Ay)+ −(Ay)
ASL [W] ASR [W] LSL [W] LSR [W] ROL [W] ROR [W] ROXL [W] ROXR [W]	(Ay) by #1 (Ay)+ by #1 −(Ay) by #1

Note: B, W, and L indicate an operand size of byte, word, or long-word.

Example 5-3

The following finds the length of a character string terminated by a null ($00) character. Assume the maximum string length is less than 256 bytes.

```
        LEA     char_str, A0    A0=Addr. of string.
        MOVE.W  #256-1,D0       Search Limit.
back    TST.B   (A0)+           Last Byte?
        DBEQ    D0, back
        SUBI.W  #255,D0         D0=string-length.
```

After the first pass, each loop iteration requires 12 clocks which compares favorably to 18 clocks on a 68000.

Example 5-4

The following moves a block of data. *N* words are moved from BLK1 to BLK2.

```
        LEA      BLK1,A0
        LEA      BLK2,A1
        MOVE.W   #N-1,D0
LOOP    MOVE.W   (A0)+,(A1)+
        DBF      D0,LOOP
```

What is the improvement of the loop mode in this case?

5.4 VIRTUAL MEMORY

In this section, we will discuss the virtual memory implementation using the 6801X. This is a big topic with a lot of information and research papers in this area. We will first cover the motivations behind virtual memory and its relevant concepts before focusing on the 6801X.

5.4.1 Motivations Behind Virtual Memory

In the early days of computing, when a program required more memory than is physically present in the memory of the system, programmers used a method called *overlaying*. This method required the programmer to cut his/her program into little pieces that would fit into available main memory. This way, the program that is stored on a relatively large secondary storage such as a hard disk can be brought into main memory in small chunks, overlaying previous parts, as required for execution. It was also the programmer's responsibility to include additional programming to transfer the overlaid pieces between the main and secondary memory.

The overlaying approach is simple, particularly because it does not require any hardware or system level support. However, it also has several drawbacks.

The most obvious is that it requires additional consideration in programming and knowledge of the main memory size. Putting the task of memory management on the user, it also makes it difficult to transport programs between such systems because of differences in disk I/O and memory sizes. Another difficulty is implementing multiprogramming (i.e., multitasking and/or multi-user) without some kind of automatic memory management by the operating system (OS), because the main memory is further divided between several programs.

A technique known as *virtual memory* was developed to automatically perform the overlay function under OS control, thus, relieving the application programmer completely from the task of overlay control. The concept of using virtual memory techniques was originally introduced in the ATLAS machine developed in the late 1950s at Manchester University. While the basic concept of virtual memory has changed very little since then, the related algorithms for memory management have expanded considerably.

Virtual memory gives the illusion to application programmers that much more memory is available than is actually present in the main memory, hence the term "virtual." The following summarizes the motivations behind virtual memory:

1. To enable running a program whose memory requirements are larger than the size of memory or that are hard to determine before execution time.
2. To make the necessary memory management needed to implement an automatic overlay of the program and data sections, completely transparent to the programmer, thus lowering programming time and costs.
3. To execute programs correctly regardless of the main memory size.
4. To support multiprogramming environments to adapt to varying demands of programs sharing the main memory. Task switching is also enhanced, as we shall discuss later.
5. Memory management required by virtual memory can also be used to provide access permission control. This is especially important in a multiprogramming environment where a software bug in one task cannot affect another task, or cannot crash the system.

In the early 1980s, virtual memory techniques found their way into high-performance microcomputers with support from microprocessors such as the 6801X, and the availability of memory management chips. One school of thought, at the time, was that as the bits-per-memory-chip is increased, it is possible to have a main memory as large as the virtual space. Even though main memory size of a few megabytes are commonplace today, up from 256 Kbytes a few years ago, the programmer's memory requirements have also increased in parallel, resulting in 32-bit microprocessors such as the 68012 and the 68020, with gigabytes of virtual address space. So, the motivations behind virtual memory have changed very little.

5.4.2 Virtual Memory Techniques

The simplified block diagram of a typical memory system using the 68010 is shown in Figure 5-7. The two important components aside from OS support are the *Memory Management Unit* (MMU) and the *two-level memory hierarchy* consisting of high-speed main memory and large secondary storage. The MMU maps the CPU addresses into available physical memory addresses using some translation tables preloaded by the OS, as illustrated in Figure 5-8. The CPU addresses are referred to as *logical* or *virtual* to distinguish them from physical memory addresses.

The high-speed main memory is limited in size because of cost considerations, whereas secondary storage, typically a hard disk with several megabytes of storage (~20 – 1,000 Megabytes) has a very low cost-per-byte but has the drawbacks that it is about 1,000 times slower and only allows sequential accesses.

The basic premise behind the virtual memory techniques is maintaining the currently active portions of a program in main memory while keeping an image of the large virtual memory space of the program on the secondary storage. As program activity shifts to other regions of the virtual space, the MMU detects when a memory location that is not currently in main memory is being accessed, thereby it suspends the execution of the user program via a bus-error exception.

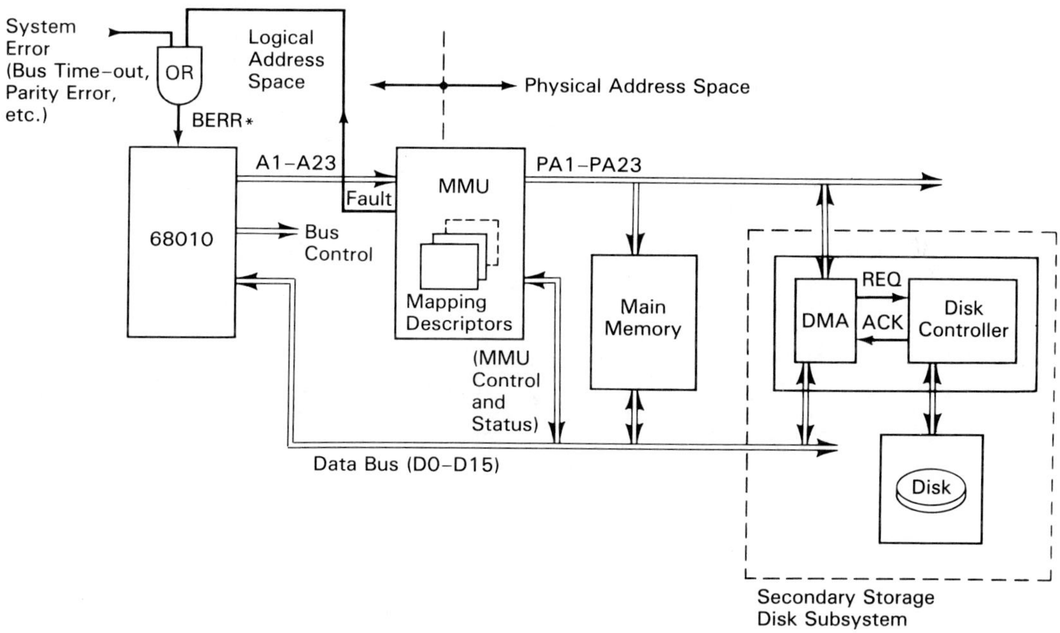

Figure 5-7 Typical 68010 Virtual System.

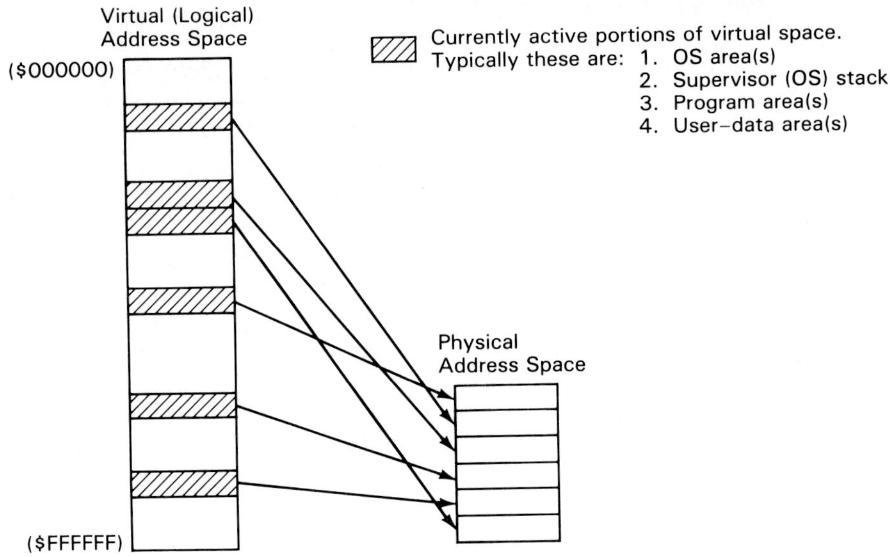

Figure 5-8 Example of Virtual-to-physical Mapping of Addresses.

The OS is then alerted, intervening and requesting that the piece of memory containing the missing location be transferred to main memory. The transfer between the two levels of memories is performed by a DMA device which transfers data faster than the CPU can, also freeing the CPU to attend to other tasks. The latter is especially important in a multitasking system, where the CPU performs another runnable task while one is suspended and waiting for the virtual I/O.

After correcting the fault condition, the OS also updates the MMU's mapping table, thus giving the illusion of a very large linear address space. Then, control is transferred back to the faulted program which continues execution from where it left off. All virtual memory management is transparent to the user.

The virtual system approximates the performance level of a system that has unlimited memory with no wait-cycles and the cost of a system using only secondary storage. This is because most programs tend to spend the majority of their execution time accessing a set of small portions of memory during any given small time period. The program code, itself, is executed sequentially, and typically in a small program loop. Accesses to operands are usually clustered to small areas of memory such as around data structures. This is called the *locality of reference*. Although locality varies from program to program, it has been shown that good programming practices (e.g., structured programming) increases the locality-of-reference characteristic of a program.

The following is an overview of relevant terminology used with regard to virtual systems:

Paged/Segmented Memory The two different types of address translation by a MMU are classified as being paged or segmented. In a paged virtual system, the memory is divided into fixed and equal size pieces called *pages*. Typically, the page size is 1 to 4 Kbytes and is usually set to be a multiple of the record size of the secondary storage to optimize transfers.

In a segmented system, memory is divided into variable-size pieces called *segments*. Segments are allowed to grow or shrink depending upon a program's code or data modules.

Although segmented systems are more flexible, a segmented MMU requires higher complexity. Paged systems are very popular because of their simpler MMU design and simpler memory management required. The word "page" is commonly used in virtual systems regardless of the actual paged/segmented memory type used, as with the next two definitions.

Paging Refers to transferring data between main memory and secondary storage.

Page Fault Refers to the condition that occurs when the accessed location is not in main memory which invokes the OS to retrieve the missing page from secondary storage.

Working Set Is the set of active pages (or segments) that are in main memory. In a multitasking system each task is allowed to keep a limited number of pages in main memory, referred to as the task's working set.

5.4.3 Virtual Memory Support of the 68000 Family

So far we have introduced virtual memory techniques without discussing how the 6801X supports the needed mechanisms required for virtual implementation. Let us assume our program is currently executing the instruction

```
MOVE.W (A0),(A1)
```

There are three possibilities in which this instruction can generate a page-fault condition. That is, during the instruction fetch and when accessing the source or destination operands. Let us say that a page fault occurred when reading the source operand. As we stated earlier, the MMU recognizes the page-fault conditions and signals this to the 6801X via the bus-error input. In response, the 6801X suspends the execution in midstream, and saves its internal state (registers and other hidden state information) on the system stack and then traps the program control to the bus-error handler (part of OS). After the page fault condition is corrected, the OS executes an RTE instruction which revives the previously suspended instruction by pulling all the state information from the stack and rerunning the same bus cycle that caused the page fault earlier. This time, though, no fault occurs because of the updated MMU mapping. The events during a page fault are illustrated in Figure 5-9. Note that a modified page has to be first written back before it is replaced.

When a bus error occurs, the 6801X suspends the execution of an instruction at the microinstruction boundary, and saves the necessary state information on the system stack to be able to revive that instruction later. This is called *instruction continuation*[1] used to support virtual memory. We will later see that newer members of the family—the 68020 and 68030 employ the same technique. The 68000 did not support virtual memory because it saved only enough information to indicate the origin of fault but not enough for instruction continuation.

Since, the page fault requires saving all CPU-state information on the supervisor stack, the 6801X virtual system requires that this stack will always reside in main memory. Otherwise, the page-fault cycle continues to repeat indefinitely.

5.4.4 68010 Virtual System and MMUs

Here we will present two commonly used MMUs in a 68010 virtual memory system. The first one is a discrete approach using a high-speed look-up table and some additional support chips to implement a paged MMU. The second system's design uses a Motorola's single-chip MMU, the '68451.

Paged MMU implementation with high-speed look-up table (LUT). Several popular 68010-based virtual systems are designed by implementing the paged MMU address translation with a high-speed look-up table (static RAM) as illustrated in Figure 5-10. The main advantage of this approach is that the address-translation time is improved over a single-chip '68451, thus requiring less wait-cycles added to each bus cycle because of MMU.

Let us assume that the page size is to be 2 Kbytes and the main memory size is to be 1 Mbytes. The logical address of the 68010 is divided into two parts. The high-order 13 bits are the page number and the low-order 11 bits are the offset within a page. The logical page number becomes the address of the translation look-up table, the main purpose of which is to translate the logical page numbers into the physical page numbers. The low-order 11 bits (10 bits plus LDS*/UDS*) are passed through without any modification. Because of the main memory size,

[1] Another method used by other microprocessors is *instruction-restart*[4].

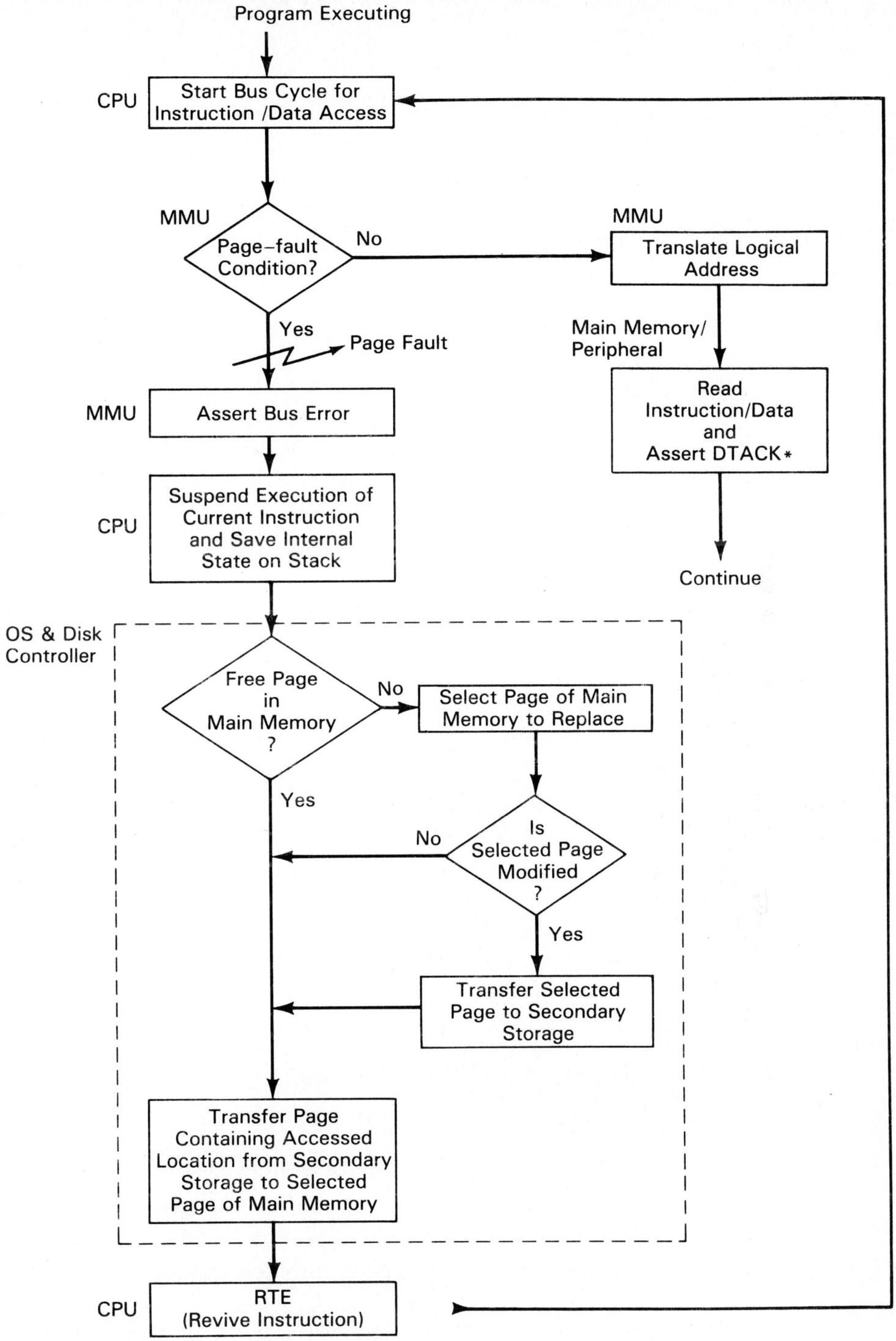

Figure 5-9 Virtual-memory Implementation Flowchart using the 6801X.

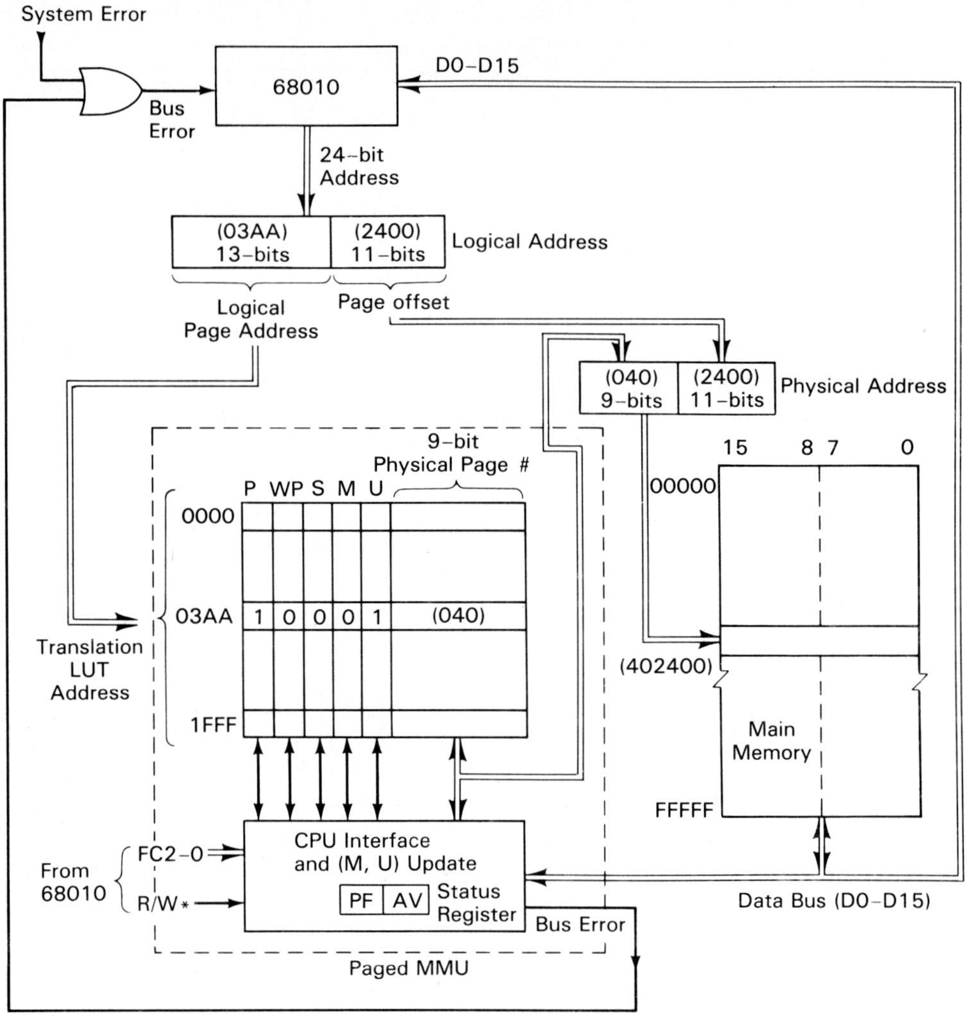

PF is set when P = 0;
AV is set when FC2 = 0 and S = 1;
M is set of referenced page when R/W* = Write and P = 1;
U is set of referenced page when P = 1.

Figure 5-10 A Paged-MMU Implementation in a 68010 Virtual System.

9 bits are required for the physical page numbers in the LUT. In addition, the following control and status bits are used for each logical page of the MMU:

P (Present) — Indicates the corresponding page is present in main memory. Since the translation LUT has 8K locations and the main memory has only 512 pages, only some

	of the P-bits are set by the OS as a page is brought into main memory.
WP (Write-protect)	This bit, when set by the OS, indicates that the corresponding page is write-protected.
M (Modified)	This bit is set by the MMU when a corresponding page is modified by the program. Pages with the M-bit set have to be written back to secondary storage before being replaced with a new page. After writing out and replacing it, the OS clears this bit.
S (Supervisor-only)	This bit, when set by the OS, indicates supervisor-only access to the corresponding page. For example, using this bit a user program is prevented from crashing the system since it cannot accidentally modify the supervisor stack or OS itself.
U (Used)	This bit is set by the MMU when a corresponding page is referenced. The purpose of this bit is to support memory management algorithms. This bit is cleared by the OS when a new page is loaded.

All 14 bits of the LUT can be read and written by the 68010 and the M- and U-bits are updated by the MMU. The MMU also maintains a global status register. Let us say that there are two bits for the 68010 to query:

PF Page-fault condition, and

AV Access Violation

as shown in Figure 5-10, even though each design differs in implementation. When a referenced page has P = 0 (not present) or when an access control is violated, the MMU asserts a bus error to the 68010. Since a bus-error condition can be due to a system error, page fault, or access violation, the OS first determines the source of the bus error by checking the MMU status register. If neither the PF or the AV is set, then it is due to a system error.

68451 MMU. The Motorola '68451 was the first MMU peripheral chip available for the 68000 family. It provides segmented address translation, write-protection of selected segments, and multitasking support. The minimum segment size is 256 bytes, so the lower seven bits of the logical address space (A1-A7) bypass the MMU and become the low-order physical address bits (PA1-PA7) as shown in Figure 5-11.

The '68451 has 32 descriptors, where each descriptor defines how a given segment of logical address space is mapped into physical memory addresses. Before the address translation, the function codes are used to reference the *Address Space Table* (AST) which stores the currently active task numbers for each address-space type as illustrated in Figure 5-12. During a memory reference, the

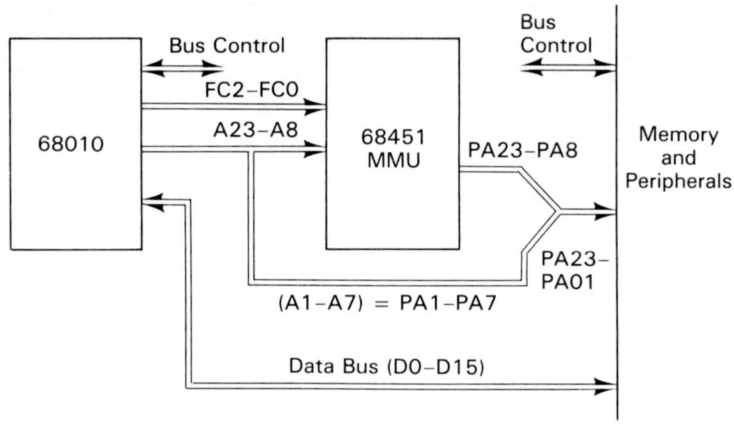

Figure 5-11 Simplified Block Diagram of a 68451 MMU System.

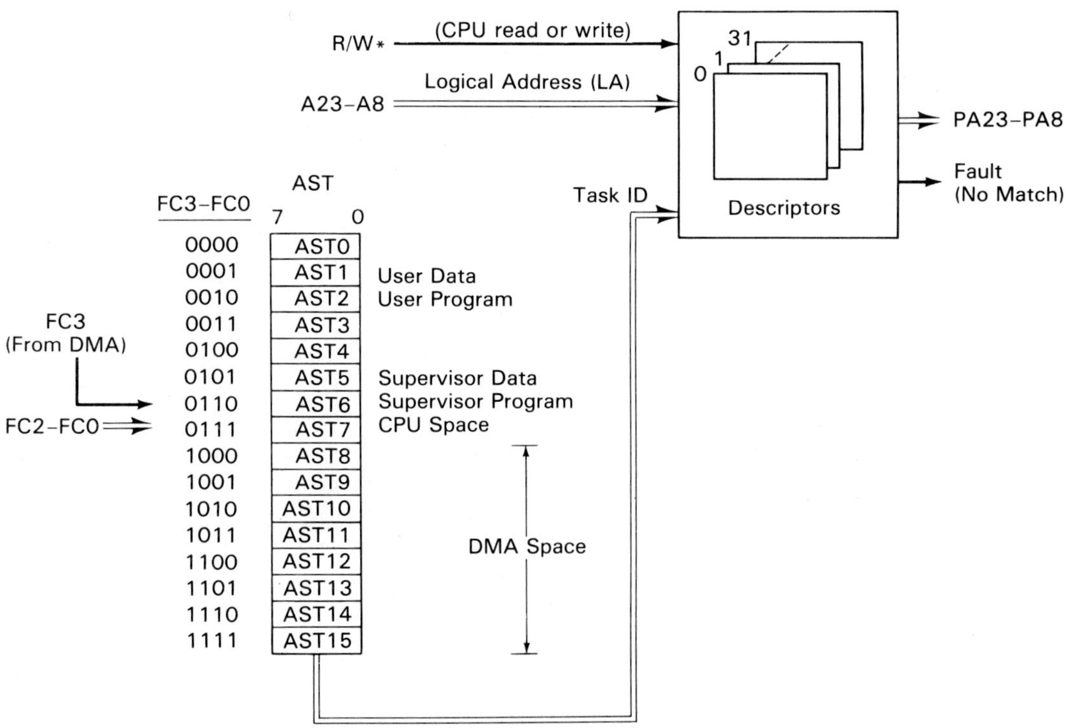

Figure 5-12 Illustration of the 68451 MMU.

corresponding entry of the AST is used to select a subset of descriptors with matching task IDs for address translation. The AST has 16 locations to allow a fourth function code (FC3) to be able to select another set of tasks with a second bus master such as DMA.

The programmer's view of descriptions is shown in Figure 5-13, where all registers can be loaded or read by the CPU. The following describes the various registers of each descriptor:

LBA (Logical Base Address) — This 16-bit register defines the starting address of a segment. The starting address of a segment is limited to 2^k boundaries.

LAM (Logical Address Mask) — This register is a 16-bit mask used in conjunction with the LBA to define the range of a segment. A logical one in the mask indicates significant bit positions, while a logical zero indicates "don't care" positions. An address range match to incoming logical address occurs when

$$\text{LAM}n \ \&\ \text{LA} = \text{LAM}n \ \&\ \text{LBA}n$$

where n is the descriptor number, and LA is the logical address. For example, to define a logical segment starting at $0A0000 and with a length of 4 Kbytes, the required LBA and LAM are

Logical Address :		A23-A20	A19-A16	A15-A12	A11-A8	A7-A4	A3-A0
LBA ($)	=	0	A	0	0	0	0
LAM ($)	=	F	F	F	0		
		← used for matching →					

ASN (Address Space Number) — Is basically the task ID assigned to a descriptor. Used in conjunction with the ASM.

ASM (Address Space Mask) — Similar to the LAM, the ASM is an 8-bit mask used to define the significant bit positions in the corresponding ASN.

The task ID (referred to as the space number in Motorola Literature) of a descriptor matches the active task number from AST, when

$$\text{task-id}_{\text{AST}} \ \&\ \text{ASM}n = \text{ASM}n \ \&\ \text{ASN}n$$

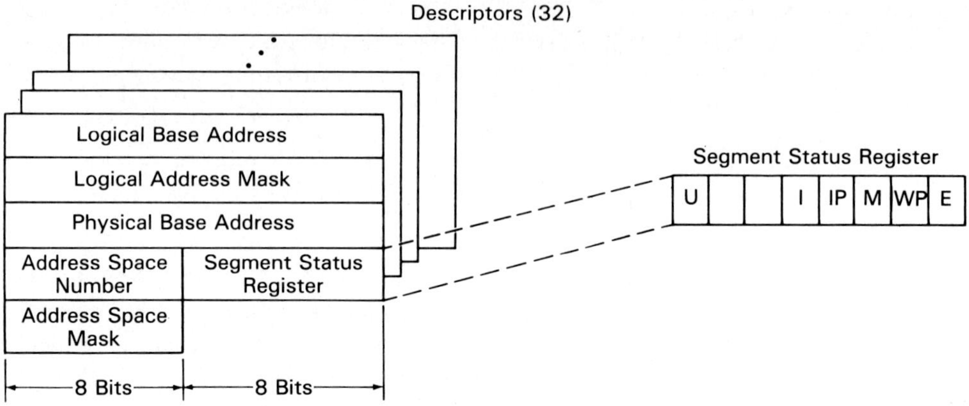

Figure 5-13 Programmer's View of Descriptors.

The main purpose behind the mask register here is to make certain segments shared by more than one task.

PBA (Physical Base Address): The 16-bit PBA is used in conjunction with the LAM register to form the physical address. The logical address is passed through to the physical address in those bit positions in the LAM which contain logical zeroes, and the PBA is gated out in those bit positions which contain logical ones, i.e.,

Physical address = LA & !LAM*n* + PBA*n* & LAM*n*
where "!" indicates logical inversion.

SSR (Segment Status Register): Each descriptor has an 8-bit SSR with the following bits:

- U (Used): Set by MMU if the corresponding segment was accessed.
- I (Interrupt): When set, generates an interrupt if the corresponding segment is accessed.
- IP (Interrupt Pending): Set by MMU, when the I-bit is set and the corresponding segment is accessed.
- M (Modified): Set by MMU when the corresponding segment has been written to.
- WP (Write-Protect): When set, the corresponding segment is write-protected, and any write attempt to that segment will cause a write violation.

E (Enable) — Is a control bit which enables a descriptor to participate in the segment matching process.

The bits U, M, and WP are very similar to the ones we used in the paged MMU. The bits I and IP are useful mainly as a debugging aid.

So far we have not addressed how the '68451 implements the address translation. The mapping of the '68451 is referred to as *associative*, because the descriptions are stored in *Associative Memory* (AM). Whereas conventional memory features access by address, AM is addressed by its contents. The information content of an AM is of the form (key, data) for which $f(\text{key}) = \text{data}$. The AM[2], also often referred to as *translation look-aside buffer* (TLB), is quite different and more complex than traditional memories because each AM cell contains a matching circuit at the bit level.

The AM of the '68451 compares the current memory reference with all 32 descriptors simultaneously. For a descriptor to match, the following needs to be true:

1. LAMn & LA = LAMn & LBAn (address range match).
2. task-id$_{\text{AST}}$ & ASMn = ASNn & ASMn (task-ID match).
3. No write violation when WP = 1.
4. E = 1 (descriptor enabled).

When a matching descriptor is found, the associated PBA is used to form the physical memory address. If no matching descriptor is found, then a fault condition is generated.

The main shortcoming of the '68451 is that 32 descriptors are not enough in a multitasking system, especially when equal-size segments are chosen to model a paged system. Even though multiple '68451s can be used to expand the number of descriptors, this is usually not favored because of the additional cost and the board space required. Also, the '68451, due to translation time, adds about two additional wait-cycles, thus lowering system performance about 50 percent. With the availability of the new Motorola MMU chip, the '68851, the above shortcomings have been eliminated and hence the '68451 will probably not be used in many new designs. Since '68851 is especially tailored for the 68020, we will discuss it in Chapter 7.

Example 5-5

Let a virtual system using the '68451 have three tasks: two users and the OS. Typically, there are several program and data areas used by each task, but here, we will

[2] There are actually two types of AM: One that returns the address, and another one that returns the associated value.

assume that each task has three segments: defining program, data, and stack areas mapped as shown in Table 5-5 at some given time by the OS. Note that mapping seems arbitrary because it is dynamicallly managed by the OS.

To switch the MMU from user A to user B, would require simply a change of AST1 and AST2 from 0 to 1. Since each user has a separate stack area, it is not possible for user A to affect user B's program. Each user thinks that his or her program is the only one running in the 16-Mbyte address space. When user A executes the instruction

```
MOVE.W D0,$30020
```

the program stores D0 at physical location $15020, and when user B executes the instruction, let's say

```
MOVE.W #01,$30020
```

the program stores $01 at physical location $60020.

5.4.5 Virtual System Performance and Memory Management

When a page fault occurs, if there is a free page in memory, then the missing page can be transferred from the secondary storage. What happens if all the pages of main memory are already occupied? In the latter case, the OS uses an algorithm to select a page of main memory for replacement. This algorithm will attempt to select a page for replacement that will not be referenced for the longest time in the future, depending on some past reference activity criteria. The underlying

TABLE 5-5 EXAMPLE MAPPING USING 68451

Task	Task-ID_{AST}	Usage	Logical Address Range	Physical Address Range[1]
OS	80_{16}	Program	F00000-F0FFFF	000000-00FFFF
		Data	C000000-C01000	12000-13000
		Stack	ED0000-E01000	13000-14000
User A	00	Program	000000-20000	A0000-C0000
		Data	30000-34000	15000-17000
		Stack	2A000-2B000	17000-18000
User B	01	Program	000000-40000	20000-60000
		Data	30000-70000	60000-A0000
		Stack	2A000-2B000	FE000-FFFFF

[1] Assume 1-Mbyte physical memory.

assumption is that the locality of reference of a program has typically temporal characteristics (i.e., will not change immediately). Comprehensive coverage of replacement algorithms is beyond the scope of this chapter, rather we will briefly describe some commonly used ones:

LRU (Least-recently Used) — The page which has not been referenced for the longest time is removed since the probability that it will soon be referenced is small.

FIFO (First-In/First-Out) — Replaces the page that has been in main memory for the longest time.

CLOCK Algorithm — A disadvantage of the FIFO method is that it may end up replacing a frequently referenced page if that page has been in memory for the longest time. This algorithm is a combination of the LRU and FIFO methods. With the CLOCK algorithm, pages of main memory are ordered as a circular queue and a usage bit (U) is associated with each page. A pointer (or clock hand) points to the last page of the circular queue that was replaced. On page fault, the pointer starts scanning, skipping over used pages (U = 1) after clearing their U-bits. The first unused page (U = 0) found is replaced.

The performance of a virtual system depends on a given replacement al-

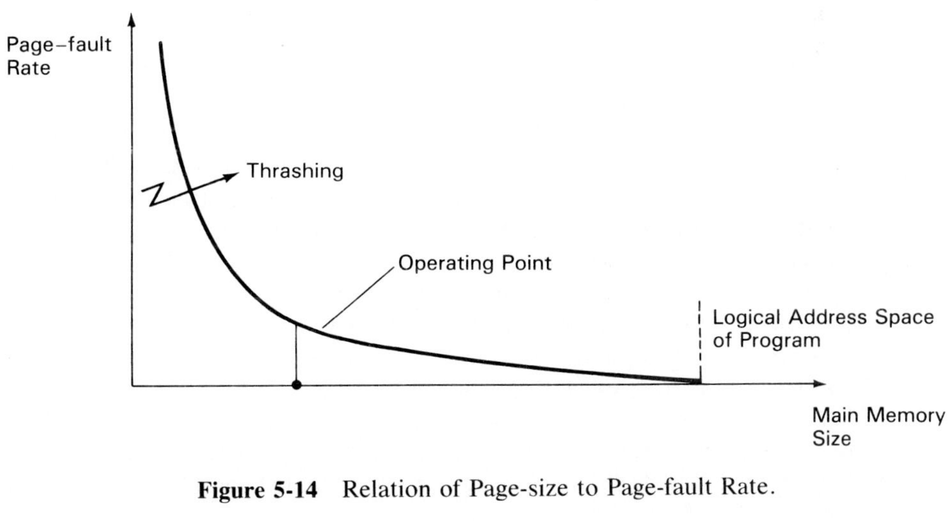

Figure 5-14 Relation of Page-size to Page-fault Rate.

TABLE 5-6 PAGING ACTIVITY FOR EXAMPLE 5-6

Page Referenced	P1	P3	P4	P9	P3	P2	P5	P2	P6	P7	P2	P9	P7	P8	P9	P10
Page Brought-in	P1	P3	P4	P9	—	P2	P5	—	P6	P7	—	P9	—	P8	—	P10
Page Removed	—	—	—	—	—	P1	P4	—	P9	P3	—	P5	—	P6	—	P2
Pages in Main Memory	P1	P1	P1	P1	P1	P2	P2	P2	P2	P2	P2	P2	P2	P2	P2	P10
		P3	P3	P3	P3	P3	P3	P3	P3	P7	P7	P7	P7	P7	P7	P7
(Working Set)			P4	P4	P4	P4	P5	P5	P5	P5	P5	P9	P9	P9	P9	P9
				P9	P9	P9	P9	P9	P6	P6	P6	P6	P6	P8	P8	P8

→ Order of Execution →

gorithm, as well as on the MMU's translation speed and size of the main memory. If the main memory is too small, the rate of page-faults becomes high as illustrated in Figure 5-14. A good trade-off between memory size and page-fault rate is to operate just below the knee of the curve. Of course, the page-fault rate varies from program to program since the locality of references of each program is different. To the left of the operating point, the system performance degrades severely which is known as *thrashing*.

Example 5-6

Let us say that task A can maintain a maximum of four pages in main memory (i.e., it has a working set of four pages) and that during execution, it references ten pages in the following order: P1, P3, P4, P9, P3, P2, P5, P2, P6, P7, P2, P9, P7, P8, P9, P10. Then, Table 5-6 illustrates paging activity using the LRU algorithm.

5.5 VIRTUAL MACHINE CONCEPT AND SUPPORT

We mentioned earlier that a program running in a virtual memory system is not aware of the actual size of the physical (main) memory. Similarly, in a multitasking system, a task cannot determine whether it has the sole use of the processor or is time sharing it with other tasks. A *virtual machine* is an extension of these concepts which supports running multiple operating systems in a system as shown in Figure 5-15. The *Governing Operating System* (GOS) that runs in the supervisor mode intercepts all I/O requests and accesses them to the supplementary supervisor registers and executes the desired operation interpretively. Such an emulation of the processor environment by the GOS makes each OS think that it is the only one in the system.

The rationale behind a virtual machine is that while one user is debugging the new release of an OS, the others can use a debugged version. Furthermore, in software development, programs can be developed and debugged for system configurations that are different from the host. For example, using a system with a 6801X, a new OS for a new 68020 system can be developed where the hardware of the 68020 system is not yet available for programming use. The debugging of the new OS is also easier because it is done under complete control of the GOS.

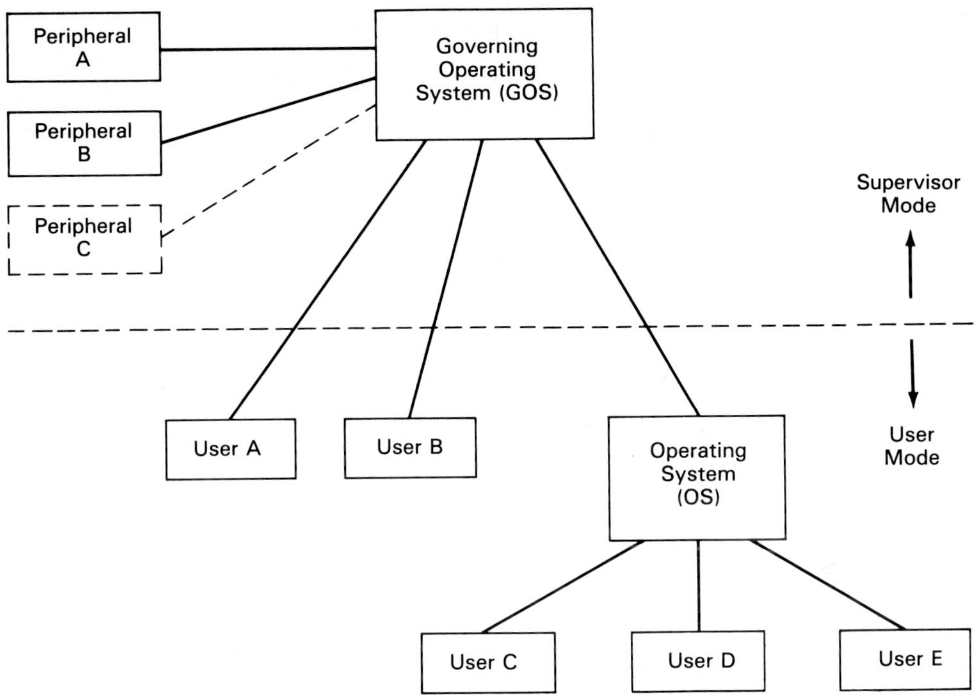

Figure 5-15 Multiple OS in Virtual Machine Environment.

The concept of a virtual machine was first introduced in the late 1960s in Cambridge, Massachusetts by the ATLAS computer. The first commercial application of the concept was the virtual machine/370 (VM/370) [13]. For a system to be classified a virtual machine, the following are required:

1. All system-level resources must be secured so that only a supervisor-level program may access them. The supervisor resources include peripherals and supplementary registers of the supervisor mode.
2. Since each OS is likely to handle exceptions differently, the GOS needs to keep a separate exception vector table for each OS.
3. Virtual memory techniques must be used so that each OS has a separate logical addressing space (i.e., the virtual machine is an extension of the virtual memory concept).
4. The system must have the ability to emulate a faulted bus cycle in software. This refers to the software re-run of the bus cycle which caused the access fault. More on this later.

One of the reasons for the 68000's lack of support of a virtual machine is that the MOVE from SR instruction was not privileged, thus, when an OS interrogated SR it could find that it is not really the only one in the system. In the user mode of the 6801X, any read or write attempt to the supplementary supervisor registers causes a privilege-violation exception. The GOS maintains a copy of the (SSP, SR, SFC, DFC, VBR) and other required information in a table for each OS. This table, also called the *control information block*, is typically kept in protected supervisor memory. During a privilege violation, the GOS intervenes and identifies the instruction that caused the violation. Let us say, the instruction

```
MOVE SR,D0
```

was attempted by the OS. Then, the GOS pulls the OS's copy of SR from the information block and passes this to the OS, just as if the instruction executed successfully. In order for this emulation to appear correct to the OS, the GOS has to concatenate the system byte of the virtual SR with the condition codes saved on the stack during the privilege-violation trap. The GOS trap handler for privilege violation is illustrated in Figure 5-16.

When a particular OS is running, the GOS loads the VBR from the control-information block so that the corresponding exception table is active. This also enables the GOS to change its emulation based on the active OS.

All I/O in a virtual machine is controlled by the GOS. When an OS attempts to access a peripheral, this will generate a bus-error condition by the MMU. There

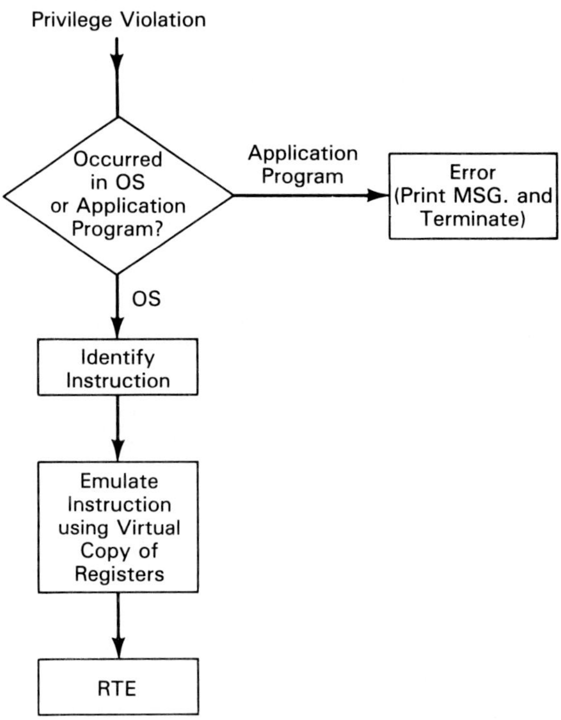

Figure 5-16 Virtual Machine Operation during Privilege Violation.

are basically two situations:

1. If the specified I/O device physically exists and has been assigned to the requesting OS, then the I/O instruction is directly executed by the GOS.
2. If the specified I/O device does not exist, then the I/O instruction is emulated using a similar I/O device.

The typical example of the latter case is the print spooler in a multi-user system where the user believes the data is going directly to the printer. Actually, the data is transferred to a temporary file on disk until the printer is available.

To support virtual machine mechanisms, it is also necessary to be able to emulate a faulted bus cycle in software. Let us consider the following example. Suppose the OS thinks a printer is mapped to \$300000-\$30000E including various control and status words. Actually, the printer is physically at \$F00000-\$F0000E. Hence, when the OS attempts to access the printer, the GOS has to intervene and use the actual addresses to emulate the desired operation. Let us say that the first thing the OS does is to check the status byte of the printer to see if it is enabled, for example

```
BTST #PRRDY,PRTSTAT
```

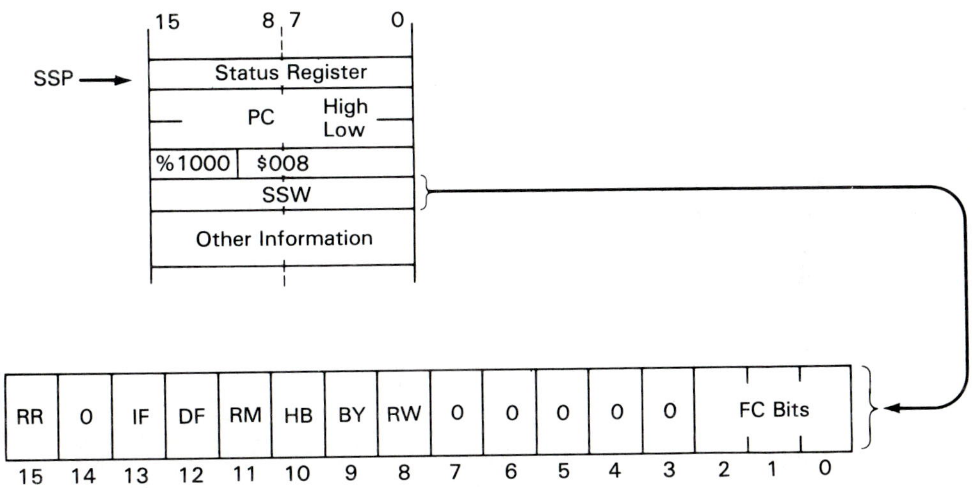

RR: Re–run flag; 0 = Processor re–run (default). 1 = software re–run
IF: Instruction fetch to the instruction input buffer
DF: Data fetch to the data input buffer
RM: Read–modify–write cycle
HB: Transfer into/out of high byte of buffer
BY: Byte transfer flag
RW: Read/write flag
FC: Funtion code of the faulted access
0: Reserved by Motorola; reads zero

Figure 5-17 Bus-error Exception Stack and Special Status Word (SSW).

where PRRDY is the bit number of the ready bit and PRTSTAT is the address of the status register in the ($300000-$30000E) range. By defining such ranges of the logical address space for devices to be emulated, a bus-error exception occurs (by MMU) when attempting to read PRTSTAT. The OS can then evaluate the fault address and identify it as the range of the printer for the OS whereby it reads the status register of the actual printer and completes the faulted access in the software.

How is a faulted bus cycle completed in software? The exception stack for a bus error includes a *special status word* (SSW) and three words for data buffers (data input, data output, and instruction input) as shown in Figure 5-17. The SSW

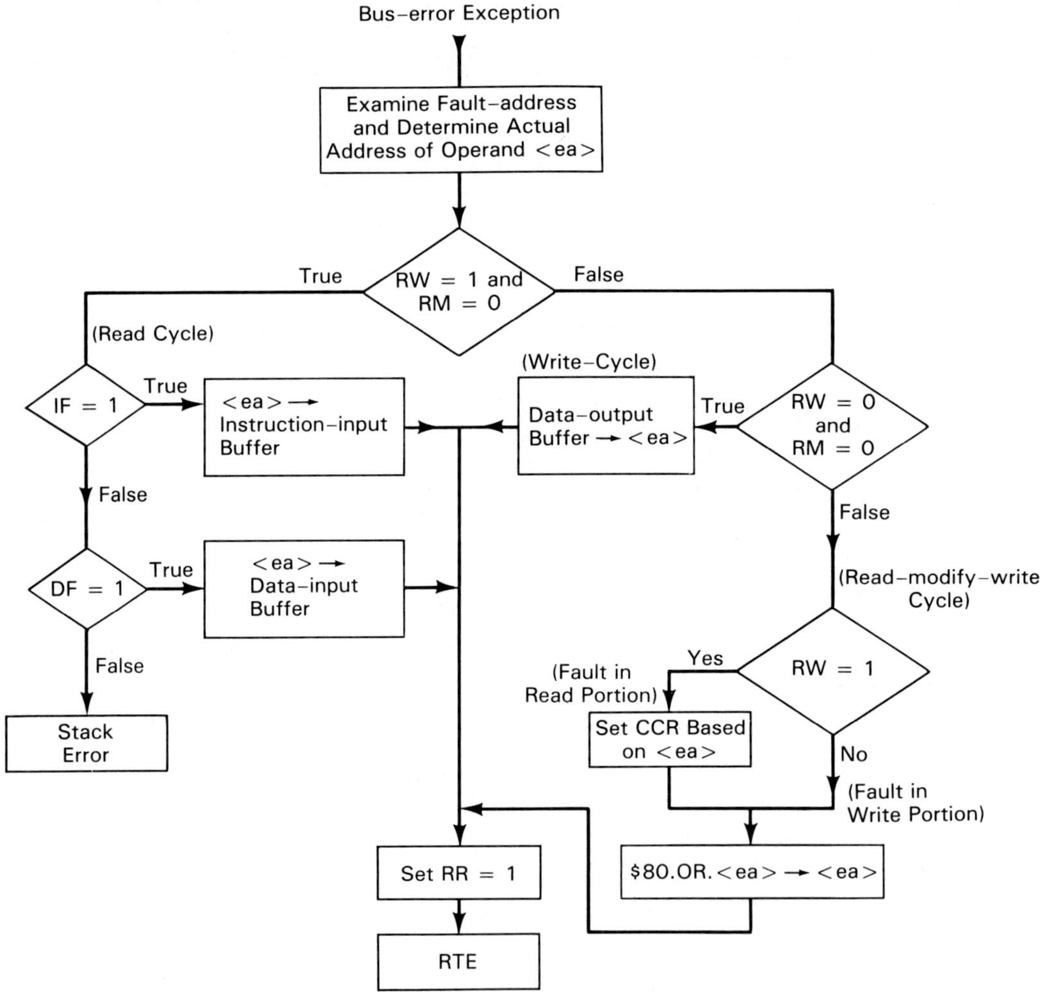

Figure 5-18 Software Re-run Operation During Bus-error Exception.

indicates the type of transfer and which buffer is to be used. For the above example, the status register value is stored in the low-byte of the data-input buffer (i.e., at 20(SP)). But then what happens when we execute RTE? Earlier, we said the 6801X will rerun the faulted bus cycle. In this case, since we performed the necessary operation in software, we simply want the instruction to continue, without re-running the faulted bus cycle and causing another bus error. The 6801X provides for this by using the *re-run* (RR) *flag* of the SSW. The RR flag defaults to re-running the bus cycle if not altered by software. When the GOS sets RR = 1, the 6801X is made to believe that the faulted bus cycle is completed normally, thus continuing with the rest of the instruction, if any. This is illustrated in Figure 5-18.

5.6 EXCEPTION PROCESSING DIFFERENCES WITH THE 68000

The exception processing of the 6801X is the same as the 68000 except for the changes required for virtual memory and virtual machine support. We stated earlier that a bus-error exception is used to suspend the execution of an instruction during a page or access fault condition. When a bus-error (or address-error) exception occurs, the 6801X saves the internal state on the system stack where the state information consists of 26 words including 15 internal execution-unit registers, instruction-pipe registers, and miscellaneous state information. After the fault condition is corrected, executing the RTE instruction restores the state of the 6801X from the stack and resumes execution of the faulted instruction.

The 68000 saves only enough state information to provide the user information about the source of the bus-error (or address-error) exception. This information is not sufficient for an instruction continuation. Furthermore, since the RTE in a 68000 expects only three words on the stack—that is SR, PC-high and PC-low—the bus-error handler first has to deallocate the additional information before executing RTE.

For the above reasons and in anticipation of other stack formats in later members of the 68000 family, the Motorola designers changed the minimum stack-frame format to include an additional word, as illustrated in Figure 5-19. The

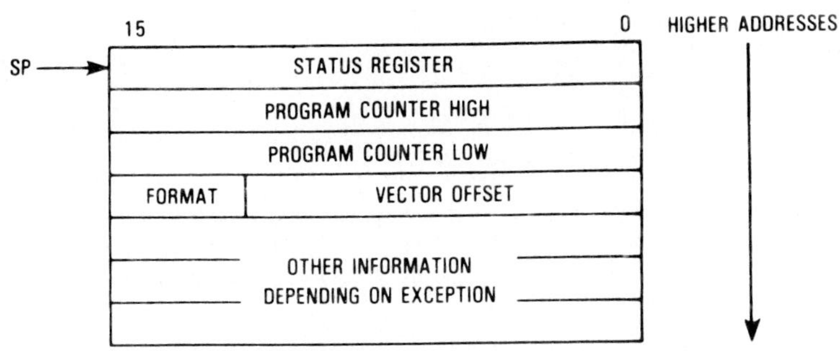

Figure 5-19 6801X Stack-frame General Format.

format number identifies the type of stack frame so that RTE can determine what information is on the stack. There are two types of stack frames allowed for the 6801X. The long format (format code = \$80) is used for bus-error and address-error exceptions (group 0 except reset, based grouping of Table 4-3) and the short-format (format code = \$00) is used for all other exceptions except Reset, as illustrated in Figure 5-20. The *vector offset* is the 8-bit vector number multiplied by four. The reason the 6801X saves this on the stack is to indicate the source of the exception to generic handlers. For example, if a handler is handling all auto-vectored interrupts, then it could quickly determine the origin of the interrupt by examining the vector offset.

Let us look at the operation of RTE instruction more closely. In a virtual-memory system, it is possible that part of the stack is on secondary storage, so it is possible to have a bus-error exception while executing an RTE instruction if the bottom of stack is not in the main memory. As we said earlier, the top of the stack always has to reside in main memory. A bus-error exception, while restoring the internal state information of the 6801X, would not be recoverable because it causes a double bus-fault condition. To avoid such a system crash, the RTE instruction checks to see if the last word of stack is resident by reading it,

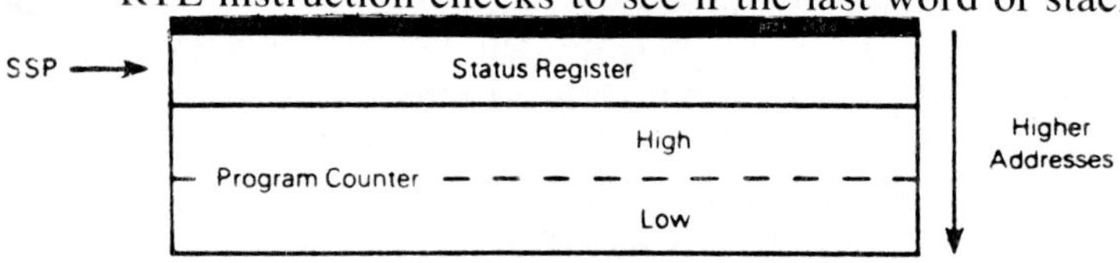

(a) Group 2 and 3 Exceptions.

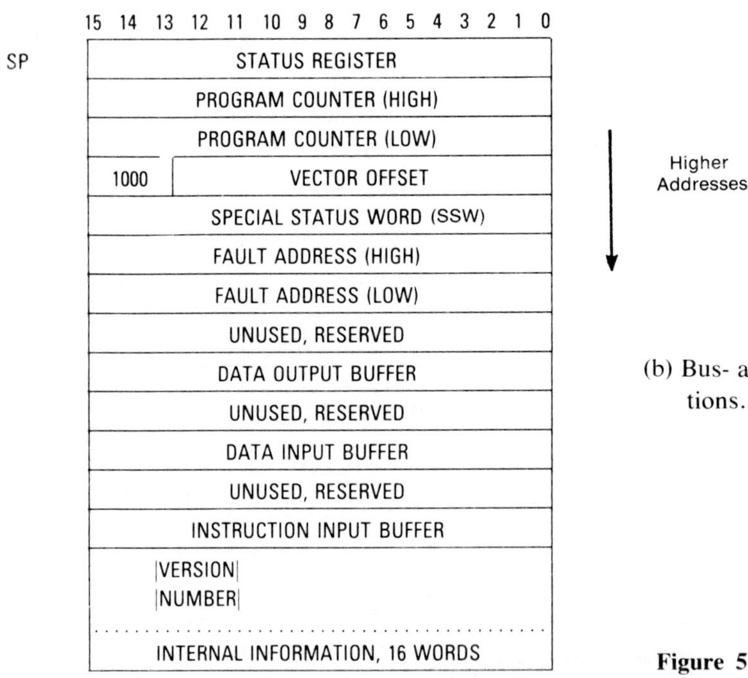

(b) Bus- and Address-error Exceptions.

Figure 5-20 6801X Stack Frames.

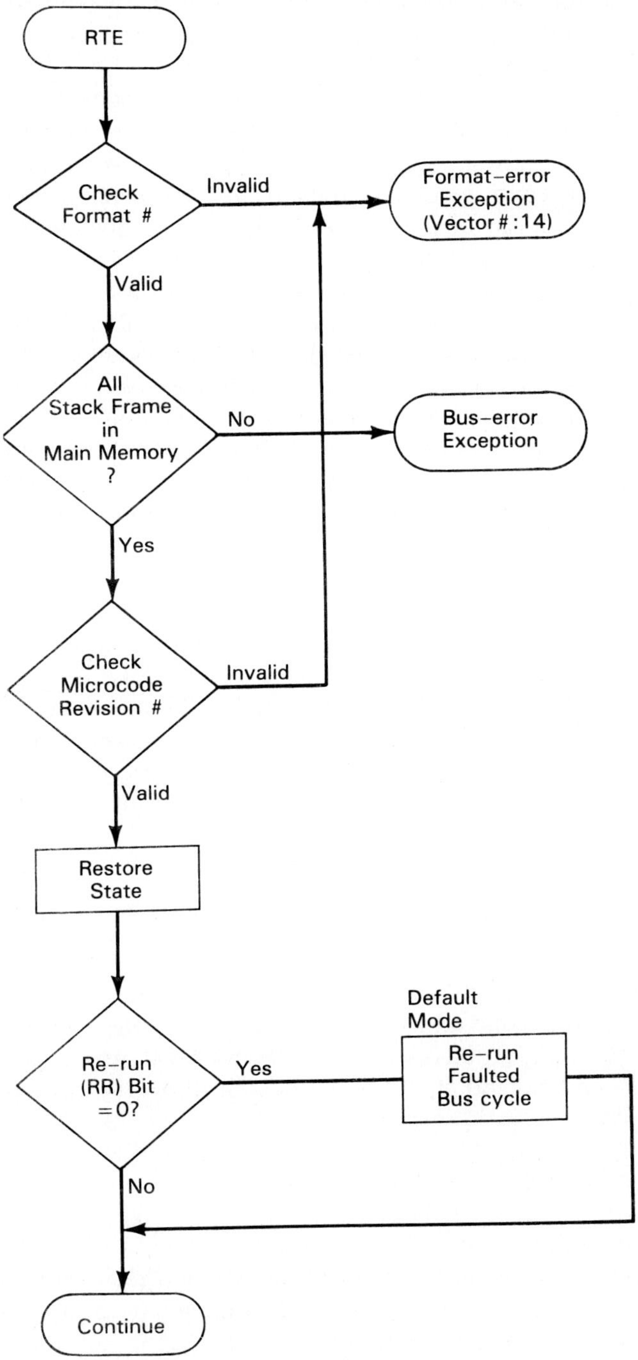

Figure 5-21 Operation of the RTE Instruction.

before it starts restoring the state information. If a bus error occurs when reading the last word of the frame, execution of the RTE is suspended, trapping to a bus handler for the OS to correct the page fault.

What if the stack frame has been corrupted because of a software bug and the RTE reads a format number other than \$0 or \$80? This generates a new type of exception called a *format exception*. An invalid format code, however, is not the only source of a format exception. Let us consider the following scenario. Suppose we have a multiprocessor system using two 68010 processors where one of the 68010s is an older version with a different microcode than the other one. A difference in microcode (i.e., the micro instructions) would not be directly apparent to the user, but it is possible that stack frame contents will be different. This is because a bus error or address error suspends the instruction execution at microinstruction boundaries. If a page fault occurs when processor A is running, and after paging, if the task is dispatched to processor B, this would cause an error or system crash. To avoid such a situation, the RTE also checks the revision number that was stored on the stack during the saving process with its own. If there is no match, this condition will also cause a format exception. The OS, in such a case, will typically put the task on hold until processor A is available, thus avciding any system crash.

The operation of the RTE instruction is illustrated in Figure 5-21. After saving the internal state, the RTE examines the RR(re-run) bit to see if the faulted bus cycle is to be re-run or not. The nice thing about the expanded RTE instruction is that it handles different stack-frame formats and various situations we discussed above and with the built-in flexibility it is also fully upward-compatible with the 68020 and the 68030. As we shall see later, these newer members of the family have additional stack-frame formats but the basic process flow of RTE is unchanged.

5.7 SOFTWARE COMPATIBILITY WITH THE 68000

Let us examine the compatibility of 68000 programs with those of the 6801X. The user-programming model is the same and the instruction set of the 6801X is a superset of the 68000. Hence, application (user-level) programs will run on a 6801X without any changes with one exception. If the application program has the instruction.

```
MOVE SR,<daea>
```

this will cause a privilege violation when run on the 6801X. One way to handle this situation is for the OS to emulate this instruction. Another and easier approach is to change the MOVE from SR instruction with the MOVE from CCR, assuming the purpose is to read the condition-code register. The latter approach can also be easily realized even if the source code of the program is not available by directly changing the load module of the program. A patch utility, typically provided by the OS, will disassemble and help locate the MOVE from SR instruction which can then be changed to the object code of MOVE from CCR (i.e., by changing \$42 to \$46).

What about compatibility of supervisor-level programs? The 6801X has three additional supervisor-mode registers. But, these registers maintain compatibility with the 68000 since the VBR is cleared to zero on power-up and function code registers are only used by the MOVES instruction. Another important change is in the stack-frame formats. Typically, an exception handler does not access data behind the top stack frame. If so, the additional word per stack frame does not create a compatibility problem. Otherwise, the offset value from the SP needs to be increased by two.

FURTHER READING

68010 and 68012

1. Hansen, Daniel J. *Programming Motorola's 32-bit Microprocessor—The 68010.*
2. MacGregor, Douglas and Mothersole, David S. *The 68010—A True Virtual Machine.*
3. MacGregor, Douglas and Moyer, Bill. "Built-in Tight-loop Mode Raises Microprocessor's Performance," *Motorola Application Note. AR-211.*
4. MacGregor, Douglas and Mothersole, David S. "Virtual Memory and the MC68010," *IEEE Micro*, Vol. 3, No. 3, June 1983, pp. 24–39.
5. Beims, Robert. *The 68010 and Virtual Memory*, ________.
6. Groepler, Paul F. *The Virtual MC68010*, ________.

Virtual Memory

7. Denning, Peter. "Virtual Memory," *Computing Surveys*, Vol. 2, No. 3, September 1970, pp. 153–189.
8. Schmitt, Stephen. "Virtual Memory for Microcomputers," *Byte*, April 1983, pp. 210–238.
9. Zehr, Gregg. "Memory Management Units for 68000 Architectures," *Byte*, November 1986, pp. 127–135.
10. Schneck, Paul B. "The Myth of Virtual Memory," *Software-Practice and Experience*, Vol. 13, 1983, pp. 537–543.
11. Schwausch, Russell E. *Making Memory Managable with the Motorola 68451.*
12. *MC68451 Memory Management Unit User Manual*, Motorola, ADI-872-R1.

Virtual Machine

13. Madnick, Stuart E. and Donovan, John J. *Operating Systems*, McGraw-Hill, 1974.

EXERCISES

New Resources

1. What is the main application of the VBR register? What is the contents of VBR after power-up reset?
2. Suppose the OS wants to return data to an application program at a location pointed to by A2. Assume the word-size data to be moved is in D0 and that address spaces are separated by a memory management unit. Write instructions to do this.
3. Using the RTE instruction, write a macro to simulate the RTD instruction. How does execution time of this macro running on a 68000 compare with the RTD instruction of the 68010. Is it possible to expand this macro to include a data register to store the words to deallocate (i.e., RTD D*n*)?
4. What is the performance improvements of the multiply and divide instruction of the 68010 with respect to the 68000?
5. What are the differences between the 68012 and the 68010 from the programmer's point of view? Please explain.
6. How does the CLR instruction of the 68010 differ from that of the 68000?
7. What is the purpose of the BKPT instruction?
8. What is a CPU-space cycle? What types of bus cycles of the 6801X classify as a CPU-space cycle?

Loop Mode of Operation

9. What is the improvement in execution of

```
BACK    CMP.W  (A0)+,(A2)+
        DBEQ   D0,BACK
```

in loop mode with respect to normal execution? Specify clock cycles per iteration with and without a loop mode of operation.

10. Make use of the loop mode of the 6801X to add two 128-bit numbers efficiently. Assume A0 points to the source operand and A1 points to a second operand which will be replaced by the result.
11. What are the conditions to exit from the loop mode of operation?

Virtual Memory

12. List the new features of the 6801X that specifically support the virtual-memory techniques.
13. What is the maximum number of page faults possible in running the following instructions?

a) `MOVE.L (A0),(A1)`

b) `MOVE.L $40(A0,D0.L),(A1)`

14. What are the different address-translation techniques used by MMUs? Please explain.
15. Can the paging method of Figure 5-10 be extended for use with the 68012? Please explain.
16. Is an MMU really necessary for virtual-memory operation? Consider a page fault on an instruction fetch and while accessing an operand.
17. When a bus error happens, how does the OS distinguish between the following three conditions?

    a) Page fault
    b) Access violation
    c) System/memory error

18. Give the value of the '68451 descriptor registers (LBA*n*, LAM*n*, PBA*n*, ASN*n*, ASM*n*) for mapping the USER A's address space given in Table 5-5.
19. Modify Example 5-6 for the FIFO algorithm.
20. Some other microprocessors use a different method to support virtual memory called the *instruction restart*. This approach restarts the faulted instruction from the beginning, and thus, is quiet different from the instruction continuation of the 68000 family. Instruction restart requires that the processor is able to restore the state of the processor and operands as they were at the beginning of the instruction. Discuss the advantages and disadvantages of both approaches.

Virtual Machine

21. List the new features of the 6801X that specifically support virtual-machine requirements.
22. Is it possible to have more than one layer of OSs under the GOS in a virtual-machine system?

Exceptions

23. How does the 6801X stack-frame format differ from that of the 68000?
24. What is a format exception?
25. How does the 6801X guarantee that the entire stack frame is in main memory before it starts restoring the internal state during an RTE instruction?

6

68020 Architecture and Programming

6.1 INTRODUCTION

In this chapter, we will focus on the architecture and programming of the 68020 processor. One of the significant features of the 68020 is that it is upwardly software compatible with the earlier members of the family. The 68020 supports all the instructions and operand addressing modes of the 6800x and the 6801x. The only instruction that is not compatible with respect to the 6800x is the MOVE from SR instruction which was changed to be privileged starting with the 68010. It is replaced with a MOVE from CCR instruction in order to be able to read condition codes in the user mode, as we saw in Chapter 5.

The significant enhancements incorporated into the 68020 are the following:

1. Three 32-bit *arithmetic units* (AUs) in the on-chip execution unit that operate concurrently for high performance.
2. A 32-bit address bus (i.e., a 4 Gigabyte addressing range).
3. A 32-bit data bus.
4. Dynamic sizing of the data bus to 8-, 16-, or 32-bits to match the size of the memory or peripheral.
5. Extended operand addressing modes.
6. Extended instruction set.
7. Coprocessor support.
8. On-chip 128-word instruction cache.
9. Extended exception processing.
10. Virtual memory/machine support extended for 32-bit buses.

We will be discussing the above enhancements during the rest of this chapter with the exception of the coprocessor support which will be discussed in detail in the next chapter.

The architecture of virtual memory/machine operation is the same as the 6801x processor. The instruction-continuation method after a page fault is used to support virtual operations. Hence, the coverage of these topics in Chapter 5 applies directly here. The 68020, however, requires a 32-bit MMU to implement a virtual memory system and also details of the emulation of an instruction in software is, of course, different since the internal structure of the 68020 is different than that of the 6801x.

68020 internal architecture. The block diagram of the 68020 architecture is shown in Figure 6-1. The microcoded control sequencer has a two-level structure (micro and nano code), similar to that used in the 68000 and provides the overall chip control. The bus controller handles all instruction prefetches and operand transfers. Transfer requests from the sequencer are queued to the bus controller allowing independent and concurrent operation of instruction execution and external bus transfers. The instruction holding register is loaded from the

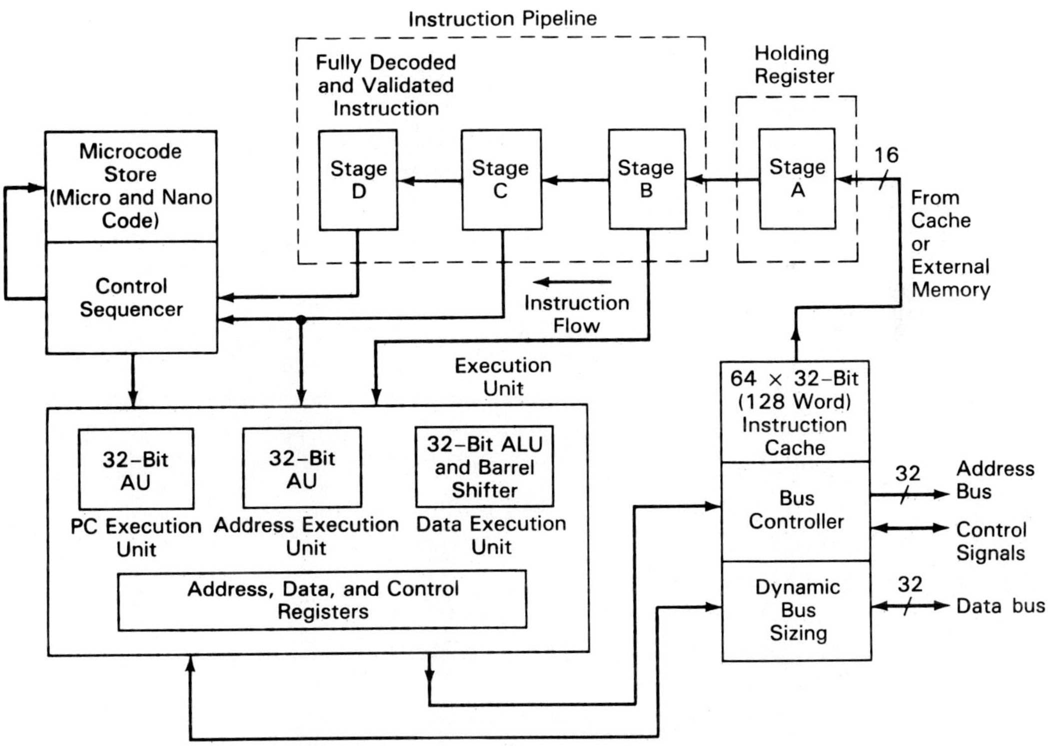

Figure 6-1 Internal Architecture of the 68020 Processor.

instruction cache if there is a cache hit (i.e., the instruction is found within the cache), or otherwise from the external memory. The instruction cache holds the most recently used instruction sequences to facilitate fast execution times without accessing the external memory.

The instructions and their extension words, if any, flow from the holding register toward stage D. As instructions are staged from B through D, they are validated (illegal instruction?) and fully decoded. Just before the execution of an instruction begins, its operation word is in stage D, and any extension words are in stages C and B. The first extension word is made available to the control unit for instructions that need further specification in order to decode an addressing mode, and so forth. The stages B and C are also connected to the execution unit to provide an operand specification that is ready to use. This is necessary for immediate operands or for operands that require effective-address calculations.

The execution unit features three separate arithmetic units for concurrent operation on effective-address calculation, program-flow control, and, most visibly to the user, data calculations. One of the AUs also has Boolean-logic capability and a 32-bit barrel shifter. The term *barrel* refers to the capability to perform any arithmetic or logical shifts or rotate-bits operations in a fixed time period (one clock period for the 68020) regardless of the shift count. In contrast, the earlier siblings of the family performed shifts iteratively, one bit to the left or right at a time, taking $2*n$ clock cycles for a shift count of n.

Such high-performance features of the 68020 result in a typical execution speed of about 2 to 3 MIPS at a 16 MHz clock speed. This makes sense because both the bus bandwidth and the clock speed are twice that of an 8 MHz 68000, which averages about 0.7 MIPS. The doubled clock frequency by itself does not translate to twofold performance mainly due to dependency on external memory access times. However, there are other factors that make up the difference, including increased internal parallelism, three AUs, and an instruction cache that contribute to the high performance of the 68020 processor.

It should also be noted that merely comparing average MIPS figures might be misleading for two reasons. First, the performance is heavily dependent on a given application program. Secondly, the amount of useful work done by one million instructions of a 68000 and a 68020 is not the same due to significant enhancements in the instruction set and the operand addressing modes of the 68020.

6.2 MEMORY ORGANIZATION

6.2.1 Data Types and Organization in Memory

The organization of memory is the same as the 68000 processor. The memory is byte addressable. The address N of a word-size operand (data or instruction) corresponds to the address of its high-order byte. The low-order byte is located at address $N + 1$. Similarly, a long-word size operand located at address N, occupies addresses N through $N + 3$, where the address $N + 3$ contains the least-significant byte. The 68000 requires that word and long-word data are to be aligned at word boundaries (i.e., at even addresses). The 68020 relaxes this restriction so that data operands may be located at any byte as shown in Figure 6-2. It is only required that the instruction and system stack words be aligned on word boundaries. A word data is said to be misaligned if it is at an odd address, and a long-word data is misaligned if the least-significant two bits of its address are not zero. In other words, a long-word is aligned if its address is on a modulo 4 address boundary. Of course, bytes are always aligned since memory is byte addressable. Figure 6-3 shows the aligned word and long-word operands. The alignment is not necessary for data operands but is still important because the most efficient data transfers occur when an operand is aligned as we shall discuss in the next section.

The operand types supported by the 68020 are the following:

Byte, word, and long-word size operands;

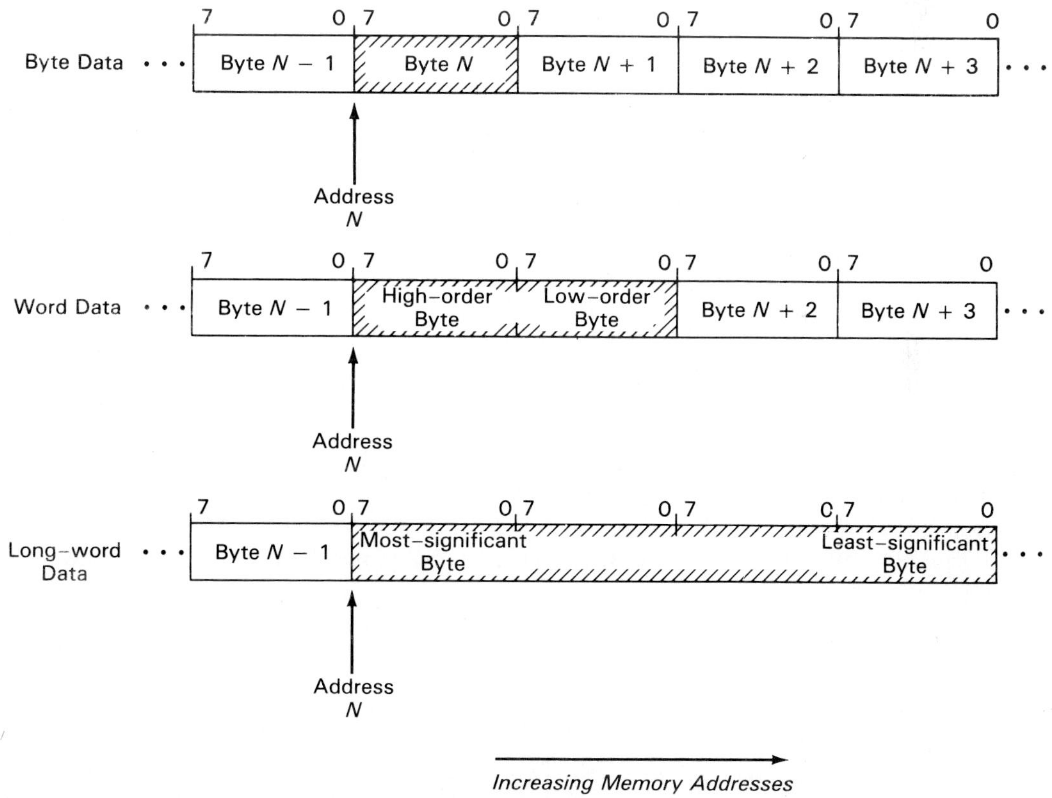

Figure 6-2 Memory Organization of Byte, Word and Long-word Operands.

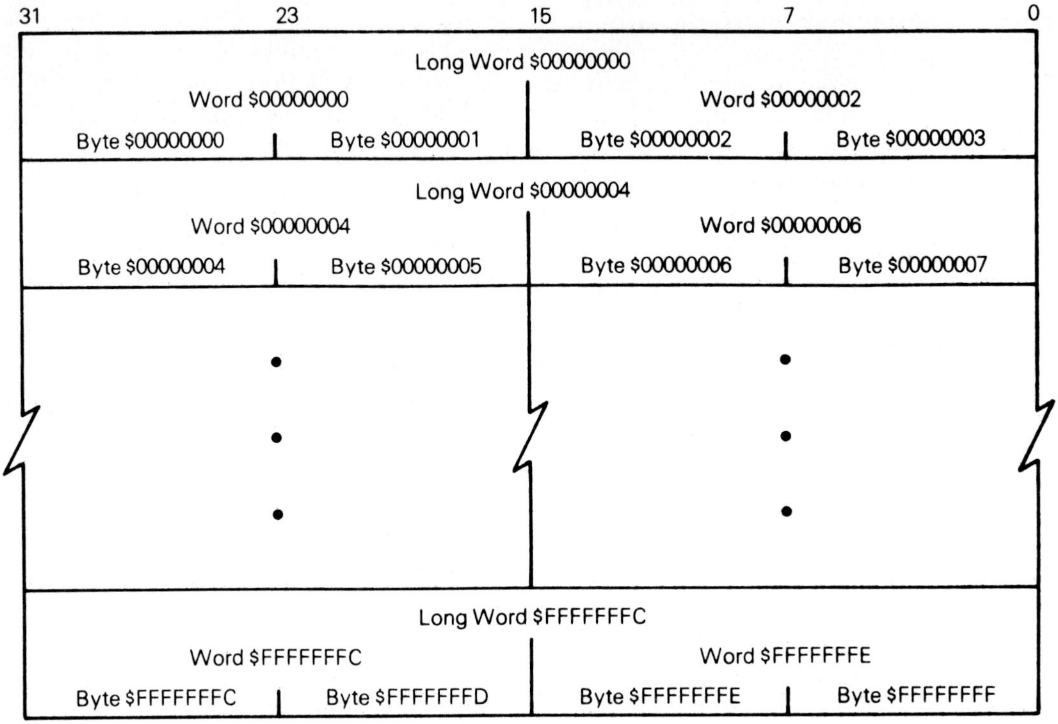

Figure 6-3 Memory Addressing of Aligned Memory Operands.

Bit data;
BCD data (packed or unpacked); and
Bit-field data.

The new operand types are unpacked BCD data and bit-field data as illustrated in Figure 6-4. The unpacked BCD contains one decimal digit per byte, whereas packed BCD contains two decimal digits. A bit-field data is a string of 1 to 32 consecutive bits, and the memory is treated as a one-dimensional array of sequential bit data. There are three parameters to specify a bit field in memory:

Base Address	Is the address of the byte which contains the base address of the bit field.
Offset	Is the number of bits to the most-significant bit of the field from the base address (i.e., the bit number of the left-most bit of the field. The allowed range is $[-2^{31}, 2^{31} - 1]$).
Width	Is the number of bits in the bit field with an allowable range of 1 to 32 bits.

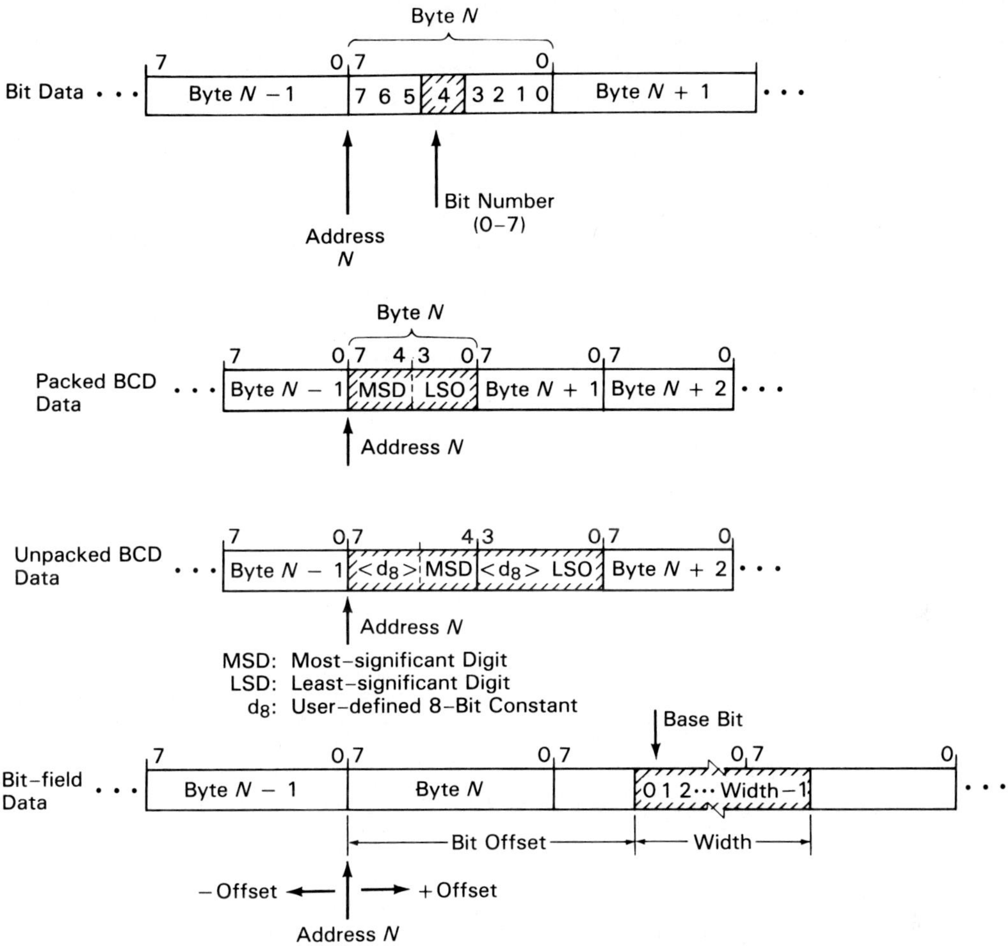

Figure 6-4 Memory Organization of Bit, BCD, and Bit-field Data Types.

An example of a bit-field is shown in Figure 6-5.

6.2.2 Dynamic Bus Sizing and Bus Operation

Figure 6-6 shows the simplified bus interface of the 68020. The signals involved in a bus operation include the following:

Address Strobe (AS*)	This signal, when asserted, indicates that there is valid address on the address bus lines A31 – A0.

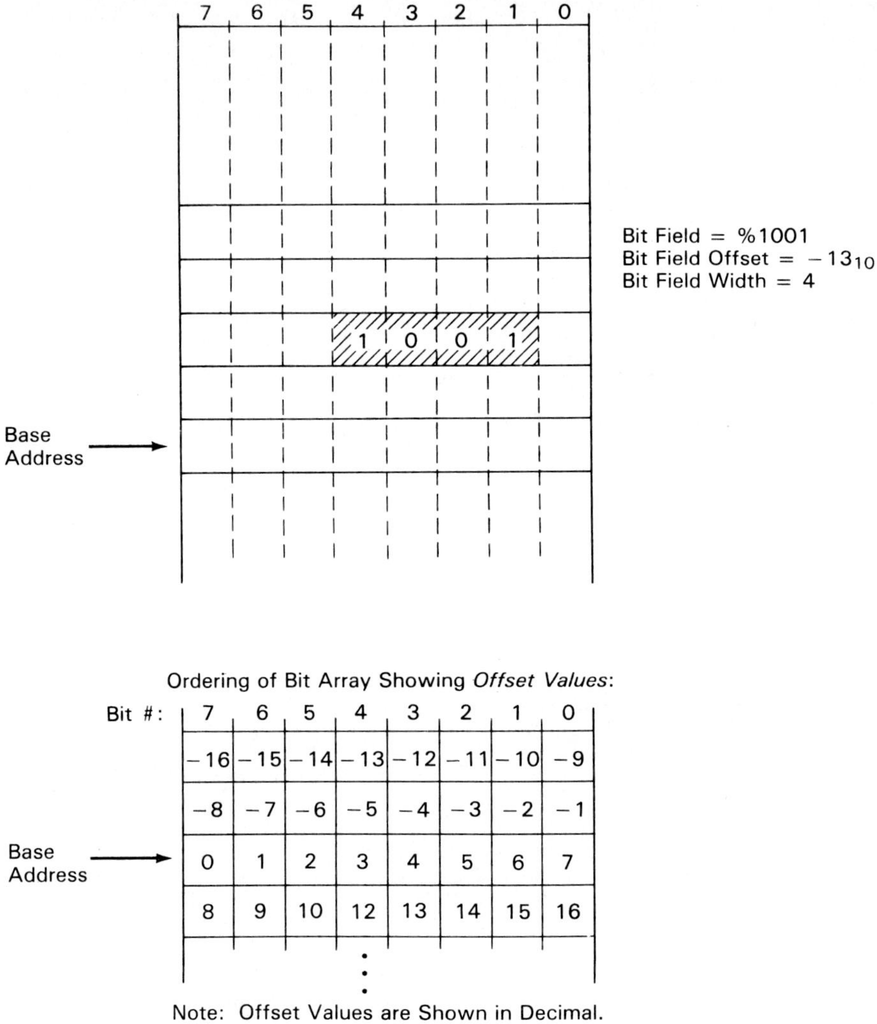

Figure 6-5 Example of Bit-field Definition.

A31 – A0	The 32-bit address lines specifying a byte address.
Data Strobe (DS*)	This signal is asserted during a read or write cycle when the data is to be transferred.
D31 – D0	The 32-bit data bus.
Read/Write (R/W*)	This signal defines the bus cycle as a read or write cycle (i.e., it defines the direction of data

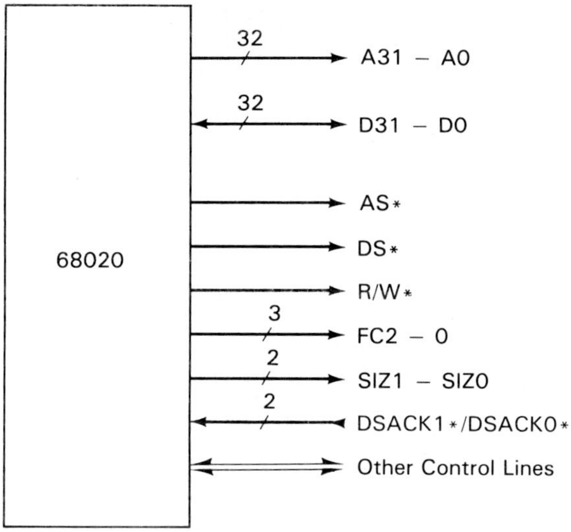

Figure 6-6 68020 Bus Interface Signal Lines.

flow on data bus). When R/W* is low, it indicates a write transfer, and when it is high it indicates a read transfer.

Function Codes (FC2-FC0) Defines the type of address space. Defined the same as for the 6801X. See Table 5-3.

The 68020 bus interface supports an important new feature called *dynamic bus sizing*. This unique feature allows the 68020 to dynamically alter the size of its data bus to match the port[1] size of a device. The port size may vary from 8 to 16, or 32 bits on a bus-cycle-by-bus-cycle basis. The following signals are used to implement dynamic bus sizing:

SIZ1, SIZ0 These two output signals indicate to external devices the *remaining* number of bytes to be transferred, which is the same or larger than the bytes of any given port size.

DSACK1*, DSACK0* These two data-transfer-and-size-acknowledge signals are an extension of the DTACK* signal used by the earlier members of the 68000 family. In addition to acknowledging a completed data transfer, the DSACKx* also indicate the size of the data port.

A1, A0 These two least-significant lines of the address bus also play a role in dynamic bus sizing, by indicating

[1] Port refers to the physical data bus interface of a peripheral device.

byte offset of an operand with respect to a long-word boundary.

The coding of the above signals are given in Table 6-1. A simplified operation of data transfers to external devices is illustrated in Figure 6-7. If the port size is 32 bits and the long-word operand is aligned, then the transfer occurs in one bus cycle. Otherwise, the 68020 may perform multiple bus cycles to transfer an operand. However, these multiple bus cycles are automatically sequenced by the 68020 and are transparent to the user, other than the additional time it takes to execute. For example, when trying to read an aligned long-word data, the 68020 first attempts to read all 32 bits at once (i.e., in one bus cycle). If the device acknowledges that it is only eight bits wide, the 68020 reads only one byte and executes three more bus cycles to read the remaining bytes.

The dynamic bus sizing of the data bus is illustrated in Figure 6-8 for operand transfers to devices with different port sizes. Note that 8-bit and 16-bit ports are required to be connected to D24 – D31 and D16 – D31, respectively. This enables the 68020 to know where to expect or place data for a given port size and is consistent with the 68000 memory organization (how?). The purpose of data routing and duplication block is twofold. First, it routes data as necessary between ports of different sizes and internal operands. Secondly, it handles all misaligned word and long-word transfers to various port sizes. Table 6-2 lists the mapping used for combinations of different port-sizes and operand offsets within a long-word.

In general, the number of bytes transferred during a bus cycle depends on

TABLE 6-1 BUS SIGNALS USED FOR DYNAMIC BUS SIZING

Signal		Description
DSACK1*	DSACK0*	Date Size and Transfer Acknowledge
H	H	Insert Wait-cycle
H	L	Complete Bus Cycle: Port Size is 8 Bits
L	H	Complete Bus Cycle: Port Size is 16 Bits
L	L	Complete Bus Cycle: Port Size is 32 Bits
SIZ1	SIZ0	Remaining Bytes to be Transferred
L	H	1 Byte
H	L	2 Bytes
H	H	3 Bytes
L	L	4 Bytes
A1	A0	Offset from Long-word Boundary
L	L	No Offset (0 Bytes)
L	H	+1 Byte
H	L	+2 Bytes
H	H	+3 Bytes

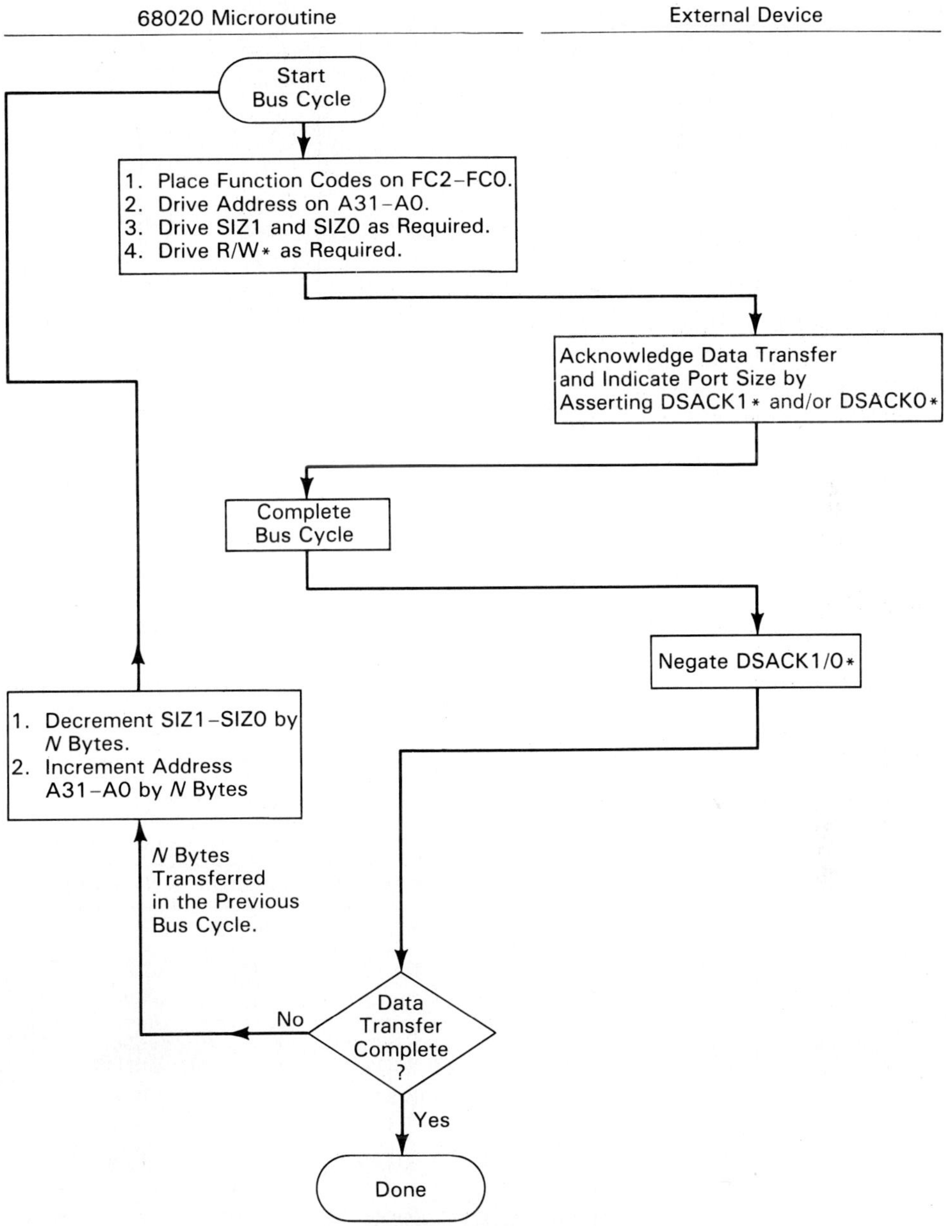

Figure 6-7 Simplified Operand Transfer Operation.

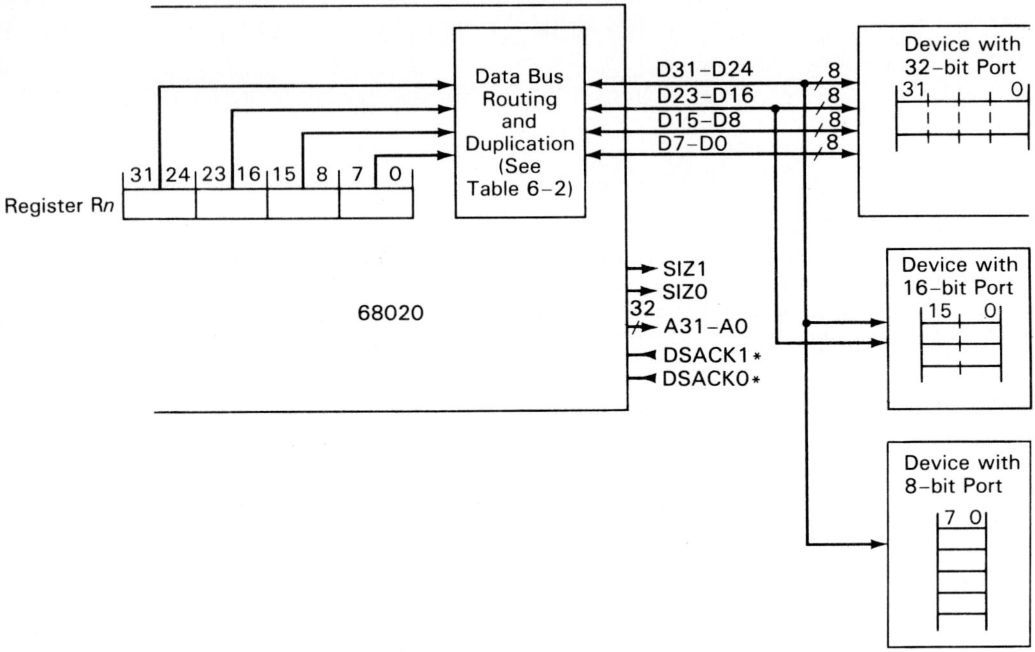

Figure 6-8 Illustration of Dynamic Bus Sizing.

TABLE 6-2 INTERNAL TO EXTERNAL ROUTING AND DUPLICATION

Transfer Size	SIZ1	SIZ0	A1	A0	Internal to External Routing/Duplication			
					D31:D24	D23:D16	D15:D8	D7:00
Byte	L	H	x	x	Rn[7:0]	Rn[7:0]	Rn[7:0]	Rn[7:0]
Word	H	L	x	L	Rn[15:8]	Rn[7:0]	Rn[15:8]	Rn[7:0]
			x	H	Rn[15:8]	Rn[15:8]	Rn[7:0]	Rn[15:8]
3 Bytes	H	H	L	L	Rn[23:16]	Rn[15:8]	Rn[7:0]	Rn[31:24]
			L	H	Rn[23:16]	Rn[23:16]	Rn[15:8]	Rn[7:0]
			H	L	Rn[23:16]	Rn[15:8]	Rn[23:16]	Rn[15:8]
			H	H	Rn[23:16]	Rn[23:16]	Rn[15:8]	Rn[23:16]
Long Word	L	L	L	L	Rn[31:24]	Rn[23:16]	Rn[15:8]	Rn[7:0]
			L	H	Rn[31:24]	Rn[31:24]	Rn[23:16]	Rn[15:8]
			H	L	Rn[31:24]	Rn[23:16]	Rn[31:24]	Rn[23:16]
			H	H	Rn[31:24]	Rn[31:24]	Rn[23:16]	Rn[31:24]

Notes: x = Don't care.
Rn = A register of 68020.

three factors: The size of the operand, the size of the port used, and the alignment of the operand. The next example will illustrate the dynamic bus sizing and handling of misaligned operands.

The main advantages of dynamic bus sizing can be summarized as follows:

1. It increases the data transfer rate to peripherals with 8- or 16-bit port sizes because one instruction can transfer four bytes.
2. The memory map of a system becomes contiguous without any interleaving unused areas. This makes it easier for system programmers by not having to have a knowledge of each device's port size. For example, the programmer's view of a 8-bit peripheral controller in a 68000 and 68020 system is shown in Figure 6-9. Note that the addresses of the registers have been changed because of dynamic bus sizing, therefore, a 68000 program in this case cannot be directly ported to the 68020 system. However, this poses no problems because the acknowledge signals (DSACK) can be asserted for a pseudo 16-bit port size in order to maintain software compatibility. The MOVEP instruction may still be used, but it works with only 16-bit ports and is mainly kept for software compatibility with earlier members.

Example 6-1.

Figure 6-10 illustrates the bus activity to transfer a long-word operand during the instruction MOVE where assume D0 = \$12345678. Three cases for different port sizes are shown. Note that DSACKx* is fixed for a given device.

6.2.3 Instruction and Operand Fetch Characteristics

There are basic differences in the way the 68020 handles data type operands and instruction words. The instruction fetch characteristics of the 68020 are as follows:

1. Instruction words are prefetched during normal execution.
2. The instructions that are prefetched from external memory are routed to the instruction pipeline and also to the instruction cache, if enabled.

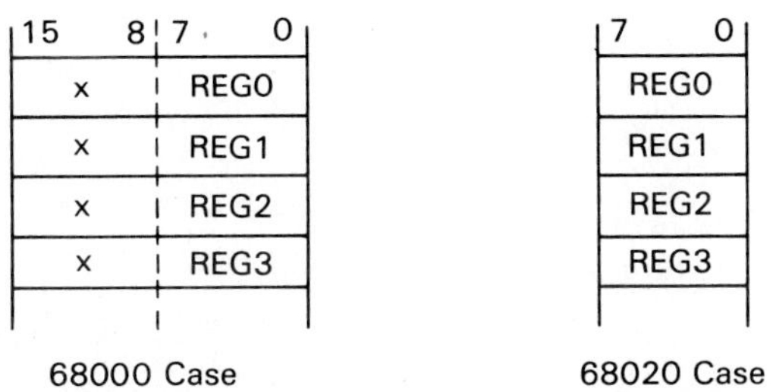

Figure 6-9 Programmer's View of an 8-bit device.

Case A. 32-bit Port. Then, DSACK1* = L and DSACK0* = L is used to acknowledge.

Instruction: MOVE.L D0,$A000

Bus Cycle #	SIZ1	SIZ0	A2 A1 A0	Data bus 31:24	23:16	15:8	7:0
1	L	L	L L L	12	34	56	78

After Execution

	31			0
A000	12	34	56	78

Instruction: MOVE.L D0,$A001

Bus Cycle #	SIZ1	SIZ0	A2 A1 A0	Data bus 31:24	23:16	15:8	7:0
1	L	L	L L H	(12)	12	34	56
2	L	H	L L L	78	(78)	(78)	(78)

After Execution

	31			0
A000		12	34	56
	78			

Case B. 16-bit Port. Then, DSACK1* = L and DSACK0* = H is used to acknowledge.

Instruction: MOVE.L D0,$A000

Bus Cycle #	SIZ1	SIZ0	A2 A1 A0	Data bus 31:24	23:16	15:8	7:0
1	L	L	L L L	12	34	(56)	(78)
2	H	L	L H L	56	78	(56)	(78)

After Execution

	15	0
A000	12	34
	56	78

Instruction: MOVE.L D0,$A001

Bus Cycle #	SIZ1	SIZ0	A2 A1 A0	Data bus 31:24	23:16	15:8	7:0
1	L	L	L L H	(12)	12	(34)	(56)
2	H	H	L H L	34	56	(34)	(56)
3	L	H	L H H	78	(78)	(78)	(78)

After Execution

	15	0
A000		12
	34	56
	78	

Case C. 8-bit Port. Then, DSACK1* = H and DSACK0* = L is used to acknowledge.

Instruction: MOVE.L D0,$A000

Bus Cycle #	SIZ1	SIZ0	A2 A1 A0	Data bus 31:24	23:16	15:8	7:0
1	L	L	L L L	12	(34)	(56)	(78)
2	H	H	L L H	34	(34)	(56)	(78)
3	H	L	L H L	56	(78)	(56)	(78)
4	L	H	L H H	78	(78)	(78)	(78)

After Execution

	7 0
A000	12
	34
	56
	78

Figure 6-10 Example Illustrating Dynamic Bus Sizing.

3. If the cache is enabled, an instruction prefetch may hit in the cache which eliminates the need to access external memory.
4. Instruction words must be aligned on word boundaries.
5. Instruction prefetches are always performed with a long-word size and at long-word boundaries. This is related to the prefetch mechanism and not the alignment requirement. For example, the BRA $2002 instruction causes the bus controller to put out $2000 and fetch two words, but only the second word is used.

On the other hand, none of the above is valid for accessing data type operands which may be transferred as part of an instruction execution with the following characteristics:

1. There are no alignment restrictions.
2. Data operands are not prefetched.
3. Data operands are never stored in the instruction cache. The only exception to this is immediate operands which are part of instruction words.
4. The system stacks are still required to be aligned on word boundaries so that the performance is not affected due to misaligned stack operations.

6.3 PROGRAMMING MODEL

The programming model of the 68020 is shown in Figure 6-11. The user-programming model stays unchanged with respect to the earlier members. In the supervisor mode, there is an additional stack pointer called the *master stack pointer* (MSP) and two cache control registers that allow control and manipulation of the instruction cache.

The 68020 maintains three different system stacks:

1. The *user stack*
2. The *interrupt stack*
3. The *master stack*

The corresponding stack pointers are the *user stack pointer* (USP), the *interrupt stack pointer* (ISP), and the MSP. The interrupt stack handles only external interrupt related events. All other exception conditions use the MSP, when enabled. The reason behind the two supervisor stacks, MSP and ISP, is to separate the asynchronous I/O related interrupt information from all other data used by supervisor level tasks. For example, this helps in setting a linked list of *task control blocks* (TCBs) on the stack. In the 68000, if interrupts do happen while saving a TCB, this results in a structure that is hard to handle because it is intermixed

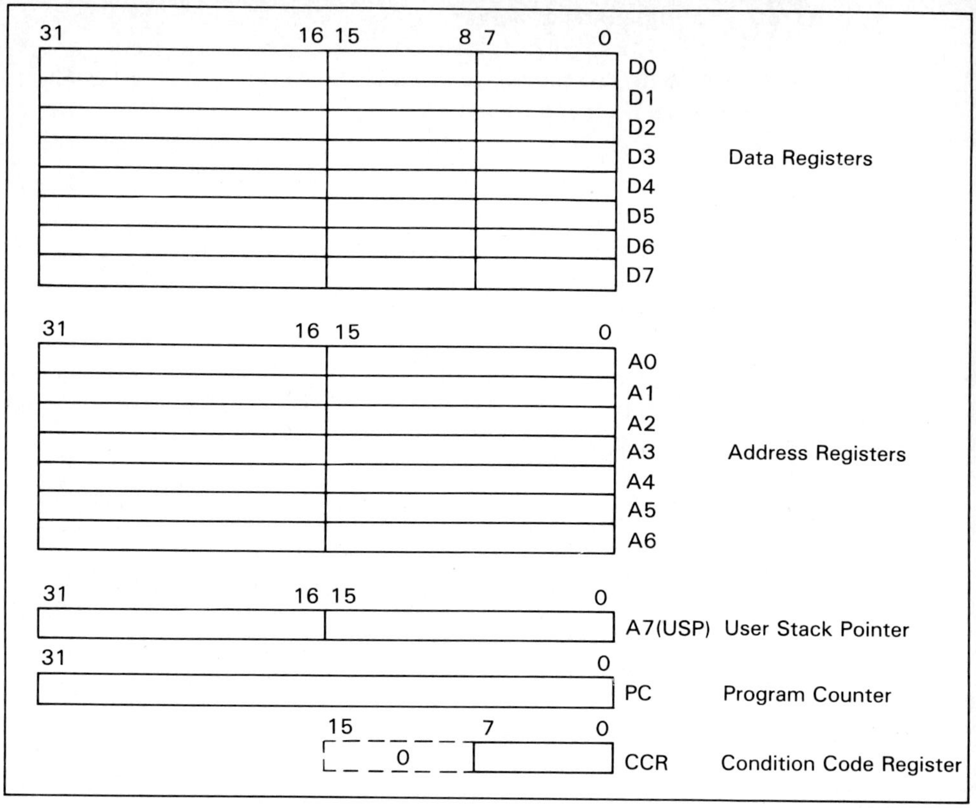

User-mode Programming Model

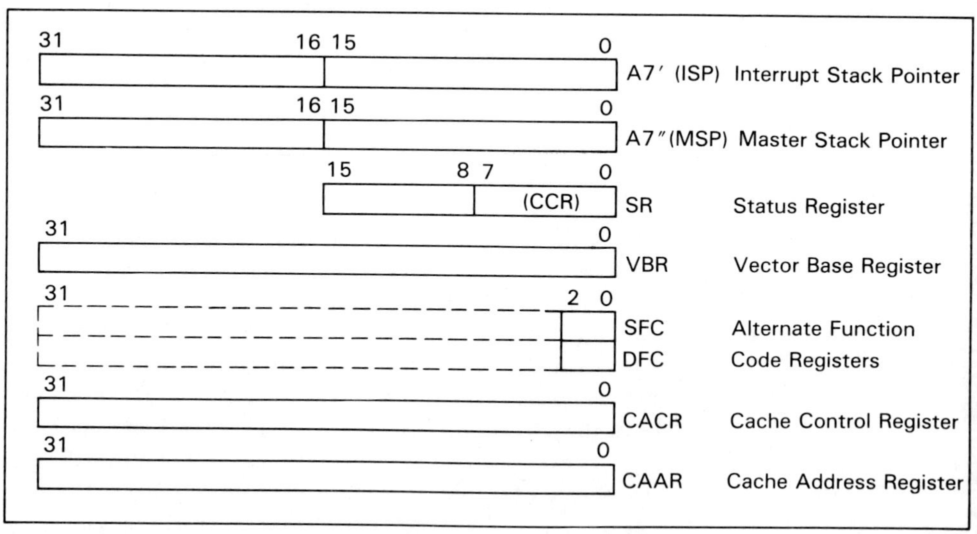

Supervisor-mode Supplementary Registers

Figure 6-11 Programming Model.

with interrupt information. The 68020 takes care of this shortcoming by having two supervisor stacks.

The status register has two new control bits, T0 and M. The addition of the T0 trace bit allows a trace exception to occur when a change of program flow is detected by the 68020. A change of flow occurs due to a branch or jump instruction or due to exception conditions and return instructions. This makes it easier to monitor a program execution at critical regions without having to single-step through each instruction. The M-bit determines which stack is active (master or interrupt) when in the supervisor mode.

The new bits of the status register are shown in Figure 6-12. After a reset condition, trace is disabled and ISP is active. A supervisor level routine may set the M-bit to enable the master stack pointer. Then, if an interrupt occurs, the 68020 will automatically clear the M-bit, process the interrupt, and the RTE instruction at the end of the interrupt service routine will restore the M-bit, as we will discuss in section 6-8-2. ISP is chosen as the default stack pointer after reset in order to maintain software compatibility with earlier 68000 system programs.

There are two registers used for controlling the instruction cache. The *CAche Address Register* (CAAR) is used to invalidate an entry of cache. The *CAche Control Register* (CACR) is used for various control functions that are described below (see Figure 6-13):

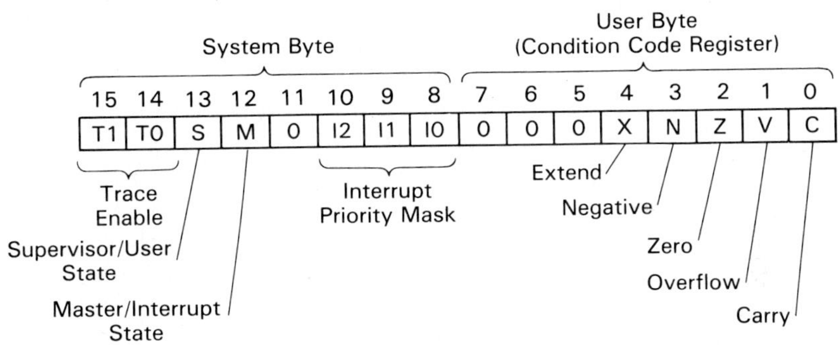

Trace Bits:	T1	T0	Description
	0	0	Tracing disabled. Reset condition.
	0	1	Trace exception on change of program flow.
	1	0	Trace exception after each instruction.
	1	1	Undefined, reserved.

Mode Bits:	S	M	Active Stack
	0	X	User stack (i.e., USP)
	1	0	Interrupt stack (i.e., ISP). Reset condition.
	1	1	Master stack (i.e., MSP)

Figure 6-12 Status Register.

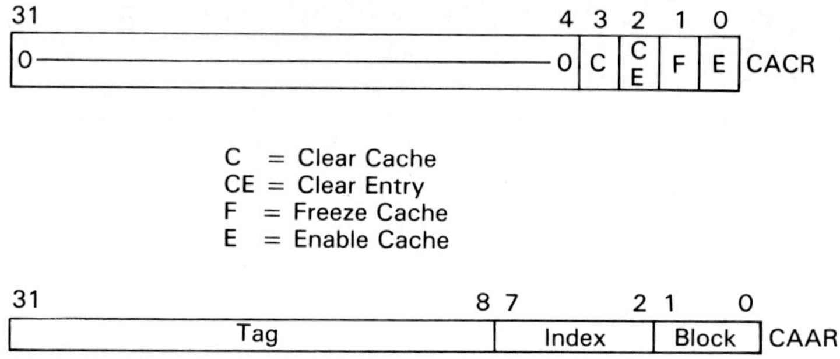

Figure 6-13 Cache Control and Address Registers.

E—Enable Cache: This bit, when set, enables the cache. During a reset operation, this bit is cleared thereby disabling the cache. The cache, when disabled, forces continuous cache misses and prevents replacing any cache entries. This may be useful for system debug and emulation purposes.

F—Freeze Cache: If the cache is enabled, (i.e., E = 1) and the F-bit is set, cache hits are read from the cache but cache misses are not allowed to update valid cache entries. The use of this bit is not necessary for proper utilization of the cache since the 68020 first checks whether the instruction is already in the cache (when E = 1). The instruction is prefetched from external memory only if it is not found in the cache. Thus, the F-bit is not typically used. A possible application is to freeze the cache by certain exception routines so as not to disturb the cache during the execution of some system utilities. This would increase the performance because it is faster to prefetch an instruction from the cache than from external memory.

CE—Clear Entry: This bit is used in conjunction with the CAAR register to invalidate a certain cache entry. The index portion of the CAAR is used to specify one of the long-word entries of cache, and the CE bit is then set to that long-word. The CE-bit is write only and will always read as zero.

C—Clear Cache: This write-only bit is used to invalidate all cache entries. It is typically used by a multitasking operating system to flush all cache entries after a *context switch*[2]

[2] Also called the *task switch*. It involves saving the state of the current task and restoring the state of the next runnable task.

is made to another ready-to-run task. This bit will always read as zero.

During a reset operation, the cache is flushed by invalidating all entries, and the E- and F-bits are cleared. Access to CACR and CAAR are provided by the MOVEC instruction. For example, to enable typical cache operation after power-up, we need to set the E-bit of CACR using the MOVEC instruction.

6.4 OPERAND ADDRESSING MODES

The 68020 retains all addressing modes of earlier members and also provides the following extensions:

Enhanced address register indirect addressing modes;
Memory indirect addressing modes; and
Enhanced program-counter relative addressing modes.

These new addressing modes are intended to perform all typical operand address calculations that are not directly supported by the 68000, as we will discuss during the rest of this section.

6.4.1 Address Register Indirect (ARI) Addressing Modes

The register indirect addressing modes of the 68020 are listed in Table 6-3. The enhanced addressing modes in this category are the two forms of ARI with an index register; one with an 8-bit displacement and the other with a base displacement. Let us examine these two modes.

Using ARI with index and 8-bit displacement, the EA is calculated as the sum of a base address in an address register, a scaled index value, and a displacement value, as shown below along with assemby syntax:

$$EA = (Am) + (Xn)_{32} * sc + d8_{32}$$

Assembly Syntax: (d8,Am,Xn.<s>*<sc>)

TABLE 6-3 ADDRESS REGISTER INDIRECT ADDRESSING MODES 1–3

Addressing Mode	Assembly Syntax
Address-register indirect	(Am)
Address-register indirect with post-increment	(Am)+
Address-register indirect with pre-decrement	-(Am)
Address-register indirect with displacement	(d16,Am)
Address-register indirect with index (8-bit displacement)	(d8,Am,Xn.<s>*<sc>)
Address-register indirect with index (base displacement)	(bd,Am,Xn.<s>*<sc>)

[1] bd: 32-bit base displacement.
[2] s: Size of index register: word (W) or long-word (L).
[3] sc: pre-scaling of index register = 1,2,4,8.

where

Am: Base address in an address register A0-A7.

Xn: An address or data register where either low-order word or entire register can be used as a dynamic index value. The index value is treated as a two's complement number and so when word-size index is used it is sign-extended to 32 bits. This is indicated by the subscript 32 in the above EA calculation.

s: Specifies the size of index register used. The allowed sizes are "W" for word, and "L" for long-word. If omitted, the index size defaults to word size.

sc: Specifies the scale value used to prescale index value. The allowed values are one (no scaling), two, four, and eight, that is used to multiply the index value. If the scale value is omitted, it defaults to no scaling.

$d8$: Specifies the 8-bit two's complement displacement value. This is sign-extended to 32 bits in the EA calculation.

This is illustrated in Figure 6-14. In this addressing mode, all three fields—the displacement, the address register, and the index register—must be specified.

The ARI with index and base displacement features an 16- or 32-bit base displacement. Then,

$$EA = (Am) + (Xn)_{32} * sc + bd_{32}$$

Assembly syntax: (<bd>,Am,Xn.<s>*<sc>)

where bd is the base displacement value. This form is very similar to the one

Instruction: ADD.W (8,A3,D0.W*4),D1

Operation: $EA = (A3) + (D0[15:0])_{32} * 4 + 8; (EA) + D1 \rightarrow D1$

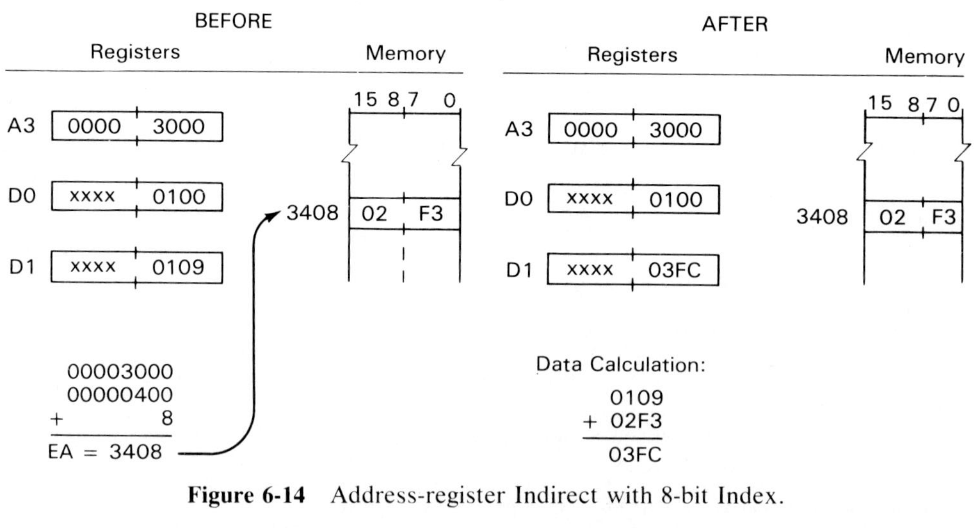

Figure 6-14 Address-register Indirect with 8-bit Index.

using the 8-bit displacement value but with two significant differences. First, the size of constant displacement is larger. Secondly, the form using base displacement allows three addends of the EA to be optional. Thus, each of the fields (A*m*, X*n*, or *bd*) may be suppressed resulting in many variations of this addressing mode, as shown in Table 6-4. The value of any suppressed field is taken as zero in the EA calculation.

Some of these variations, such as (D*n*) and (*bd*, D*n*), are especially interesting. These could be considered as data-register indirect addressing modes where data register contains an address value. But, it is better to think of these in terms of orthogonal forms, (X*n*) and (*bd*, X*n*), where any address or data register is alllowed. Another special case is (*bd*) which is the same as absolute addressing modes.

An optimizing assembler chooses the best addressing mode and the proper size of the displacement to use. For example, the operand addressing mode (disp, A*m*) will be assembled using the ARI with 16-bit displacement mode if disp can fit into 16 bits since this requires a smaller number of clock periods to calculate EA. Otherwise, the (*bd*, A*m*) mode will be used because it can support a larger displacement. Therefore, the programmer usually need not be concerned about what native addressing mode is actually being used.

As a general rule, any address that is not already 32 bits is first sign-extended before use. That means a data register would also be sign-extended in calculating the source address as in the case

```
MOVE.W  (D0),(A0)
```

where source is sign-extended since default is D0.W.

A typical application of ARI with an index is in accessing elements of an array. In accessing one-dimensional arrays, we would have A*m* or *bd* pointing to the beginning of array and X*m* would contain the variable index. The scale would be used to scale the index by the number of bytes per element of the array in

TABLE 6-4 VARIATIONS OF (bd,Am,Xm.<s>*<sc>)

Assembly Syntax	Description
(bd,Am,Xn.<s>*<sc>)	None of the fields are suppressed.
(Am,Xn.<s>*<sc>)	bd is suppressed.
(bd,Xn.<s>*<sc>)	Am is suppressed.
(bd,Am)	Extended displacement form of (*d*16,A*m*)
(Xn.<s>*<sc>)	Both bd and Am are suppressed. Could be (D*n*) and so on.
(bd)	Same as absolute addressing mode.

order to offset to element *i*, as illustrated in Figure 6-15 for an array of long-word numbers.

In accessing two-dimensional numbers, *bd* can be used to point to the beginning of the array. We could not do this with the 68000 because displacement was limited to only 8 bits. Then, A*m* can be used to point to the beginning of row of elements, and X*m* will have the subscript value within a row of elements. There are considerable gain in calculating the effective address if number of elements in each row is a power of two. This reduces time-costly multiplications to a shift operation as illustrated in Figure 6-16. Of course, since *bd* is a constant, this approach is useful for accessing an two-dimensional array at a fixed location, such as in graphics or image display memories. Otherwise, it is of limited use because it would not generate position-independent code.

6.4.2 Memory-indirect Addressing Modes

This new addressing mode provides one level of memory indirection where a location in memory contains the address of the operand. An intermediate effective address (IEA) is calculated from which a long-word base address value is fetched

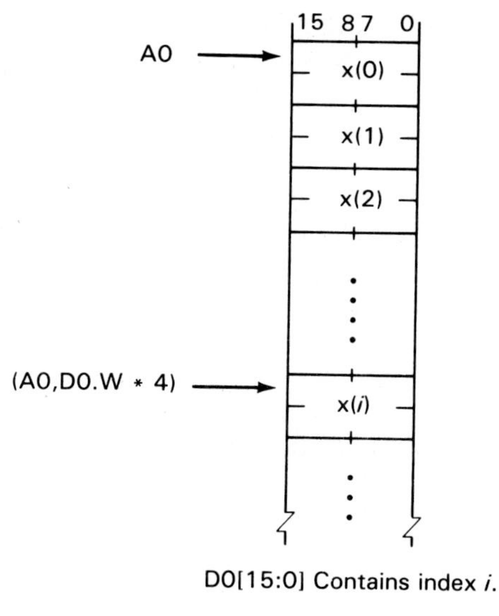

68000			68020		
LSL.W	#2,D0		MOVE.L	(A0,D0.W*4),D1	x(i) → D1
MOVE.L	0(A0,D0.W),D1	x(i) → D1			

Figure 6-15 Accessing a One-dimensional Array.

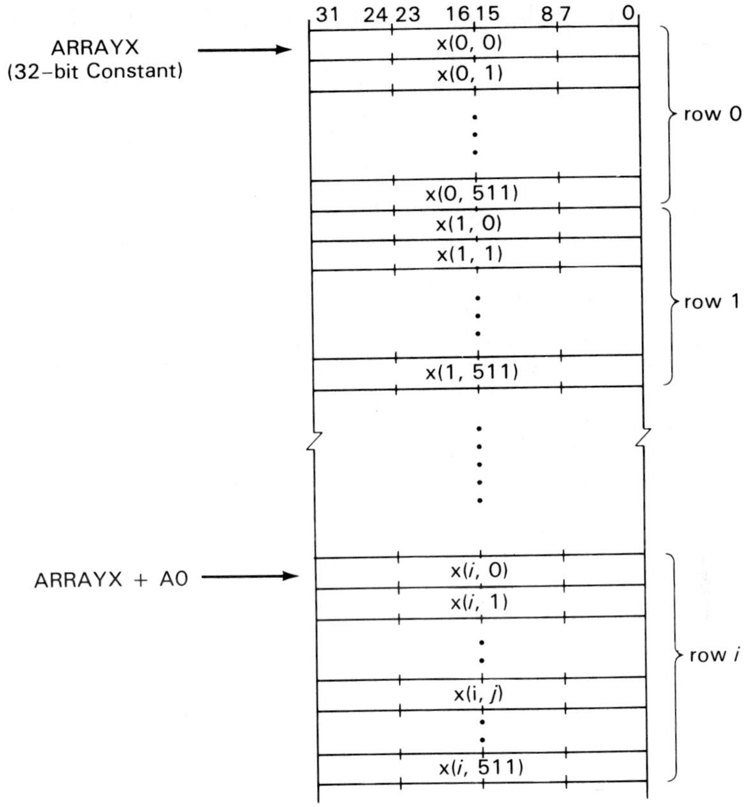


```
* Initially, assume the following register contents:
* D0[15:0] has row index i.
* D1[15:0] has column index j.
* D2[15:0] = 9
* Number of elements per row = 512 (= 2**9).
*
      EXT.L    D0                           Clear bits D0[31:16].
      LSL.L    D2,D0                        Multiply by 2**9
      MOVE.L   D0,A0                        A0 = Offset to beginning of row i.
      MOVE.L   (ARRAYX,A0,D1.W*4),D1        D1 = x(i,j).
```

Figure 6-16 Accessing a 2-D Array Located at a Fixed Location.

which is then used in calculating the effective address of the operand. Two different constant displacements may be specified: The base displacement (*bd*) is used before the memory indirection and the outer displacement (*od*) is used after the indirection. Furthermore, a scaled index register may be used before or after the intermediate memory access, referred to as pre-indexed and post-indexed modes, respectively. The address of the operand is calculated as follows:

$$\text{Pre-indexed:}\quad \text{IEA} = bd + (\text{A}m) + (\text{X}n)_{32} * sc$$

$$\text{EA} = (\text{IEA}) + od$$

$$\text{Post-indexed:}\quad \text{IEA} = bd + \text{A}m$$

$$\text{EA} = (\text{IEA}) + (\text{X}n)_{32} * sc + od$$

where

bd: Specifies a 16- or 32-bit base displacement.

A*m*: One of the address registers, A0-A7.

X*n*: Specifies one of the address or data registers used as an index register. Either the low-word or the entire register may be used as the index value, using the "W" or "L" suffix, consistent with the rest of the assembly syntax.

sc: Specifies the scale value that multiplies the index value. The scale value may be 1, 2, 4, or 8.

od: Specifies the 16- or 32-bit outer displacement value.

As with other addressing modes, any addend with less than 32 bits is sign-extended, considering it as a two's complement number. The general assembly syntax of memory-indirect addressing modes are

Pre-indexed: ([bd,Am,Xn.<s>*<sc>],od)

Post-indexed: ([bd,Am],Xn.<s>*<sc>,od)

where memory indirection is denoted by braces "[ ]". The address specification within braces is evaluated as IEA as illustrated in Figure 6-17. The reader might have noted that the assembly syntax of the 68020 is different from that of the 68000 in that the displacements are specified within the parentheses—that is, for example, (*d*16, A*m*) instead of *d*16(A*m*). This is to avoid any confusion in more complex addressing modes, such as in memory indirect.

All four fields of the memory-indirect addressing mode (*bd*, A*m*, X*n*, and *od*) are optional and can be suppressed resulting in the variations shown in Table 6-5. In the extreme case, suppressing everything will yield ([]) which means fetch-

TABLE 6-5 VARIATIONS OF MEMORY-INDIRECT ADDRESSING MODES

No Index	Pre-index	Post-index
([bd])	([Xn.<s>*<sc>])	([bd],Xn.<s>*<sc>)
([Am])	([bd,Xn.<s>*<sc>])	([Am],Xn.<s>*<sc>)
([bd,Am])	([Am,Xn.<s>*<sc>])	([bd,Am],Xn.<s>*<sc>)
([bd],od)	([bd,Am,Xn.<s>*<sc>])	([bd],Xn.<s>*<sc>,od)
([Am],od)	([Xn.<s>*<sc>],od)	([Am],Xn.<s>*<sc>,od)
([bd,Am],od)	([bd,Xn.<s>*<sc>],od)	([bd,Am],Xn.<s>*<sc>,od)
	([Am,Xn.<s>*<sc>],od)	
	([bd,Am,Xn.<s>*<sc>],od)	

Instruction: `ADD.W ([$400000,A0,D0.W * 2],8),D1`

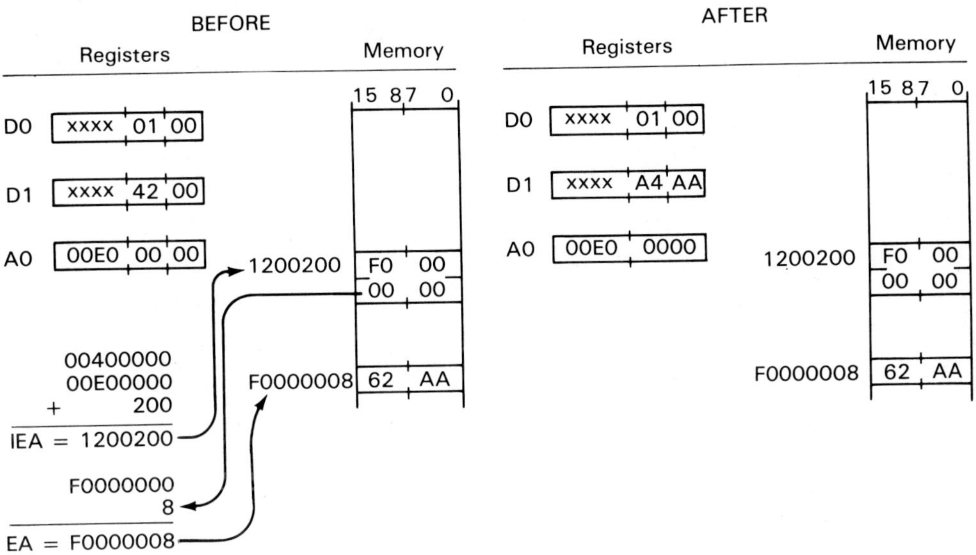

(a) *Pre-index Mode*

Instruction: `ADD.W ([$400000,A0],D0.W * 2,8),D1`

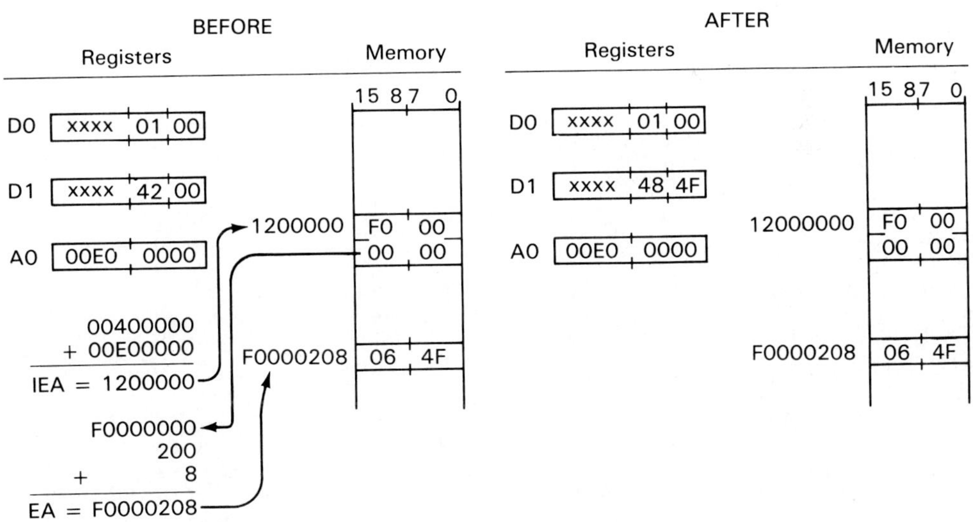

(b) *Post-index Mode*

Figure 6-17 Illustration of Memory-indirect Addressing Modes.

ing the effective address from address \$0. The programmer does not need to remember all these permutations because of their regular and consistent structure with no exceptions. It will suffice to know the general form and that each element can be suppressed.

Example 6-2

The following gives examples of memory-indirect addressing modes.

Part	Instruction	Description
A.	`MOVE.W #$1234,([A0])`	Moves the constant \$1234 to the address contained in address that is pointed to by A0. See Figure 6-18-a.
B.	`BTST #0,([A4,D0.W*4],3)`	Accesses the third register of a peripheral device via a device address table that is pointed to by A4. See Figure 6-18-b.
C.	`MOVE.W ([ARRAYX,SP],D0.W*2),D1`	Fetches the D0'th element of an one-dimensional array whose address is passed on the stack as shown in Figure 6-19. This form is efficient only if random accesses are required to the array. Otherwise, using LEA to fetch the base address followed by sequential accesses using post-increment or pre-decrement addressing mode would be more efficient.

6.4.3 Program-counter Relative Addressing Modes

The *program-relative addressing modes* incorporate the capabilities of all ARI addressing modes. The PC functions as the base register replacing A*m* as shown in Table 6-6. All memory references are made with respect to the word following the instruction's operation word since the PC always points to the next word when

TABLE 6-6 PC-RELATIVE ADDRESSING MODES 1–3

Addressing Mode	Assembly Syntax
PC indirect with displacement	(d16,PC)
PC indirect with index (8-bit displacement) PC indirect with index (base displacement)	(d8,PC,Xn.<s>*<sc>) (d8,PC,Xn.<s>*<sc>)
PC, memory indirect with pre-index PC, memory indirect with post-index	([bd,PC],Xn.<s>*<sc>,od) ([bd,PC,Xn.<s>*<sc>],od)

[1] bd: 32-bit base displacement.
[2] s: Size of index register: word (W) or long-word (L).
[3] sc: pre-scaling of index register = 1,2,4,8.

TABLE 6-7 VARIATIONS OF (bd,PC,Xm.<s>*<sc>)

Assembly Syntax	Description
(bd,PC,Xn.<s>*<sc>)	None of the fields are suppressed.
(PC,Xn.<s>*<sc>)	bd is suppressed.
(bd,ZPC,Xn.<s>*<sc>)	PC is suppressed.
(bd,PC)	Extended displacement form of (*d*16,PC)
(ZPC,Xn.<s>*<sc>)	Both bd and PC are suppressed.
(bd,ZPC)	Same as absolute addressing mode but program space.
(PC)	A simple variation.

the execution of an instruction starts. One of the limitations of the 68000 with regard to a position-independent code was that all references were limited to ± 32K bytes of PC using the (*d*16, PC) mode. Since this was not general enough, compilers had to use multiple instructions. The availability of 32-bit displacements with the 68020 eliminates these additional instructions.

As with ARI and memory-indirect addressing modes, any field of the PC-relative with base displacement or memory-indirect addressing modes may be suppressed, with many resulting variations as shown in Table 6-7 and 6-8.

To distinguish between the suppressed PC and suppressed A*m* variations of corresponding addressing modes, the symbol ZPC (zero PC) is used when PC is suppressed indicating a zero PC value is to be used in the EA calculation.

There are two important differences between PC-relative and ARI addressing modes:

1. All PC-relative addressing modes use program space whereas ARI modes use data space unless they are used by a JMP or JSR instruction. The particular address space indicated by function codes is important especially when there is an MMU. For example,

```
MOVE.W   ($A000),D0        Uses data space.
MOVE.W   ($A000,ZPC),D0    Uses program space.
```

TABLE 6-8 VARIATIONS OF PC-RELATIVE WITH MEMORY-INDIRECT ADDRESSING MODES

No Index	Pre-index	Post-index
([bd,ZPC])	([ZPC,Xn.<s>*<sc>])	([bd,ZPC],Xn.<s>*<sc>)
([PC])	([bd,ZPC,Xn.<s>*<sc>])	([PC],Xn.<s>*<sc>)
([bd,PC])	([PC,Xn.<s>*<sc>])	([bd,PC],Xn.<s>*<sc>)
([bd,ZPC],od)	([bd,PC,Xn.<s>*<sc>])	([bd,ZPC],Xn.<s>*<sc>,od)
([PC],od)	([ZPC,Xn.<s>*<sc>],od)	([PC],Xn.<s>*<sc>,od)
([bd,PC],od)	([bd,ZPC,Xn.<s>*<sc>],od)	([bd,PC],Xn.<s>*<sc>,od)
	([PC,Xn.<s>*<sc>],od)	
	([bd,PC,Xn.<s>*<sc>],od)	

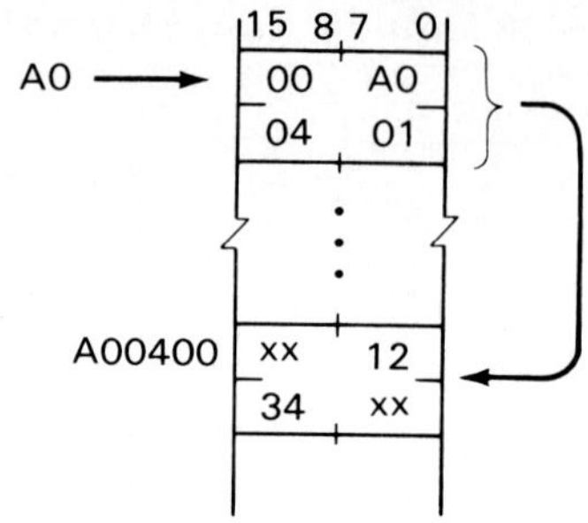

(a) Illustration of MOVE.W #$1234,([A0]).

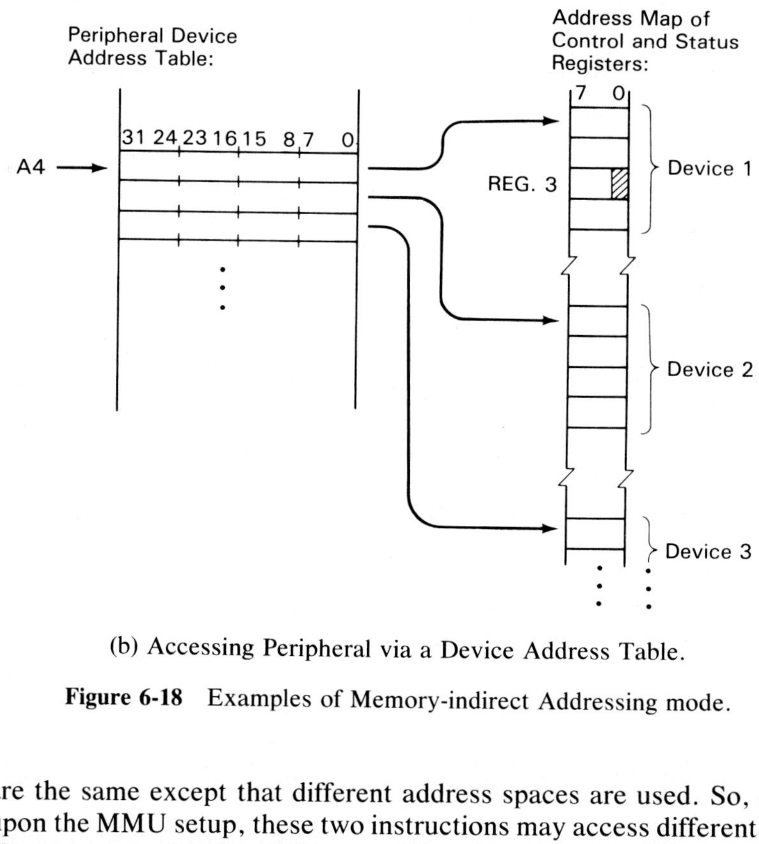

(b) Accessing Peripheral via a Device Address Table.

Figure 6-18 Examples of Memory-indirect Addressing mode.

are the same except that different address spaces are used. So, depending upon the MMU setup, these two instructions may access different operands. However, as with the 68000, we still cannot write an operand using a PC-relative addressing modes as the destination (i.e., PC-relative operands are not alterable).

2. When using the PC-relative addressing modes, the assembler will evaluate the symbols *d*16 or *bd* relative to the PC value. The only exception to this

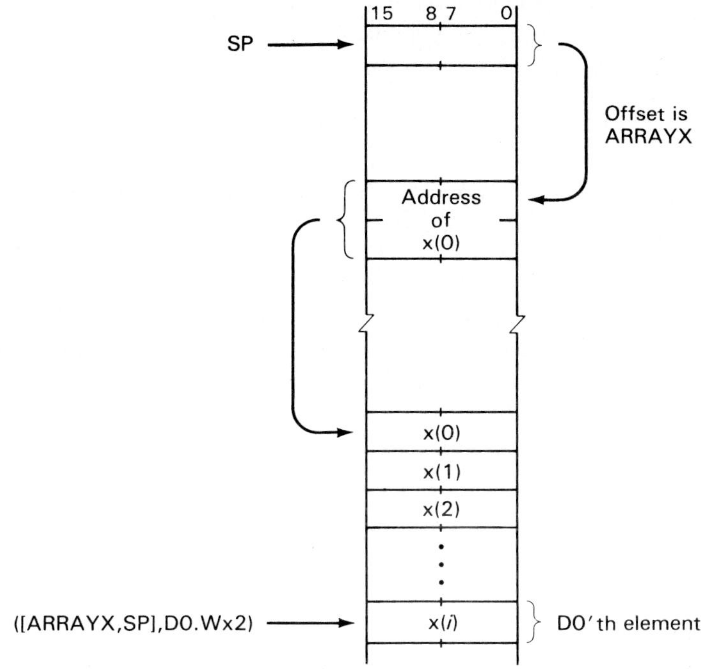

NOTES: 1. x(i) is 1-D Array of Word-size Numbers.
2 D015-D00 Contains Index i.

Figure 6-19 Accessing an Array Whose Address is on Stack.

is when ZPC is used, then *bd* is not assembled as an offset from the current PC. The outer displacement (*od*) is never calculated as an offset from the PC. On the other hand, the displacement *d*16 or *bd* is always taken as an absolute value in (*d*16, A*m*) or (*bd*, A*m*).

Example 6-3

A jump table may simply be programmed using

```
       JMP   ([JMPTBL,D0.W*4])
       .
       .
       .
JMPTBL DC.L ROUTINE1     Index D0 = 0.
       DC.L ROUTINE2     Index D1 = 1.
       .
       .
       .
       DC.L ROUTINEN     Index D0 = N-1.
```

In addition to the obvious benefit of a decreased number of instructions with respect to the 68000 (see Figure 3-43), note that the 68020 implementation uses only register D0.

6.4.4 Summary of Addressing Modes

Table 6-9 summarizes the addressing modes of the 68020. The significant enhancements to the 68000 addressing modes are *memory indirect modes*, a *scaled index*, and *larger displacements*. Furthermore, the variations of addressing modes create a regular and consistent structure. These addressing modes, coupled with the enhanced instruction set we are going to discuss in the next section, not only improves the performance directly but also, due to the more orthogonal structure, makes compiler-generated code much more efficient. For example, any addressing mode with a displacement allows 16- and 32-bit offset sizes and an optimizing assembler will automatically choose the most efficient variation. Thus, the pro-

TABLE 6-9 SUMMARY OF ADDRESSING MODES

Addressing Category/Mode	EA Syntax	AddressGroup[1] D	M	C	A	Space
Register Direct Addressing						
Data Register Direct	Dn	x	—	—	x	—
Address Register Direct	An	—	—	—	x	—
Absolute Data Addressing						
Absolute Short	<label>	x	x	x	x	D/P[2]
Absolute Long	<label>	x	x	x	x	D/P[2]
Immediate Data Addressing	#<value>	x	x	—	—	Prog.
ARI Addressing						
Register Indirect	(An)	x	x	x	x	D/P[2]
Postincrement Register Indirect	(An)+	x	x	—	x	Data
Predecrement Register Indirect	-(An)	x	x	—	x	Data
Register Indirect With Offset	(d16,An)	x	x	x	x	D/P[2]
With Index and 16-bit Offset	(d16,An,Xm.<s>*<sc>)	x	x	x	x	D/P[2]
With Index and 16/32-bit Offset	(bd,An,Xm.<s>*<sc>)	x	x	x	x	D/P[2]
Memory Indirect						
Pre-indexed	([bd,Am,Xn.<s>*<sc>],od)	x	x	x	x	Data
Post-indexed	([bd,Am],Xn.<s>*<sc>,od)	x	x	x	x	Data
Program Counter Relative Addressing						
With 16-bit Offset	(d16,PC)	x	x	x	—	Prog.
With Index and 8-bit Offset	(d8,PC,Xn.<s>*<sc>)	x	x	x	—	Prog.
With Index and 16/32-bit Offset	(bd,PC,Xn.<s>*<sc>)	x	x	x	—	Prog.
Memory Indirect with Post-index	([bd,PC],Xn.<s>*<sc>,od)	x	x	x	—	Prog.
Memory Indirect with Pre-index	([bd,PC,Xn.<s>*<sc>],od)	x	x	x	—	Prog.

[1] D (Data), M (Memory), C (Control), A (Alterable).

[2] D/P: Classified as DATA reference except with JMP and JSR instructions. Then, it is classified as PROGRAM reference.

grammer can concentrate on his or her work without having to consider a lot of special cases and limitations.

6.5 INSTRUCTION SET

In this section, we will examine the instruction set extensions of the 68020. These extensions include enhancement of some of the 6801X instructions as well as the addition of some new ones. The instruction groups for logical, shift, and bit manipulation instructions stay unchanged. The other groups include new and/or enhanced instructions. Also provided is a new group of instructions to handle manipulation of the bit-field data type.

The 68020 user's manual gives specific details of each instruction. For example, the ADD instruction is listed as shown in Figure 6-20. As before, the attributes imply the allowed operand sizes. Explicitly, the assembly syntax is:

```
ADD.<s>     <ea>,Dn
ADD.<s>     Dn,<ea>
```

where `s` is the operand size. Omitting the size specification usually defaults to word size. But we recommend that size be specified explicitly when there is more than one size possible for an instruction.

While instruction variations (−A, −Q, −X, and so on) stay unchanged, the object code format is affected due to extension in addressing modes and instruction set as shown in Figure 6-21. A 68020 instruction with the longest object code requires 11 words. However, this is not typical since it is used, for example, by the MOVE instruction when both source and destination uses the full format of memory-indirect addressing where both *bd* and *od* are 32-bit displacements.

The extension-word format of the 68020 is shown in Table 6-10 on page 265. Normally, a programmer does not need to be concerned about instruction encoding unless writing a compiler or verifying the correct assembly of an instruction.

6.5.1 Data and Address Movement Instructions

Table 6-11 summarizes the movement instructions where the only extension is the enhanced LINK instruction. In earlier members, LINK was limited to 32 Kbytes of displacement. This restriction is relieved by the 68020 allowing long-word displacements for local data and parameter areas of subroutines.

The MOVEP instruction loses some of its usefulness, since it was intended to work with 8-bit peripherals on the 16-bit data bus of the 68000. As we discussed earlier, the dynamic-bus sizing of the 68020 automatically takes care of this. However, MOVEP is kept to maintain software upgradability of 68000 programs.

ADD — Add — ADD

Operation: Source + Destination → Destination

Assembler Syntax: ADD <ea>,Dn
ADD Dn,<ea>

Attributes: Size = (Byte, Word, Long)

Description: Add the source operand to the destination operand using binary addition, and store the result in the destination location. The size of the operation may be specified to be byte, word, or long. The mode of the instruction indicates which operand is the source and which is the destination as well as the operand size.

Condition Codes:

X	N	Z	V	C
*	*	*	*	*

N Set if the result is negative. Cleared otherwise.
Z Set if the result is zero. Cleared otherwise.
V Set if an overflow is generated. Cleared otherwise.
C Set if a carry is generated. Cleared otherwise.
X Set the same as the carry bit.

Instruction Format:

15	14	13	12	11	10	9	8	7	6	5	4	3	2	1	0
1	1	0	1	Register Dn			Op-Mode			Effective Address Mode			Effective Address Register		

Instruction Fields:

Register field — Specifies any of the eight data registers.
Op-Mode field —

Byte	Word	Long	Operation
000	001	010	<ea> + <Dn> → <Dn>
100	101	110	<Dn> + <ea> → <ea>

Effective Address Field — Determines addressing mode:
a. If the location specified in a source operand, the all addressing modes are allowed as shown:

Figure 6-20 ADD Instruction as Shown in the User Manual.

ADD

Add

ADD

Addr. Mode	Mode	Register	Addr. Mode	Mode	Register
Dn	000	reg. number:Dn	(xxx).W	111	000
An*	001	reg. number:An	(xxx).L	111	001
(An)	010	reg. number:An	#<data>	111	100
(An)+	011	reg. number:An			
−(An)	100	reg. number:An			
(d_{16},An)	101	reg. number:An	(d_{16},PC)	111	010
(d_8,An,Xn)	110	reg. number:An	(d_8,PC,Xn)	111	011
(bd,An,Xn)	110	reg. number:An	(bd,PC,Xn)	111	011
([bd,An,Xn],od)	110	reg. number:An	([bd,PC,Xn],od)	111	011
([bd,An],Xn,od)	110	reg. number:An	([bd,PC],Xn,od)	111	011

*Word and Long only.

b. If the location specified is a destination operand, then only alterable memory addressing modes are allowed as shown:

Addr. Mode	Mode	Register	Addr. Mode	Mode	Register
Dn	—	—	(xxx).W	111	000
An	—	—	(xxx).L	111	001
(An)	010	reg. number:An	#<data>	—	—
(An)+	011	reg. number:An			
−(An)	100	reg. number:An			
(d_{16},An)	101	reg. number:An	(d_{16},PC)	—	—
(d_8,An,Xn)	110	reg. number:An	(d_8,PC,Xn)	—	—
(bd,An,Xn)	110	reg. number:An	(bd,PC,Xn)	—	—
([bd,An,Xn],od)	110	reg. number:An	([bd,PC,Xn],od)	—	—
([bd,An],Xn,od)	110	reg. number:An	([bd,PC],Xn,od)	—	—

Notes: 1. If the destination is a data register, then it cannot be specified by using the destination <ea> mode, but must use the destination Dn mode instead.
2. ADDA is used when the destination is an address register. ADDI and ADDQ are used when the source is immediate data. Most assemblers automatically make this distinction.

Figure 6-20 (cont'd)

6.5.2 Integer Arithmetic Instructions

Table 6-12 summarizes the arithmetic instructions where TST, CMPI, MUL*x*, and DIV*x* are enhanced, and CMP2 and EXTB are new instructions. Even though TST and CMPI does not affect the contents of the destination operand, program-counter relative modes were not supported by the 68000. The 68020 allows all effective address (ea) modes. The programmer, therefore, does not need to read

15 ... 0
Operation Word (One Word, Specifies Operation and Modes)
Special Operand Specifiers (If Any, One or Two Words)
Immediate Operand or Source Effective Address Extension (If Any, One to Five Words)
Destination Effective Address Extension (If Any, One to Five Words)

Figure 6-21 Object Code Format of 68020 Instructions.

operand into a data register before using TST or CMPI in order to write a position-independent code.

The multiply and divide instructions support word, long-word, and quad-word size operands as illustrated in Figure 6-22. For example, multiplying two 32-bit numbers or dividing a 64-bit number by a 32-bit divisor can be performed in a single instruction. A quad-size operand is held in any pair of data registers indicated by the syntax `Dn:Dm`. In a division operation, the V-bit is set if an overflow is detected, that is, if the quotient size is not large enough to hold the result. As with previous members, when an overflow is detected the operands are unchanged, and division by zero causes exception processing. In a multiplication operation, the only possibility for overflow is 32×32 multiply yielding a 32-bit product. Otherwise, the V-bit is always cleared.

The EXTB instruction sign-extends a byte to long-word directly. In the 68000, this required two steps: EXT.W followed by EXT.L.

The CMP2 instruction compares an operand to both a lower and upper bound and sets the condition codes accordingly. The bound pair is stored in the memory with the lower bound pointed to by the effective address and the upper bound following it as illustrated in Figure 6-23. The Z-bit is set if X*n* is equal to either bound and the C-bit is set if X*n* is out of range. This instruction can be used with both unsigned or two's complement numbers. The processor automatically evaluates the bounds and since the lower bound should be arithmetically smaller in value, it performs bounds checking as either a signed or unsigned operation.

The main application of CMP2 is checking the range of a parameter as the next example will illustrate.

Example 6-4

It is good practice to verify the validity of each parameter at the beginning of a subroutine and return an error status if an out-of-range condition exists. The following illustrates checking the proper range of a parameter PARM1 that is passed to the subroutine on the stack.

TABLE 6-10 LIST OF ADDRESSING MODES THAT REQUIRE EXTENSION WORD(S)

Addressing Category/Mode	Extension Word(s)
Absolute data addressing Absolute short Absolute long	 One word containing 16-bit address Two words containing 32-bit address
Immediate data addressing	One or two words of immediate value.
Register indirect addressing ARI with offset ARI or memory-indirect with index	 One/two words containing displacement. One word defining address mode + 0,1, or 2 words for base displacement (*bd*)+ 0,1, or 2 words for outer displacement (*od*)
Program counter relative addressing Relative with offset Relative with index and offset	 One/two words containing displacement. Same as ARI or Memory-indirect with Index

TABLE 6-11 DATA AND ADDRESS MOVEMENT INSTRUCTIONS

Instruction	Syntax	Size	Operation
EXG	`EXG Rn,Rm`	(L)	R*n* ↔ R*m*
LEA	`LEA <cea>,An`	(L)	⟨*cea*⟩ → A*n*
LINK[6]	`LINK An,#<d16/d32>`	—	SP-4 → SP; A*n* → (SP); SP → A*n*; SP + (*d*16 or *d*32) → SP
MOVE MOVEA	`MOVE.<s> <ea>,<daea>` `MOVEA.<s> <ea>,An`	B,W,L W,L	Source → Destination Source → Destination (long-word)
MOVEM	`MOVEM.<s> <list>,<caea>` `MOVEM.<s> <cea>,<list>`	W,L W,L	Listed Registers → Destination Source → Listed Registers
MOVEP	`MOVEP.<s> Dn,d16(Am)` `MOVEP.<s> d16(Am),Dn`	W,L W,L	D*n* → (Byte-wide Peripheral.) (Byte-wide Peripheral) → D*n*
MOVEQ	`MOVEQ #<d8>,Dn + 1`	—	8-bit Data → D*n* (sign-extended)
PEA	`PEA <cea>`	(L)	SP − 4 → SP; ⟨*cea*⟩ → (SP)
UNLK	`UNLK An`	—	A*n* → SP; (SP) → A*n*; SP + 4 → SP

[1] ⟨*s*⟩ is operand size (B, W, L).
[2] *d*16: 16-bit constant.
[3] *d*8: 8-bit constant.
[4] *d*32: 32-bit constant.
[5] ⟨*daea*⟩: data-alterable addressing modes;
⟨*ea*⟩: All addressing modes;
⟨*cea*⟩: Control addressing modes;
⟨*caea*⟩: Control-alterable addressing modes.
[6] Enhanced Instruction

TABLE 6-12 INTEGER ARITHMETIC OPERATIONS

Instruction	Syntax	Size	Operation
ADD ADDA	ADD.<s> Dn,<amea> ADD.<s> <ea>,Dn ADDA.<s> <ea>,An	B,W,L B,W,L W,L	source + destination → destination
ADDI ADDQ	ADDI.<s> #<data>,<daea> ADDQ.<s> #<1-8>,<aea>	B,W,L B,W,L	Data + destination → destination
ADDX	ADDX.<s> Dn,Dm ADDX.<s> -(An),-(Am)	B,W,L B,W,L	Source + destination + X → destination.
CLR	CLR.<s> <daea>	B,W,L	0 → destination.
CMP CMPA	CMP.<s> <ea>,Dn CMPA.<s> <ea>,An	B,W,L W,L	Destination − source
CMPI[1]	CMPI.<s> #<data>,<dea>	B,W,L	Destination − data
CMPM	CMPM.<s> (An)+,(Am)+	B,W,L	Destination − source
CMP2[1]	CMP2.<s> <cae>,Xn	B,W,L	Lower Bound ⇐ X*n* ⇐ Upper Bound
DIVS[1]	 DIVS.W <dea>,Dn DIVS.L <dea>,Dn DIVS.L <dea>,Dn:Dm DIVSL.L <dea>,Dn:Dm	 Mixed Mixed Mixed Mixed	Signed Divide: 32/16 Bits → D*n* = 16*r*:16*q* 32/16 Bits → D*n* = 32*q* 64/32 Bits → D*n* = 32*r*, D*m* = 32*q* 32/32 Bits → D*n* = 32*r*, D*m* = 32*q*
DIVU[1]	 DIVU.W <dea>,Dn DIVU.L <dea>,Dn DIVU.L <dea>,Dn:Dm DIVUL.L <dea>,Dn:Dm	 Mixed Mixed Mixed Mixed	Unsigned Divide: 32/16 Bits → D*n* = 16*r*:16*q* 32/16 Bits → D*n* = 32*q* 64/32 Bits → D*n* = 32*r*, D*m* = 32*q* 32/32 Bits → D*n* = 32*r*, D*m* = 32*q*
EXT	EXT.W Dn EXT.L Dn	W L	Sign extend D*n*[7:0] → D*n*[15:0]. Sign extend D*n*[7:0] → D*n*[31:0].
EXTB[1]	EXTB Dn	L	Sign extend D*n*[7:0] → D*n*[31:0].
MULS[1]	MULS.W <dea>,Dn MULS.L <ea>,Dn MULS.L <ea>,Dh:Dl	W L L	Signed Multiply: 16 × 16 → 32-bits Signed Multiply: 32 × 32 → 32-bits Signed Multiply: 32 × 32 → 64-bits
MULU[1]	MULU.W <dea>,Dn MULU.L <ea>,Dn MULU.L <ea>,Dh:Dl	W L L	Unsigned Multiply: 16 × 16 → 32-bits Unsigned Multiply: 32 × 32 → 32-bits Unsigned Multiply: 32 × 32 → 64-bits
NEG	NEG.<s> <daea>	B,W,L	0 − destination → destination
NEGX	NEGX.<s> <daea>	B,W,L	0 − destination − X → destination
SUB SUBA	SUB.<s> <ea>,Dn SUB.<s> Dn,<amea> SUBA.<s> <ea>,An	B,W,L B,W,L W,L	Destination − source → destination
SUBI SUBQ	SUBI.<s> #<data>,<daea> SUBQ.<s> #<1-8>,<daea>	B,W,L B,W,L	destination − data → destination
SUBX	SUBX.<s> Dn,Dm SUBX.<s> -(An),-(Am)	B,W,L B,W,L	Destination − source − X → destination
TST[1]	TST.<s> <ea>	B,W,L	Destination tested, affecting CCR

[1] New or enhanced arithmetic instructions.

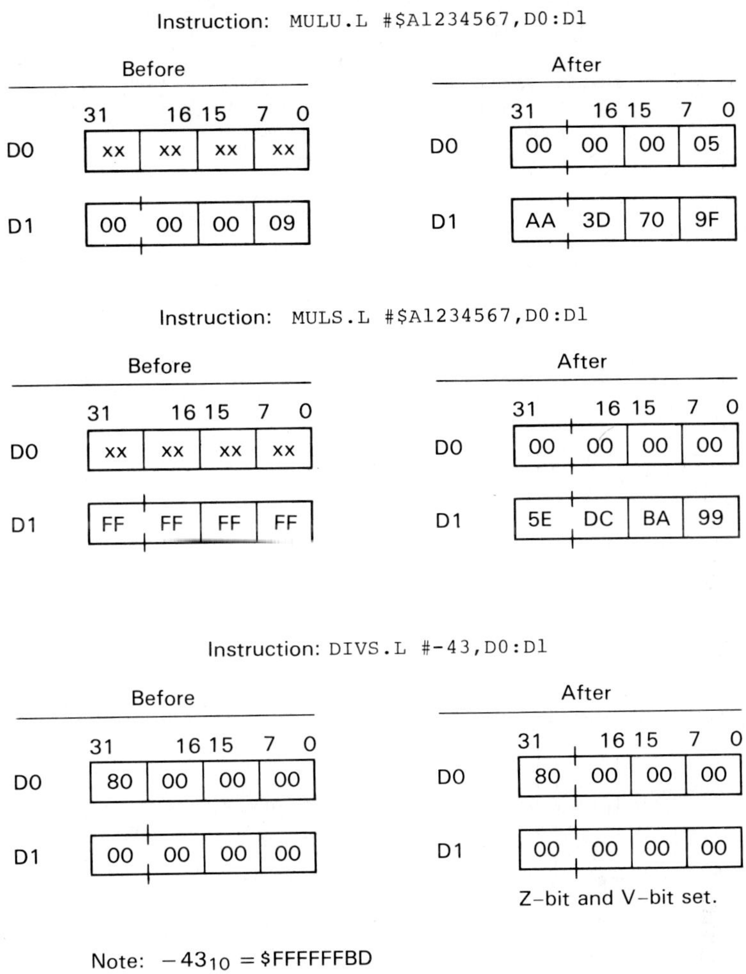

Figure 6-22 Example of MUL*x* and DIV*x* Instructions.

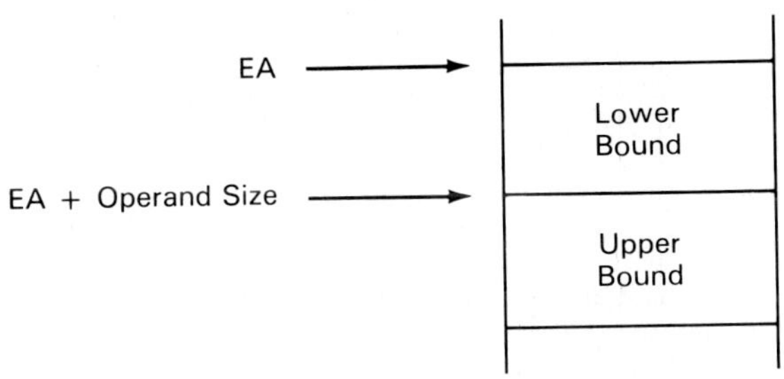

CMP2.<s> <ea>, Xn

Figure 6-23 CMP2 Instruction.

```
* Range Definitions:
*
P1_RANGE    DC.W    -16                 Lower Bound
            DC.W     16                 Upper bound
            .
            .
            .
* Main Body of Subroutine:
*
            .
            .
            .
            MOVE.W (PARM1,A6),D0    Get PARM1 from stack.
            CMP2.W P1_RANGE,D0      P1 is out of range?
            BCS    ERR_BNDS         If so, return with error status.
            .
            .
            .
```

6.5.3 Program Control Instructions

Table 6-13 shows the program-flow control instructions. The enhanced instructions (BRA, BSR, and B⟨*cc*⟩ allow a displacement size of 32 bits in addition to 8 and 16 bits. Since displacement is a two's complement number relative to the

TABLE 6-13 PROGRAM-FLOW CONTROL INSTRUCTIONS

Type	Instruction	Assembly Syntax	Notes
Conditional	B⟨*cc*⟩	B<cc> <label>	1,2,3
	DB⟨*cc*⟩	DB<cc> Dn,<label>	1,2,3
	S⟨*cc*⟩	S<cc> <ea>	2,3
Unconditional	BRA	BRA <label>	1
	BSR	BSR <label>	1
	CALLM	CALLM #<data>,<ea>	4
	JMP	JMP <cea>	1
	JSR	JSR <cea>	1
	NOP	NOP	1
Returns	RTD	RTD #<offset>	5
	RTM	RTM	4
	RTR	RTR	1
	RTS	RTS	1

[1] 68000 instruction. Discussed in detail in Chapter 3.
[2] The condition codes (*cc*'s) discussed in Chapter 3.
[3] Optional displacement size specification is not shown.
[4] New 68020 instruction.
[5] Introduced with the 68010. Discussed in Chapter 5.

word that follows the operation word of branch instruction, the maximum range is ∓ 2 Gigabytes.

The size of the displacement is usually determined by the assembler depending on the range or assembler directives that force a given size. The size of a branch displacement may also be explicitly specified using a size suffix as shown below:

```
B<cc>.<s>   <label>
BRA.<s>     <label>
BSR.<s>     <label>
```

where the optional displacement size specification is

s = B or S for byte,
s = W for word,
s = L for long-word.

In an object code, the 32-bit displacement is coded by using $FF in the 8-bit displacement field as shown in Figure 6-24.

Example 6-5

The following shows examples of branch instructions:

```
BRA     LOOP1        Branch size determined by assembler.
BNE.S   TRY_AGAIN    Small loop uses 8-bit offset.
BSR     GETLIN       Branch size determined by assembler.
BSR.L   GETLIN       32-bit offset is used.
```

If GETLIN is an external subroutine (i.e., not part of current program module) the assembler will choose the long form unless otherwise directed. The displacement will then be determined during the linkage of modules.

CALLM (call module) and RTM (return from module) instructions. These two new instructions are intended for better support of modular programming. As we discussed earlier, a subroutine call requires that the address of the subroutine be known at assembly or link time. This might be a problem for modules

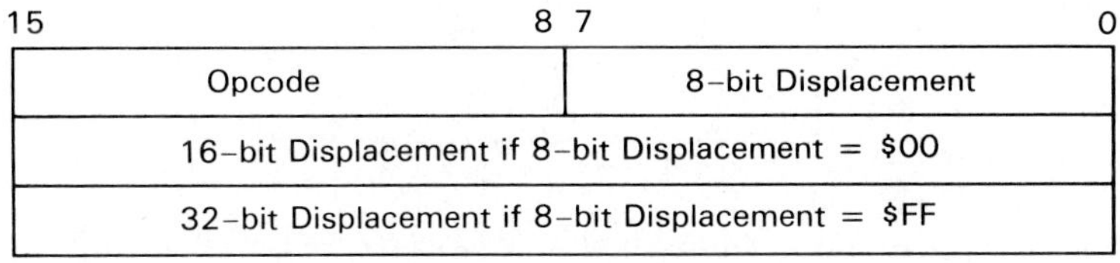

Figure 6-24 Object Code of BSR, B⟨*cc*⟩, and BRA Instructions.

that are relocated at run-time. Alternatively, a module descriptor can be used to call a program module as illustrated in Figure 6-25. Only the beginning address of the descriptor then must be known at assembly or link time. The address of the called module can be set dynamically by the governing operating system in a virtual memory system.

The CALLM and RTM pair handles all passing of parameters and their deallocation upon return automatically. This is illustrated in Figure 6-26. The first word of the called module indicates which register is to be used as the called module's data area pointer. The selected register is saved on the stack and is then

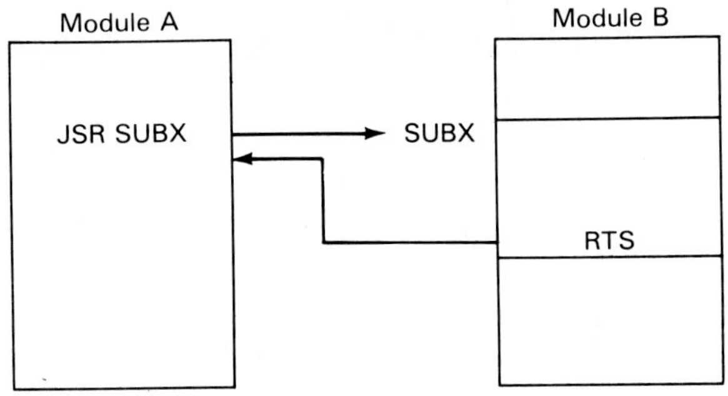

(a) A Subroutine Call.

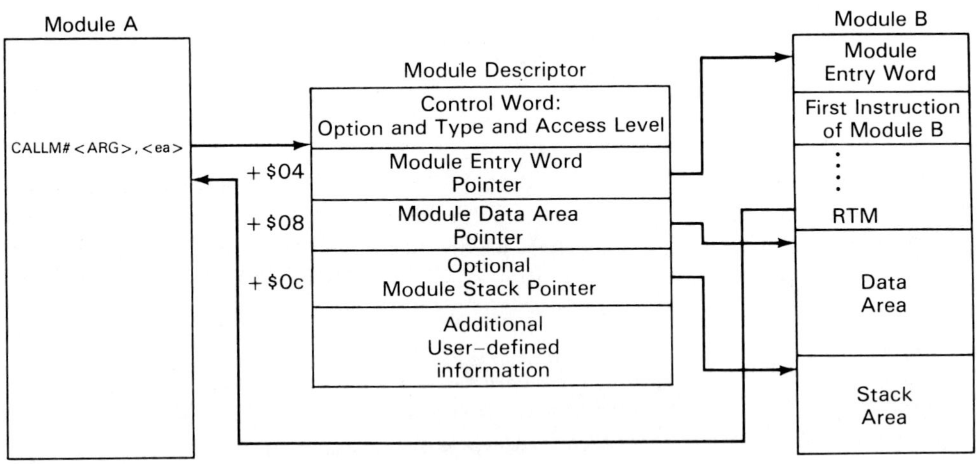

(b) Module Call Using CALLM and RTM.

Figure 6-25

```
* Example of CALLM and RTM Instruction Pair.
*
*MODULE CALL:
        PEA      <parm1>             Address of first parameter
        PEA      <parm2>             Address of second parameter.
*       CALLM    #2*4,(A0)           8 bytes of parameters pushed,
*                                    and A0 → Desc. block.
*         .
          .
          .
*       CALLED MODULE:
        DC.W     $F000               Module Entry word.
        MOVE.L   (PARM1,SP),D0       Get first parameter.
          .
          .
          .
        RTM                          Return to calling program module.
```

Figure 6-26 Example Module Call.

loaded from the module descriptor block. The format of this entry word is shown in Figure 6-27.

These two instructions also provide a mechanism for subdividing the user state into 256 levels of privilege. Similar to a TRAP instruction or any exception that changes the privilege level from the user to supervisor mode, CALLM may be used to increase the user access level. This hierarchical protection provides the ability to control accesses to system modules with finer granularity than just user and supervisor modes.

The information contained in a module descriptor includes the address of the called module, the address of the module's data area, an optional stack-pointer value to be used by the module, module type, options, and the associated access level. There are two types of module descriptors. The simple type (type = 0) supports simple module calls without any hierarchical levels. For type 0 there is no change in stack pointer and arguments are not copied. The second type involves complex module calls and requires the support of an external device for access-privilege control. For example, the 68851 PMMU registers and microcode support

15	14 13 12	11 10 9 8 7 5 6 4 3 2 1 0
D/A	Reg. #	← 0 →

D/A = 1 for address register,
= 0 for data register.
Reg. # = register number.

Figure 6-27 Module Entry Word Format.

such module calls. Thus, the operation of CALLM and RTM depend upon the type of descriptor block.

Since control access levels are supported by the microcode of CALLM and RTM and by the 68851 PMMU, this would increase the performance of an operating system. However, this requires that the call and return mechanism of the entire operating system and all system programs such as a compiler be restructured and reprogrammed—a formidable task. Thus, the CALLM-RTM instruction pair is rarely used and we refer the reader to the programmer's manual for further discussion of the module support of the 68020.

6.5.4 Bit-Field Instructions

This category of instructions provides the ability to directly manipulate variable-width bit fields. A bit-field operand in a data register or in memory map may be cleared, set, complemented, extracted, inserted, scanned, or tested as we shall discuss in this section. The instruction mnemonic is of the form BF⟨*opr*⟩ where ⟨*opr*⟩ specifies the operation code as listed in Table 6-14. A bit-field operand is defined by the syntax of the form `<ea>{<offset>:<width>}` where:

- `ea` Specifies the effective address of the byte which contains bit zero of the bit array.
- `offset` Specifies the number of bits to the first bit of the field from the effective address (i.e., the bit number of the left-most bit of the field). The allowed range is $[-2^{31}, 2^{31} - 1]$. For memory operands, the offset is given with respect to the most significant bit of the byte specified by the effective address. For an operand in a data register, the offset is with respect to D*n*[31], and is treated as modulo 32.
- `width` Is the number of bits in the bit field with an allowable range of 1 to 32 bits. The width can be given as an immediate value or contained in a data register. In the latter case, it is evaluated as modulo 32. The width values 0 and 1 − 31 specifies field width of 32 and 1 − 32, respectively.

A constant offset or width value requires no "#" sign since the assembler can easily make the distinction. Figure 6-28 illustrates a bit-field operation using the BFCHG instruction. Note that the direction of the bit-field offset is the opposite of usual bit numbering.

Supported by the barrel shifter of the arithmetic unit, the bit-field instructions provide a convenient and efficient way of dealing with a mixture of bit-field operands that are often packed in memory. For example, suppose an application requires an array of data words, each word containing four fields of packed data as shown in Figure 6-29. Using the instruction set of previous members of the

TABLE 6-14 BIT-FIELD INSTRUCTIONS

Type	Instruction Syntax	Operation[2]
Test and Change	BFTST <cea>{<offset>:<width>} BFTST Dn{<offset>:<width>}	Test and affect CCR only.
(See Note 1)	BFCLR <cea>{<offset>:<width>} BFCLR Dn{<offset>:<width>}	Clear bit field.
	BFSET <cea>{<offset>:<width>} BFSET Dn{<offset>:<width>}	Set all bits in bit field.
	BFCHG <cea>{<offset>:<width>} BFCHG Dn{<offset>:<width>}	Complement all bits in bit field.
Movement	BFEXTU <cea>{<offset>:<width>},Dn BFEXTU Dn{<offset>:<width>}	Extract & Zero-extend → D*n*[31:0]
	BFEXTS <cea>{<offset>:<width>},Dn BFEXTS Dm{<offset>:<width>},Dn	Extract & Sign-extend → D*n*[31:0]
	BFINS Dn,<caea>{<offset>:<width>} BFINS Dn,Dm{<offset>:<width>}	Move bit-field D*n*[width-1:0] → Destination.
Scanning	BFFFO <cea>{<offset>:<width>},Dn BFFFO Dm{<offset>:<width>},Dn	Search for first "1". The offset of the first most significant bit set → D*n*. If there are no set bits, then offset + width → D*n*.

[1] The CCR is affected as follows:
MSB of operand → N-bit.
Z-bit is set if all bits of field are zero.

[2] The operand size of these instructions are 1 − 32 bits.

68000 family, we would require the following statements to extract and zero extent the type bit field and to move the lower bits of D0 to the type bit field.

```
FETCH   MOVE.W   #$3C00,D0    D0 = Mask.
        AND.W    <ea>,D0      Type field.
        LSR.W    #8,D0        Right-justify field value
        LSR.W    #2,D0
and
STORE   LSL.W    #8,D0        Justify with Type Field.
        LSL.W    #2,D0
        MOVE.W   #$C3FF,D1    D1 = Mask.
        AND.W    <ea>,D1      Clear Type field.
        OR.W     D0,D1        Insert Field.
        MOVE.W   D1,<ea>      Store back to destination.
```

The above instructions, especially shifts, are slow and cumbersome. In the

Instruction: `BFCHG D0{3:4}`

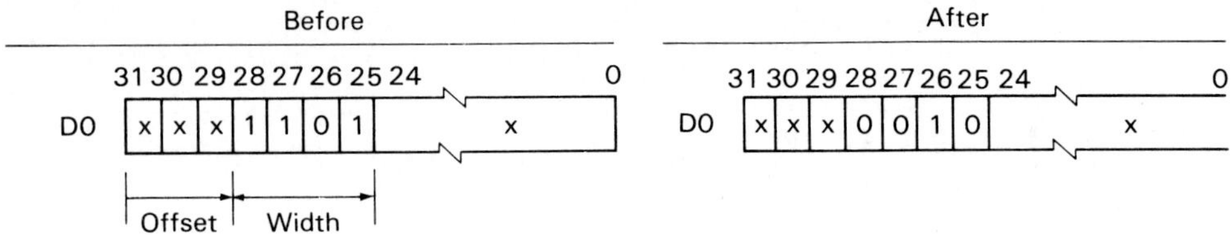

(a) Operand in a Register.

Instruction: `BFCHG (A0){3:4}`

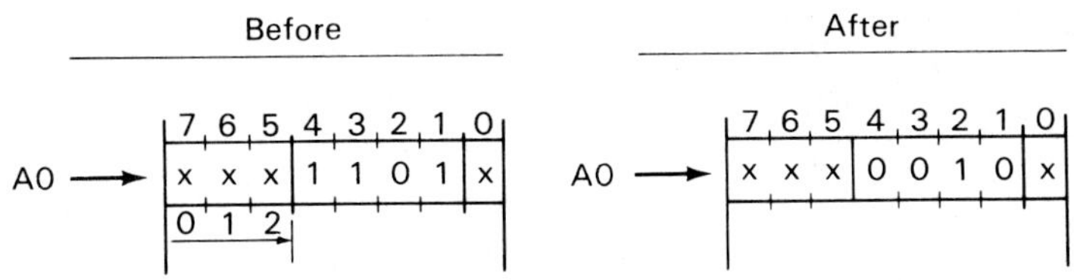

(b) Operand in Memory.

Figure 6-28 Illustration of the BFCHG Instruction.

68020, each access can be replaced by a single bit-field instruction as follows:

```
FETCH   BFEXTU   <ea>{2:4},D0
```

and

```
STORE   BFINS    D0,<ea>{2:4}
```

These instructions have the further advantage that no intermediate registers are used. Remember that bit fields are not required to be aligned with any memory

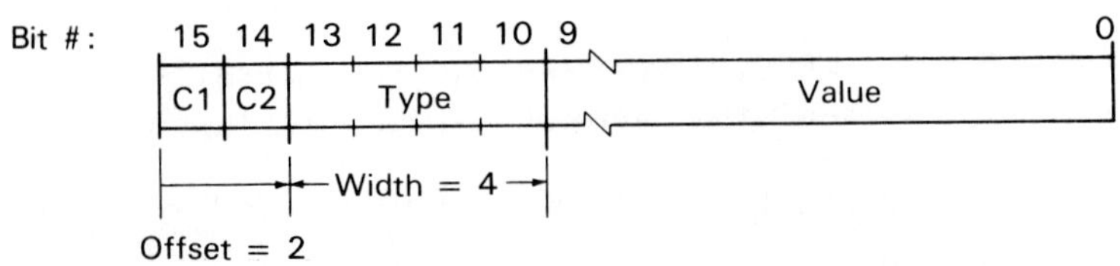

Figure 6-29 Example Bit Field Assignments in a Packed Data Word.

boundaries. The 68020 will perform one or more bus cycles as required depending upon the alignment and size of the bit field and the port size of memory.

The following lists the most common applications of the bit-field instructions:

1. The data storage requirements are reduced by packing data fields together where the bit-field instructions provide an efficient access mechanism. This is especially important in applications such as graphics or digital image processing because of the amount of data (see Example 6-6). Similarly, in representing Boolean logic, bits can be used instead of bytes.
2. In hardware control applications, the bit-field instructions provide a convenient way of manipulating various control and status registers.
3. The BFFFO instruction is particularly useful in managing memory blocks and disk storage. For example, it can be used to find the first unused page in a virtual memory system.
4. The bit-field instructions can significantly increase the efficiency of high-level languages such as C or ADA. These languages support bit-field structures which could be directly translated to single bit-field instructions. For example, in C language, the packed data structure of Figure 6-29 can be defined as follows:

```
struct   packed_struct
   {
    unsigned int c1:1;
    unsigned int c2:1;
    unsigned int type:4;
    unsigned int value:10;
   };
.
.
.
struct packed_struct packed_value; /* Define variable packed_value. */
```

Then, the statement that sets the type field to 2 given by

```
packed_value.type= 3;
```

will translate to assembly language as follows:

```
BFINS     #3,PACKED_VALUE(A6){2:4}
```

where we assume the destination address points to the desired data word.

5. There are other, simple but efficient applications of the bit-field instructions. For example, to move bits [12:23] of a data register to a memory location pointed by A0, we can simply use the instruction BFEXTU D*n*{8:12},(A0). This is much more efficient than shifting followed by a MOVE instruction.

Example 6-6

Suppose an image processing application requires picture elements (called *pixel* for short) to be logically organized as 512 × 512. If each pixel is 6 bits, then storing one element per byte would require 262,144 bytes. Alternatively, we can pack all elements together reducing the storage requirements to $512^2*6/8$ or 196,608. If pixels x(i, j) are stored in row-sequential format, we can make use of the bit-field instructions in order to efficiently access an element as shown in Figure 6-30. The image data is treated as a string of bits and the bit field offset with respect to the beginning of the array is given by

```
(i*512 + j) * 6 bits.
```

We have avoided doing any multiplies using MULx, since it is faster to perform shift operations.

Example 6-7

Suppose we have 16 long-words of data that we wish to scan to find the position of the first bit which is "1." This could be simply programmed using BFFFO as shown in Figure 6-31. At the end, if D1 = −1, then no "1" is found. Otherwise, D0 indicates the offset to the first bit which is set.

6.5.5 BCD Instructions

Table 6-15 summarizes the BCD instructions. The two new instructions in this category are PACK and UNPK. PACK takes a word-size operand, adds a 16-bit constant adjustment word to it, and then writes the second and fourth hex digits of the result to the 8-bit destination as illustrated in Figure 6-32. With displacement equal to zero, it could simply be used to pack two unpacked BCD digits into a byte. It also provides the ability to easily convert two decimal digits (i.e., 0-9)

```
* Assume the following register contents initially:
* A0 → Beginning of data array.
* D0[31:0] = Row-index i.
* D1[31:0] = Column-index j.
*
      LSL.L    #8,D0             Calculate 512 * i.
      LSL.L    #1,D0
      ADD.L    D1,D0             Add j.
      MOVE.L   D0,D2             Calculate *6 as (*4 + *2).
      LSL.L    #1,D2
      LSL.L    #2,D0
      ADD.L    D2,D0
      BFEXTU   (A0){D0:6},D2     D2 = x(i,j).
```

Figure 6-30 Accessing a 2-D Array of 6-bit Pixels.

```
* A0 → Beginning of Data.
*
     MOVE.W  #16-1,D1           D1 is loop counter.
     CLR.L   D0                 Initialize as zero offset.
LOOP BFFFO   (A0)(D0:31),D0
     DBNE    D1,LOOP
```

Figure 6-31 Example of BFFFO Instruction.

TABLE 6-15 BCD ARITHMETIC INSTRUCTION

Instruction	Syntax	Size	Operation
ABCD	ABCD Dn,Dm ABCD -(An),-(Am)	B B	$Dn_{10} + Dm_{10} + X \rightarrow Dm$ $(An - 1)_{10} + (Am - 1)_{10} + X \rightarrow (Am - 1)$
NBCD	NBCD <daea>	B	$0 - (daea)_{10} - X \rightarrow (daea)$
PACK[1]	PACK -(Am),-(An),#<d16> PACK Dm,Dn,#<d16>	W → B	Unpacked $(Am - 2) + d16 \rightarrow$ Packed $(An - 2)$ Unpacked $Dm[15:0] + d16 \rightarrow Dn[7:0]$
SBCD	SBCD Dn,Dm SBCD -(An),-(Am)	B	$Dn_{10} - Dm_{10} - X \rightarrow Dm$ $(An - 1)_{10} - (Am - 1)_{10} - X \rightarrow (Am - 1)$
UNPK[1]	UNPK -(Am),-(An),#<d16> UNPK Dm,Dn,#<d16>	B → W	Packed $(Am - 2) + d16 \rightarrow$ Unpacked $(An - 2)$ Packed $Dm[7:0] + d16 \rightarrow Dn[15:0]$

[1] New Instructions

coded in ASCII[3] or EBCDIC[4] to a packed BCD byte. The adjustment required is \$CFD0 and \$0F10 for ASCII and EBCDIC, respectively. This is illustrated in Figure 6-33.

The UNPK instruction takes a byte-size operand, forms an intermediate word-size extension by placing the first BCD digit into bits [11:8], and the second one into bits [3:0]. As with PACK, a 16-bit constant adjustment is added before the result is written to the destination as illustrated in Figure 6-34. This could be used to unpack two BCD digits that are stored in a byte by just using a zero adjustment. Also, it could simplify conversion of packed BCD digits to two bytes of ASCII or EBCDIC code using constants \$3030 and \$F0F0, respectively.

[3] *The American Standard Code for Information Interchange* (ASCII) is commonly used to code standard character set and special control functions such as *carriage return* (CR).

[4] *The Extended Binary Coded Decimal Interchange Code* (EBCDIC) was developed by IBM for use on the IBM System/360.

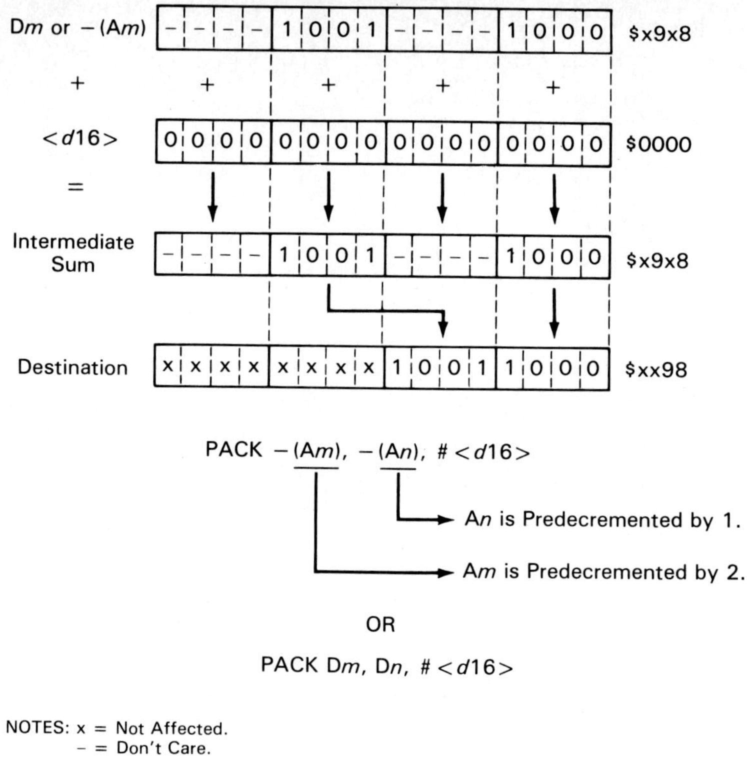

Figure 6-32 Illustration of PACK Instruction.

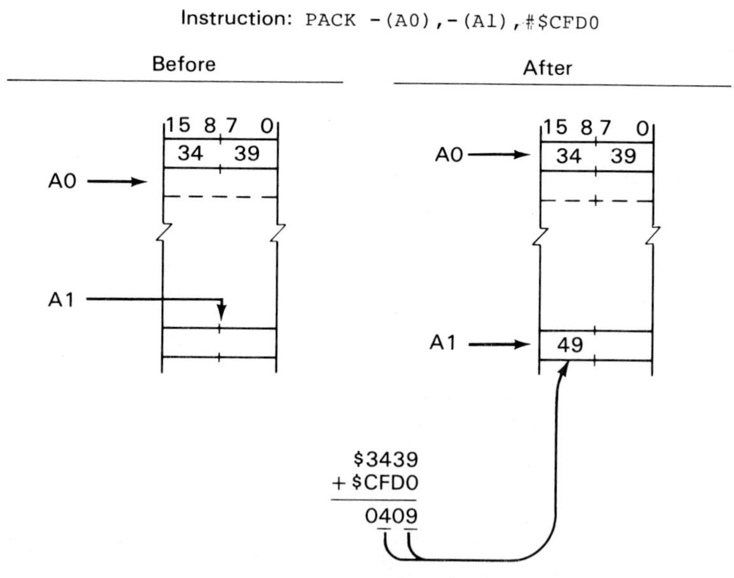

Figure 6-33 Example of ASCII-to-BCD Conversion using PACK.

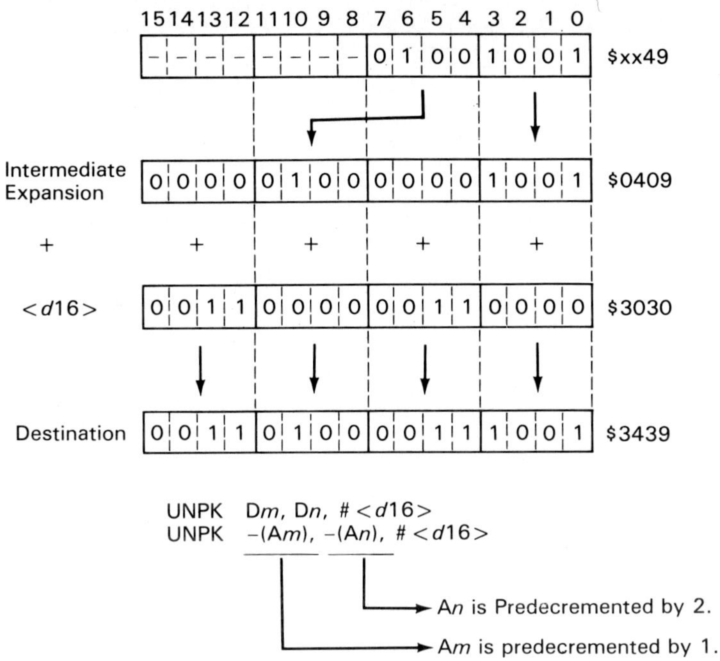

Figure 6-34 Illustration of the UNPK Instruction.

6.5.6 System Control Instructions

Table 6-16 summarizes the system control instructions. MOVEC and BKPT are enhanced and two new instructions, CHK2 and TRAP⟨*cc*⟩, have been added to this category.

MOVEC is extended to include access to the four additional control registers, namely, CACR, CAAR, MSP, and ISP. As before, the transfer size is always 32 bits even though fewer bits may actually be required. Since immediate addressing mode is not supported, setting up a control register is a two-step operation. For example, enabling the cache after power-up requires

```
MOVE.L      #1,D0
MOVEC       D0,CACR.
```

The bounds checking instruction, CHK2, is very similar to the CMP2 except CHK2 causes an exception to occur in addition to setting the condition codes. When the value is out of bounds it traps using the same exception vector as the CHK instruction.

TRAP⟨*cc*⟩ is a conditional trap instruction which causes exception processing to occur if the specified condition is true. If the condition is false, control

TABLE 6-16 SYSTEM CONTROL INSTRUCTIONS

Instruction Syntax	Size	Operation
Privileged		
ANDI #<data>,SR	W	Immediate data AND SR → SR.
EORI #<data>,SR	W	Immediate data EOR SR → SR.
MOVE <dea>,SR	W	Operand → SR.
MOVEC Xc,Xn[3]	L	Read Control Register Xc → Xn.
MOVEC Xn,Xc[3]	L	Write Xn → Control Register Xc.
MOVES.<s> Xn,<aea>	B,W,L	Xn → ⟨aea⟩ using DFC addr. space.
MOVES.<s> <ea>,Xn	B,W,L	⟨ea⟩ → Xn using SFC addr. space.
MOVE An,USP	L	An → USP.
ORI #<data>,SR	W	Immediate data or SR → SR.
RESET	—	Assert RESET* for 512 clocks periods.
RTE	—	(SP) → SR; SP + 2 → SP; (SP) → PC; SP + 4 → SP.
STOP #<data>	W	Immediate data → SR; Stop.
Trap Generating		
BKPT #<data>[3]	—	Breakpoint Instruction (see text).
CHK.<s> <dea>,Dn	W,L	If Dn < 0 or Dn > ⟨dea⟩, then CHK exception.
CHK2.<s> <dea>,Xn[3]	B,W,L	If Xn is out of bounds, then CHK exception.
TRAP #<data>	—	TRAP exception #(data = 1 − 16)
TRAP<cc>[3]	—	If ⟨cc⟩ is true, then TRAP⟨cc⟩ exception.
TRAP<cc>.<s> #<data>[3]	W,L	Same as TRAP⟨cc⟩ except immediate data that follows.
TRAPV	—	If V = 1 then TRAPV exception.
Condition Code Register		
ANDI #<data>,CCR	B	Immediate data AND CCR → CCR.
EORI #<data>,CCR	B	Immediate data EOR CCR → CCR.
MOVE <dea>,CCR	B(W)[1]	Operand → CCR.
MOVE CCR,<daea>	W[2]	CCR → Operand.
ORI #<data>,CCR	B	Immediate data OR CCR → CCR.

[1] Is a word operation, but only CCR is affected. The upper byte is ignored.
[2] Is a word operation, but only low-byte contains CCR. The upper byte is all zeros.
[3] New or enhanced instructions.

is passed to the next instruction. Any of the 16 condition codes used by DB⟨*cc*⟩ are allowed including TRAPT (trap always) and TRAPF (never trap). The latter form, although generally not so useful, may be used for downward compatibility with the 68000 programs since then it causes an illegal-instruction trap.

The alternate form of TRAP⟨*cc*⟩ also allows a 16- or 32-bit value to be embedded following the operation word. This immediate value has no significance to the processor, but instead, is passed as a reference to the exception handler, or it can be the address of a parameter block. For example, TRAPT.W #1 can be used instead of

```
TRAPT
DC.W     1
```

Since the program counter points to the next instruction, this also eliminates the need for the exception handler to change the saved program counter value to skip over the immediate value.

Breakpoint operation (BKPT instruction). Suppose we wish to set a breakpoint in a program loop so that the program is interrupted only after *N*-iterations through the loop. Assuming the program code is stored in read/write memory, the operating system can temporarily replace the operation word where a breakpoint is desired with a BKPT instruction and save the replaced operation word. When BKPT is encountered in the 6801X, it causes a trap to the illegal-instruction exception handler thus allowing the operating system to handle it. Such intervention by the OS in a break-after-*N*-times situation has the disadvantage that it slows down the execution of the program being debugged or tested. The 68020 extends the BKPT to provide more real-time program debug support. This requires the support of external hardware where the iteration count and the saved operation word are stored for up to 8 breakpoints[5] as illustrated in Figure 6-35. The OS replaces the operation word with one of the BKPT instructions shown in Table 6-17, saves the operation word in the corresponding register of external breakpoint support hardware, and sets the iteration count. Each time the BKPT instruction is encountered while executing the target program, the 68020 generates a special CPU-space cycle called a *breakpoint cycle*. During this cycle (see Figure 6-36), the breakpoint number is placed on the address bus. The breakpoint hardware, if it exists, recognizes this cycle and responds by decrementing the corresponding iteration counter and placing the operation word on the data bus. The 68020 reads this operation word and continues execution as if no breakpoint had been encountered. When the same BKPT instruction is executed for the *N*th time, external hardware asserts the bus error (BERR*) signal causing an illegal instruction trap. This flow is illustrated in Figure 6-37.

6.5.7 Multiprocessor Instructions

In addition to TAS, the 68020 provides two new instructions (CAS and CAS2) that allow secure updating of shared resources as given in Table 6-18. While it may be appropriate to discuss also the generic coprocessor instructions here, we will postpone that until the next chapter.

As we discussed in Chapter 3, a semaphore can be associated with any

[5] This feature is included in the 68851 PMMU.

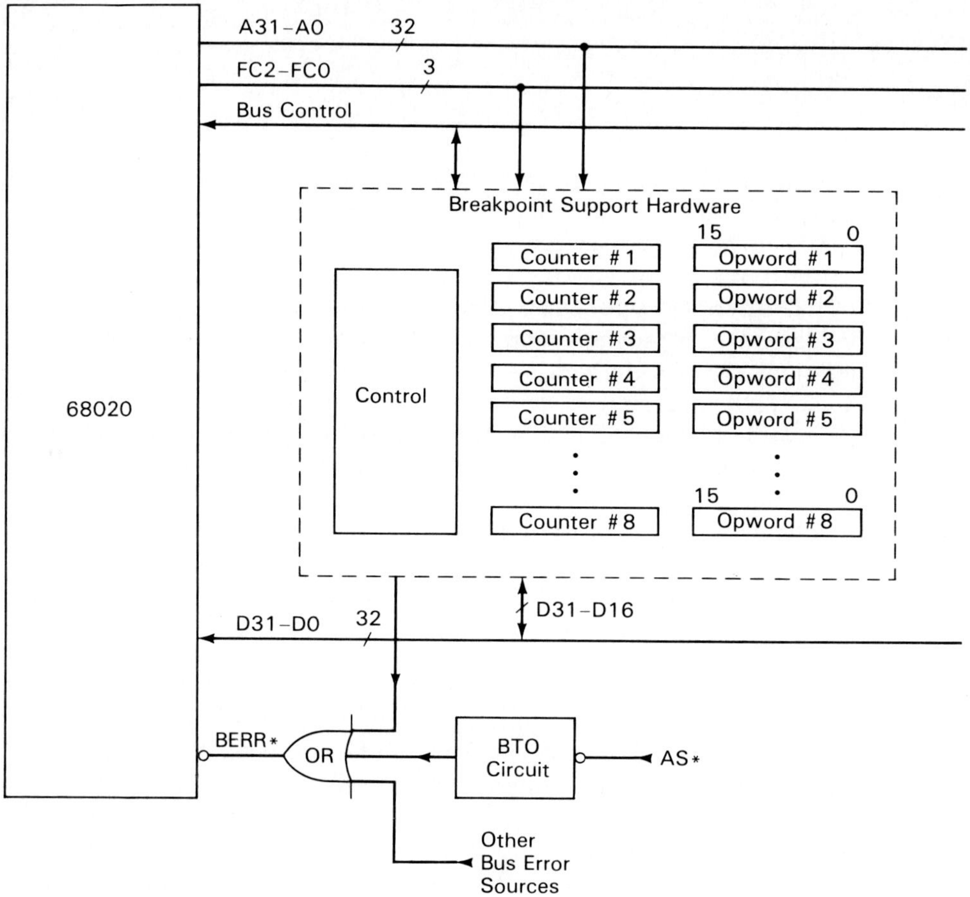

Figure 6-35 Breakpoint Block Diagram.

TABLE 6-17 BREAKPOINT INSTRUCTIONS

Instruction	Object Code	Breakpoint
BKPT #0	$4848	0
BKPT #1	$4849	1
BKPT #2	$484A	2
BKPT #3	$484B	3
BKPT #4	$484C	4
BKPT #5	$484D	5
BKPT #6	$484E	6
BKPT #7	$484F	7

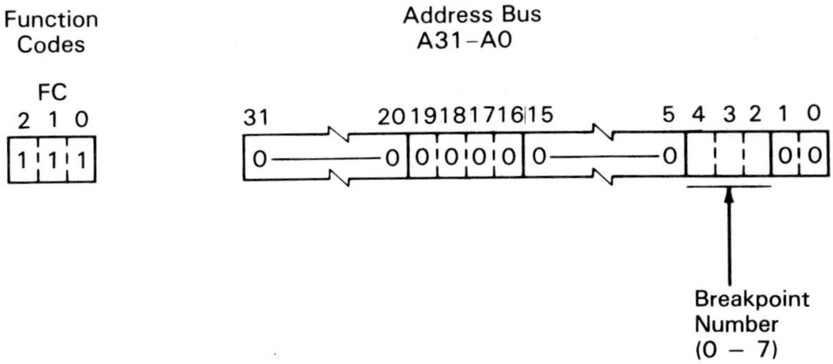

Figure 6-36 Breakpoint CPU-Space Cycle.

resource that assigns its ownership to only one task or processor in the system at any given time. The shared resource can be a printer interface, small blocks of read/write memory, system variables, and so on. In a multitasking but single processor system we can use either TAS or BSET to test if a resource is currently allocated and, if not, "lock" it to prevent accesses by all other tasks. On the other hand, in a multiprocessor system, only TAS may be used to control semaphores since hardware arbitration of access to shared resources is performed on a bus cycle-by-bus-cycle basis. Because TAS executes the read-modify-write operation as a special indivisible bus cycle it prevents other processors from accessing the semaphore while one is accessing by using a TAS instruction.

The TAS instruction of the 68000 stays unchanged as we have noted above. In a multiprocessor system, there are usually many resources that are globally shared and that could be independently manipulated. The TAS instruction is general in that it could be used to control access to any such resource. However, this requires that each independent system resource have an individual semaphore register. To prevent this additional overhead of manipulating semaphores, the 68020 provides two special instructions—CAS and CAS2. These instructions also use an indivisible bus cycle similar to TAS in order to perform a compare-and-swap operation as described in Figure 6-38.

TABLE 6-18 MULTIPROCESSOR SYNCHRONIZATION INSTRUCTIONS

Instruction	Syntax	Size
TAS (Test And Set)	TAS <daea>	B
CAS (Compare And Swap)[3]	CAS.<s> Dc,Du,<aea>	B,W,L
CAS2 (Compare And Swap 2 operands)[3]	CAS2.<s> Dc1:Dc2,Du1:Du2,(Xn):(Xm)	B,W,L

[1] Dc, Dc1, Dc2, Du, Du1, and Du2 are data registers.
[2] Xn and Xm are data or address registers.
[3] New instructions.

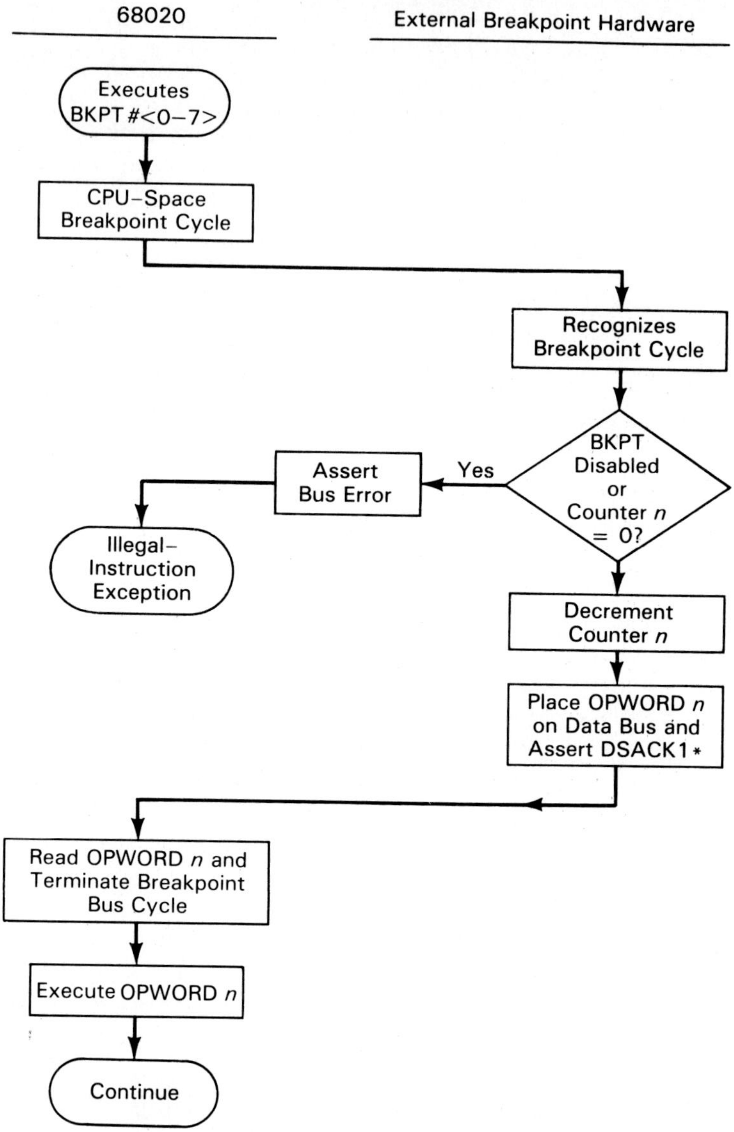

Figure 6-37 Breakpoint Flow Diagram.

The CAS and CAS2 allow for the secure update of system variables and globally shared pointers. This is useful in a multiprocessor system because bus cycles for operand accesses are indivisible by hardware arbitration. Furthermore, unlike TAS, there is no equivalent of these instructions. They are also useful, therefore, in an interrupt-driven multitasking but single processor environment since a single instruction cannot be interrupted in midstream.

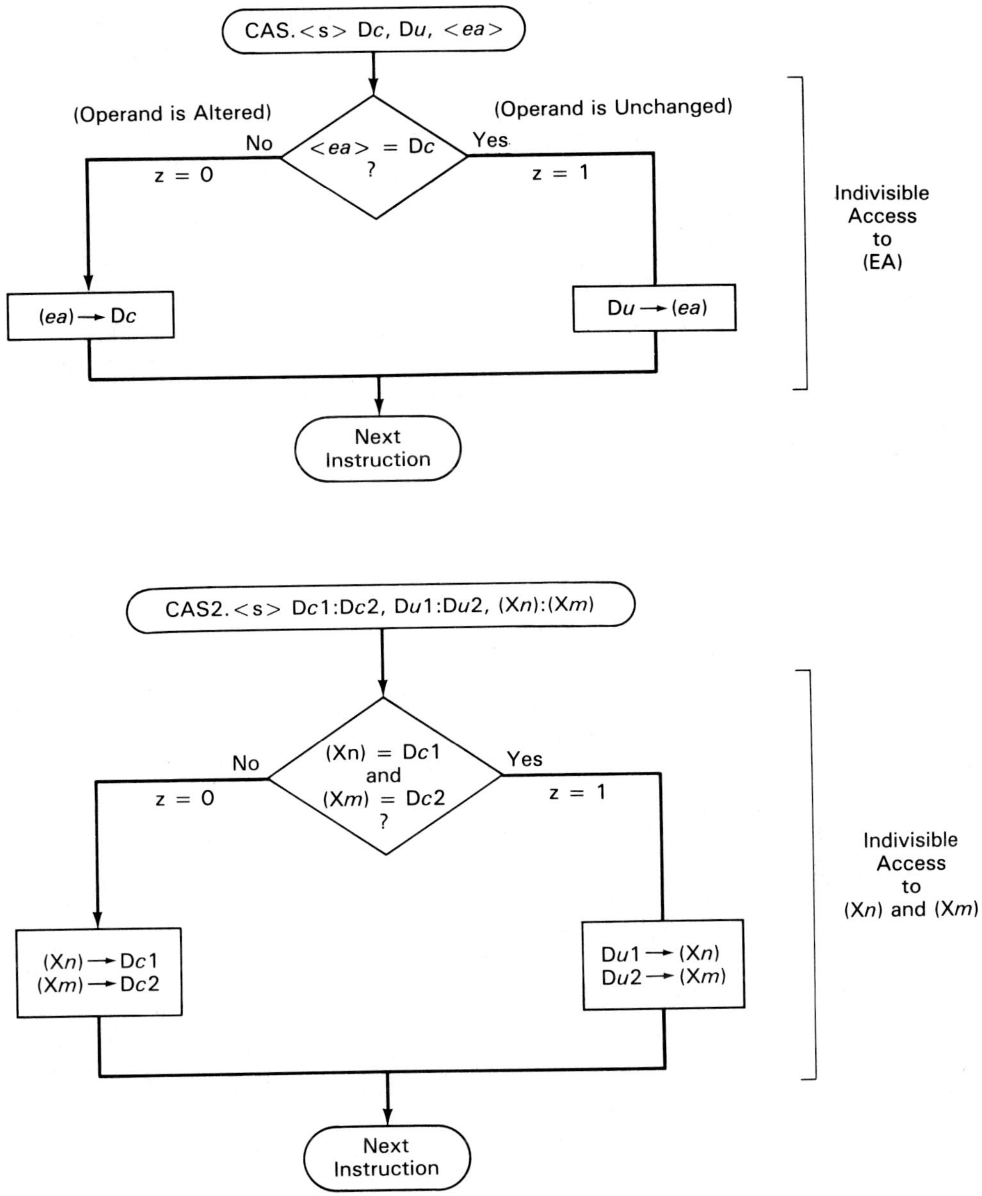

Figure 6-38 Operation of CAS and CAS2 Instructions.

For example, to manipulate a shared system variable, let us say SYSVAR, we can read it into a data register and modify its value as desired. To write the value back to SYSVAR, we must use CAS. Thus, the program code looks as follows:

```
        MOVE.<s>        SYSVAR,Dc         Get SYSVAR value. Dc is D0-D7.
LOOP    <Manipulate Dc>
        .
        .
        .
        CAS.<s>         Dc,Du,SYSVAR      If unchanged, update SYSVAR.
        BNE             LOOP
        .
```

When the CAS is executed, one of the following conditions are true:

1. In the meantime, another processor or task changed the value of SYSVAR.
2. The SYSVAR is unchanged.

In the first case, the comparison will fail and the write will not take place. Instead, CAS will read the new value of SYSVAR into register D*c* in order to prepare for another try. In the second case, the comparison passes, so the new value is written to SYSVAR.

CAS2 is similar to CAS except it performs two comparisons to make sure that neither of the *two* operands have been changed before updating them. Otherwise, it reads the two operands again in order to redo the manipulation. This is useful, for example, for handling doubly linked lists that require manipulation of two pointers.

Example 6-8

Let us consider manipulation of a Last-In-First-Out(LIFO) queue, where only the last entry pointed to by a variable (let us call it HEAD) may be controlled. In a single processor and single task environment in order to insert an element to a queue, all we need is to establish a forward link for the new element and update HEAD using the following statements:

```
MOVE.L   HEAD,(NEXT,A0)
MOVE.L   A0,HEAD
```

where NEXT is the displacement between the beginning of a queue element and its pointer to the next element. However, this would generate intermittently erroneous results in a multitasking or multiprocessor environment as illustrated in Figure 6-39. This is due to the possibility that control may be transferred after the first instruction to another task which may happen to execute the same two instructions. Such a transfer is possible due to an interrupt to switch context in a multitasking situation or due to hardware arbitration to allow access to another processor in a multipro-

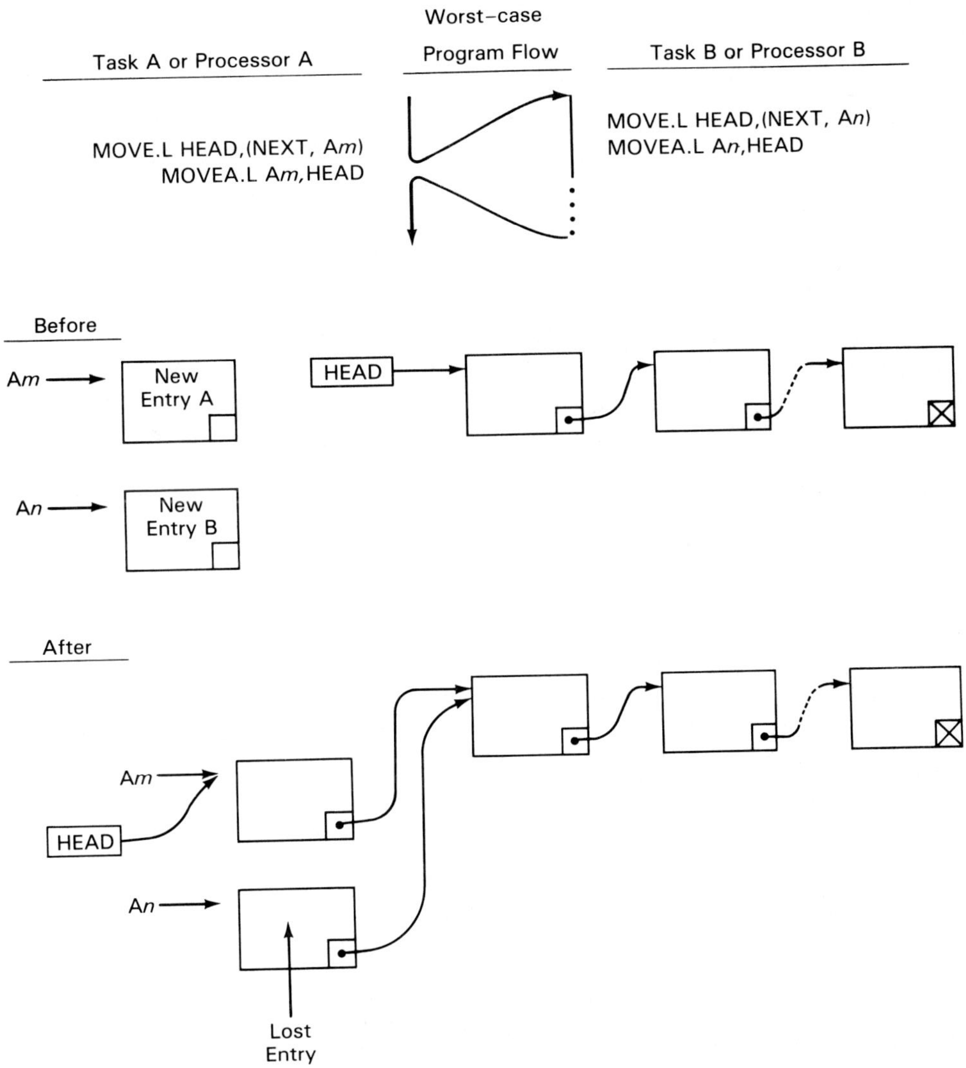

Figure 6-39 Intermittently Erroneous Insert Operation to a Queue.

cessing environment. If there is such an intervention, it results losing the entry that was inserted by the other task or processor.

The use of the CAS instruction remedies this situation by first verifying whether HEAD is changed. If there was no intervention, CAS will update HEAD to point to the new entry. Otherwise, CAS will simply read the new HEAD value to reattempt the insert operation. This is illustrated in Figure 6-40.

Task A/B or Processor A/B

```
     MOVE.L      HEAD,D0          Read Current HEAD VALUE.
     MOVE.L      (Aj),D1          New HEAD value needed in a
*                                 data register.
LOOP MOVE.L      D0,(NEXT,Aj)     Establish forward link.
     CAS.L       D0,D1,HEAD       Update HEAD, if unchanged.
     BNE         LOOP             Otherwise, HEAD → D0, and try
*                                 again.
     .
     .
     .

j: m or n.
```

Figure 6-40 Correct Insert Operation.

Example 6-9

Suppose we wish to increment a system counter, SYSCNT, that resides in shared memory in order to keep count of some system operation. In a single-processor environment (multitasking, or not), we can simply use:

```
ADDQ.W   #1,SYSCNT
```

In a multiprocessor environment, we can either use a semaphore and TAS instruction to control accesses or we may use CAS without any semaphores as illustrated in Figure 6-41.

```
WAIT         TAS      SEM_SYSCNT       Allocate.
             BNE      WAIT             If busy, wait till done.
             ADDQ.W   #1,SYSCNT        SYSCNT + 1
             CLR.B    SEM_SYSCNT       Unlock SYSCNT.
             .
             .
             .
```

(a) Using TAS and a Semaphore.

```
             MOVE.W   SYSCNT,D0
TRY_AGAIN    MOVE.W   D0,D1
             ADDQ.W   #1,D1
             CAS.W    D0,D1,SYSCNT
             BNE      TRY_AGAIN
             .
             .
             .
```

(b) Using CAS.

Figure 6-41 Two Ways of Incrementing a Shared SYSCNT Variable.

6.6 INSTRUCTION CACHE

As we stated earlier, the 68020 features a 256-byte on-chip cache memory that holds the most recently used instructions. The program loops residing within this cache will execute faster because on-chip cache access requires only two clock cycles. This is 33 percent faster than the minimum three cycle, zero wait-cycle access to external memory as illustrated in Figure 6-42. Furthermore, it allows simultaneous accesses for instruction fetches from cache and operand transfers from external memory.

The cache is limited to instructions only since this avoids any stale data problems and, thereby, simplifies its implementation. The cache is organized as 64 long-words as illustrated in Figure 6-43. Since there is only one comparator, it is referred to as *direct mapped* or *set associative* with a set size of one. Each entry contains two instruction words and has a *valid* (V) *bit* and *tag bits* associated with it. The tag consists of address bits A31-A08 and also FC2 which provides supervisor- versus user-mode distinction. In fetching an instruction, index bits A7-A2 select one of the 64 cache entries. If the high-order address bits and address space matches the tag field, then it is a cache hit and the instruction word is read from the on-chip cache memory. Otherwise, it is fetched from external memory which also replaces the selected cache entry. This is illustrated in Figure 6-44. The hit ratio is typically between 40 and 70 percent.

The 68020 provides no direct means to explicitly access the contents of the instruction cache. Entries and their handling are affected only through manipulating CACR and CAAR registers by using the privileged MOVEC instruction. For example, a cache entry containing a breakpoint, (i.e., a BKPT instruction) may be invalidated to remove the breakpoint. Upon the reset operation, all cache entries are invalidated. Also, a bus error during a prefetch causes an invalid entry in the cache.

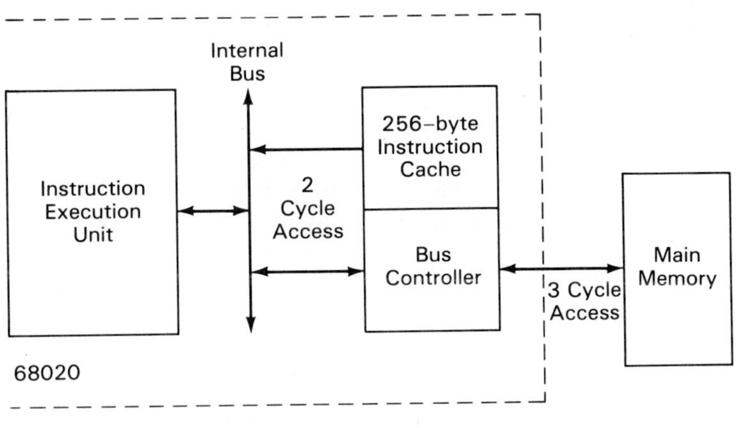

Figure 6-42 Instruction Cache.

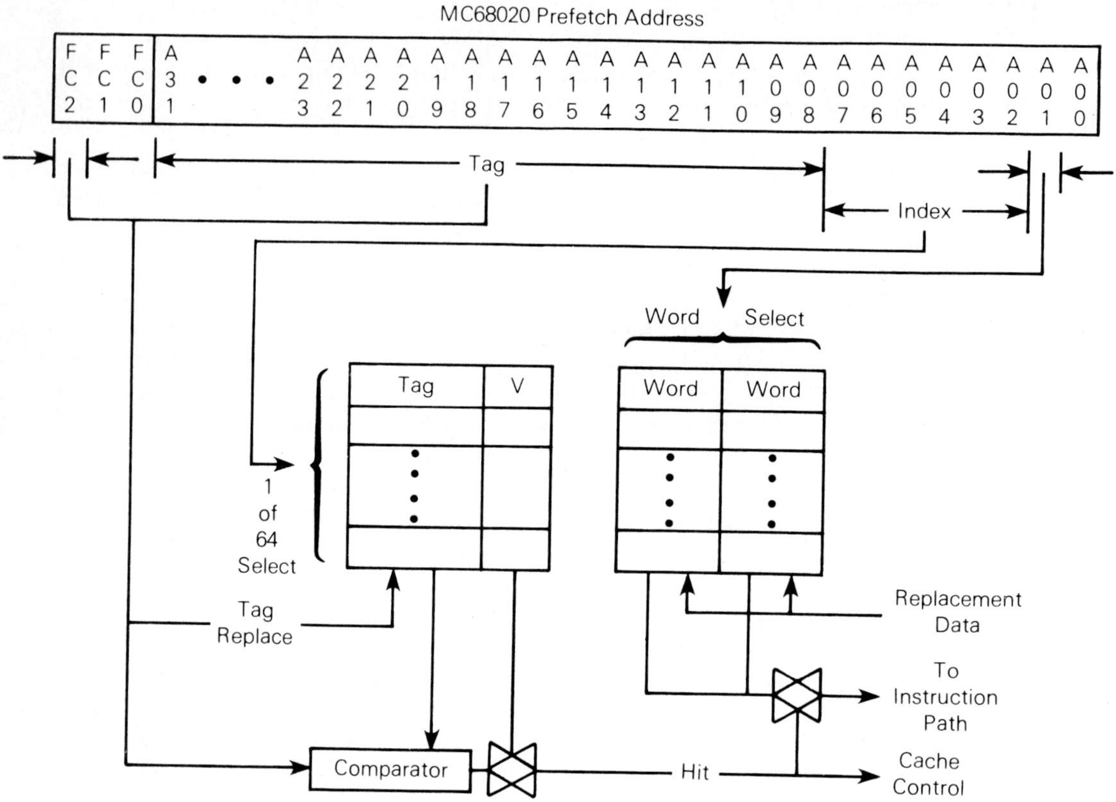

Figure 6-43 Organization of the 68020 Instruction Cache.

It is not possible to fool the 68020 to cache a data word. For example, MOVES ⟨*ea*⟩,D0 with SFC pointing to program space still fetches from external memory.

6.7 INSTRUCTION TIMING

The instruction timing estimation of the 68020 is significantly more complex with respect to earlier members of the family. This is basically due to the instruction cache, the flexible operand alignment, and the parallelism between the internal sequencer and the bus controller. The features that affect the timing of an instruction include the following:

1. Speed of the 68020 clock (e.g., 20 MHz, 25 MHz).
2. Cache enabled or disabled and cache hit or miss.

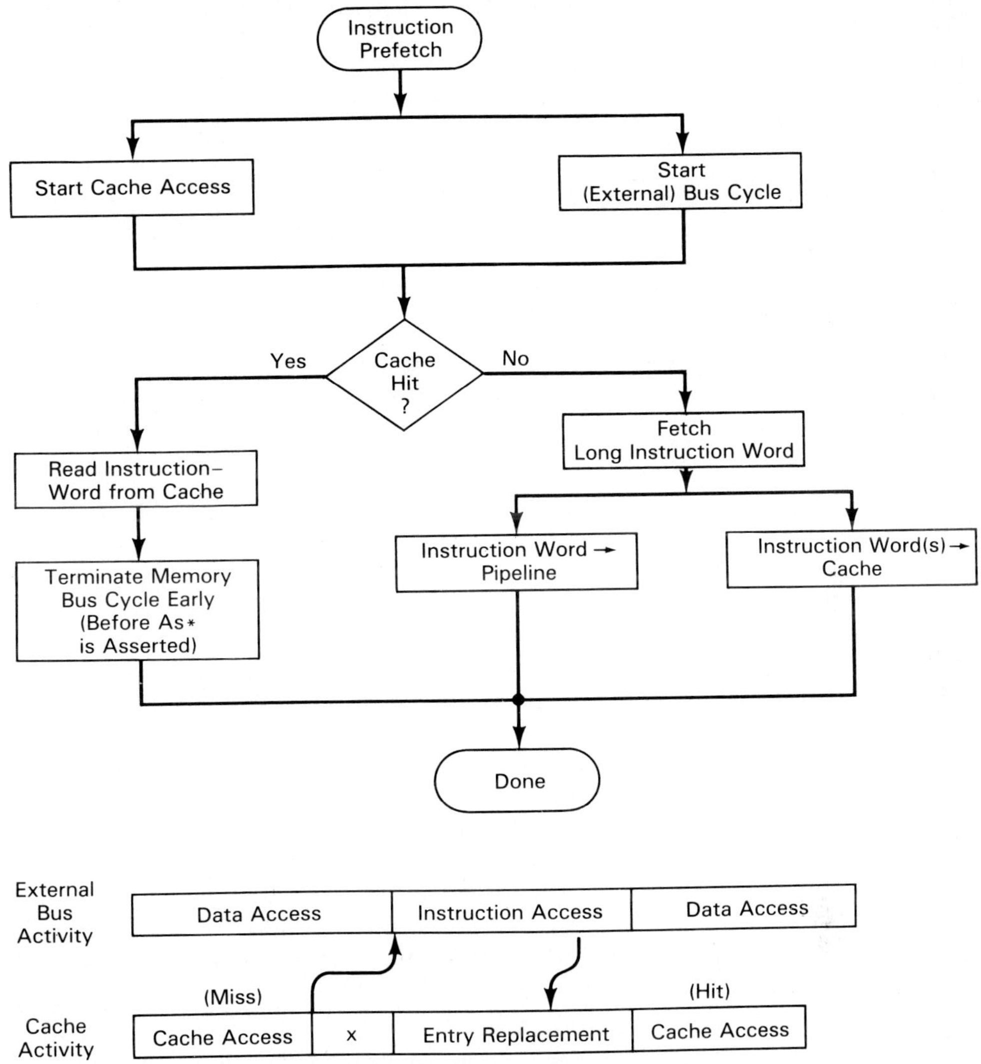

Figure 6-44 Cache Operation.

3. Operand alignment (i.e., misaligned or not).
4. The memory or peripheral port size.
5. Addressing mode used.
6. Speed of bus cycles (i.e., number of wait-cycles, if any).
7. Instruction alignment to even or odd word.
8. Possible overlap in execution of consecutive instructions.

Of these, let us examine the last one. For example, let us take the instruction sequence

```
MOVE.L  D0,(A0)
ADD.W   D0,D1
MOVE.L  (A1),D2
ADD.L   D1,D2
```

where we will assume:

1. The data bus is 32 bits wide.
2. Zero wait-cycles for all accesses.
3. The cache is enabled and all instructions already reside in the cache.

The sequencer will transfer D0 to the bus controller and instructs it to write at the address pointed to by A0. The write will take three clock cycles. This gives enough time for the sequencer to also complete the execution of the next instruction. That is, the second instruction, the ADD, executes effectively in zero time. On the other hand, the same parallelism is not possible for the last two instructions. This is because D2 has to be read before the addition can be performed. In general, a read bus cycle is the synchronization point between the sequencer and the bus controller. In other words, no scoreboard is kept about actual usage of registers.

In addition to a read bus cycle, a single NOP instruction may be used to synchronize the bus controller and sequencer in order to avoid any instruction overlap. The NOP instruction keeps the sequencer idling until all pending bus cycles are completed. This second purpose of a NOP is intended for rare cases when the sequential model of execution falls apart. For example, a NOP or a dummy read cycle may be required in some cases of interrupts, as discussed in Exercise 6-39.

The timing tables in the 68020 user manual specifies instruction timing for three cases:

Best Case:	A. Instructions in cache and cache is enabled.
	B. Maximum overlap between instructions.
Cache Case:	A. Instructions in cache and cache is enabled.
	B. No overlap between instructions.
Worst Case:	A. Instructions not in cache or cache is disabled.
	B. No overlap between instructions.

An example of instruction timing is given in Figure 6-45. The timing tables, as shown in the user manual, assume the following:

Arithmetic/Logical Operations Timing Table

Instruction	Best Case	Cache Case	Worst Case
ADD* <*ea*>, D*n*	0(0/0/0)	2(0/0/0)	3(0/1/0)

*Add Fetch Effective Address Time
Format: 3(0/1/0)

- Number of Operand Write Cycles
- Number of Instruction Access Cycles
- Number of Operand Read Cycles
- Total Number of Clock Cycles

Effective Address Calculation Timing Table

Address Mode	Best Case	Cache Case	Worst Case
(A*n*)+	2(0/0/0)	2(0/0/0)	2(0/0/0)

ADD •<*s*> (A*n*) + D*n* Total Time: Best Case: 2 Clock Cycles
Cache Case: 4 Clock Cycles
Worst Case: 5 Clock Cycles

Figure 6-45 Example Timing of ADD Instruction.

1. All external devices have a 32-bit port size.
2. All operands and instructions are long-word aligned.
3. Zero wait-cycles.

6.8 EXCEPTION PROCESSING

During program execution, anything out of the ordinary such as privilege violation or an illegal instruction causes an exception condition. The exception processing of the 68020 is very similar to earlier members but includes extensions necessary for the new features provided. Following the 68000 family evolution, it most resembles the 6801X. Basically, some exceptions are enhanced in functionality, and some new exception types are added. There are also changes in exception processing sequence and stack frame formats. However, most of these changes are transparent to the application programmer.

6.8.1 Internal Exceptions

The internal exceptions originate due to conditions detected within the 68020. These include instructions that may cause exceptions, address errors, and trace mode as shown in Table 6-19. The new exceptions are shown in italics. Of these, the most significant is the coprocessor-dependent exceptions. These depend on the particular coprocessor. For example, the *floating-point coprocessor* (FPCP) may cause a floating-point divide-by-zero condition. Such an exception condition, including the vector number, is communicated to the 68020 via the coprocessor interface. We have considered coprocessor exceptions as internal because co-

TABLE 6-19 OVERVIEW OF 68020 EXCEPTIONS

Caused By	Exception(s)	Description
Instructions	Privilege Violation	Occurs when a privileged instruction is executed in user mode.
	Format Error	Occurs due to incorrect stack frame format detected by RTE, RTM, CALLM, or ⟨cp⟩RESTORE instructions.
	TRAP #⟨*n*⟩	Causes unconditional exception to one of the sixteen exception vectors.
	TRAPV, *TRAP⟨cc⟩*, *⟨cp⟩TRAP⟨cc⟩*	Causes an exception to occur if the condition is true.
	CHK, *CHK2*	Causes an exception if out-of-bounds condition is detected.
	Divide by Zero	Divide-by-zero condition.
	Coprocessor-Dependent	Caused by conditions detected by coprocessor(s).
	Illegal Instruction	Caused by two conditions: A. Unimplemented instruction opcodes. B. BKPT #⟨*n*⟩ instruction.
Instruction Prefetch from an odd address	Address Error	Typically caused by an incorrect jump address e.g., JMP (A0) where A0 is odd.
Trace Mode	Trace Exception	T1 T0 Trace Mode 0 0 Disabled 0 1 Exception on change of flow (e.g., BRA, JMP, RTE, and so on). 1 0 Exception after each instruction. 1 1 Undefined, reserved.

processor instructions appear as extensions of the 68020 instruction set and any communication between the 68020 and a coprocessor is done as transparent to the programmer at the microcode level.

The format exception, first introduced in the 6801X is expanded to cover additional stack frame formats. It may occur when executing the RTE, CALLM, RTM, and ⟨cp⟩RESTORE instructions.

The trace exception is also expanded so that an exception may occur either when change of program flow is detected or at the end of each instruction. For example, in the following instruction sequence with T1-T0 = 01,

```
BACK   ADD.W   (A0)+,D0
         .
         .
       DBF     D0,BACK
```

at the completion of the DBF instruction, a trace exception will occur if the branch is to be taken. The OS executes a trace service routine, possibly displaying PC and/or other registers for debugging purposes. At the end of the exception handler, the execution of RTE will resume program execution beginning with the ADD instruction.

The internal exception processing sequence is illustrated in Figure 6-46. Note that exception related information is saved on the stack and the trace mode is disabled during the exception processing.

6.8.2 External Exceptions

The external exceptions are due to external events such as an interrupt request from a peripheral. The three sources of external exceptions are interrupts, a bus-error condition, and CPU reset operation as we shall discuss next.

Reset exception. The reset exception occurs when RESET* input is asserted to initialize the 68020. Typically, this occurs after a system power-up or a system reset. This exception initializes 68020 control registers as follows:

Initialization	Description
S = 1	Supervisor state.
T1, T0 = 0,0	Tracing is disabled.
VBR = 0	Exception vector table offset is zero.
M = 0	Master stack is disabled.
I2, I1, I0 = 111	Interrupt mask level is set to seven.
CACR = 0	Cache is invalidated and disabled.

As before, the reset exception is not to be confused with the RESET in-

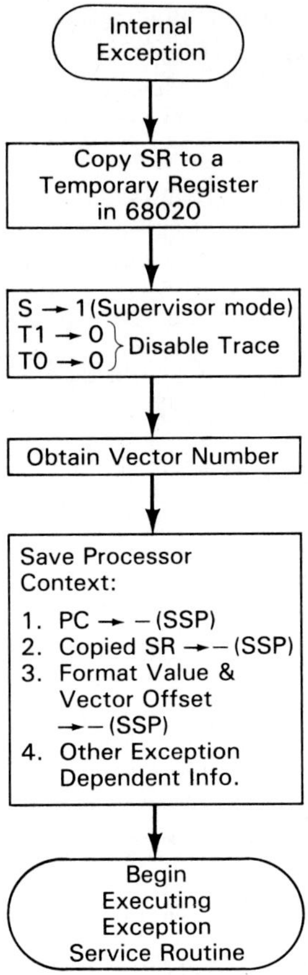

Figure 6-46 Internal Exception Processing Sequence.

struction where the latter only affects the peripherals. After the above initialization, the 68020 fetches initial ISP and PC values from vector 0 and 1 contents, respectively, and program execution starts. This is illustrated in Figure 6-47. If a bus error or address error occurs before the first program instruction is fetched, a double bus fault condition occurs halting the 68020 until another reset exception occurs. That is, any bus or address-error condition before the 68020 starts executing the first instruction is considered a catastrophic system failure. In general, the double-bus-fault condition occurs in the following cases:

1. When a bus or address error occurs during a reset exception.
2. When a bus error occurs during processing of a bus or address-error exception.
3. When an address error occurs during processing of a bus or address-error exception.
4. When restoring the internal state information during a RTE instruction.

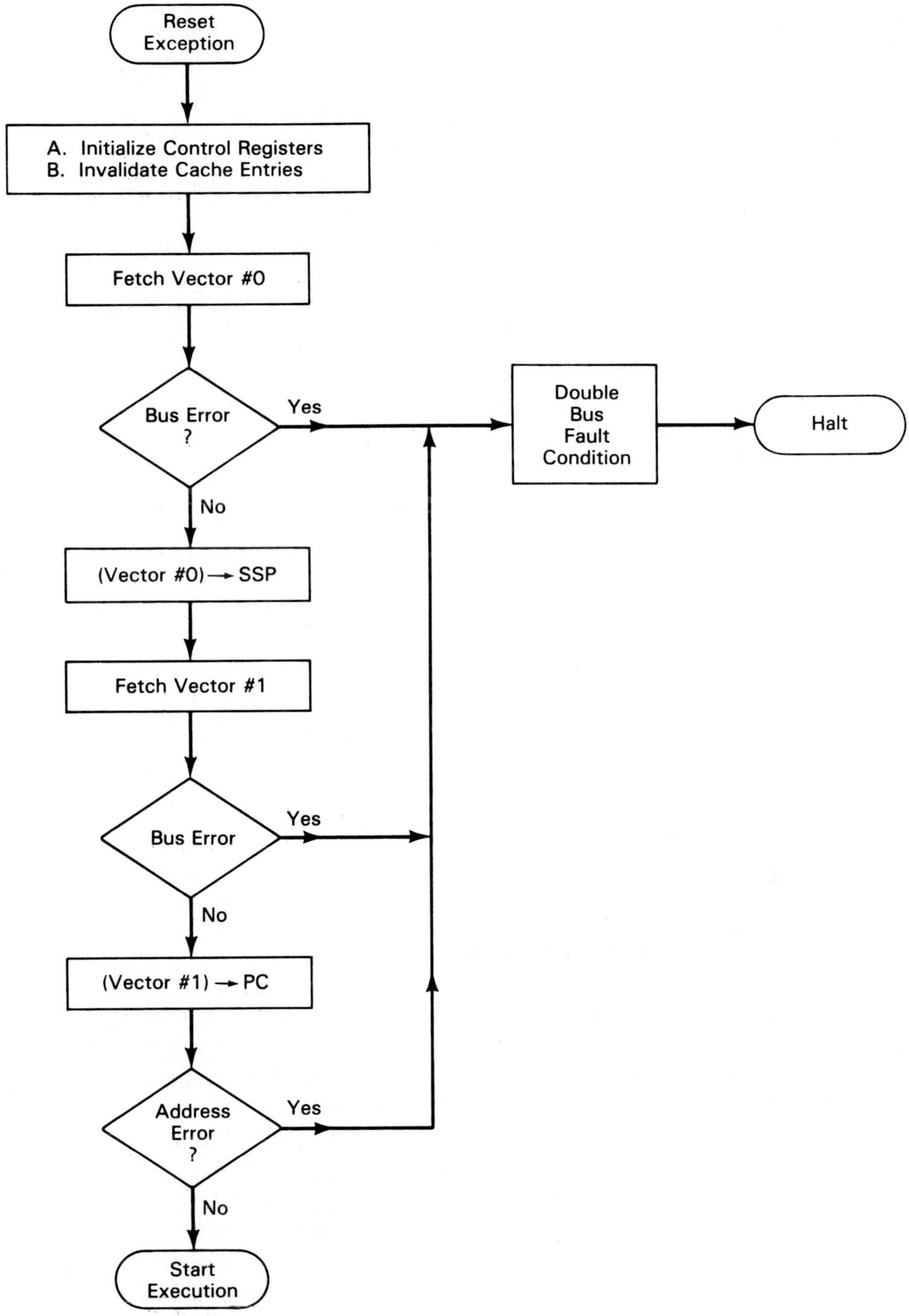

Figure 6-47 Reset Exception Processing Sequence.

For example, if the initial PC vector contents are set to an odd address, this will cause an address error, and thereby to a double bus fault condition.

Bus error exception. When a problem is detected with a bus cycle, external logic asserts the bus error (BERR*) input of the 68020 causing a bus-error exception. Typically, it is encountered in the following cases:

1. Due to a hardware error, the addressed device does not respond with DSACK*n** causing external a Bus Time Out (BTO) circuit to assert BERR*.
2. Due to a software error, an attempt is made to access a nonexistent device or memory, thus causing BTO to assert BERR*.
3. In a virtual-memory system, MMU detects a page fault condition or privilege violation and asserts BERR*.
4. In a virtual-machine system, MMU asserts BERR* to emulate a nonexistent device in software.
5. External hardware detects an error condition with the current bus cycle, such as parity error and asserts BERR*.

The exception processing sequence during a bus-errors exception is illustrated in Figure 6-48.

The 68020 distinguishes two types of bus errors. If a bus error occurs due to an instruction fetch, then exception processing is deferred until the execution of that instruction begins. If, on the other hand, a bus error occurs due to an operand fetch, then exception processing begins immediately.

Virtual memory/virtual machine support. The virtual memory and machine implementation of the 68020 is a simple extension of the 6801X that we discussed in detail in Chapter 5. The only difference is in the stack frame formats due to differences in the hardware architecture of the 68020.

In a virtual-memory system, when the MMU detects a page fault condition, a bus-error exception occurs. The bus-error condition may stop execution in the middle of an instruction. For example, a page fault may occur when fetching the source operand of MOVE.W (A0),D0. The 68020, then saves its internal state on the system stack and starts exception processing. If the bus error occurs in prefetching the next instruction (i.e., on an instruction boundary) a short bus-error stack is used because the amount of information required to continue is less. Otherwise, a long bus-error stack is saved that includes all necessary internal state information to be able to resume instruction execution. These two stacks have different format values as shown in Figure 6-49 and 6-50.

As illustrated in Figure 6-51, after the page fault condition is fixed, the execution of the RTE instruction causes the faulted bus cycle re-run and instruction to resume where it left off. In case of a read-modify-write cycle, the entire cycle will be re-run.

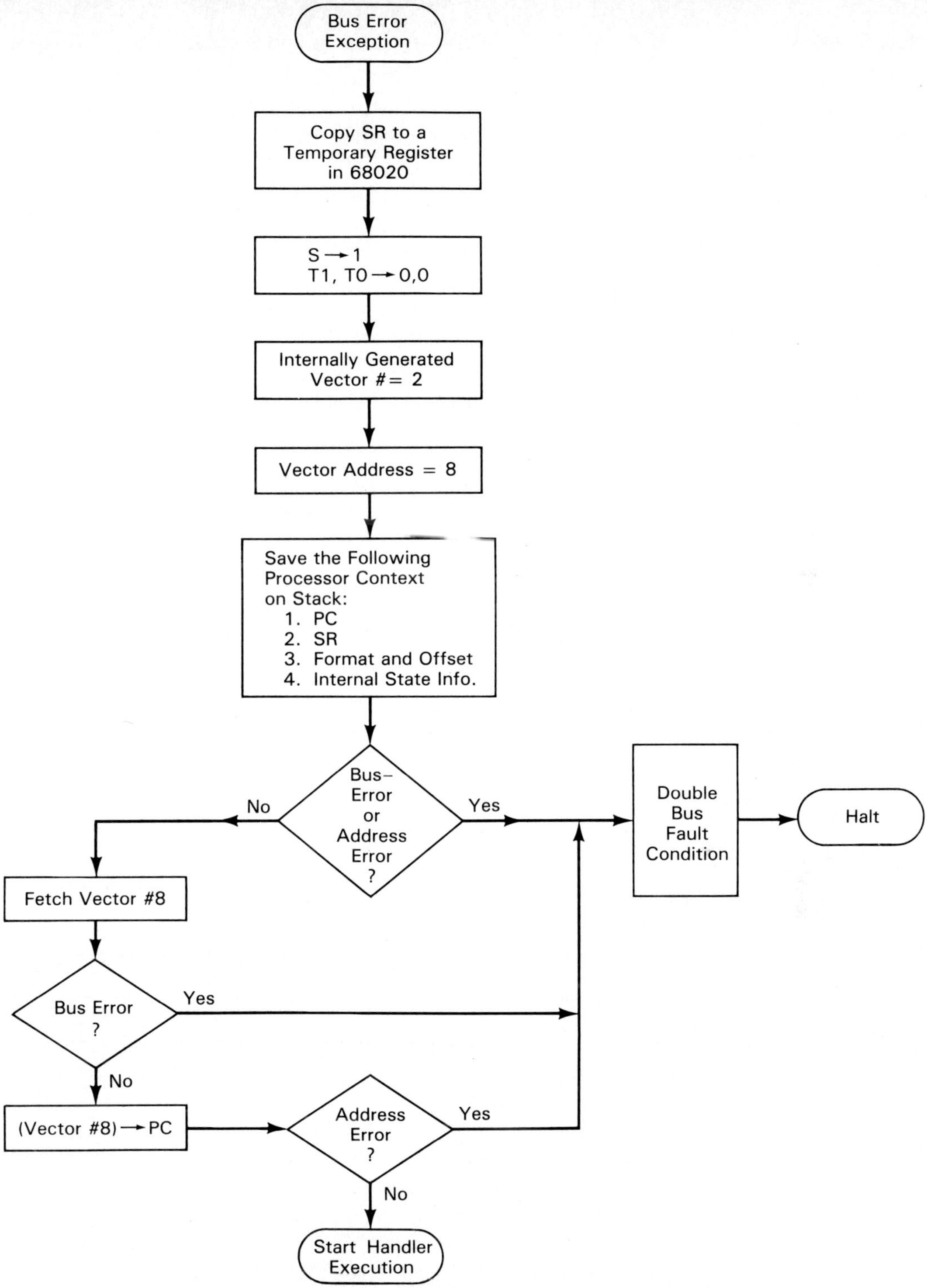

Figure 6-48 Bus-error Exception Processing Sequence.

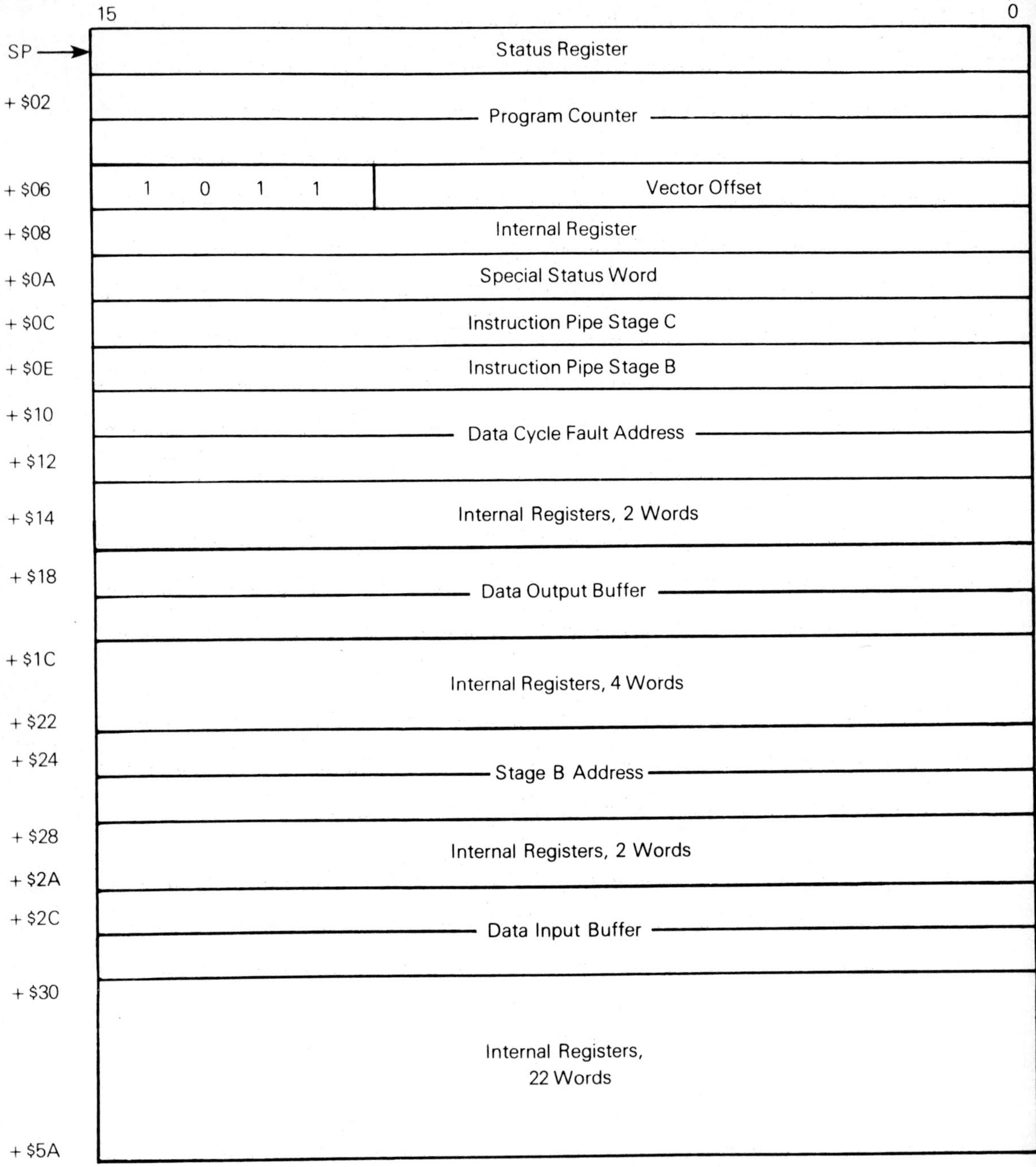

Figure 6-49 Long Bus-error Stack Frame Format.

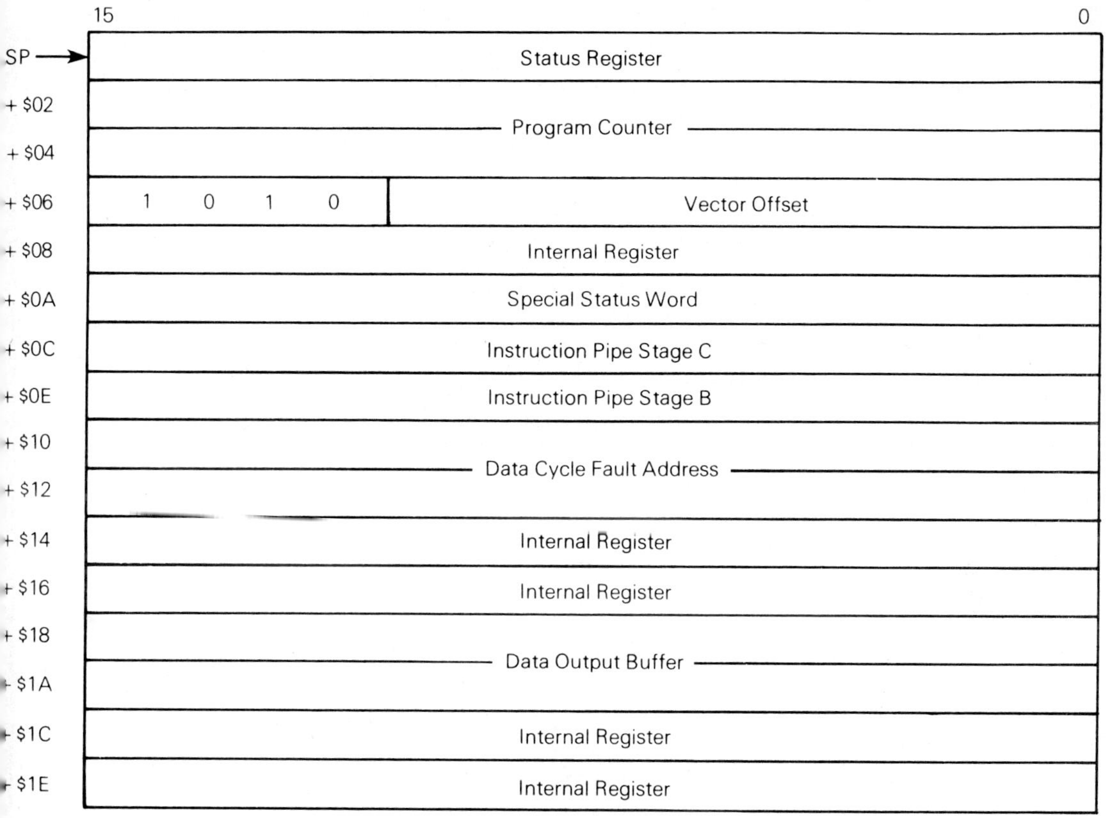

Figure 6-50 Short Bus-error Stack Frame Format.

For a virtual-machine implementation, software could emulate system functions by manipulating the *Special Status Word* (SSW) and other stack contents as illustrated in Figure 6-52. In this case, software clears the re-run bit DF and, thus, the faulted cycle will not re-run since it is emulated in software.

Example 6-10

Let us examine the long bus-error stack frame format. Figure 6-53 illustrates the long format using the instruction

```
MOVE.W  (A0),D0
```

where we set A0 so that a bus error occurs in attempting to fetch the source operand. Intentionally, we set A0 to point to an unoccupied address location thereby generating a BTO condition. Note the values of SP, PC, and A0 before we attempt to single step over the MOVE instruction.

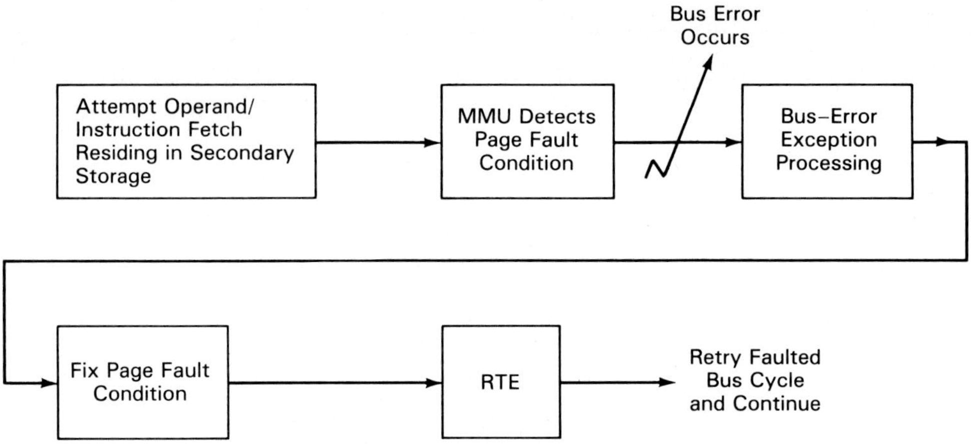

Figure 6-51 Virtual-memory Support.

Example 6-11

We ran Example 6-10 on Motorola's MVME 133 module. Figure 6-54 shows the display when bus error occurs. Attempting to access a nonexistent device causes a bus time out transferring control to the OS (MVME133B BUG, in this case) displaying all relevant information to help the programmer.

Interrupts. The interrupt request lines (IPL2∗, IPL1∗, IPL0∗) and priority level encoding is the same as previous members. If an interrupt request has a higher priority level than the mask level, the 68020 will initiate exception processing at the end of the current instruction (see Table 4-4).

Figure 6-55 illustrates the interrupt processing flow of the 68020. First, SR is copied into a temporary register so that it could later be saved on the stack. The mode is changed to supervisor level and trace modes are disabled. The interrupt mask is raised to the priority level of the interrupt being processed.

The 68020 supports both user- and auto-vectored interrupts. In a user-vectored interrupt, the interrupting peripheral asserts DSACK1/0∗ and provides the exception vector number. If the port size is byte, which is typically the case for an interrupter, the vector number is read from data lines D31-D24. In this case, only DSACK0∗ needs to be asserted. It is also possible that the interrupting peripheral responds with a port size of word or long-word even though only a byte is required. In this case, the 68020 reads the vector from D23-D16 and D7-D0 for long-word and word size ports, respectively.

If the interrupting peripheral is not able to provide a vector number, it asserts the *Auto Vector* (AVEC∗) signal of the 68020 to indicate auto vectoring.

The other possibility is that no device responds by asserting DSACK1/0∗ or AVEC∗. The external BTO circuit will then assert BERR∗ causing a spurious

15	14	13	12	11	10	9	8	7	6	5	4	3	2	1	0
FC	FB	RC	RB	0	0	0	DF	RM	RW	SIZ		0	FC2-FC0		

FC — Fault on Stage C of the Instruction Pipe
FB — Fault on Stage B of the Instruction Pipe
RC — Rerun Flag for Stage C of the Instruction Pipe*
RB — Rerun Flag for Stage B of the Instruction Pipe*
DF — Fault/Rerun Flag for Data Cycle*
RM — Read-Modify-Write on Data Cycle
RW — Read/Write for Data Cycle – 1 = Read, 0 = Write
SIZ — Size Code for Data Cycle
FC0-FC2 — Address Space for Data Cycle
*1 = Rerun Faulted Bus Cycle, or Run Pending Prefetch
0 = Do Not Rerun Bus Cycle

(a) SSW Format

```
IF DF = 1 THEN
  IF RW = 1 THEN
    DIB {44} = (FAULT ADDRESS {16})
  IF RW = 0 THEN
    (FAULT ADDRESS {16}) = DOB {24}
  DF = 0

IF FB = 1 THEN
  IF 6(SP) = 1010x--x THEN
    INSTRUCTION PIPE STAGE B = (PC + 4)
  ELSE
    INSTRUCTION PIPE STAGE B = (STAGE B ADDRESS {36})
  RB = 0

IF FC = 1 THEN
  IF 6(SP) = 1010x--x THEN
    INSTRUCTION PIPE STAGE C = (PC + 2)
  ELSE
    INSTRUCTION PIPE STAGE C = (STAGE B ADDRESS {36} - 2)
  RC = 0
RTE
```

(b) Recovery Using Software Emulation

Figure 6-52 Virtual-machine Support.

interrupt exception. This is possible due to either a hardware error or due to negation of the interrupt request just before it is acknowledged. Normally, it is required that any interrupt request be held until it is acknowledged.

We mentioned earlier that the 68020 can maintain two separate supervisor stacks, one of which is used only for interrupt related information. The two su-

Before		After	
PC	= $1000	PC	= $1006
SR	= $2700	SR	= $2700
USP	= $4000	USP	= $4000
MSP	= $5000	MSP	= $5000
ISP	= $6000	ISP	= $5FA4
VBR	= 0	VBR	= $0
A0	= $FFF000	A0	= $FFF000
D0	= $0	D0	= $0

Stack After Bus Error:

	15 0
ISP → (SR)	2700
(PC)	0000
	1000
(Format and offset)	B008
Internal register)	0EAC
(SSW)	0165
	4AFC
	4E71
	00FF
	F000
	00FF
	F000
	0000
	2D98
	3010
	3010
	0000
	1006
	0000
	1004
	0000
	1002
	0000
	0000
	⋮

Figure 6-53 Example of Long Bus-error Stack Frame Format.

pervisor level stacks (using ISP and MSP) makes it easy for the system programmer to work with stack data. How does this work? After a reset operation, the M-bit is cleared, and so, if the user choose not to use both supervisor stacks, this automatically allows full compatibility with earlier members. If the master mode is entered (M = 1), the 68020 will then maintain both interrupt and master stack separately.

In the master mode, during interrupt processing, transition is automatically made so that ISP is used for asychronous I/O data, and the RTE at the end of the interrupt handler restores the mode back to master status. To implement this mechanism, the 68020 stores two stack frames during interrupt processing when the M-bit is set. The first frame saved is the normal four-word stack frame shown in Figure 6-56. The second stack frame is necessary to save the state of the M-bit so that upon executing RTE, it will be restored (see Figure 6-57). Since this stack frame does not carry any other useful information, it is called a *throwaway stack frame*.

(a)

Figure 6-54 MVME133B BUG Display When Bus Error Occurs. (Courtesy of Motorola.)

```
Effective address: 00001002
Effective address: 00001000

Local Bus Time-out

Exception: Long Bus Error
Format/Vector=B008
SSW=0165 Fault Addr.=00FFF000 Data In=00000000 Data Out=00001002
PC   =00001000 SR   =2706=TR:OFF_S._7_..ZV.
USP  =00004000 MSP  =00005000 ISP* =00005FA4 VBR  =00000000
SFC  =0=XX     DFC  =0=XX     CACR =0=..     CAAR =00000000
D0   =00000000 D1   =00000000 D2   =00000000 D3   =00000000
D4   =00000000 D5   =00000000 D6   =00000000 D7   =00000000
A0   =00FFF000 A1   =00000000 A2   =00000000 A3   =00000000
A4   =00000000 A5   =00000000 A6   =00000000 A7   =00005FA4
00001000 7FFF                 DC.W       $7FFF
133Bug>md 1000:4;di
00001000 7FFF                 DC.W       $7FFF
00001002 4E71                 NOP
00001004 FFFF                 DC.W       $FFFF
00001006 FFFF                 DC.W       $FFFF
133Bug>
```

(b)

Figure 6-54 *(continued)*

Example 6-12

Let us take the instruction sequence

```
ADD.W   D2,D0    Interrupt processed after this instruction.
MOVE.W (A0),D1   This is the first instruction after ISR.
```

where we assume the following before an interrupt occurs:

1. ADD instruction resides at address $1000.
2. Interrupt request level = 4, auto vectored with vector offset equal to $070.
3. SR = $32XX (S = 1, M = 1, Mask = 2)

Figure 6-58 illustrate the stack frame contents before the first instruction of the interrupt handler is executed. Note that the same program counter and vector offset is saved on both stacks.

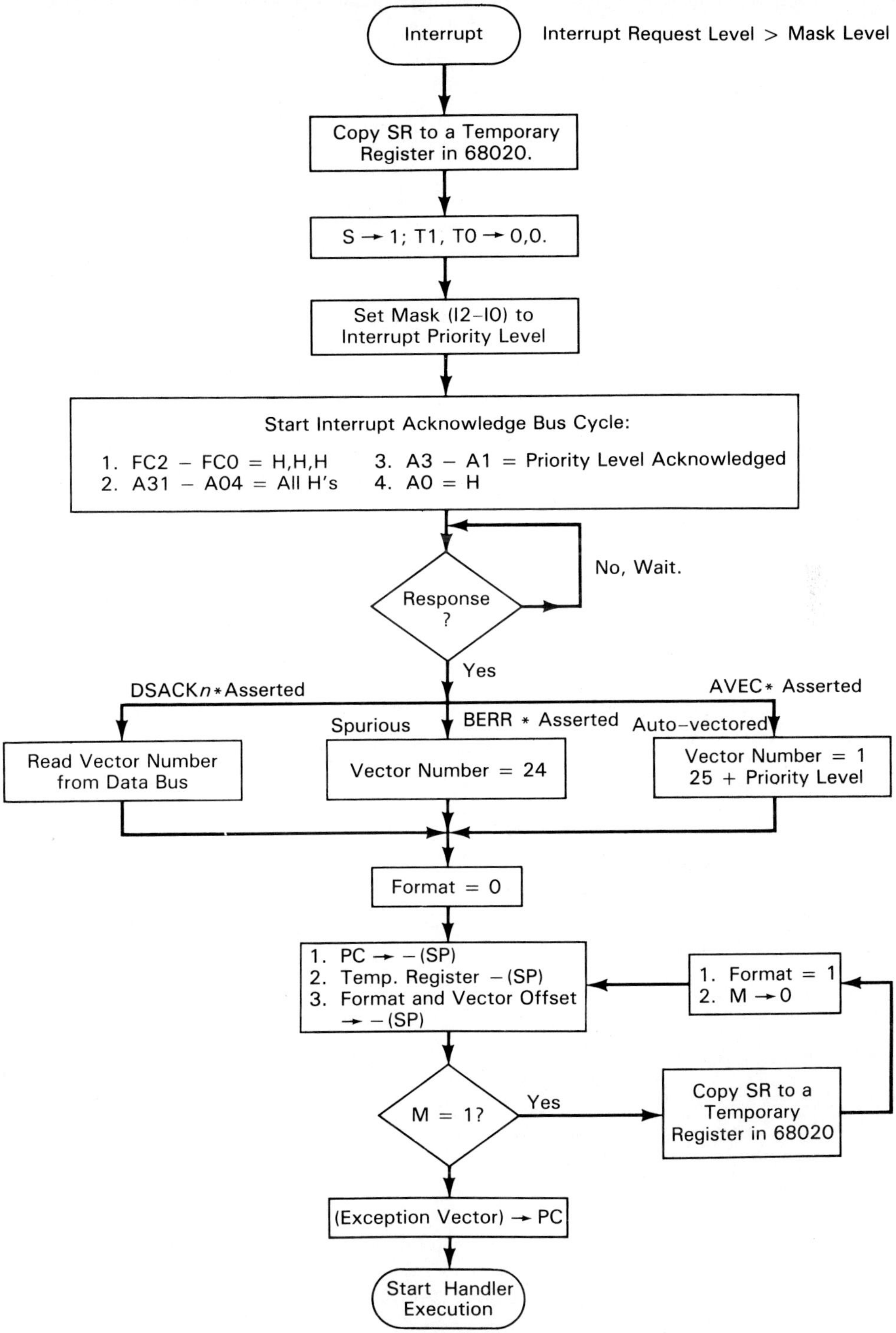

Figure 6-55 Illustration of Interrupt Processing Sequence.

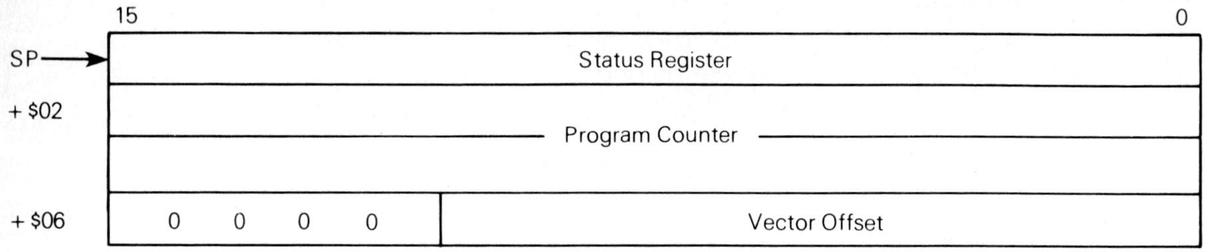

Figure 6-56 Normal Four-word Stack Frame Format.

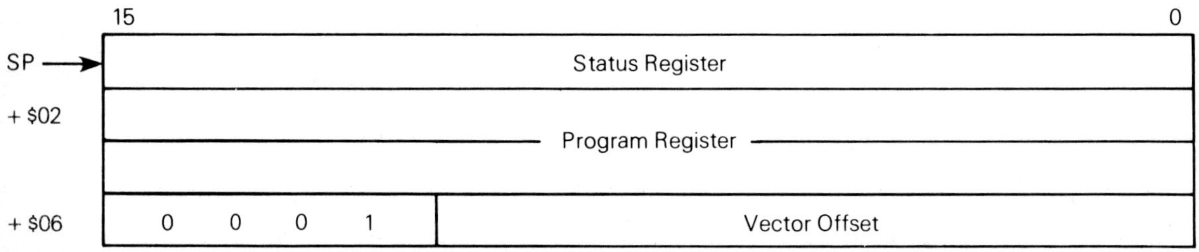

Figure 6-57 Throwaway Stack Frame Format.

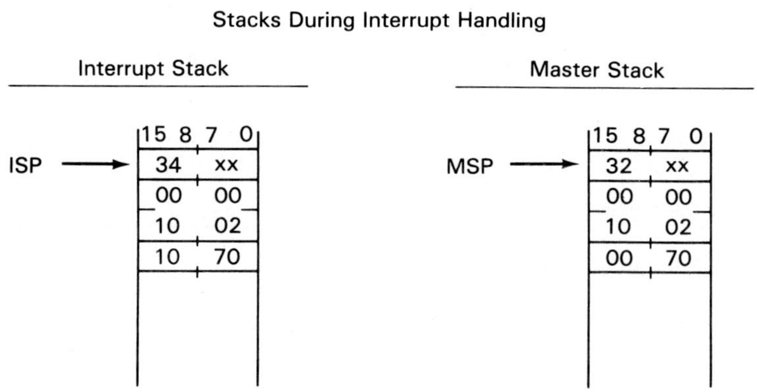

Figure 6-58 Example of Interrupt Stack Frame Formats.

6.8.3 Exception Vectors

The exception vector table of the 68020 has minor additions to that of the 6801X's vector assignments as shown in Table 6-20. New vector numbers are assigned for coprocessor exceptions, and some previous ones, such as TRAPV, are shared with the new exception types.

The vector table also indicates which numbers are generated internally and which numbers are obtained externally. An external device, an interrupter or coprocessor, normally has vector numbers within the ranges defined in the table. However, the 68020 has no range checking mechanism internally. So, it is possible to have an interrupter invoke the bus-error handler, for example. This is not a good practice and the programmer should be aware of it only for debugging purposes.

The vector base register (VBR) points to the beginning of the 1,024 byte exception vector table. In general, we have

$$\text{Vector Offset} = 4 * \text{Vector Number}$$

$$\text{Exception Handler Address} = (\text{VBR} + \text{Vector Offset})$$

where, as usual, ( ) indicates "the contents of" (see Figure 5-2). The exception handler address always points to a 32-bit PC value.

Note that the reset vector is always fetched from address zero since VBR is zero following a reset operation. The reset exception is a special case also because it requires two vectors, the initial ISP and initial PC values. Moreover, the reset vector resides in the supervisor program space, whereas all other vectors reside in supervisor data space.

6.8.4 Exception Grouping and Priorities

When multiple exceptions occur simultaneously, the 68020 uses a priority relation to determine which exception is processed first. The exception priorities are listed in Table 6-21 in decreasing order of priority where group 0 has the highest priority and group 4.2 has the lowest priority.

If there are two simultaneous exceptions, A and B (where A has higher priority), the 68020 first goes through the exception processing sequence of A. For example, if A is a TRAP exception, then the 68020 copies SR to an internal temporary register, sets the S-bit, disables the trace mode, and saves current PC and SR on stack. If B is an interrupt, then before the first instruction of the trap handler is executed, the 68020 starts the processing of the interrupt exception. In other words, the interrupt handler is executed first, even though TRAP has a higher priority. In general, this is true. That is, the handler of lowest priority is executed first.

Table 6-22 shows the recognition times of exceptions. These times indicate

TABLE 6-20 EXCEPTION VECTOR ASSIGNMENTS

Vector #	Source of Vector #	Vector Offset (Hex)	Assignment
0 (1)	Internal	0 4	Reset: Initial ISP Reset: Initial PC
2	Internal	8	Bus Error
3	Internal	C	Address Error
4	Internal	10	Illegal Instruction
5	Internal	14	Zero Divide
6	Internal	18	CHK, CHK2 Instruction
7	Internal	1C	TRAPV, ⟨*cp*⟩TRAP⟨*cc*⟩, TRAP⟨*cc*⟩
8	Internal	20	Privilege Violation
9	Internal	24	Trace
10	Internal	28	Line 1010 Emulator
11	Internal	2C	Line 1111 Emulator
12		30–33	(Unassigned, Reserved)
13	Internal	34	Coprocessor Protocol Violation
14	Internal	38	Format Error
15	External	3C	Uninitialized Interrupt Vector
16–23		40–5C	(Unassigned, Reserved)
24	Internal	60	Spurious Interrupt
25	Internal	64	Level 1 Interrupt Autovector
26	Internal	68	Level 2 Interrupt Autovector
27	Internal	6C	Level 3 Interrupt Autovector
28	Internal	70	Level 4 Interrupt Autovector
29	Internal	74	Level 5 Interrupt Autovector
30	Internal	78	Level 6 Interrupt Autovector
31	Internal	7C	Level 7 Interrupt Autovector
32–47	Internal	80–BC	Trap Instruction Vectors (16)
48	Coprocessor	C0	FPCP Branch or Set on Unordered Condition.
49	Coprocessor	C4	FPCP Inexact Result

TABLE 6-20 EXCEPTION VECTOR ASSIGNMENTS (*continued*)

Vector #	Source of Vector #	Vector Offset (Hex)	Assignment
50	Coprocessor	C8	FPCP Divide by Zero.
51	Coprocessor	CC	FPCP Underflow.
52	Coprocessor	D0	FPCP Operand Error.
53	Coprocessor	D4	FPCP Overflow.
54	Coprocessor	D8	FPCP Signalling NAN.
55		DC	(Unassigned, Reserved)
56	Coprocessor	E0	PMMU Configuration.
57	Coprocessor	E4	PMMU Illegal Operation.
58	Coprocessor	E8	PMMU Access Level Violation.
59–63		EC–FC	(Unassigned, Reserved)
64–255	External	100–3FC	User Interrupt Vectors (192)

the earliest time when processing an exception may start. For example, a pending interrupt can only be processed at the end of the current instruction. If the current instruction happens to be MOVEM, it will be a few bus cycles before it is processed. This delay between an interrupt request and an acknowledgment of the request is called *interrupt latency*.

TABLE 6-21 EXCEPTION PRIORITIES

Group	Priority	Exception
0	0	Reset
1	1.0 1.1	Address Error Bus Error
2	2.0	BKPT, CALLM, CHK, CHK2, Divide by Zero, RTE, RTM, TRAP, TRAPV, TRAP⟨*cc*⟩, ⟨*cp*⟩TRAP⟨*cc*⟩, ⟨*cp*⟩Mid-instruction, ⟨*cp*⟩Protocol Violation.
3	3.0	Illegal Instruction, Line A and F, Privilege Violation, ⟨*cp*⟩Pre-instruction
4	4.0 4.1 4.2	⟨*cp*⟩Post-instruction Trace Interrupts

TABLE 6-22 RECOGNITION TIMES OF EXCEPTIONS

Recognition Time	Exception
End of Clock Cycle	Reset
End of Bus Cycle	Address Error, Bus Error
Before the Beginning of Next Instruction	Illegal Instruction Privilege Violation
End of an Instruction Cycle	Trace Exception Interrupts
Within an Instruction Cycle	TRAP, TRAP⟨*cc*⟩, TRAPV, ⟨*cp*⟩TRAP⟨*cc*⟩, CHK, CHK2, Divide by Zero, Format Error.

6.8.5 Exception Stack Frames and the RTE Instruction

The general stack frame format is the same as used by the 6801X (see Figure 5-19). The vector offset specifies the relative address within the exception vector table. The reason for the vector offset is to indicate the source of exception. The format number indicates the type of stack frame that is used.

We have already seen stack frame formats $0, $1, $A, and $B. The other two stack frame formats the 68020 uses are a six-word stack frame that is used by instruction exceptions and a coprocessor mid-instruction exception stack frame as shown in Figure 6-59. Table 6-23 shows the usage of stack frame formats by different exception types. Note that depending upon the exception, the saved PC may be pointing to different instructions.

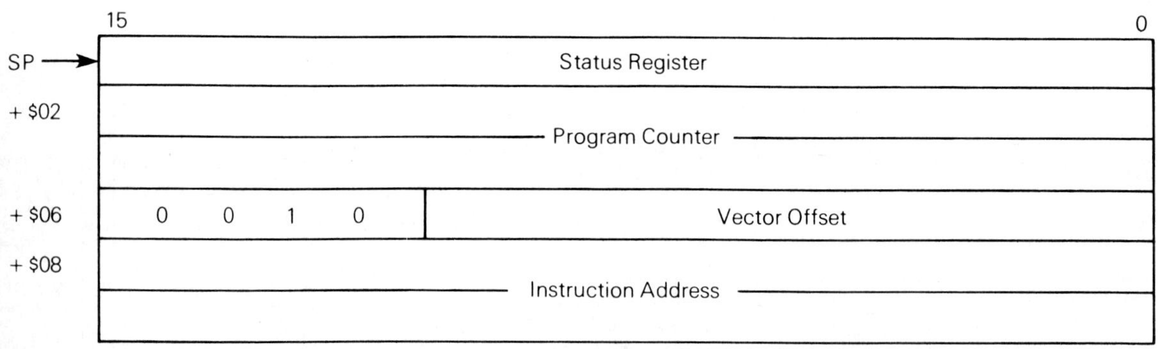

(a) Format $2: Normal Six-word Stack Frame.

Figure 6-59 Formats $2 and $9 Stack Frame Formats.

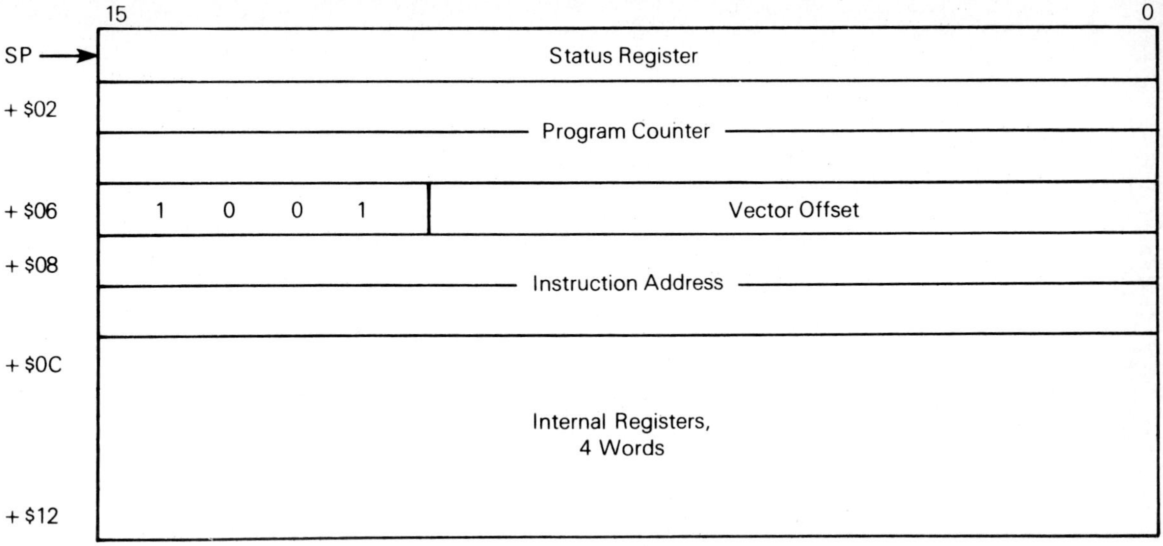

(b) Format $9: Coprocessor Mid-instruction Stack Frame.

Figure 6-59 *(continued)*

TABLE 6-23 STACK FRAME USAGE

Exception	Stack Frame	Format Number	Stack PC Points to
Reset	None	—	—
Bus Error	Short (16)	A	Next Instruction
	Long (46)	B	Present Instruction[2]
Address Error	Short (16)	A	Next Instruction
	Long (46)	B	Present Instruction[2]
Illegal Instruction	Normal (4)	0	Illegal Instruction
Zero Divide	Normal (6)	2	Next Instruction
CHK, CHK2	Normal (6)	2	Next Instruction
⟨*cp*⟩TRAP⟨*cc*⟩, TRAP⟨*cc*⟩, TRAPV	Normal (6)	2	Next Instruction
Privilege Violation	Normal (4)	0	Present Instruction[1]
Trace	Normal (6)	2	Next Instruction
Line 1010 Emulator	Normal (4)	0	A-Line Instruction
Line 1111 Emulator	Normal (4)	0	F-Line Instruction
Protocol Violation	Mid-instruction (10)	9	Next Word of Instruction Stream
Format Error	Normal (4)	0	Detecting Instruction
Interrupts	Normal (4)	0	Next Instruction
Interrupts (Master State)	Throwaway (4)	1	Next Instruction
TRAP #*n*	Normal (4)	0	Next Instruction
Pre-instruction	Normal (4)	0	Present Instruction
Mid-instruction	Mid-instruction (10)	9	Next Word of Instruction Stream
Post-instruction	Normal (6)	2	Next Instruction

[1] First word of instruction that caused privilege violation.
[2] Address of instruction in execution when fault occurred. This may not be the instruction that caused the faulted bus cycle.

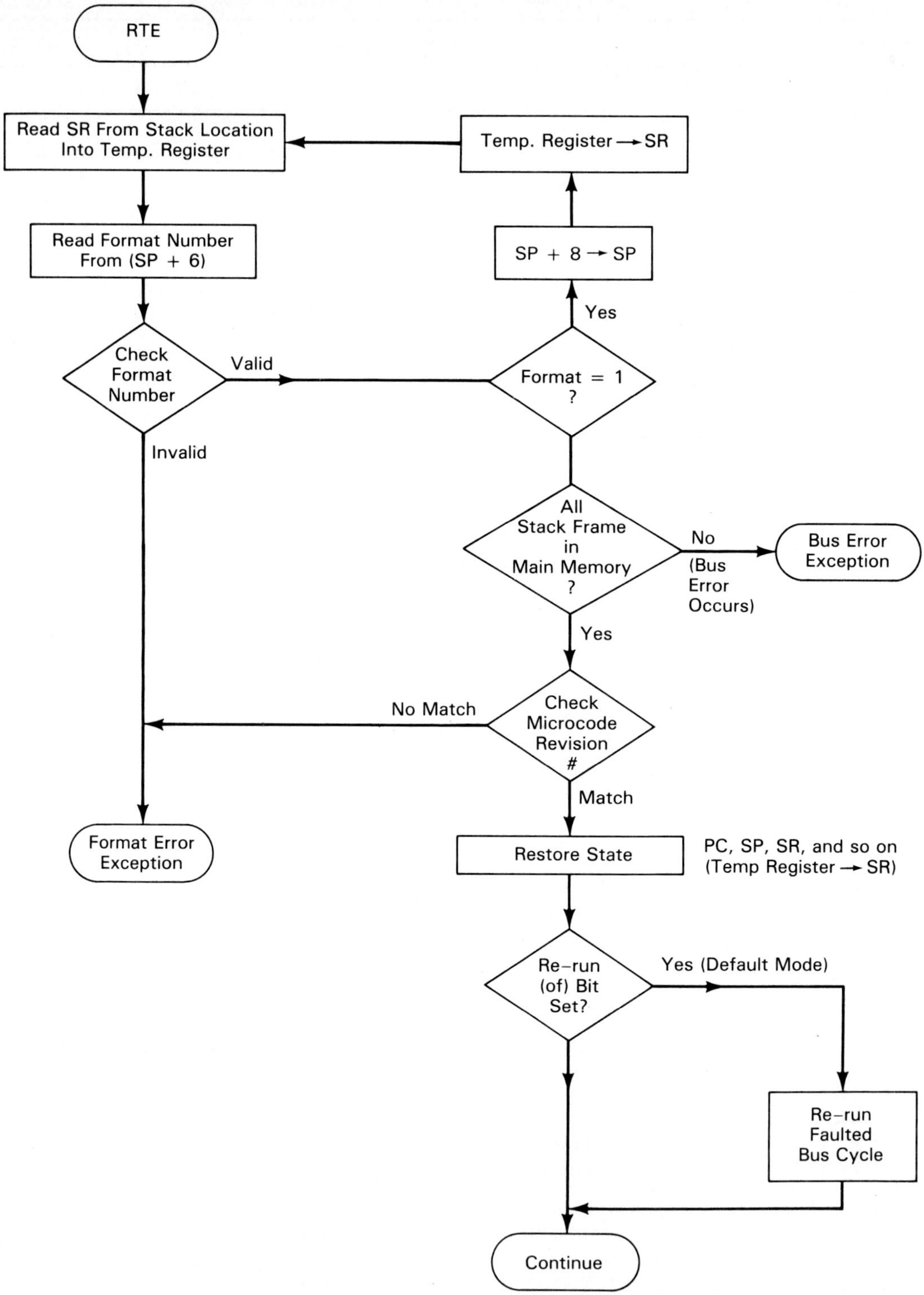

Figure 6-60 Operation of the RTE Instruction.

The RTE instruction is enhanced to handle the new stack frame formats, as well as the new master stack as illustrated in Figure 6-60. It is otherwise very similar to the RTE of the 6801X. RTE first verifies that the format number is a valid one and that all of the stack frame resides in main memory. The latter is necessary to support virtual-memory systems so that if part of the stack happens to be on secondary storage, the OS can handle this situation before re-running the faulted instruction. The microcode revision number is also checked to see if it matches the revision number of the particular 68020. This is necessary in a multiprocessor system using two or more 68020s with different microcode versions. Although such a microcode difference is transparent to the user it is possible that the saved processor state information is different.

In the case of a read-modify-write cycle, RTE will re-run the entire bus cycle to maintain the integrity of data. This ensures that semaphores are handled correctly and that no collisions occur in a multiprocessor system.

6.9 68030 ENHANCEMENTS

As we discussed in Chapter 2, the 68030 is simply a subset of the 68851 PMMU and the 68020 merged on a single chip. A data cache is added and a dual internal bus structure is used, as shown in Figure 6-61, to approximately double the aggregate bus throughput with respect to the 68020. The dual bus structure allows

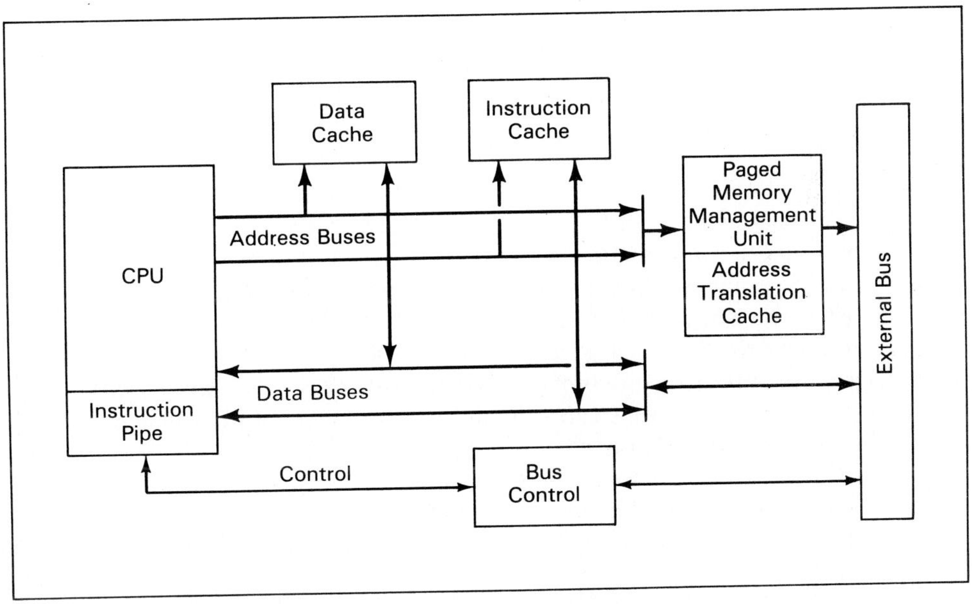

Figure 6-61 Block Diagram of the 68030 Architecture.

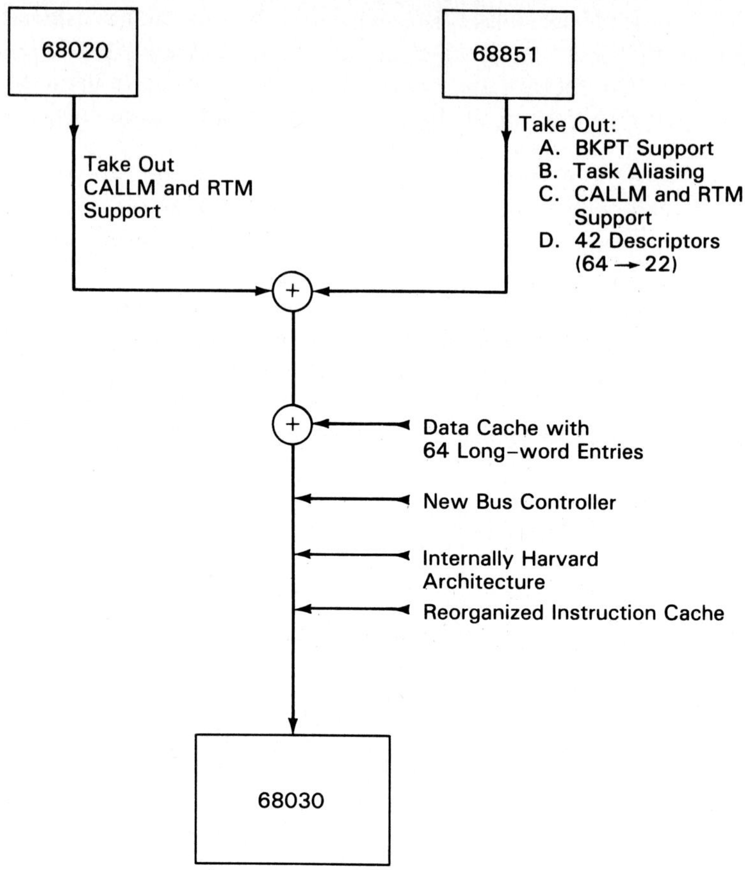

Figure 6-62 68030 Enhancements and Differences.

parallel access to instructions and data. Such a separate bus structure for data and instructions eliminates bottlenecks since it eliminates any collisions or contentions that would arise on a single bus for concurrent instruction and operand accesses. This dual bus architecture that used to be used in mainframe computers is called the *Harvard style architecture* due to its origin. The 68030 has Harvard architecture only on-chip since there is still a single external bus.

Figure 6-62 illustrates the differences between the 68020 and the 68030. The CALLM and RTM instruction pair of the 68020 is taken out. Similarly, the PMMU support for breakpoint, task aliasing, and CALLM-RTM is deleted. The task aliasing is removed because the number of descriptions is decreased from 64 to 22, a number too small for multiple task descriptors to co-reside in the ATC. Therefore, the 68030 instruction set and addressing modes are the same as the 68020 minus CALLM-RTM and plus a subset of PMMU's privileged instructions. The user-programming model remains unchanged.

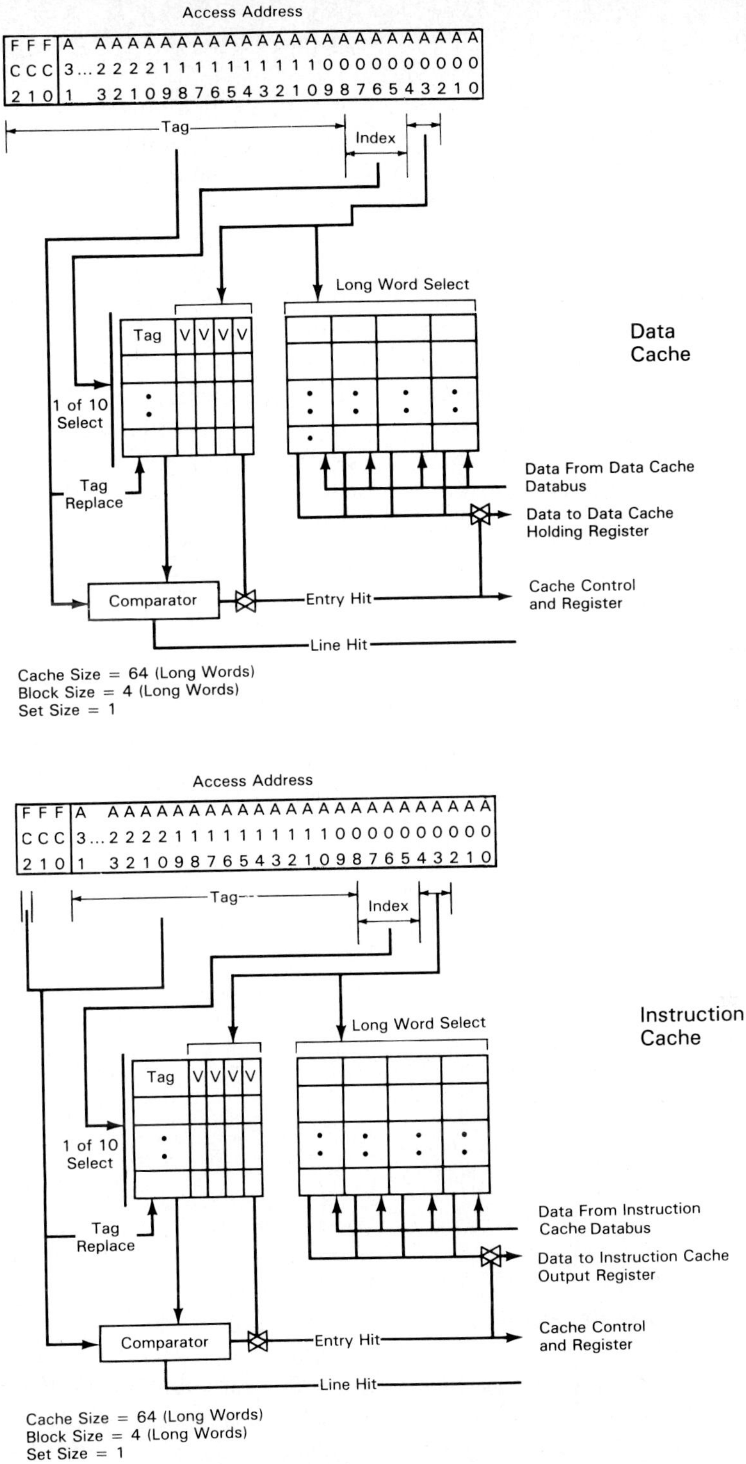

Figure 6-63 68030 Instruction and Data Caches.

A data cache with 64 long-word entries in addition to a similarly configured instruction cache further enhances performance and reduces bus activity as compared to the 68020. Both are logical caches, and are organized as four long-words per entry as shown in Figure 6-63. If a cache hit occurs during an operand write cycle, both the data cache entry and external memory are updated with new data. This eliminates any cache coherency or stale data problems. Such a data cache implementation is said to feature a *write-through* mechanism. Its disadvantage is that every write requires a main memory access time in case of a cache miss. An alternate approach for data cache is *write-back* or *copy-back* mechanisms which perform writes to cache only, and on task switch or interrupt writes back the changed cache locations to main memory. The 68030 features a write-through data cache because its implementation is simpler and does not have any complications in a multiprocessor system. The 68030 caches has one clock cycle access time versus the two clock cycle time of the 68020.

FURTHER READING

1. MacGregor, Doug (Motorola), and Rubinstein, Jon (Hewlett-Packard). "A Performance Analysis of MC68020-based Systems," *IEEE Micro*, December 1985, pp. 50–70.
2. Beims, Bob (Motorola). "The MC68020 32-Bit MPU: Opening New Application Doors," *Motorola Application Note AR232*, May 1986.
3. Cooper, Thayne C. et al., (Sperry). "A Benchmark Comparison of 32-bit Microprocessors," *IEEE Micro*, August 1986, pp. 53–58. Also available as *Motorola Application Note AR242*.
4. Beims, Bob (Motorola). "Multiprocessing Capabilities of MC68020 32-bit Microprocessor," *Motorola Application Note AR220*, May 1986.
5. Beims, Bob (Motorola). "The MC68020 and System V/68," *Motorola Application Note AR219*, May 1986.
6. Macgregor, Doug, Mothersole, Dave and Moyer, Bill (Motorola). "The Motorola MC68020," *IEEE Micro*, August 1984, pp. 101–118. Also available as *Motorola Application Note AR217*.
7. *Using the MC68020 as a Dedicated DMA Controller, A Motorola Design Concept Document*, DC003/D, September 1987.

EXERCISES

Internal Architecture

1. How does the internal architecture of the 68020 differ from the 68000? List all new architectural features.

2. What is the length of the 68020 instruction pipeline? When the instruction execution flow is changed, what happens to the instructions that are already in the pipeline?

3. What is the reason for three arithmetic units within the execution unit?
4. What is a barrel shifter?
5. What are the two architectural features of the 68020 that contributes most to its performance increase over the 68000?

Memory Organization

6. What are the new data types supported by the 68020?
7. Indicate whether the operand stored by the following instructions are aligned or misaligned.
   a) `MOVE.W D0,$A0002`
   b) `MOVE.W D0,$1001`
   c) `MOVE.L D0,$A0002`
   d) `MOVE.L D0,$F000C`
   e) `MOVE.B D0,$1001`
   f) `MOVE.B D0,-(SP)`

   Note: The 68020 handles the stack the same as the 68000.
8. What are the restrictions, if any, on the operand alignment in the 68020?
9. What are the differences between operand and instruction fetches?
10. Draw a map of memory showing the bit field defined as follows:

    Bit Field = $4A9

    Width = 12

    Offset = 17

    Base Address = $1000
11. What are the allowed ranges for offset and width parameters of a bit field?
12. What are the differences in the bus interface of the 68020 with respect to the 68000? What are the equivalent signals for the 68000's LDS* and UDS*?
13. Answer the following questions regarding dynamic bus sizing.
    a) Does it apply to both instruction and operand fetches?
    b) How does the 68020 determine the port size during a bus cycle?
    c) Which data lines must be connected to an 8-bit peripheral?
    d) Which data lines must be connected to a 16-bit peripheral?
14. Show the details of bus cycles during the operand fetches of instruction

```
MOVE.L    #$11223344,$F00003
```

    for port sizes of 8, 16 and 32 bits. Use format of Example 6-1.
15. How many bus cycles are required for an instruction prefetch operation? Consider byte, word, and long-word port sizes for long-word and odd word alignment cases.
16. Assume SR = $5500. What mode is the processor in? Which stack pointer is active? Which interrupt levels will the processor respond to?

Operand Addressing Modes

17. Identify the following addressing modes:
    a) `(A2)+`
    b) `($A,A0)`
    c) `($49FFFE,A0)`
    d) `($E0000,A0,D0.L*4)`
    e) `([D0])`
    f) `([$400000])`
    g) `(D0)`
    h) `([$400000],D0)`
    i) `($F00000,PC)`
    j) `(PC)`
    k) `(PC,D0.L*2)`
    l) `([-80,PC,D2.W],$2000)`
18. What is the effective address (EA) for source and destination operands of the following instructions? Assume

    A0 = \$E0000

    D0[15:0] = \$800

    (\$E2400) = \$10FFAB00

    TST instruction is located at \$1000.

    a) `MOVE.L (-100,A0, D0.W*4),D1`
    b) `MOVE.W ($E000,D0.W*2),D1`
    c) `SUB.L ([$400,A0,D0.W*4]),D1`
    d) `TST.B ($400,PC)`
    e) `TST.B ([$D23FE,PC],3)`
19. What is difference between (*d*16, PC) and (*d*16, ZPC)? How is *d*16 coded in each case?

Instruction Set

20. Is the 68020 object code compatible with earlier members of the family? Please explain.
21. Figure out the object code of instruction

```
MOVE.W     ([$4000,A0,D0.W*2],$30),D0
```

22. a) What is the difference between CMP2 and CHK2 instructions?
    b) How does CMP2 distinquishes between signed and unsigned arithmetic?
23. What are the possible error conditions that may arise during a multiply or divide instruction. Which condition code bit is affected? How does destination get affected in case of an error condition?
24. What are the advantages and disadvantages of CALLM-RTM pair with respect to JSR-RTS?

25. Show the memory map displaying the destination after the following instruction executed.

```
BFSET   $1000{-22:4}
```

26. Regarding Example 6-7, answer the following:
   a) What is the resultant value in D0 if all 16 long-words are zero?
   b) What is the resultant D0 if the second long-word is $00100000?

27. Indicate whether SFC and/or DFC is used for the following instructions:
   a) `MOVES.L <ea>,D0`
   b) `MOVES.L D0,-<ea>`

28. Write a program to convert a string of *N* packed BCD digits to a ASCII string. Assume the following:

A0 → Last byte of packed BCDs.

A1 → Last byte of ASCII string destination.

D0 = Loop count.

29. What happens during the execution of a BKPT instruction if there is no external breakpoint logic?

30. What is the possible application of TRAPT instruction?

31. Suppose you want to read the parameter of TRAP.W #⟨*n*⟩ instruction within a trap handler routine. Specify a MOVE instruction to do this (in one instruction)?

32. Write a small program that deletes the first entry in a linked list. Consider a multitasking/multiprocessor environment, and also the case when list is empty.

Instruction Cache and Timing

33. List the advantages that the 68020 cache provides.

34. What is the total number of memory bits required by the on-chip cache implementation?

35. Answer the following questions regarding the 68020 cache as true or false. If false, please explain why.
   a) To be able to utilize cache, consecutive instructions within a 128 word size must reside within the cache.
   b) Cache is implemented using a fully-associative memory (i.e., all tags are compared in parallel).
   c) The best-case external bus-cycle timing of the 68020 is three clock cycles.
   d) The cache access time is one clock cycle.
   e) Cache is enabled after a reset operation.
   f) To be able to use cache, freeze (F) bit has to be continually manipulated by software.
   g) An external bus cycle is started only if there is cache miss.

36. Discuss complications that would arise if an on-chip data cache were implemented. Consider the multiprocessing case.

37. Estimate the execution time to calculate the sine of an angle as defined in Example 3-15. Consider best, cache, and worst-case timings including call and return overhead. How much speed improvement could be gained if it were changed to be an in-line routine using a macro?
38. What is the affect of a NOP instruction on internal parallelism?
39. Assume an interrupter requires a write operation to clear an interrupt condition. Describe what problem may occur in the following instruction sequence:

```
IRQ_HNDLR  .                                  Interrupt Handler
           .
           .
           MOVE.B   #CLRIRQ,CTLREG           Clear Interrupt.
           ANDI     #$F8FF,SR                Clear interrupt mask level.
           .
           .
           .
           RTE
```

Use a NOP instruction to fix the above program.

Exception Processing

40. What is the active stack after a reset exception?
41. List the new exception types of the 68020.
42. List the enhanced exception types in the 68020.
43. List the conditions that would cause a double bus fault.
44. Assume VBR is $1000 before a system reset (i.e., reset exception). What is the address from which the initial ISP and PC values are fetched?
45. Indicate what exception occurs in the following cases:
    a) Bus-time-out occurs in attempting to access a nonexistent device.
    b) Format value is found to be invalid when RTE is executing.
    c) During interrupt acknowledge no device responds.
    d) SR = $F700
    e) BRA $200FB
    f) Microcode revision numbers do not match when RTE is executing.
    g) BKPT #0
    h) TRAPEQ instruction.
    i) VBR is set to $A000D.
46. Repeat Example 6-12 for SR = $22XX and SR = $02XX.

7

Coprocessor Support

While a general-purpose 32-bit microprocessor like the 68020 provides an adequate level of performance, this may not be enough for some applications. For example, floating-point arithmetic, in the absence of special-purpose hardware, is typically performed using large and time-consuming software packages. Similarly, other special applications such as graphics or *Digital Signal Processing* (DSP) may also require a level of performance that cannot be met alone by a general-purpose microprocessor. That is where a companion of the microprocessor, termed as *coprocessor*[1], comes into the picture. Unlike the microprocessor, a coprocessor is a special-purpose hardware device that is optimized to perform one particular task, such as floating-point calculations. Using a modular approach with one or more coprocessors, a system designer can tailor the functionality and performance level to match the requirements of a particular application.

The 68020 is the first processor in the 68000 family to provide inherent support for coprocessors. There are currently three coprocessor chips designed by Motorola for the 68000 family and that can be directly interfaced to the 68020 and later members of the family. The first one introduced was the *68881 Floating-Point Coprocessor* (FPCP). The 68881 is a VLSI implementation of the IEEE standard for *Binary Floating-Point Arithmetic* (P754). The second one is the paged MMU, the 68851 (PMMU) that was introduced in 1986. The PMMU supports address translation and virtual memory management, and has special coprocessor instructions to implement paging algorithms and access protection. Figure 7-1

[1] One of the earlier coprocessors is Intel's 8087 floating-point coprocessor for the Intel 8086 Microprocessor.

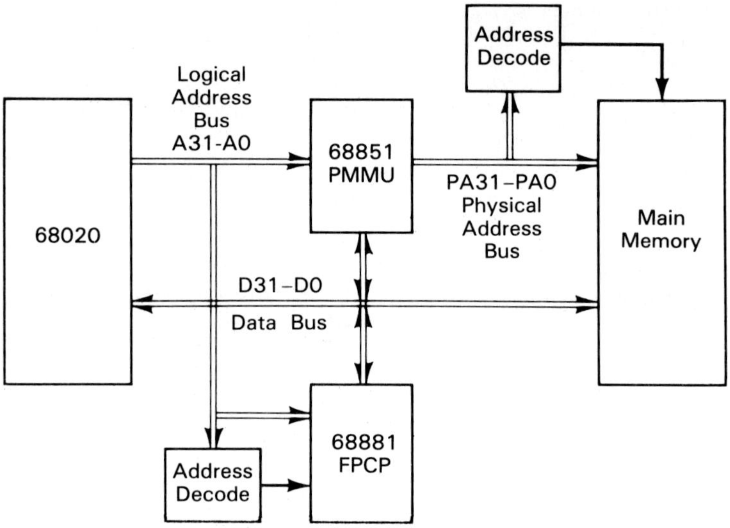

Figure 7-1 A 68020 System With FPCP and PMMU Coprocessors.

shows the block diagram of a 68020 system using both FPCP and PMMU coprocessors. The third coprocessor, the 68882, is an enhanced version of the first FPCP. It is optimized to provide approximately 50 percent more performance, but its programmer's model and instruction set are the same as the 68881.

7.1 COPROCESSOR INTERFACE

The coprocessor interface designed by Motorola defines the hardware interface and communication protocol between the main processor (the 68020 or later members) and the coprocessors in the system. The communication protocol that is used to transfer commands and data are implemented at the microcode level on both the main processor and on each coprocessor, and thus, is completely transparent to the programmer. A programmer only needs to know the programmer's model and instruction set of a given coprocessor to utilize its functions. In other words, from programmer's point of view, a coprocessor makes it look as if the programmer's model is extended and additional instructions and processing capability are available on the main processor.

We will next discuss the architecture of the 68000 family coprocessor interface, before our discussion of the FPCP and PMMU in the following sections. For applications that require implementation of a user-specific coprocessor, further details are necessary that are discussed in the 68020 user manual.

7.1.1 Hardware Interface

The coprocessor interface requires no special signal lines as shown in Figure 7-2. Only a subset of the standard bus-interface signals are used. Coprocessors are mapped in the CPU-space (i.e., FC1-FC0 = HHH), and standard CPU-space read and write cycles are used to transfer commands and data between the main and coprocessors (see Figure 7-3). As we discussed earlier, CPU-space cycles are for special processor related functions. The 68020 supports four types of CPU-space cycles that consist of acknowledgment of an interrupt or breakpoint, access level control using the CALLM instruction, and communication with a coprocessor. The address lines A19 through A16 determine the type of CPU-space, and for coprocessor communications, the lines A15 through A13 contains the coprocessor

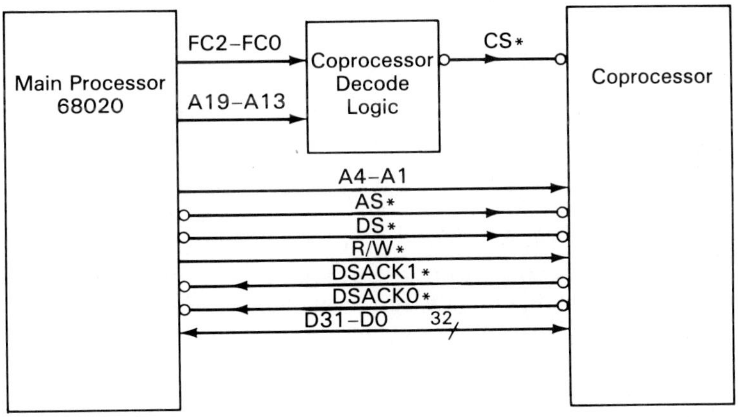

Figure 7-2 Coprocessor Interface Signals.

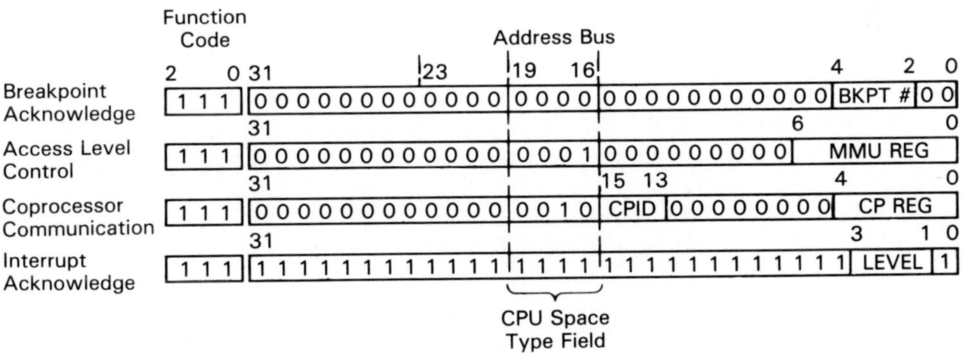

Figure 7-3 CPU Space Cycle Types.

identification code which selects one of the eight possible coprocessors in the system. This leaves 8 Kbytes of addressing range reserved for each coprocessor, but actually, only the first 32 bytes of this range are used by the communication protocol. Since the interactions between the main processor and a coprocessor are handled at the hardware level, these interface registers are not visible to the programmer.

The coprocessor identification codes are allocated as shown in Table 7-1. As we are going to see later, this 3-bit identification code is encoded as part of a coprocessor instruction word. The Motorola assembler will by default use the codes 0 and 1 for PMMU and FPCP, respectively.

7.1.2 Coprocessor Instructions

The coprocessor instructions are implemented by using the line-F operation words, with object code format as shown in Figure 7-4. A line-F operation word contains ones in bit positions 15 through 12, as we stated earlier. The remaining bits of the operation word contains the coprocessor identification and the type of coprocessor operation to be performed. This operation word may be followed by one or more extension words that contains additional information for the execution of a coprocessor instruction. For example, an effective address specification may require extension words.

The coprocessor architecture of the 68000 family defines seven generic instruction types that may be functionally divided into three categories: coprocessor defined, conditional, and system control, as shown in Table 7-2. The "⟨*cp*⟩" at the beginning of an instruction selects the desired coprocessor. For example, all FPCP and PMMU instruction mnemonics used by Motorola assembler start with "F" and "P", respectively. Of course, the specific syntax depends on the particular assembler used.

The "⟨*cpgen*⟩" instruction is used to implement a general group of instructions for data movement and processing for a given coprocessor. For example, FMOVE and FSIN are two floating-point instructions of FPCP that are implemented using the general cpgen instruction as illustrated in Figure 7-5.

The conditional coprocessor instructions are similar to their counterparts in the 68000 family instruction set. The condition codes (⟨*cc*⟩), however, are defined

TABLE 7-1 COPROCESSOR IDENTIFICATION CODES

Identification Code	Coprocessor
0	68851 PMMU
1	68881 or 68882 FPCP
2–5	Reserved for Motorola
6–7	Reserved for User Designs

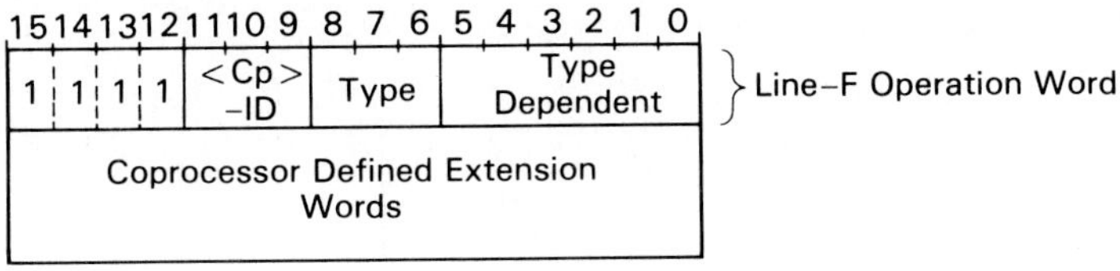

Figure 7-4 Object Code Format of Coprocessor Instructions.

by the coprocessor and have no meaning to the main processor. During execution, a code is passed to the coprocessor to select and evaluate one of the condition codes, and then action is taken based on the binary result (true or false) returned by the coprocessor.

The system control instructions, ⟨*cp*⟩SAVE and ⟨*cp*⟩RESTORE, are used to save and restore the internal state of a coprocessor. As we shall discuss in the next section, an exception handler must be enveloped by ⟨*cp*⟩SAVE and ⟨*cp*⟩RESTORE pair for the enhanced FPCP 68882 coprocessor. Also, these instructions are necessary to implement instruction-continuation for a coprocessor instruction in a virtual-memory system.

7.1.3 Concurrency of Execution

The coprocessor interface supports concurrency of execution for the main processor and its coprocessors. If a coprocessor instruction affects only a destination

TABLE 7-2 GENERIC COPROCESSOR INSTRUCTIONS

Category	Instruction(s)	Syntax	Operation
Coprocessor Specific	⟨*cpgen*⟩	(Coprocessor defined)	Defines a set of operations
Conditional	⟨*cp*⟩B⟨*cc*⟩	`<cp>B<cc>.<s> <label>`	If ⟨*cc*⟩ is true: PC + ⟨*disp*⟩ → PC
	⟨*cp*⟩DB⟨*cc*⟩	`<cp>DB<cc> <label>,Dn`	Same as DB⟨*cc*⟩ except uses coprocessor defined condition codes.
	⟨*cp*⟩S⟨*cc*⟩	`<cp>S<cc> <ea>`	Same as S⟨*cc*⟩ except uses coprocessor defined condition codes.
	⟨*cp*⟩TRAP⟨*cc*⟩	`<cp>TRAP<cc>` `<cp>TRAP<cc> #<data>`	Same as TRAP⟨*cc*⟩ except uses coprocessor defined condition codes.
System Control	⟨*cp*⟩SAVE ⟨*cp*⟩RESTORE	`<cp>SAVE <ea>` `<cp>RESTORE <ea>`	Save internal state of a given coprocessor at specified EA. Restore internal state of a given coprocessor from specified EA.

Instruction Format:

15	14	13	12	11	10	9	8	7	6	5	4	3	2	1	0
1	1	1	1	Coprocessor ID			0	0	0	Effective Address Mode			Effective Address Register		
0	R/M	0	Source Specifier			Destination Register			0	0	0	1	1	1	0

FSIN

Instruction Format:

15	14	13	12	11	10	9	8	7	6	5	4	3	2	1	0
1	1	1	1	Coprocessor ID			0	0	0	Effective Address Mode			Effective Address Register		
0	R/M	0	Source Specifier			Destination Register			0	0	0	0	0	0	0

FMOVE

Figure 7-5 Object Code Format of FMOVE and FSIN.

register in the coprocessor, it may ask the main processor to proceed with the next instruction. If the next instruction does not involve the same coprocessor, then execution proceeds concurrently by the main processor and one or more coprocessors. This requires no special attention by the programmer, because all synchronization are performed at the microcode level to make it look as if a nonconcurrent execution model is supported. For example, the *floating-point sine* (FSIN) instruction of the FPCP takes about 50 microseconds to execute. After the source operand is transferred to the FPCP, the 68020 is released to execute the next instruction, if the trace bit T1 is not set. Upon completion, the sine value of the operand is stored in a floating-point data register of the FPCP. Hence, during most of the time the FPCP is busy calculating the sine, the 68020 can execute many other instructions that do not involve the same coprocessor. If another floating-point instruction is encountered before the FPCP completes the sine calculation, it will instruct the 68020 to wait, so that the 68020 and the FPCP will synchronize before proceeding with the next instruction.

7.1.4 Communication Protocol

When the 68020 recognizes a line-F instruction, it initiates coprocessor communication by reading or writing one of the interface registers of the selected coprocessor. If the selected coprocessor is optional and does not exist in the system, then external hardware asserts a bus-error signal. The bus error exception handler may either emulate the desired operation in software or handles it as an error condition. If the coprocessor does exist, it then acknowledges (using DSACK*n**) and sets up a response primitive using an interface register called the *response register*. The response may be a simple "come again, I am busy now," if the coprocessor is still busy with the previous instruction. In general, the response from a coprocessor contains primitive commands that are summarized in Table 7-3. The 68020 microcode supports and performs these primitive actions

TABLE 7-3 OVERVIEW OF COPROCESSOR PRIMITIVE COMMAND SET

Category/Primitive Command	Description
Processor Synchronization	
Busy	Indicates coprocessor is still busy with the previous instruction.
Null	Communicates coprocessor status to the main processor. Indicates whether any pending interrupts is to be serviced; any further service required from main; and whether coprocessor instruction is completed.
General Operand Transfer	
Evaluate and Transfer EA	The EA is calculated and transferred to coprocessor.
Evaluate EA and Transfer Data	Operand is transferred between the specified EA and the coprocessor.
Write to Previous EA	Transfers an operand from coprocessor to the previously evaluated EA.
Take Address and Transfer Data	Transfer an operand between the coprocessor and an address given by the coprocessor.
Transfer To/From Top of Stack	Transfers an operand between the coprocessor and the top of active system stack.
Register Transfer	
Transfer a Register	Transfers an operand between a main processor and coprocessor.
Transfer Multiple Main Processor Registers	Transfers data between multiple address and/or data registers of main and the coprocessor.
Transfer Multiple Coprocessor Registers	Multiple operands are transferred between the EA specified in coprocessor instruction and the coprocessor.
Instruction Manipulation	
Transfer Operation Word	Operation word is passed to coprocessor.
Transfer Words from Instruction	Transfers operand(s) from the instruction to the coprocessor.
Exception Handling	
Supervisor Check	Allows coprocessor to verify the main processor is in the supervisor state. If not, the main will start privilege violation exception.
Request Exception Processing	The main processor will initiate exception processing/using a coprocessor supplied exception vector.

requested by a coprocessor. Thus, during the communication between the main processor and a coprocessor, called as a *dialog*, the main processor becomes a slave to the coprocessor, until it is released to proceed with the next instruction. As we said earlier, all dialog between the main processor and coprocessor is transparent to the programmer.

For example, using the Null primitive response a coprocessor may allow the main processor to process any pending interrupts while it is busy. Figure 7-6 illustrates the general flow of operation during this communication protocol. The primitive command set also allows the coprocessor to access some important resources resident on the main processor. These resources facilitate effective-address calculations, operand transfers, and exception processing, so that these functions do not have to be duplicated on the coprocessor. For example, a coprocessor may direct the main processor to calculate the effective address and fetch the operand. Any exception conditions that are detected by the coprocessor are passed over to the main processor via primitive commands. In other words, all exception processing are handled by the main processor using the exception vector passed by the coprocessor. For example, if an exception condition arose during the execution of a coprocessor instruction while the 68020 is concurrently executing other instructions, then this condition is communicated to the 68020 at the beginning of next coprocessor instruction.

7.1.5 Coprocessor Types

There are two types of coprocessors: *non-DMA type* and *DMA type*. The non-DMA type coprocessors always operate as bus slaves. Therefore, any operand transfers must be handled by the main processor using a temporary register and in two bus cycles. For example, to read an operand from a memory address to a coprocessor register, the main processor first reads it into a temporary register and then uses a second bus cycle to write it to the appropriate interface register of coprocessor. This is, of course, not very efficient when the number of required transfers is large. Its advantage, on the other hand, is that it does not require any bus arbitration and bus-master circuitry. For example, the 68881/68882 FPCP are non-DMA type coprocessors. The DMA type is advantageous when the required bus bandwidth is high. For example, this might be the case for a special graphics coprocessor. In order to save the second bus cycle, the DMA type coprocessor may take control of the bus to perform one or more bus cycles for execution of the coprocessor instruction. However, both DMA and non-DMA types operate as bus slaves during a dialog with the main processor.

7.2 FLOATING-POINT COPROCESSORS 68881 AND 68882

The *floating-point coprocessors*, or FPCP's, extend the integer data processing capabilities of the 68020 processor by providing a floating-point arithmetic unit and a set of floating-point data registers. There are currently two FPCP available—

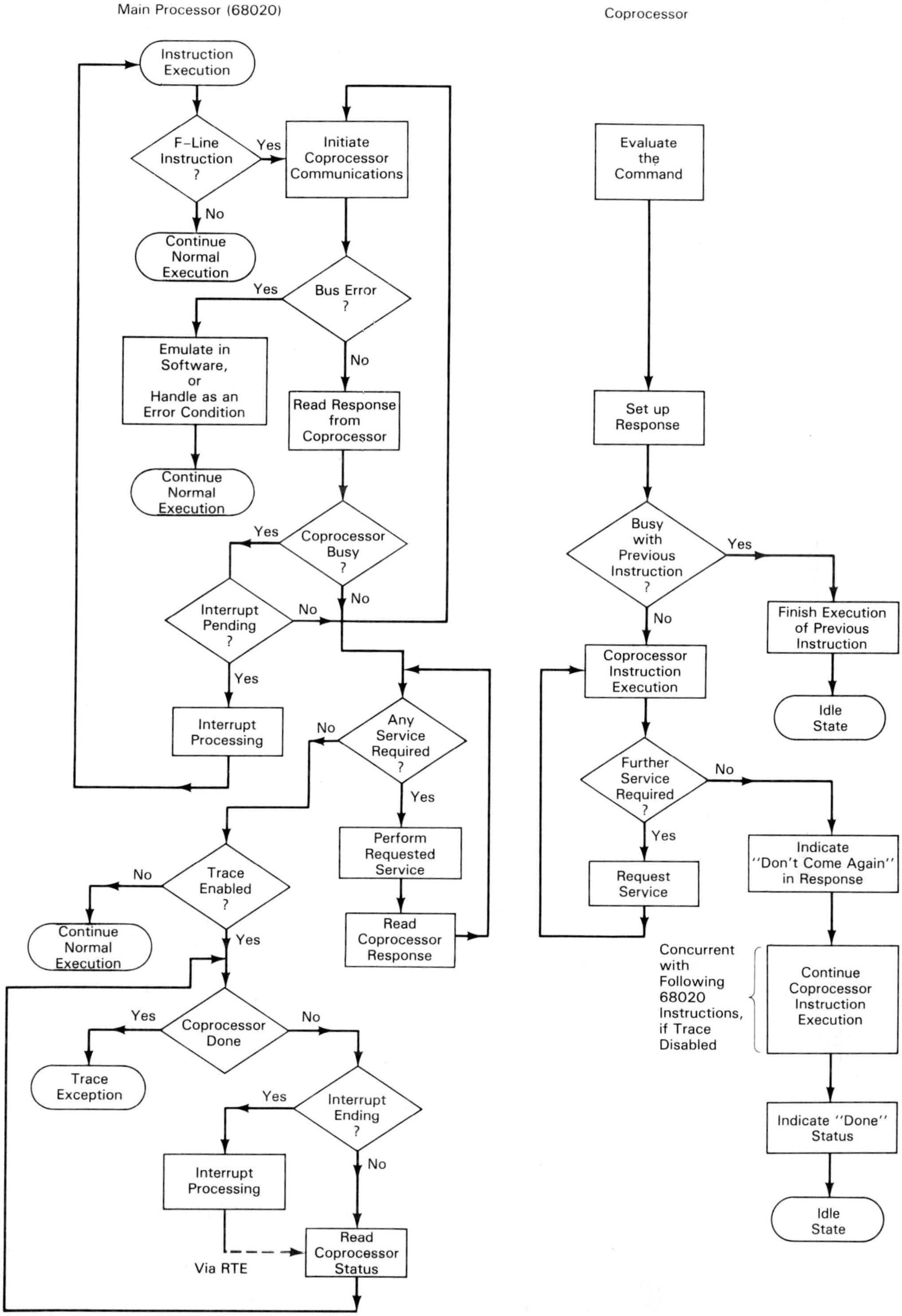

Figure 7-6 Overview of Coprocessor Interface Protocol.

the 68881 and the enhanced 68882, both from Motorola. In addition to the full support of IEEE P754 floating-point arithmetic functions, these two FPCPs also implement a complete set of trigonometric and transcendental functions.

Figure 7-7 illustrates the internal architecture of the 6888x FPCPs. The *Bus Interface Unit* (BIU) interfaces to the local 680xx bus and contains the interface registers to implement the coprocessor communication protocol. The *Microcoded Control Unit* (MCU) consists of a two-level microcoded sequencer similar to the one used by the 680xx family of processors to control the *Execution Control Unit* (ECU). The ECU contains a 67-bit ALU for quick manipulation of mantissa and exponents and a 67-bit barrel shifter for high-speed scaling used for normalizing and so forth. The ECU also includes a set of general purpose 80-bit floating-point registers (64-bit mantissa plus a sign-bit and a 15-bit exponent), and a *Read-Only Memory* (ROM) that stores various constants such as pi or e. The enhanced FPCP (the 68882) also features additional internal parallelism. For example, while one floating-point arithmetic operation is being performed by the ECU, the CCU can start the dialog of the next FPCP instruction including any necessary conversion between internal and external formats. This, in fact, enables the 68882 to execute two floating-point instructions concurrently while maintaining the sequential-instruction execution model. Otherwise, from the programmer's point of view, both FPCPs are the same.

7.2.1 Programmer's Model

As we stated earlier, a coprocessor performs as a logical extension of the main processor where to the programmer it is as if this additional functionality is resident on the main processor. The user's programmer's model of the 68020 and 6888x FPCP is shown in Figure 7-8. All registers in the programmer's model of the FPCP may be accessed in the user-mode. Eight 80-bit floating-point data registers (FP0-FP7) are analogous to the integer data registers (D0-D7) in that they are completely general purpose. In other words, any instruction that requires the use of a floating-point data register may select any one of them.

The control register (FPCR) contains enable bits for each exception condition that may be detected by the FPCP, and also an 8-bit mode control bits to select various rounding and precision modes of operation. The status register (FPSR) contains floating-point condition codes, quotient bits that are set by modulo arithmetic, and exception status bits. The *Instruction-Address Register* (FPIAR) contains the address of the floating-point instruction that may generate an exception condition. The FPCP automatically loads the FPIAR with the address of any FPCP instruction that may potentially cause an exception condition at the beginning of instruction execution. This is necessary so that the exception handler can locate the instruction that caused the exception. We will discuss the above control registers further during our discussion of system-control instructions.

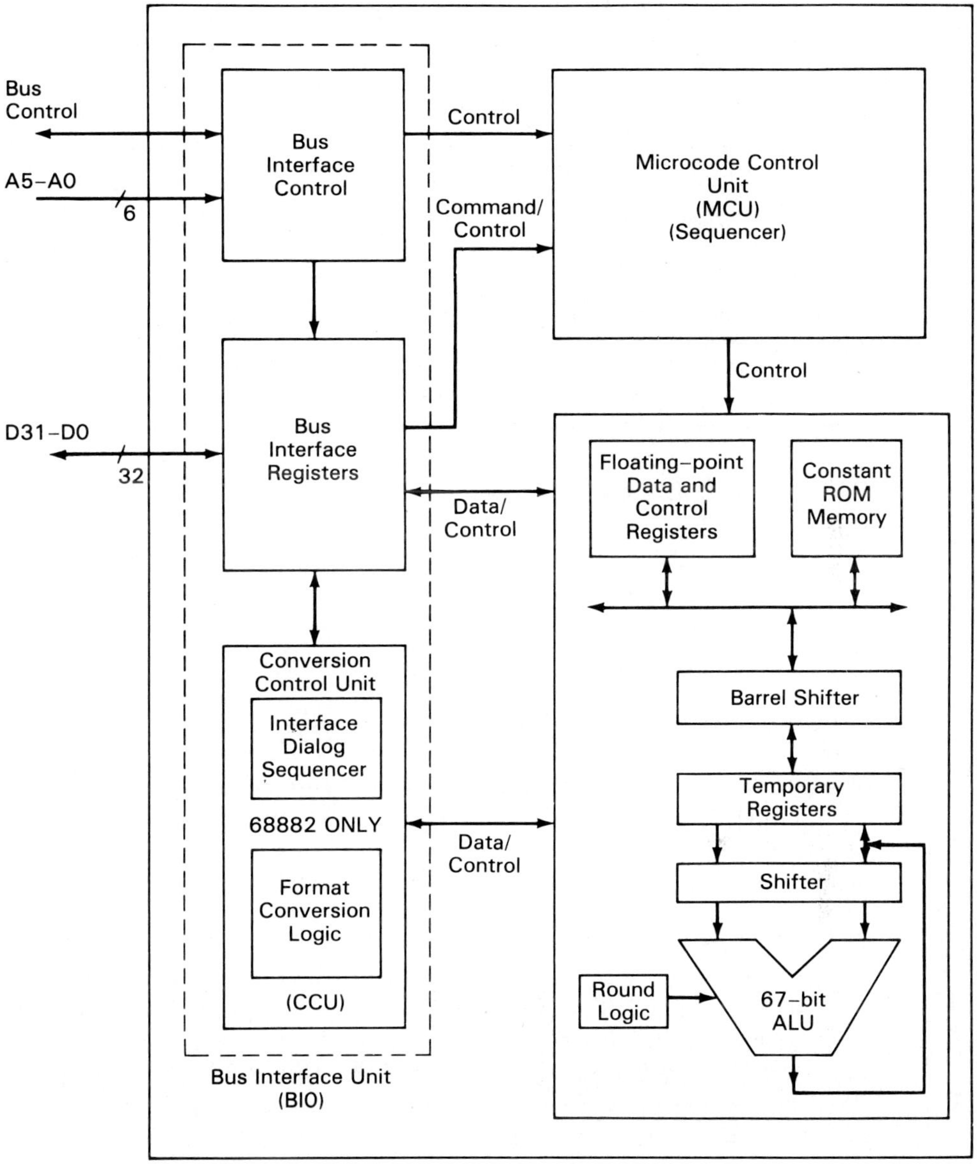

Figure 7-7 Block Diagram of 68881 and 68882 Coprocessors.

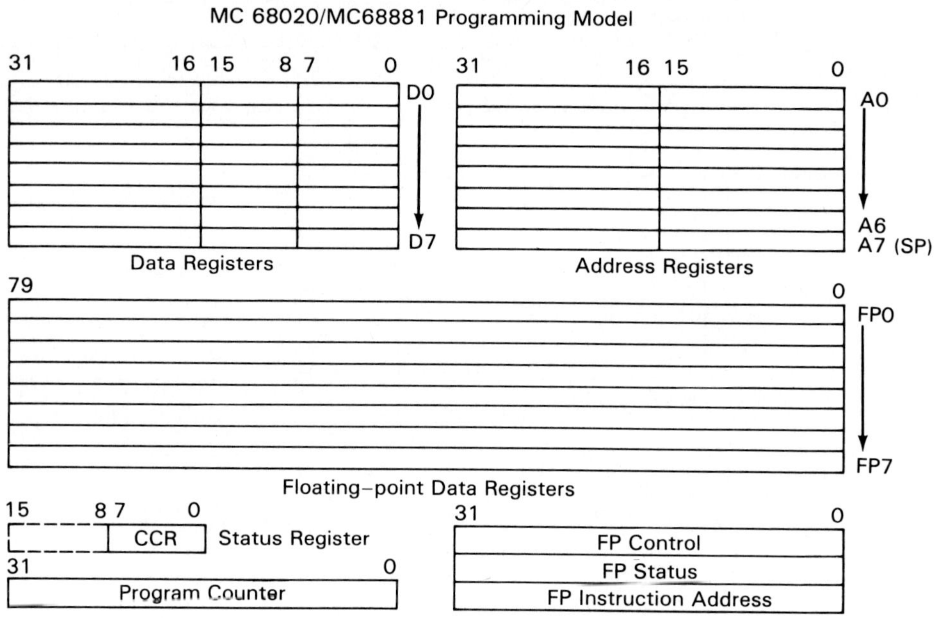

Figure 7-8 User Programming Model of the 68020 and 68881/68882.

7.2.2 Review of Floating-point Notation and the IEEE P754 Standard

Thus far we have only discussed how integer operands are stored and manipulated by the 68000 family. We have seen that the 68000 family supports integer or fixed-point operands of byte, word, and long-word sizes. A fixed-point operand, where an implicit point is assumed, is used to represent fractional numbers. For example,

$$(0010\ 1010.0110\ 0000)_2 = 42.375_{10}$$

using a word-size operand with the binary point in the middle. The main processor, of course, is not aware where the implicit binary point is, and processes numbers as though they are all integers. As long as the results are interpreted with the appropriate implicit point, they are correct. This has the advantage that fixed-point operands can be handled fast by the main processor without the need for an additional coprocessor. However, such representation also requires that the programmer be aware of and keep track of the implicit location of the binary point. Furthermore, the fixed-point format cannot represent a large dynamic range of a number with relatively few bits.

The floating-point representation includes a scale factor as part of the number to eliminate the above shortcomings. It has the general form

$$\text{Mantissa} \times \text{Base}^{\text{exponent}}$$

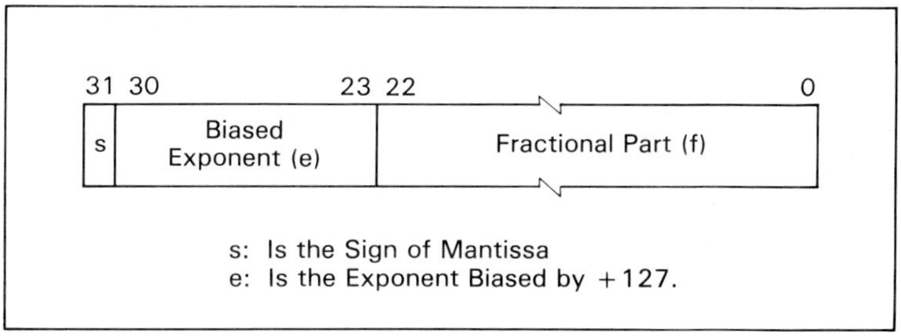

Figure 7-9 Memory Format of IEEE Single-precision Real Number.

as typically used in scientific notation, such as 3.78×10^{-7}. A number represented in such a form is called a *real*[2] or *floating-point number* to distinquish it from integer numbers. In computer arithmetic, base of 2 or 16 is used. For example,

$$\begin{aligned} 34.375_{10} &= (10\ 0010.0110)_2 \\ &= (1.0\ 0010\ 0110)_2 \times 2^5. \end{aligned}$$

A binary floating-point number is said to be *normalized* if the most-significant digit of its mantissa is one (e.g., $(1.0\ 0010\ 0110)_2 \times 2^5$) unless the number is zero. By convention, all floating-point operations are performed on normalized operands and generate normalized numbers. The purpose of this is to retain the maximum possible precision (i.e., the number of significant digits) of the mantissa throughout a sequence of operations.

The IEEE standard binary floating-point format for single-precision numbers have a long-word size, and has the memory format illustrated in Figure 7-9. This format is chosen for the following reasons. First, the sign-bit is in the most-significant bit position to make it easy to test for a positive or a negative number. Second, the exponent is positioned in higher order bits with respect to the mantissa to make easy comparison of two real numbers. This is because, if the two numbers A and B are normalized, we can determine that A is greater than B if the exponent of A is greater than the exponent of B. If the exponents are equal, then A is greater than B if the mantissa of A is greater than the mantissa of B. Thus, the CMP instruction may be used to compare real numbers.

Since we may assume that all real numbers are normalized under normal conditions (i.e., without any overflow, and so forth), the first bit of the mantissa can be discarded or "hidden" since it is always one. The IEEE standard assumes a mantissa where the binary point lies to the right of the hidden bit (i.e., of the form (1.f)). The 8-bit exponent value is biased or has an offset to its midrange to

[2] We will use the terms "real" and "floating-point" interchangably during the rest of our discussion.

eliminate the need for an additional sign-bit. Thus, the real number represented as

$$(-1)^s \times 1.f \times 2^{(e-127)}$$

for a non-zero number. Zero is represented as a special case with e = \$00 and f = \$0. Before any floating-point operation, the hidden bit is added and the bias of exponent is removed. Thus,

$$1 \leq \text{mantissa} < 2$$

Example 7-1

The real number, $80459_{10} = 13A4B_{16}$, is represented as shown in Figure 7-10 using single precision.

Operations that require additional precision and dynamic range may use double precision (64 bits) or extended precision (96 bits) with memory formats as shown in Figure 7-11. The exponent bias values for double and extended precision are +1023 and +16383, respectively. The extended-precision format has bits 65 through 80 as zeros, and also contains integer bit of mantissa that is hidden in single- and double-precision formats. Table 7-4 summaries these binary floating-point data formats.

It is not always possible to represent the result of an operation in normalized numbers. The normalized numbers include all directly representable real values other than zero and are between the overflow and underflow thresholds. If a resultant exponent of a floating-point operation is less than the minimum value, the mantissa is denormalized to sacrifice some precision to prevent underflow. Such numbers are called *denormalized numbers* in the IEEE standard and are indicated by e = 0 and f equal to a non-zero pattern. If, on the other hand, the resultant exponent is larger than the maximum exponent value, then overflow is detected, and the result is represented using the infinity form that has e equal to its maximum value and f equal to zero.

Sometimes the result of an operation has no mathematical meaning. For example, calculating x^y or x/y when both x and y are zero or infinity cannot produce

f = \$003A4B
e = 16 + 127
= 143
= \$8F
s = 0

31   0
47 80 3A 4B

Figure 7-10 Floating-point representation of 80459_{10}.

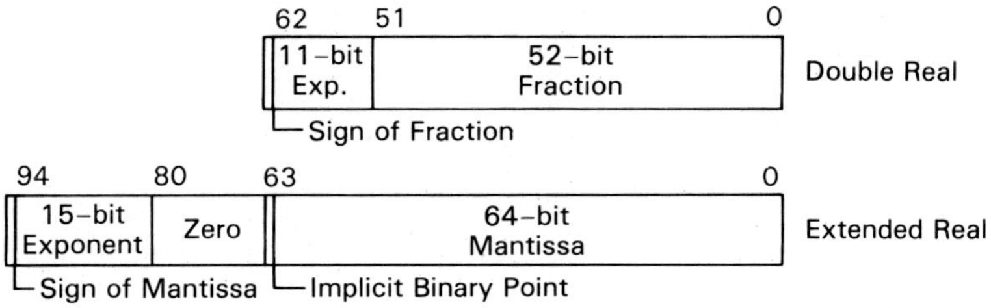

Figure 7-11 Memory Formats Double and Extended Precision Numbers

TABLE 7-4 SUMMARY OF FLOATING-POINT DATA FORMATS

Format	Features
Single Precision	Memory format: s: Sign-bit e: 8-bit biased exponent. f: 23-bit fraction value. Normalized numbers: Representation: $(-1)^s \times 2^{(e-127)} \times 1.f$ Mantissa = 1.f Range of e: $0 < e <$ \$FF Maximum positive number = 3.4×10^{38} Minimum positive number = 1.2×10^{-38}
Double Precision	Memory format: s: Sign-bit e: 11-bit biased exponent. f: 52-bit fraction value. Normalized numbers: Representation: $(-1)^s \times 2^{(e-1023)} \times 1.f$ Mantissa = 1.f Range of e: $0 < e <$ \$7FF Maximum positive number = 18×10^{307} Minimum positive number = 2.2×10^{-308}
Extended Precision	Memory format: s: Sign-bit e: 15-bit biased exponent. u: 16-bit zero field that is reserved. j: 1-bit integer part of mantissa. f: 63-bit fraction value. Normalized numbers: Representation: $(-1)^s \times 2^{(e-16383)} \times j.f$ Mantissa = j.f Range of e: $0 < e <$ \$7FFF Maximum positive number = 6×10^{4931} Minimum positive number = 8×10^{-4933}

any meaningful results. In such cases, a special format, called *Not A Number* (NAN), is used. A NAN number is represented using the maximum value of e and a non-zero f value. Table 7-5 summarizes the above operand types.

7.2.3 FPCP Operand Data Types

All internal FPCP arithmetic is performed using the extended-precision format. Thus, the floating-point registers of the FPCP use the extended-precision format except that the 16 zero bits are not included. Actually, the intermediate results are calculated using three additional bits beyond the extended precision (i.e., using a 67-bit mantissa to minimize error propagation due to round-off errors). This conforms to the IEEE P754 maximum allowable error specifications.

The FPCP supports seven different operand formats including three two's complement integer types as shown in Table 7-6. The single-letter instruction suffix indicates the format of operands. Since all internal arithmetic is performed at extended precision, this indicates what type of conversion is necessary for external operands. For example, `FADD.W (A0),FP0` reads a two's complement word-size operand pointed by A0, converts it to extended precision, and adds it to the FP0 register. The nice thing about this is that mixed-mode arithmetic that involves different operand formats are handled automatically, without any special attention by the programmer.

The packed *Binary Coded Decimal* (BCD) representation of real numbers is also supported by the FPCP, with the format shown in Figure 7-12. It consists of a 17-digit mantissa and 3-digit exponent. This format is very useful for I/O operations allowing the FPCP to convert efficiently to and from decimal scientific notation without additional software.

All operand types are stored in memory consistent with the general memory organization of the 68000 family. That is, the most significant byte of the operand is located at the specified effective address, and each following byte at successive byte addresses. The *Define Constant* (DC) and *Define Storage* (DS) directives are extended to support real operands. If a memory operand, regardless of its

TABLE 7-5 REPRESENTATION OF OPERAND DATA TYPES

Precision	Normalized	Denormalized[1]	Zero	NAN	Infinities
Single	0 < e < \$FF Mantissa = 1.f	e = \$00 Mantissa = 0.f	e = \$00 f = 0	e = \$FF f is non-zero.	e = \$FF f = 0
Double	0 < e < \$7FF Mantissa = 1.f	e = \$000 Mantissa = 0.f	e = \$000 f = 0	e = \$7FF f is non-zero.	e = \$7FF f = 0
Extended	0 < e < \$7FFF Mantissa = j.f	e = \$0000 Mantissa = 0.f	e = \$0000 f = 0	e = \$7FFF f is non-zero.	e = \$7FFF f = 0

[1] Represents the following real numbers: Single precision: $(-1)^s \times 2^{(-126)} \times 0.f$
Double precision: $(-1)^s \times 2^{(-1022)} \times 0.f$
Extended precision: $(-1)^s \times 2^{(-16383)} \times 0.f$

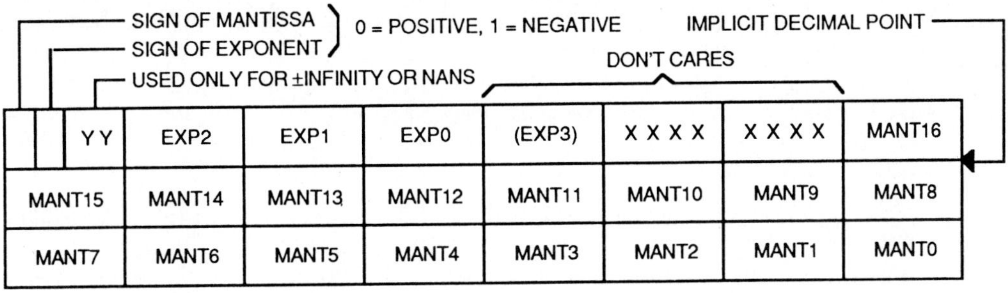

MANTn Is the nth digit of the mantissa.
EXPn Is the nth digit of the exponent. EXP3 is generated only during a move out operation if the source operand exponent exceeds the magnitude of a three digit exponent; otherwise, it is a don't care. Only EXP0-EXP2 are used for input.
XXXX Are don't care bits, which are zero on output and ignored on input.

Figure 7-12 Packed BCD Floating-point Data Format.

type, is not a normalized real number, it will be normalized during conversion to extended precision.

7.2.4 FPCP Instruction Set

The FPCP instruction set can be functionally divided into four categories:

1. Data-movement instructions
2. Floating-point arithmetic instructions
3. Program control instructions
4. System control instructions

Next, we will discuss each of these instruction groups. The reader should refer to the *FPCP User's Manual* for a detailed description and coding of each coprocessor instruction.

Data-movement instructions. This group of instructions handle all operand moves between external memory or 68020 registers and FPCP registers as

TABLE 7-6 FPCP OPERAND DATA TYPES

Operand Type		Instruction Suffix
Integers:	Byte size	B
	Word size	W
	Long-word size	L
Real Numbers:	Single precision	S
	Double precision	D
	Extended precision	X
	Packed BCD	P

shown in Table 7-7. On all moves to a floating-point data register, the operand with a specified format is converted to extended-precision data format. Similarly, when a floating-point data register is moved to a memory destination or the 68020 data register, it is converted to the specified format.

The third operand, called the *k-factor*, is required for packed real BCD moves in order to specify the format of decimal string. If k-factor is in the range [−64, 0], then it specifies the number of significant digits to the right of the decimal point before conversion. If k-factor is in the range [1, 17], it specifies the total number of significant digits. For example, if FP0 contains the decimal value +12345.6789, then Figure 7-13 illustrates the result of two different k-factors.

The FMOVECR instruction provides a convenient way to load a register with some commonly used constants such as e, pi, or even zero that are stored (at extended precision) within the read-only memory of the FPCP. The FPCP uses certain numbers that correspond to particular constants. For example, 0 corresponds to π and \$0E corresponds to e. Table 7-7 shows only a subset of these constants predefined by the FPCP. The instruction FMOVECR.X #0F,FP0 is, of course, more efficient than FMOVE.X #0,FP0.

In addition to data operands, FMOVE is also used to read and modify the contents of three control registers, FPCR, FPSR, and FPIAR. For example, the instruction FMOVE.L #0,FPCR clears all bits of the FPCR register.

TABLE 7-7 FPCP DATA MOVEMENT INSTRUCTIONS

Instruction	Syntax	Operand Type(s)	Description
FMOVE	FMOVE.X FPm,FPn	X	Source → Destination
	FMOVE.<s> <ea>,FPn	B,W,L,S,D,X,P	
	FMOVE.<s> FPm,<aea>	B,W,L,S,D,X	
	FMOVE.P FPm,<aea>{#k}	P	
	FMOVE.P FPm,<aea>{Dn}	P	
	FMOVE.L <ea>,FPcr	L	
	FMOVE.L FPcr,<aea>	L	
FMOVECR	FMOVECR.X #\$00,FPn	X	π → FP*n*
	FMOVECR.X #\$0B,FPn		log10(2) → FP*n*
	FMOVECR.X #\$0E,FPn		e → FP*n*
	FMOVECR.X #\$0F,FPn		0.0 → FP*n*
	FMOVECR.X #\$30,FPn		l*n*(2) → FP*n*
	FMOVECR.X #\$31,FPn		l*n*(10) → FP*n*
	(etc.)		(etc.)
FMOVEM	FMOVEM.<s> <mea>,<list>	L,X	Source → FP*n* or FP*cr* register list
	FMOVEM.X <mea>,Dn	X	
	FMOVEM.<s> <list>,<amea>	L,X	FP*n* or FP*cr* register list → Destination
	FMOVEM.X <Dn>,<amea>	X	

k-factor	Source Operand Value	Destination Value
−3	12345.6789	1.2345679×10^4
+6	12345.6789	1.23457×10^4

Figure 7-13 Illustration of k-factors.

The FMOVEM instruction transfers a selected list of floating-point registers (FP0-FP7) to or from a specified effective address. It is analogous to the MOVEM instruction of the 68000 family in its usage and assembly syntax. One significant difference, though, is that the register list may be dynamically specified by using a main processor data register. Since the purpose of this instruction is to save or restore the internal status of the FPCP, no data type conversion is performed. Actually, this is the only transfer instruction that moves data between an FPCP and external memory without any conversion or affecting any status or condition bits.

FPCP Control Registers. Figure 7-14 shows the details of the control and status registers where both the exception status and exception enable bytes have the same bit allocation. Upon power-up or system reset, all three control registers are cleared to zeros (i.e., FPCR = \$00000000). That is, all exception classes are disabled, rounding mode is "to-nearest", and rounding precision is extended. This corresponds to the IEEE standard defaults.

When a certain exception condition is detected by the FPCP, it sets the corresponding bit in the exception-status byte. If the associated enable bit is already set, then exception processing starts. Sometimes an error condition triggers multiple exception bits of the status register to be set. In this case, only the highest-priority enabled exception will be processed and the other exception conditions will be ignored. Thus, the exception handler should examine the FPSR to determine all relevant exception conditions.

Sometimes, it is desirable to disable all FPCP exception traps and instead poll the exception-status register. To allow for this without having to check the status byte after each floating-point operation, the IEEE P754 standard defines five "sticky" exception bits that are part of FPCP's accrued-exception byte. The programmer can check the status of these bits after a series of floating-point operations to see if an error condition has occurred. Any new exception-condition is logically OR'ed with the corresponding accrued-exception bit as shown below:

$$
\begin{aligned}
IOP &= IOP \vee (BSUN \vee SNAN \vee OPERR)_{EXC} \\
OVFL &= OVFL \vee OVFL_{EXC} \\
UNFL &= UNFL \vee (UNFL \vee INEX2)_{EXC} \\
DZ &= DZ \vee DZ_{EXC} \\
INEX &= INEX \vee (INEX1 \vee INEX2 \vee OVFL)_{EXC}.
\end{aligned}
$$

These sticky bits are cleared only after a reset or with a FMOVE instruction.

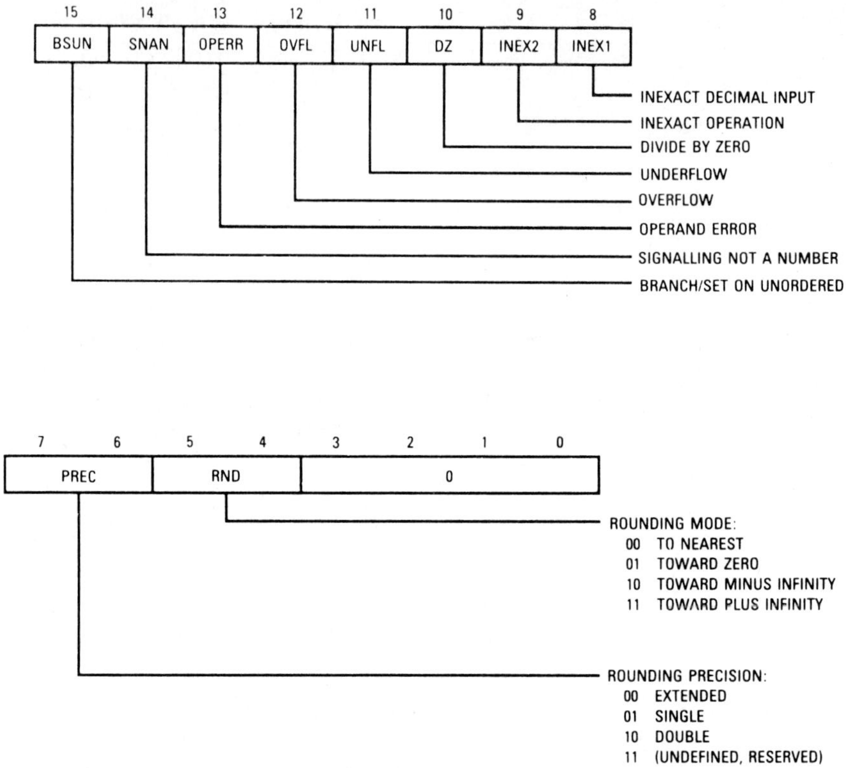

Figure 7-14-a FPCP Control Register.

Floating-point arithmetic instructions. The FPCP supports floating-point operations with one or two input operands. The operations that require one input operand, such as sine, are referred to as *univariate* or *monadic*. The operations, such as multiply or add, that require two operands are called *bivariate* or *dyadic*. The formats of monadic operations are as follows:

```
F<monadic-op>.<s> <ea>,FPn
F<monadic-op>.X   FPm,FPn
F<monadic-op>.X   FPn
```

where $\langle s \rangle$ = B, W, L, S, D, X, or P. The first two forms calculate the specified function of the source operand and stores the result in FP*n*. The last form uses the same register for both source and destination values.

The only exception to the above formats is the FSINCOS instruction, which calculates both sine and cosine of the source operand, thus two destination registers are needed as shown below:

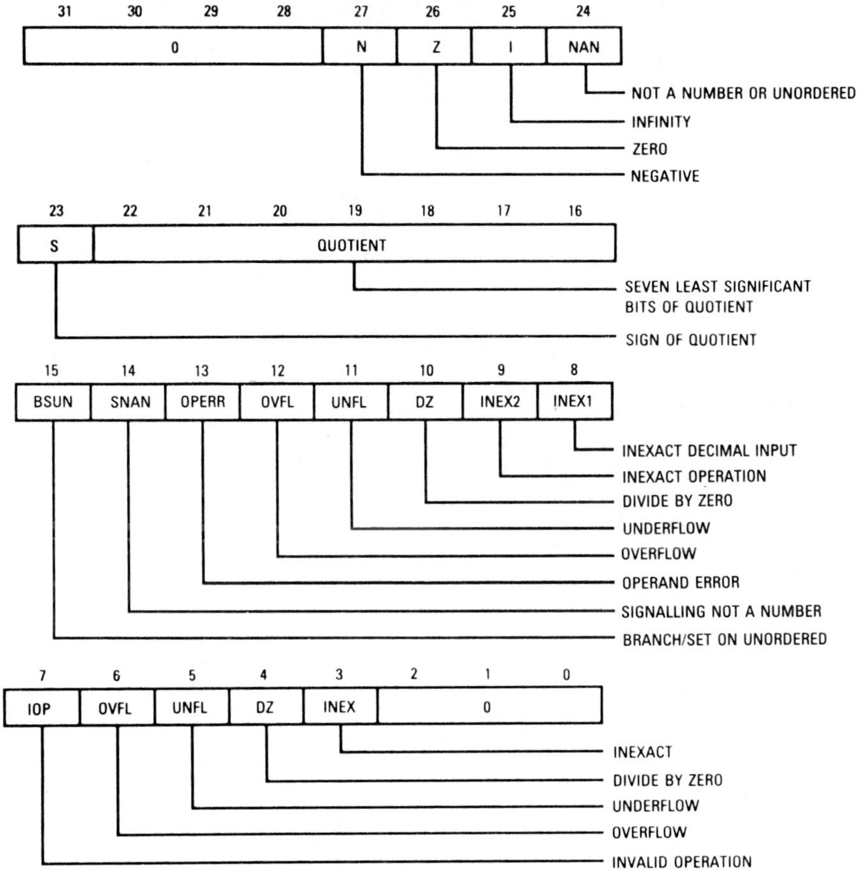

Figure 7-14-b FPCP Status Register.

```
FSINCOS.<s> <ea>,FPc:FPs
FSINCOS.X   FPm,FPc:FPs
```

where the FP*c* and FP*s* registers contain the cosine and sine values, respectively.

The dyadic operation format is as follows:

```
F<dyadic-op>.<s> <ea>,FPn
F<dyadic-op>.X   FPm,FPn
```

where $\langle s \rangle$ = B, W, L, S, D, X, or P. For example, FMUL.S (A0),FP0 multiplies the FP0 register with the single-precision floating-point number pointed to by A0, and stores the result back in FP0.

Table 7-8 lists the floating-point arithmetic instructions.

TABLE 7-8 FPCP ARITHMETIC INSTRUCTIONS

Type	Instruction	Function
Monadic	FABS	Absolute value.
	FACOS	Arc cosine.
	FASIN	Arc sine.
	FATAN	Arc tangent.
	FATANH	Hyperbolic arc tangent.
	FCOS	Cosine.
	FCOSH	Hyperbolic cosine.
	FETOX	exp(x)
	FETOXM1	exp(x) − 1
	FGETEXP	Extract exponent.
	FGETMAN	Extract mantissa.
	FINT	Extract integer part.
	FINTRZ	Extract integer part, rounded to zero.
	FLOGN	$ln(x)$
	FLOGNP1	$ln(x + 1)$
	FLOG10	log10(x)
	FLOG2	log2(x)
	FNEG	Negate.
	FSIN	Sine.
	FSINH	Hyperbolic sine.
	FSQRT	Square root.
	FTAN	Tangent.
	FTANH	Hyperbolic tangent.
	FTENTOX	10**x
	FTWOTOX	2**x
Dyadic	FADD	Add.
	FCMP	Compare.
	FDIV	Divide.
	FMOD	Modulo remainder.
	FMUL	Multiply.
	FREM	IEEE remainder.
	FSCALE	Scale exponent.
	FSGLDIV	Single-precision divide.
	FSGLMUL	Single-precision multiply.
	FSUB	Subtract.

Example 7-2

Multiplication of two complex numbers usually requires four floating-point multiplications and two floating-point additions. That is,

$$(a + b*j) * (c + d*j) = (a*c - b*d) + (b*c + a*d)*j.$$

Let constants {a, b, c, d} be single-precision numbers stored in that order in consecutive memory locations, with the constant a pointed to by A0. Figure 7-15 illustrates the programming of complex multiplication, where the result is stored in the location pointed to by A1.

```
FMOVE.S    (A0),FP0
FMUL.S     8(A0),FP0        FP0 = a*c
FMOVE.S    4(A0),FP1
FMUL.S     12(A0),FP1       FP1 = b*d
FSUB.X     FP1,FP0          FP1 = a*c - b*d
FMOVE.S    FP0,(A1)+        Store real part.
FMOVE.S    4(A0),FP0
FMUL.S     8(A0),FP0        FP0= b*c
FMOVE.S    (A0),FP1
FMUL.S     12(A0),FP1       FP1 = a*d
FADD.X     FP1,FP0          FP0 = b*c + a*d
FMOVE.S    FP1,(A1)         Store imaginary part.
```

Figure 7-15 Complex Multiplication Example.

Example 7-3

Let us consider evaluation of a polynomial at x0 using the first $N + 1$ elements as shown below:

$$y0 = c(0) + c(1) * x0 + c(2) * x0^2 + \cdots + c(N) * x0^N$$

where, c(0), c(1), . . . , c(N) are single-precision floating-point constants stored in a table. The subroutine shown in Figure 7-16 calculates the value of such a polynomial.

Program control instructions. The program control instructions shown in Table 7-9 are directly analogous to their counterparts in the 68020 instruction set. The condition code syntax and evaluation, however, are determined by the FPCP. Interestingly, the four condition code bits are used for 32 different conditional tests. As shown in Table 7-10, these tests are divided into three groups. The first group is called *IEEE-Nonaware* because the NAN-bit of the condition code byte is not included as part of the evaluation. Since, in a comparison operation involving a NAN-type operand, the less than, greater than, or equal condition cannot be assessed, this group generates an exception condition by setting the BSUN bit when the NAN bit is set. The second group, called the *IEEE-aware tests*, assumes the programmer is familiar with the IEEE P754-defined operand types, and thus, do not cause an exception. The third group of tests include various miscellaneous ones.

System control instructions. The FPCP has three system control instructions shown in Table 7-11. FTRAP⟨*cc*⟩ instruction is analogous to the TRAP⟨*cc*⟩ instruction except it uses one of the 32 FPCP conditional tests. If the selected condition is true, exception processing is started, typically to call the operating system to handle an error condition.

The privileged instructions FSAVE and FRESTORE are used respectively to save and restore the internal state of the FPCP that is not user visible. Any

```
* SUBROUTINE POLYNOM
*
* Purpose: This subroutine calculates the value of a polynomial at a given point.
*          (Also see exercise 8)
* Inputs:   x0 :  Specifies the address of single-precision value where polynomial
*                 is to be evaluated.
*       CTABLE :  Specifies the address of coefficient table.
*
* Outputs:  y0 :  Specifies the address where the value of the polynomial is to be
*                 stored in single-precision.
*
* Sample Call  :
*                 PEA      X0          Push Address of x0.
*                 PEA      Y0          Push Address of y0.
*                 MOVE.W   #N,-(SP)    The order of polynomial.
*                 PEA      CTABLE      Coefficient table address.
*                 JSR      POLYNOM
*
* Main Body of POLYNOM:
*
POLYNOM     LINK      A6,#0                 A6 is frame pointer.
            MOVEM.L   A0/D0,-(SP)           Save used registers.
            FMOVEM.X  FP0-FP3,-(SP)
```

```
*
*           FP0 = x0
*           FP1 = Partial sum
*           FP2 = x0**J
*           FP3 = C(J)*x0**J
            MOVE.W    PARM_N(A6),D0         Get N value.
            MOVE.L    PARM_CTABLE(A6),A0    A0 → CTABLE.
            FMOVE.S   [PARM_X0(A6)],FP0     FP0 = x0.
            FMOVE.S   (A0)+,FP1             FP1 = c(0).
            FMOVE.B   #1,FP2                FP2 = 1.
*
LOOP        FMOVE.S   (A0)+,FP3            c(j)*x0**(j)
            FMUL.X    FP2,FP3
            FADD.X    FP3,FP1               FP1 = y0
            FMUL.X    FP0,FP2               x0**J.
            DBF       D0,LOOP               Loop N times.
*           FMOVE.S   FP1, [PARM_Y0(A6)]    Store the result.
            FMOVEM.X  (SP)+,FP0-FP3         Restore register values.
            MOVEM.L   (SP)+,A0/D0
            UNLK      A6
            RTS
```

Figure 7-16 Polynomial Evaluation Example.

TABLE 7-9 PROGRAM FLOW CONTROL INSTRUCTIONS

Instruction	Syntax	Operation
FB⟨*cc*⟩	`FB<cc>.<s>   <label>`	If ⟨*cc*⟩ is true, then PC + $d \rightarrow$ PC. s = W for 16-bit displacement, s = L for 32-bit displacement.
FDB⟨*cc*⟩	`FDB<cc>   Dn,<label>`	Same as DB⟨*cc*⟩ except uses FPCP condition.
FNOP	`FNOP`	No operation.
FS⟨*cc*⟩	`FS<cc>   <ea>`	Similar to S⟨cc⟩ except uses FPCP condition.
FTST	`FTST.<s>   <ea>` `FTST   FPn`	Sets FPSR condition codes. s = B,W,L,S,D,X,P

exception handlers related to FPCP execution are bounded by FSAVE and FRESTORE for the following possible applications:

1. In a virtual memory system, it is necessary to implement instruction continuation for FPCP instructions. That is, if a page fault occurs in addressing a floating-point operand, it is necessary to suspend the execution of that FPCP instruction temporarily.
2. In a multitasking system when a task time-out may occur in the middle of a FPCP instruction, it is necessary to suspend the operation of the FPCP.
3. In a 68882 FPCP system, it is necessary that all FPCP exception handlers be bounded by FSAVE and FRESTORE. This is necessary due to the concurrency between control and execution units (CCU and ECU) of the 68882. When exception processing starts because of an exception condition detected by the ECU, the CCU may be in the middle of the next FPCP instruction. Thus, before any other FPCP instructions are executed to gather more information about the exception, the internal state must be saved using the FSAVE instruction. The inclusion of FSAVE and FRESTORE would, therefore, make upgrading from the 68881 to the 68882 simpler.

The state information saved on the system stack during FSAVE is called a *state frame* and depends upon the status of the FPCP as follows:

Null-state Frame — Indicates that the FPCP state has not been changed since the last FRESTORE instruction or power-up reset condition.

Idle-state Frame — This state frame is used when the FPCP is currently not executing any instructions. It includes status information and any pending exception conditions of the FPCP.

TABLE 7-10 FPCP CONDITIONAL TESTS

Type	⟨*cc*⟩ Mnemonic	Definition
IEEE-Aware	EQ	Equal
	NE	Not Equal
	OGT	Ordered Greater Than
	ULE	Unordered or Less or Equal
	OGE	Ordered Greater Than or Equal
	ULT	Unordered or Less Than
	OLT	Ordered Less Than
	UGE	Unordered or Greater or Equal
	OLE	Ordered Less Than or Equal
	UGT	Unordered or Greater Than
	OGL	Ordered Greater or Less Than
	UEQ	Unordered or Equal
	OR	Ordered
	UN	Unordered
IEEE-Non-aware	EQ	Equal
	NE	Not Equal
	GT	Greater Than
	NGT	Not Greater Than
	GE	Greater Than Or Equal
	NGE	Not Greater Than or Equal
	LT	Less Than
	NLT	Not Less Than
	LE	Less Than Or Equal
	NLE	Not Less Than or Equal
	GL	Greater or Less Than
	NGL	Not Greater or Less Than
	GLE	Greater, Less or Equal
	NGLE	Not Greater, Less or Equal
Miscellaneous	F	False
	T	True
	SF	Signalling False
	ST	Signalling True
	SEQ	Signalling Equal
	SNE	Signalling Not Equal

TABLE 7-11 SYSTEM CONTROL INSTRUCTIONS

Instruction	Syntax	Operation
FRESTORE	FRESTORE <aea>	Restore internal state.
FSAVE	FSAVE <ea>	Save internal state.
FTRAP⟨*cc*⟩	FTRAP<cc>	If ⟨*cc*⟩ is true, then trap.
	FTRAP<cc>.W #<d16>	Contain a user defined operand
	FTRAP<cc>.L #<d32>	with 16- or 32-bit size.

Busy-state Frame: This state frame is used when the FPCP is currently busy executing an instruction. It includes the address of the microprogram counter, temporary register values, and exception information.

The null-state frame is common to all 68000 family coprocessors. The other two state formats indicate the version number of the FPCP and state-frame size in the most significant word of the first word of the frame. The exception handler must recognize that 68882 state frames are 32 bytes longer than the 68881 due to additional internal complexity.

7.3 VIRTUAL-MEMORY MANAGEMENT COPROCESSOR—THE MC68851

The Motorola MC68851 is a high-performance *paged memory management unit* (PMMU) that is designed to function as a coprocessor to the 68020. The MC68851 chip, or PMMU as we shall call it hereafter, provides complete support to implement a virtual memory environment in a 68020 processor system. We will next give an overview of the PMMU's features and implementation. The system designer should refer to the PMMU's user manual for further details.

The PMMU's primary function is, of course, the fast translation of 68020 32-bit logical addresses into physical addresses of main memory. A 16 MHz PMMU performs address translation in 45nsec, which corresponds to less than one clock cycle delay[3]. The PMMU also provides access protection to either certain areas or selected pages of physical memory. For example, it can trap unauthorized accesses by a user-level program to reserved operating system areas, or certain pages can be write-protected. In addition, the PMMU supports the BKPT #⟨*n*⟩ instruction of the 68000 family by including on-chip hardware for break-after-*N*-iteration function. Eight simultaneous breakpoints are supported.

7.3.1 Address Translation Mechanism

Figure 7-17 illustrates the block diagram of a 68020/68851 system where the logical and/or physical sides of address space may have alternate bus masters. The low-order 8-bits of the logical address bus is always bypassed without any translations, thereby limiting the minimum page size to 256 bytes. The address translation tables containing page descriptors are stored in main memory. This has the advantage that the table size is not limited, and can be configured according to system requirements. However, accessing external translation tables during each bus cycle would be unacceptably slow. Therefore, the PMMU features an on-chip *address-translation cache* (ATC) that stores the most recently used page descrip-

[3] This translates to zero wait-cycles for 25nsec or faster access-time physical memory or 1 wait-cycle for physical memory with 80nsec or faster access time for a 16 MHz 68020.

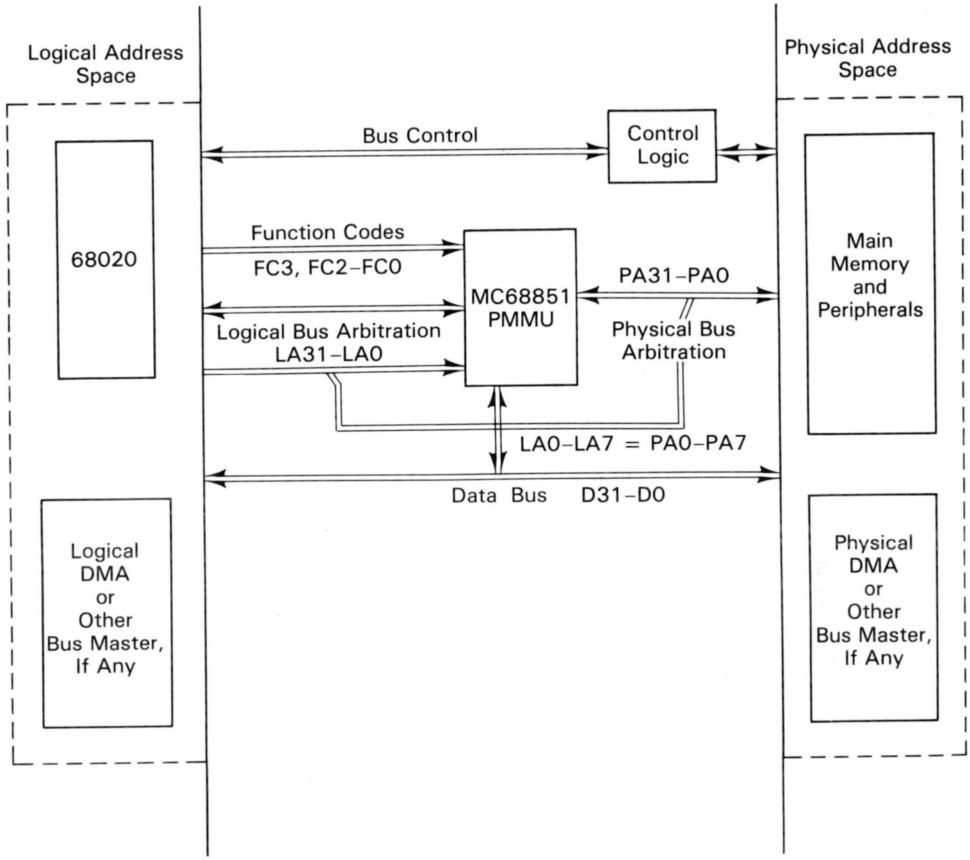

Figure 7-17 Simplified Block Diagram of 68020/68851 System.

tors. During an address translation, the PMMU first checks to see if there is a matching descriptor in the ATC. If not, it will automatically search and load the descriptor residing in main memory. Because page descriptors are loaded on demand into the ATC, the PMMU is also referred to as demand-paged MMU.

How do we store the descriptors into main memory in the first place? The 68020 can disable the address translation function by clearing an enable bit in a translation control register of the PMMU, or the reset operation will also clear this enable bit. During system initialization, the 68020 will transfer the address translation tables into main memory, and then indicate to the PMMU where they are by writing a pointer to the beginning of the table called a *root pointer* in the PMMU's user manual, as shown in Figure 7-18.

When the translation mechanism of the PMMU is enabled, it compares an incoming logical address and function codes against all ATC entries. If a matching

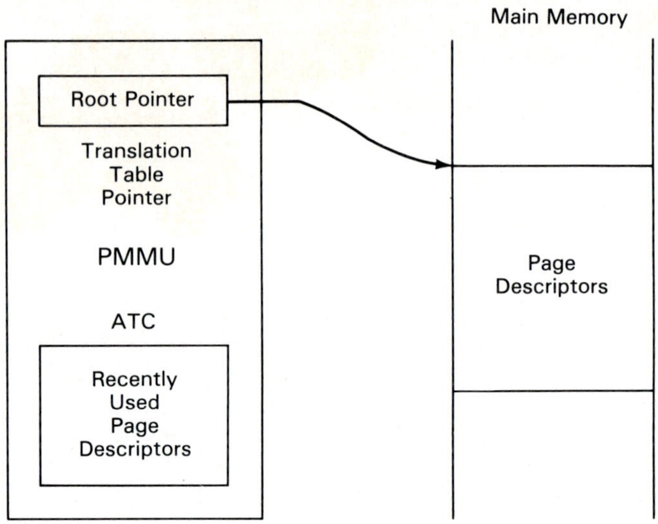

Figure 7-18 PMMU's Page Descriptors.

ATC entry is found, the PMMU places the corresponding physical address on the output bus, if there is no access-protection violation. If the PMMU is not currently the physical bus master, then it will request and wait until it regains control of the bus. As illustrated in Figure 7-19, if there is no matching entry found in ATC, then the PMMU asserts BERR* and HALT* signals to the 68020 to retry the same bus cycle and simultaneously requests the mastership of the logical bus.[4] The latter is done for two reasons. First, the 68020 will wait before retrying while the PMMU fetches the decriptor from main memory. Secondly, this is done so that the PMMU can take over the data bus during this search operation without using additional buffering of buses.

If no descriptor is found during the table search or if access is denied to such an address range, a special *unmappable* descriptor type is generated. Another case is a read-modify-write cycle with no matching entry found in the ATC. Then, the PMMU always asserts BERR*, because the bus cycle will be interrupted due to the table search. There are two other exceptions to the above. First, if the bus cycle addresses one of the PMMU's registers, then the PMMU transfers the requested register data and performs any necessary action. Second, if the bus cycle is a CPU-space type but does not access the PMMU, then the logical address is transferred to physical address outputs without any translation.

The ATC has 64 entries and consists of two parts: the fully associative *Content-Addressable Memory* (CAM), and corresponding RAM array containing the physical addresses, access protection, and status information. The CAM part contains the logical address mask, address-space information, and task number

[4] It also requests the physical bus if the PMMU is currently not the master.

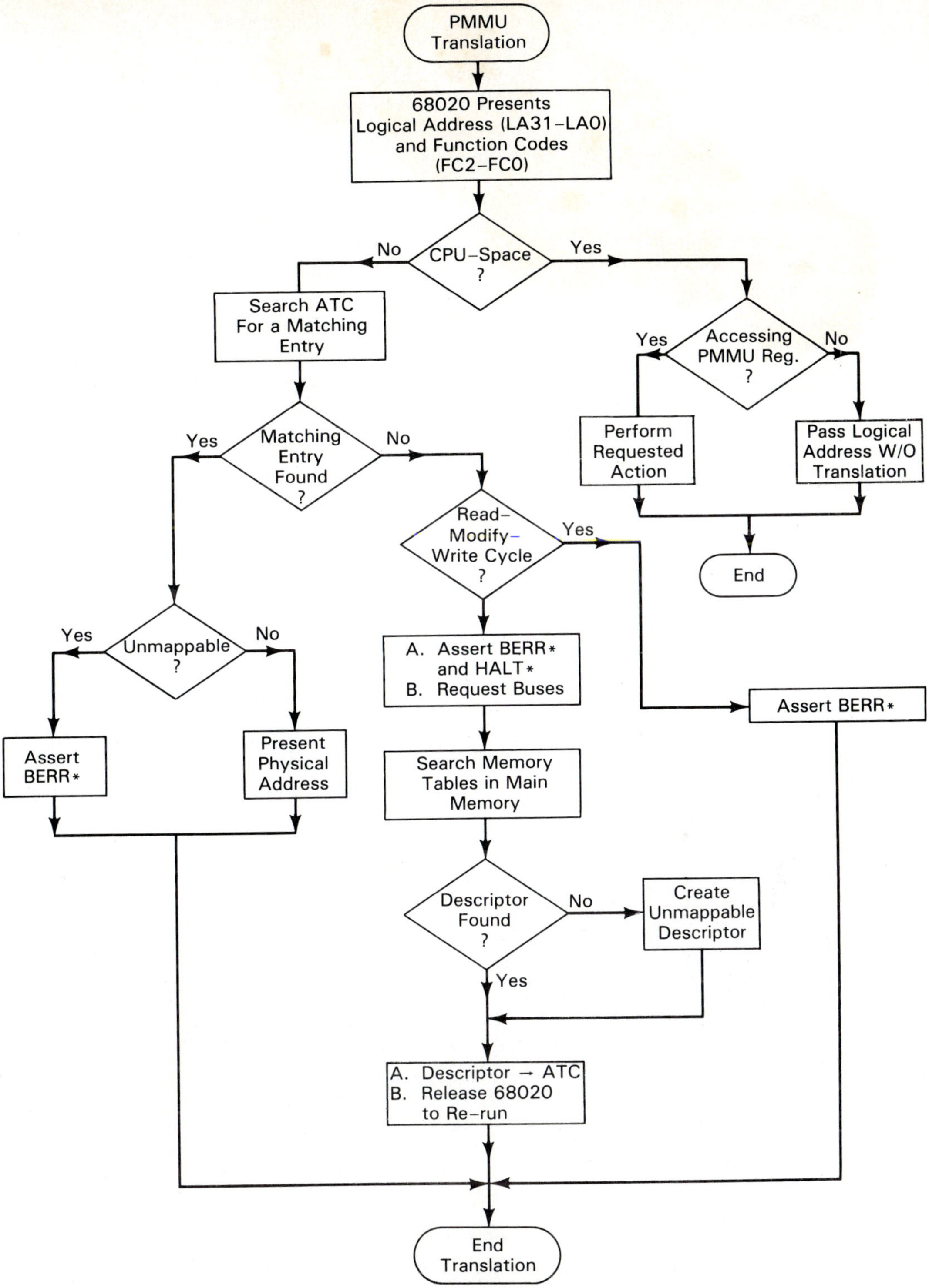

Figure 7-19 Address-translation Mechanism of PMMU.

(see Figure 7-20). The address-space field is compared against the incoming function codes, FC3-FC0. The fourth function code input, FC3, enables selecting a different set of descriptors when a DMA has mastership of the logical bus. The task number (TA2-TA0) is compared with the currently active task number, TA_{ACT}.

Any time a descriptor is loaded into the ATC, it is assigned a 3-bit unique number (TA2-TA0), called a *task alias*, dependent on a given root pointer. These task-alias bits allow translation descriptors for multiple tasks to co-reside in the ATC. For example, if the root pointer is modified to point to task B, a different task-alias is used by the PMMU. The task-aliases for eight recently used tasks are maintained in a different table called a *root-pointer table* (RPT). The assignment of these unique task aliases are performed by the PMMU without any software intervention. If a new entry to the RPT table overwrites a task-alias that has been previously assigned to another task, the PMMU automatically flushes or invalidates all corresponding entries in the ATC.

A CAM entry generates a match condition when both the logical address and FC field exactly matches the current bus cycle, and also the task alias field,

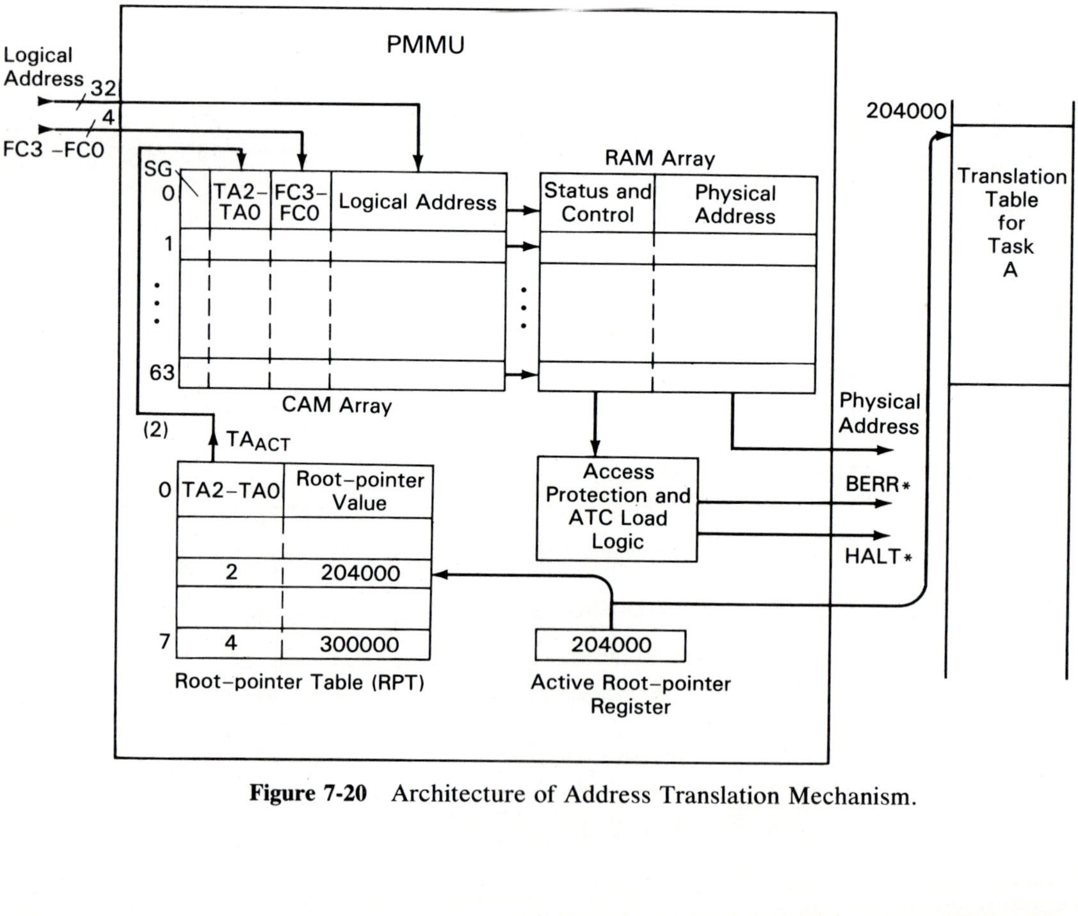

Figure 7-20 Architecture of Address Translation Mechanism.

TA2-TA0 must be equal to TA_{ACT} (i.e., the entry must belong to the active task). The only exception to this is when a descriptor or ATC entry is to be shared by all tasks. This is selected by the SG-bit selected in the page descriptor.

Both ATC and RPT are automatically maintained by PMMU circuitry, and neither is directly accessible by the programmer. The PMMU uses a *least-recently-used* (LRU) type algorithm to decide which entry to replace, if there are no invalid or unused entries. To exempt an ATC entry from being replaced, a lock (L) bit may be set in the page descriptor. Similarly, the SG-bit prevents an RPT entry from being replaced.

7.3.2 Translation Table Structure

The translation tables are stored in a tree structure with up to five levels as illustrated in Figure 7-21. This hierarchical structure contains page descriptors at

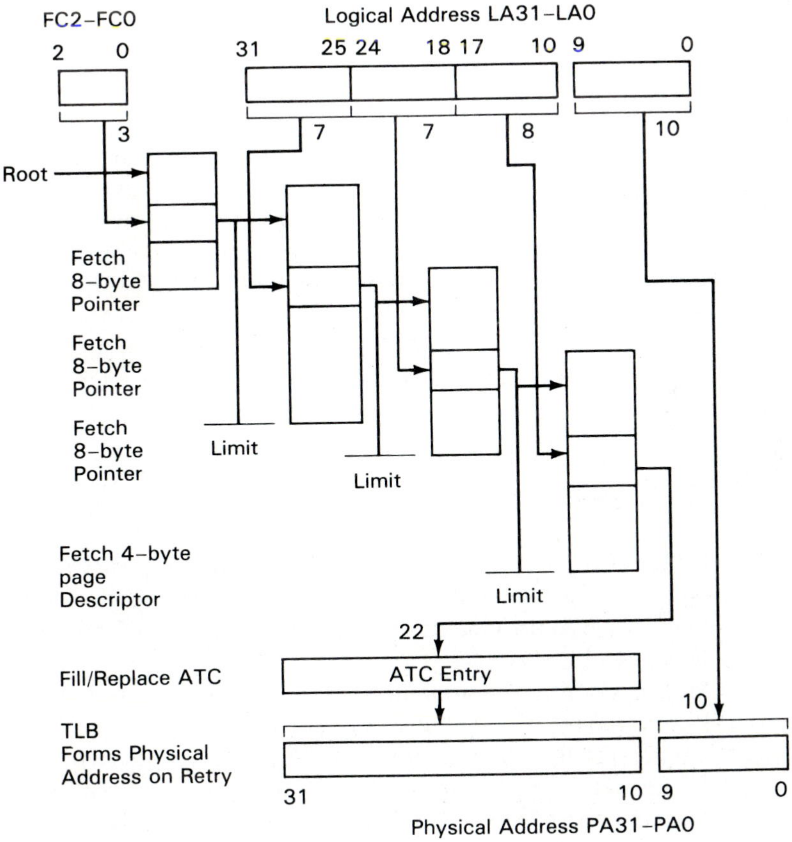

Figure 7-21 Translation Table Structure.

its lowest level. The logical address is partitioned into one to four fields. The width of each field, given by TIA through TID, is configured using a translation control register of the PMMU. The *initial shift* (IS) field indicates the number of high-order bits of logical address to skip before the TIA field is extracted. It is required that

$$\text{page size (PS)} = 32 - (\text{IS} + \text{TIA} + \text{TIB} + \text{TIC} + \text{TID})$$

and the following ranges are permitted:

Field	Starting Bit Position	Width
TIA	31-IS	1-15
TIB	31-IS-TIA	0-15 (if zero, then TIC = TID = 0 is required)
TIC	31-IS-TIA-TIB	0-15 (if zero, then TID must be also zero)
TID	31-IS-TIA-TIB-TIC	0-15

The advantage of this tree structure over a linear table is the reduced memory size required for page descriptors. For example, a paged virtual system using a linear table to map 2^{32} bytes would require 2^{32-10} translation table entries for a 1K byte page size. That is, even if a page is not currently in memory, an entry is needed to indicate this. On the other hand, the PMMUs flexible translation table structure allows an invalid type of table descriptor that may be used at any level of the structure to indicate large unmapped areas of memory. This will cause an unmappable descriptor that has the bus-error (B) bit set to be loaded into the ATC, thereby generating a page fault.

7.3.3 Breakpoint Support

The PMMU also provides support for up to eight different breakpoints. Although this function is not related to the virtual memory support, the PMMU was a convenient place to provide this capability, since a 68020 microcomputer will also typically have an MMU.

An 8-bit counter is maintained for each of the eight breakpoints so that break-after-*N*-iterations can be conveniently implemented, where *N* is less than or equal to 255. When the 68020 encounters a BKPT #⟨k⟩ instruction, it executes a breakpoint-acknowledge bus cycle, as we saw in Chapter 6. The PMMU detects this bus cycle, and decrements the *k*'th breakpoint counter and also responds by either providing a replacement opcode prestored in the *k*'th opcode register of PMMU, or by asserting the bus-error signal if the breakpoint count is decremented to zero or if it is disabled. The latter case cause an illegal instruction exception.

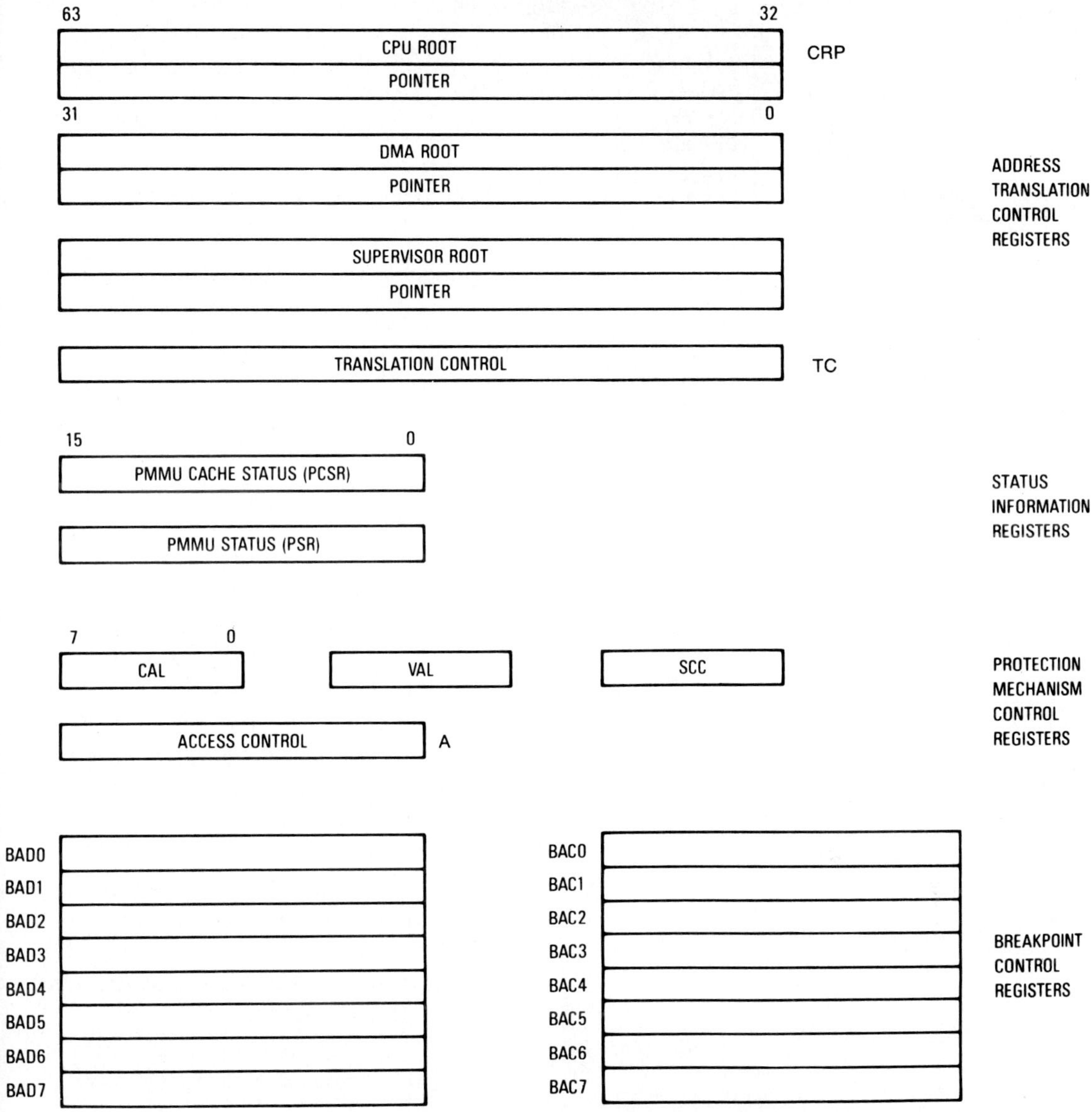

Figure 7-22 Programming Model of PMMU.

7.3.4 Programmer's Model and Instruction Set

The PMMU programming model is shown in Figure 7-22 and consists of the following registers:

Root Pointers (CRP, SRP, DRP) The PMMU has three root-pointer registers that point to different trans-

TABLE 7-12 SUMMARY OF PMMU INSTRUCTIONS

Instruction	Function
PMOVE	Transfers data to/from a PMMU register.
PDB⟨*cc*⟩	Is a looping primitive similar to DB⟨*cc*⟩ but uses a PMMU condition.
PFLUSH	Invalidates all or selected entries of the ATC.
PLOAD	Load an entry into the ATC.
PRESTORE	Restore internal state of PMMU from stack. Includes certain programmer registers.
PSAVE	Is the inverse of PRESTORE.
PS⟨*cc*⟩	Similar to S⟨*cc*⟩ of 68020, but uses PMMU condition.
PTEST	Searches translation tables to determine mapping information of a given logical address.
PTRAP⟨*cc*⟩	Similar to TRAP⟨*cc*⟩, but uses PMMU condition.
PVALID	Verifies access rights of a given address. Intended to support CALLM-RTM access levels.

Note: All instructions are privileged.

	lation tables associated with the user and supervisor modes and for logical DMA accesses. These registers contain a 32-bit actual address pointer and other information such as descriptor type (e.g., long format, short format, and so on).
Translation Control (TC) Register	This 32-bit register contains configuration information that includes bits allocated to each level of the translation tree, the page size (PS), initial shift (IS), and translation enable bit.
Cache Status Register (PCSR)	This is a read-only 16-bit register that contains the status of the ATC and RTP caches. For example, the currently active task-alias may be read from this register.
PMMU Status Register (PSR)	This register indicates the cause of PMMU-detected fault conditions.
Protection Mechanism Control Registers (CAL, VAL, SCC, AC)	These registers are intended to support the CALLM-RTM multiple access level protection mechanism.
Breakpoint Control Registers (BAD0-BAD7, BAC0-BAC7)	These registers control breakpoint functions.

The above registers appear as an extension to the 68020 supervisor programming model and may be accessed using the PMMU's coprocessor instructions. The PMMU instructions can load or read a PMMU register, control various virtual-memory functions, and save or restore the PMMU's internal state as summarized in Table 7-12.

EXERCISES

1. Discuss the advantages and disadvantages of incorporating coprocessor features onto the main processor.
2. What is the difference between a coprocessor and a peripheral device? Discuss 68020 bus interface differences.
3. What are the different CPU-cycles supported by the 68020?
4. What are the advantages and disadvantages of DMA and non-DMA type coprocessors?
5. Discuss why sign-magnitude instead of two's complement form is choosen for the IEEE floating-point format.
6. What is the representation of 10492_{10} in IEEE single-precision floating-point format?
7. What is the interrupt latency of the 68020 when a FSIN instruction is executing?
8. Example 7-3 is incomplete because the constant offset values PARM_N, PARM_CTABLE, and PARM_X0 that define parameter values on the stack are not specified. Add EQU statements for these.

8

Hardware Design with the 68000 and 68010

8.1 INTRODUCTION

In this chapter we are going to focus on the hardware design using the 68000. From a hardware perspective, the only difference between the 68000 and the 68010 is that the 68010 provides a more flexible bus-error (BERR*) signal timing. We will note the details of this difference in our discussion of the system control signals in Section 8.5.2. Otherwise, everything we discuss here about the 68000 also directly applies to using the 68010.

Figure 8-1 shows the block diagram of minimum circuitry that is necessary for a microcomputer or controller using the 68000. During the rest of this chapter, we will discuss the design of the submodules shown on this figure and we will examine possible design approaches, tradeoffs, and critical issues, instead of simply giving cookbook recipes.

Programmable logic devices (PLDs) will be used in some of our example designs and exercises due to their many advantages. Therefore, an introduction to designing with PLDs will also be given in this chapter. Another related item of interest we will discuss in this chapter is the possible circuit hazards to avoid such as metastability (we will define this term later).

We have studied the MC6800 peripheral control signals (VPA*, VMA*, and E) of the 68000 in Chapter 1. With the exception of the VPA* signal, we will not discuss these control signals further in this chapter. These control signals are seldom used; other than the VPA*, that is used to signal auto-vectoring during a interrupt-acknowledge cycle. This is due to the availability of many 68000 peripheral chips that provide higher performance and easier interface (see Table 2-3).

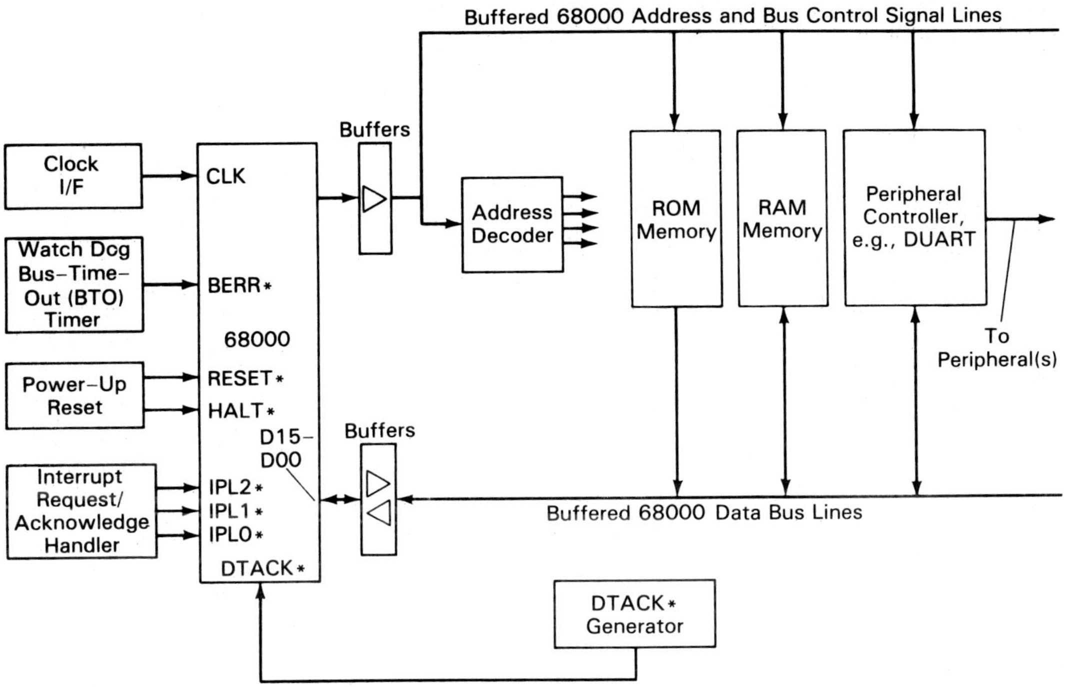

Figure 8-1 Simplified Block Diagram of a 68000-based Design.

To avoid any confusion, we will adopt the following notation in our discussion of various timing parameters:

t⟨*nn*⟩: Refers to a 68000 timing parameter, where the parameter number *nn* is the same number that is used by Motorola in their databook.

$T_{\langle xxxx \rangle}$: This refers to a timing parameter of a device other that the 68000 family processor. As a suffix, we will adopt the commonly used abbreviations when possible. For example, T_{dw} refers to data set-up time of a static RAM device.

Furthermore, to simplify our discussion, we will give values of timing parameters for the 10 MHz 68000 (MC68HC000⟨*pt*⟩10 where *pt* indicates package type). The parameter values differ for other speeds and are summarized in Appendix A.

8.2 DC-ELECTRICAL CHARACTERISTICS AND SIGNAL BUFFERING

Table 8-1 gives the DC-electrical characteristics of the 68000. An important parameter is the maximum current that the 68000 output drivers can sink. This characteristic is defined by the parameter I_{ol}, which is only 3.2 mA for the address

TABLE 8-1 DC-ELECTRICAL CHARACTERISTICS OF THE MC68HC000[1] (COURTESY OF MOTOROLA). V_{CC} = 5V + −5%.

Characteristic		Symbol	Min	Max	Unit
Input High Voltage		V_{IH}	2.0	V_{CC}	V
Input Low Voltage		V_{IL}	GND − 0.3	0.8	V
Input Leakage Current @ 5.25 V	BERR*, BGACK*, BR*, DTACK*, CLK, IPL0–IPL2*, VPA* HALT*, RESET*	I_{In}	— —	2.5 20	μA
Three-State (Off State) Input Current @ 2.4 V/0.4 V	AS*, A1–A23, D0–D15, FC0–FC2, LDS*, R/W*, UDS, VMA*	IT_{SI}	—	20	μA
Output High Voltage (I_{OH} = −400 μA)	E, AS*, A1–A23, BG*, D0–D15, FC0–FC2, LDS*, R/W*, UDS*, VMA*	V_{OH}	V_{CC} −0.75	—	V
Output Low Voltage (I_{OL} = 1.6 mA) (I_{OL} = 3.2 mA) (I_{OL} = 5.0 mA) (I_{OL} = 5.3 mA)	 HALT* A1–A23, BG*, FC0–FC2 RESET* E, AS*, D0–D15, LDS*, R/W*, UDS*, VMA*	V_{OL}	 — — — —	 0.5 0.5 0.5 0.5	V
Current Dissipation*	f = 8 MHz f = 10 MHz f = 12.5 MHz f = 16.67 MHz	I_D	— — —	25 30 35 50	mA
Power Dissipation	f = 8 MHz f = 10 MHz f = 12.5 MHz	P_D	— — —	0.13 0.16 0.19 0.26	W
Capacitance (V_{In} = 0 V, T_A = 25°C, Frequency = 1 MHz)**		C_{In}	—	20.0	pF
Load Capacitance	HALT* All Others	C_L	— —	70 130	pF

* Currents listed are with no loading.

** Capacitance is periodically sampled rather than 100% tested.

[1] CMOS Version.

bus, and 5.3 mA for the bus control signals and the data bus. At this current level, the output voltage (V_{ol}) is 0.5 volts, thus leaving 0.3 volts for the TTL-logic noise margin. Similarly, the outputs can source 400 microAmps (I_{oh}) in driving a high level of TTL-logic where the minimum output voltage will be 2.4 volts (V_{oh}). This provides a worst-case high-state noise immunity of 0.4 volts.

Let us look at the fan-out capability to drive 74Fxxx type logic (referred to as FAST). For the address bus we have

$$\begin{aligned} \text{Logic L Output Fanout} &= I_{ol} \text{ of 68000 output (max)}/I_{il} \text{ of ``F'' Input (max)} \\ &= 3.2 \text{ mA}/0.6 \text{ mA per Input} = 5 \text{ inputs.} \end{aligned}$$

Logic H Output Fanout = I_{oh} of 68000 output (max)/I_{ih} of "F" Input (max)
= 400 microAmp./20 microAmp per Input = 20 inputs.

where

I_{oh} (max) = Maximum high-level output current that the driver can supply.
I_{ol} (max) = Maximum low-level current that the driver can sink.
I_{ih} (max) = Maximum high-level input current of a buffer or gate.
I_{il} (max) = Maximum low-level input current of an input.

Since the minimum of the two above figures is five, the fanout is in the order of five to drive F-type logic for the 68000 address-bus drivers. We said "in the order of" because not all F-logic have the same loading. If, internally, multiple input structures are tied together, then the input current values also multiply. For example, the 'F244 buffer chip has a loading given by

$$I_{il} = 1.6 \text{ mA and } I_{ol} = 20 \text{ microAmp.}$$

which would reduce the fanout to two inputs. If, on the other hand, ALS-, HCT-, or FCT-type logic is driven by the 68000, the fanout is significantly higher. The designer has to choose the appropriate logic and decide what 68000 output signals to buffer based on the fanout, circuit speed, and power-consumption requirements. Due to the limited drive capability of the 68000, however, it is usually necessary to buffer the signal lines as shown in Figure 8-2. Using the 'ALS244 and 'ALS245 buffer chips provide an Iol of 24 mA to peripheral devices, thus increasing the fanout significantly.

At minimum, it is often necessary to buffer the AS* and R/W* signal lines. We will hereafter refer to buffered version of signals using the CPU_⟨*xxxx*⟩ or B⟨*xxxx*⟩ prefixes. For example, we will use CP_AS*/CPU_AS1* and CPU_WRITE* to indicate buffered AS* and R/W*, respectively. If the 68000 is the only bus master (i.e., if there are no DMA type devices), these buffers can drive the local bus all the time. In other words, we may connect the BUFEN* to ground in this case. However, if the local bus is to be shared with another bus master, then we could use the BGACK* input of the 68000 to control turning-on the external buffers only when the 68000 is the bus master—that is when BGACK* is negated. The BGACK* is asserted by a secondary bus master when it takes over the 68000 bus. We will discuss the operation of BGACK* further in the bus-arbitration section of this chapter.

A potential circuit problem may occur at the beginning of a write bus cycle. The R/W* is asserted before the output buffers of the 68000 are turned on as shown in Figure 8-3. However, the time between the assertion of R/W* and data bus driven is only 20 nanoseconds for a 10 MHz 68000 as specified by the timing parameter t55. This time is reduced to zero nanoseconds for the 16 MHz 68000.

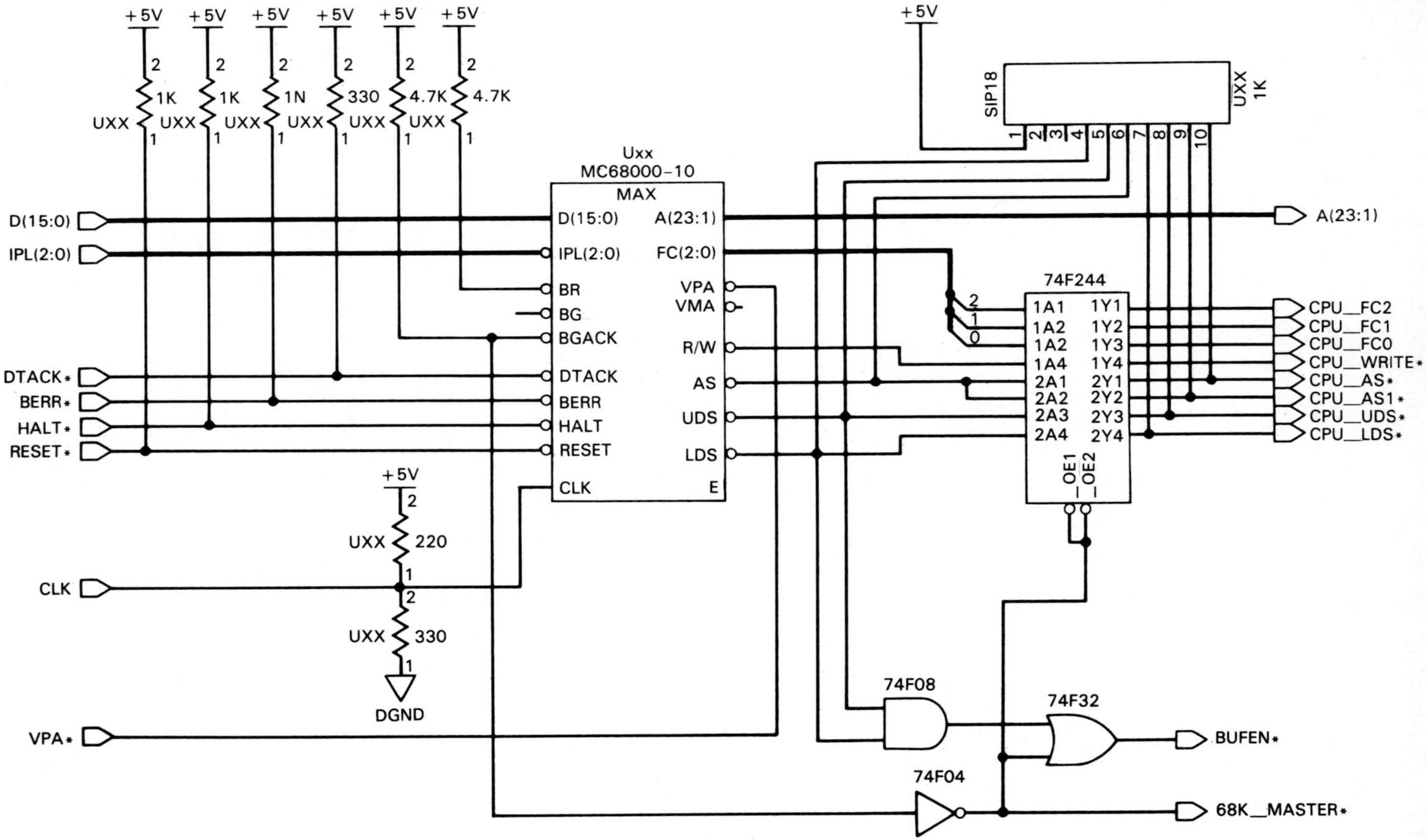

Note: _SIGNAL is equivalent to SIGNAL * or $\overline{\text{SIGNAL}}$.

Figure 8-2 Example Buffering of the 68000 Signal Lines.

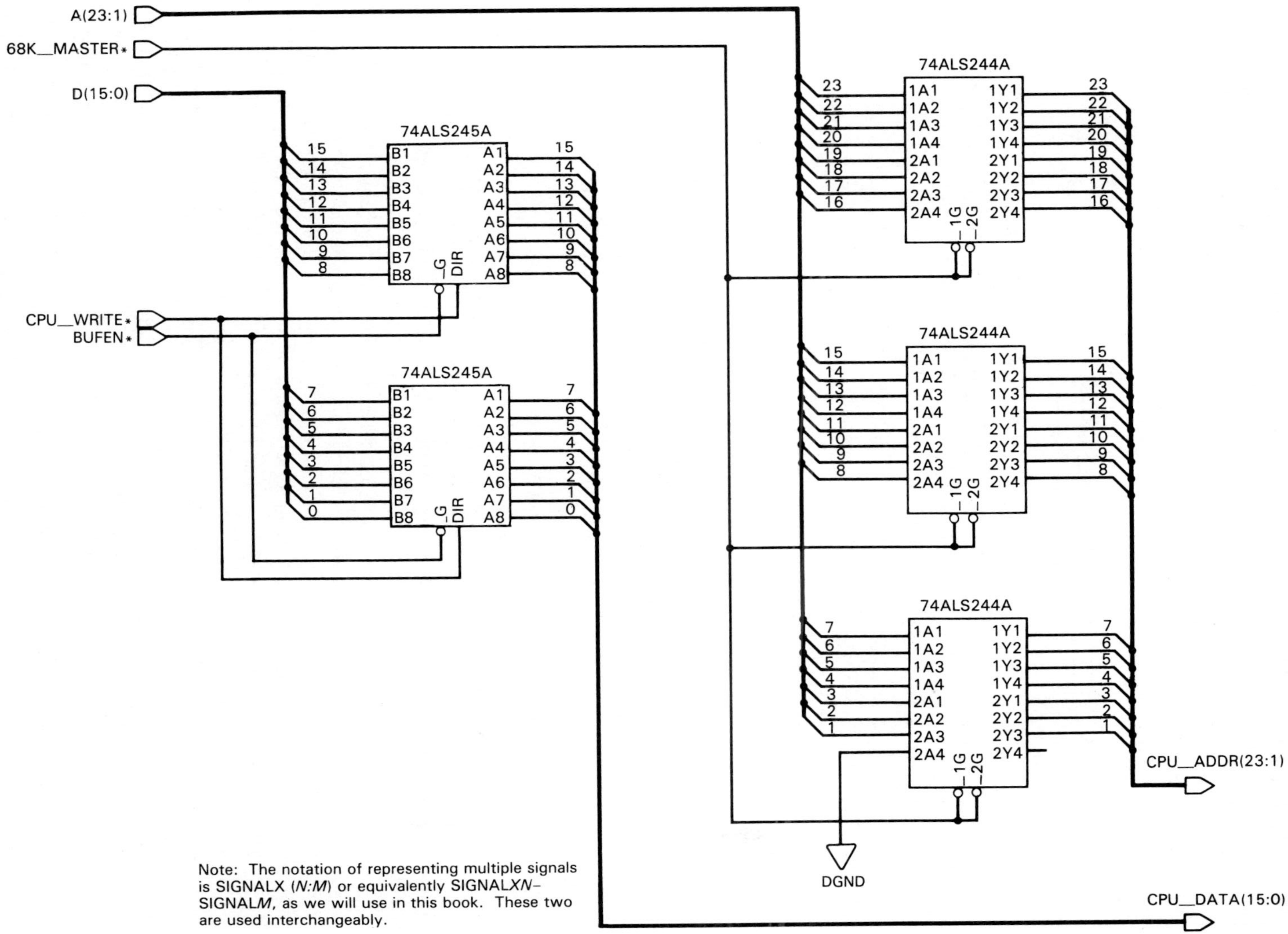

Note: The notation of representing multiple signals is SIGNALX (*N:M*) or equivalently SIGNALX*N*–SIGNAL*M*, as we will use in this book. These two are used interchangeably.

Figure 8-2 (cont.) Example Buffering of the 68000 Signal Lines.

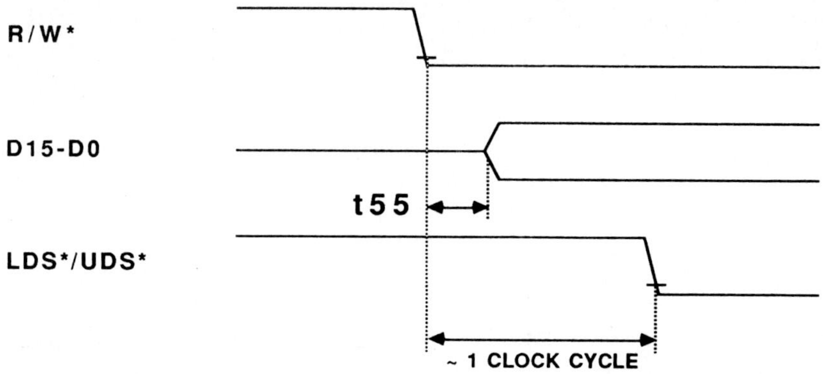

Parameter	Characteristic	Min	Max	Units
t55	R/W* Asserted to Data bus Driven	20	—	nsec.

Figure 8-3 Timing of Data Buffer Control.

If the external bidirectional buffers were unable to change their direction in this time period, this would cause a bus conflict or contention between the 68000 output data buffers and the external bidirectional 'ALS245 buffers. One way to ensure that this will not happen is to turn off the external data buffers until one or both of the data strobes, LDS*/UDS* are asserted. Since, during a write bus cycle, the data strobes are asserted about one clock cycle after the R/W*, this will prevent any such bus conflict.

All unused inputs of the 68000 *must* be pulled high. Typically, a pull-up resistor of 1K to 10K connected to +5 volts is sufficient. Since the input leakage current of the 68000 is less than 20 micro-Amps, the voltage drop over the pull-up resistor will be negligible in the worst case.

In the case of used 68000 inputs, there is another design consideration. The TTL device output drivers have a typical characteristic impedance in the order of tens of ohms, whereas the inputs of the 68000 have an impedance in the order of megaohms. If the transition time of the signal is less than the propagation time from the driver output to the 68000 input, this causes a voltage-doubling effect when the line switches state[1]. This is similar to a unterminated transmission line type problem, and thus is more likely to occur with fast AS- or F-type driver devices. The close placement of drivers to the 68000 inputs will also help prevent or reduce such "ringing" or undershoots. The allowed worst-case input voltage for the 68000 is −0.3 to 6.5 volts (from Table 8-1). We could use resistive termination in order to avoid any excessive undershoot that could easily violate the input voltage range of the 68000. One approach is to use a series resistor at the output of the external driver, typically 33 or 47 ohms. However, such a resistor

[1] See references 24, 35, 36 for further reading.

may present problems when used with an in-circuit emulator for the 68000. A safer approach in this case is using a pull-up with 330 ohms or utilizing a dual-ended termination with 220 ohm pull-up and 330 ohm pull-down.

An ideal design, however, will have impedance controlled signal traces and RC-type terminations, where typically R is 47 ohms and C is 56 pF. The R and C are connected in series between the input and the ground. R is matched to the impedance of the trace, and as such they provide a perfect termination.

Here, due to its simplicity we will use the 330 ohm pull-up for important control inputs such as DTACK* and use the dual-ended termination for the clock input.

The address outputs may also be pulled high, because they are in high-impedance state between bus cycles or when there is no bus activity. This is especially necessary when CMOS logic devices are being driven directly by the 68000. The input of CMOS devices, if left floating without any pull-up, may result in significantly increased power consumption, and could also cause oscillatory and unpredictable behavior. This is because a CMOS gate input is actually the open-gate input of a MOSFET transistor.

8.3 CLOCK SIGNAL AND INTERFACE

The 68000 requires a TTL-compatible clock input as shown in Figure 8-4. The clock input must meet the specified rise and fall times, as well as the limits on low and high width times. The 68000 also places a minimum limit on the clock frequency because of the refresh requirements of the dynamic memory[2] used on the chip.

Figure 8-5 shows an example clock interface circuit. The crystal oscillator output is divided by two to guarantee approximately 50–50% high-and-low duty cycle, and the clock input is buffered such that other logic inputs will not load the 68000 clock input, thus ensuring that its rise and fall time requirements are met. Since the rise and fall times are small, the clock interface circuit should be located close to the 68000 in order to eliminate the possibility of any reflections and ringing in the clock signal.

Internally, the 68000 operates synchronously with the clock input using both positive- and negative-going edges of the clock signal. This means that all external output signals are asserted or negated at specific clock times. The 68000, however, does not require any of its external inputs to be synchronous with the clock signal. Therefore, all external control inputs are synchronized internally to the 68000 clock before being used.

Since an asynchronous input has no fixed relationship to the 68000's clock input, it may be changing at sampling time. The input synchronizers always resolves the state of the input to a logic level one or zero, so that the rest of the

[2] In dynamic memory the data bits are stored as a charge on capacitor that must be periodically recharged.

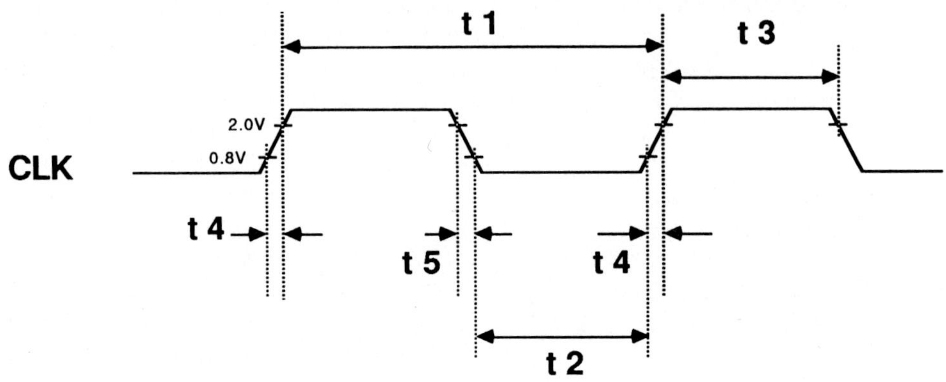

Parameter	Characteristic	Min	Max	Units
	Frequency of Operation (1/t1 or 1/tcyc)	4	10.0	MHz
t1 or tcyc	Clock Period	100	250	nsec.
t2, t3	Clock Pulse High or Low Width	45	125	nsec.
t4, t5	Clock Rise and Fall Times	—	10	nsec.

Figure 8-4 Clock Timing Requirements.

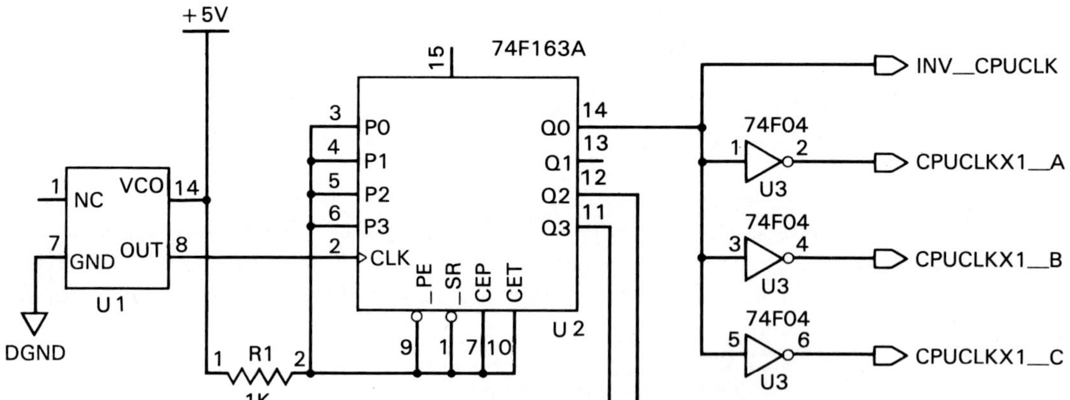

Figure 8-5 Example Clock Circuit.

internal circuit always receives a valid logic level, and not an indeterminate state[3]. To accomplish input synchronization and reliable operation, the 68000 uses three *transparent* latches as shown in Figure 8-6. These latches allow an input to propagate to its output like a buffer when E (Enable) is high. When E is low, the input is latched. So, the control inputs are sampled at the negative edge of the clock signal. These three latches causes a delay of one clock cycle before an asynchronous control input is acted upon by the 68000. The high-gain characteristics of the devices compromising these latches quickly resolves a marginal signal into a valid state.

If an input signal meets the asynchronous input setup time, specified by parameter t47, then it will be recognized as asserted as illustrated in Figure 8-7. If an input violates the setup time by making a transition during a sample window, the logic level recognized by the processor is not predictable, but as we said earlier, will always be resolved to a high or low logic level by the 68000. If a changing input signal is not recognized during a sample window or if it is asserted after the sample window, then it will be recognized during the next sample window as long as it stays asserted.

A bus cycle with no wait-cycles consists of eight internal states called S0 through S7. For slow peripherals, wait-cycles are added when the internal state machine is in state 4 (S4). We will show these added clock cycle(s) as a pair of wait-states, SW. The high clock period of SW is equivalent to S4 with the exception of added wait-cycles. This is illustrated in Figure 8-8.

8.4 ASYNCHRONOUS BUS OPERATION

8.4.1 Asynchronous Bus Control Signals and Bus Operation

Figure 8-9 shows the asynchronous bus control signals of the 68000. The address strobe, AS*, is the earliest control signal indicating a 68000 bus cycle has begun. Its timing with respect to the 68000 clock is shown in Figure 8-10. The timing

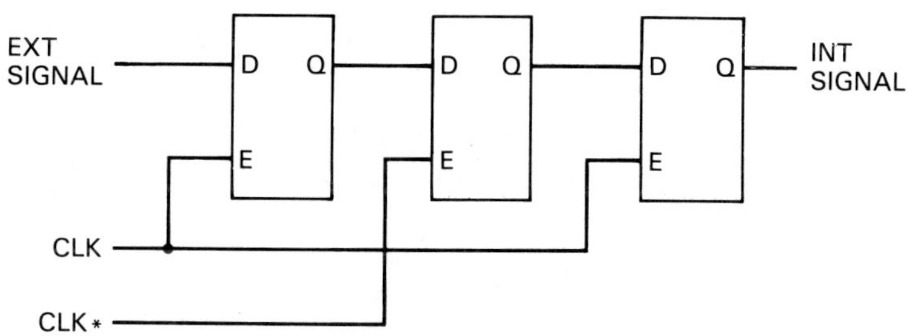

Figure 8-6 68000 Input Synchronizers. (Courtesy of Motorola).

[3] Such a indeterminate or oscillatory state is called a *metastable state*. More on this later.

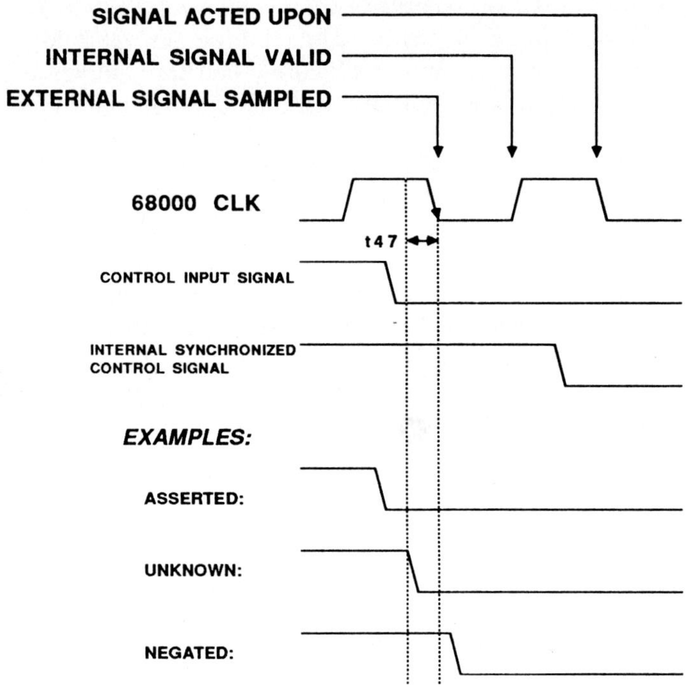

Parameter	Characteristic	Min	Max	Units
t47	Asynchronous Input Setup Time	10	—	nsec.

Figure 8-7 Asynchronous Control Input Recognition.

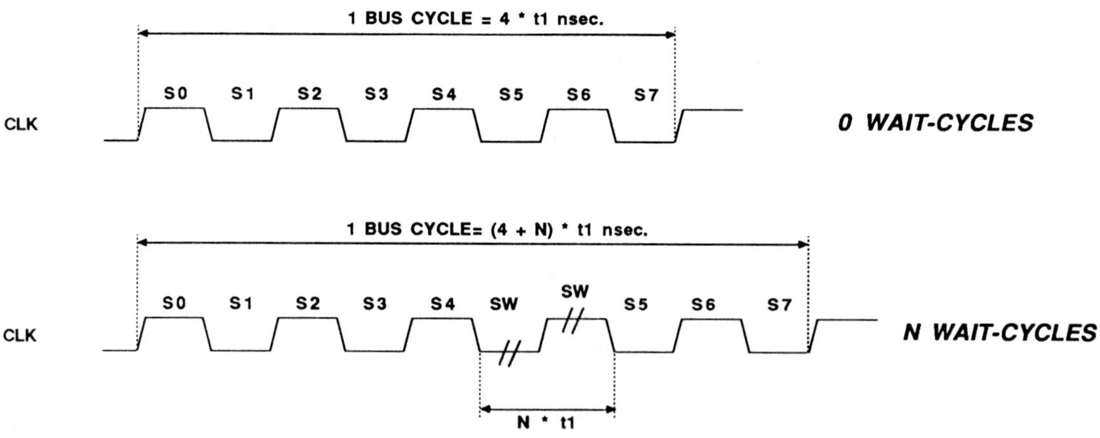

Figure 8-8 Bus-cycle States of the 68000.

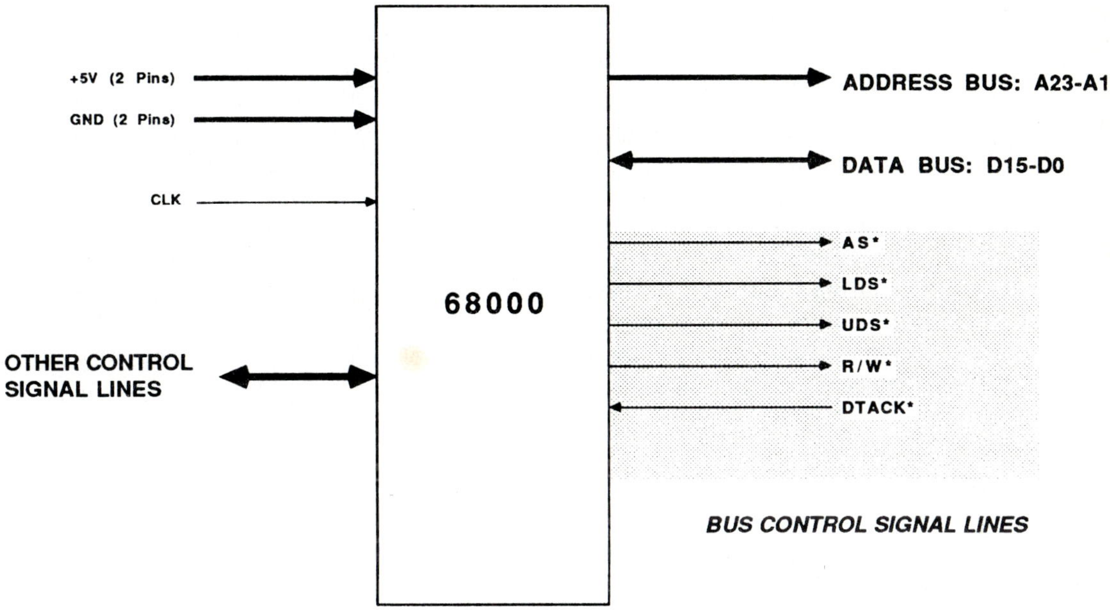

Figure 8-9 Asynchronous Bus Control Signals.

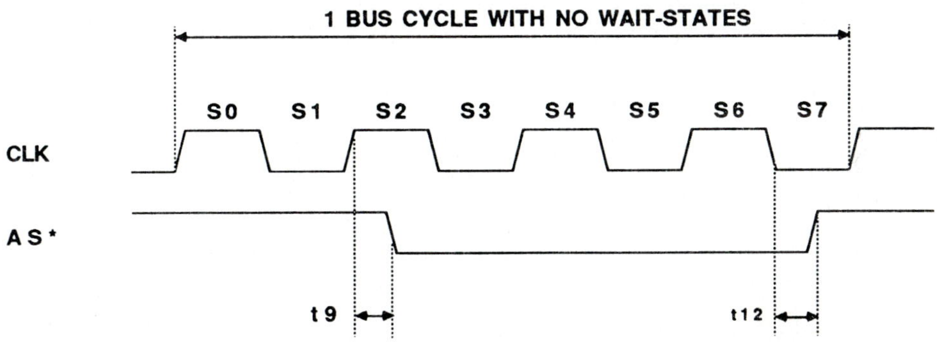

Parameter	Characteristic	Min	Max	Units
t9	Clock High to AS*/LDS*/UDS* Asserted.	3	50	nsec.
t12	Clock Low to AS*/LDS*/UDS* Negated.	—	50	nsec.

Figure 8-10 AS* Timing.

parameter t9 specifies when AS* is asserted after the positive-going edge of state S2. For a 10 MHz 68000, we have

$$t9\ (max) = 50\ nsec.$$

$$t3\ (min) = 45\ nsec.$$

This means, in the worst case, the assertion of AS* may coincide with the beginning of state S3. At the end of the cycle, the AS* is negated with a timing of t12 after the negative-going edge of state S6. Similarly, the worst-case timing figures indicate that the negation of AS* may coincide with the end of state S7.

The timing of the AS*, address lines, and function code signals are the same for both read and write bus cycles (see Figure 8-11). Valid function codes are driven during state zero, t6a after the positive-going edge of S0, and are maintained until the end of the bus cycle.

When there is no bus activity, the address signal lines A23-A1 are in the high-impedance state. When a bus cycle begins, a valid address is placed during

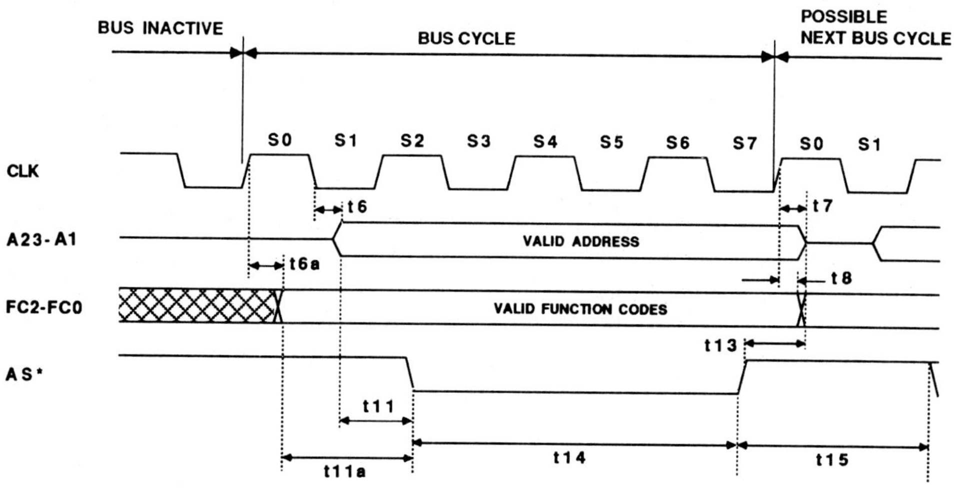

Parameter	Characteristic	Min	Max	Units
t6	Clock Low to Address Valid	—	50	nsec.
t7	Clock High to Address bus in High-Impedance	—	70	nsec.
t8	Clock High to Address and FC2-FC0 Invalid	0	—	nsec.
t11	Address Valid to AS* asserted.	20	—	nsec.
t11A	FC2-FC0 Valid to AS* asserted.	70	—	nsec.
t13	AS* negated to Address and FC2-FC0 Invalid	30	—	nsec.
t14	AS* Width asserted.	195	—	nsec.
t15	AS* Width negated.	105	—	nsec.

Figure 8-11 Timing of Address and Function Code Signals.

state S1 and stays unchanged through the end of the bus cycle. Note that the beginning of a valid address and the function codes are specified with respect to both clock and address strobe signals.

DTACK∗ recognition. Using the DTACK∗, peripheral devices signal the 68000 to terminate the bus cycle, indicating that the data transfer is complete or will be completed before the cycle is completed. The first sample window of the DTACK∗ is on the falling edge of state S4. If the DTACK∗ is asserted and meets the setup time t47 before this falling edge, then it is guaranteed that the 68000 will recognize it and will terminate the bus cycle without inserting any wait-cycles at the end of state S7. If DTACK∗ is asserted in the middle of the sample window, it may or it may not be recognized by the 68000. If it is not recognized during the first sampling window, the 68000 will assert one wait-cycle and will sample DTACK∗ again at the falling edge of next clock cycle. This assumes that VPA∗ or BERR∗ is not asserted in lieu of or before DTACK∗, because any one of {DTACK∗, BERR∗, VPA∗} will terminate a bus cycle. Normally and typically, a bus cycle is terminated by DTACK∗ assertion. The BERR∗ indicates an error condition, as we discussed earlier. The different cases of DTACK∗ recognition are illustrated in Figure 8-12.

There is no time limit imposed by the 68000 on the return of the DTACK∗. It will wait and insert wait-cycles indefinitely until DTACK∗ or one of the other bus-cycle termination signals is received.

At the end of the bus cycle, the 68000 requires that the peripheral device negates DTACK∗ after AS∗ or one of the data strobes (LDS∗/UDS∗) are negated.

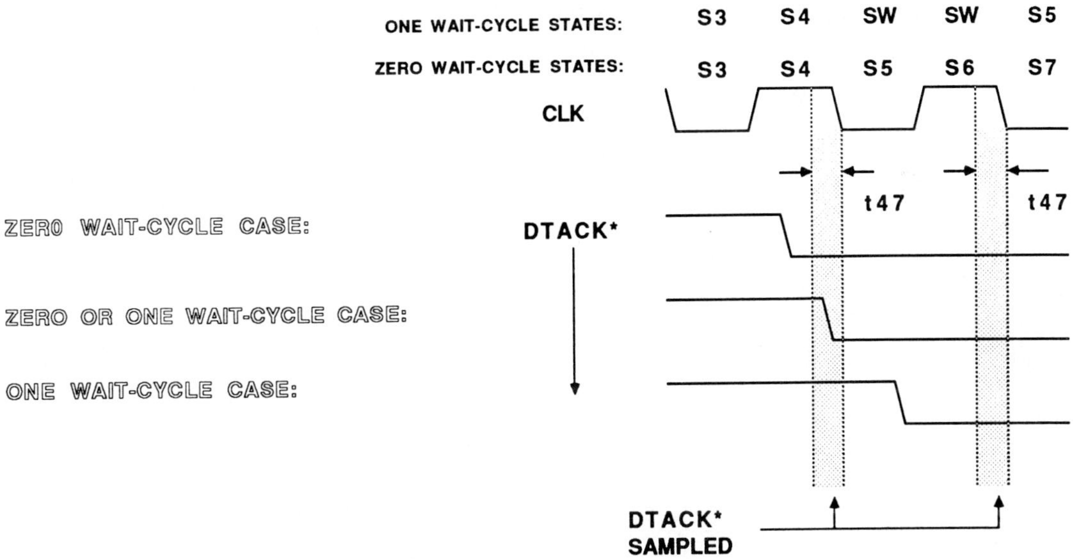

Figure 8-12 DTACK∗ Recognition.

The maximum time specified for negation is given by parameter t28, as shown in Figure 8-13. The purpose of this is to avoid early misdetection of DTACK* in a consecutive bus cycle. For example, if we are running the 68000 with one wait-cycle, and if the DTACK* is not negated for 200 nanoseconds after the AS* is negated, then the next bus cycle will detect the DTACK* from the previous bus-cycle during its first sampling window, causing an error. Otherwise, there is no restriction to negate DTACK* at the end of each bus cycle. For example, if all devices are running at zero wait-cycles, the DTACK* input may be permanently grounded. However, this is very seldom the case.

The minimum time for t28 represents the hold time for DTACK*. This parameter value is zero, meaning that we cannot negate DTACK* before one of the AS*/LDS*/UDS* is negated.

8.4.2 Read Bus Cycle

During a read bus cycle, the 68000 reads a byte or word size operand from external memory or other type of peripheral device. The bus timing is shown in Figure 8-14 where the signal lines {R/W*, LDS*/UDS*, D15-D0} are highlighted because their timing differ between read and write bus cycles. The following define the state of bus control signals with respect to the state of the 68000 clock:

STATE 0 (S0) The bus cycle starts in S0, during which the clock is high. After the rising edge of S0, the valid function codes are placed on the FC2-FC0 lines and the R/W* is driven high. Also, the address bus placed in the high-impedance state.

STATE 1 (S1) The address of the accessed location in memory map is placed on the address lines A23-A1.

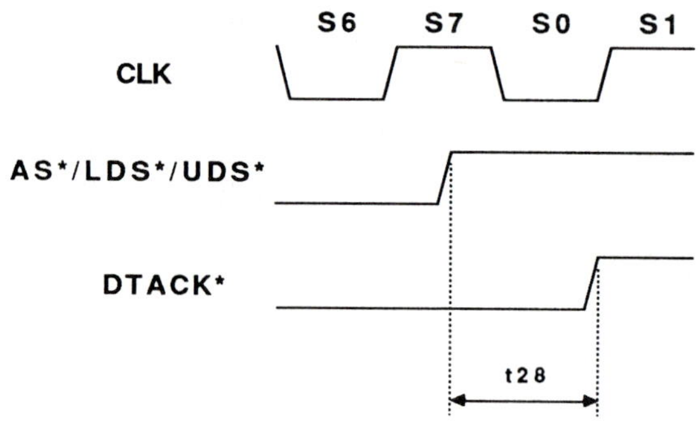

Parameter	Characteristic	Min	Max	Units
t28	AS*/LDS*/UDS* Negated to DTACK* Negated.	0	190	nsec.

Figure 8-13 DTACK* Negation Timing.

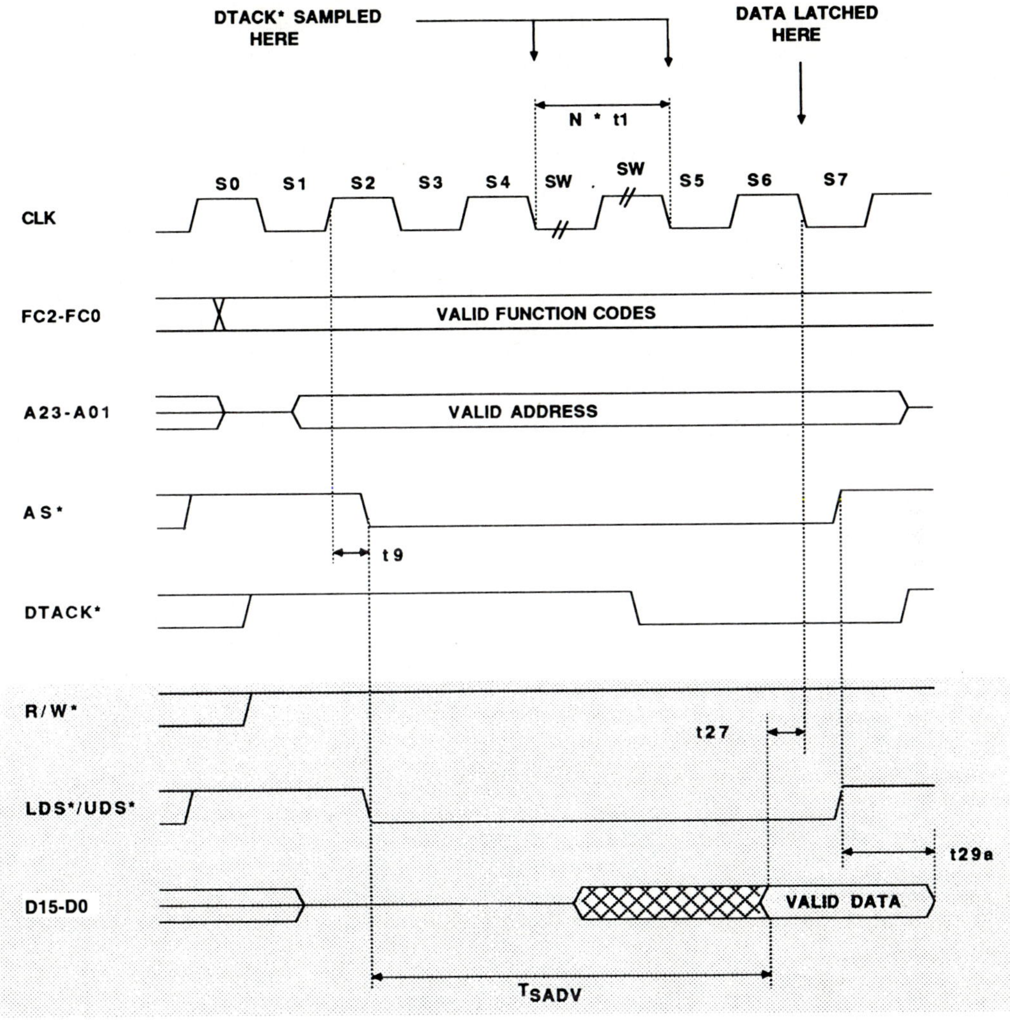

Parameter	Characteristic	Min	Max	Units
t12	Clock Low to AS*, LDS/UDS* Negated	—	50	nsec
t17	R/W* Hold Time At the End of Bus Cycle.	30	—	nsec
t18	Clock High to R/W* High.	0	45	nsec
t27	Data Setup Time.	10	—	nsec
t29a	AS*, LDS*/UDS* Negated to Data In Hi-Z.	—	150	nsec

Figure 8-14 Read Bus-cycle Timing.

STATE 2 (S2) After the rising edge of S2, the AS* and LDS*/UDS* are asserted.

STATE 3 (S3) No 68000 bus control output signals are altered in this state.

STATE 4 (S4) DTACK* is sampled at the end of this state. If DTACK* is not recognized as asserted, a wait-cycle is asserted. The 68000 stays in state S4, although we refer to this as wait-cycles or SW, until one of the bus termination signals is recognized.

STATE 5 (S5) The 68000 proceeds to S5 when a bus termination signal is recognized. No 68000 output signals are altered in this state.

STATE 6 (S6) At the end of this state, the 68000 latches the data inputs. The data has to be stable at the 68000 data pins with a setup time of t27 before the falling edge of S6.

STATE 7 (S7) After the beginning of S7, the 68000 negates the AS* and LDS*/UDS* with a delay of t12. The valid address and data are held until the end of this state.

The parameter t29a specifies the maximum time by which the read data has to be removed from the bus after the completion of a read bus cycle. The worst case allowed value (120 nsec. in the case of 10 MHz 68000) is specified so that the data outputs of the current bus cycle do not collide with the next bus cycle's read or write data.

To understand the maximum time available to make a read access, we can define the following parameter:

$$T_{SADV} = \text{Strobe-Asserted-to-Data-Valid}$$

This gives the time window starting when AS* is asserted to when the data has to be valid at the 68000 data inputs, meeting the setup time t27. As such, it includes external buffer delays, propagation time of the chip-select decode logic, and mainly the device access time. Examining the timing diagram with respect to clock edges, we have

$$T_{SADV} = (2 + N) * t1 + t3 - t9 - t27$$

where N is the number of wait-cycles ($N = 0, 1, 2, \ldots$). Using worst-case design rules, we have

$$N = 0 : T_{SADV} = 175 \text{ nsec.}$$

$$N = 1 : T_{SADV} = 275 \text{ nsec.}$$

and so on. However, we have to bear in mind that T_{SADV} gives the overall access time only for read cycles. We will examine the write cycle access-timing considerations in the next section.

8.4.3 Write Bus Cycle

The write bus-cycle timing is shown in Figure 8-15. The write cycle differs from the read cycle in that the R/W∗ is asserted at the beginning of the bus cycle, and the 68000 places the data to be written on the bus and then asserts the LDS∗/UDS∗. The following describe the activity of write cycle during each of the eight bus-cycle states:

STATE 0 (S0)	The write cycle starts in S0 during which the clock is high. After the rising edge of S0, the valid function codes are placed on FC2-FC0, and R/W∗ is driven high. Also, the address bus is placed in the high-impedance state.
STATE 1 (S1)	The address of the accessed location in memory map is placed on the address lines A23-A1.
STATE 2 (S2)	After the rising edge of S2, the AS∗ and R/W∗ are asserted. The R/W∗ is driven low with a delay of t20 after the clock edge.
STATE 3 (S3)	During S3 the 68000 places the data to be written on the bus. The data becomes valid with a delay of t23 after the clock edge. The timing parameter t55 specifies the minimum delay from R/W∗ asserted to the time the data output buffers of the 68000 are enabled. The purpose of t55, as we saw in Figure 8-3, is to allow time for the direction of peripheral's bidirectional data buffers to be changed before the 68000 starts driving the data bus.
STATE 4 (S4)	During this state, the 68000 asserts the LDS∗/UDS∗ with a delay of t9 after the clock edge. The parameter t26 specifies the minimum time from data-out-valid to when the LDS∗/UDS∗ is asserted (i.e., the data setup time before the data strobes). DTACK∗ is sampled at the end of this state, and the 68000 inserts wait-cycles until a DTACK∗ or one of the other termination signals is recognized. This is the same as the read cycle.
STATE 5 (S5)	The 68000 proceeds to S5 when a DTACK∗ and/or BERR∗ is detected at the end of S4. No 68000 output signals are altered in this state.
STATE 6 (S6)	No signals are altered during this state.
STATE 7 (S7)	After the beginning of S7, the 68000 negates AS∗ and LDS∗/UDS∗. The valid address and data are held until the end of this state.

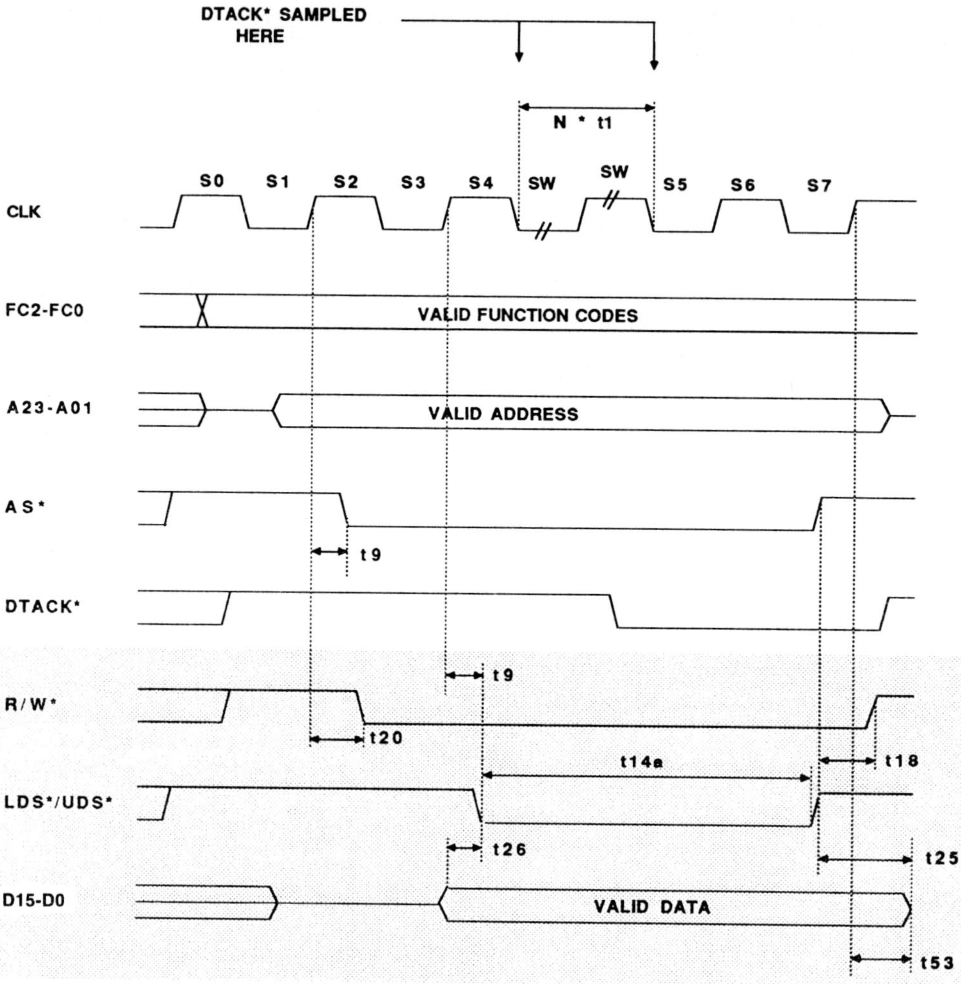

Parameter	Characteristic	Min	Max	Units
t14a	LDS*/UDS* Asserted Width.	95	—	nsec.
t20	Clock High to R/W* Low.	0	45	nsec.
t23	Clock Low to Data-out Valid	—	50	nsec.
t25	AS*, LDS*/UDS* Negated to Data Invalid	30	—	nsec.
t26	Data-out Valid to LDS*/UDS* Asserted.	30	—	nsec.
t53	Data-out Hold Time from Clock High.	0	—	

Figure 8-15 Write Bus-cycle Timing.

As we discussed earlier, during a write bus cycle the 68000 asserts one or both of the data strobes signals (LDS* and/or UDS*) depending upon the operand size and alignment. For a byte-size operand, the 68000 uses the internal address bit A0 to determine which strobe to assert (see Table 1-2). Thus, we cannot initiate a write access to a device until LDS*/UDS* are asserted because the external logic has no indication whether one or both of the bytes will be written. The disadvantage of this is that the LDS*/UDS* are asserted rather late in a write bus cycle in state S4. Let us look how much time we have to complete a write operation. The parameters t26 and t25 specify the minimum valid data-output setup and hold times with respect to LDS*/UDS*/AS*, respectively. The parameter t14a specifies the minimum time LDS*/UDS* stays asserted. In general, (t14a + *N*), where *N* is the wait-cycles gives us a good idea about the overall write access-time requirements. For example, t14a is 95 nanoseconds for a 10 MHz 68000. Accounting for buffer and other interface logic delays, this would approximately require a 55 nanosecond version of a static RAM memory to access with no wait-cycles. This shows the discrepancy between the read and write cycle access requirements (e.g., 95 nanoseconds versus 175 for read).

8.4.4 Asynchronous Versus Synchronous Types of Bus Interface

The physical bus interface of the 68000 to the outside world is referred to as an *asynchronous bus interface*. The term asynchronous in this context carries two different and important meanings. First and primarily, it means that the processor starts a bus cycle and the external world determines the duration of the access using the DTACK* signal. Such a handshake maximizes the data throughput by matching the processor speed to that of the memory or other peripheral devices. For example, a high-speed static RAM memory array can be accessed with no wait-cycles while another relatively slow peripheral device does not impose significant performance penalty on the entire 68000 system.

The second meaning of the term asynchronous addresses the fact that all external input signals to the 68000 may be asynchronous to its clock signal. As we saw in Section 8.3, the 68000 internally synchronizes all of its control inputs. This means that in designing the bus control interface logic, there are three possible approaches as we will describe next.

Fully asynchronous interface. In this case, the 68000 input signals such as DTACK* generated by the interface logic has no fixed relationship to the clock input of the 68000. Furthermore, the interface logic has no knowledge about the clock frequency of the 68000. This approach ensures full clock frequency independence at the system level and is used by most of the 68000 peripheral chips.

This means that the 68000's clock signal is not used by the interface logic. Also, we can make no assumptions about the timing between the different handshake signals. For example, we cannot assume that the minimum data setup time before the LDS*/UDS* is asserted is 30 nanoseconds for parameter t26 because its value actually varies between 40 and 15 nanoseconds for different speed versions of the 68000 (see Appendix A).

In this mode of interface, AS* is used to indicate the start of a bus cycle, and for a write operation LDS*/UDS* indicates valid data is placed on the data bus. DTACK* must be returned by the addressed device *after or as soon as* the data transfer (read or write) is completed. This is illustrated in Figure 8-16.

Pseudo-asynchronous interface. This is the same as the fully asynchronous interface except that the clock frequency of the 68000 is known. This means that we know the timing relationship between the bus signals. An important parameter in this case is the DTACK*-Asserted-to-Data-in-Valid time specified by t31 for a read bus cycle. In other words, the timing specifications allow DTACK* to precede valid data by the maximum amount of time given by t31. Meeting this parameter ensures the validity of data that is latched by the 68000.

Synchronous interface. In the synchronous operation of the interface logic, the 68000 clock signal is used to generate DTACK* and other bus control input signals. Thus, these input signals have a fixed phase relation to the 68000's clock signal. DTACK* has to meet the setup time t47 of a sampling window, and also for a read cycle, the valid data has to meet the setup time t27 of the next

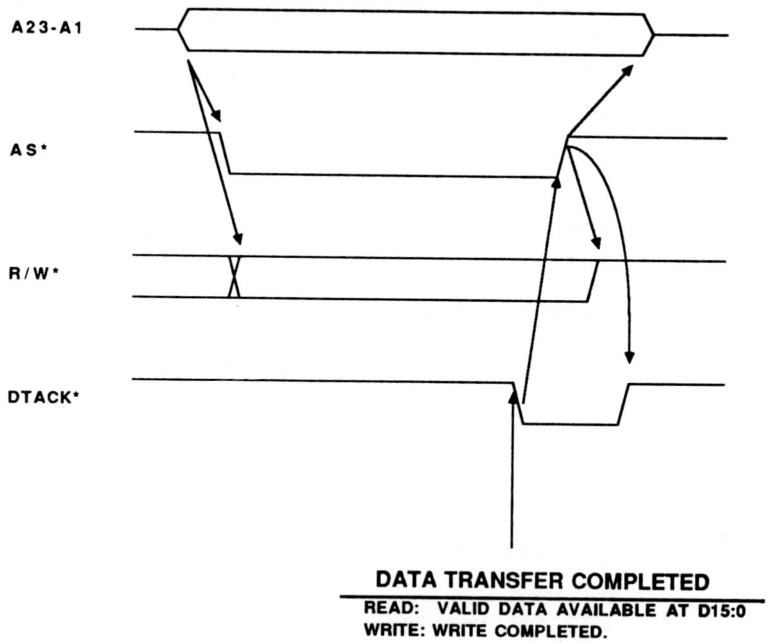

Figure 8-16 Illustration of Fully Asynchronous Bus Cycles.

falling edge of the clock signal. Figure 8-17 illustrates the synchronous versus pseudo-asynchronous interface requirements.

Comparison of interface approaches and summary. The above synchronous operation of the bus interface should not be confused with the synchronous bus control signals, {VPA*, VMA*, E}, which are intended to be used in interfacing to the 8-bit 6800 peripheral chips.

Let us clarify another area of possible confusion. The type of interface used does not affect the operation of the 68000 other than possibly the number of wait-cycles. In other words, the 68000 does not know whether our interface is working synchronously with its clock or otherwise. For example, during a read cycle, if DTACK* is recognized during S4 then the data will be latched at the end of state

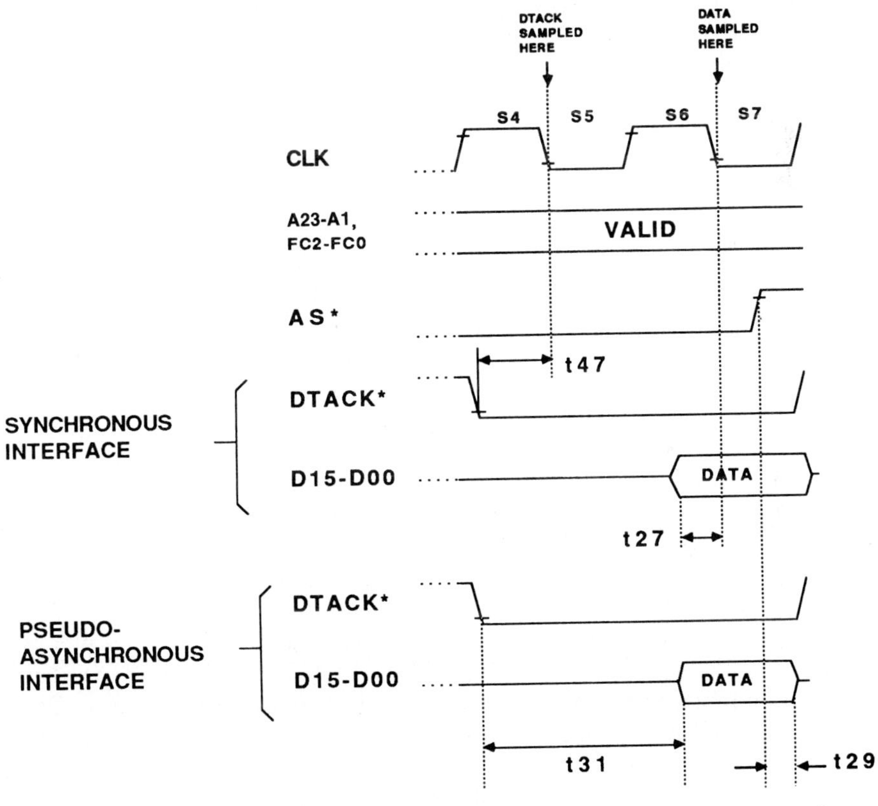

Parameter	Characteristic	Min	Max	Units
t31	DTACK* Asserted to Data-in Valid (Read).	—	65	nsec.

Figure 8-17 Synchronous versus Pseudo-asynchronous Interfaces.

S6 regardless of the type of interface logic used. One may note that, because the sampling of DTACK* and data are one clock cycle apart, there is potentially one wait-cycle difference between the synchronous and fully asynchronous types of interfaces.

The type of interface a designer uses depends primarily on the peripheral device types. For example, the 68000 family peripheral chip '68681 DUART internally operates at a different clock and thus uses a fully asynchronous interface. A significant advantage of this is that it allows the same 68000-family peripheral chips to be interfaced to the 68000 of different clock speeds and also different processors of the 68000 family. Another advantage of this approach is that the clock frequency of the 68000 can be upgraded without affecting any of the peripheral or interface logic.

The memory type devices, on the other hand, are usually interfaced using synchronous operation, because the synchronous mode is closely coupled to the internal operation of the 68000, and as such, it provides optimal performance (i.e., the minimal number of wait-cycles).

The 68000 supports the different methods of interface by specifying most of its timing signals to *both* clock edges and other related signals. For example, the assertion of AS* is specified with respect to the rising edge of S2 (t9), and also with respect to the valid address on the bus (address setup time of t11).

8.4.5 Types of Bus Cycles

In addition to the read and write bus cycles we have already discussed, the 68000 has two other transfer cycles: A read-modify-write bus cycle and an interrupt-acknowledge bus cycle. Any 68000 bus cycle can be classified in one of the four categories.

Read-modify-write bus cycle. During the bus cycle, the 68000 first reads a given byte location, modifies it, then writes it back to the same address. Only one 68000 instruction, namely TAS, uses this bus cycle type, thus it is not frequently encountered. This type of bus cycle works only with byte-size transfers, due to the definition of the TAS instruction.

The read-modify-write cycle timing is similar to a read bus cycle, followed by a write bus cycle except the addresses A23-A1 stay unchanged and the address strobe remains asserted throughout the entire cycle as shown in Figure 8-18. This cycle is referred to as *indivisible* because it cannot be interrupted by exceptions other than system reset and bus error. As we saw earlier, this is necessary to implement a software semaphore in a multiprocessor environment.

Interrupt-acknowledge bus cycle. The purpose of this cycle is to read the vector number of the interrupting device. During this bus cycle, the 68000 sets the function codes to all highs (i.e., FC2-FC0 = {HHH}). This is the only indication to distinquish this type of bus cycle.

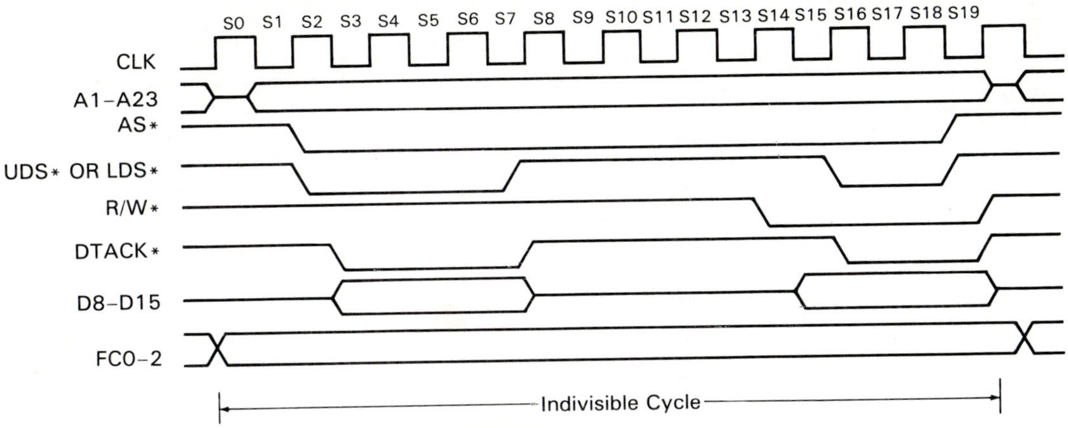

Figure 8-18 Read-modify-write Bus Cycle. (Courtesy of Motorola.)

We are going to discuss the further details of interrupt acknowledge in Section 8.11 under the interrupt operation.

8.5 SYSTEM CONTROL SIGNALS

The three control signals shown in Figure 8-19 provides various utility functions for a 68000-based system. Based on the combination of these signals that are active, the 68000 performs the following operations:

RESET*	BERR*	HALT*	Resulting Operation
L	H	L	Reset the 68000.
H	L	H	Bus Error Exception.
H	H	L	Halt the 68000.
H	L	L	Re-run the current bus cycle.
H	H	H	Normal program execution.

Next we will discuss the timing for these signals.

8.5.1 Reset Operation

When both RESET* and HALT* signal lines are asserted by external logic, this is recognized as a reset operation for the 68000 and its peripherals. The reset operation is necessary at power-up time, after a double-bus fault which causes the 68000 to halt until reset or simply to restart the system for some other reason. As shown in Figure 8-20, after power-up, HALT* and RESET* have to be asserted for a minimum of 100 milliseconds. Other times 10 clock cycles will be sufficient unless a RESET instruction happens to be executed. In the latter case, the

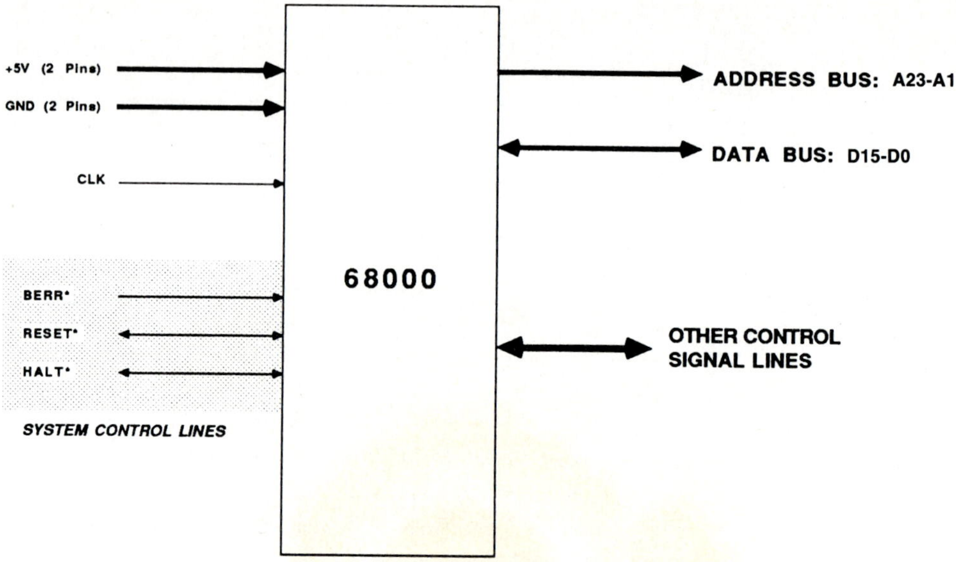

Figure 8-19 System Control Signal Lines.

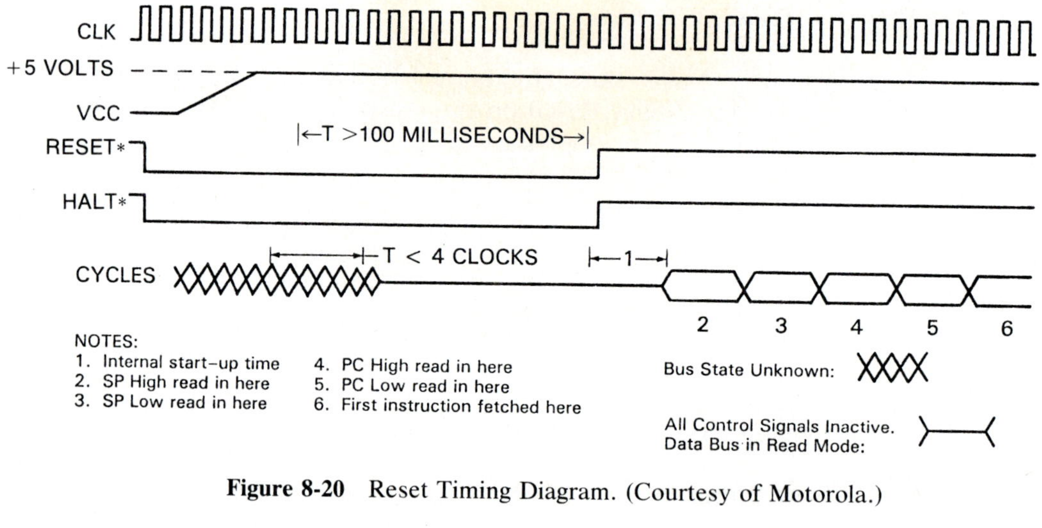

Figure 8-20 Reset Timing Diagram. (Courtesy of Motorola.)

RESET* and HALT* have be asserted for a minimum of 134 clock cycles because the RESET instruction asserts the bidirectional RESET* line for 124 clock cycles. During this time, any external reset input will go unnoticed by the 68000.

In general, it is safer to assert RESET* and HALT* much longer than the required minimums. An example reset circuit is shown in Figure 8-21 where the '555 compatible timer provides more than 200 millisecond reset time for both power-up and manual reset operation. The 1N4001 diode is used to detect any

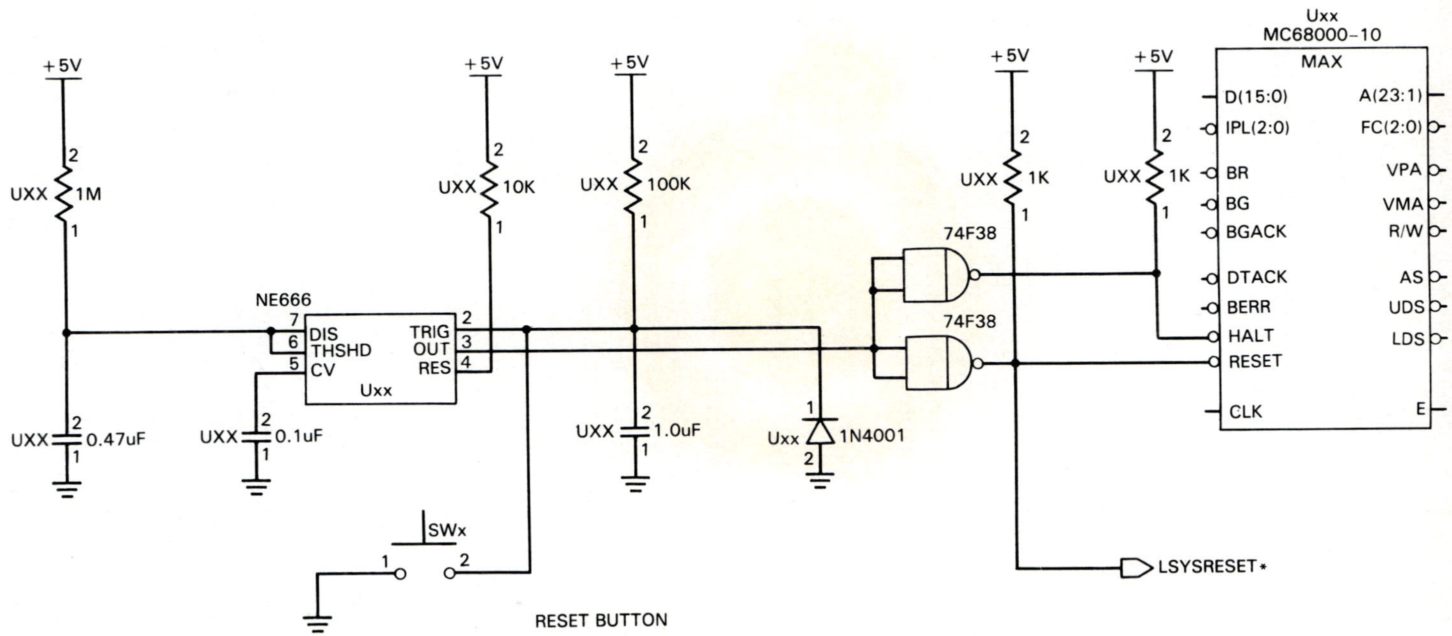

Figure 8-21 An Example Reset Circuit.

power glitches. When power is momentarily interrupted, this diode quickly discharges the timing capacitor. This triggers the '555, causing a reset operation.[1]

The 68000 responds, after an internal start-up time, by reading and initializing the SSP and PC from address $000000 and $000004, respectively. Since both of these exception vectors are long-words, the first four bus cycles of the 68000 are always used to fetch these values. Thereafter, the 68000 starts running at the address pointed by the PC.

8.5.2 Bus Error Operation

A bus cycle can be terminated by asserting the bus error (BERR*) input of the 68000 in lieu of the DTACK*. This indicates an error condition and the 68000 will consequently start bus error exception handling. When BERR* is asserted with no DTACK*, its timing requirements are the same as DTACK* in normal operation. Therefore, we can interface to BERR* input using synchronous, pseudo-synchronous, or fully asynchronous timing as we discussed earlier for DTACK* recognition.

The timing requirements for the BERR* input differ for the 68000 and 68010 when DTACK* is also asserted. The different cases of BERR* recognition are shown in Figure 8-22. The 68010 allows late bus-error recognition *after* the DTACK* is asserted.

In a virtual memory/machine system bus-error termination occurs during page faults and for access violation and so forth. In general, the most typical use of the bus error is when the 68000 attempts to access an unpopulated address space. In this case, a *Bus Time Out* (BTO) circuit asserts BERR* after a certain time-out on the bus. Such a circuit is also sometimes referred to as a *Watch Dog Timer* because it ensures that the 680XX never waits indefinitely for DTACK* in case of a problem. It is better for the 68000 to report the problem, if possible, instead of "hanging" the system.

Another typical use of the bus error is the detection of RAM access errors. This is only applicable in the presence of an external parity error checking or error-correction circuit. The bus error, in this case, indicates a non-correctable error condition.

An example BERR* interface circuit is shown in Figure 8-23. All possible bus-error conditions are ORed to generate the BERR* input signal of the 68000. The BTO circuit is implemented using an 8-bit counter 'LS393 that counts with a one MHz clock when the AS* is asserted. A jumper is also provided to disable the BERR* input. This is useful in debugging the circuit because all bus signals stay frozen if no DTACK* is received, thus allowing one to probe the signals as to why no DTACK* is generated.

[1] The time that the '555 output is high is given by the equation $T = 1.1 \times R_a \times C$. For more information refer to Motorola Linear and Interface Integrated Circuits Databook, MC1455, pp. 11-4 to 11-10, DL128, Rev. 2.

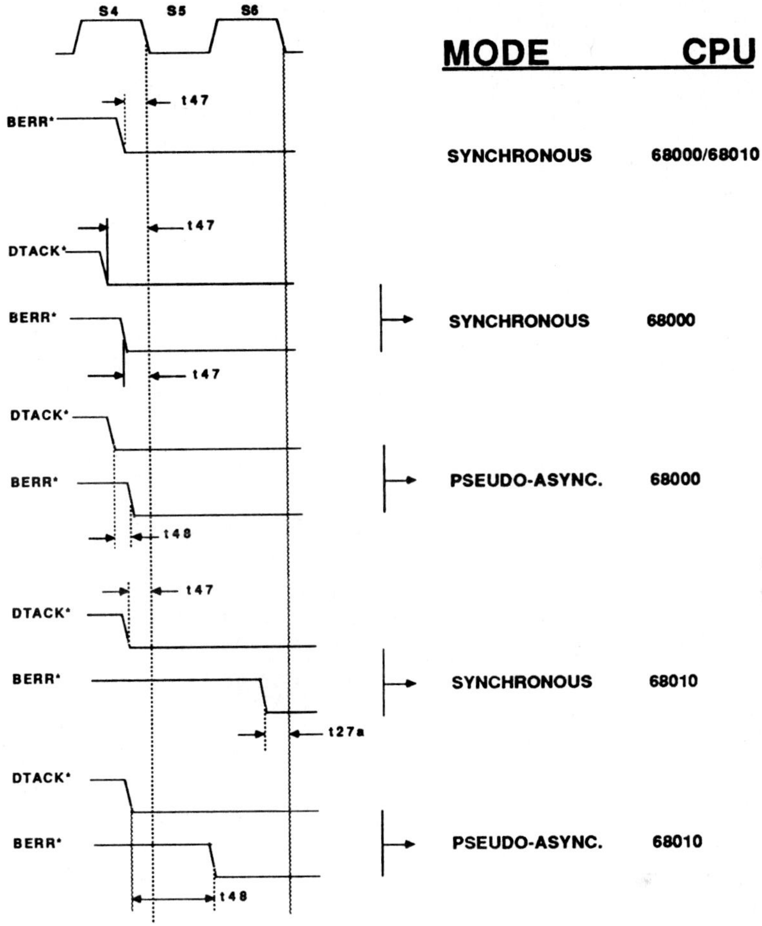

Parameter	Characteristic	Min	Max	Units
t27a	Late BERR* Asserted to CLK low.	45	—	nsec.
t48	68000: BERR* asserted to DTACK* asserted.	20	—	nsec.
	68010: DTACK* asserted to BERR* asserted.	—	55	nsec.

Figure 8-22 Different Cases of BERR* Recognition.

An application of bus error is checking the system configuration. For example, the bus error condition when trying to access an optional system peripheral indicates uninstalled feature since no DTACK* will be returned from such an unpopulated space. This, of course, requires a BTO circuit.

Although the setting of bus time out is somewhat arbitrary, it must be determined such that the time-out period is longer than any normal bus cycles,

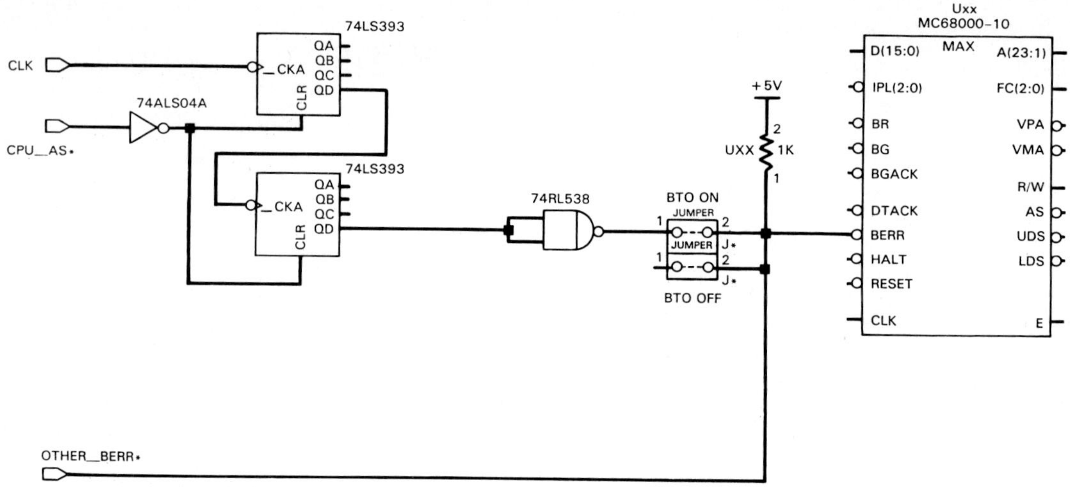

Figure 8-23 Example BERR* Interface Circuit.

considering all connected devices with slow accesses and worst-case bus cycles. On the other hand, too long a time-out could slow-down finding system configuration, diagnostics, and so on.

8.5.3 HALT Operation

The HALT* signal line, when used in conjunction with the DTACK* signal, performs halt/run/single-step function as shown in Figure 8-24. After HALT* is asserted, the processor first finishes the current bus cycle and then halts (i.e., does nothing while the HALT* is asserted). When the 68000 recognizes that HALT* is negated on the falling edge of clock, it resumes bus activity after 1.5 clock cycles of internal start-up time. For proper halt operation, it is necessary that

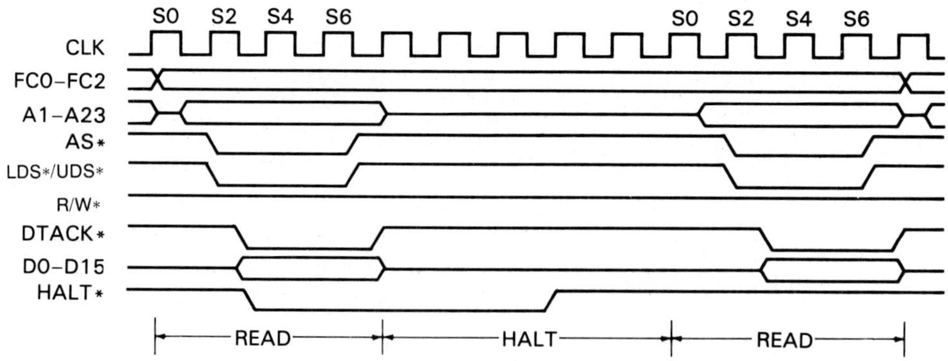

Figure 8-24 Halt Timing Diagram. (Courtesy of Motorola.)

HALT* is asserted at the same time or before the DTACK* and while the BERR* remains negated.

Single-stepping through bus cycles is a typical application of the halt operation. In such a single-step mode, the HALT* signal normally stays asserted. To initiate a single bus cycle, HALT* is negated until the processor starts a bus-cycle, then re-asserted to halt at the end of that cycle. Note that this single-stepping is different than the instruction single-stepping (such as using the trace mode: T = 1).

During the halt mode, the address and data bus drivers are turned off and the bus control pins are negated. However, the bus arbitration control signals are still functional.

Re-run operation. When a bus error condition is detected, external logic can simply assert the BERR* signal and handle the error condition in the software as we have seen earlier. However, in an interface where the same error might not recur again, it is possible to request running the same bus cycle again. To do this, HALT* and BERR* must be asserted in lieu of, at the same time as, or before the DTACK* signal as shown in Figure 8-25. HALT* must stay asserted for at least one clock cycle after negation of BERR* but may stay asserted as long as necessary before the cycle is re-run.

8.6 INTRODUCTION TO PROGRAMMABLE LOGIC DEVICES

8.6.1 PLD Concept

Programmable logic devices (PLDs) are an extension of the fusible link technology pioneered by Monolithic Memory (MMI that is now acquired by AMD) and Harris for use in bipolar programmable read-only memories called PROMs for short.

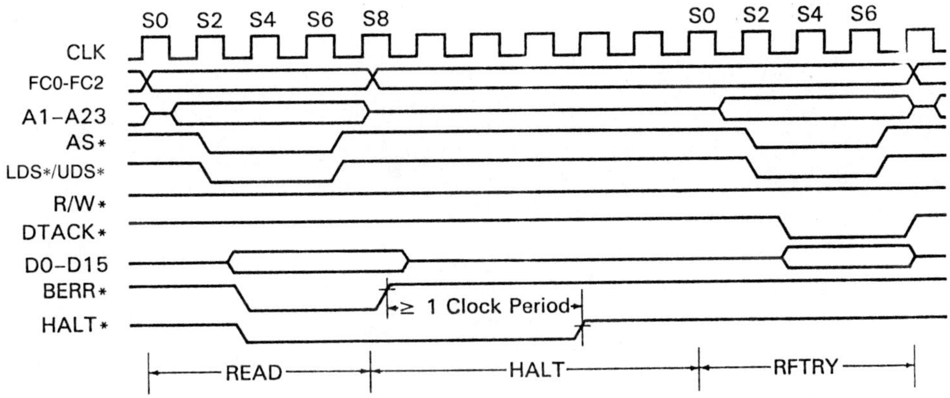

Figure 8-25 Bus-cycle Re-run Timing Diagram. (Courtesy of Motorola.)

The PROM enables a designer to quickly and easily customize the chip to fit his or her requirements. In a few seconds, a PROM can be programmed to contain a custom look-up table, a microprogram, or logic equations. The PLDs extend this flexibility to implement user-defined complex logic functions.

Let us first look at the notation used to represent its structure. An AND gate with multiple inputs is represented with a single line for all of its inputs as illustrated in Figure 8-26. The purpose of this is to make complex PLD internal diagrams readable. The vertical lines represent possible input lines to an AND gate and unprogrammed fuse links are shown with "X". An unprogrammed or unblown fuse makes contact between a vertical line and an input of the AND gate. The "X" is removed to indicate a fuse that is blown (i.e., no contact). Initially, none of the fuses are blown.

The output of such an AND gate is referred as *product term*. The PLDs have the basic AND-OR array structure as shown in Figure 8-27 for N-inputs and M-outputs. The input buffer section receives the N-inputs (I_1-I_N) and outputs that are fed back (Q_1-Q_M).

The input buffers provide both true and inverted polarities of each signal to the AND array. The OR array combines the various product terms to implement the desired sum-of-product terms. Note that the number of OR gates is the same as the outputs, but the number of product terms is independent of the number of inputs or outputs. If an input of an OR gate is not used, all the fuses of the corresponding product term are left intact. This produces a logic low on the product line because the "true" inputs are ANDed with their complements.

The output section varies significantly between PLDs. Usually it provides a programmable output polarity (i.e., active-high or active-low output) and may also include a flip-flop to register outputs.

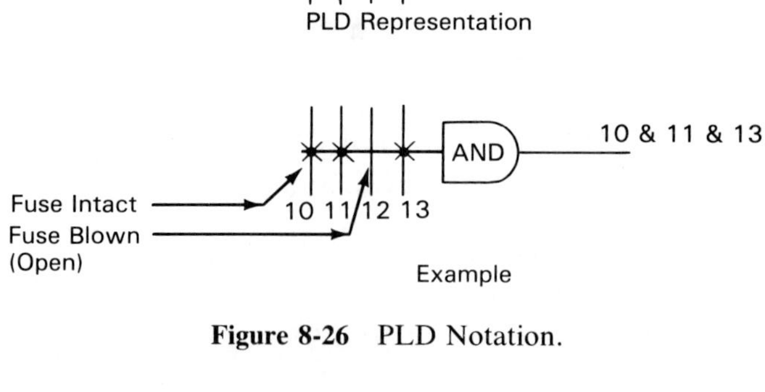

Figure 8-26 PLD Notation.

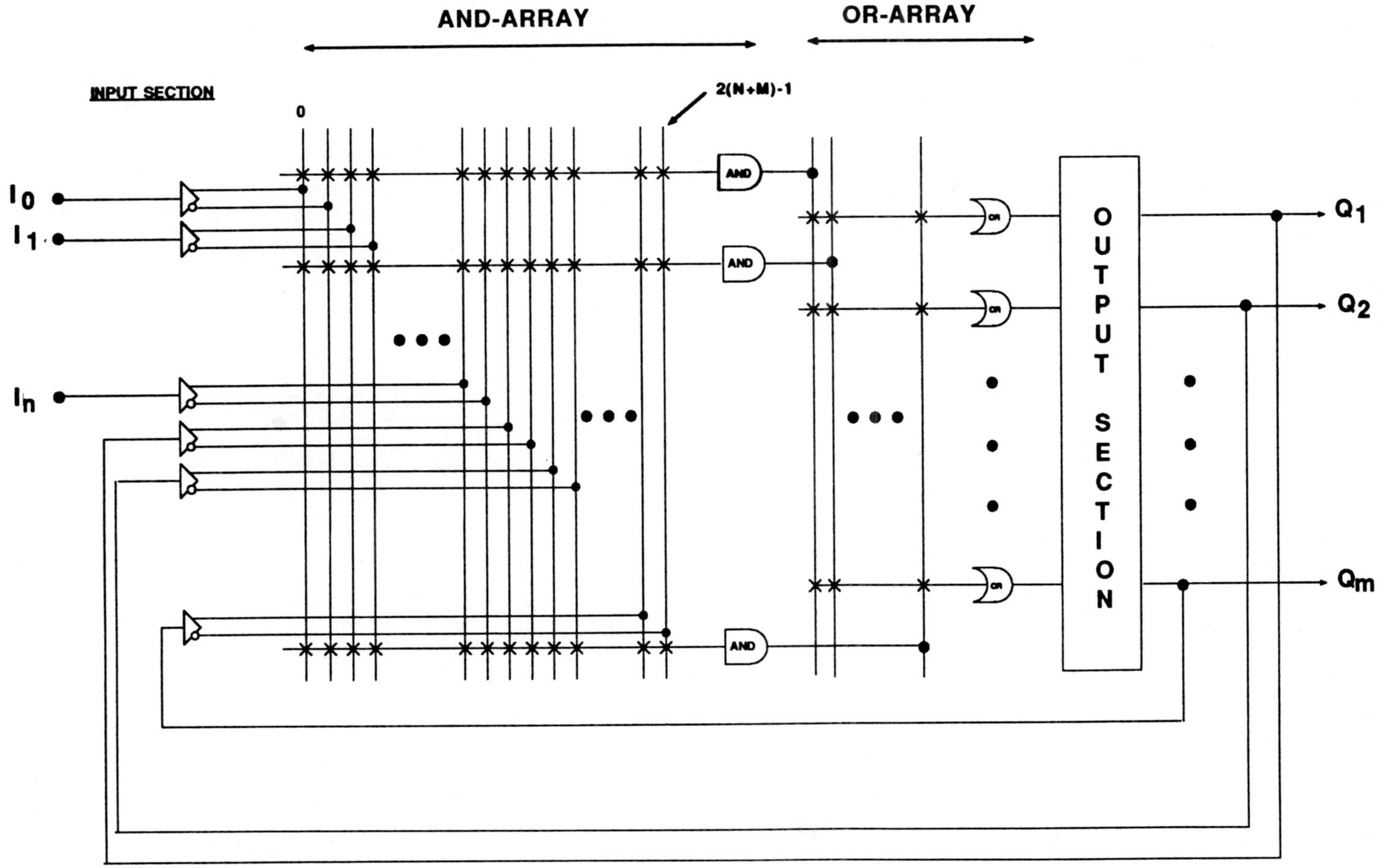

Figure 8-27 Illustration of PLD Structure.

The three distinct members of the PLD family are *Programmable Array Logic* (PAL), *Programmable Logic Array* (PLA), and PROMs. The nomenclature is confusing and is not indicative of the differences. Actually, the main difference between these three lies in what is programmable as shown in Table 8-2. The PAL, the most commonly used PLD, has a programmable AND array and a fixed OR array. This requires that certain product-term lines are connected to specific outputs, typically eight product terms per output. The PLA, on the other hand, is the most flexible. It provides both a programmable AND array and a programmable OR array. However, this additional flexibility slows the speed of the PLD about 10 nanoseconds compared to PAL because a signal has to propagate through two fuses. Moreover, most applications do not require the flexibility of a programmable OR array.

The PROM is the opposite of the PAL. It has fixed a AND array and a programmable OR array. The fixed AND array is often called the *address decoder*, while the programmable OR array stores the memory bits. The advantage of PROMs over PALs and PLAs is that all possible combinations of input lines are decoded. For N-inputs or address lines and M-outputs, this means that M different output signals are generated where each output signal line is independent and can represent any combinatorial function of the N-input lines. This, of course, requires 2^N product terms and an OR array that is M-lines wide. For example, a PROM with 10 inputs and 4 outputs requires 4,096 fuse locations. Adding two more inputs would quadruple the array size to 16,384 bits or fuses. The PAL and PLA have the advantage that they do not have such exponential dependency on the number of their inputs, but the number of product terms for each output is significantly less than 2^N. For example, an 8-input PAL typically has a maximum of 8 product terms per output (i.e., we have $8 \ll 2^8$).

Let us next look at a commonly used PLD—the '22V10. We will use this PAL in the example designs during the rest of this book.

8.6.2 The PAL '22V10

At the time of this writing, the '22V10 is one of the most commonly used PALs. It is multi-sourced by several manufacturers[4] and is built using bipolar (both TTL and ECL) and CMOS technologies. The cover page of the Cypress '22V10 datasheet is shown in Figure 8-28.

TABLE 8-2 COMPARISON OF PLD TYPES

PLD Type	AND Array	OR Array	Output Section
PROM	Fixed	Programmable	Fixed (registered or non-registered)
PLA	Programmable	Programmable	Programmable
PAL	Programmable	Fixed	Programmable[1]

[1] Typical of second generation PALs.

[4] Including TI, Cypress, and AMD/MMI.

Features

- **Advanced second generation PAL architecture**
- **Low power**
  - **— 55 mA max "L"**
  - **— 90 mA max standard**
  - **— 120 mA max military**
- **CMOS EPROM technology for reprogrammability**
- **Variable product terms**
  - **— 2 × (8 thru 16) product terms**
- **User programmable macro cell**
  - **— Output polarity control**
  - **— Individually selectable for registered or combinatorial operation**
  - **— "15" commercial & industrial**
    10 ns t_{CO}
    10 ns t_S
    15 ns t_{PD}
    50 MHz
  - **— "20" military**
    15 ns t_{CO}
    17 ns t_S
    20 ns t_{PD}
    31 MHz
- **Up to 22 input terms and 10 outputs**
- **Enhanced test features**
  - **— Phantom array**
  - **— Top Test**
  - **— Bottom Test**
  - **— Preload**
- **High reliability**
  - **— Proven EPROM technology**
  - **— >2000V input protection**
  - **— 100% programming and functional testing**
- **Windowed DIP, windowed LCC, DIP, LCC, PLCC available**

Functional Description

The Cypress PAL C 22V10 is a CMOS second generation Programmable Logic Array device. It is implemented with the familiar sum-of-products (AND-OR) logic structure and a new concept, the "Programmable Macro Cell".

The PAL C 22V10 is executed in a 24 pin 300 mil molded DIP, a 300 mil windowed Cerdip, a 28 lead square ceramic leadless chip carrier, a 28 lead square plastic leaded chip carrier and provides up to 22 inputs and 10 outputs. When the windowed CERDIP is exposed to UV light, the 22V10 is erased and then can be reprogrammed. The Programmable Macro Cell provides the capability of defining the architecture of each output individually. Each of the 10 potential outputs may be specified to be "REGISTERED" or "COMBINATORIAL". Polarity of

PAL® is a registered trademark of Monolithic Memories Inc.

Logic Symbol and Pinout

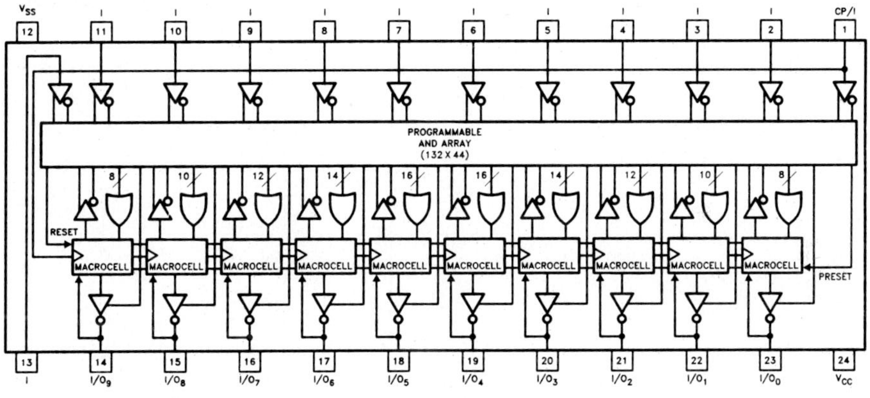

0023-1

LCC and PLCC Pinout

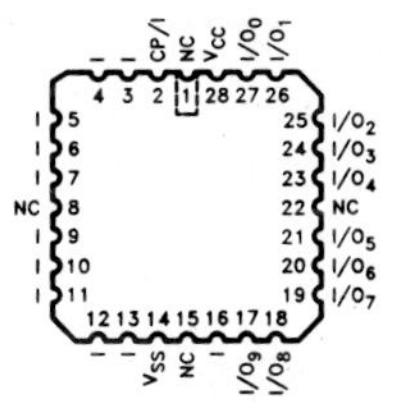

0023-10

Figure 8-28 Cover Page of Cypress '22V10 Datasheet. (Courtesy of Cypress Semiconductor Corporation.)

The '22V10 has twelve dedicated input lines and ten programmable I/O macrocells. Each output macrocell independently allows combinations of registered/non-registered active-high/active-low outputs as shown in Figure 8-29. Also, a feedback line is provided for each output. This allows each of the 10 macrocell outputs to be used as an input-only, output-only, or as a bidirectional signal line using the separate product term that is used to enable each output buffer. Note that the manufacturer's numbering "22" signifies the maximum number of possible inputs, "V" for variable product terms for each output, and "10" is the maximum number of outputs. Of course, if we use all 22 inputs, we would have no outputs! So, in the limiting cases, either it has 12 inputs and 10 outputs or 21 inputs and one output.

Varying number of product terms are assigned to each output, ranging from eight to sixteen per output. This provides an efficient utilization of the '22V10, by assigning the outputs based on product-term requirements.

Figure 8-30 shows the internal logic diagram of the '22V10. The "X"s for fuses are omitted for the sake of readability. Note that the number of total product terms is 132. The product terms are distributed as (8,10,12,14,16,16,14,12,10,8). Also, there is one OE product term per output, and AR and SP terms for 10 outputs.

The first input can be used as a general-purpose input and/or clock input. Note that as a clock input to output flip-flops, its input polarity cannot be inverted.

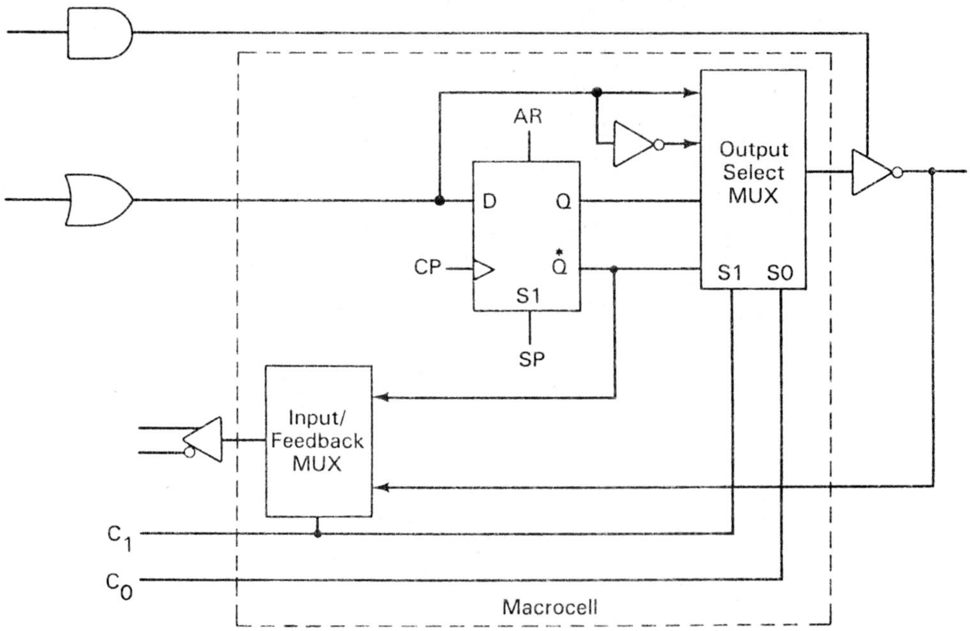

Figure 8-29 The '22V10 Output Macrocell. (Courtesy of Cypress Semiconductor Corporation.)

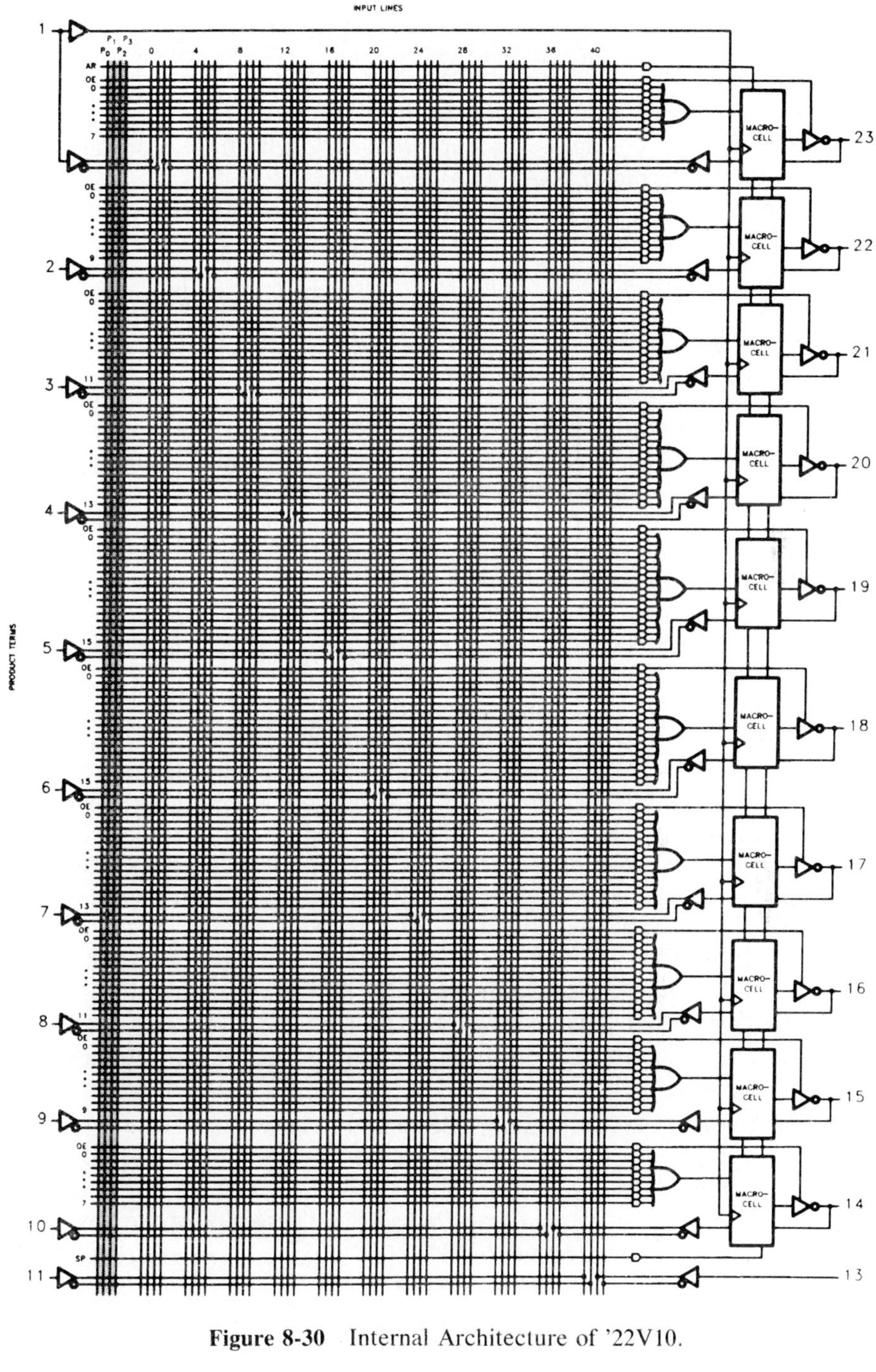

Figure 8-30 Internal Architecture of '22V10.

In addition to the clock line, the output macrocells also share a common *asynchronous reset* (AR) and *synchronous preset* (SP) line. A single product term is assigned to AR and SP that is connected to *all* macrocells. This sharing of output control signals may present a limitation in certain applications. There are other PLD types that provide independent clocking, reset, and set capability of each flip-flop using a separate product term for each of these signals. These type of PLDs are referred to as *asynchronous PLDs* due to their support of multiple clock inputs. Their disadvantage is that they are relatively slower and more complex to design (and to debug).

8.6.3 Advantages of PLDS and Their Affects on Design Methodology

Traditionally, digital circuit designers used ''pre-designed'' chips that have a fixed and permanent function once they leave the factory. Examples are the 74-Series TTL chips. A favorite catalog was the hard-bound TTL databook from Texas Instruments. Digital design involved primarily selecting, mixing, and matching these TTL chips so that design goals are met with a minimum possible number of chips. This was more of an art and did not require much circuit theory as new graduates found out. As John Birkner, the coinventor of the PAL device, puts it, ''Designers who had studied switching theory, information theory, Boolean algebra, and Quine–McCluskey minimization at college soon found that their textbooks would not be of much use.''[5] Since, most of the time, existing TTL chips did not exactly match the functionality required by the designer, a design would require a lot of SSI/MMSI chips and consume a large board space.

A distinct advantage of PLDs is that they can be programmed to meet a designer's exact specifications. This allows the integration of multiple TTL functions onto a single programmed chip to reduce board space, cost, power consumption, and to improve reliability. The following lists the other advantages of PLDs:

1. A PLD has the fastest design cycle of any form of custom logic. It can be specified and programmed at the user's site. Furthermore, the designer may also simulate the logic prior to programming an actual device.
2. High-speed PLDs run faster or equal to the best of the other bipolar logic devices.
3. PLDs protect proprietary designs. PLDs are like ''black boxes'' on a schematic and one cannot understand the operation of a circuit without knowing the functionality of PLDs. PALs and PLAs have a security fuse which, when blown, disables reading or copying the fuse plot of the device.
4. PLDs reduce the number of different parts a company has to stock.

[5] Reference 17.

The PLD chips require a different design methodology similar to what we learned in school. A PLD design specification usually requires a set of Boolean equations and pin definitions. These are translated by a PLD compiler software package into a fuse plot that can be downloaded into a device programmer. Examples of PLD development software include CUPL (which stands for Universal Compiler for Programmable Logic) from Assisted Technology, ABEL from DATA I/O Corporation, AMAZE from Signetics, and PALASM from MMI/AMD. We will adapt the CUPL notation for our examples in this book as defined in Figure 8-31. An in-depth discussion of CUPL features is outside the scope of this book and therefore, we will only cover the features we will be using in our examples.

The PLD design process is shown in Figure 8-32. The two important files generated by the CUPL software are ⟨*filename*⟩.DOC and ⟨*filename*⟩.JED. The DOC file documents the design showing expanded logical equations, product-term usage, and pin definitions. The JED stands for JEDEC file. The JEDEC file format JC-42.1, as defined by the *Joint Electron Device Engineering Council* (JEDEC), is the most commonly used file format that can be read by most PLD programming hardware. The JEDEC file also contains a fuse checksum field. The checksum is evaluated as a 16-bit hexadecimal value that is the sum of consecutive 8-bit hex values of the fuse-link data. The checksum is verified by the programmer after down-loading the JEDEC file. Typically, it is also a unique value that can be used to identify the revision level a PLD.

After the PLD is programmed, it is usually tagged with the following information:

Company's Part Number:	This is unique for each programmed part and is different from the number that is assigned to the unprogrammed parts.
Location:	Indicates where the PLD is located on a given board.
Checksum	PLD checksum value.

Example 8-1

Figure 8-33 shows a sample PLD specification using CUPL notation, as entered by the designer. The function that is implemented here is basically an 8-bit counter that counts up and periodically requests a refresh operation for a memory module that we are going to discuss in the next chapter. When a count value of 233 detected, the REFCYC_REQ* output is asserted. This output is negated when the REFCYC* input is asserted.

```
Logic Operation Symbols

            & : Logical AND
            # : Logical OR
            $ : Logical Exclusive-OR
            ! : Logical Negation

Comments /* : Start of Comment.
         */ : End of Comment.

Equations

      [!]variable[.ext] = expression ;

      where

      []            :     optional field.
      variable      :     Is a single or list of variables. In the
                          latter case, the expression is assigned to
                          each variable.
      ext           :     Associates the equation with a major node
                          inside the PLD. One of the following is used:

            D       :     Registered type output.
      (no ext)      :     Defines combinatorial type output.
            AR      :     Assigns equation to AR input of output(s).
            SP      :     Assigns equation to SP input of output(s).
            OE      :     Assigns equation to OE (output enable) of an
                          output.

Pin Definitions

      Pin pin_no = [!]variable ;

            where

            pin_no    : Is the pin number assigned.
            !         : Optional input or output inversion.

Short-Hand References

            List Notation:

            Rather than [A6, A5, A4, A3, A1, A0] we may use [A6..0].
```

Figure 8-31 CUPL PLD Notation Overview.

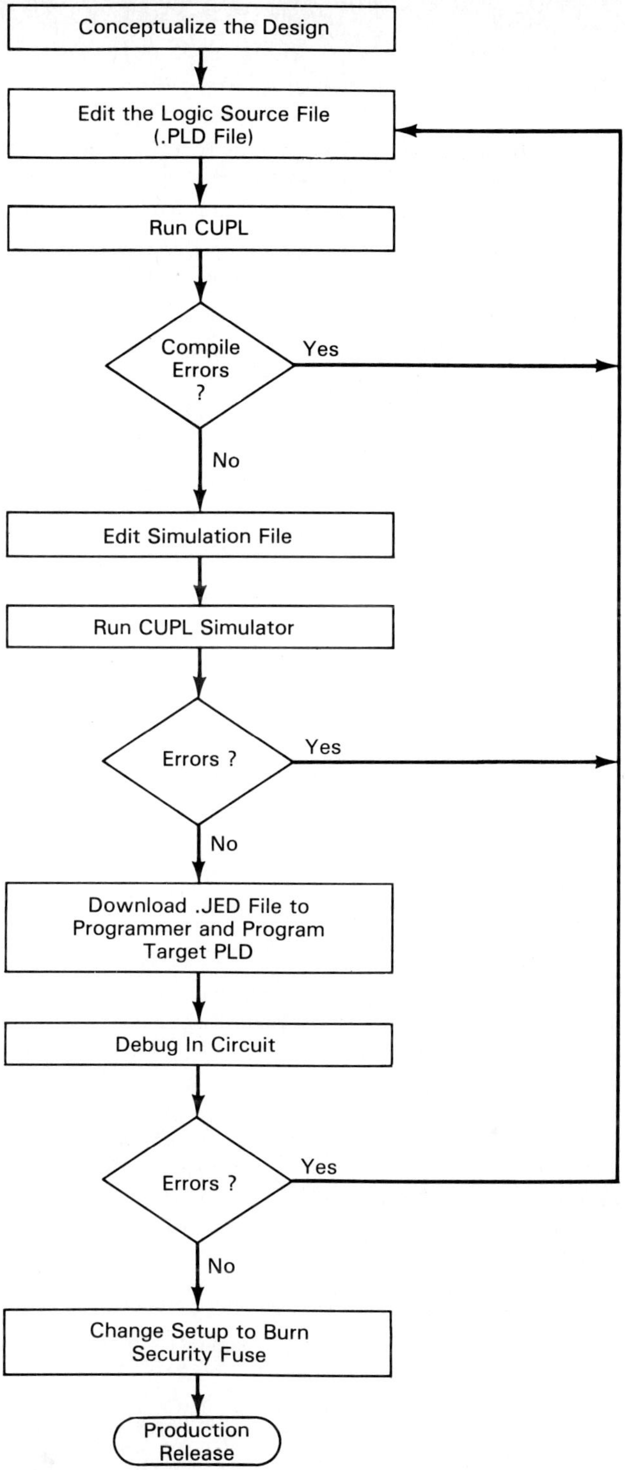

Figure 8-32 PLD Design Process.

The following provides some guidelines in using PLDs:

1. In choosing a PLD, first check whether the number of I/O fits the requirements. Second, check that the internal structure, i.e., the number of product terms and the types of output meet design requirements.
2. Choose a part that is available by more than one manufacturer. This ensures availability of the part. It will also likely have a lower cost than single-sourced devices.
3. Do not use exotic or state-of-the-art PLDs unless there is a very strong reason. These are usually not cost effective. Instead, try to find a way to use commonly available PLDs. Do not get stuck with a given design approach. Try a different implementation approach, if necessary.
4. Use slow-speed versions of parts when possible. The slower versions consume less power and are usually less expensive.
5. As a rule of thumb, use the TTL-logic counterparts if a PLD does not seem to replace the functionality of at least 3 regular TTL chips. This is because

```
Name        DRAMREFG.PLD;
Partno      XXXX;
Date        XX/XX/XX;
Revision    XX;
Designer    Tibet Mimar;
Company     CLI;
Assembly    X.21;
Location    4F;

/*****************************************************************/
/* Purpose: This device generates refresh cycle requests for the */
/*          DRAM memory. A refresh cycle is requested every 14   */
/*          microseconds, and the request is negated as soon as  */
/*          a refresh cycle starts. Since the counter is running */
/*          with 60 nanosecond clock period, this translates to  */
/*          a count of 233 before a refresh cycle is generated.  */
/*****************************************************************/
/*  Allowable Target Device Types: 22V10                         */
/*****************************************************************/

/*  Inputs  **/

Pin   1  = !CPUCLKX1_B   ;   /* Inverted CPU Clock.              */
Pin   2  = !REFCYC       ;   /* Indicates a refresh cycle.       */
```

Figure 8-33 Example PLD Source File.

```
/**   Outputs   **/

Pin  23  = !REFCYC_REQ  ;   /* Indicates a refresh cycle request. */
Pin  22  = !Q0          ;   /* Refresh Request Timer Output Q0.   */
Pin  21  = !Q1          ;   /* Refresh Request Timer Output Q1.   */
Pin  20  = !Q2          ;   /* Refresh Request Timer Output Q2.   */
Pin  19  = !Q3          ;   /* Refresh Request Timer Output Q3.   */
Pin  18  = !Q4          ;   /* Refresh Request Timer Output Q4.   */
Pin  17  = !Q5          ;   /* Refresh Request Timer Output Q5.   */
Pin  16  = !Q6          ;   /* Refresh Request Timer Output Q6.   */
Pin  15  = !Q7          ;   /* Refresh Request Timer Output Q7.   */
Pin  14  = !RESET       ;   /* Asserted during Timer Reset.       */

/**   Logic Equation   **/


Q0.D = (!Q0) & !RESET ;
Q1.D = (Q1 $ Q0) & !RESET ;
Q2.D = (Q2 $ Q1 & Q0) & !RESET ;
Q3.D = (Q3 $ Q2 & Q1 & Q0) & !RESET ;
Q4.D = (Q4 $ Q3 & Q2 & Q1 & Q0) & !RESET ;
Q5.D = (Q5 $ Q4 & Q3 & Q2 & Q1 & Q0) & !RESET ;
Q6.D = (Q6 $ Q5 & Q4 & Q3 & Q2 & Q1 & Q0) & !RESET ;
Q7.D = (Q7 $ Q6 & Q5 & Q4 & Q3 & Q2 & Q1 & Q0) & !RESET ;

RESET.D = (Q7 & Q6 & Q5 & !Q4 & Q3 & !Q2 & !Q1 & !Q0) ;

REFCYC_REQ.D =  RESET & !REFCYC  # REFCYC_REQ & !REFCYC ;
```

Figure 8-33 (cont.) Example PLD Source File.

PLDs are usually 2 to 3 times more expensive than the standard TTL-family devices.

6. In a PLD design, always provide some unused input and output pins. This is useful in limiting the affect of design changes or upgrades. For example, let us assume a change causes the product terms of an output to become insufficient. In this case, the feedback from an unused output can be used as an intermediate signal to gain additional product terms. Secondly, adding another input or output will not require the addition of another chip, but only one wire.
7. Define the PLD such that all internal signals are active-high. It is much simpler to conceptualize in terms of active-high signals when writing the logical equations.
8. PLDs are usually put in sockets to allow easy upgrades.

8.7 CIRCUIT HAZARDS TO WATCH

There are three circuit hazards that we will discuss in this section. These are *glitches, critical race conditions*, and *metastability*. As we are going to see, these hazards are not always avoidable but must be taken into account during the design so that they do not cause any circuit malfunction or other operational errors.

8.7.1 Glitches

The propagation delay differences in different paths of combinatorial circuits may cause the generation of an unwanted pulse or a logic spike usually called a *glitch*. The classic example of this is the two-input multiplexer shown in Figure 8-34. For the input conditions X = Y = H, the select input S changing from H to L causes a glitch in the output of the multiplexer. This is caused by the delay of the inverter.

A glitch in a control signal line (e.g., chip select of a RAM memory device) or in other lines such as address or data when the qualifying control signal is asserted must be avoided. One way this could be accomplished is to draw the Karnaugh map (K-map in short) of the circuit, and to add additional logic for such hazard coverage. This could be done by overlapping the adjacent couples on the K-map. In this particular example, adding another gate such that

Q = X & S # Y & !S # X & Y

will eliminate the glitch without changing the functionality of the circuit. However, this approach is hardly practical for large and complex circuits. Furthermore, it

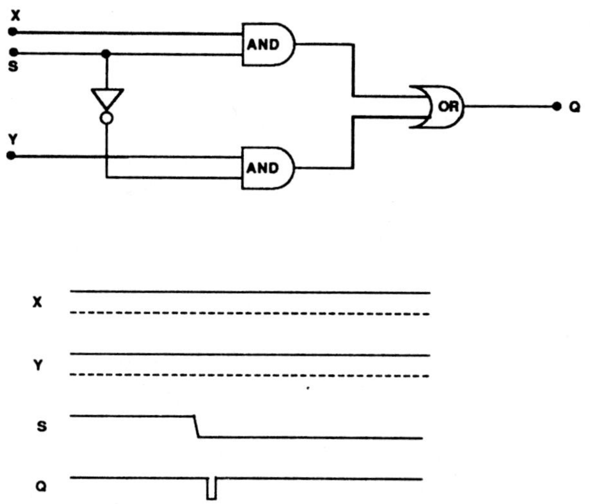

Figure 8-34 Illustration of a Circuit Glitch.

is not supported by commonly used logic families. For example, in the logic diagram of the 'F157 shown in Figure 8-35, the quad 2-input multiplexer does not provide any such built-in protection against glitching. There is a second and more practical way of preventing glitches. But, before we discuss this, let us first look at the two types of glitches. A *static glitch* is a momentary transient in the output signal that should have remained static in response to an input change [34] such as the one in our above example. The *dynamic glitch* condition, on the other hand, is when an output signal has multiple momentary transients, when it should have changed only once in response to an input change as shown in Figure 8-36. It can be shown that the dynamic glitch condition is really caused by static glitches.

There are two practical approaches to prevent circuit malfunction due to glitching. First, we can use synchronous logic whereby all inputs and outputs of a combinatorial logic block are latched by the same clock edge as shown in Figure 8-37. In this case, we would not care any glitches in the outputs of the combinatorial logic, as long as all transient conditions are ended T_{su} before the next clock edge. In other words, if we are operating below the frequency limit of the circuit given by

$$F_{max} = 1/(T_{dl} + T_{comb} + T_{su} - T_{skew}) \qquad \text{(Eq. 8-1)}$$

then, any glitches of combinatorial logic block are of no significance, where

T_{dl}: Is the maximum clock-to-output propagation delay of the latch(es).

T_{comb}: Is the worst-case delay of combinatorial logic, using the longest path (critical signal path) and maximum possible signal delays.

T_{su}: Is the input setup time of latch(es).

T_{skew}: Is the worst-case clock skew between the input and output latches.

When it is not desirable (possibly due to time delay) or practical to use latches around the combinatorial circuit, we can use a qualifier or enable signal instead. The enable signal would be asserted after the other inputs, allowing sufficient time to avoid any momentary transients in the outputs. Such an enable input is commonly provided by most logic families, including the 'F157 device we saw. This is illustrated in Figure 8-38. The input setup time required before the enable is asserted is not directly specified in data sheets, but can be calculated from the inequality

$$T_{en} > T_{i\text{-}to\text{-}q} - T_{en\text{-}to\text{-}q} \qquad \text{(Eq. 8-2)}$$

where

$T_{i\text{-}to\text{-}q}$: Maximum propagation delay from input to output.

$T_{en\text{-}to\text{-}q}$: Maximum propagation delay from enable input to output.

T_{en}: Minimum delay necessary from input signals valid and stable to enable asserted.

LOGIC DIAGRAM, '157A

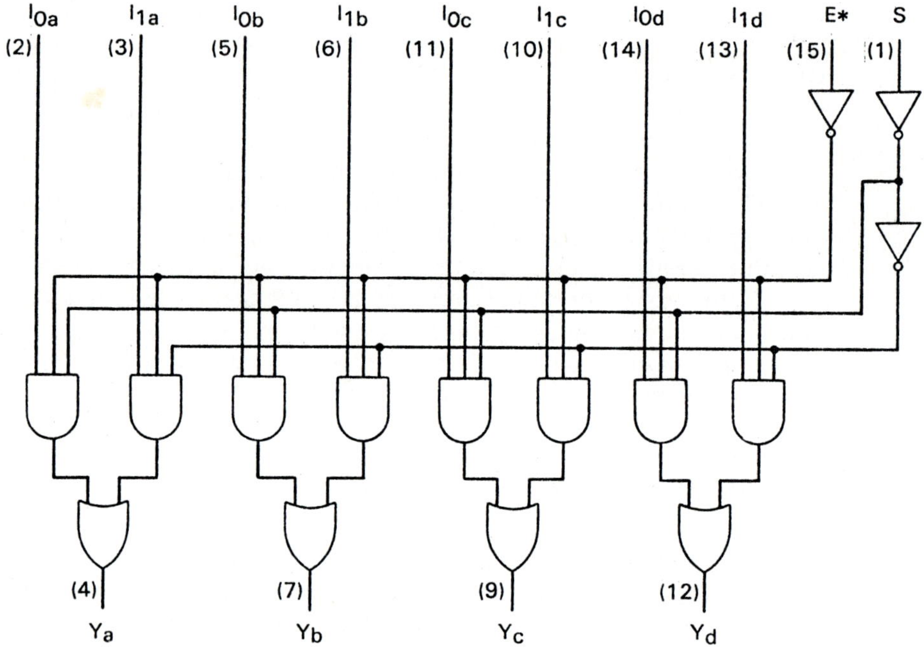

V_{CC} = Pin 16
GND = Pin 8

FUNCTION TABLE, '157A

Enable	Select Input	Data Inputs		Output
E*	S	I_0	I_1	Y
H	X	X	X	L
L	H	X	L	L
L	H	X	H	H
L	L	L	X	L
L	L	H	X	H

H = High voltage level
L = Low voltage level
X = Don't care

Figure 8-35 'F157 Logic Diagram. (Courtesy of Signetics.)

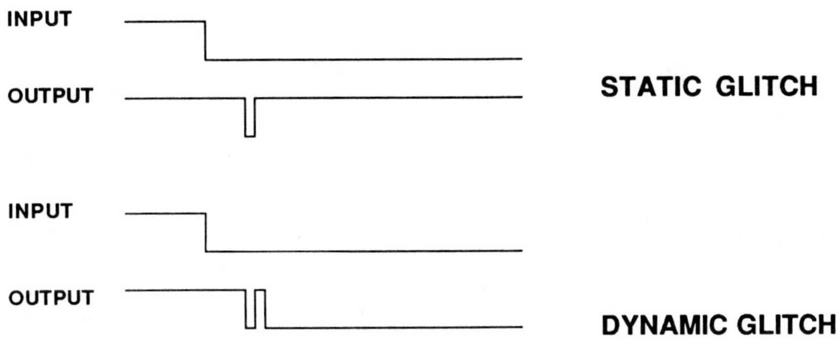

Figure 8-36 Types of Glitch Conditions.

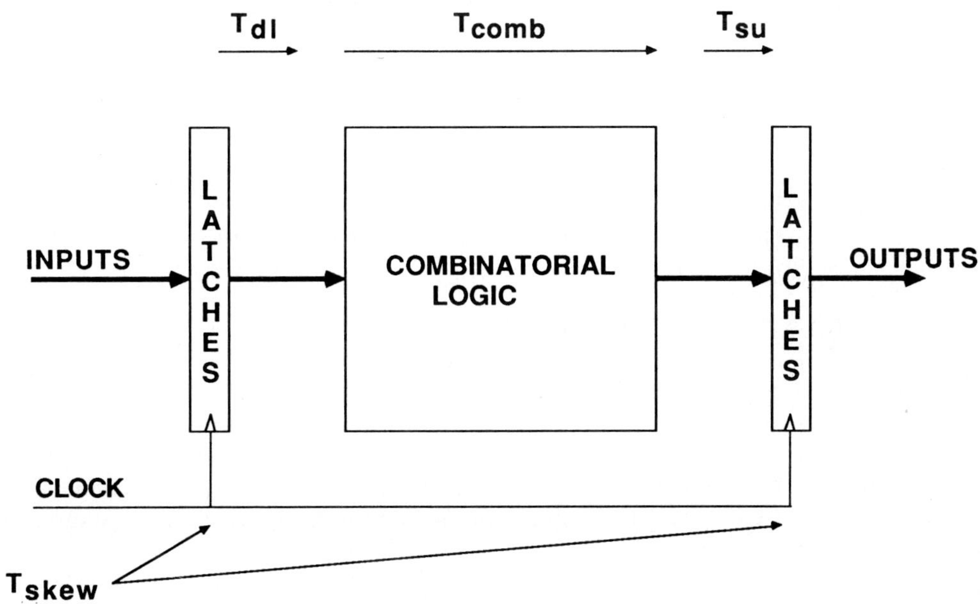

Figure 8-37 Latches to "Hide" Circuit Glitches.

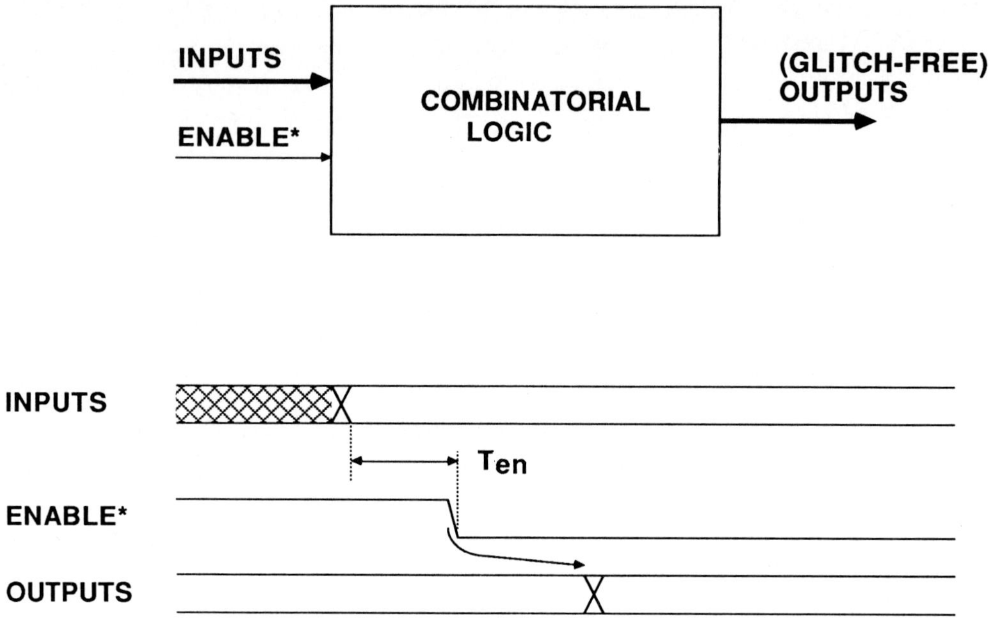

Figure 8-38 Use of Enable Signal to Prevent Glitches.

Example 8-2.

Let us consider an address decoder for the 68000 using the 'F138 as shown in Figure 8-39. The AS* is used as the enable signal. The device select signals are glitch free since the address-valid-to-AS*-asserted (parameter t11 of the 68000) satisfies the minimum T_{en} required (Exercise 8-29).

8.7.2 Critical Race Condition

Let us consider the circuit of Figure 8-37 again. If the latched input signal propagates to the output latch and violates its hold time, this is called a *critical-race condition*. Because, in general, when a synchronous circuit is clocked, we must ensure that each sequential device determines its next state on the basis of inputs as they existed during the previous clock period. To avoid a critical race condition, we must have

$$T_{dl(min)} + T_{comb(min)} - T_{skew} > T_{hold} \qquad \text{(Eq. 8-3)}$$

where T_{hold} is the minimum hold time of the output latches. The minimum propagation time is usually not specified in data books, but as a rule of thumb, we can assume it is one-third the maximum value. The simplest way to avoid such a critical race condition is to put some extra logic, such as an 'ALS244 in between the two latches to increase the value of $T_{comb(min)}$.

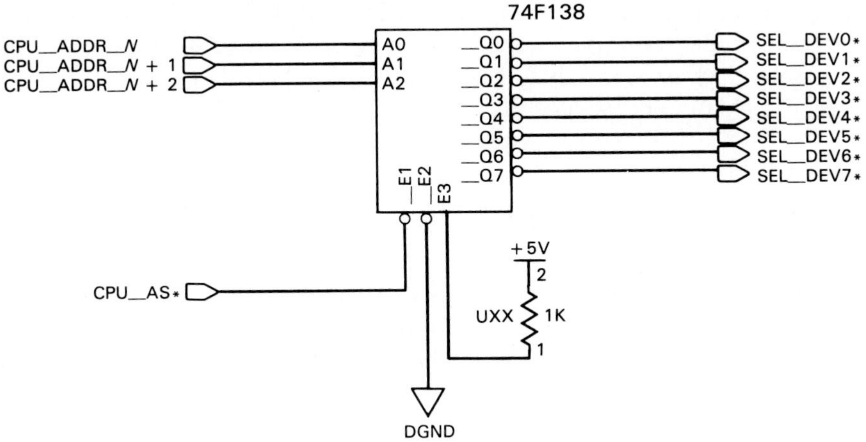

Figure 8-39 Example Address Decoder Without Any Glitches.

8.7.3 Metastability

A D-type flip-flop has a predictable output state only if the manufacturer's specifications are followed. The data input must meet the required setup and hold times (i.e., it is required to be stable over a sample window with respect to the clock edge) as shown in Figure 8-40. However, in reality it is seldom possible to guarantee that the setup and hold time requirement will always be met. The most typical example of this is an asynchronous input fed into synchronous logic such as a state machine.

A flip-flop may exhibit anomalous behavior when the setup or hold time requirement is violated. In such a case, the output of the flip-flop hesitates, analogous to rolling a ball toward a bell-shaped obstacle, where the ball almost stops at the top of the obstacle that is an unstable equilibrium point. If the ball has

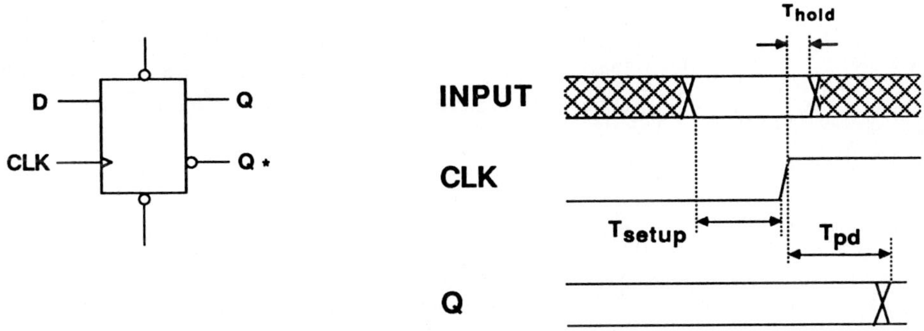

Figure 8-40 The Setup and Hold-time Requirements.

enough energy, it will pass the obstacle, otherwise it will fall back, but if it happens to have just the right amount of energy, it could stop on top of the obstacle until some disturbance (noise) causes it to fall one way or another.

This condition is called a *metastable state*, a greek word meaning "in-between." If a flip-flop enters a metastable state, one of the four possible events listed below occurs[26]:

- Case 1 The output starts to make a transition, but snaps back to its original state (i.e., fails to register the data input).
- Case 2 The output makes a complete transition but the maximum delay specification of the device is exceeded.
- Case 3 The output oscillates and then returns to its previous state (i.e., fails to register the input data).
- Case 4 The output oscillates and then changes its state.

As illustrated in Figure 8-41, the flip-flop snaps out of the metastable state in a short period of time even though theoretically this condition can last indefinitely. The time to snap out of metastability is called the *decision time*. It is important to note that if the output changes to an incorrect state, then the correct output state will definitely be registered in the next clock edge assuming the data remains the same.

The time to snap out of a metastable condition depends on a given IC and its speed rating, where generally the faster ICs settle quicker. Typically, the decision time is 15 to 20 nanoseconds for most ICs. Unfortunately, manufacturers seldom specify device characteristics for metastability. According to a study of AMD/MMI [26], we have the relation given by

$$\text{Failure rate} = (K1 * F_{\text{clock}} * F_{\text{data}}) * \exp(-K2 * [T\text{-}T0]) \text{ counts/sec.} \qquad \text{(Eq. 8-4)}$$

where

T: Defines the time when the output Q of a flip-flop is sampled after the clock edge that caused a metastable state.

K1,K2,T0: Are constants that define the metastability characteristics of a given device. For example, for a PAL16R4A we have [26]:

$$K1 = 1 \times 10^{-7} \text{ (sec.)}$$

$$K2 = 4.3 \text{ nsec}^{-2}.$$

$$T0 = 34.5 \text{ (nsec.)}$$

F_{clock}: System clock frequency (Hz).

F_{data}: Asynchronous data frequency (Hz).

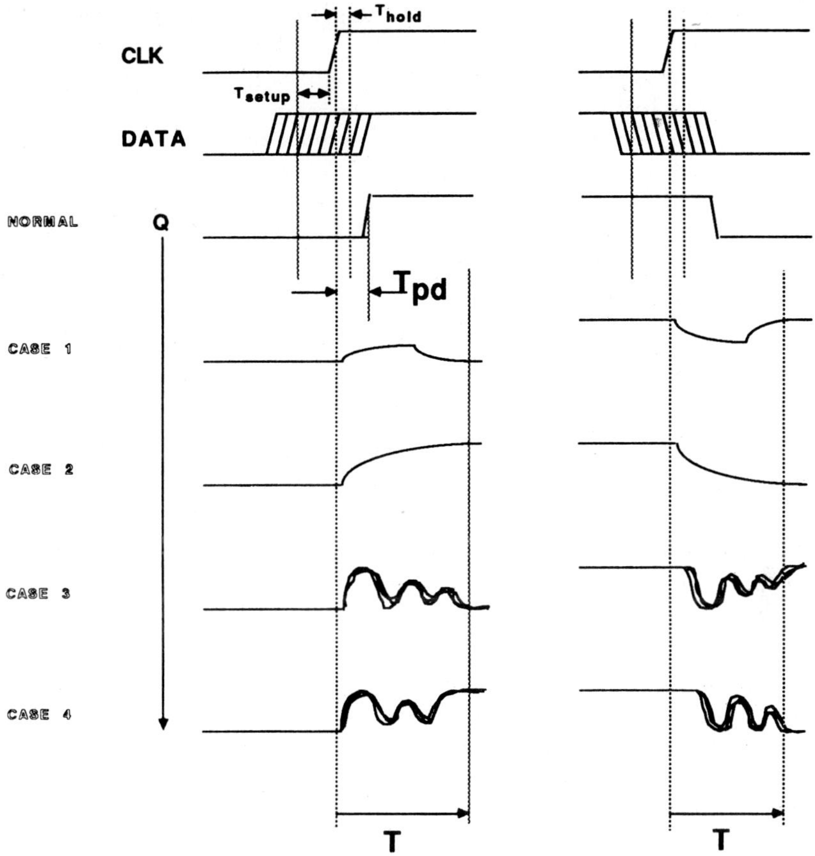

Figure 8-41 Illustration of Metastable State.

The above failure rate calculation gives the probability of a failure for a given sampling time. The parameter T0 defines the knee of the failure-rate curve. For example, if we specify T = 100 nanoseconds, the above equation gives the number of times per second that the allowed decision time will not be adequate. Note that the failure rate decreases exponentially when T is greater than T0, but there is always a finite possibility that the flip-flop is still in a metastable state even if a long time is allowed. We have to allow sufficient time for the probability of late toggling or oscillatory behavior due to metastability to become adequately low.

In effect, the failure rate shows when we can reliably use the output signal. For example, if the output of a first flip-flop is connected to a second one via some combinatorial logic, and both are connected to the same clock, we have

$$F_{clock(max)} = 1/(T + T_{comb} + T_{setup}) \qquad \text{(Eq. 8-5)}$$

where T_{comb} and T_{setup} are the propagation delays of the combinatorial logic and the setup time of the second flip-flop, respectively (see Figure 8-42). In the case the output of the first flip-flop is still toggling/oscillating when the allowed decision time is reached, this may cause the second flip-flop to also enter a metastable state. In the worst-case scenario, the metastability ripples through the synchronous logic and causes circuit malfunction. Considering that the circuit may be operating in the MHz range, we cannot allow any such malfunction even if it is one per day or week (Would once a month be acceptable?).

We recommend the following guideline for reliable designs that handle the metastability condition:

1. It is a good practice to synchronize any asynchronous inputs before they are used as part of synchronous logic. As a rule of thumb, allow a T of 60 nanoseconds or larger. The maximum operating frequency of the system must allow the additional delay during a metastability.
2. To further reduce the probability of metastability, use two flip-flops as shown in Figure 8-43.
3. Allow only one flip-flop to be affected by an asynchronous input. For example, in the case of a synchronous state machine with an asynchronous input that is not synchronized, allow only one registered output or state bit to be affected [31]. Another common mistake is to synchronize an asynchronous input at multiple places in the circuit. This may cause one synchronization flip-flop to go into a state different from others which may subsequently cause circuit failure.

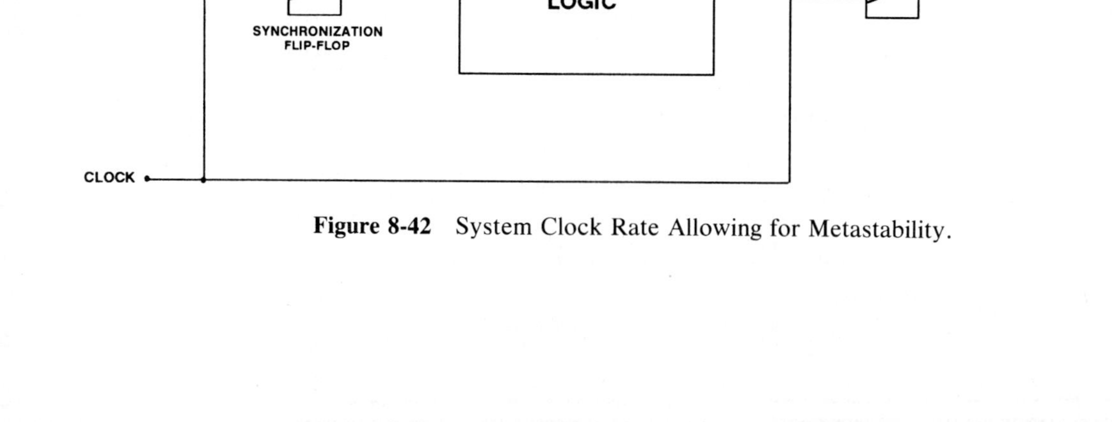

Figure 8-42 System Clock Rate Allowing for Metastability.

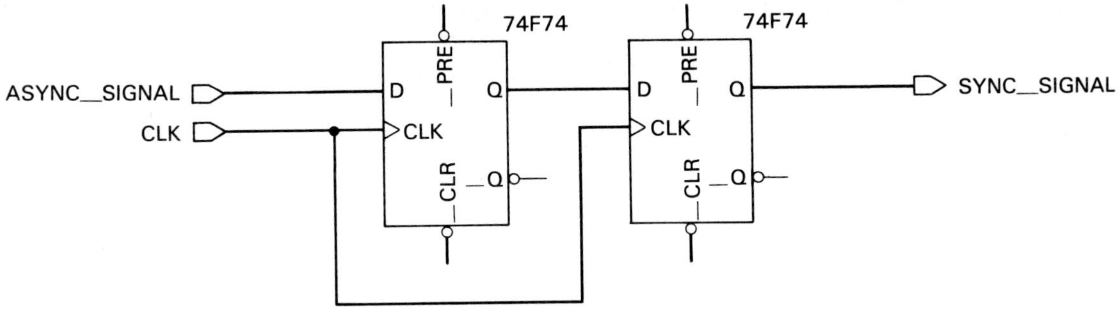

Figure 8-43 Double Synchronization.

8.8 ADDRESS DECODER DESIGN

The purpose of the address decoder is to enable the device that is to be accessed. As illustrated in Figure 8-44, the address-decode logic decodes the address bits A23-A⟨N⟩ for a device that spans the address range of $0{:}2^N$-1. We called the decode signal as DECODE_⟨*device_name*⟩* for clarity. The address decoder also looks at the function codes so that no devices are decoded during an interrupt-acknowledge bus cycle (i.e., when FC2-FC0 are {HHH}).

The first step in designing an address decoder is defining the memory map, an example of which is shown in Table 8-3. We have the following considerations in preparing this table. First, the reset vector has to be stored in non-volatile memory such as PROM. This means that we may locate the PROM at the beginning of memory map, and put the RAM memory area following it. The disadvantage of this is that the rest of the exception-vector table also ends up in the

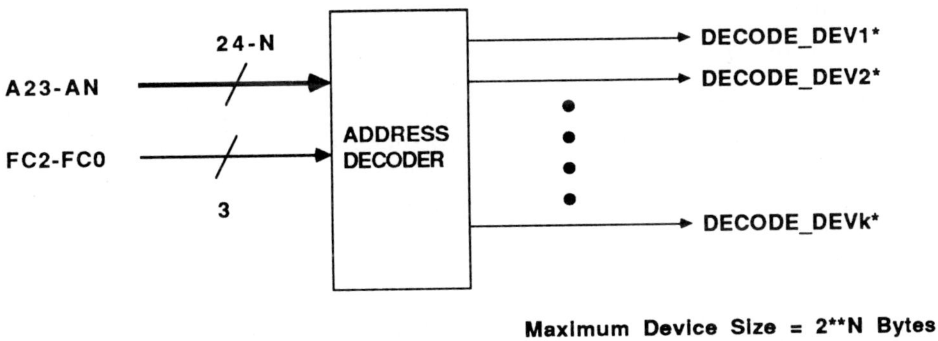

Figure 8-44 Block Diagram of Address Decoder.

TABLE 8-3 EXAMPLE MEMORY MAP OF 68000

Memory Area	Device	Address Space (Hex)	Size (Bytes)
Memory Devices	EPROM	000000–000007	8
	RAM	000008–01FFFF	128K
	Non-volatile RAM	180000–187FFF	32K
	Reserved for Expansion	200000–2FFFFF	(To 1M)
	EPROM	300008–33FFFF	256K
Peripheral Controllers	DUART # 1	F00000–F0000F	16
	RTC	F00010–F0001F	16

PROM, thus we cannot change the exception-vector entries in a program. A more flexible approach is to divide the decoding of the PROM into two parts. First eight bytes of the PROM will contain the reset vector, and will be accessed when the 68000 accesses locations zero through seven. The rest of the exception vectors will reside in RAM, which the 68000 has to initialize immediately after a reset operation. The remaining locations of the PROM can be located somewhere else in the memory map, typically after the RAM area.

An address decode limitation we have should be noted. Devices must be placed on address boundaries equal to their size (e.g., an 8K byte device on 8K address boundary).

A well-organized memory map usually has separate areas of address space assigned to memory type devices, peripheral controllers, and so on. It is also a good practice to reserve some address space between devices. This allows possible expansion of memory sizes and additional peripherals without relocation of other devices.

Qualifying with AS*. Thus far we have not qualified the address decode signal DECODE_DEVX* with the address strobe AS*. Qualifying the address decode with address strobe is necessary so that an access is made only when there is a valid bus cycle.

In qualifying the address decode with the AS* we may simply AND the active-high version of these signals such as

```
AS & DECODE_DEVX
```

which is equivalent to a negative-OR, such as using a 'F32. Let us call the qualified address decode signal SEL_DEVX* to distinquish it from DECODE_DEVX*. The SEL_DEVX* signal could be used to select devices, (i.e., can be connected to CS* of a DUART).

One potential problem, however, with qualifying the AS* *after* the address decode is that such a SEL_DEVX* may glitch if decode is completed after the AS* is asserted. From section 8.7, it is required that

$$T_{decode} < t11$$

where the t11 is 20 nanoseconds for a 10 MHz 68000 and gets smaller for higher clock rates. This equation is difficult to meet, therefore we can do one of two things to avoid any glitches in device select signals as illustrated in Figure 8-45. First, instead of qualifying at the end of address decode, we can make AS* part of the address decode, so we meet Equation 8-2 and generate SEL_DEVX* in one step. This is the simplest approach, but may not be optimal for performance. Secondly, we may qualify the address decode with a delayed version of the AS*, let us call it DAS* (for delayed AS*).

There are several ways we can delay the address strobe:

1. We may use a delay line.
2. We can use a D-type flip-flip and use the rising edge of state S3 (why not falling edge of S2?).
3. We can delay with logic that asserts the DAS* after the falling-edge of S2 such as

   ```
   DAS = AS & !CLK # DAS & AS;
   ```
   (Eq. 8-6)

   where the first is the "turn-on" term, and the second term maintains DAS* as asserted until AS* is negated.

In the approach 3 we assume that the address decode is completed by the end of state S2.

Alternatively, we can directly generate the select signal at the beginning of state S3 such as

```
SEL_DEVX = AS & !CLK & DECODE_DEVX # SEL_DEVX & AS;
```
(Eq. 8-7)

instead of using the DAS* from approach 3.

Example address decoder. An example decoder logic using the '22V10 PLD is given in Figure 8-46. The address and function code inputs to this decoder could be the corresponding 68000 output signals or their buffered versions.

The peripheral control devices are slow, and so optimizing the address decode does not really make any difference in access time. The AS* is used by the

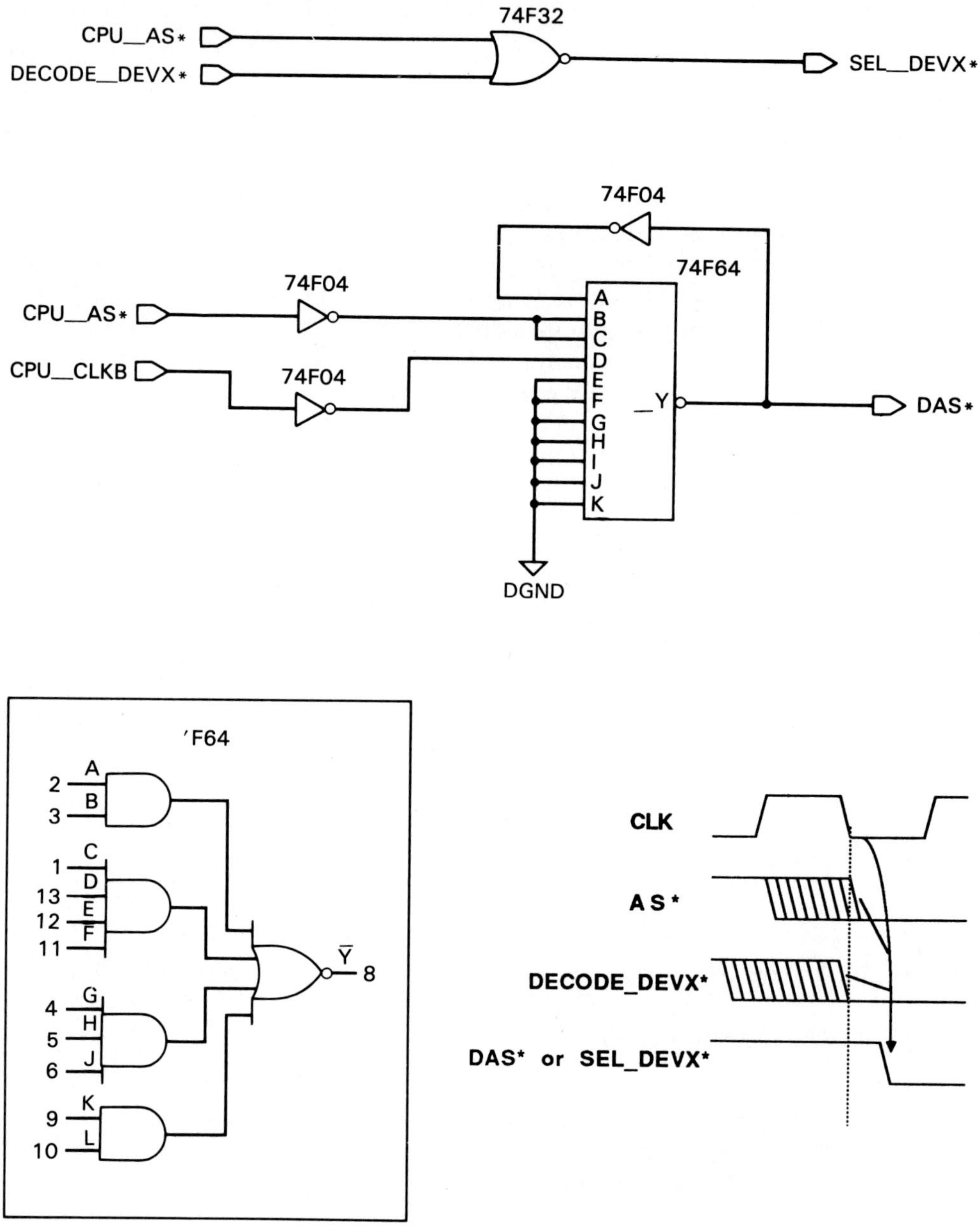

Figure 8-45 Qualifying Address Decode with AS*

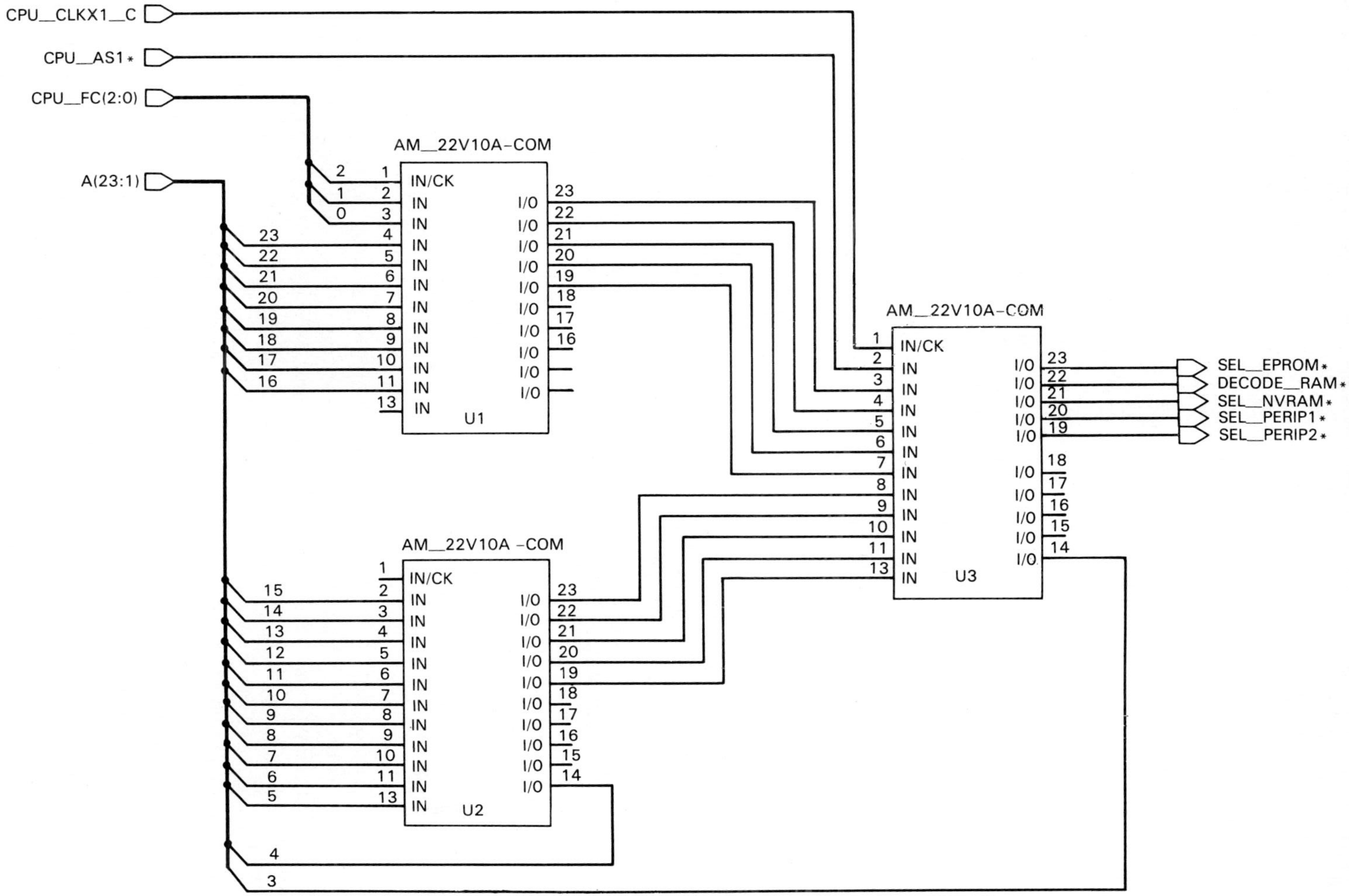

Figure 8-46 Schematic of Address Decoder.

U3 PLD to qualify the address decode and also, the SEL_PERIPx* are negated as soon as possible at the end of the cycle to avoid any potential contention with the next bus cycle.

The PLD files for this circuit is shown in Figure 8-47.

8.9 DTACK* GENERATION LOGIC

The DTACK* generation logic ensures that the correct number of wait-cycles are inserted into all bus cycles. In general, a data-transfer-acknowledge signal is generated for each peripheral device that is on the 68000 bus and these signals are ORed before driving the DTACK* input of the 68000. During a bus cycle, the address decode logic will select a peripheral to be accessed, which, in turn, initiates the generation of DTACK* for that peripheral. If no devices are selected and if it is not an interrupt-acknowledge bus cycle, no DTACK* is generated. In this case, a bus-error exception is generated, if there is a *bus-time-out* (BTO) circuit. Otherwise, the bus will "freeze" indefinitely.

There are two types of peripheral devices with regard to DTACK* generation. The 68000 family peripheral controller devices such as the '68681 DUART interface fully asynchronously with the 68000 and provide a DTACK* output that can be directly passed to the 68000. This is shown in Figure 8-48. Other peripherals do not have a DTACK* output that we can readily use. These include memory type devices and other peripheral chips (e.g., a *real-time clock/calendar* (RTC) chip). The DTACK* circuitry, in this case, generates a fixed amount of delay after the beginning of the bus cycle before asserting the DTACK* to the 68000.

To generate a fixed delay, we may use the address strobe (AS*) to qualify the address decode signal (i.e., for device X, we start counting the delay after the AS* is asserted and qualify it with DECODE_DEVX* before we "return" DTACK*). To implement a delay logic, we can use a counter or a shift-register as shown in Figure 8-49. The 'F164 shift register provides an 8-bit shift, at the positive edge of the clock, of its two ANDed inputs as shown in Figure 8-50. Its outputs can be cleared asynchronously.

The output of the 'F164 is either jumper-selected or hard-wired to choose the number of wait-cycles. However, there are two shortcomings of the above circuit. First, the access time requirements for read and write bus cycles are different, as we saw in Sections 8.5 and 8.6. This means, for example, accessing a memory device may require no wait-cycles for read and one wait-cycle for write. Using the above DTACK* circuit, we have to choose one wait-cycles for both read and write which is not optimal.

Secondly, this DTACK* circuit does not support the *read-modify-write* (RMW) bus cycles used by the TAS instruction. As we saw earlier, the address strobe stays asserted throughout the RMW bus cycle, but a separate DTACK* is needed for the read and write subcycles. The DTACK* will stay asserted using

```
U1 PLD:

/* Inputs */

Pin [1..3]    = [FC2..0] ;
Pin [4..11]   = [A23..16] ;

/* Outputs */

Pin 23 = !U1_EPROM        ;   /* Asserted when EPROM is decoded by
                                  this PLD.                          */
Pin 22 = !U1_RAM          ;   /* Partial RAM Decode.                 */
Pin 21 = !U1_NVRAM        ;   /* Partial NVRAM Decode.               */
Pin 20 = !U1_PERIP        ;   /* Partial Peripheral Area Decode.     */
Pin 19 = !RESET_VECTOR    ;   /* Partial Decode for Reset Vector.    */

/* Logical Equations */

U1_EPROM =   !A23 & !A22 &  A21 &  A20 &      /* Addr= 30xxxx        */
             !A19 & !A18 & !A17 & !A16 ) &
             !(FC2 & FC1 & FC0)               /* Not CPU Space.      */

RESET_VECTOR =(!A23 & !A22 & !A21 & !A20 &    /* Addr= 00xxxx        */
               !A19 & !A18 & !A17 & !A16 ) &
              !(FC2 & FC1 & FC0)              /* Not CPU SPACE.      */

U1_RAM    = (!A23 & !A22 & !A21 & !A20 &      /* Addr= (00-01)xxxx   */
             !A19 & !A18 & !A17 ) &
             !(FC2 & FC1 & FC0)               /* Not CPU Space.      */

U1_NVRAM = (!A23 & !A22 & !A21 &  A20 &       /* Addr= 18xxxx        */
              A19 & !A18 & !A17 & !A16 ) &
             !(FC2 & FC1 & FC0)               /* Not CPU Space.      */

U1_PERIP = ( A23 &  A22 &  A21 &  A20 &       /* Addr= F0xxxx        */
             !A19 & !A18 & !A17 & !A16 ) &
             !(FC2 & FC1 & FC0)             ; /* Not CPU Space.      */

U2 PLD:

/* Inputs */

Pin [2..11]  = [A15..6] ;
Pin [13..14] = [A5..4]  ;
```

Figure 8-47 Address-decoder PLD-file Examples (File Headers Not Shown).

```
/* Outputs */

Pin 23 = !ADDR_xx000x ;
Pin 22 = !ADDR_xx001x ;
Pin 21 = !EXPANSION1  ;  /* Future expansion/change.     */
Pin 20 = !EXPANSION2  ;  /* Future expansion/change.     */
Pin 19 = !EXPANSION3  ;  /* Future expansion/change.     */

/* Logical Equations */

ADDR_xx000x = !A15 & !A14 & !A13 & !A12 & /* Addr= xx0000xx.   */
              !A11 & !A10 & !A9  & !A8  &
              !A7  & !A6  & !A5  & !A4  ;

ADDR_xx001x = !A15 & !A14 & !A13 & !A12 & /* Addr= xx0001xx.   */
              !A11 & !A10 & !A9  & !A8  &
              !A7  & !A6  & !A5  & !A4  ;
```

U3 PLD:

```
/* Inputs */

Pin  1 =  CPU_CLK    ;    /* Buffered 68000 Clock.       */
Pin  2 = !CPU_AS1    ;    /* Buffered 68000 AS* Signal. */
Pin  3 = !U1_EPROM   ;
Pin  4 = !U1_RAM     ;
Pin  5 = !U1_NVRAM   ;
Pin  6 = !U1_PERIP   ;
Pin  7 = !RESET_VECTOR ;
Pin  8 = !ADDR_xx000x ;
Pin  9 = !ADDR_xx001x ;
Pin 10 = !EXPANSION1  ;
Pin 11 = !EXPANSION2  ;
Pin 13 = !EXPANSION3  ;
Pin 14 = A3

/* Outputs */

Pin 23 = !SEL_EPROM   ;
Pin 22 = !DECODE_RAM  ;
Pin 21 = !SEL_NVRAM   ;
Pin 20 = !SEL_PERIP1  ;
Pin 19 = !SEL_PERIP2  ;
```

Figure 8-47 (cont.) Address-decoder PLD-file Examples (File Headers Not Shown).

```
/* Logical Equations */

SEL_EPROM = CPU_AS1 & !CPU_CLK &
            (U1_EPROM # RESET_VECTOR & ADDR_xx000x & !A3) #
            SEL_EPROM & CPU_AS1 ;

DECODE_RAM = U1_RAM ;

SEL_NVRAM  = CPU_AS1 & !CPU_CLK & U1_NVRAM # SEL_NVRAM & CPU_AS1;

SEL_PERIP1 = CPU_AS1 & !CPU_CLK & U1_PERIP & ADDR_xx000x #
             SEL_PERIP1 & CPU_AS1 ;

SEL_PERIP2 = CPU_AS1 & !CPU_CLK & U1_PERIP & ADDR_xx001x #
             SEL_PERIP2 & CPU_AS1 ;
```

Figure 8-47 (cont.) Address-decoder PLD-file Examples (File Headers Not Shown).

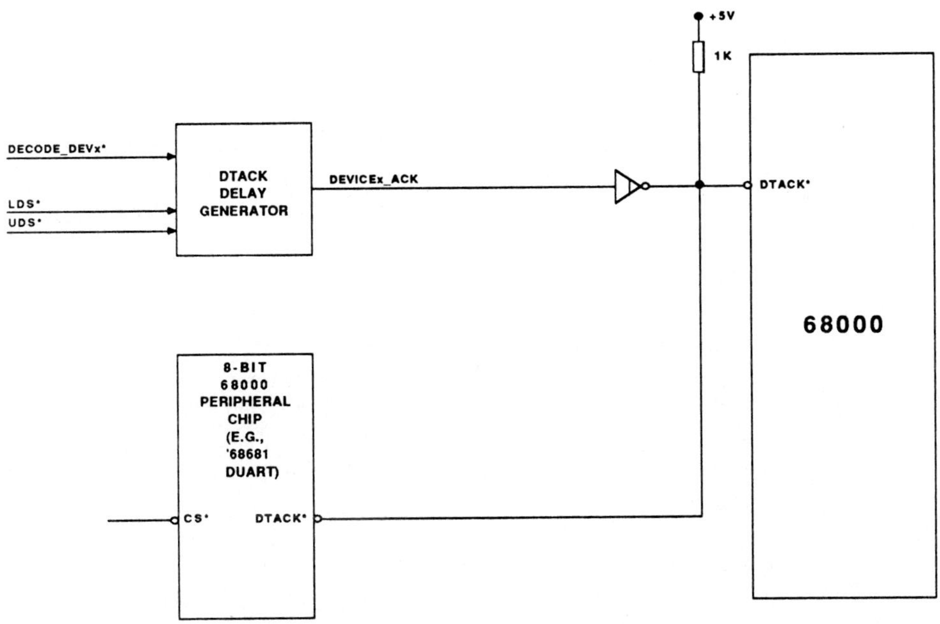

Figure 8-48 Illustration of DTACK* Generation.

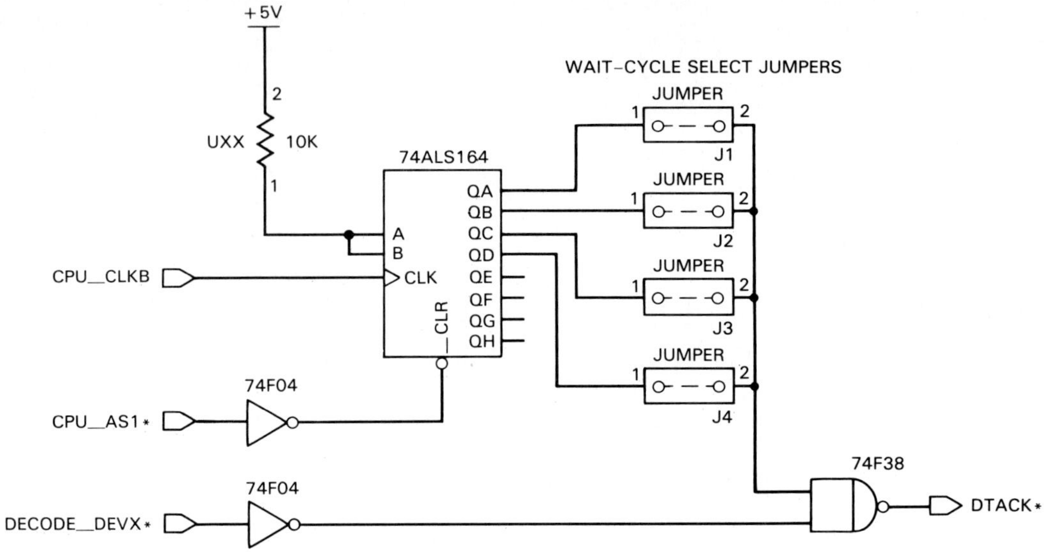

Figure 8-49 Incorrect DTACK* Generation.

the above delay circuit, which will only work if both read and write portions of access can work with zero wait-cycles.

We can resolve both of these shortcomings by modifying the circuit as shown in Figure 8-51. This circuit uses the logical OR of LDS* and UDS* to initiate the DTACK* delay generation. Since the data strobes are asserted one clock cycle later for the write bus cycle, there will be automatically one-wait-cycle difference between read and write accesses. Furthermore, the LDS*/UDS* is strobed during the read and write subcycles of the RMW bus cycle, thus causing DTACK* to be generated twice.

Since the 'F164 uses the positive-edge of the clock and LDS*/UDS* is asserted during the high portion of the clock cycle, this ensures that the Qa output will go high after the next rising edge of clock. To have the same number of wait-cycles during multiple accesses to a given device, we have to make sure that the DTACK* setup time t47 is always met. In our example, we have

$$t47 = t2 - (T_{f164} + T_{F38}) \qquad \text{(Eq. 8-8)}$$

where

T_{f164}: Is the clock-to-output propogation delay of 'F164. From the datasheet summary, this is 11 nanoseconds worst case.

T_{F38}: Is the high-to-low output propagation delay of 'F38, which is 5.5 nanoseconds from Figure 8-52.

LOGIC DIAGRAM

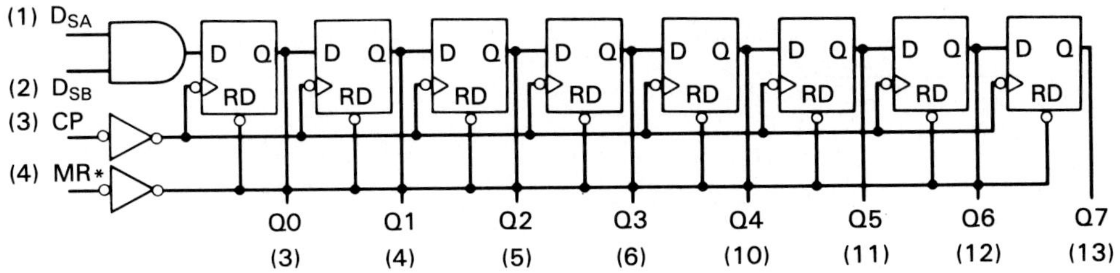

Vcc = Pin 14
GND = Pin 7

MODE SELECT—TRUTH TABLE

Operating Mode	Inputs				Outputs	
	MR*	CP	D_{sa}	D_{sb}	Q0	Q1 – Q7
Reset (clear)	L	X	X	X	L	L – L
Shift	H	↑	l	l	L	q0 – q6
	H	↑	l	h	L	q0 – q6
	H	↑	h	l	L	q0 – q6
	H	↑	h	h	H	q0 – q6

H = High voltage level.
h = High voltage level one setup time prior to the low-to-high clock transition.
L = Low voltage level.
l = Low voltage level one setup time prior to the low-to-high clock transition.
q = Lower case letters indicate the state of the referenced input (or output) one setup time prior to the low-to-high clock transition.
X = Don't care.
↑ = Low-to-high clock transition.

Characteristic	Min	Max	Units
Clock to Output Propagation Delay.	2.5	11	nsec.
Reset to Output Propagation Delay.	4	11.5	nsec.
Inputs A/B Setup Time.	7	—	nsec.
Recovery Time: Reset to Clock Input.	7	—	nsec.

Figure 8-50 'F164 Shift-register Datasheet Summary. (Courtesy of Signetics.)

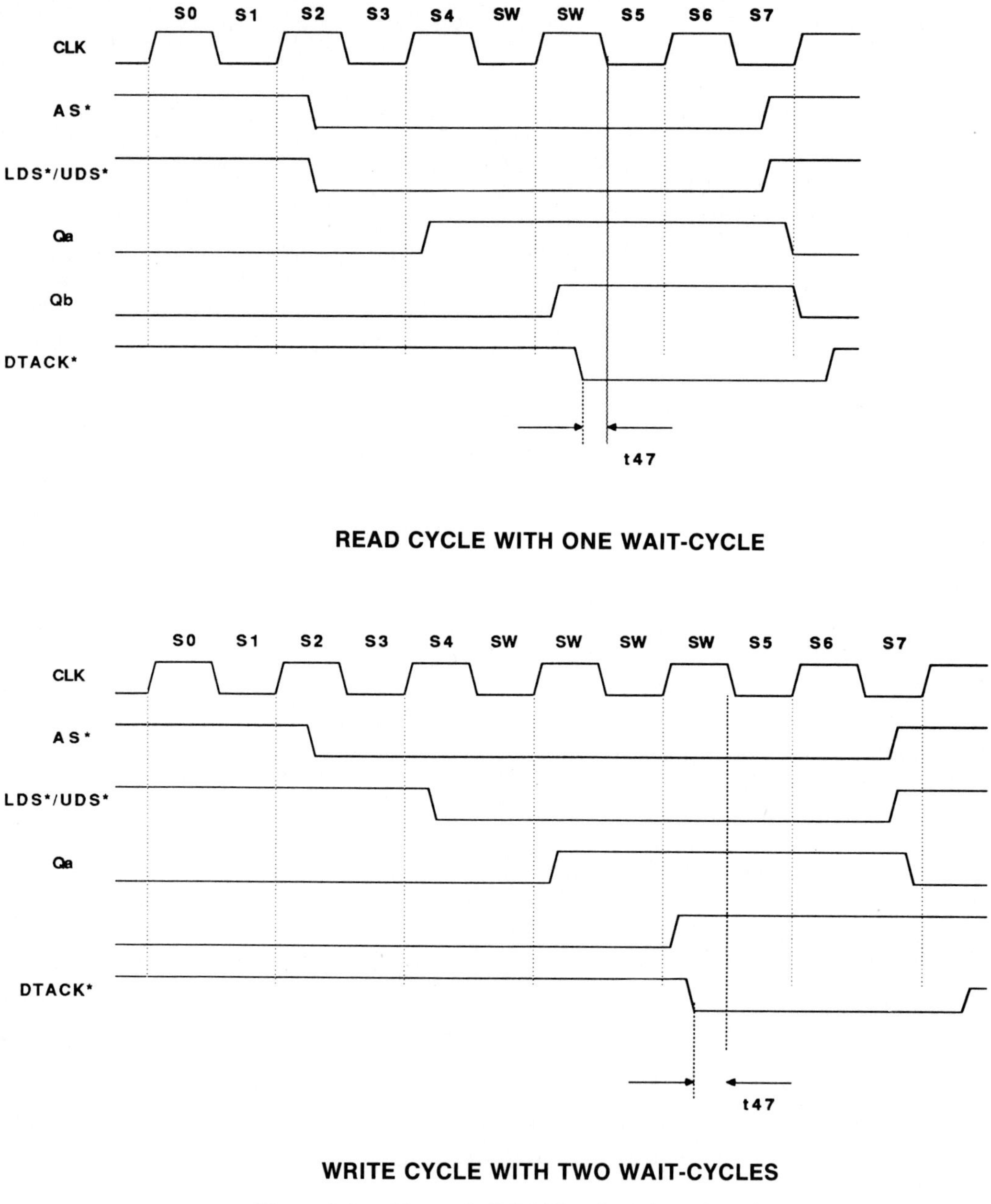

Figure 8-51 Example DTACK* Interface Circuit.

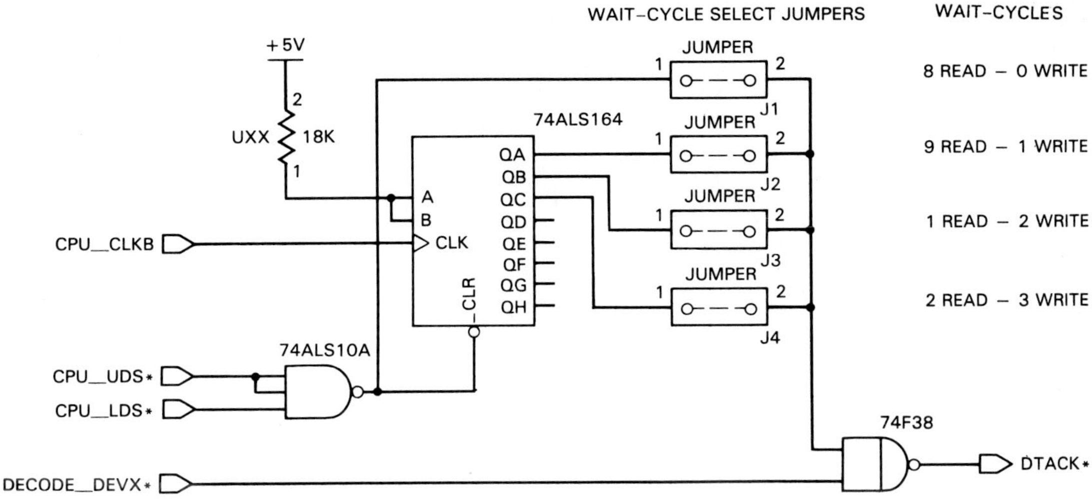

Figure 8-51 (cont.) Example DTACK* Interface Circuit.

Thus, we have

$$t47 = 28.5 \text{ nsec.}$$

which is greater than the minimum requirement of 10 nanoseconds for a 10 MHz 68000.

So far, we have discussed DTACK* circuitry for only one device. To generate DTACK* for multiple devices, we could repeat the circuit of Figure 8-51 for each device that does not provide a DTACK* output. A more efficient approach is to use the 'F164 shift register or a counter as a delay generator shared by multiple devices. Such a circuit is shown in Figure 8-53. The wait-cycle selection for each device is independent.

The other alternative is to use a PLD to replace the circuit in Figure 8-53 with a circuit of Figure 8-54. The wait-cycles, in this implementation, are programmed for each device into the PLD equations. In this example, we also chose to OR all "transfer-acknowledge" signals within this PLD, where the 68000 peripheral controller chip's DTACK* outputs are brought in as inputs to this PLD. This necessitates pull-up resistors for each of the open-drain DTACK* outputs of these devices. The PLD equations for this example are given in Figure 8-55.

Other than meeting the setup time, we also have to be careful about the timing of DTACK* negation. The requirement is to negate DTACK* within the maximum limit of parameter t28, we we discussed earlier. The t28 is 150 nanoseconds for a 10 MHz 68000, which is easily met by both the 'F164 and PLD implementations discussed here (exercise 8-33).

One final note on the DTACK* circuit is that the performance of the 68000 is dependent on how the system clock frequency and the number of wait-cycles

AC ELECTRICAL CHARACTERISTICS

Symbol	Parameter	Test Conditions	74F38					Unit
			$T_A = +25°C$, $V_{CC} = +5.0V$, $C_L = 50pF$, $R_L = 500\Omega$			$T_A = 0°C$ to $+70°C$, $V_{CC} = +5.0V \pm 10\%$, $C_L = 50pF$, $R_L = 500\Omega$		
			Min	Typ	Max	Min	Max	
t_{PLH} t_{PHL}	Propagation delay A, B to Y*	Waveform 1	7.5 1.5	10 3.0	12.5 5.0	7.5 1.5	13 5.5	ns

AC WAVEFORM

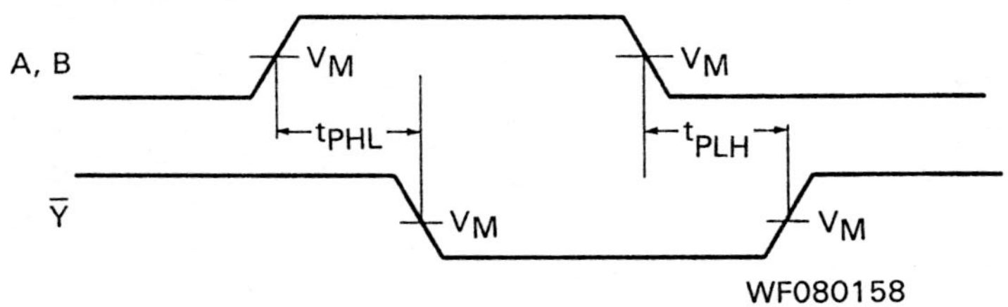

NOTE: For all waveforms, V_M = 1.5V.

Figure 8-52 Signetics 'F38 Datasheet Summary.

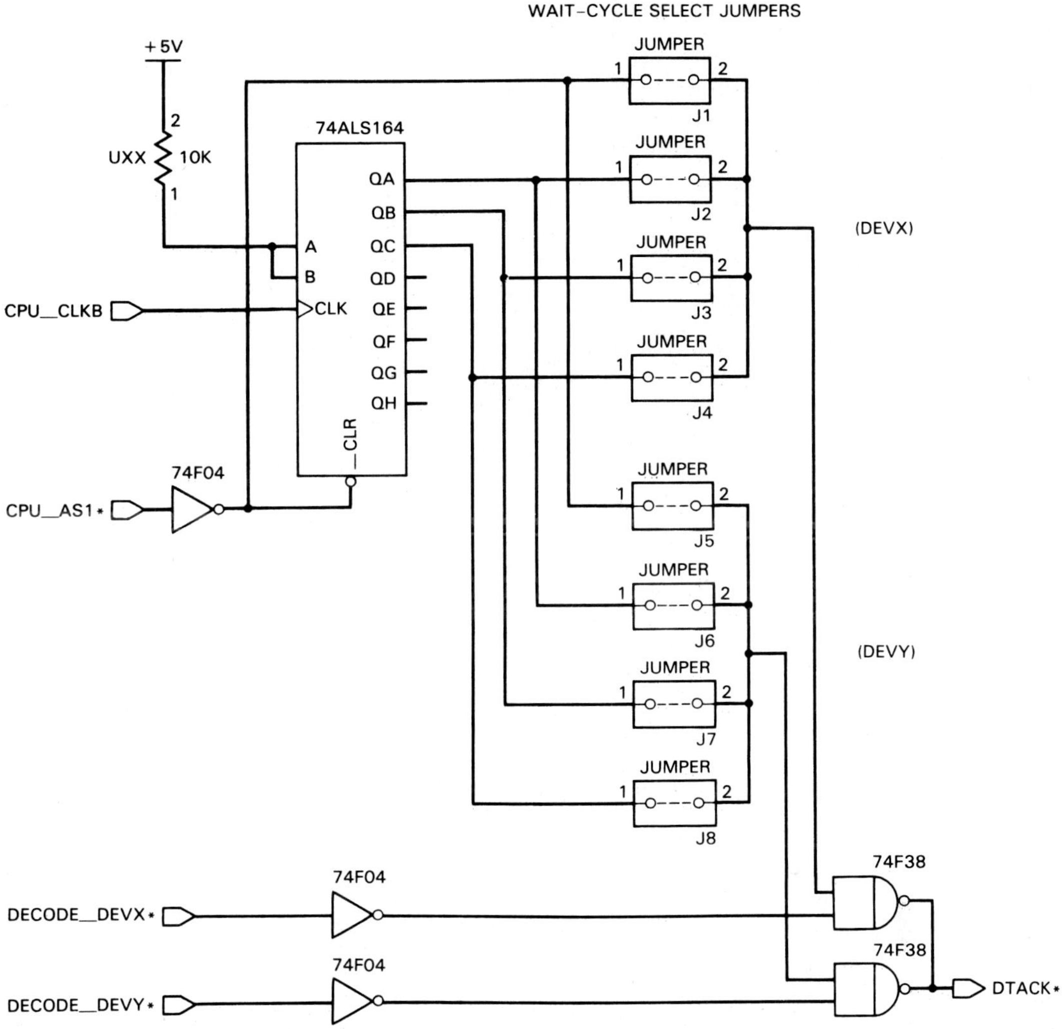

Figure 8-53 DTACK* Generator for Multiple Devices.

are chosen. Instead of simply using the maximum possible 68000 clock frequency, we have to watch the number of wait-cycles. In other words, it may provide higher performance to run the 68000 slower than its maximum rated speed. For example, let us assume that the system memory is heavily accessed and requires 1 wait-cycle when we run the 68000 at 10 MHz. If reducing the clock frequency, let us say by 10 percent results in running with no wait-cycles, it is preferable. This is because it results in an increase of overall system performance by 15 percent even

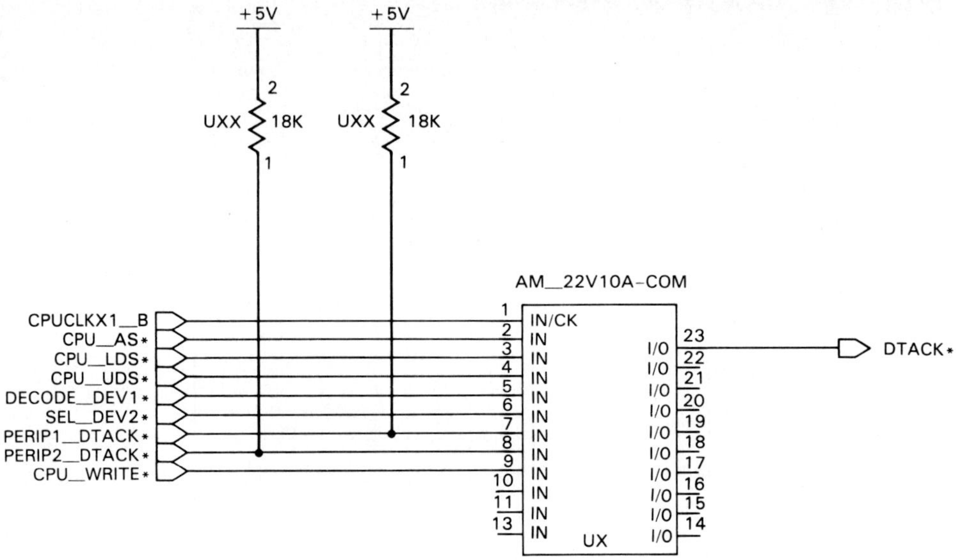

Figure 8-54 PLD Implementation of Circuit of Figure 8-53.

```
Name         DTACK.PLD;
Partno       XXXX;
Date         XX/XX/XX;
Revision     XX;
Designer     XXXXX;
Company      XXXXX;
Assembly     XXXXX;
Location     XXXXX;

/*******************************************************************/
/* Purpose: This device generates DTACK* signal for four devices. */
/*                                                                 */
/*           Device     READ WAIT_CYCLES    WRITE WAIT_CYCLES      */
/*            DEV1            0                   1                */
/*            DEV2            2                   2                */
/*            PERIP1          See note            See note         */
/*            PERIP2          See note            See note         */
/*                                                                 */
/* The Device #1 uses a address decode signal that is not          */
/* qualified with the AS*. The Device #2 uses the SEL_DEV2*,       */
/* which is already qualified with the AS*.                        */
/* The Peripherals, PERIP1 and PERIP2, are two peripheral          */
/* controllers of the 68000 family that provide a DTACK* signal.  */
/*******************************************************************/
/*  Allowable Target Device Types: 22V10                           */
/*******************************************************************/
```

Figure 8-55 Sample PLD Source File for the DTACK* PLD.

```
/**  Inputs  **/

Pin  1  = CPUCLKX1_B    ;       /* CPU Clock.                    */
Pin  2  = !CPU_AS       ;       /* Buffered Address Strobe.      */
Pin  3  = !CPU_LDS      ;       /* Buffered High Data Strobe.    */
Pin  4  = !CPU_UDS      ;       /* Buffered Low Data Strobe.     */
Pin  5  = !DECODE_DEV1  ;       /* Device #1 Decode Signal.      */
Pin  6  = !SEL_DEV2     ;       /* Device #2 Select Signal.      */
Pin  7  = !PERIP1_DTACK ;       /* DTACK* from PERIP1.           */
Pin  8  = !PERIP2_DTACK ;       /* DTACK* from PERIP2.           */

/**  Outputs  **/

Pin  23 = !DTACK        ;       /* DTACK* Output.                */
Pin  22 = !Qa           ;       /* An intermediate output.       */
pin  21 = !Qb           ;       /* An intermediate output.       */

/**  Logic Equations  **/

Qa.D = (CPU_LDS # CPU_UDS) ;

Qb.D = Qa & CPU_AS ;

Qc.D = Qb & CPU_AS ;

DTACK = ( Qa & DECODE_DEV1 #
          Qb & DECODE_DEV2 & !CPU_WRITE #
          Qa & DECODE_DEV2 &  CPU_WRITE #
          PERIP1_DTACK  #
          PERIP2_DTACK ) & CPU_AS ;
```

Figure 8-55 (cont.) Sample PLD Source File for the DTACK* PLD.

though we actually slowed down the clock! This approach is used by some popular personal computers such as the MacIntosh SE.

8.10 INTERFACE TO MEMORY DEVICES

Before we discuss interfacing the 68000 to memory devices, let us briefly look at the different types of semiconductor memories. The following gives an overview of memory types:

Read-only Memory (ROM)	This is what the name says. It is not very commonly used, other than for very high production volumes because it requires programming by the semiconductor manufacturer per user's requirements.

Programmable Read-only Memory (PROM)	This is similar to ROM, but can be programmed at the user's site using a programmer. Once programmed, its contents are not erasable.
Erasable PROM (EPROM)	This type of device is commonly used as non-volatile storage. It can be programmed by the user, and it is also UV-light erasable. At the time of this writing, EPROM chips are available with up to 2 Megabits per chip.
Static Random-Access Memory (SRAM)	This name is a misnomer because it really refers to a static read/write memory. A SRAM memory device uses a bistable flip-flop as its basic storage cell and, therefore, no clocking or refresh action is required after the data is written in order to retain data. Hence, the word static.
Dynamic Random-access Memory (DRAM)	A DRAM device uses capacitors to store information (binary 1 and 0 for the presence and absence of charge). Its memory cell consists of one gating transistor and a storage capacitor. Its simple memory cell structure, compared to the four transistors of a SRAM cell, results in significantly higher memory capacities per chip. This is shown in Figure 8-56. On the other hand, DRAM has the disadvantage that its cell capacitors need to be frequently recharged because of leakage currents. Hence, the term dynamic.
Electrically Erasable PROM (EEPROM)	Referred to as *E-square PROM*. This is similar to EPROM except it is programmable in an operational circuit. The write accesses are slow (about 2 to 10 milliseconds to complete) and the number of write operations are limited (to about 10,000 times). However, it allows fast reads.
Non-volatile RAM (NVRAM)	This is a low-power SRAM memory device that is externally battery backed-up. The battery, typically Lithium, maintains stored information in SRAM during system power-down periods. It has the advantage over EEPROM that both fast reads and writes are allowed and without any limitation in the number of writes. However, it requires external support circuitry and a battery.

Multiport RAM Memory	This is a shared memory that can be accessed by multiple processors. Each processor "views" the memory as a simple SRAM memory (i.e., separate address, data, and control bits are provided for each port). The memory manages and arbitrates between multiple and concurrent accesses to its locations. In its simplest form, it has two ports and is referred to as Dual-port RAM (DPRAM).

8.10.1 SRAM Memory Design

Characteristics of a typical SRAM memory device. An example of a typical SRAM device is the μPD43256A that is manufactured by NEC. This SRAM has 256 K-bit storage capacity that is organized as 32 K-words by 8-bits as shown in Figure 8-57. We have choosen the '43256 because it is also second-sourced by other manufacturers such as Fujitsu and Hitachi. As a general rule, the designer should always try to choose parts that are multi-sourced, when possible, because it ensures the availability and usually lower costs. Even though the 32K by 8 SRAMs sourced by different manufacturers have different part numbers, they are usually compatible in pinouts and AC-electrical characteristics for a given speed rating. The address pinouts may differ but this is not important (why?).

As shown in the logic block diagram, the chip-select (CS*) is the primary control signal that enables a read or write access. It is also referred to as enable

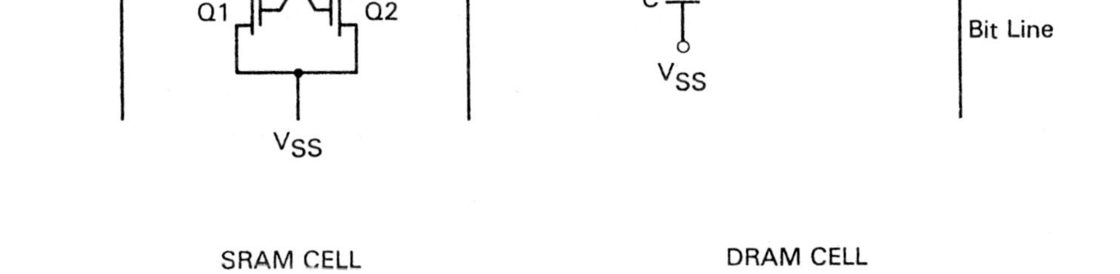

Figure 8-56 SRAM and DRAM Memory Cells.

Description

The μPD43256A is a 32,768-word by 8-bit static RAM fabricated with advanced silicon-gate technology. Its unique circuitry, using CMOS peripheral circuits and N-channel memory cells with polysilicon resistors, makes the μPD43256A a high-speed device that requires very low power and no clock or refreshing to operate.

Minimum standby power is drawn when $\overline{CS}$ is at a high level, independent of the other inputs' levels. Data retention is guaranteed at a power supply voltage as low as 2 V. The μPD43256A is available in standard 28-pin plastic DIP or 28-pin plastic miniflat packaging.

Features

- ☐ Single +5-volt power supply
- ☐ Fully static operation—no clock or refreshing required
- ☐ TTL-compatible inputs and outputs
- ☐ Common I/O using three-state outputs
- ☐ One $\overline{CS}$ pin and one $\overline{OE}$ pin for easy application
- ☐ Data retention voltage: 2 V minimum
- ☐ Standard 28-pin plastic DIP or miniflat packaging

Ordering Information

Part Number	Access Time (max)	Data Retention Current (max) $T_A = 0\text{-}70°C$	Package
μPD43256AC-85L	85 ns	50 μA	28-pin plastic DIP (600 mil)
C-10L	100 ns		
C-12L	120 ns		
C-15L	150 ns		
μPD43256AC-85LL	85 ns	20 μA	28-pin plastic DIP (600 mil)
C-10LL	100 ns		
C-12LL	120 ns		
C-15LL	150 ns		
μPD43256AGU-85L	85 ns	50 μA	28-pin plastic miniflat
GU-10L	100 ns		
GU-12L	120 ns		
GU-15L	150 ns		
μPD43256AGU-85LL	85 ns	20 μA	28-pin plastic miniflat
GU-10LL	100 ns		
GU-12LL	120 ns		
GU-15LL	150 ns		

Pin Configuration

28-Pin Plastic DIP or Miniflat

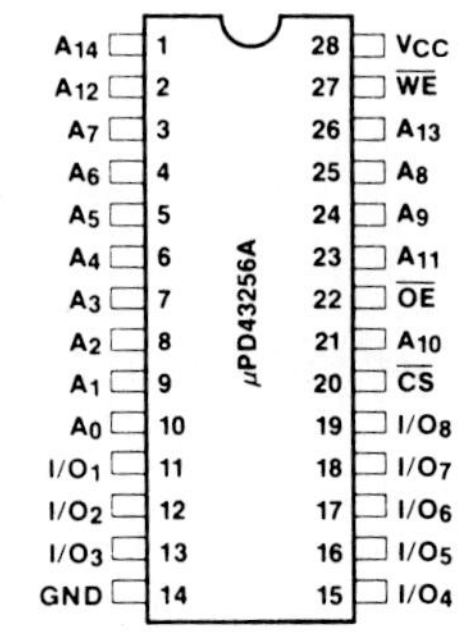

Pin Identification

Symbol	Function
A_0-A_{14}	Address inputs
I/O_1-I/O_8	Data inputs/outputs
$\overline{CS}$	Chip select
$\overline{OE}$	Output enable
$\overline{WE}$	Write enable
GND	Ground
V_{CC}	+5-volt power supply

Truth Table

$\overline{CS}$	$\overline{OE}$	$\overline{WE}$	Mode	I/O	I_{CC}
H	X	X	Not selected	High-Z	Standby
L	H	H	Not selected	High-Z	Active
L	L	H	Read	D_{OUT}	Active
L	X	L	Write	D_{IN}	Active

Notes:

(1) X = don't care.

Figure 8-57 Example SRAM Device. (Courtesy of NEC.)

(E*) or chip-enable (CE*) by other manufacturers. The write-enable (WE*) indicates a write operation to SRAM when asserted and read operation when negated. The output enable (OE*) signal controls the enabling of data-output buffers, and thus carries significance only for read accesses. This means that the OE* may permanently be connected to digital ground, whereby the data-output buffers will be controlled by CE* and WE*.

The '43256 comes in four different speed versions: 85 nsec. (−85 version), 100 nsec. (−100), 120 nsec. (−120), and 150 nsec. (−150). The reader should examine the full datasheet of this SRAM that is included in AppendixH. The slowest version that is allowed by the design requirements should be used, since higher speed versions cost significantly more and also consume more power.

Read Cycle The read cycle timing requirements of the '43256 are shown in Figure 8-58. As shown, there are two types of read cycles we can use. The first one is called the *address-controlled read-cycle* and involves continuously asserting the OE* and CS* while WE* is high. This type of access is useful when SRAM is used as a *Look-up Table* (LUT), where Q = func(addr.), assuming the SRAM contents are already loaded. The second type of read access represents the typical read cycle used in interfacing to a microprocessor.

The *read cycle time* (T_{rc}) specifies time for a read operation during consecutive read accesses. In other words, the cycle time includes any recovery time needed between consecutive accesses. As such, the cycle time defines the maximum possible access throughput of a SRAM device. In an optimized SRAM device, read and write cycle and access times are all equal to each other.

The read access timing from CS* assumes that addresses (A14-A0) become valid prior to or coincident with the assertion of CS*. It is important that WE* is high before the CS* is asserted. The data output becomes valid after the minimum of parameters T_{aa}, T_{acs}, and T_{oe} have been satisfied. If, for example, the CS* is asserted 100 nsec. after the address become valid, and the OE* is always asserted, then the data output is guaranteed to be valid 100 nanoseconds plus T_{acs} after the valid address. Note, however, the SRAM starts driving its data outputs before this time (i.e., T_{clz} after the CS* is asserted). In other words, T_{acs} minus T_{clz} is the time from when the data buffers are enabled to when the data becomes valid. For the 100 nsec. version, the above time is 90 nsec. in the worst case.

Once again let us emphasize proper design rules. The operating parameters of a given part are typically significantly better than the worst-case specifications guaranteed by its manufacturer (especially at room temperature). This is why a prototype design may work in the lab with no problems, but may have problems in production of high quantities due to variations in the part's timing parameters. In order to avoid this, worst-case design rules *must* be applied consistently.

At the end of a normal read cycle, the data output buffers can be turned-off using the OE* and/or CS*. The turn-off delay is specified by T_{chz} and T_{ohz}, respectively, and is controlled by the one that is satisfied first.

ADDRESS CONTROLLED:

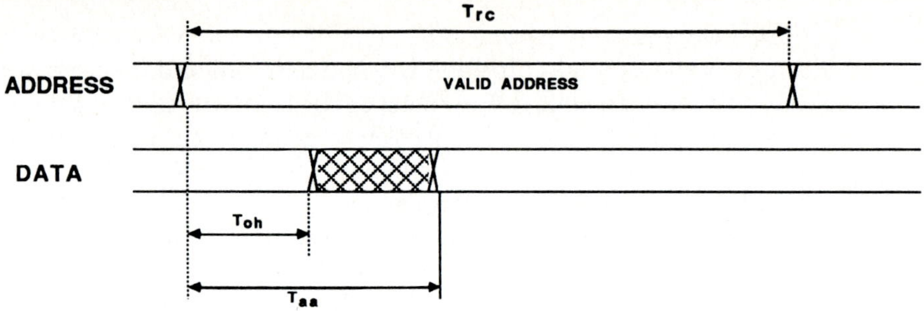

CHIP-SELECT CONTROLLED:

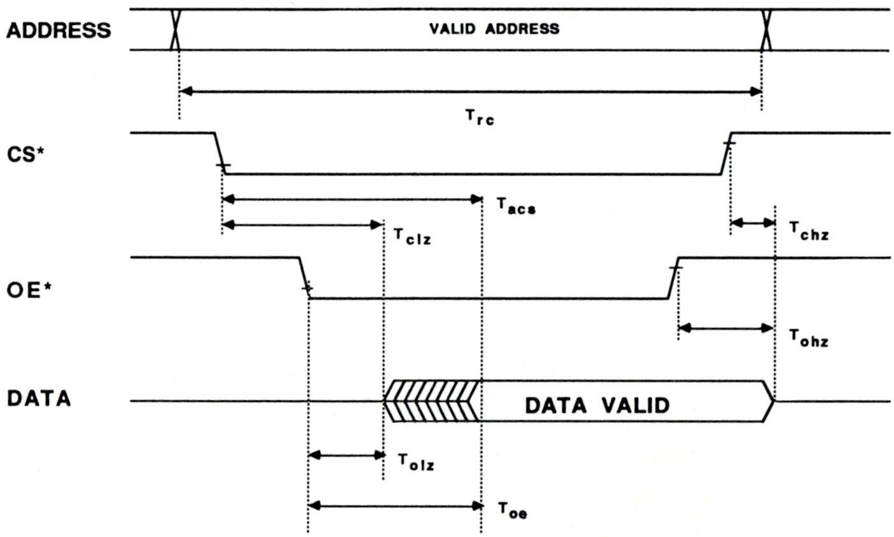

Notes: **1. WE* = H for read cycle.**
2. Address Valid before or at the same time as CS*.

Parameter	Characteristic	Min	Max	Units
T_{rc}	Read Cycle Time.	100	—	nsec.
T_{aa}	Address Access Time.	—	100	nsec.
T_{acs}	Chip-select Access Time.	—	100	nsec.
T_{oe}	Output-enable to Output Valid.	—	50	nsec.
T_{oh}	Output Hold from Address Change.	10	—	nsec.
T_{clz}	Chip-select Asserted to Output Enabled.	10	—	nsec.
T_{olz}	Output-enable Asserted to Output Enabled.	5	—	nsec.
T_{chz}	Chip-select Negated to Output in Hi-Z.	—	35	nsec.
T_{ohz}	Output-enable Negated to Output in Hi-Z.	—	35	nsec.

Note: Values shown for the 100 nsec. version.

Figure 8-58 SRAM Read Cycle Requirements.

Write Cycle

The write cycle is more critical because a circuit error results in erroneously changing the contents of the SRAM. The internal write access of the SRAM occurs during the overlap of both CS* and WE* asserted. A write operation starts at the latest transition of CS* or WE* getting asserted and is terminated when either of these two control signals is negated. If the CS* is asserted after WE* and is negated before WE*, this type of write cycle is called *CS*-controlled*. If, on the other hand, the WE* is asserted after the CS*, and negated before, then the write cycle is *WE*-controlled*. The timings of these two types of write cycles is shown in Figure 8-59.

The address inputs of the SRAM must have a valid address before the CS* or WE* that controls the write operation is asserted. The parameter T_{as} defines the required address setup time. In the case of '43256, the minimum setup time is zero, meaning the address-valid can be coincident with the assertion of CS*. Violating the T_{as} is likely to result in changing the contents of another location, as well as the location accessed.

An important feature to note about the operation of SRAMs is that a write access may be started before the data-to-be-written is actually available. It is only required that the valid data meets the setup and hold-time requirements, T_{dw} and T_{dh}, with respect to the termination of the write cycle.

A potential circuit hazard in interfacing to SRAM devices may happen during a write cycle if a bus conflict or contention occurs on the data bus between the device driving the data lines and the SRAM's bidirectional I/O buffers. Let us consider the following case. If the WE* is asserted after the CS*, then the SRAM will initially interpret this as a read bus cycle and starts turning on its data output buffers. If, at the same time, the device supplying the data-to-be-written is already driving the data bus, there will be a bus conflict until T_{whz} after the WE* is asserted. Even though the duration of this conflict may be small, this must not be allowed for proper and reliable circuit operation. However, this is only an issue for the WE*-controlled write accesses. For example, in interfacing the 68000 to SRAM devices using CS*-controlled writes and R/W* connected to WE* of SRAM(s), this potential problem will not occur, because the R/W* is asserted before the LDS*/UDS* is asserted. Since these strobe signals will be used in generating the CS* inputs, this insures that no such bus conflict occurs.

For a successful write operation, we must also meet the minimum pulse width requirements for the CS* and WE*, given by parameters T_{cw} and T_{wp}, respectively. Another important parameter of the write cycle is the write recovery time at the end of the access. This is defined by the parameter T_{wr} which specifies the minimum amount of time the valid address must be held after the termination of the write operation.

SRAM interface design. Figure 8-60 shows the block diagram of the 68000 interface to SRAM memory. We have already discussed the address-decode logic and DTACK*-generation circuit. The SRAM memory consists of one or

CS* - Controlled

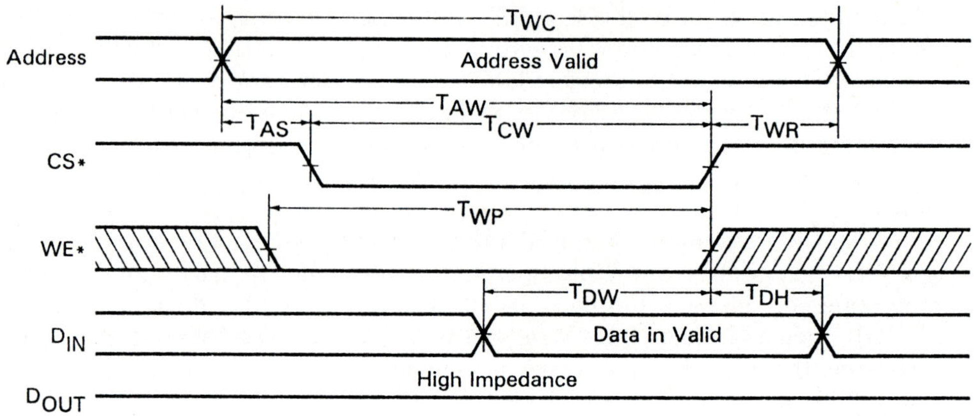

Notes:
(1) A write occurs during the overlap of a low CS* and a low WE*.
(2) CS* or WE* must be high during address transition.
(3) If OE* is high, the I/O pins remain in a high-impedance state.

WE* - Controlled

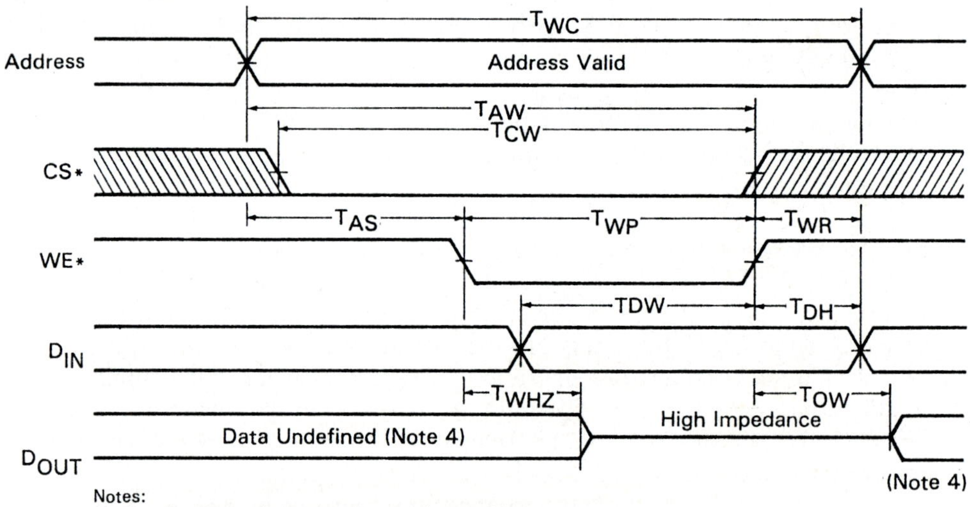

Notes:
(1) A write occurs during the overlap of a low CS* and a low WE*.
(2) CS* or WE* must be high during address transition.
(3) If OE* is high, the I/O pins remain in a high-impedance state.
(4) During this period, the I/O pins may be in the output state; therefore, input signals of opposite phase to the outputs must not be applied.

Figure 8-59 Write Cycle Timing Requirements.

Parameter	Characteristic	Min	Max	Units
T_{wc}	Write Cycle Time.	100	—	nsec.
T_{cw}	Chip-select Asserted to Write Complete.	80	—	nsec.
T_{aw}	Address Valid to End of Write.	80	—	nsec.
T_{as}	Address Setup Time.	0	—	nsec.
T_{wp}	Write Pulse Width.	70	—	nsec.
T_{wr}	Write Recovery Time.	5	—	nsec.
T_{dw}	Data Valid to End of Write.	40	—	nsec.
T_{dh}	Data Hold Time.	0	—	nsec.
T_{whz}	Write Enable to Outputs Disabled.	—	35	nsec.
T_{ow}	Outputs Enabled From End of Write.	10		nsec.

Note: Values shown for the 100 nsec. version.

Figure 8-59 (cont.) Write Cycle Timing Requirements.

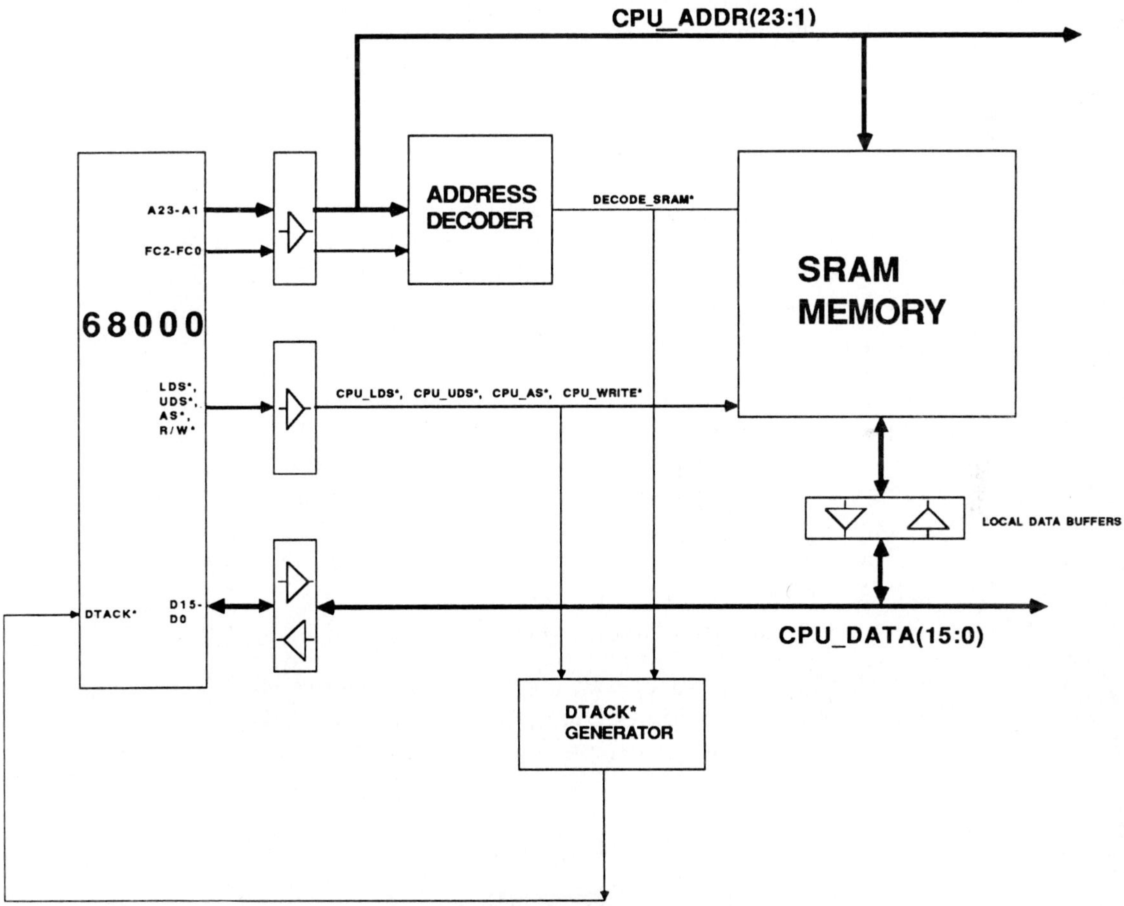

Figure 8-60 Simplified Block Diagram of SRAM Interface.

more SRAM memory devices, control logic, and local data buffering, if necessary. CMOS devices have a limited drive capability (e.g., I_{ol} = 2-4 mA), and therefore usually require local data buffer to drive all the devices on the 68000 data bus.

As an example of SRAM memory design, let us consider 128 Kbytes of SRAM that are organized as 64 Kwords by 16-bits. This could be implemented using four 32K × 8 SRAM devices as shown in Figure 8-61. The memory has two banks, where each bank consists of two SRAM devices connected as 32K × 16-bits. The respective data I/O pins of the two banks are connected together before the 'ALS245 data buffers. The buffered 68000 address signals, CPU_ADDR(15:1), are connected to address pins A14-A0 of all SRAM devices. The OE* of all SRAMs are grounded, and all WE* inputs are connected to CPU_WRITE*, which as we defined earlier is the buffered R/W* signal of the 68000.

A control PLD designated U1 generates all the necessary interface signals. The DECODE_SRAM* is not qualified with the AS* or data strobes LDS*/UDS*. Therefore, DECODE_SRAM* will, at times, be asserted, during address transitions when there is really no valid access to the SRAM address range. We will use the beginning of state S3 to qualify the address decoding, assuming DECODE_SRAM* is stable by the end of state S2 as shown in Figure 8-62.

SRAM access timing. The SRAM read bus-cycle timing is shown in Figure 8-63. Since a CS* is asserted $T_{pd(22v10)}$ after the beginning of state S3, we can write the following inequality by adding the timing parameters from S3 through S6,

$$(2 + N_r) * tcyc >= T_{pd(22V10)} + T_{acs} + 2 * T_{als245} + t27 \qquad \text{(Eq. 8-9)}$$

where N_r = 0, 1, 2, . . . is the number of wait-cycles during a SRAM read cycle. The above inequality establishes the relation between the number of wait-cycles and the characteristics of the external devices used. It is, of course, dependent on our example design. Typically, we have N_r given as a design requirement and we select the speed of the SRAM and interface logic accordingly.

The write bus-cycle timing of the SRAM memory is shown in Figure 8-64. We have, in this case,

$$t14a + N_w * tcyc >= T_{cw} \qquad \text{(Eq. 8-10)}$$

where N_w is the number of wait-cycles during a SRAM write bus cycle. In addition, for reliable operation we must also meet or exceed the data setup and hold times and address-recovery requirements. We have

$$T_{dw} = T_{cw} \qquad \text{(Eq. 8-11)}$$

$$t25 - (T_{F244} + T_{pd(22V10)}) >= T_{dh} \qquad \text{(Eq. 8-12)}$$

$$t13 - (T_{F244} + T_{pd(22V10)}) >= T_{wr} \qquad \text{(Eq. 8-13)}$$

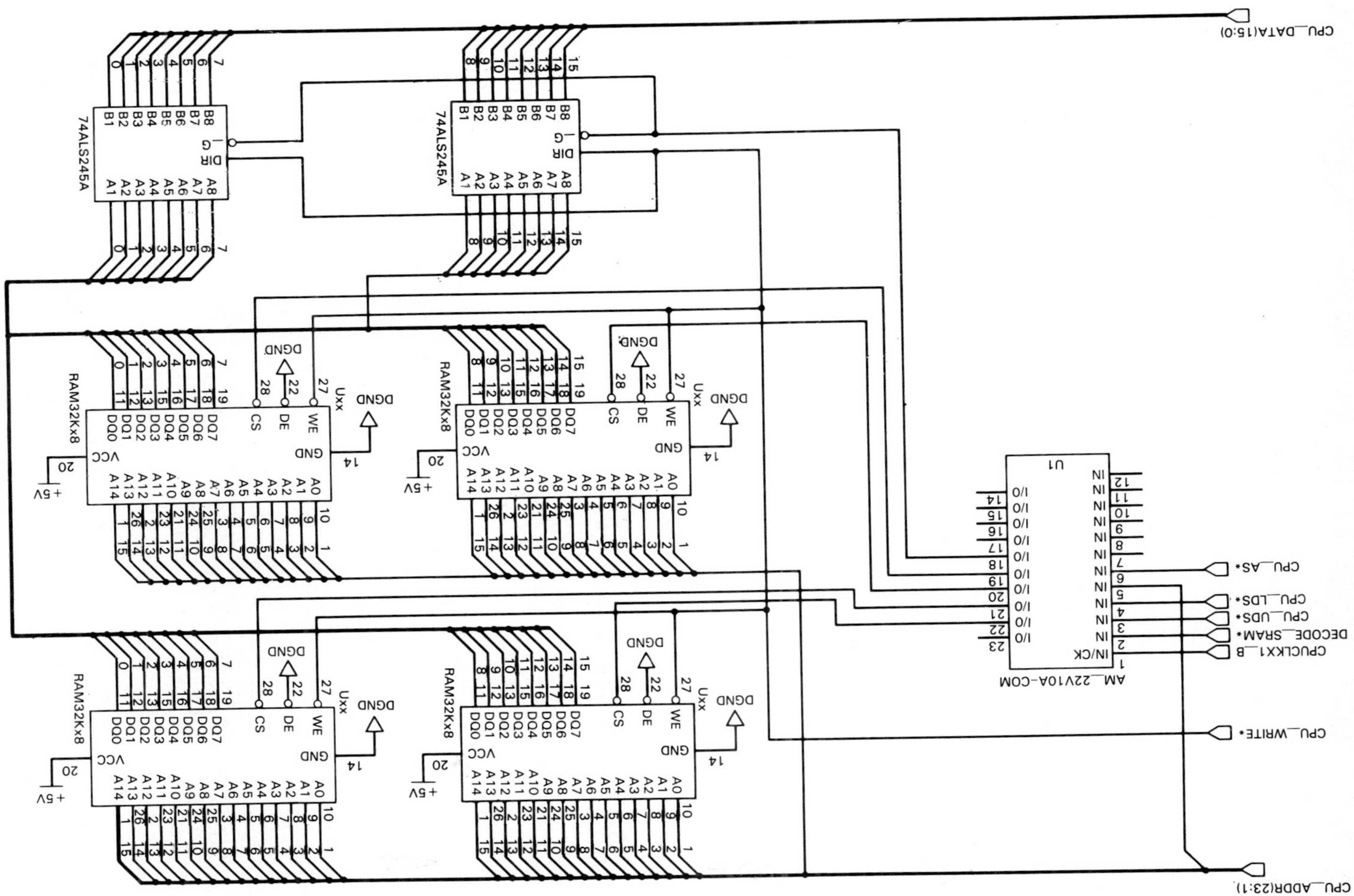

Figure 8-61 SRAM Memory Design Example.

```
/* Inputs */
Pin  1 = CLK         ;
Pin  2 = !DECODE_SRAM ;
Pin  3 = !CPU_UDS ;
Pin  4 = !CPU_LDS ;
Pin  5 = A16      ;
Pin  6 = !CPU_AS  ;

/* Outputs */
Pin 22 = !BANK0_CS_HIGH ;  /* CS* of Bank 0 and high-byte. */
Pin 21 = !BANK0_CS_LOW  ;  /* CS* of Bank 0 and low-byte.  */
Pin 20 = !BANK1_CS_HIGH ;  /* CS* of Bank 1 and high-byte. */
Pin 19 = !BANK1_CS_LOW  ;  /* CS* of Bank 1 and low-byte.  */
Pin 18 = !DATA_BUFEN    ;  /* Enables SRAM data buffers.   */

/* Logic Equations */

SRAM_ACC = !CLK & DECODE_SRAM & AS # SRAM_ACC & AS ;
 /* This is intermediate output that will be used by CUPL.
    Asserted at the beginning of S3.  */

BANK0_CS_HIGH = SRAM_ACC & CPU_UDS & !A16    ;

BANK0_CS_LOW  = SRAM_ACC & CPU_LDS & !A16    ;

BANK1_CS_HIGH = SRAM_ACC & CPU_UDS &  A16    ;

BANK1_CS_LOW  = SRAM_ACC & CPU_LDS &  A16    ;

DATA_BUFEN = DECODE_SRAM & AS ;      /* It is okay for this signal to glitch. */
```

Figure 8-62 SRAM Interface PLD Source File (without header).

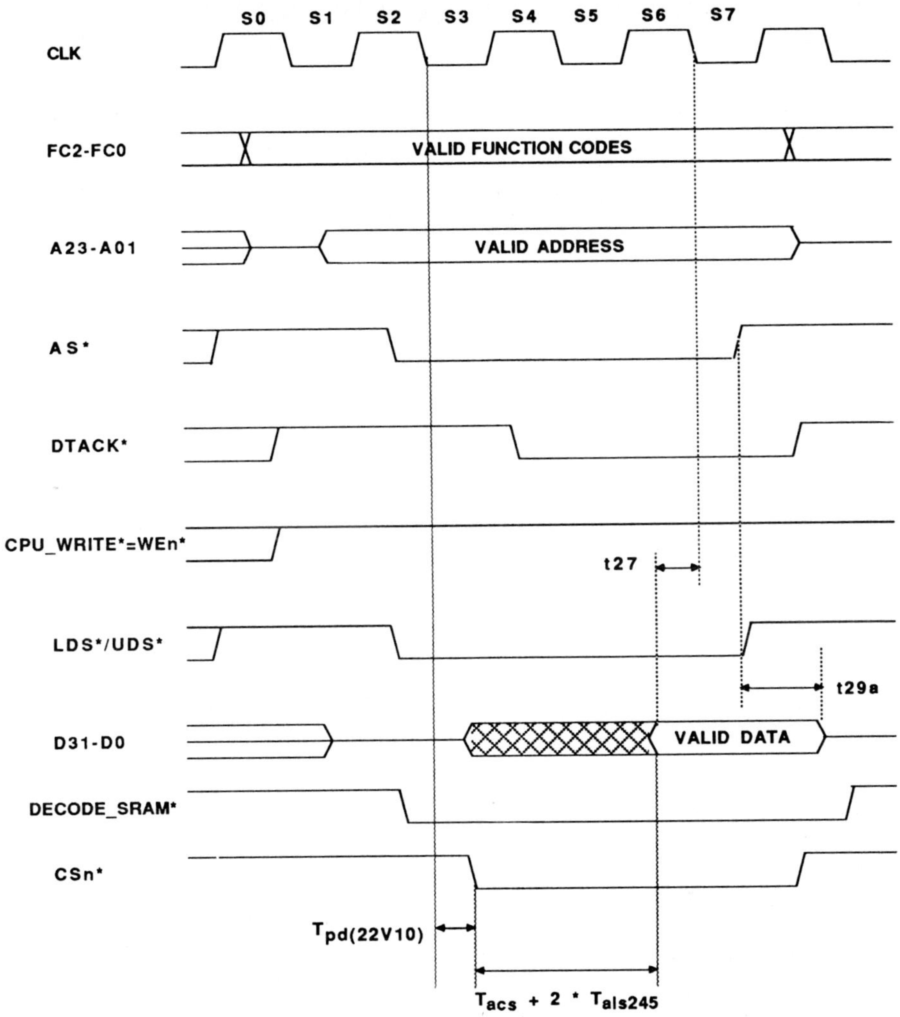

Figure 8-63 SRAM Interface Read Bus-cycle Timing.

The data hold-time calculation assumes that the buffer's propagation and turn-off delays are zero for absolute worst-case considerations. In reality, these delays help extend the actual data hold time, as seen by the SRAM devices.

In evaluating the above, we have to be careful in using the worst-case values for all parameters. This usually requires choosing the minimum or maximum values to represent the worst-case, as the next example will illustrate.

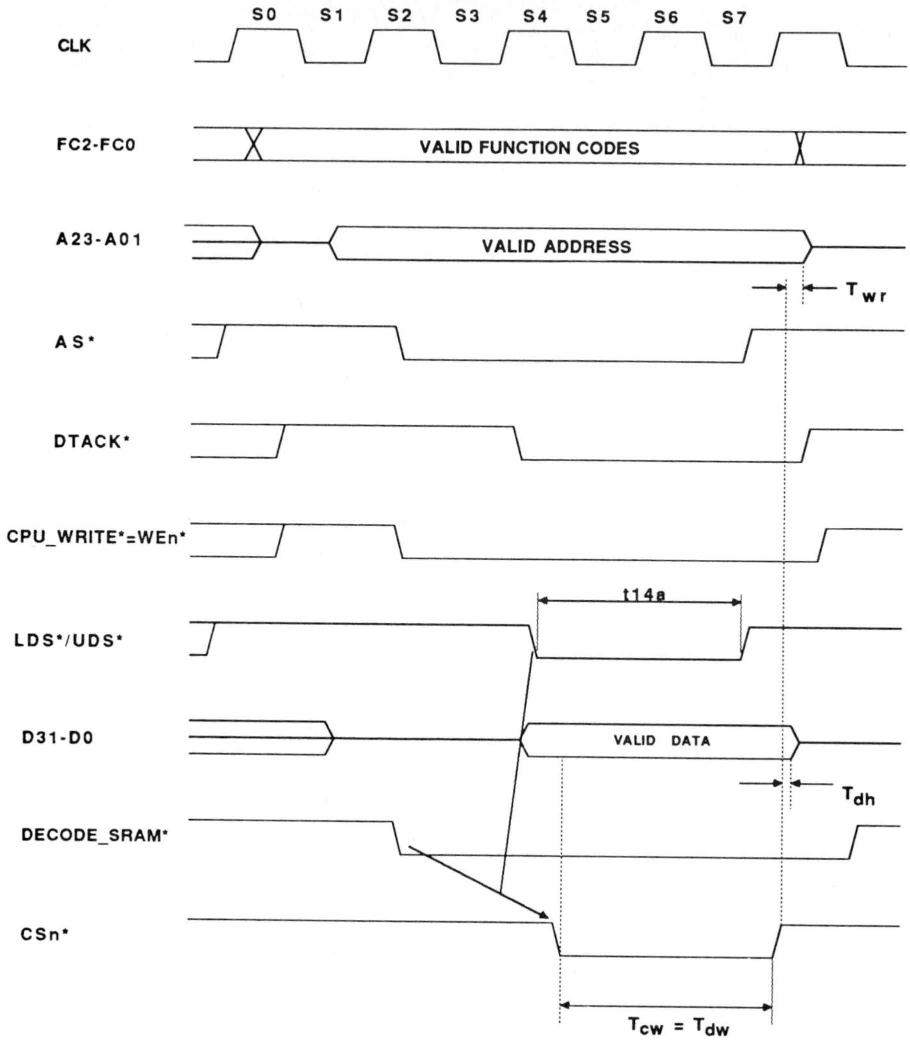

Figure 8-64 SRAM Write Access Timing.

Example 8-3

Let us evaluate the equations given above to determine the SRAM access time requirements and the selection of other component's speed ratings. Initially, let us assume that we use the '22V10-25, including for the address decoder and the −10 (100 nsec.) version of SRAMs. Also, we have

$$T_{als245}\ (\text{max}) = 20\ \text{nsec. (From TI databook)}$$

$$T_{als245}\ (\text{min}) = 5\ \text{nsec. (From TI databook)}$$

$$T_{F244}\text{ (max)} = 6.5\text{ nsec. (From Signetics/Philips databook)}$$

$$T_{F244}\text{ (min)} = 2.5\text{ nsec. (From Signetics/Philips databook)}$$

Therefore,

Read Cycle: $(2 + N_r) * 100 >= 25 + 100 + 2 * 20 + 10 = 175$ nsec.

Write Cycle: $95 + N_w * 100 >= 80$

assuming a 10 MHz 68000. This indicates that both read and write can be run with zero wait-cycles. Calculating the other write cycle requirements, we have

Eq. 8-12: $30 - (6.5 + 25) = -1.5$ nsec.

which is not greater than the required zero value (i.e., this violates the T_{dh} of SRAMs). Similarly,

Eq. 8-13: $30 - (6.5 + 25) = -1.5$ nsec.

which violates the address recovery time. In order to satisfy these equations, we have to use the 15 nanosecond version of the interface PLD. Then, we have

Eq. 8-9: $(2 + N_r) * 100 >= 165$ nsec.

Eq. 8-10: Unchanged.

Eq. 8-12: 8.5 nsec. $> T_{dh}(\text{min}) = 0$

Eq. 8-13: 8.5 nsec. $> T_{wr}(\text{min}) = 5$ nsec.

Examining the above equations, we can conclude the following:

1. The SRAM interface PLD has to be the −15 version. The address decoder can stay as a −25 or even a slower version.
2. $N_r = N_w = 0$, i.e., no wait cycles.
3. We can even use the 120 nanosecond version of the SRAMs without violating any worst-case conditions.
4. Changing the 'ALS245's to 'F245's will allow the use of 150 nanosecond SRAMs, but such "F" devices may cause excessive "ringing" in data lines due to fast signal transition times, and thus requires additional attention to routing of signal traces.

8.10.2 NVRAM Design

Battery backup circuit and requirements. *Nonvolatile Memory* (NVRAM) is simply a SRAM that is battery backed up. When the power (+5V) that is being supplied from the primary energy source is removed, the power supply of SRAMs is automatically switched to battery power, thus retaining the memory contents. The block diagram of a NVRAM design is shown in Figure 8-

65. The goal of the battery backup circuit is to guarantee memory data retention for days, months, or years. The voltage detector and switching circuit provides power-fail detection and controls switching to battery power. The memory array deselect circuit isolates the chip-select inputs of SRAMs from the interface logic when a power-fail condition is detected. The battery backup circuit is usually an integral part of the memory, i.e., all placed on the same printed-circuit board (PCB).

The following are the basic requirements to implement NVRAM memory:

1. Not all SRAM devices are appropriate to implement NVRAM. It is necessary to select a SRAM memory device that features a low-power data retention mode. Typically, this means that the SRAM will maintain its contents for a supply voltage as low as 2 volts and will require 100 microAmps or less in the data retention mode.

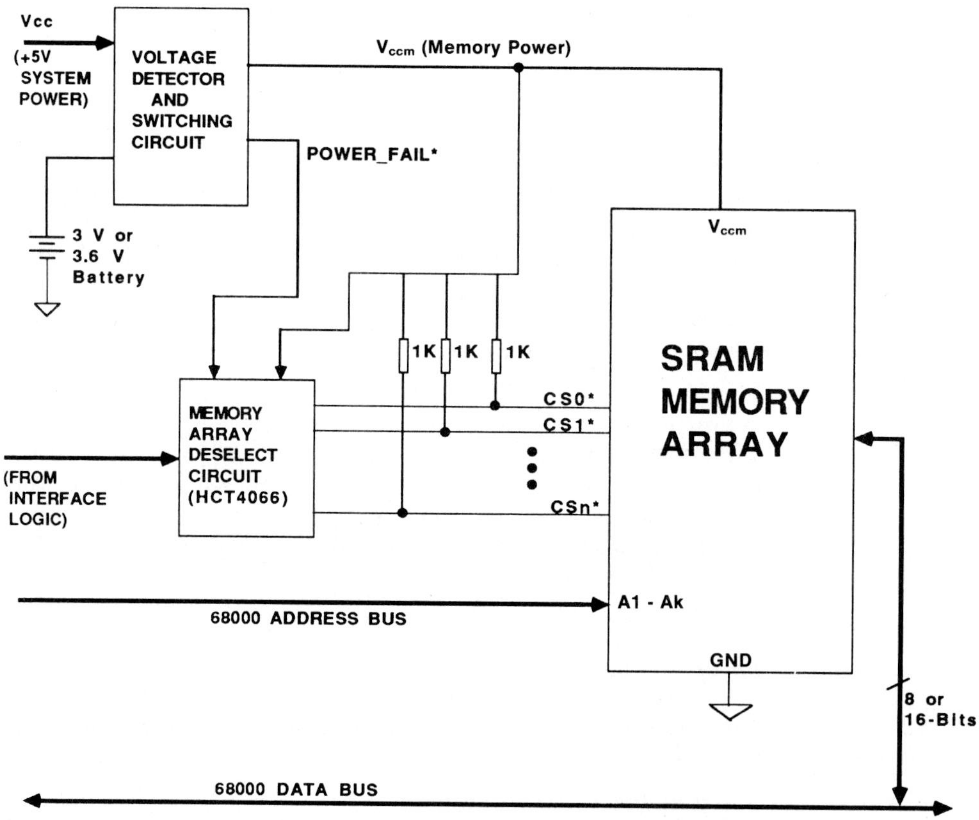

Figure 8-65 Block Diagram of NVRAM.

2. To enable the data retention mode of a SRAM device, it is usually necessary to pull-up CS* of the SRAM very close to its supply voltage level. The usual requirement for the data retention mode is $V_{cs} >= V_{ccm} - 0.2$, where V_{ccm} is the supply voltage of the SRAM. Most of the SRAMs with a low-power data-retention mode require only the CS* input to be pulled up to near its supply voltage, where other inputs can be floating during the data-retention mode. If this feature is not provided, then all other inputs must also be pulled up to minimize power consumption.
3. In general, we cannot assume that the interface logic that CS* is connected to is going to be in a high-impedance state when not powered up, because this is usually not specified in data sheets. More importantly, as the system is powered up and down, the microprocessor and other surrounding interface logic can produce spurious control signals. It is the function of the memory-deselect circuit to isolate the SRAM's CS* inputs from such illegal control signals in order to prevent erroneous writes. In other words, SRAM accesses must be inhibited until power is restored and stabilized again. This could be implemented using a digitally controlled analog switch such as the HCT4066 to isolate the CS* inputs when power-fail is detected.

One such low-power SRAM device is the NEC '43256 we studied earlier. As shown in Figure 8-66, this device requires a data retention current of 50 microAmps. This represent worst-case, since it is specified over the commercial temperature range of 0-70 degrees Celsius. The retention current degrades significantly with temperature (i.e., the loading of this SRAM is significantly less under typical standby conditions). The LL version guarantees a maximum current of 20 microAmps over 0-70 C and only 3 microAmps over 0-40 C.

In its simplest form, the NVRAM consists of a single low-power SRAM device and the battery backup circuit. Larger memory sizes can be designed using multiple SRAM devices in an 8-bit or 16-bit wide organization for the 68000.

Battery selection. The *Nickell-Cadmium* (Ni-Cad) or *Lithium* (Li) type batteries are usually used as the backup power source. The characteristics of these two batteries are compared in Table 8-4. Both of these battery types offer high-energy density. The Ni-Cad batteries have the advantage that they are rechargeable. Therefore, while system is powered up, they can be charged in the circuit and supply power to backed up SRAMs when the primary power is turned off. This means that they do not have to be replaced during the life of the equipment. However, they assume certain cycling of system power, because the charge retention of Ni-Cad's are very short compared to Lithium batteries. The Lithium batteries offer slightly higher energy densities and provide charge retention for 10 years.

The Lithium battery cells are, in general, more suitable for battery backup applications. A single cell with 3 or 3.6 volt is sufficient, and provides a very stable supply voltage. This gives approximately one volt margin for the minimum

LOW V_{CC} DATA RETENTION CHARACTERISTICS
T_A = 0 to 70°C

Parameter	Symbol	Limits Min	Limits Typ	Limits Max	Unit	Test Conditions
Data retention supply voltage	V_{CCDR}	2.0		5.5	V	CS ≥ V_{CC} − 0.2 V
Data retention supply current	I_{CCDR}		1	50	μA	V_{CC} = 3.0 V; CS ≥ V_{CC} − 0.2 V (Notes 1, 2)
Chip deselection to data retention	t_{CDR}	0			nsec.	
Operation recovery time	T_R	T_{RC}			nsec.	

Notes:
(1) For μPD43256A-LL, I_{CCDR} = 20 μA (max) for T_A = 0 to 70°C and 3μA (max) for T_A = 0 to 40°C.
(2) For μPD43256A-L, I_{CCDR} = 15 μA (max) for T_A = 0 to 40°C.

DATA RETENTION TIMING CHART

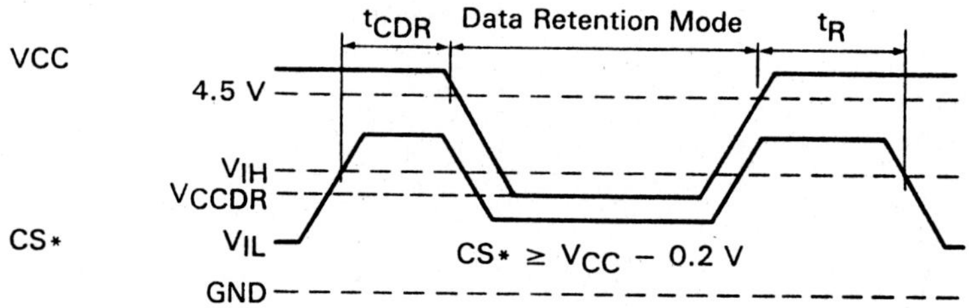

Note:
(1) The other inputs (Addresses, OE*, WE*, I/Os) can be in a high-impedance state.

Figure 8-66 '43256 Data Retention Characteristics and Timing. (Courtesy of NEC.)

TABLE 8-4 LITHIUM VERSUS NI-CAD BATTERY CHARACTERISTICS

Characteristic	Lithium	Nickel-Cadmium
Charge Retention	10 Years	6 Months
Rechargable	No	Yes
Energy Density	Very High	High
Cost	Moderate	Moderate
PCB-Compatible	Yes	Yes

2 volts needed in the data-retention mode of SRAMs. Different kinds of Lithium batteries are available that can be placed in a low-profile socket on the PCB, or with solder pin connections, as shown in Figure 8-67. The soldered cells offer more reliability because, with replaceable batteries in a socket, the battery and connector contacts must be kept thoroughly clean to avoid unreliable and erratic operation.

In choosing a Lithium battery an important parameter we need to define is the *battery capacity*. The battery capacity specifies the output capability over a period of time in *Ampere-hours* (Ah). We can determine the capacity using the following equation:

$$\text{Battery Capacity (mAh)} = I_{bat}\,(\text{mA}) + \langle\text{Time in backup mode}\rangle(\text{hours/day}) * 365\,(\text{days/year}) * \langle\text{Number of years}\rangle \qquad \text{(Eq. 8-14)}$$

where I_{bat} is the total battery current in the absence of system power. This current includes the battery backup circuit, pull-up resistors and the backed up SRAMs.

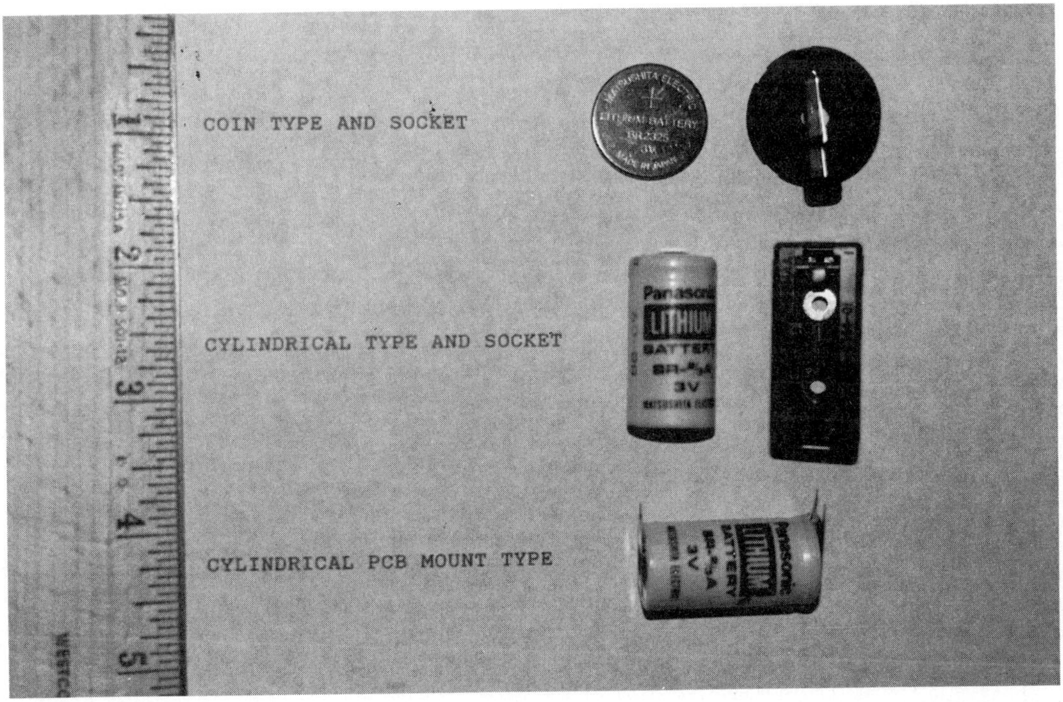

Figure 8-67 Lithium Batteries and Sockets.

For example, if the worst-case battery current requirement is 100 microAmps and the battery's backup period is assumed to be 5 years at 14 hours-per-day, we have

$$\text{Battery Capacity (mAh)} = 0.1 \text{ mA} * 14 \text{ h/day} * 365 \text{ days/year} * 5 \text{ years}$$
$$= 2555 \text{ mAh.}$$

We have to use the closest standard size that is larger than this figure. Alternatively, we can use the battery selector charts provided by some manufacturers.

The other consideration regarding the battery capacity depends on how the battery is mounted on the PCB. The Lithium batteries with welded terminals could be hand soldered, but this is hardly practical for high-production quantities. The use of PCB dip-soldering (also called wave-soldering) is usually used, but causes a temporary short of the battery terminals when dipped in the solder bath. This is acceptable, since, compared to conventional Alkaline or Ni-Cad batteries, the Lithium batteries have a higher internal impedance. This results in less current when short-circuited. However, the reduction in battery capacity is unavoidable. We can calculate this as follows:

$$\text{Used Capacity (mAh)} =$$
$$\text{Battery Capacity (mAh)} * \langle\text{Short Time}\rangle \text{ (sec)} * 1/60 * 1/60 \quad \text{(Eq. 8-15)}$$

For 10 seconds of short-circuit time, the capacity is reduced by about 2 to 3 percent, a negligible amount. Other conditions for soldering by the manufacturer must also be met, such as the solder tank temperature and the dipping time (short-circuit time) of leads.[6]

The other important design consideration is the battery protection. The commonly observed UL standards specify the following two requirements:

1. Since Lithium batteries are not rechargeable, during the presence of system power, the leakage charge current into the battery from the main power supply must be limited to 1 percent of the battery capacity. This can be calculated as follows:

$$\begin{aligned}\text{Leakage Charge Current} = {} & 0.01 * \langle\text{Battery Capacity}\rangle \text{ (mAh)}* \\ & \langle\text{System Power Up Time}\rangle \text{ (hours/day)} * \\ & 365 \text{ (days/year)}* \\ & \langle\text{Number of Years}\rangle\end{aligned} \quad \text{(Eq. 8-16)}$$

[6] Extreme care must be exercised also not to drop the battery into solder bath during automatic soldering since it would cause an explosion.

Using our example values from above, we have 0.6 microAmps for a 1,000 mAh standard battery size.

2. In case the circuit that protects the Lithium battery from getting charged is damaged, the maximum charging current is specified as 5 mA. We can use a current-limiting resistor for this purpose. The resistor value we need is

$$R(\text{ohms}) = 1.1 * (5.5V - 2V)/5mA = 770 \qquad \text{(Eq. 8-17)}$$

for the worst-case conditions of maximum system voltage and minimum battery voltage, and 10 percent resistor value variation.

Battery backup circuit design considerations. Let us examine the voltage detector and switching circuit. The requirements on this circuit are twofold. First, it isolates the main system power line V_{cc} from the battery, so that battery power is only used for the SRAMs and the backup circuit. Second, it must be able to sustain the maximum operating current of the SRAM array, while providing minimum voltage drop. For example, if the recommended operating supply voltage range of the SRAM is 4.5 to 5.5 volts for a system power supply in the 4.75 to 5.25 range, the maximum voltage drop must be less than 0.25 volts.

The simplest possible voltage detector and switching circuit is shown in Figure 8-68. The D1 diode isolates the SRAM memory power from the rest of the system during power-down. A Schottky diode is chosen because it provides a relatively small forward voltage drop (V_f) and sufficient load current. For example, the Motorola's 1N5820 has a voltage drop of approximately 0.2V (worst-case) at 150 mA load current. Its leakage current is 1 microAmps for a reverse voltage of less than four volts at 75 degrees C (see *Motorola Rectifiers and Zener Databook*, DL125, Rev. 3, pp. 3-51 to 3-54).

The D2 diode prevents the Lithium battery from getting charged when system power is on. The reverse leakage current parameter through this diode is more important because the V_f is small due to a small forward current during power-down. An additional series current limiting resistor is provided for extra protection per the UL standard. To reduce or eliminate the leakage charge current through this diode, a bleeder resistor R2 is also provided. The lithium battery, in this case, always discharges very slowly through R2 even when the main power source is active.

Design example. Figure 8-69 shows a 32 Kbytes of NVRAM that is organized as byte-wide. As a battery backup circuit we used a nonvolatile controller chip. This controller chip, the DS1210 shown in Figure 8-70, replaces several components (thus, saves space and increases reliability), and also provides the following additional functionality:

1. It uses a precision comparator for a more precise power-fail detection. When power-fail is detected, the *chip-enable output* (CEO*) is inhibited, and it is pulled to within 0.2 volts of the battery supply voltage. This gives a con-

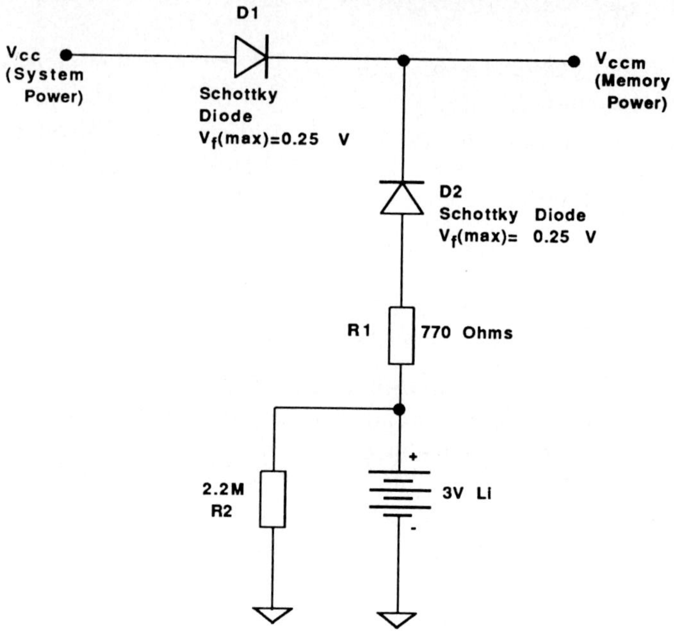

Mode	V_{cc}	V_{ccm}
Normal Operation	5.0V	4.75V
	4.75V	4.5V
Data Retention	0V	2.75V

Figure 8-68 Simple Power-down Detect and Switching Circuit.

```
PLD:
/* Inputs */
Pin 1 = CPUCLKX1_C    ;
Pin 2 = !SEL_NVRAM    ;
Pin 3 = !CPU_WRITE    ;

/* Outputs */
Pin 23 = !NVRAM_ACC   ;   /* Asserted during NVRAM Accesses. */
Pin 22 = Qa           ;   /* Used to build a shift-register, */
Pin 21 = Qb           ;   /* for fixed delay until state S6. */
Pin 20 = Qc           ;

/* Logic Equations */
Qa.D = SEL_NVRAM ;
Qb.D = Qa & SEL_NVRAM ;
Qc.D = Qb & SEL_NVRAM ;
NVRAM_ACC = !CPU_WRITE & SEL_NVRAM #
             CPU_WRITE & SEL_NVRAM & !Qc;
```

Figure 8-69 Example NVRAM Design.

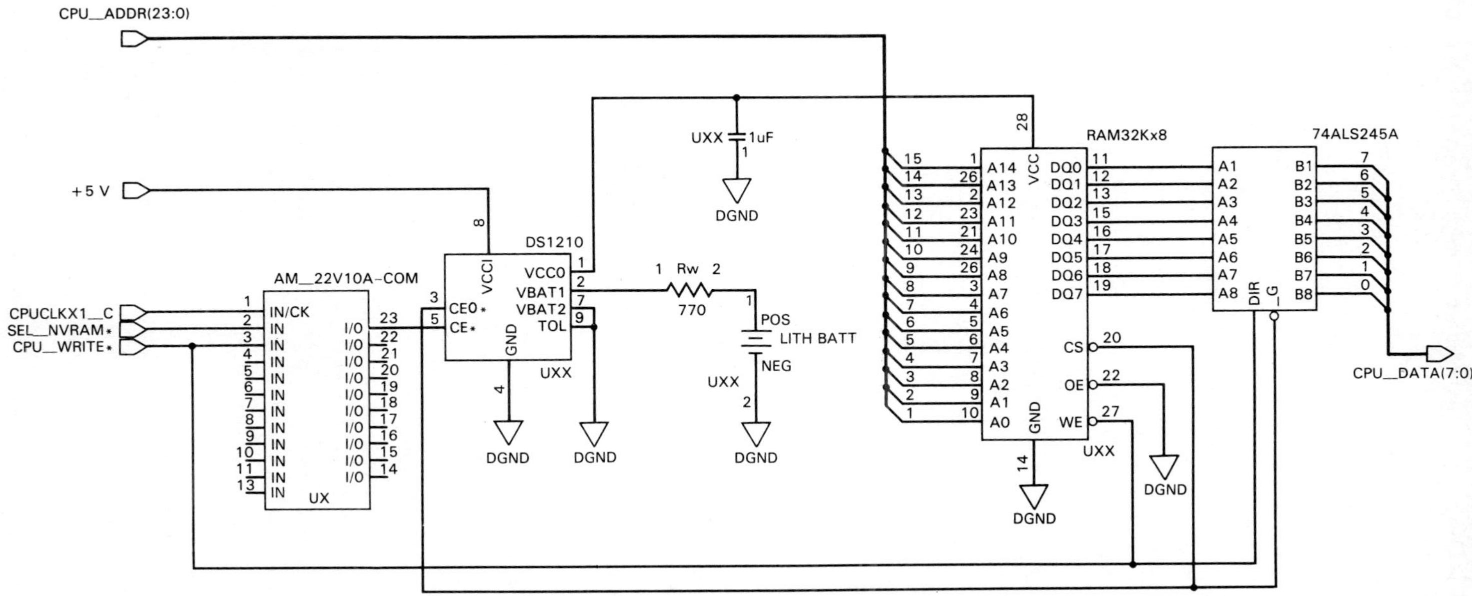

Figure 8-69 (cont.) Example NVRAM Design.

FEATURES

- Converts CMOS RAMs into nonvolatile memories
- Unconditionally write protects when V_{CC} is out of tolerance
- Automatically switches to battery when power fail occurs
- Space saving 8-pin DIP
- Consumes less than 100 nA of battery current
- Tests battery condition on power up
- Provides for redundant batteries
- Optional 5% or 10% power fail detection
- Low forward voltage drop on the V_{CC} Switch
- Optional 16-pin SOIC surface mount package

PIN CONNECTIONS

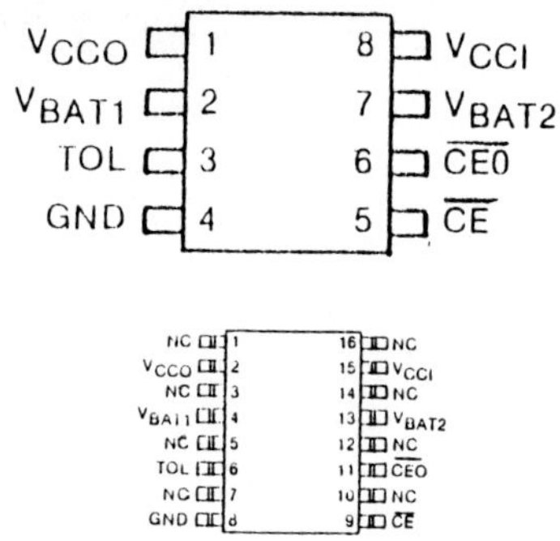

PIN NAMES

V_{CCO}	- RAM Supply
V_{BAT1}	- + Battery 1
TOL	- Power Supply Tolerance
GND	- Ground
$\overline{CE}$	- Chip Enable Input
$\overline{CEO}$	- Chip Enable Output
V_{BAT2}	- + Battery 2
V_{CCI}	- + Supply
NC	- No Connect

Figure 8-70 Cover Page of DS1210 Datasheet. (Courtesy of Dallas Semiconductor.)

venient way to handle the CS* input of SRAMs, as well as other backup circuit requirements.

2. The DS1210 provides the capability to test the battery condition. This enables us to detect the battery-low condition before a NVRAM failure occurs. Each time the system power is turned on, a precision comparator tests if the battery voltage is less than 2 volts. If it is, the *second* NVRAM access cycle is inhibited. This allows software to test the battery condition after power-up as follows:

   a) Read a location of the NVRAM (first access).
   b) Write to the same location (second access).
   c) Read back the same location to verify if the write was successful.

   The battery is low if the write was not successful.

The DS1210 has a voltage drop of less than 0.25 volts, can supply 80 mA, according to its datasheet (see Appendix C). The maximum operating supply current of the '43256 is 40 mA, which is within the limits of what the DS1210 can supply.

Let us assume that we use the LL version of the SRAMs which has a maximum data retention current of 20 microAmps at 3 volts over the commercial temperature range. The retention current would be much higher if the battery voltage were 5 volts. This is one of the reasons why 3 volts is chosen as the backup voltage. Another reason is that it makes it easier to detect the removal of system power.

The total retention current drawn from the battery is then

$$20 \text{ microAmp} + 0.1 \text{ microAmp} = 20.1 \text{ microAmps.}$$

To maintain data retention for four years at 16 hours per day power-down time, the battery capacity required is given by

Battery Capacity (mAh)

$$= 0.0201 \text{ mA} * 16 \text{ hrs/day} * 365 \text{ days/year} * 4 \text{ years} = 469 \text{ mAh}$$

So, we choose the 500 mAh Li size.

The maximum battery current a DS1210 can supply is 50 microAmps from its datasheet. This is larger than the 20 microAmps required by an SRAM device.

The usually overlooked design parameters are the data hold and address recovery times (T_{dh} and T_{wr}) of the SRAM. In this case, the delay through the DS1210 is 20 nanoseconds maximum. If we did not terminate the write access of the SRAM earlier, we would have the following data hold time as seen by the SRAM device. Assuming the address strobe is buffered by an 'F244 type device and the address decode PLD ('22V10) is a 15 nanosecond version, it is easy to calculate that the CS* would have been negated after data becomes invalid, thus it would not meet the T_{dh} requirement of the SRAM. In other words, we would have

$$T_{dh} \text{ (nsec.)} = t25 - (20 + T_{F244}(\text{max}) + 15) + T_{als245}(\text{min})$$

The above value of T_{dh} is -6.5 nanoseconds, which violates the worst-case requirements (equals to zero for '43256 from Figure 8-59).

Therefore, in our example design the CS* of NVRAM is negated in approximately 2 clock cycles after the SEL_NVRAM* is asserted for write bus cycles. The purpose of this is to terminate the write access to the SRAM before the end of the bus cycle while the data is still valid. This ensures that the T_{dh} is met with a good margin. The reader should verify that this also meets the T_{dw} requirement of SRAM.

The reader may note that we did not use LDS*/UDS* in generating the chip-select signal. Although generally this would be necessary to enable which byte(s) are to be written, in our example case the memory is only byte wide, and thus, this is not necessary. (See Exercise 52 for a 16-bit design.)

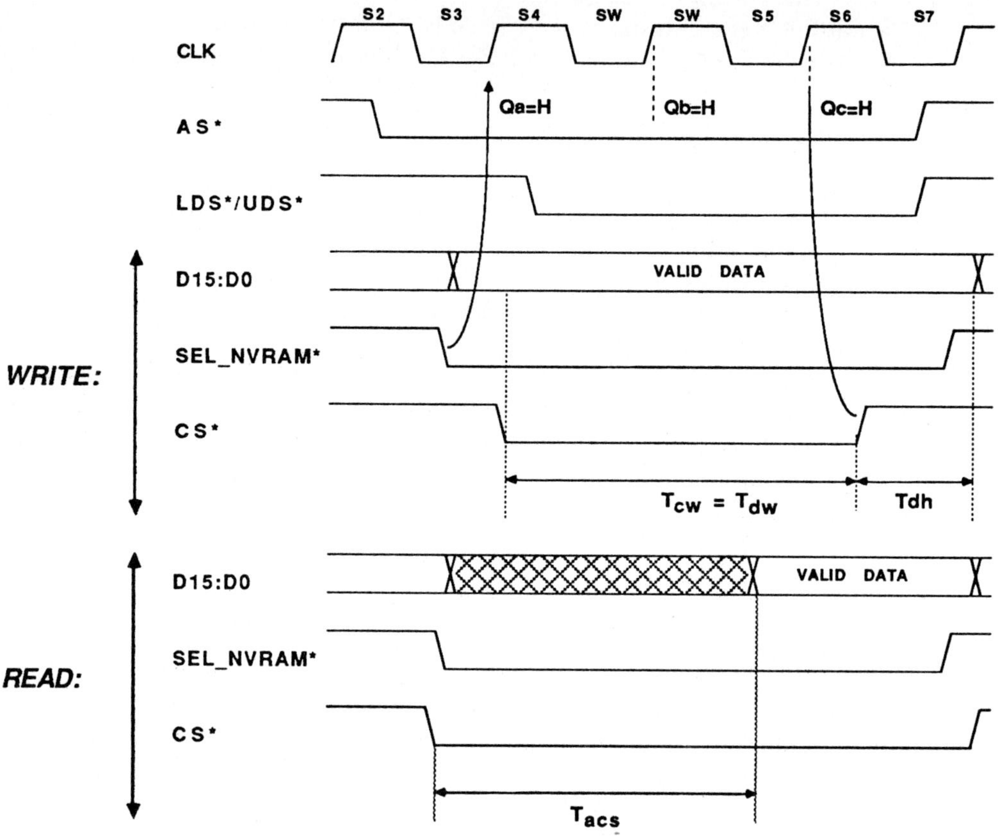

Figure 8-71 NVRAM Access Timing Using the '43256-100.

8.10.3 EPROM Memory Design

The EPROM memory interface is basically the same as the SRAM interface, but only the read operation is valid. This simplifies the design significantly, because there is no longer the possibility of incorrectly modifying the memory contents. The major consideration is for the read data to meet the setup time at the 68000 data pins before the falling edge of state S6.

Figure 8-72 shows the cover page of a 1 Megabit EPROM that we are going to use in our example design here. The Am27c010 is manufactured by AMD and also second sourced from other manufacturers, but with different part numbers. The EPROM is organized as 128 Kbytes (131,072 × 8 bits exactly), and comes in different access speeds ranging from 150 to 300 nanoseconds. The program input (PGM*) is only used by the programmer before the EPROM is placed in its operational circuit, where it must be pulled high with a resistor.

The access timing of the Am27c010 is shown in Figure 8-73. Both the chip-enable (CE*) and output-enable (OE*) control signals must be asserted to obtain valid data at the outputs. The CE* controls the device selection, and when it is negated, puts the EPROM in standby mode, whereby the current drawn by the

PRELIMINARY

Am27C010

Advanced Micro Devices

DISTINCTIVE CHARACTERISTICS

- High-performance CMOS technology
- Fast access time — 150 ns
- Low power dissipation
  - 100 μA maximum standby current
- Easy upgrade from 28-pin JEDEC EPROMs
- Compact 32-pin DIP package requires no hardware change for upgrades to 8 Mbit
- TTL- and CMOS-compatible inputs
- Ceramic DIP and LCC packages

GENERAL DESCRIPTION

The Am27C010 is a 1,048,576-bit ultraviolet-light-erasable, programmable read-only memory (UV EPROM) device organized as 128K bytes of 8 bits each. Its pin compatibility with byte-wide JEDEC EPROMs allows easy upgrades from 512K through 8-Mbit densities. AMD's CMOS process technology provides high-speed and low power consumption.

The standard Am27C010 offers access times as fast as 150 ns, allowing operation with high-speed microprocessors without any wait states. The Am27C010 also offers separate Chip Enable ($\overline{CE}$) and Output Enable ($\overline{OE}$) controls, which eliminates bus contention in a mulitple-bus microprocessor system.

BLOCK DIAGRAM

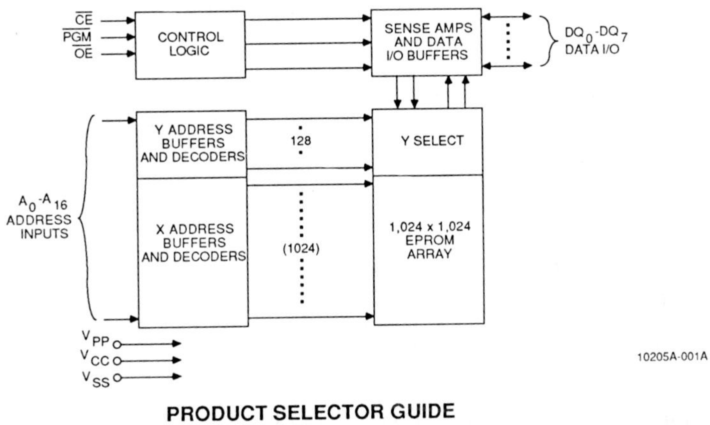

PRODUCT SELECTOR GUIDE

Family Part No.	Am27C010				
Ordering Part No:					
V_{cc} ± 5%	−155	−175	−205	−255	−305
V_{cc} ± 10%	—	−170	−200	−250	−300
Max. Access Time (ns)	150	170	200	250	300
$\overline{CE}$ Access Time (ns)	150	170	200	250	300
$\overline{OE}$ Access Time (ns)	65	65	75	100	100

Publication # 10205 Rev. A Amendment /0
Issue Date: April 1988

Figure 8-72 Example 1 Megabit EPROM Characteristics (Courtesy of AMD).

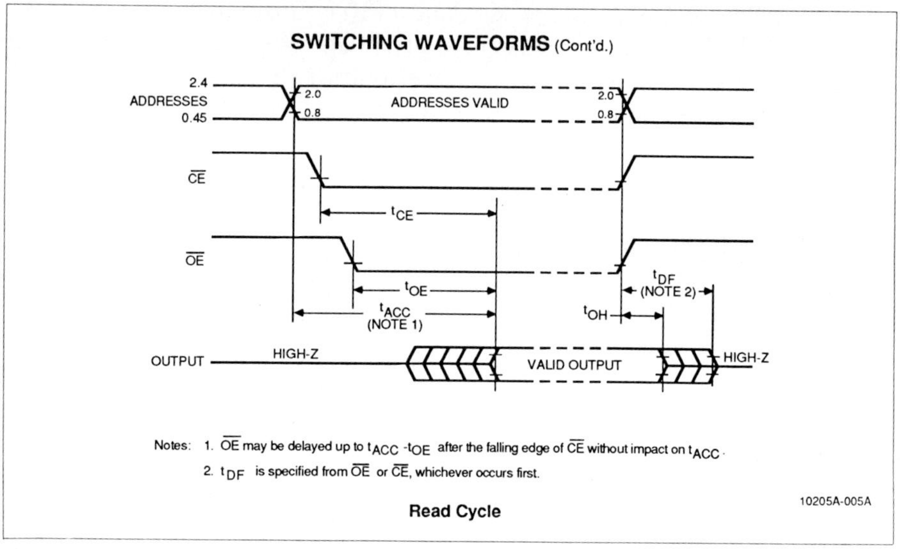

Figure 8-72 (cont.) Example 1 Megabit EPROM Characteristics (Courtesy of AMD).

Parameter	Characteristic	Min	Max	Units
T_{ce}	Chip-select Asserted to Output Valid.	—	200	nsec.
T_{oe}	Output-enable Asserted to Output Valid.	—	75	nsec.
T_{acc}	Address Valid to Output Valid.	—	200	nsec.
T_{df}	Outputs Disabled from OE* Negated.	0	60	nsec.
T_{oh}	Output Hold Time from CE*, OE* or Ann.	0	—	nsec.

Note: Values shown for the 200 nsec. version.

Figure 8-73 Am27C010 Read Access Timing. (Courtesy of AMD.)

EPROM is significantly reduced. The OE* controls enabling the data output drivers when CE* is asserted. Typically, the CE* is used as the primary device-selection control, while OE* is made common to all EPROM devices and connected to CPU_WRITE* line of the CPU bus. This ensures that the EPROM buffers will not be turned on for any accidental or erroneous write access, thereby preventing any conflict of multiple drivers on the bus.

An example EPROM design is shown in Figure 8-74. The SEL_EPROM* signal is from the address decoder, and is already qualified with AS*. When selected, both high and low-byte of EPROMs are enabled, regardless of word or byte access. This is acceptable, because the 68000 reads only the required byte(s) (see Table 1-2). External data buffers are provided because of the limited drive capability of EPROM devices.

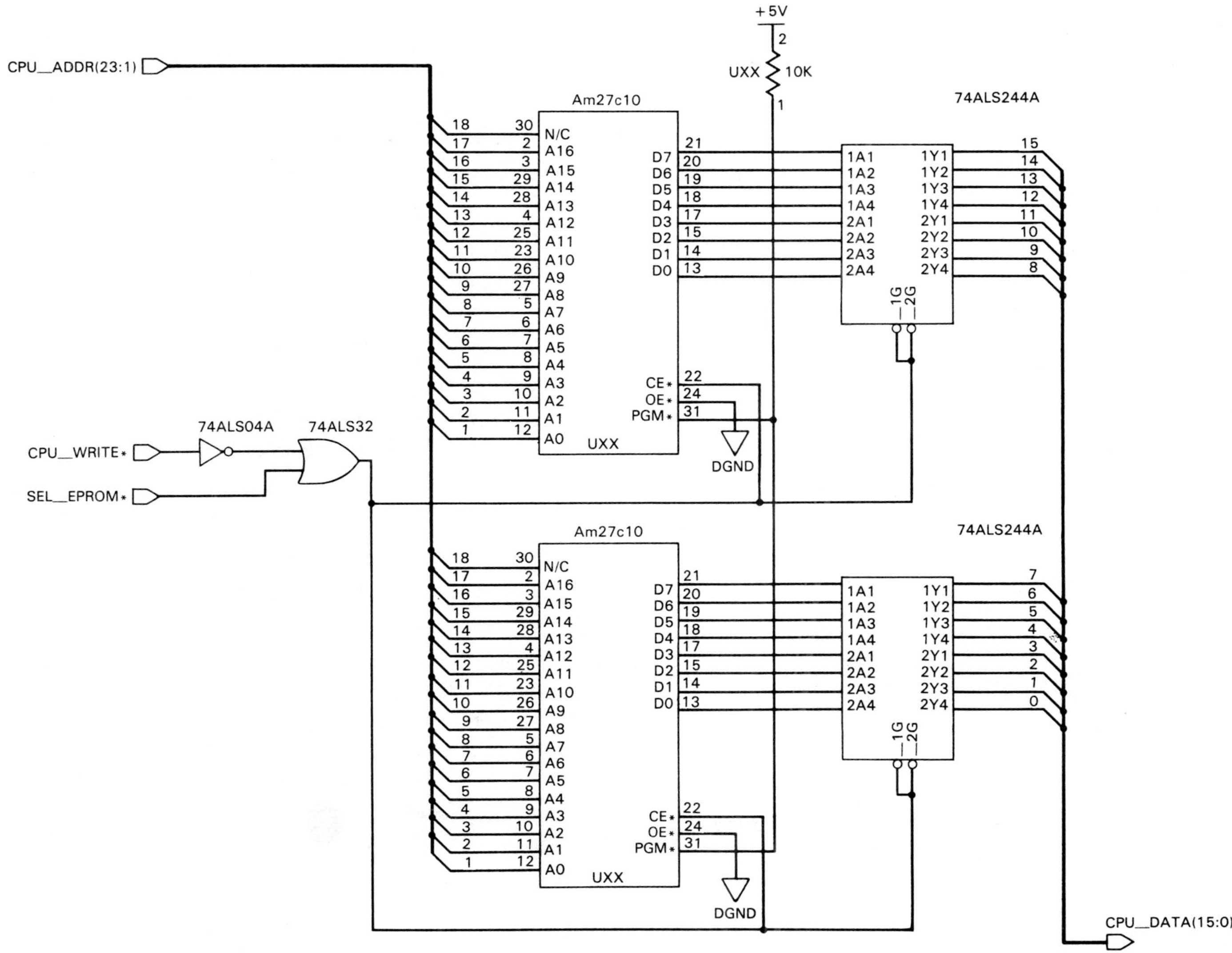

Figure 8-74 Example 68000 EPROM Interface.

For faster access timing we can make use of the fact that only read cycles are valid. Thus, we can enable the EPROMs all the time by connecting their CE*'s to ground, and connecting the SEL_EPROM* only to buffer enables, as shown in Figure 8-75. The advantage of this is that the EPROM access time is cut approximately in half, because T_{oe} is typically about half of T_{ce}. The disadvantage of this approach is increased power consumption since the EPROMs are never in a standby mode, even when they are not being accessed. We can also use a combination of these two above approaches, as discussed in Exercise 47.

8.10.4 Dual-port RAM Design

When the processing speed of one processor is not adequate for some given task or requirements, we may use multiple processors to obtain the necessary computational power. Each processor either executes the same program[7] on a different portion of data, or executes completely different but related tasks. An example of the former is in a digital image processor where multiple processors can execute the same program on different portions of the image data. An example of the latter is a front-end processor that handles some or most of the I/O related tasks. This unloads the main processor from such tasks, and allows it to concentrate on data processing.

In any of the above multiprocessing schemes there is a need for shared memory, by means of which we can pass commands and data between the processors. For example, in the case of the image processing example we usually need to pass boundary information between the image areas allocated to each processor. In the case of the I/O processor, the main processor writes commands to a shared memory area, sometimes referred to as *mail-box*.

Getting back to our main topic of interest here, if the shared memory has two ports then it is called a *dual-port RAM* (DPRAM). Both processors can read or write to all locations of the DPRAM, just as if it is a RAM dedicated to themselves. The DPRAM consists of SRAM or DRAM devices and interface logic that arbitrates access requests from both of the processors. We are going to examine the implementation of an SRAM-based DPRAM here, but the concept could easily be extended to DRAMs.

An example DPRAM circuit is shown in Figure 8-76. Here we assume that both processors accessing the DPRAM will be 68000s. Since the SRAM can only provide one access at any given time, both address and data signals of the SRAM need to be buffered for each port. The access arbiter is implemented as a PLD-based state machine, which takes access requests from both 68000s and allows only one of them to access the SRAM at any one time. This state machine controls enabling the buffers, and also returning DTACK* to each processor when access is completed.

[7] We still assume that each processor has a separate program memory, because each processor could be at different points of the program.

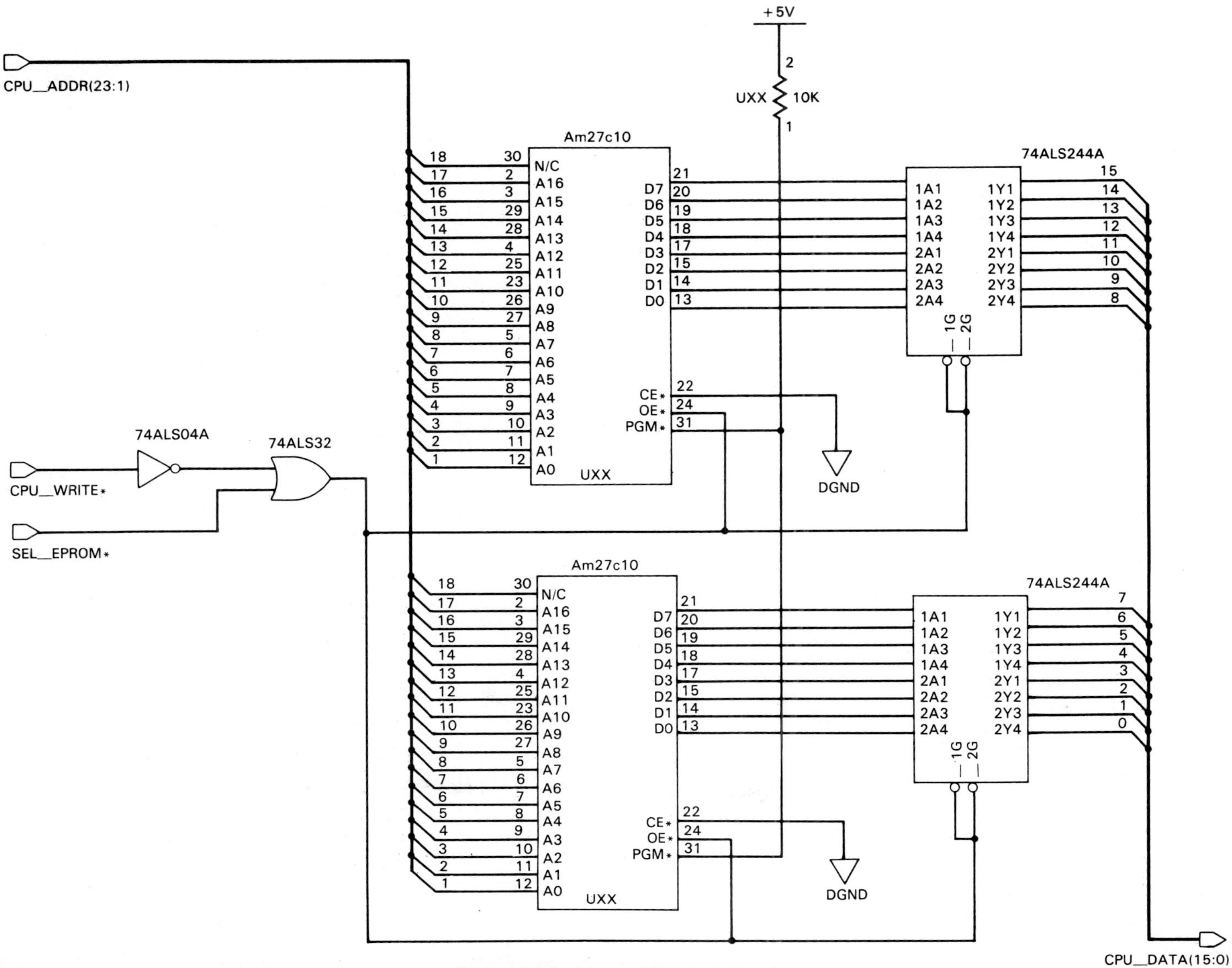

Figure 8-75 Faster EPROM Interface.

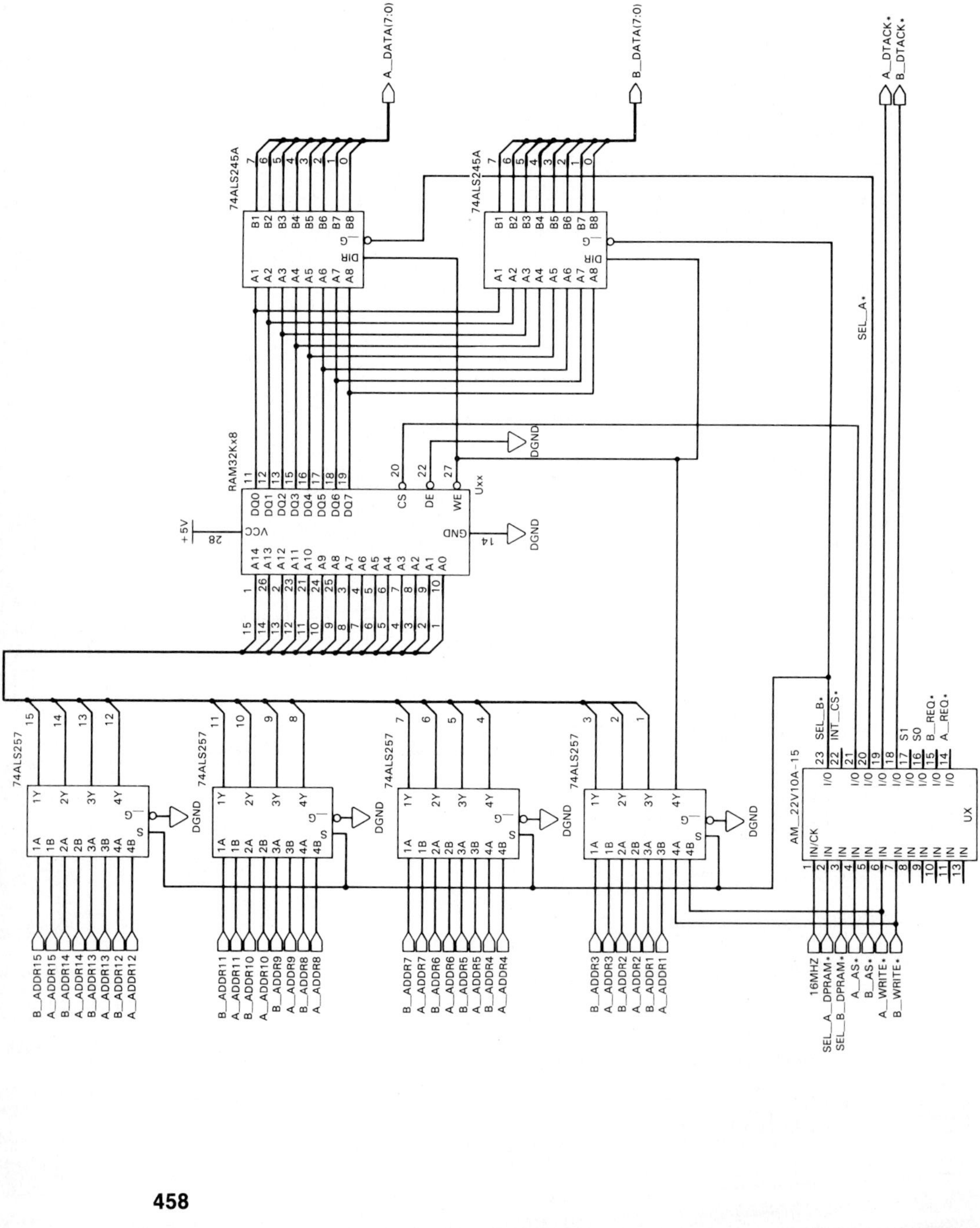

Figure 8-76 PLD Based Dual-port RAM.

The flow diagram of the state machine is shown in Figure 8-77. The state machine idles in state 0 until one or both of the 68000's request access to the DPRAM. The access request from each processor is simply an address decode signal that is qualified with the corresponding AS*. Depending on the system configuration, one or both of these request signals may be asynchronous with respect to the clock of the state machine. To prevent any state-machine errors, each processor request is first registered (i.e., synchronized) by the PLD. The synchronized request signals are called A_REQ* and B_REQ*. For our example design here, let us assume that both of the 68000s are running at 10 MHz and the state machine clock is 16 MHz (66 nanoseconds).

When only one of the processors makes a request, it is granted access within two clock cycles. For example, as soon as A_REQ* is detected by the state machine, it moves to state 1 and enables the control, address, and data buffers for the A-side. Then, the state machine unconditionally proceeds to states 2 and 3. Assuming we use 120 nanosecond SRAMs, this means we can assert DTACK*

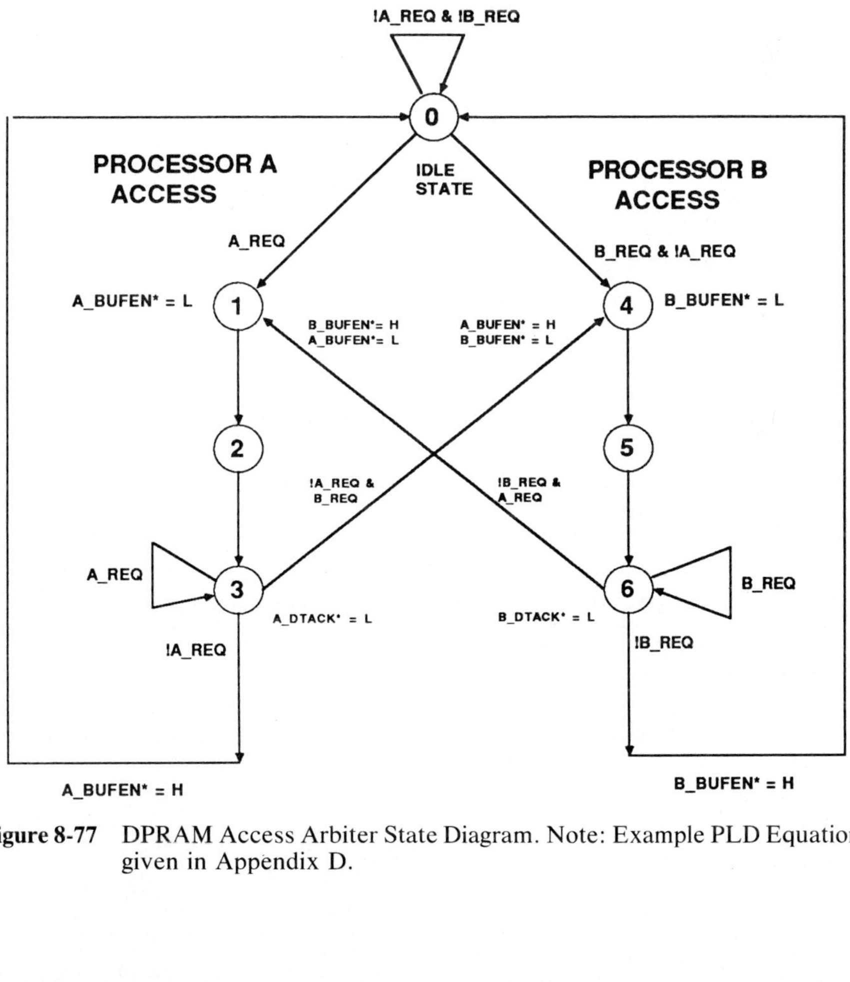

Figure 8-77 DPRAM Access Arbiter State Diagram. Note: Example PLD Equations given in Appendix D.

after two clock cycles of the state machine using the fully asynchronous interface type. There are no control state changes in state 2 but it is inserted to meet the access time of the SRAMs.

The state machine waits in state 3 until the processor A signals the end of bus cycle. We have to be careful about how we terminate the access for the following reason. If we use A_REQ* to terminate the access, then we may violate the t28 and/or t29a parameters of the 68000. This is due to the "flushing out" time due to the following. When AS* is negated, it may take 1 clock cycle (66 nsec.) in the worst-case for the A_REQ* to be negated. Then, it takes another clock cycle for the state machine to go back to state 0 and turn-off all buffers. In our case, we used the A_AS* or B_AS* to turn off the data buffers and DTACK* outputs as early as possible. This allows us to meet t28 and t29a parameters.

If both access requests are detected simultaneously, then processor A side is given priority. To prevent the situation that A side does not "hog" the DPRAM, the requests are acknowledged in a round-robin format. This avoids the side with low priority from having a bus time-out, while the other side is continuously accessing the DPRAM. Such a round-robin grant of accesses is accomplished by checking any access requests from the other processor, after completion of access of one processor.

One final note is that we should have valid read/write signal present at the SRAM WE* pin before the CS* is asserted. As we discussed earlier, this prevents any conflict between the drivers during a write bus cycle. To realize this, the chip-select signal is passed through an intermediate output of the U1 PLD (INT_CS*). This additional delay of CS*'s is sufficient to ensure that, in the worst case, they will be coincident with WE* at the SRAM devices, accounting for possible different PCB delay paths for CS* and WE*.

8.11 INTERRUPT OPERATION AND INTERFACE LOGIC

8.11.1 Interrupt Control Signals and Interrupt Acknowledge

The interrupt control signal lines of the 68000 are IPL(2:0)* for interrupt requests, and VPA* to signal auto-vectoring as shown in Figure 8-78. The VPA* input signal has dual usage, as we discussed earlier. During a bus cycle to transfer operands, it indicates that the device being accessed is an 8-bit 6800-type peripheral. During an interrupt-acknowledge bus cycle, the VPA* indicates to the 68000 to use auto-vectoring. The vector number used in this case is determined by the priority of the interrupt being acknowledged (See Table 4-2).

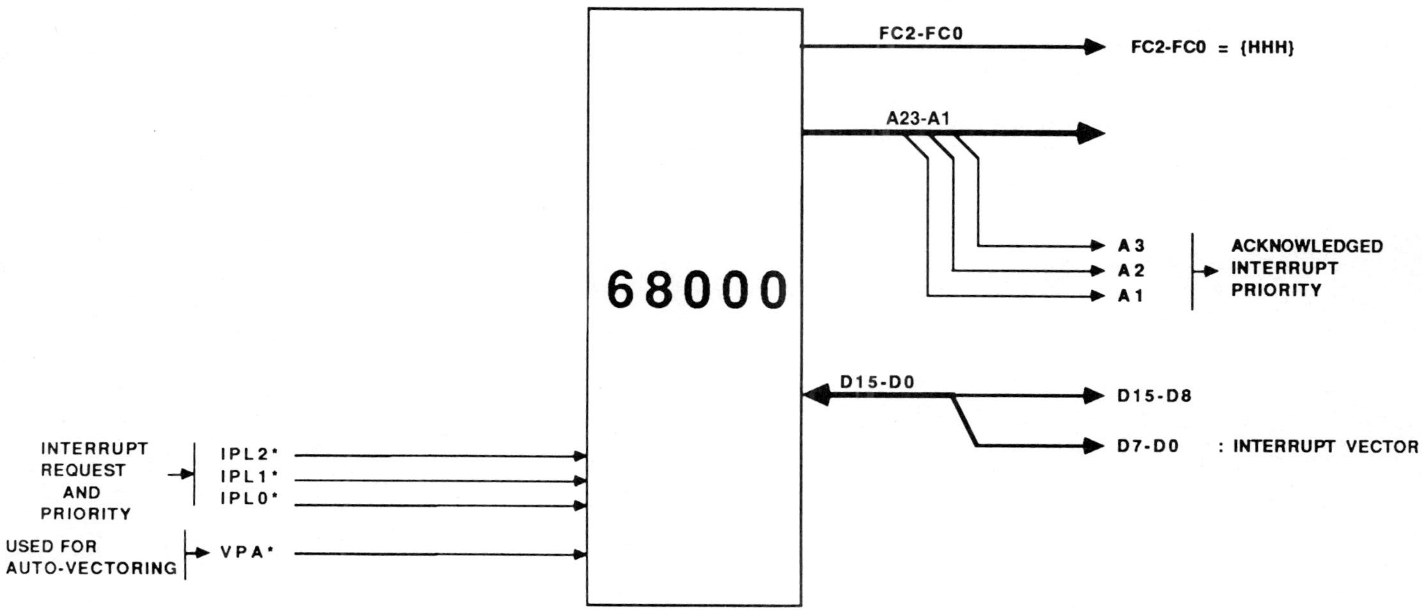

Figure 8-78 Interrupt Control and Acknowledge Signal Lines.

The interrupt control signals, IPL(2:0)*, indicate the encoded priority of interrupt requests from peripheral devices. Since the encoded priority level is inverted (as indicated by "*"), IPL(2:0)* equal to {HHH} means level zero or no interrupt and {LLL} means that request level is seven which is the highest priority interrupt (refer back to Table 4-4).

When an interrupt level with a priority of 1 through 6 is requested, the interrupt will be acknowledged and serviced only if the request level is *higher* than the mask level of register SR. The difference between levels one through six and level seven is that level seven is edge sensitive, whereas other levels are level sensitive. This means that a level seven interrupt is not maskable, and thus is called a *Non-Maskable Interrupt* (NMI). Any transition to the level seven request from a lower level will cause a level seven interrupt to be serviced by the 68000. Therefore, if a level seven interrupt persists, the 68000 will recognize this interrupt only once, unless the interrupt mask level is lowered in software.

Since the interrupt request levels one through six are level sensitive, the interrupt request for these levels must be removed when they are serviced. Otherwise, if the same interrupt request remains, it will cause another interrupt acknowledge after executing the RTE instruction.

The following are the other signals that are used in acknowledging an interrupt request:

A3-A1	These three low-order bits of the 68000 address bus indicates the priority of the interrupt request being acknowledged. The other address lines remain high during an interrupt acknowledge cycle.
FC2-FC0	Is {HHH} to indicate an interrupt acknowledge bus cycle.
D7-D0	The low-order byte of the data bus is used to fetch the interrupt vector from the interrupting peripheral.
AS*, LDS*, DTACK*	Are the bus control signals that are used in reading the interrupt vector.
VPA*	If the interrupter does not have the capability to provide an interrupt vector, it will assert VPA*, thereby causing the 68000 to internally generate the vector number.

The interrupt acknowledge bus cycle has the same timing as a read bus cycle, but is distinguished by the function code signals being all high. Also, in the case of auto-vectoring, it is terminated by VPA* being asserted, instead of DTACK*. The interrupt-acknowledge bus cycle is shown in Figure 8-79. Even though only the low-order byte is used, both LDS* and UDS* are asserted by the 68000.

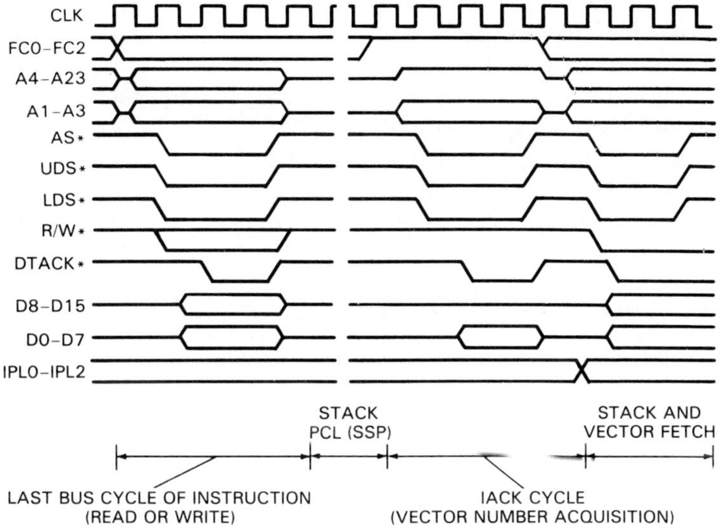

*Although a vector number is one byte, both data strobes are asserted due to the microcode used for except processing. The processor does not recognize anything on data lines D8 through D15 at this time.

User-Vectored

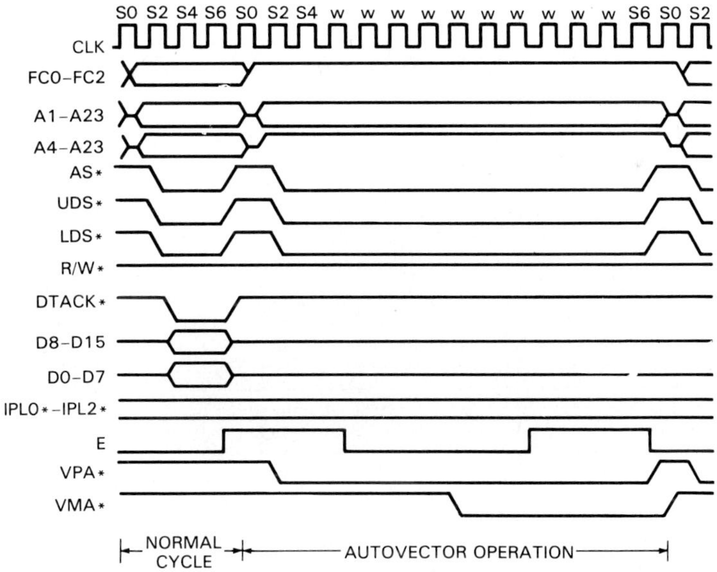

Auto-Vectored

Figure 8-79 Interrupt-acknowledge Bus Cycle. (Courtesy of Motorola.)

8.11.2 Interrupt Request Logic

The seven interrupt request levels can be encoded from peripheral device request signals, IREQ(7:1)*, as shown in Table 8-5. The external interrupt request logic not only encodes the interrupt request signals, but also prioritizes them, where it presents the highest priority encoded request to the 68000. For example, if both IREQ6* and IREQ4* are asserted, then the IPL(2:0)* is {LLH}. Such a priority encoder can be implemented using a 74ALS148, as shown in Figure 8-80. The inputs of the '148 are pulled high with a resistor pack. This is usually necessary because most interrupting peripherals have open-drain or open-collector type driv-

TABLE 8-5 PRIORITY ENCODING OF INTERRUPT REQUESTS

IREQ7*	IREQ6*	IREQ5*	IREQ4*	IREQ3*	IREQ2*	IREQ1*	IPL2*	IPL1*	IPL0*
L	X	X	X	X	X	X	L	L	L
H	L	X	X	X	X	X	L	L	H
H	H	L	X	X	X	X	L	H	L
H	H	H	L	X	X	X	L	H	H
H	H	H	H	L	X	X	H	L	L
H	H	H	H	H	L	X	H	L	H
H	H	H	H	H	H	L	H	H	L
H	H	H	H	H	H	H	H	H	H

X: Don't Care, i.e., H or L.

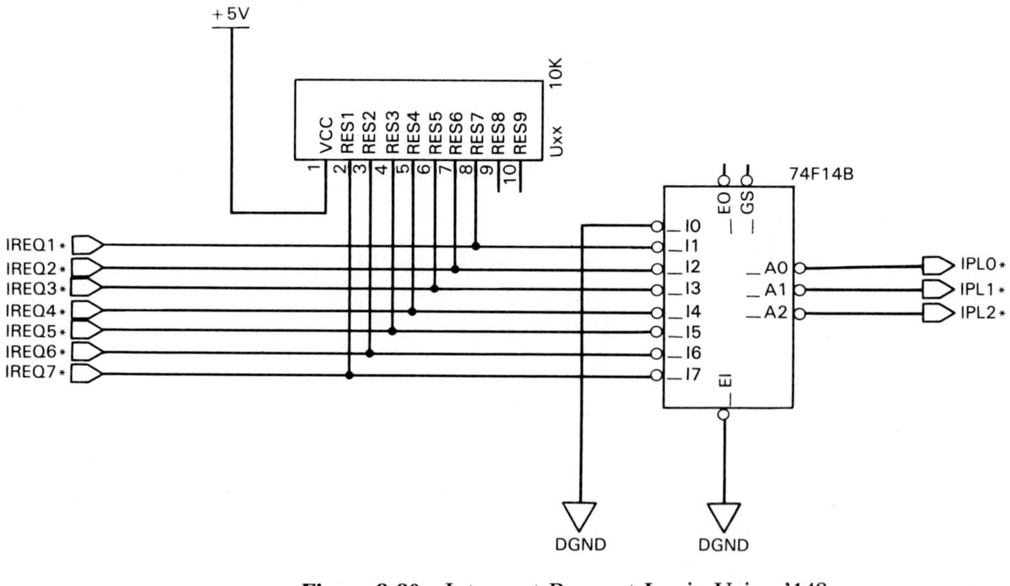

Figure 8-80 Interrupt Request Logic Using '148.

ers for interrupt requests that can be readily wire-ORed with other devices. Also, the unused interrupt request signals must be pulled high to ensure that they are inactive or negated.

The 68000 synchronizes the encoded IPL(2:0)* input internally so that the designer does not have to worry about asynchronous nature of the interrupt request signals. With the earlier versions of the 68000, it was left to external logic to synchronize interrupt request inputs against incorrect sampling in case these inputs change during the sampling window. This is no longer true. The 68000 verifies that the request level remains the same for two consecutive clock cycles to be considered valid.

The interrupt request logic can also be implemented using a PLD, as shown in Figure 8-81. Note that each product term is shown on a different line to increase readability. All equations are written using positive-logic, and signal inversions to negative logic are done at the inputs and outputs of the PLD as indicated by "!". Compilers usually do not complain about this because a terminator such as ";" is used at the end of each equation. The PLD, in this case, is not justified just to replace a '148 unless it incorporates other and possibly unrelated logic.

8.11.3 Interrupt Recognition

Once an interrupt request is asserted, it should be held asserted until the 68000 acknowledges that interrupt request. If an interrupt request is removed just before it is acknowledged, this will cause a spurious interrupt exception (how?). The 68000 samples the IPL(2:0)* interrupt control pins and compares it to the interrupt mask level at a given point within the execution of each instruction. An instruction may take a few bus cycles to execute, and the particular bus cycle in which the IPL(2:0)* are sampled is instruction dependent. It is possible that an interrupt is held for as short as two-clock cycles of the 68000 to be recognized. In general, however, it is neither possible nor necessary to predict which interrupt will be acknowledged with multiple pending interrupt requests. For example, suppose the mask level is set to three, and a level four interrupt is present for two clock cycles. Then a level six interrupt is requested and remains pending. Which interrupt will be recognized first? [4].

Our discussion of interrupts so far addressed the request phase, and therefore applies equally to user- and auto-vectored interrupts. An important consideration is the time between when an interrupt request is made and when the first instruction of its service routine is executed. As we discussed in Chapter 6, this time span is called the *interrupt latency*. The maximum value of interrupt latency is important to ensure that no data loss occurs in servicing any peripherals. For the 68000 the worst case occurs when we have a MOVEM.L instruction followed by a DIVS [4]. The interrupt request pins are sampled at the beginning of MOVEM, but for DIVS they are sampled at the end of instruction execution. Thus, if an interrupt request is made just after the beginning of MOVEM, we have the latency given by

MOVEM:	146 clock periods +	Any wait-cycles
DIVS:	174 clock periods +	Any wait-cycles
Interrupt Acknowledge:	58 clock cycles	(for auto-vector operation)
Maximum interrupt latency:	378 clock periods +	Any wait-cycles.

If polling is used to determine the source of an interrupt, then the polling time must also added to the above figures. It is very important for a reliable system design to take into consideration the worst-case interrupt latency, because any data loss in such a case can cause system malfunction, but can be quite intermittent (i.e., may not be detected during system debugging).

8.11.4 Interrupt Acknowledge Interface Logic

Peripheral chips of the 68000 family supporting the user-vectored interrupts typically have an interrupt request output (open-drain type) and an interrupt-acknowledge input. Assuming there is only one interrupting device per priority level, an interrupt acknowledge circuit can decode which interrupter is currently being acknowledged, and assert the interrupt-acknowledge input of that interrupter. The peripheral then places its vector number on the low-byte of the data bus and asserts DTACK* to request termination of the interrupt-acknowledge bus cycle.

Figure 8-82 illustrates the interrupt request and acknowledge interface of the 68000 with three interrupters. The interrupt-acknowledge signal for a given priority level, let us call it IACKn* for level n, is derived from address lines A3-A1, qualified with FC2-FC0 equal to {HHH} and AS* asserted. We can use the 74ALS138, one-of-eight decoder chip with three enable inputs, to generate IACKn*, as shown in Figure 8-83. The PLD equivalent of this circuit is shown in Figure 8-84.

Let us consider the following scenario: The 68000 responds to an interrupt request and the IACKn* input of the corresponding peripheral is asserted by the logic we discussed above. However, suppose that, possibly due to an error condition, that the peripheral does not have a pending interrupt and does not respond with a DTACK*. Assuming there is a BTO circuit, the BERR* is asserted after time-out causing a spurious-interrupt exception. This is fine because the detection of a spurious exception provides an error detection mechanism for the user-vectored interrupts. In the case of auto-vectored interrupts, on the other hand, there is no such built-in protection. We may use the corresponding IREQn* to qualify the IACKn* for auto-vectored interrupts, but this will not work if the IACKn* actually clears the interrupt request in hardware. A more general approach for auto-vectored interrupts is to verify the interrupt condition at the beginning of its service routine.

Example 8-4

The following is an example of the DUART peripheral ('68681) interface. The interface of a '68681 DUART to the 68000 is simple as shown in Figure 8-85. The '68681 is typical of 68000 peripherals, and supports the asynchronous bus structure

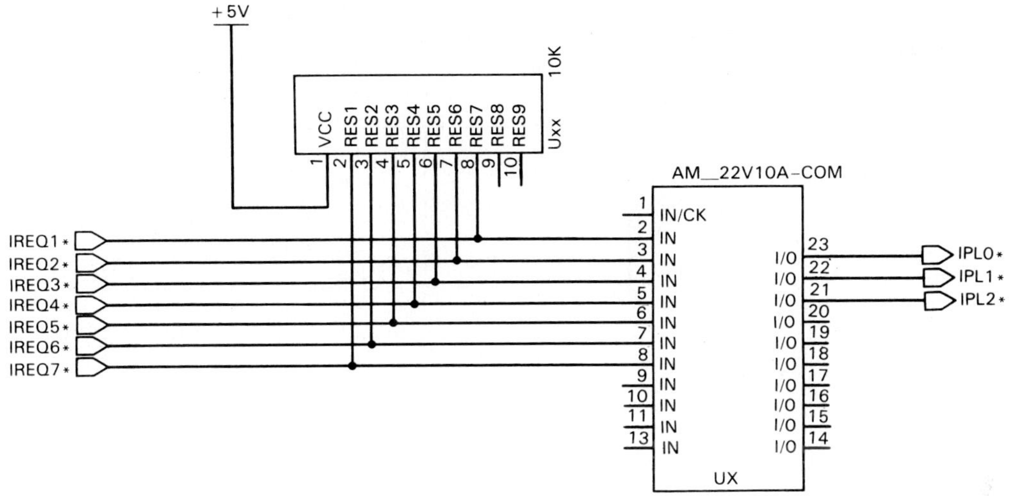


```
/* Inputs */
Pin [2..8] = ![IREQ1..7] ;

/* Outputs */
Pin 23 = !IPL2 ;
Pin 22 = !IPL1 ;
Pin 21 = !IPL0 ;

IPL0 = IREQ7 #
      !IREQ6 &  IREQ5 #
      !IREQ6 & !IREQ4 &  IREQ3 #
      !IREQ6 & !IREQ4 & !IREQ2 & IREQ1 ;

IPL1 = IREQ7 #
       IREQ6 #
      !IREQ5 & !IREQ4 &  IREQ3 #
      !IREQ5 & !IREQ4 &  IREQ2 ;

IPL2 = IREQ7 #
       IREQ6 #
       IREQ5 #
       IREQ4 ;
```

Figure 8-81 Interrupt Requester Using a PLD.

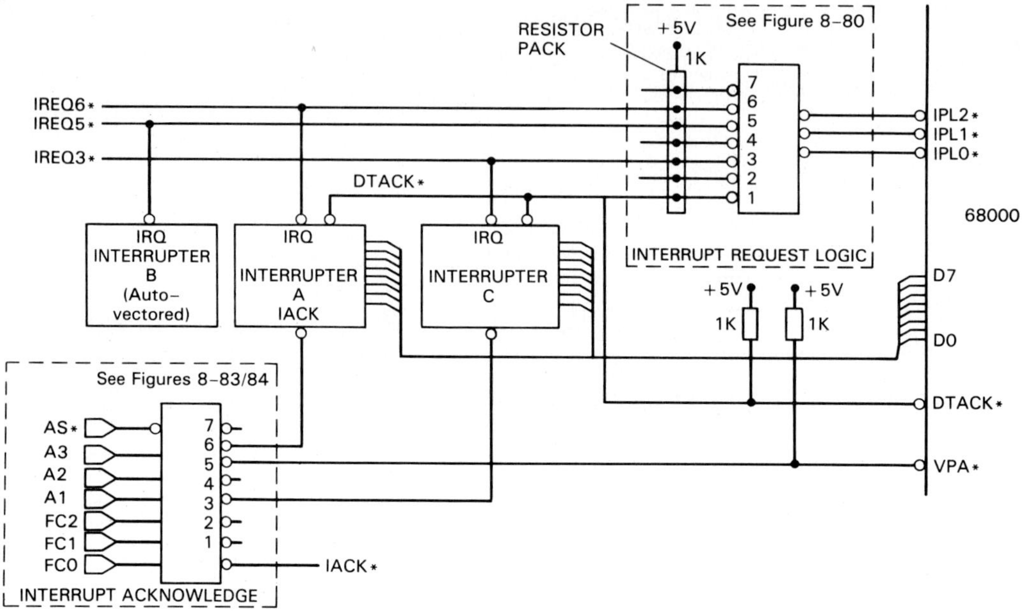

Interrupter	Priority Level	User- or Auto-Vectored
Peripheral A	6	User-vectored
Peripheral B	5	Auto-vectored
Peripheral C	3	User-vectored

Figure 8-82 Illustration of Interrupt Circuit.

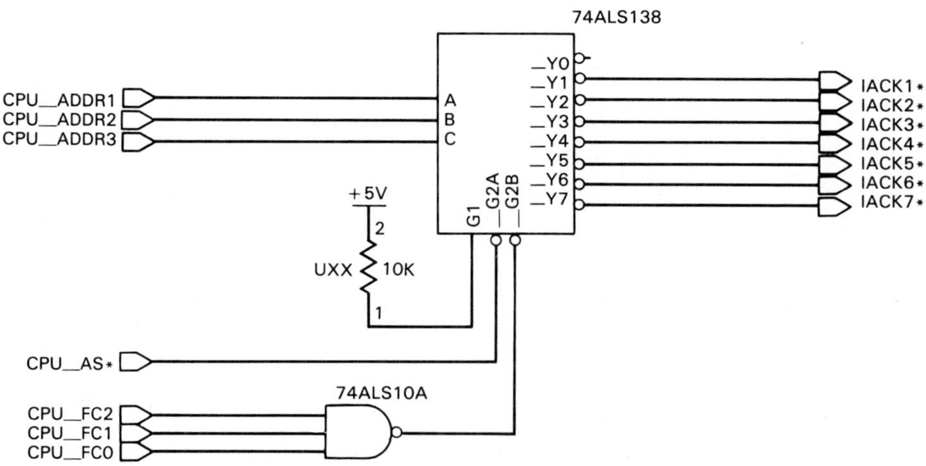

Figure 8-83 Interrupt-acknowledge (IACK) Generation Circuit.

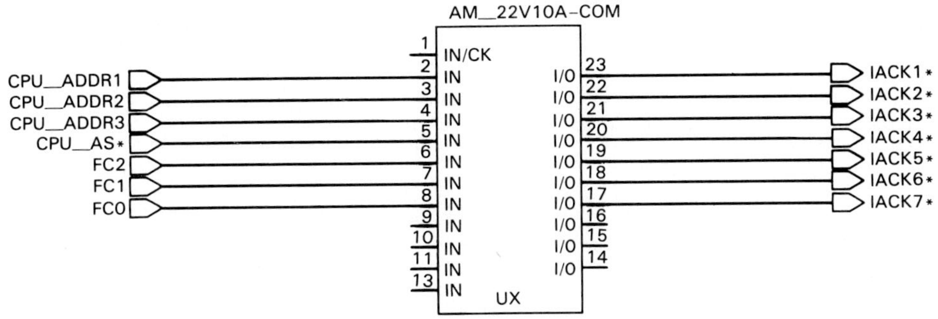

Figure 8-84 PLD Implementation of IACK Circuit.

and user-vectored interrupts of the 68000. The RESET* signal is used to initialize the DUART to its default state and configuration.

The '68681 is also quite versatile. Each communication channel compromises a full-duplex asynchronous receiver/transmitter (UART) with many software programmable features (see *68000 Family Reference Manual*). Our purpose for the DUART here is to connect, let's say, two RS-232C ports to our SBC: a terminal and a printer interface.

We can connect the DUART to the high or low byte of the 68000 data bus, but the user-vectored interrupts expect the vector number in the low-byte position. Therefore, the DUART is connected to the low 8-bits of the 68000 data bus.

8.11.5 Daisy-chaining of Interrupts

In the above discussion, we assumed that there are, at most, seven interrupt generating devices with a maximum of one interrupter per each level. This assumption simplifies the interrupt acknowledge circuit. But, what happens if there are more than seven interrupts?

The answer is that more than one interrupter can share the same interrupt request line in a wired-OR configuration (i.e., using open-drain drivers). The interrupters within a given priority level can be sub-prioritized by daisy-chaining the interrupt-acknowledge lines as IACK*n*_IN*X** and IACK*n*_OUT*X** as illustrated in Figure 8-86. In this notation *n* indicates the priority level, and *X* indicates the interrupter within a chain connection. Thus, the only change to the previous circuit of Figure 8-82 is the addition of daisy-chain logic.

The concept drawing of the interrupt daisy-chain logic is shown in Figure 8-87. When an interrupt for priority level *n* is acknowledged, IACK*n** is asserted, as we discussed before. The first element in the daisy-chain passes this acknowledge to the next one, only if it does not have a pending interrupt. To pass the acknowledge, it asserts the IACK*n*_OUTA*. If device A does have a pending interrupt, then IACK*n*_OUTA* is not asserted. In this case, the device A completes the bus cycle by returning DTACK* or VPA* for auto-vectored operation.

In practice, the circuit of Figure 8-87 cannot be used because it has a race

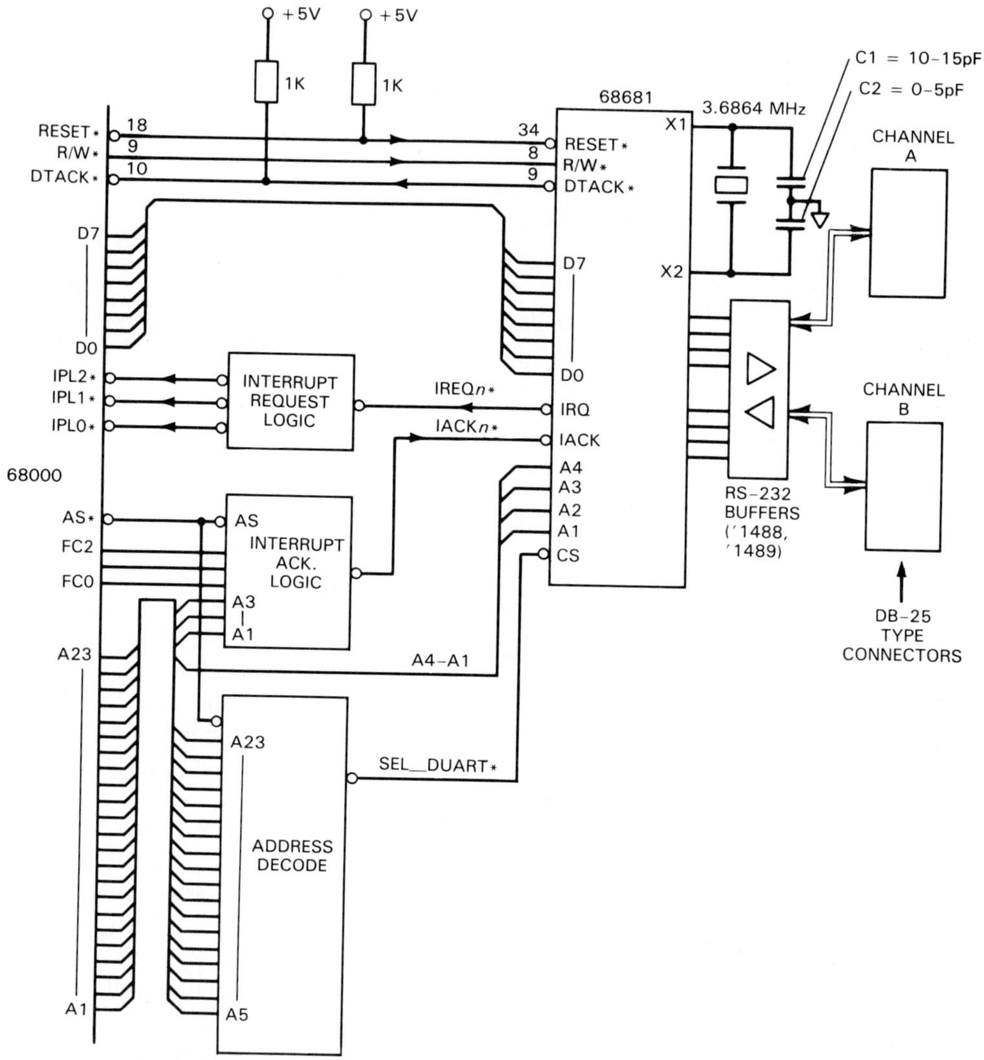

Note: C1 or C2 stray capacitance < 5pF. This requires board layout where these capacitors and crystal are very close to the pin of the DUART.

Figure 8-85 '68681 DUART Interface Example.

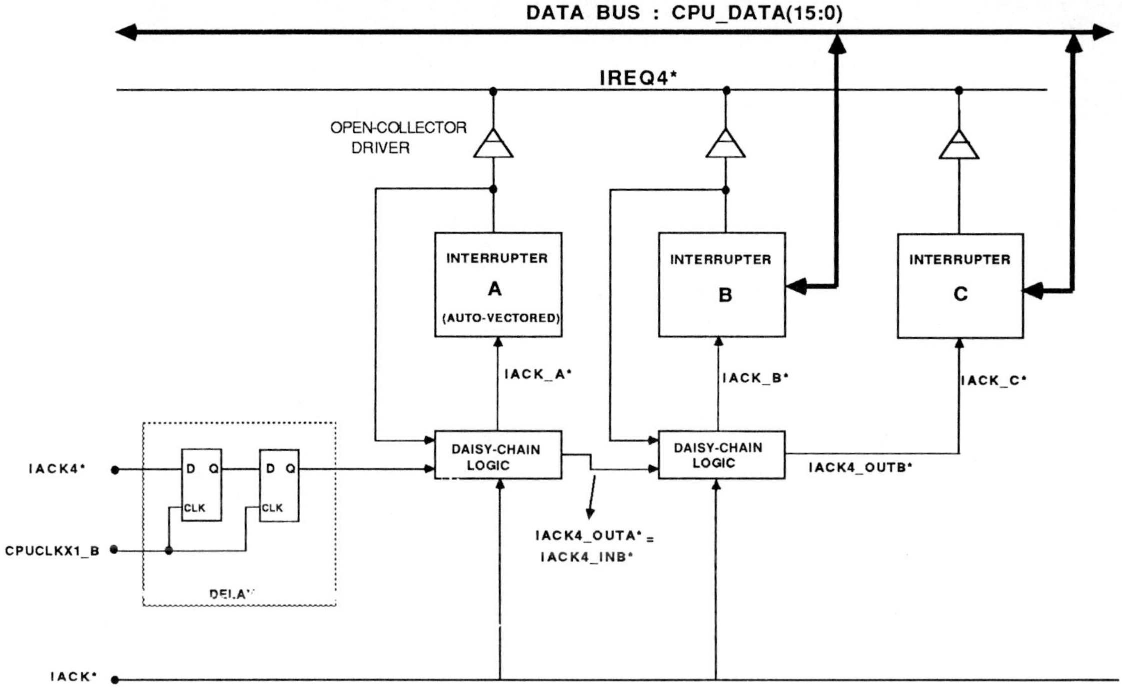

Figure 8-86 Illustration of Daisy-chain Interrupts.

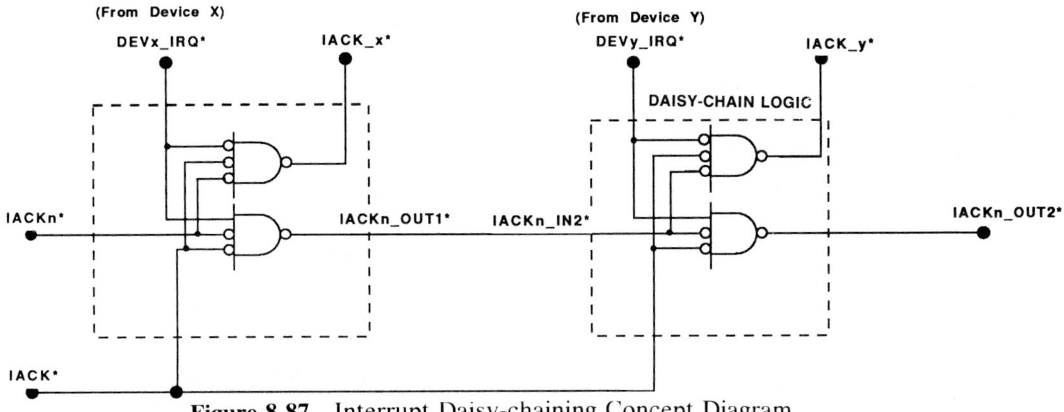

Figure 8-87 Interrupt Daisy-chaining Concept Diagram.

condition. For example, suppose an element in the daisy-chain passed the IACKn_INX* to IACKn_OUTX*, because there was no pending interrupts from interrupter X. What if this interrupter requests an interrupt, immediately after an acknowledge is passed through. This will likely cause two devices to acknowledge the interrupt at the same time (i.e., a circuit malfunction). To prevent such a situation, all interrupt requests presented to the daisy-chain logic must be frozen as soon as an interrupt-acknowledge cycle begins—that is when IACK* is asserted. A transparent latch may be used to freeze the interrupt requests, as shown in Figure 8-88. The IACKn* is delayed using two flip-flops and connected to the IACKn_INX* input of the first element, so that the output of the transparent latch is stable when the pass or no-pass decision is made. This circuit can also be implemented using a '22V10 as follows:

```
LATCHED_DEVx_IRQ  =  !IACK & DEVx_IRQ #
                      IACK & LATCHED_DEVx_IRQ ;
                      *This implements a transparent latch*/


IACKnOUT_X  =  !LATCHED_DEVx_IRQ & IACK & IACKn_INX ;
```

using active-high logic.

Summary of interrupt interface logic design. The first step in the design of interrupt interface logic should be the definition of interrupts and how they are handled. This means defining the interrupt priority level and the type of interrupt for each device that can generate an interrupt to the 68000, as in the example given in Table 8-6. The listing of interrupts in decreasing order of priority will

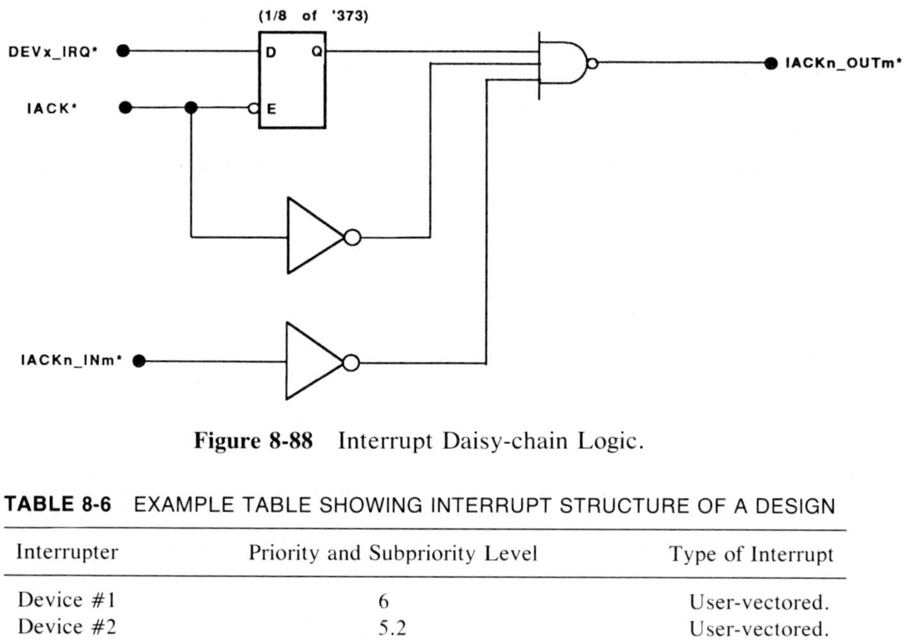

Figure 8-88 Interrupt Daisy-chain Logic.

TABLE 8-6 EXAMPLE TABLE SHOWING INTERRUPT STRUCTURE OF A DESIGN

Interrupter	Priority and Subpriority Level	Type of Interrupt
Device #1	6	User-vectored.
Device #2	5.2	User-vectored.
Device #3	5.1	User-vectored.
Device #4	4	User-vectored.
Device #5	3	Auto-vectored.
Device #6	2	Auto-vectored.
Device #7	2	Auto-vectored.
Device #8	1.0	User-vectored.

also enable showing the daisy-chain structure within any given level. For example, we can note that there are two interrupters in level five that are user-vectored. This means that these two must be daisy-chained. Similarly, there are two interrupters in level two. The daisy-chain circuit, however, cannot be used in the case of more than one auto-vectored interrupter for a given priority level. Instead, it requires polling in software the status of each possible auto-vectored interrupt for that level. The order of polling, in this case, determines the order or subpriority of polled interrupts.

8.12 BUS ARBITRATION

In our discussions so far we considered that the 68000 drives its local busses all the time (i.e., it is the only bus master). In some systems, there may be more than one device that is capable of doing the data transfers over the same bus. The most common application of this is the use of the *Direct-Memory-Access* (DMA) method whereby a secondary or alternate bus master gains control of the bus to transfer a block of data between a peripheral and the processor's external RAM memory. This is illustrated in Figure 8-89.

While the secondary bus master has control of the bus, the 68000 turns-off its bus drivers, and no data passes through the 68000. Obviously, the bus timing generated by the alternate bus master must meet the timing specifications of the 68000 (i.e., it must emulate 68000's timing).

Even though the 68000 is not, at some time, the bus master, it may still continue its processing internally, until it needs the use of the bus again for operand transfers or instruction prefetches. For example, it may be executing a multiply instruction while another bus master uses the bus.

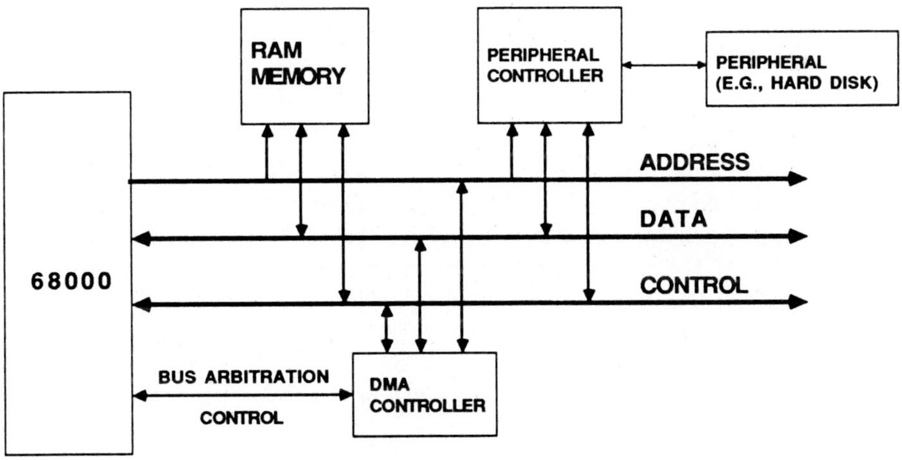

Figure 8-89 A 68000 System With DMA Controller.

With the DMA technique, it is possible to realize a relatively high data transfer rate, because, otherwise, the 68000 has to execute a MOVE and a BRA instruction. This is especially slow since the 68000 does not have an instruction cache. Using the DMA controller, the 68000 will request the transfer of a block of data and will receive completion notice, typically via an interrupt, when the entire block has been moved. The DMA controller may transfer the entire block in a single burst, but this has the disadvantage that the processor is virtually halted, if it needs access to the bus at the same time—and usually it does. Alternatively, the DMA transfers can be interleaved with processor accesses to the bus. This is referred to as *cycle stealing*. It makes the DMA activity transparent to the processor, but the transfer rate is reduced. Some of the DMA controllers provide control of the percentage of bus activity or bus bandwidth for the DMA operation. For example, the '68450 DMA controller chip allows defining the DMA burst time and what portion of bus cycles is available to the DMA transfers.

In a multiprocessor system, a mechanism called *bus arbitration* is used to determine which device is to be the next bus master. The 68000 supports bus arbitration with three control signals as shown in Figure 8-90. If there is no other bus master beside the 68000, all we need to do is to pull-up the BR* and BGACK* inputs. In a multi-master system, when another device wants to become the bus master, it asserts the 68000's Bus Request (BR*) input. The 68000 treats the BR* as an asynchronous input and synchronizes it internally to its clock. After recognizing the BR* input, the 68000 asserts the Bus Grant (BG*) output to indicate that the bus *will* be granted. Receiving the BG* does not mean that the alternate bus master can immediately start using the bus. It simply means that the bus will be released at the end of the current bus cycle. The requesting device must wait until the following conditions are all true:

1. AS* is negated. This indicates that the 68000 or other previous bus master has completed its bus cycle.
2. DTACK* is negated. This indicates that the previous device being accessed has stopped driving the bus (i.e., DTACK* and data lines D15-D0 in case of read).
3. BGACK* is negated. This indicates that the previous bus master has relinquished the bus (i.e., the address and control signal lines). In other words, a bus master will assert BGACK* during its bus mastership, and will negate BGACK* only when it wants to give up the bus. To further clarify this, let us assume that there are three possible bus masters: The 68000, peripheral-A and peripheral-B. If peripheral A is currently the bus master (i.e., asserting BGACK*) and peripheral B makes a request by asserting the BR*, then the 68000 will still respond by asserting the BG*. But, this does not mean that at the end of the current bus cycle, peripheral-B will take over the bus. The peripheral B can become the bus master only after peripheral-A negates BGACK*.

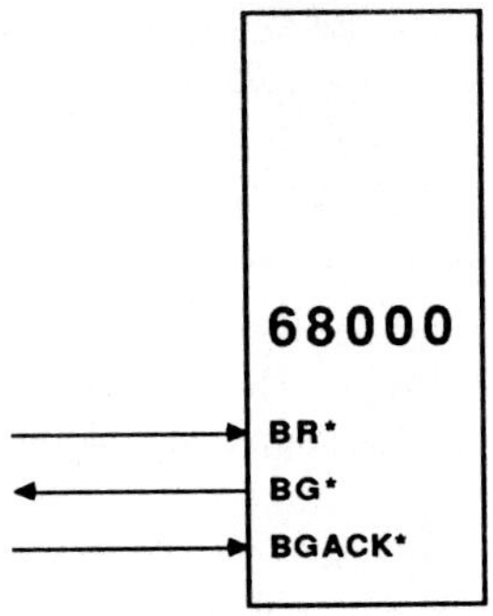

BR* : BUS REQUEST
BG* : BUS GRANT
BGACK* : BUS-GRANT ACKNOWLEDGE

Figure 8-90 Bus Arbitration Control Signals.

The bus arbitration timing is shown in Figure 8-91. After all of the above conditions are met, the device requesting the bus must assert BGACK*. This informs the arbitration logic of the 68000 that another bus master has taken control of the bus. Note that the 68000 does not wait for BGACK* before actually turning

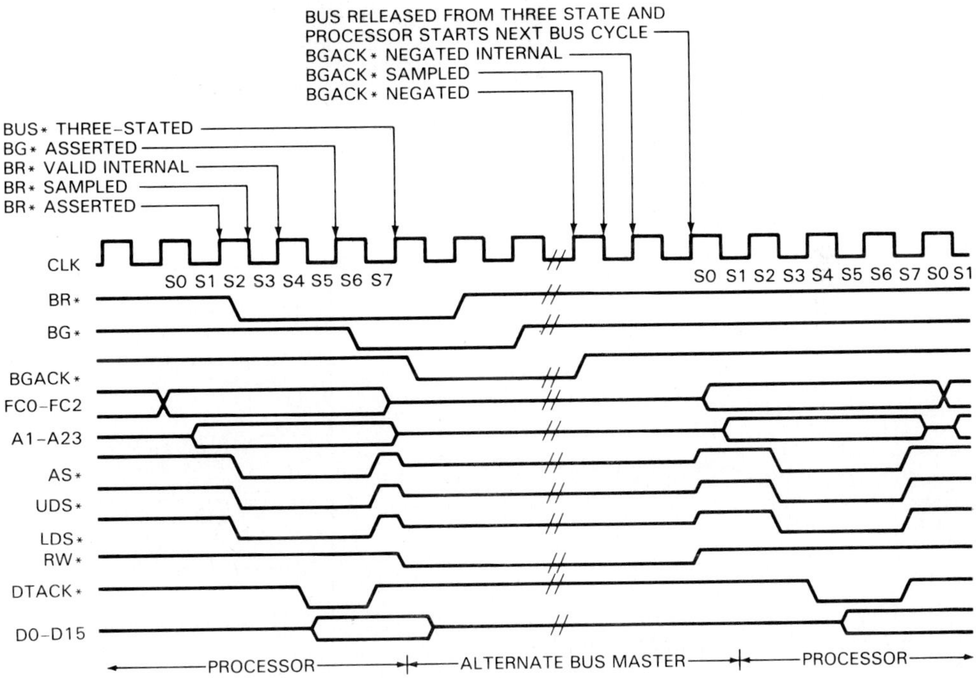

Figure 8-91 Bus Arbitration Timing Diagram. (Courtesy of Motorola.)

off its bus drivers. In this diagram, the bus activity of the alternate bus master is not shown to focus on the condition of the 68000 signal lines.

Unlike the interrupt request lines, a bus request to the 68000 cannot be masked. A bus request is always acknowledged at the end of the current bus cycle or within 3.5 clock cycles if the bus is inactive. In other words, the 68000 is at a lower priority than any other device requesting the use of the bus.

The sequence of bus arbitration is shown in Figure 8-92. There are two possible cases—only one secondary bus master and multiple alternate bus mas-

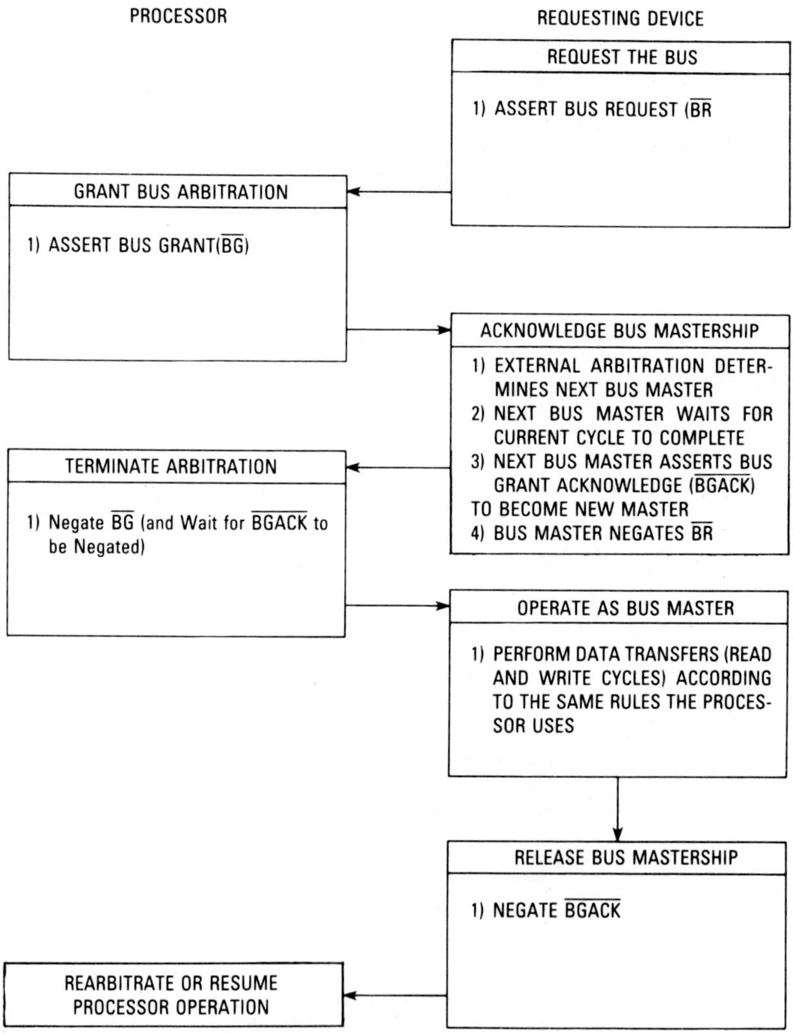

Figure 8-92 Bus Arbitration Cycle Flowchart. (Courtesy of Motorola.)

ters, as shown in Figure 8-93. In the first case, minimum or no external logic is needed for the bus arbitration. In the second case, we can implement a arbitration logic by daisy-chaining the Bus Grant (BG*), where BR* and BGACK* are bussed using wired-OR signals. Actually, the logic for daisy-chaining interrupts can also be used here.

Finally, the timing of the bus-arbitration control signals are shown in Figure 8-94. It is important to note that, in the case of non-overlapping requests, the parameter t37a specifies that the BR* cannot be removed until after BGACK* is asserted.

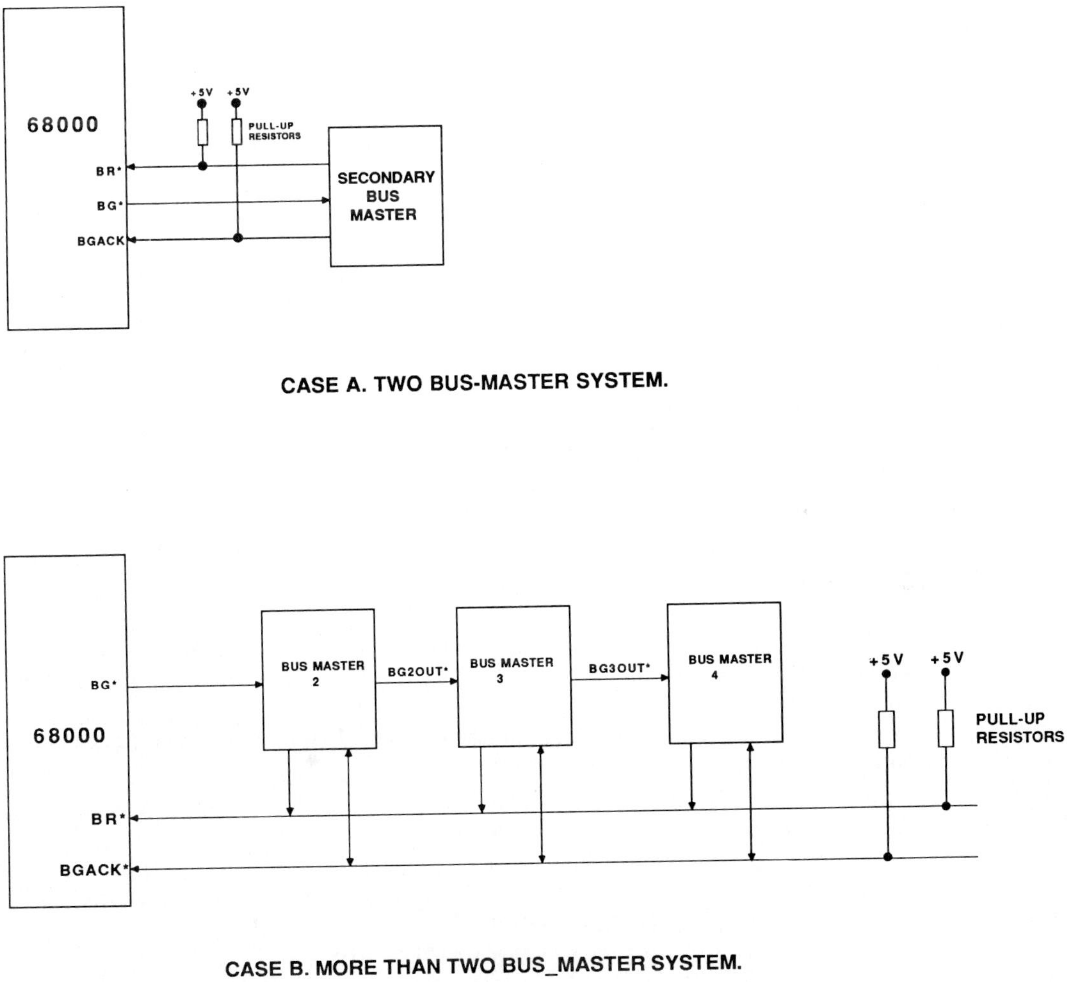

Figure 8-93 Bus Arbitration Control.

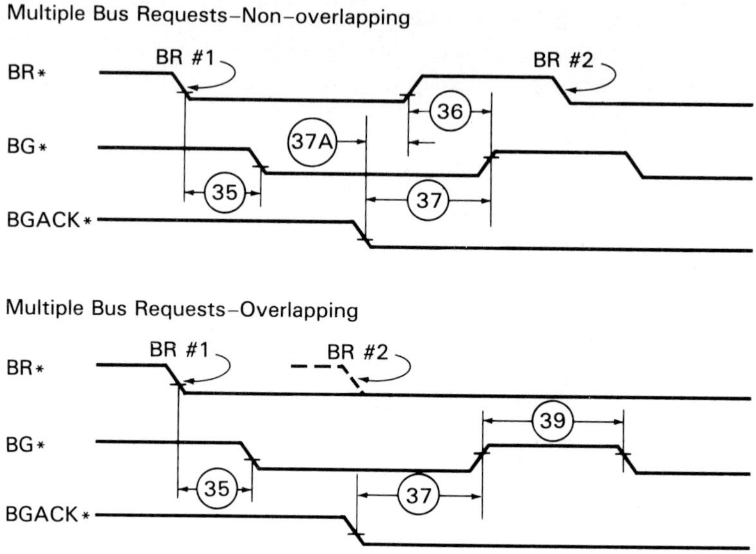

Parameter	Characteristic	Min	Max	Units
t35	BR* asserted to BG* asserted.	1.5	3.5	clks.
t36	BR* negated to BG* negated.	1.5	3.5	clks.
t37	BGACK* asserted to BG* negated.	1.5	3.5	clks.
t37a	BGACK* asserted to BR* negated.	20 nsec	1.5	clks.
t39	BG* width negated.	1.5	—	clks.

Figure 8-94 Bus Arbitration Timing Parameters. (Courtesy of Motorola.)

FURTHER READING

Designing with 68000

1. Harper, Kyle. "A Terminal Interface, Printer Interface, and Background Printing for an MC 68000-based System using the MC68681 DUART," *Motorola Application Note: AN899*, 1984.
2. West, Trey. "A High Performance MC68000L12 System with NO Wait States," *Motorola Application Note: AN867*, 1982.
3. Brown, Geoff. "Serial I/O, Timer, and Interface Capabilities of the MC68901 Multi-function Peripheral," *Motorola Application Note: AN896A*, 1984.
4. Taylor, Mitchell B. "A Discussion of Interrupts for the MC68000," *Motorola Engineering Bulletin: EB97*, 1983. The second revision of this is printed as a *Motorola Application Note AN1012/D* in 1988.
5. West, Trey. "Dual-Ported RAM for the MC68000 Microprocessor," *Motorola Application Note: AN881*, 1983.

6. Vaglica, John. "The Bisync Protocol and a Bisync Data Link Between Two MC68000 MPU Based Systems," *Motorola Application Note: AN882*, 1982.
7. Morales, Arnold J. "Interfacing M6800 Peripheral Devices to the MC68000 Asynchronously," *Motorola Application Note: AN808*, 1981.
8. Reddy, Al. "Dynamic Memory Refresh Considerations," *Motorola Application Note: AN887*, 1983.
9. Tavana, Danesh. "68000 Interrupt Controller," *Monolithic Memories Application Note: AN119*.
10. Scherer, Victor A. and Peterson, William G. "The MC68230 Parallel Interface/Timer Provides an Effective Printer Interface," *Motorola Application Note: AN854*, 1982.
11. Graden, Duane. "Software Refreshed Memory Card for the MC68000," *Motorola Application Note: AN816*, 1981.
12. Brown, Geoffrey and Harper, Kyle. "MC68008 Minimum Configuration System," *Motorola Application Note: AN897*, 1984.
13. "The interrelationship Between Access Time and Clock Rate in a MC68000 System," *Motorola Engineering Bulletin, EB-83A*, 1982.
14. "The Interrupt Controlling Capabilities of the MC68901 and the MC68230," *Motorola Application Note AN975/D*, 1988.
15. "Motorola MMT8 (68000) Course Notes," *MTT8 CN, Rev 1.*, June 1987.

Designing with PLDs

16. *PAL Handbook*, Monolithic Memories Inc., Third Edition (1983).
17. *Programmable Array Logic*, Advanced Micro Devices, 1984.
18. *Systems Design Handbook*, Monolithic Memories Inc., Second Edition.
19. *Programmable Logic Data Manual*, Signetics, 1986.
20. The Technical Staff of Monolithic Memories, Inc., *Designing with Programmable Array Logic*, McGraw-Hill, 1981.
21. "Programmable Hardware," pp. 194–263, *Byte*, Vol. 12, Number 1, January 1987. This issue of Byte has a section of various comprehensive articles on using and designing with PLDs.

Circuit Hazards

22. "IC Markers Grapple with Metastability," *EDN*, August 1988, pp. 30.
23. Sokal, Nathan O. *EDN*, "Use of Check List Prevents Problems in TTL Systems," November 1986, pp. 253–262.
24. Sokal, Nathan O. "Check Lists Help You Avoid Trouble With MOS and Memory ICs," *EDN*, November 27, 1986, pp. 229–235.
25. "Metastable Characteristics," section 3-4 of *Texas Instruments Designer's Handbook*, May 1988, pp. 3-29 to 3-36.
26. "Metastability, AMD/MMI Technical Article," *PAL Device Data Book*, 1988, pp. 3-164 to 3-169.

Memories

27. Prince, Betty and Due-Gundersen, Gunnar. *Semiconductor Memories*, John-Wiley and Sons, 1983.
28. NEC, "Battery Backup Circuits for SRAMs," *Application Note 50*, Can be found NEC's Memory Products databook of 1989, pp. 6-51 to 6-61.
29. Panasonic Battery Sales Division, *Panasonic Lithium Batteries Tecnical Handbook, 88/3*, March 1988.
30. "Message Passing With Dual-Ported RAMs," *Electronic Products*, January 15, 1987, pp. 24–29.

Circuit Design

31. Fletcher, William. *An Engineering Approach to Digital Design*, Prentice-Hall, Inc., 1980.
32. Peatman, John B. *Digital Hardware Design*, McGraw-Hill Book Company, 1980.
33. Blakeslee, Thomas R. *Digital Design with Standard MSI and LSI, Second Edition*, Wiley-Interscience Publication, 1979.
34. Johnson, E. L. and Karim, M. A. *Digital Design—A Pragmatic Approach*, PWS Engineering, 1987.
35. Ritchey, Lee W. Controlled Impedance PCB Design, Printed Circuit Design, pp. 23–28, June 1989.
36. Del Corso, D., et al. Microcomputer Buses and Links, Academic Press, 1986.
37. Kogge, Peter M. The Architecture of Pipelined Computers, McGraw-Hill Book Company, 1981.

EXERCISES

DC Electrical Characteristics and Signal Buffering

1. What is the fanout under the following conditions:
   a) When the 68000 address bus directly drives FCT type logic devices?
   b) Same as A except for ALS type logic devices.
   c) When a peripheral device with I_{ol} of 2 mAmp (max.) drives ALS type logic devices?

2. How many power and ground pins does the 68000 have? Do all power and ground pins need to be connected?

3. What is the maximum current and power consumption of the 68000?

4. Why have we used LDS*/UDS* instead of the AS* for the data buffer enable control?

5. **a)** Calculate the value of the pull-up resistor needed for the unused inputs of the 68000.
   b) In Figure 8-2, why do we need the pull-up resistors at some of the inputs and outputs of the 'F244?

Clock Timing Requirements

6. What are the clock high, low, and transition time requirements for the 16.67 MHz 68000?
7. What layout precautions do we need to take with the clock circuit of the 68000?
8. What are the internal clock states in a bus cycle with one wait-cycle? Indicate the sampling windows for asynchronous inputs.
9. Define the following terms: clock state, clock cycle, bus cycle, and instruction cycle.

Bus Control Signals and Bus Operation

10. What is the primary control signal that indicates a 68000 bus cycle? What is the minimum time this signal stays negated between consecutive bus cycles? Why is this important?
11. Draw the timing diagram of signals CLK, AS*, and DTACK* for zero wait-cycles.
    a) Indicate the maximum variation of AS* timing with respect to the CLK signal for a 10 MHz 68000.
    b) Indicate where DTACK* is sampled.
    c) What happens if DTACK* is asserted during its sample window?
    d) Repeat a)-c) for 2 wait-cycles.
12. What happens if DTACK* is not negated according to the parameter t28?
13. What are the bus control signals whose timing differ for a read and write bus cycle?
14. For proper operation, do we have to ensure that the DTACK* always meets the t47 setup time?
15. What are the differences between the fully asynchronous, pseudo-asynchronous, and fully synchronous types of 68000 bus interface logic?
16. In a read cycle, can we assert DTACK* before the valid data is actually placed on the bus? Please explain.
17. Calculate T_{sadv} for a 16.67 MHz 68000. What is the write access time available for the same 68000? How does the required read and write access times compare? Consider zero and one wait-cycles.
18. What are the different bus cycle types supported by the 68000?

System Control Signals

19. When are the following bidirectional signals driven as outputs by the 68000?
    a) HALT*
    b) RESET*
20. What is the purpose of a BTO circuit? What is the time-out period of the circuit given in Figure 8-23?
21. What are the first four bus cycles used for after a system power-up?

22. a) Calculate the reset timing of the circuit shown in Figure 8-21. Modify the circuit so that instead of a manual reset, a TTL-compatible signal is used to initiate a 68000 reset operation.
    b) What is the worst-case leakage current of a 1N4001 diode? Based on this leakage current, what RC values can be chosen if we wanted to double the reset time.

Designing With PLDs

23. Replace the BTO circuit of Figure 8-23 with a '22V10 PLD. Define pin numbers and specify logic equations using the CUPL format.
24. What can we do when more than one product term is necessary to control the OE, AR, or SP of a '22V10?
25. What is the maximum number of product terms of an output of a '22V10? What can we do if additional product terms are needed?
26. Modify the Example 8-1 PLD so that the counter counts down from an initial fixed value, and reloads upon reaching zero.

Circuit Hazards

27. A combinatorial type PLD output generates a glitch on its Q output, where

$$Q = X \ \& \ Y;$$

when both X and Y transition at the same time. Describe at least two different ways by which we can avoid a glitch on the Q output.
28. Calculate the metastable failure rate per year for 16R4A for a 10 MHz clock and 5 MHz data frequency. What would be failure rate if the input signal were registered twice using the 16R4A outputs.
29. What is the value of T_{en} for the example 8-2. Assume a 10 MHz 68000 is used, and the buffer delays for address and AS* are the same.

Address Decoder Design

30. a) Why is it necessary to use the function code signals as part of the address decode?
    b) Implement the memory map given in Table 8-3 using AND, OR, and NOT gates.
    c) Apply DeMorgan's theorem to Equation 8-6 to see if it could be implemented in less number of devices than shown in Figure 8-45.
31. Modify the circuit in Figure 8-46 so that for the first four bus cycles after a reset operation, the EPROM is always enabled. In other words, the memory map is changed to the following after the reset vectors are fetched:

```
RAM:    000000 - 01FFFF

EPROM:  030000 - 06FFFF
```

32. How can you increase the effective addressing range of the 68000 to 64 Mbytes using the function codes, FC2-FC0? Please explain the disadvantages, if any, of this approach.

DTACK* Generation

33. What is the DTACK* negation time after the AS* or LDS*/UDS* for the following:
    a) 'F164 circuit given in Figure 8-53.
    b) PLD circuit given in Figure 8-54.
34. a) What is the speed rating of a PLD we have to use to meet the t47 time requirement of a 10 MHz 68000.
    b) Same as A, except for a 16.67 MHz 68000.
35. Modify the circuit of Figure 8-53 to use a 'F163.
36. For a system which runs with no wait states for all devices, would it be simpler just to ground DTACK? Please discuss.
37. Modify the PLD equations given in Figure 8-55 for the following:
    Device # 1 : Read : 2 wait-cycles.
    Write: 3 wait-cycles.
    Device # 2 : Read/Write : 1 wait-cycles.

Memory Design

38. Find two SRAM devices that are compatible with the NEC '43256.
39. a) Modify the circuit of Figure 8-60 to four banks of 32K × 8 memories.
    b) Specify the PLD pin definitions and equations for the changes of A.
    c) Assuming DEV1 is the SRAM in PLD shown in Figure 8-55 make necessary changes to it to run without any wait-cycles for both read and write accesses to the SRAM.
    d) Verify that a 120 nsec version of the SRAM can be used without any performance degradation.
40. How would the access times of a SRAM memory be affected if we use the AS* as part of the address decode (i.e., if SEL_SRAM* was used instead of DECODE_SRAM* in the example design of Figure 8-60).
    a) Assume the address decode time is 15 nanoseconds after AS* is asserted.
    b) Assume the address decode time is 35 nanoseconds after AS* is negated.
41. Re-evaluate Example 8-3 for the 16.67 MHz 68000 timing.
42. A two-processor 68000 configuration uses a RAM communication area that can be both read from or written to by both processors as shown below. The SRAM is only byte wide and is connected to the low-byte of both processors. To gain write access, processors use the TAS instruction. Furthermore, both processors are run at 10 MHz and one is interfaced synchronously with the DPRAM arbiter (i.e., the arbiter is using the 10 MHz clock).
    a) Explain how the TAS instruction can be used to gain access.
    b) The block diagram on page 484 has two important oversights. What are these?
    c) Modify the PLD equations of Figure 8-75 for this case. What are the DTACK* and data hold times? Are these within the specification for both of the 68000s?
    d) What are the data setup and hold times for the SRAM?

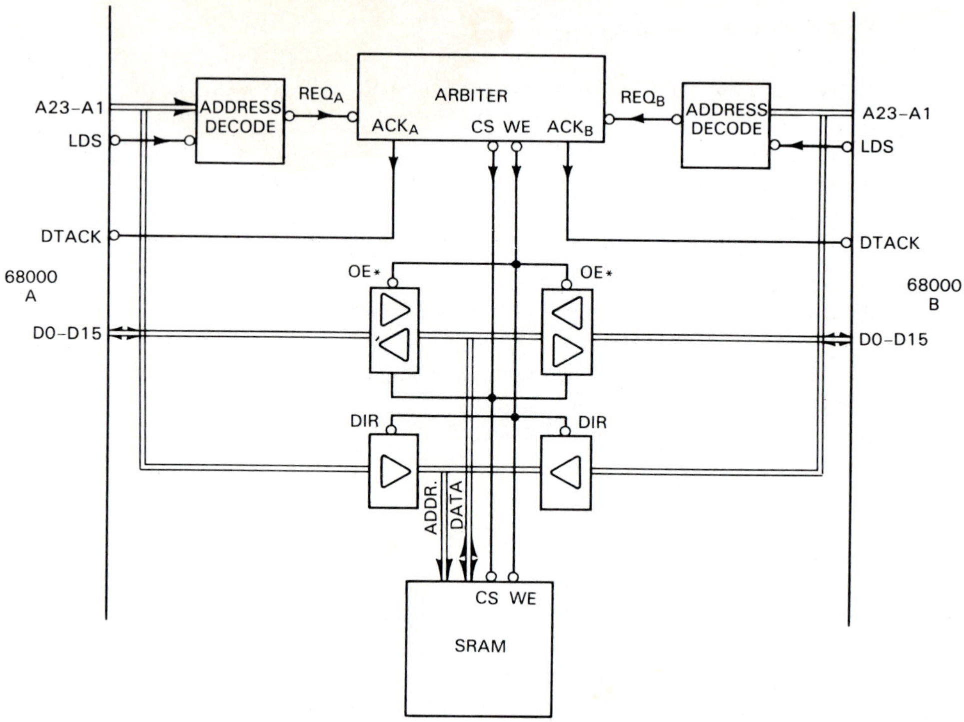

Block Diagram of DPRAM for Exercise 42.

43. Replace the DPRAM circuit of the previous exercise with a single DPRAM device from Cypress Semiconductor or Integrated Device Technology (IDT). Look up the data sheet of one of these devices and draw the interface circuit diagram.

44. What is the difference between the current levels of a '43256 at standby and the data retention modes.

45. In our battery backup circuit, we can put a large capacitor across a Lithium battery so that we may change the battery without loosing the SRAM contents. Calculate the capacitor size for a 30 seconds changing time. Assume the load is 40 microAmps.

46. What happens if we have a system power failure in the middle of a NVRAM access? (Hint: How long does it take for the +5V to go out of working range. Also look at the DS1210 data sheet.)

47. Modify the circuit of Figure 8-73 using a '22V10 PLD to control the CE∗ of EPROMs and the BUFEN∗ signal with the following specifications:

a) EPROMs are normally in the standby condition.

b) When two consecutive accesses to the EPROM is detected, the EPROMs are enabled for 16 clock cycles (CE∗'s asserted). The standby is then resumed if there are no further consecutive accesses.

c) The interface PLD returns an EPROM_ACK∗ that will be combined with the other DTACK∗ signals in a wired-OR configuration.

48. Change the EPROM circuit of Figure 8-74 for the following:

a) Update so that 2 Mbit EPROM devices are usable with a PLD change.

b) Update for two banks of EPROMs.

49. a) Draw the timing diagram for the circuit of Figure 8-74.

b) Calculate the parameter t29a to see if it is violated for a 10 MHz 68000.

50. Modify the DPRAM of Figure 8-76 to a 16-bit configuration.

51. Modify the state flow chart of Figure 8-77 assuming 55 nanosecond SRAMs and 10 MHz 68000s.

52. Modify the circuit of Figure 8-69 for 32K × 16 configuration using two 32K × 8 SRAMs.

a) Draw the updated circuit diagram, including the address-decode circuit. (Hint: Decoding has to be changed to use LDS*/UDS*).

b) Draw the timing diagram for the updated circuit.

c) Provide the updated PLD equations.

d) Verify that the critical timing parameters are met.

e) What is the SRAM access time required for 0 wait-cycle need and 1 wait-cycle writes?

Interrupts

53. Calculate the data throughput (in bytes/second) for an 8-MHz 68000 interfaced to an 8-bit and single-buffered peripheral for interrupt I/O.

54. Write the logic equations for the PLD shown in Figure 8-84.

9

Hardware Design with the 68020

In this chapter we will study the hardware design using the 68020 microprocessor. The 68020 has more features, runs at higher clock speeds, and has reduced bus-cycle times as compared to the earlier members of the 68000 family. This makes the hardware design more critical.

We can overview our coverage in this chapter in three main areas. Our first focus is the bus operation of the 68020. This is a topic that is oftentimes not fully understood with regard to the operation of the 68020 and the design trade-offs involved. We will discuss the necessary support circuitry needed in order to make a 68020-based system work; such as the DSACK generation and dynamic-bus sizing logic. Our second focus is the interfacing of memory devices to the 68020 including SRAM, EPROM, and DRAMs. In this chapter, we will also include a comprehensive background on the operation of DRAMs. And finally, our third area of focus is the possible circuit hazards we should be aware of in designing a 68020-based system. Examples are *bus contention* and *metastable states* in inferfacing to peripherals that can cause circuit malfunctions.

Let us first look at the main differences between the 68020 and the earlier members from a hardware point of view. Figure 9-1 gives an overview of the 68020's signal lines. The address and data buses are nonmultiplexed and 32 bits each. The bus control signals are expanded mainly to support the dynamic bus sizing feature. Note the absence of 6800-peripheral interface signals. They are no longer supported due to the availability of ample peripheral chips designed specifically for the 68000 family. The interrupt and system control signals have some minor changes, as we are going to discuss, but the bus arbitration control signals remain unchanged. The bus arbitration of the 68020 is the same as the 68000 that we already covered in Chapter 8.

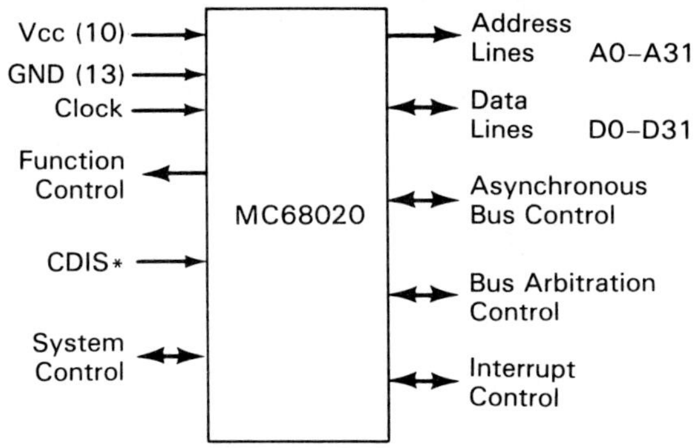

Figure 9-1 Overview of the 68020 Signal Lines.

There is also a signal to control the instruction cache. The *Cache-Disable* (CDIS*) input disables the on-chip instruction cache. This hardware function is intended mainly to be used by the in-circuit emulators which need to disable the cache in order to capture and disassemble an instruction trace.

In discussing the various timing parameters of the 68020, we will use the same timing parameter numbers that are used in the Motorola's *68020 Databook*. This should facilitate easy cross-referencing. Furthermore, to distinguish between the 68020 and other device parameters, we will adopt the notation that $t\langle nn\rangle$ represents a 68020 parameter and $T\langle_{xxx}\rangle$ (i.e., with capital "T") represents another device parameter. Also, to simplify our discussion, we will only specify the timing parameters for the 16.7 MHz 68020 (MC68020RC16). The parameter values differ for parts tested for other speeds such as the 20 MHz MC68020RC20.

9.1 CLOCK SIGNAL AND INTERFACE

The clock input requirements of the 68020 are shown in Figure 9-2 for the 16 MHz 68020. Note that the rise and fall times must be 5 nanoseconds, or less. The clock is a continuous (non-gated) signal and the clock interface circuitry used for the 68000 (see Figure 8-4) may be used without any changes. There are, however, two disadvantages of this clock circuit. First, it does not provide any "times-two" clock with edges that coincide with the CPU clock. This is due the clock-to-output propagation delay of the 'F163. Second, there is no support for a device known as an *Automated Test Equipment* (ATE). An ATE requires a way of disabling the CPU clock and a way of inserting its own clock because it cannot work at the clock rates of the 68020. The circuit shown in Figure 9-3 provides both of these features. The only trade-off here is that we have to use a "times-four" clock oscillator, whereby the PCB layout requires attention in locating these components closely.

All signals that are internally used by the 68020 are synchronous to the clock signal and use both the positive and the negative edges for various operations.

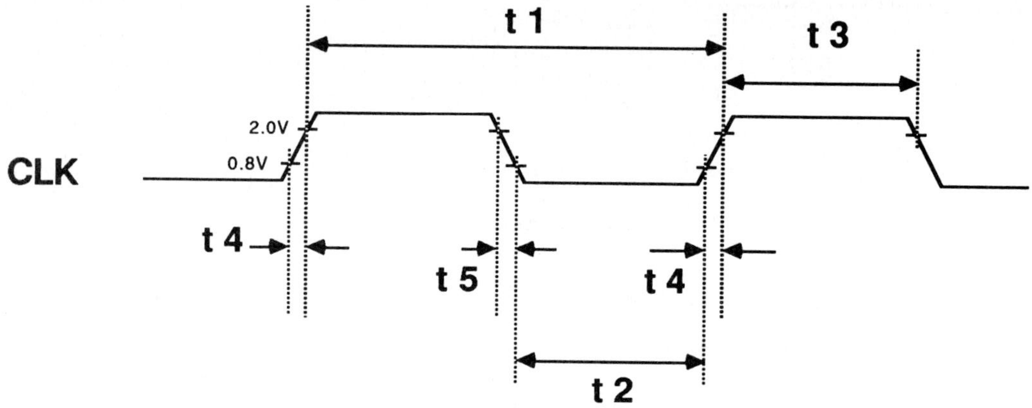

Parameter	Characteristic	Min	Max	Units
	Frequency of Operation (1 / t1)	8	16.67	MHz
t1	Clock Period	60	125	nsec.
t2,t3	Clock Pulse High or Low Width	24	95	nsec.
t4,t5	Clock Rise and Fall Times	—	5	nsec.

Figure 9-2 Clock Timing Requirements.

An asynchronous input signal such as DSACKn*, is first internally synchronized to the clock signal. Furthermore, asynchronous inputs are sampled only during a window where the processor latches the input. To ensure recognition, an asynchronous input signal must meet the setup and hold timings with respect to a given clock edge. If the signal changes in the middle of a sample window, then the level recognized is not predictable but is always resolved to a high or low level by the 68020. In other words, no indeterminate metastable state is generated.

This explains the pseudo-asynchronous nature of the 68020. That is, the external interface may generate the input signals without a fixed relation to the 68020's clock signal. Hence, the term "asynchronous."

There are three possibilities that may occur when an input signal is asynchronous:

1. The input signal meets the asynchronous setup and hold times and is recognized correctly during the first sample window.
2. The input signal changes in the middle of a sample window to the active state (such as assertion of DSACKn*) but happens to be recognized correctly.
3. The signal changes in the middle of a sample window to the active state but is not recognized. In this case, it will be recognized in the next sample window if it stays asserted.

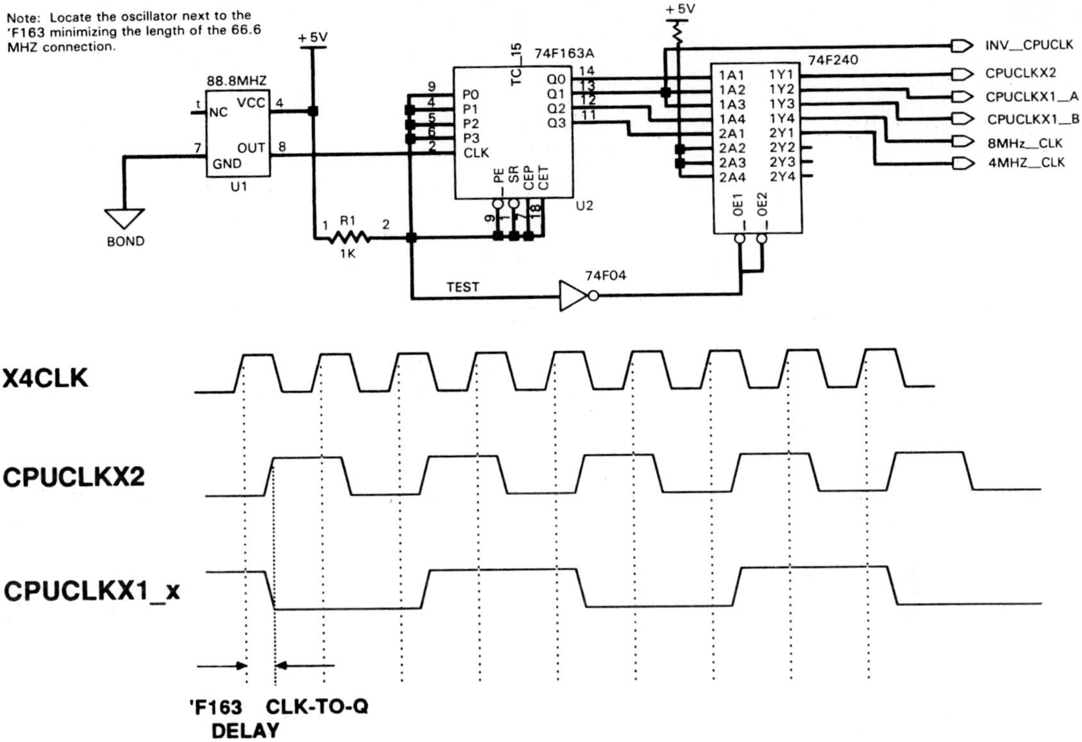

Figure 9-3 Improved Clock Interface Circuit and Timing.

A no-wait-state 68020 bus cycle is three clock cycles long that is composed of 6 internal states. As illustrated in Figure 9-4, the first sample window is at the negative-going edge of state S2. The setup time t47a is important since we will use this parameter frequently. All control signals are active-low and, in general, an asynchronous input signal must be maintained from state S2 through S5 or results will be unpredictable. Therefore, the hold time, t47b, does not have much significance because it is usually automatically satisfied.

9.2 BUS CONTROL SIGNALS AND BUS OPERATION

9.2.1 Bus Control Signals and Timing

Figure 9-5 shows the bus control signals of the 68020. We have studied most of these in Section 6.2.2 already, except the following signals:

Data Buffer Enable (DBEN*) — This output signal is intended to be optionally used to enable any external data buffer chips used with the 68020.

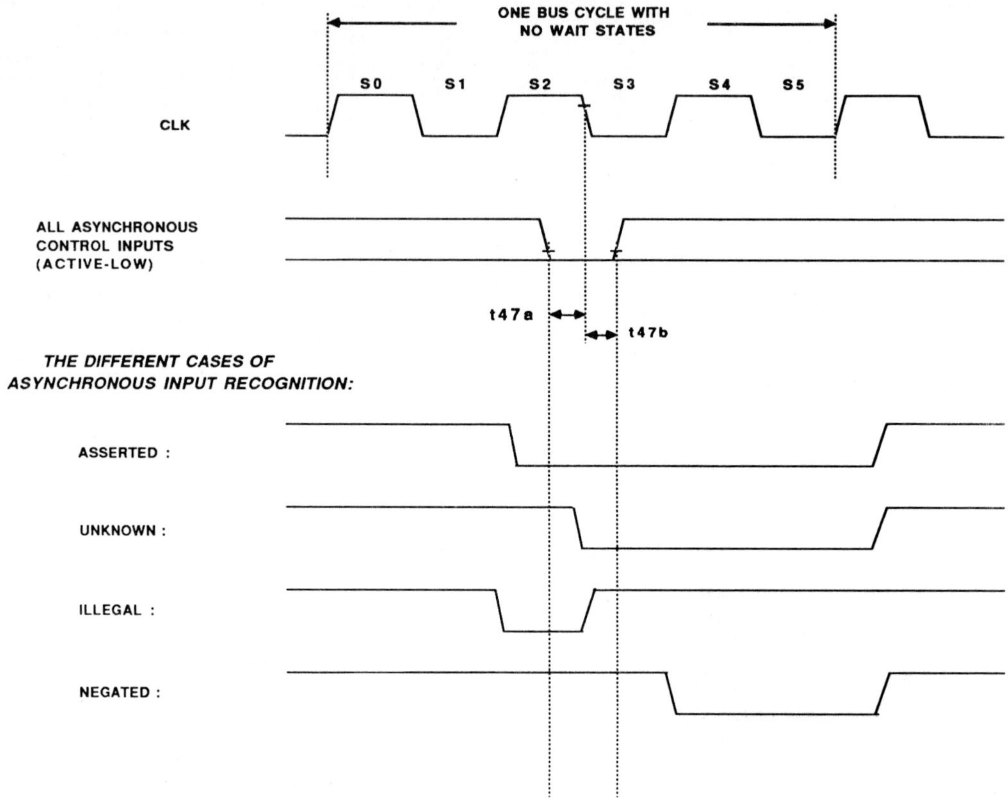

Parameter	Characteristic	Min	Max	Units
t47a	Asynchronous Input Setup Time	5	—	nsec.
t47b	Asynchronous Input Hold Time	15	—	nsec.

Figure 9-4 Asynchronous Control Input Recognition.

Its timing is such that it is asserted after the R/W* is asserted, thereby eliminating the possibility of any buffer contention between the 68020 and the buffer chips. This is illustrated in Figure 9-6, including the DBEN* timing specification

The DBEN* is a tri-state signal that is in a high-impedance state when the 68020 grants the bus to another bus master. The external pull-up resistor ensures that the data buffers are turned

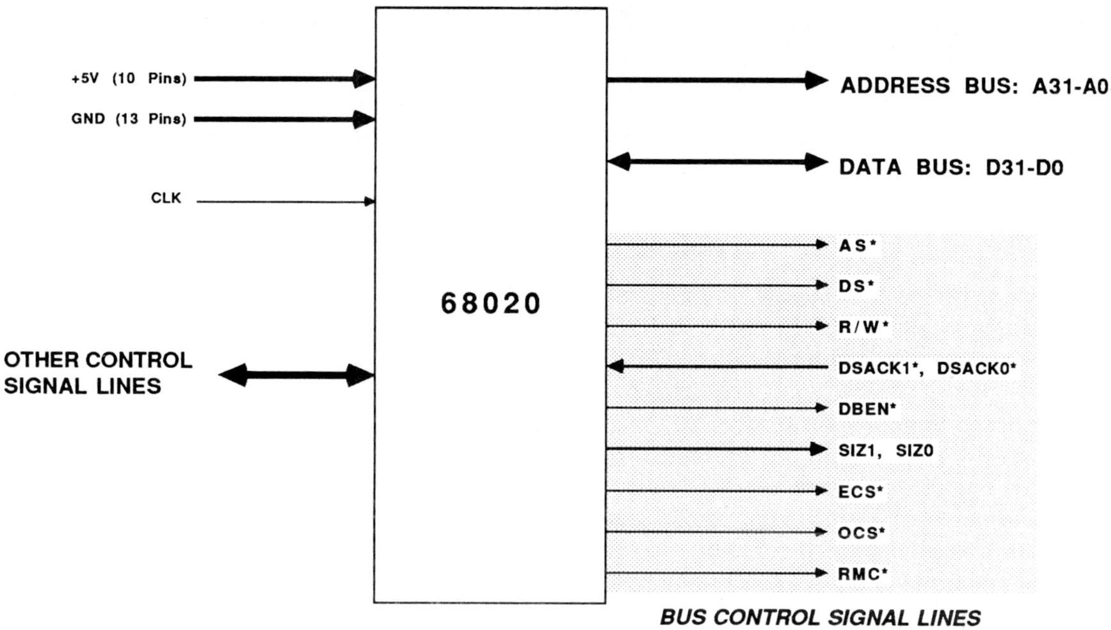

Figure 9-5 Bus Control Signals of the 68020.

off when the 68020 is not the bus master.

It is important to note that if DBEN∗ is used to enable external data buffers, no peripheral devices can be connected between these buffers and the 68020 (i.e., to unbuffered D31-D0).

Early Cycle Start (ECS∗) This output signal is asserted during the first half a clock cycle of every bus cycle in order to provide the earliest indication that the 68020 *may* be starting a bus cycle. For example, during an instruction fetch, the 68020 may initiate a bus cycle and place valid address, size, and function codes on the bus and then assert the ECS∗. In the case of cache hit, the bus cycle is aborted and the AS∗ is not asserted. Therefore, to guarantee that a bus cycle is in progress, the ECS∗ has to be later validated by the AS∗.

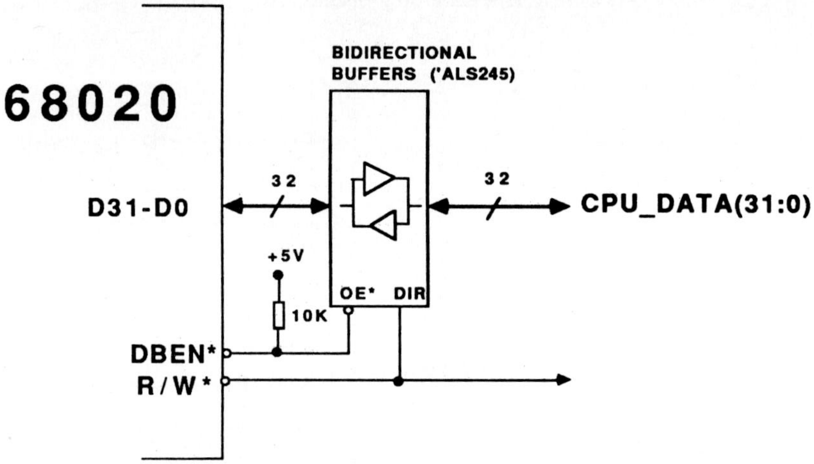

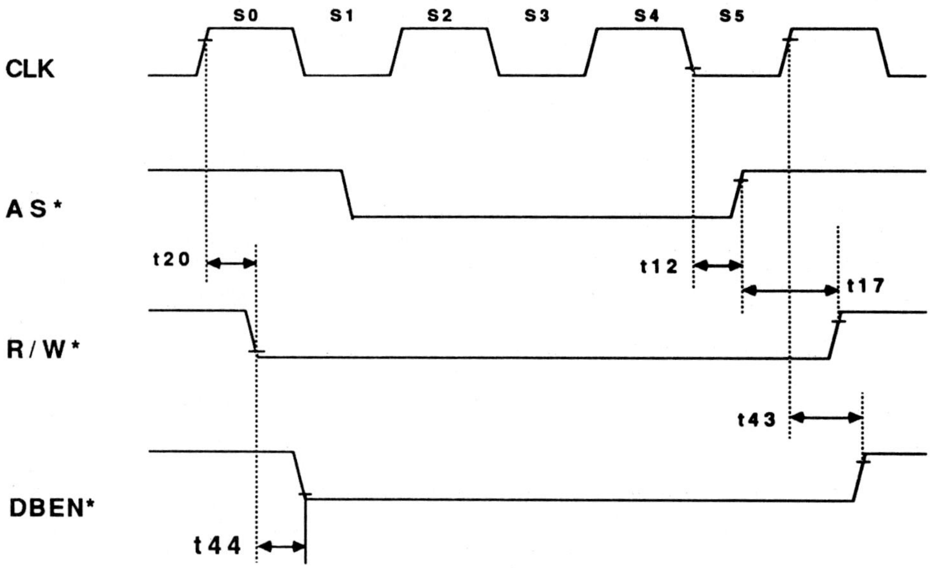

WRITE BUS-CYCLE

Parameter	Characteristic	Min	Max	Units
t12	Clock Low to AS* Negated	0	30	nsec.
t17	AS* Negated to R/W* High	15	—	nsec.
t20	Clock High to R/W* Low	0	30	nsec.
t43	Clock High to DBEN* Negated (Write)	0	30	nsec.
t44	R/W* Low to DBEN* Asserted (Write)	15	—	nsec.

Figure 9-6 The DBEN* Operation and Timing.

Operand Cycle Start (OCS*)	This output signal is similar to the ECS* and has the same timing, except it is asserted only during the first bus cycle of a multiple bus cycle operand transfer. For example, if a 32-bit operand is being read from a 16-bit port in two consecutive bus cycles, then the ECS* is asserted at each bus cycle, but the OCS* is asserted only during the first one.
Read-Modify-Write Cycle (RMC*)	This output signal indicates that the current bus cycle is an indivisible transfer cycle. This signal stays asserted during the entire read-modify-write operation. This type of special bus cycle is used only by the multiple processor instructions—the TAS, the CAS, and the CAS2. The use of this signal was necessary because during a CAS2 instruction, multiple addresses are used so the AS* cannot stay asserted. The RMC* signal is intended to ensure operand integrity in a multiple processor environment.

Figure 9-7 gives the timing of the 68020 bus control output signals that have the same timing for both the read and write bus cycles. Since all outputs of the 68020 are synchronous to the clock input, the CLK signal is also shown here. The primary signal that defines a bus cycle and stays asserted for most of its duration is the *address strobe* (AS*). The address lines, function, and size codes have the same timing and become valid before the address strobe with a setup time of t11. They are held for t13 after the address strobe is negated.

The minimum clock period for the 16.7 MHz 68020 is 60 nanoseconds. This leaves 25 nanoseconds for a clock-low or high period for a perfectly symmetric clock waveform assuming the maximum rise and fall times. The parameter t6 is within the range zero to forty nanoseconds. This means that the address, function, and size codes can actually become valid as late as the state S1. Similarly, the address strobe is typically asserted at the beginning of state S1 but can be as late as the positive-going edge of state S2. These points will be important to remember in generating the DSACKn* and in optimizing for performance.

The *early-cycle-start signals*, ECS* and OCS*, are asserted around the negative-going edge of state S0 with a setup time of (t2–t6a) and a hold time of t12a. There is no timing relation given between the ECS* and the address, function, and size code signal lines. For example, in the worst case, the ECS* may be

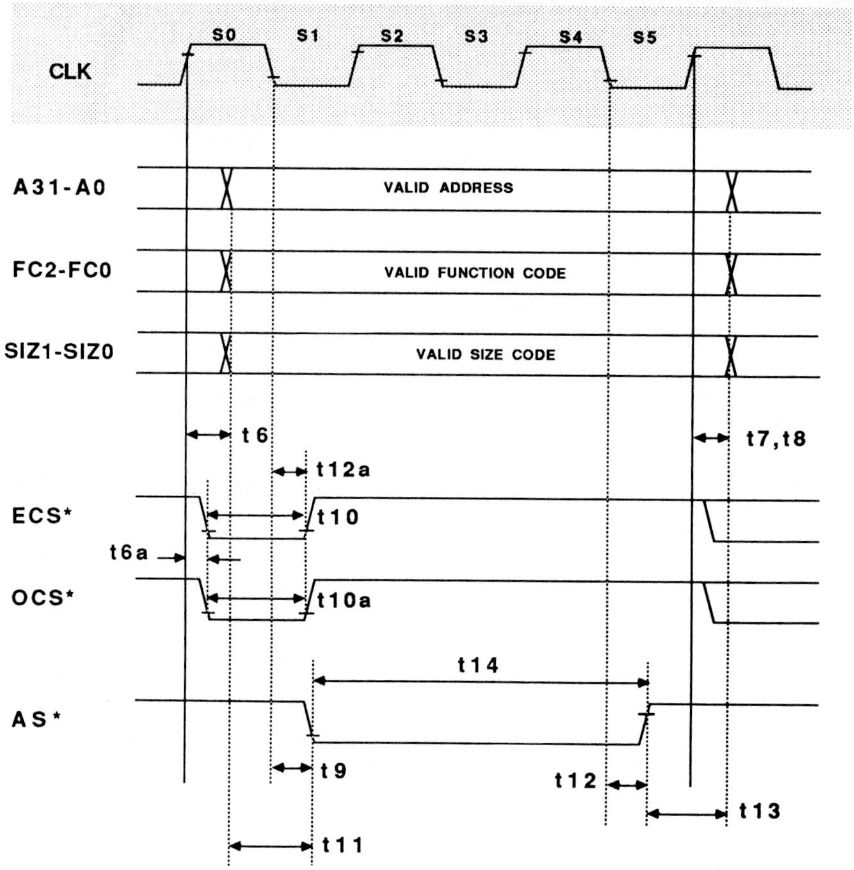

Parameter	Characteristic	Min	Max	Units
t6	Clock High to Address/FC/Size Valid	0	30	nsec.
t6a	Clock High to ECS*, OCS* asserted.	0	20	nsec.
t7	Clock High to Address/FC/Size in Hi-Z.	0	60	nsec.
t8	Clock High to Address/FC/Size invalid.	0	—	nsec.
t9	Clock Low to AS* Asserted.	3	30	nsec.
t10	ECS* Width Asserted.	20	—	nsec.
t10a	OCS* Width Asserted	20	—	nsec.
t11	Address/FC/Size Valid to AS* Asserted.	15	—	nsec.
t12	Clock Low To AS* Negated.	0	30	nsec.
t12a	CLK Low to ECS*/OCS* Negated.	0	30	nsec.
t13	AS* Negated to Address/FC/Size Invalid.	15	—	nsec.

Figure 9-7 68020 Output Signals Common to Read and Write Bus Cycles.

asserted at the beginning of S0, but the address lines become valid in state S1. This limits the usefulness of the ECS* and OCS* since we cannot initiate any address decoding or device access before {A31-A0, FC2-FC0, SIZ1-SIZ0} become valid.

All control inputs must be negated after the strobes {AS*, DS*} are negated with a timing of t28 as shown in Figure 9-8. This prevents misdetection of these signals in the next bus cycle. Otherwise, although not usual practice, an input signal such as DSACKn* may stay low for consecutive bus cycles when it is guaranteed that there are no wait cycles for any access.

It is usually necessary to buffer the output control signals, AS* and R/W*, (at least) because they will be used most by the peripheral circuits (see Figure 9-9). During the rest of our discussion in this chapter, we will use BAS* or CPU_AS* and CPU_WRITE* to refer to the buffered AS* and R/W*, respectively. It is also useful to have a "run" indicator that indicates that the 68020 is fetching operands and instructions. The "run" actually indicates an active bus cycle and it is displayed when the AS* is asserted.

DSACKn* Input Recognition. As we discussed in Chapter 6, the DSACKn* signals are driven by the addressed device to indicate two things to the 68020. When one or both of them are asserted, they signal that the data transfer is completed or will be completed shortly. Secondly, depending on the combination of {DSACK1*, DSACK0*} asserted, it indicates the port size of the device (refer to Table 6-1). For example, for 32-bit port, both DSACK1* and DSACK0*

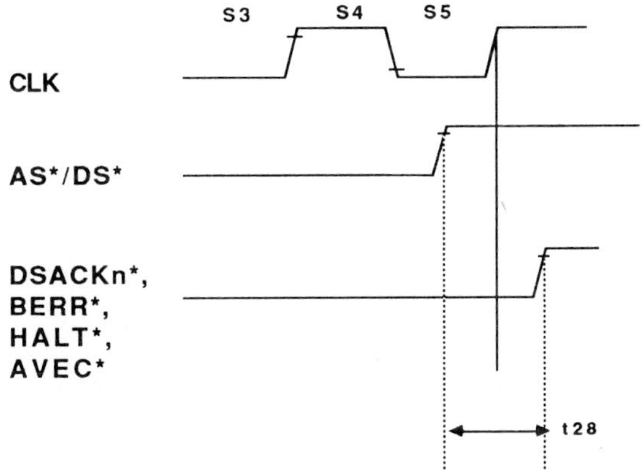

Parameter	Characteristic	Min	Max	Units
t28	AS*/DS* Negated to DSACKn*, BERR*, HALT*, AVEC* Negated.	0	80	nsec.

Figure 9-8 Negation Timing of Input Control Signals.

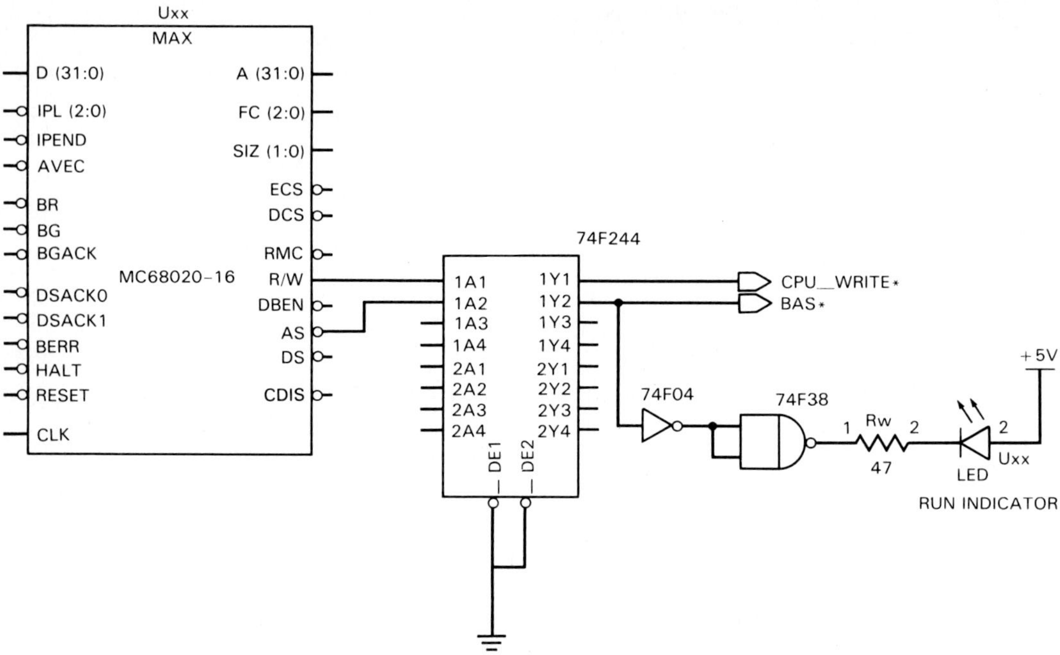

Figure 9-9 Buffering of AS*, R/W*, and "RUN" Indicator.

are asserted. The recognition of DSACKn* is illustrated in Figure 9-10 using the 32-bit port example. Only one of the two DSACKn* signals needs to meet the asynchronous setup time, t47a, of the 68020. The second one must meet the maximum skew requirement, t31a, which is 15 nanoseconds for the 16.7 MHz 68020. The skew requirement does not need to be met if *both* DSACKn* satisfy the setup time t47a (i.e., are stable during the sample window).

If the access time requirements cannot be met with zero wait-cycles, then the DSACKn* is delayed so that one or more wait-cycles are asserted. The next sample window of DSACKn* is during the next negative-going clock edge after S2 as illustrated in Figure 9-11.

9.2.2 Asynchronous Versus Synchronous Operation of Bus Cycles

As in the case of earlier members of the 68000 family, all the inputs of the 68020 may be synchronous or asynchronous with respect to the clock input. An asynchronous input has no fixed phase relationship to the CLK input and does not always meet the asynchronous setup and hold times of a sample window (t47a and t47b). Motorola specifies the timing parameters so that the designer may choose to operate their interface logic in synchronous or asynchronous manner as illustrated in Figure 9-12.

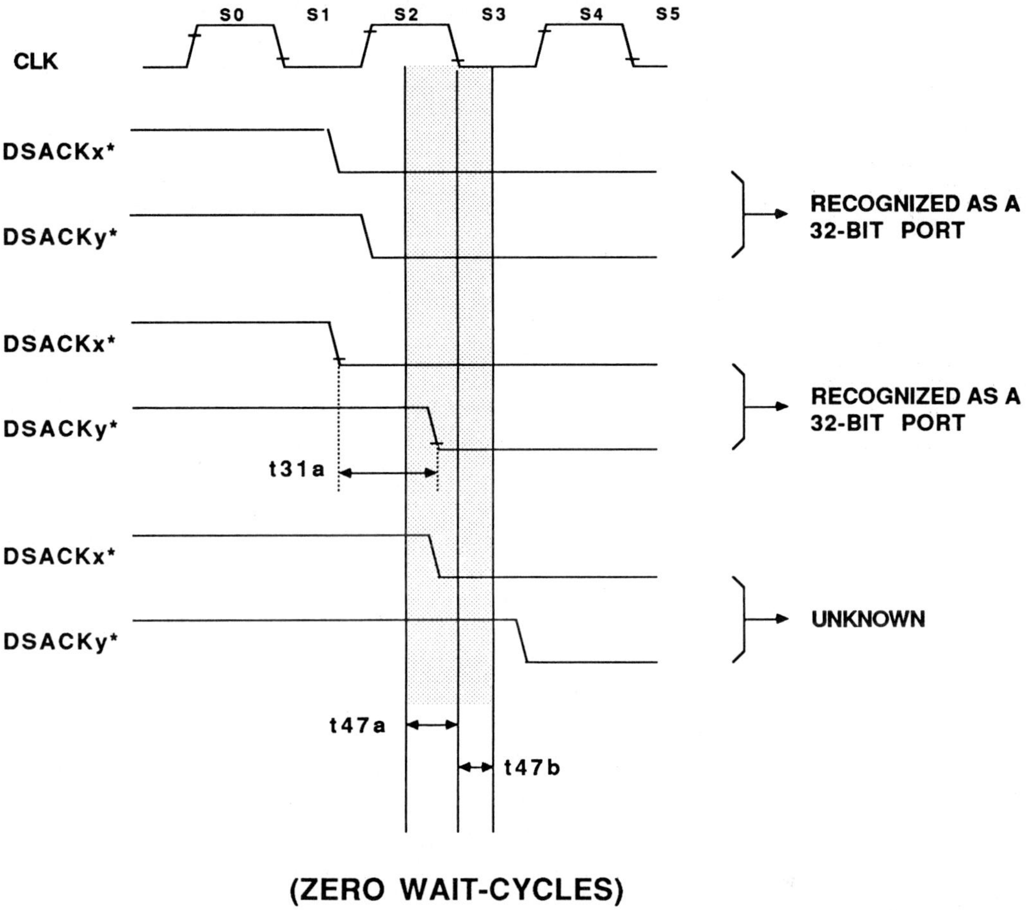

Parameter	Characteristic	Min	Max	Units
t47a	Asynchronous Input Setup Time.	5	—	nsec.
t47b	Asynchronous Input Hold Time.	15	—	nsec.
t31a	DSACKx* Asserted to DSACKy* Asserted.	—	15	nsec.

Figure 9-10 Recognition of the DSACKn* Inputs.

There are two requirements in the synchronous operation of a read bus cycle with no wait-states. First, the DSACKn* has to meet the setup and hold time requirements of t47a and t47b during its first sample window (negative-going edge of S2). Second, the read data has to be stable at the data pins of the 68020 with a setup time of t27 before the negative-going edge of S4. The synchronous interface requires that the CLK signal is used to guarantee both the DSACKn* and data meet the minimum setup times.

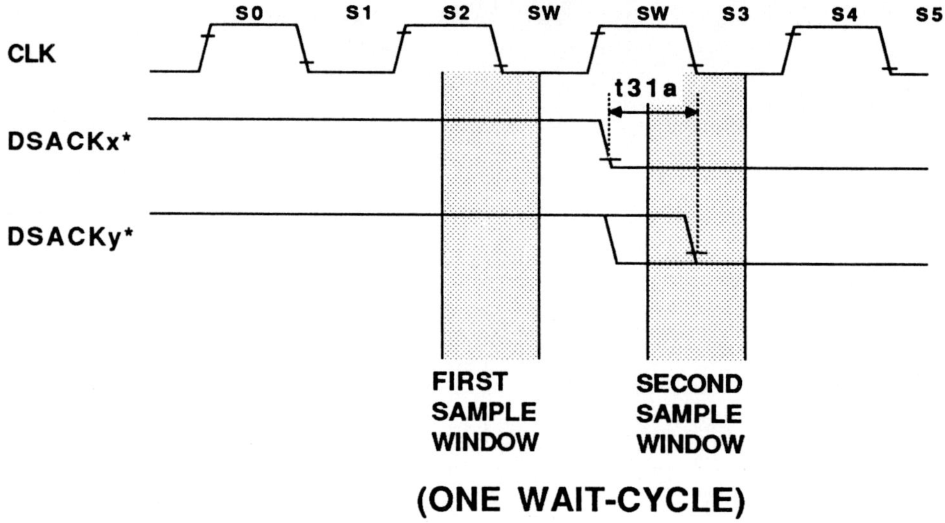

Figure 9-11 The DSACK Recognition With One Wait-Cycle.

On the other hand, in the pseudo-asynchronous operation of a read cycle, DSACKn* do not need to bear any relationship to the CLK input. However, it is required that DSACKn* do not precede the data by more than t31 and that the data is held valid until the address strobe AS* is negated (parameter t29). If the DSACKn* is not recognized in the first sample interval, then wait-cycles will be inserted until it is recognized as asserted. In other words, an asynchronous interface logic uses only the signal lines {AS*, DS*, R/W*, DSACKn*, BERR*, HALT*} to control a read or write cycle (i.e., the CLK is not used). As we discussed in Chapter 8, we used the term "pseudo" if we know the clock speed of the 68020, and therefore we can make certain assumptions about its timing parameter values. Otherwise, the interface is fully asynhronous.

Each approach has its advantages. These include:

1. It is usually easier to design and debug synchronous logic.
2. Since a synchronous interface logic is tightly coupled to the 68020's internal clock and operation, it will yield better performance with less interface logic.
3. In a synchronous design, it is more difficult to upgrade to a faster 68020. It is much simpler to upgrade in a pseudo-asynchronous design where the 68020 has a separate clock oscillator, assuming the parameter t31 is still met.
4. Asynchronous interface is necessary in accessing peripherals operating at a different clock frequency. For example, a disk controller chip or a DUART will require asynchronous interface.

It is important to remember that the interface logic such as the DSACKn* generation depends on the particular type of device we are interfacing to. Thus,

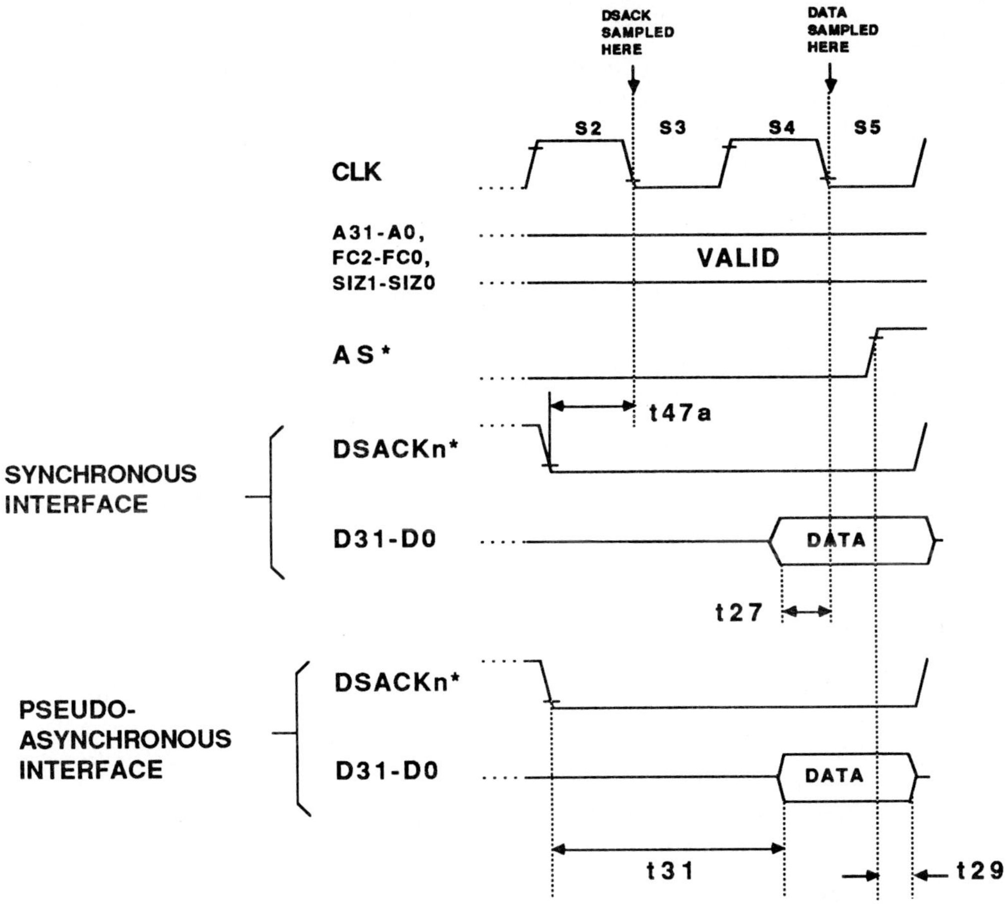

Parameter	Characteristic	Min	Max	Units
t27	Data-In Valid to Clock Low (Data Setup).	5	—	nsec.
t29	AS*/DS* to Data Invalid (Hold Time).	0	—	nsec.
t31	DSACKn* asserted to Data-in Valid.	—	50	nsec.

Figure 9-12 Synchronous versus Asynchronous Interface During a Read Bus Cycle.

in a typical system, there is usually a combination of synchronous and asynchronous interfaces.

The asynchronous operation parameter t31 does not guarantee that there are no wait cycles. It only ensures that the captured data is valid because t27 would be automatically met. It may be confusing that the DSACKn* is asserted in the middle of the sample window in the worst-case timing of asynchronous operation. This is because

$$t27 + t31 = 55 \text{ nsec.}$$

for a 16.67 MHz clock frequency (t1 = 60 nsec.). Therefore, t31 does not guarantee that the DSACKn* will be recognized in the first sample window. However, such a specification of timing parameters are necessary for the capture of data in asynchronous operation. For example, consider the case when the DSACKn*-to-Data-Valid is equal to

$$65 \text{ nsec.} > t31 = 50 \text{ nsec.}$$

Since we do not know when the DSACKn* are asserted with respect to the clock edge, this may cause incorrect operation. The error occurs when the DSACKn* is asserted in the middle of the sample window but is still recognized. Then, the data setup time of t27 would not be met.

9.2.3 Read Bus Cycle

The read cycle timing is shown in Figure 9-13. The signal lines (R/W*, DS*, D31-D0} are highlighted to indicate their timing during the read bus cycles. These three are the only signal lines that differ between a read and a write cycle assuming the same number of wait-cycles for both.

The data strobe, DS*, is asserted concurrently with the address strobe with a skew of t9a for their assertion. The R/W* is set high typically during the state S0 but may be as late as state S1. It is guaranteed to be held high for t17 after the strobes {AS* and DS*} are negated.

Before we can initiate an access to a device, we need a minimum of {A31-A0, FC2-FC0, SIZ1-SIZ0, R/W*} signal lines to be valid. For a 16 MHz 68020, this means

$$\max(t6_{max}, t18_{max}) = 30 \text{ nsec.}$$

The other important parameter is the address strobe which must qualify any bus access. The worst-case timing for the AS* is

$$t9_{max} = 30 \text{ nsec.}$$

for 16 MHz 68020. In accessing a memory type device, it is useful to calculate the two following parameters:

$$t_{AVDV} = \text{Address-Valid-to-Data-Valid.}$$

$$t_{SADV} = \text{Address-Strobe-Asserted-to-Data-Valid.}$$

These timing parameters are measured at the pins of the 68020 and include the following factors:

1. Address/data and other control signal external buffer propagation delays.
2. Address decoding time.
3. Memory/device access time.

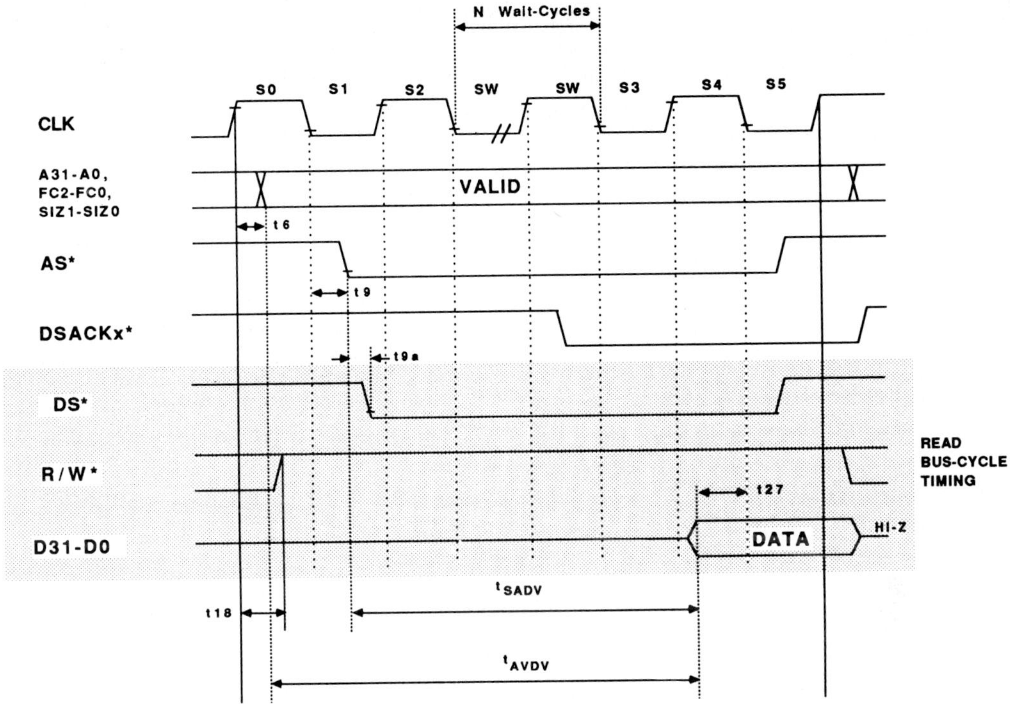

Parameter	Characteristic	Min	Max	Units
t9a	AS* to DS* Assertion During Read Cycle	–15	+15	nsec.
t17	R/W* Hold Time after AS*/DS* Negated.	15	—	nsec.
t18	Clock High to R/W* High.	0	30	nsec.
t21	R/W* High to AS* Asserted.	15	—	nsec.

Figure 9-13 Read Bus Cycle Timing.

In general, we have the following for a read cycle:

$$t_{AVDV} = (3 + N) * t1 - t6 - t27 - t2 - t4 \quad \text{(Eq. 9-1)}$$

and

$$t_{SADV} = (2 + N) * t1 - t27 - t9 \quad \text{(Eq. 9-2)}$$

where:

N: Is the number of wait-cycles. N = 0, 1, 2, and so on.

The parameter t_{AVDV} is typically more important in accessing static memory devices since a read access to these devices can be started and may later be validated by the address strobe. For the dynamic devices, however, t_{SADV} is more critical because a bus cycle must be validated with the address strobe before an access can be initiated. Table 9-1 gives the values for these parameters for zero to two wait-cycles.

9.2.4 Write Bus Cycle

The write bus cycle is similar to the read bus cycle, except that the R/W* is asserted at the beginning of the bus cycle and the data strobe DS* is asserted after the 68020 places the data on the bus. The write bus cycle timing is shown in Figure 9-14. The 68020 provides a data setup time of t26 before asserting the DS*, and the data is held valid for t25 after the {AS*, DS*} are negated. The data strobe is asserted one clock cycle after the address strobe, t9 after the negative-going edge of state S2. This allows ample time to do address decoding qualified with the AS* with respect to the read cycle.

There are two types of peripheral devices. Some devices require that the data be valid before an access can be started. The majority of the peripheral devices allow the starting of an access before the data is placed on the bus. The system performance is typically determined by the latter category.

The critical parameters for write access time are

$$t_{DVASH} = \text{Data-Valid to Address-Strobe High.}$$

$$t14 = \text{AS* Low Time.}$$

The parameter t_{DVASH} is important for interfacing to SRAM devices. This is because SRAM devices require a certain data setup time before their chip-select signal is negated.

The minimum t14 is 100 nanoseconds for a zero wait-cycle. We saw in the previous section that the total access time requirement is 85 nanoseconds for read bus cycle with zero wait-cycles. This means that the read and write cycle access time requirements are about the same. This is important because it means that we could design such that read and write bus cycles have the same number of wait-cycles.

TABLE 9-1 READ CYCLE ACCESS TIMES FOR MC68020RC16

Parameter	$N = 0$	$N = 1$	$N = 2$	Units
t_{AVDV}	116	176	236	nsec.
t_{SADV}	85	145	205	nsec.

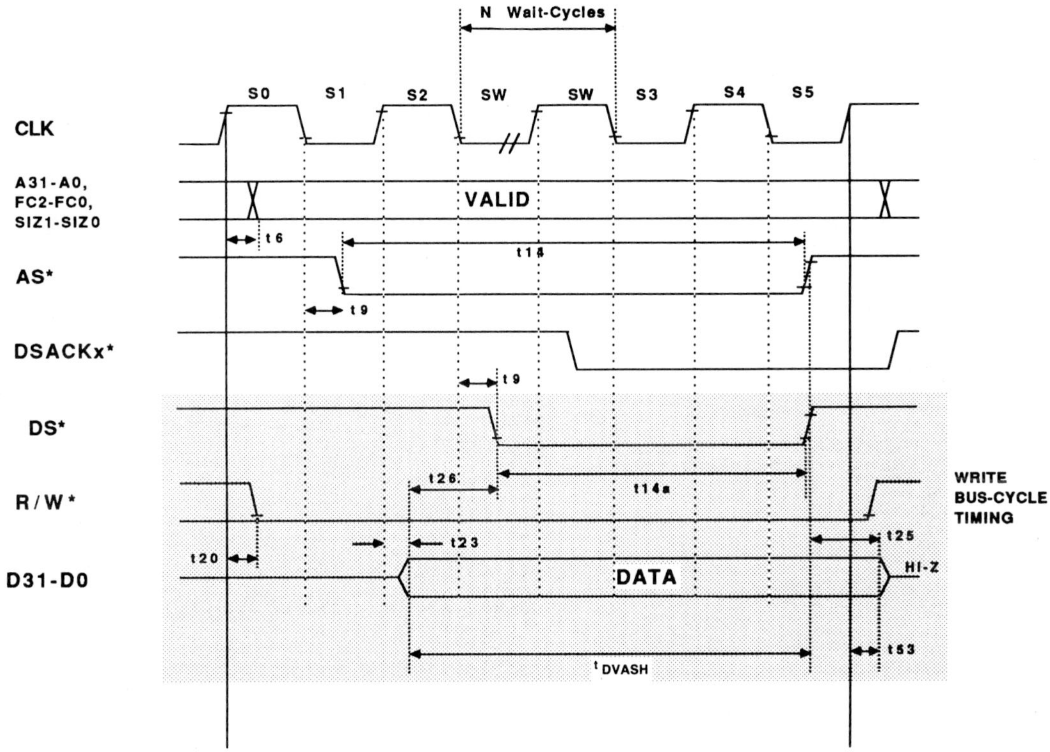

Parameter	Characteristic	Min	Max	Units
t9	Clock Low to AS*/DS* Asserted.	3	30	nsec.
t14a	DS* Low Duration During Write.	40	—	nsec.
t17	R/W* Hold Time after AS*/DS* Negated.	15	—	nsec.
t20	Clock High to R/W* Low.	0	30	nsec.
t23	Clock High to Data-out Valid.	—	30	nsec.
t25	DS* Negated to Data-out Invalid.	15	—	nsec.
t26	Data-out Valid to DS* Asserted.	15	—	nsec.
t53	Data-out Hold From Clock High.	0	—	nsec.

Figure 9-14 Write Bus Cycle Timing.

9.3 TYPES OF BUS CYCLES AND FUNCTION CODE SIGNAL LINES

The 68020 has four types of bus cycles. These are:

Read Bus Cycle	This type of bus cycle is used to read a data operand or to fetch an instruction from an external device.
Write Bus Cycle	This is used to write a data operand to an external device.
Read-Modify-Write Bus Cycle	This is basically a read followed by a write bus cycle. There are two inactive clock cycles in between the read and write as shown in Figure 9-15. This type of bus cycle is only used by the multiprocessor instructions. The RMC* is asserted for the duration of this bus cycle to indicate that this is an indivisible bus cycle. To ensure data integrity, no bus grant is asserted when there is a bus request. Also note that due to dynamic bus sizing the read and/or write might take multiple bus cycles each.
CPU Space Cycles	This is the same as a read or write bus cycle except it is used for special CPU operations that are listed below: a) Breakpoint acknowledge during a BKPT instruction. b) Access level control when using the CALLM-RTM instruction pair. c) Coprocessor communications that are transparent to the programmer. d) During interrupt acknowledge in order to read the user-vector number.

The 68020 indicates the type of bus cycle by the signal lines {FC2-FC0, R/W*, RMC*}. Note that the function codes are unchanged with respect to the 6801X as shown in Figure 9-16. The CPU-space cycles are recognized from all other bus cycles by the function codes (i.e., when FC2-FC0 = {HHH}). It is necessary to decode the CPU_SPACE* signal so that normal device accesses are disabled during the CPU-space bus cycles as we will see in the next section. Types of CPU space cycles are recognized by the coding of address lines as shown in Figure 9-17.

Generally, the FC2 reflects the status of the S-bit of the status register SR. Less importantly, the function codes also classifies a bus operation as program

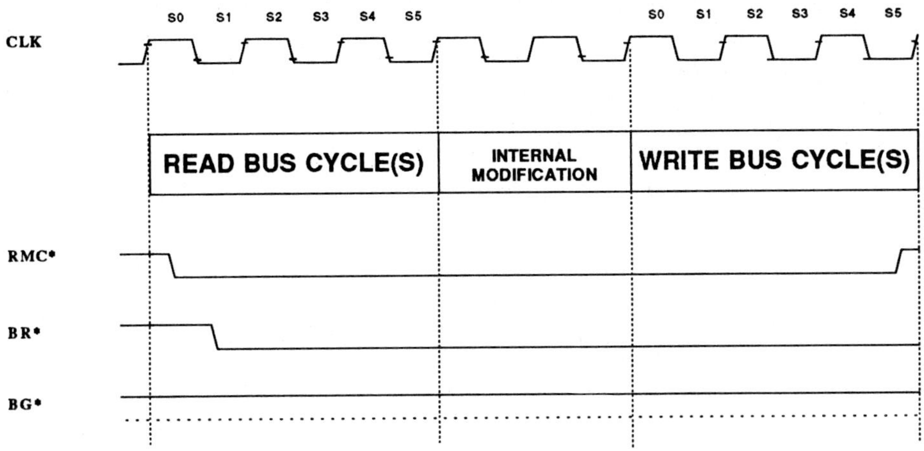

Figure 9-15 Read-Modify-Write Bus Cycle.

Function Code FC2	FC1	FC0	Reference Type
L	L	L	Unassigned, Reserved
L	L	H	User Data
L	H	L	User Program
L	H	H	Unassigned, Reserved[1]
H	L	L	Unassigned, Reserved
H	L	H	Supervisor Data
H	H	L	Supervisor Program
H	H	H	CPU Space

[1] Reserved for user definition.

Figure 9-16 Function Code Outputs of the 68020.

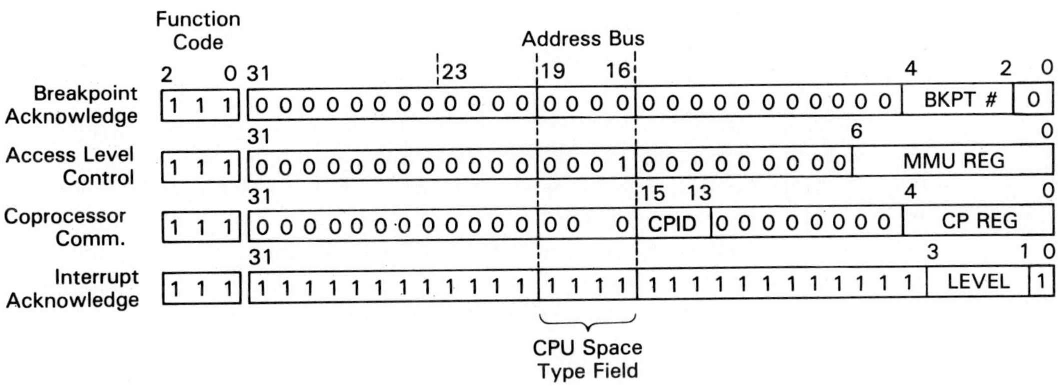

Figure 9-17 CPU-space Address Encoding.

or data accesses. Fetching reset vectors PC and SSP, instruction fetches including immediate data, fetches of operands of JSR/JMP instructions, or operands with PC-relative addressing modes are classified as program space accesses.[1] All other accesses are classified as data-space type.

9.4 ADDRESS DECODING

The 32-bit address bits select a location of the address space to be accessed during a bus cycle. The purpose of the address decoding is to select and enable the external device for a given address. If a device spans addresses of range $(0:2^N - 1)$, then it uses the address lines A0 through $A[N-1]$ to select a particular location of that device. Let the address decode signal of such a device be DECODE_DEVn*. In general, the DECODE_DEVn* is a function of the address bits, function codes, i.e.,

$$\text{DECODE\_DEVn*} = \text{FUNC}(\text{A31-A}[N], \text{FC2-FC0}) \qquad \text{(Eq. 9-3)}$$

as illustrated in Figure 9-18. The function codes are necessary so as not to decode any devices during the CPU-space cycles, other than for special CPU operations.

It is important to note that we did not use the AS* as part of the address decoding. Instead, we will qualify it after the address decoding with one of the strobes (AS* or DS*), as part of a device interface logic. This is usually necessary to meet the timing requirements of memory chips because this speeds up turning off or deselecting the addressed device at the end of a bus cycle. Generally, it also has another advantage. Since the address and function codes become valid before the AS*, this provides address decoding to proceed before the AS* is asserted, thereby reducing the overall access time requirements.

In general, a device decode signal, DECODE_DEVn* may cover multiple chips of the same kind. For example, one megabyte RAM will typically require more than one chip. This requires further decoding of addresses, and in this case, the DECODE_DEVn* should not be confused with the chip select (CS*) signal of the addressed device. Such further decoding also depends on the memory configuration (i.e., whether memory is 8-, 16-, or 32-bits wide as we are going to discuss later).

In decoding the device select, if a subset of the A31-A[N] address lines are used, it is referred to as *partial address decoding*. This means that the device will appear multiple times in the memory map of the 68020. Alternatively, we can choose to decode all address lines so that a device spans a single and unique location in the memory map. The advantage of partial address decoding is that it requires less logic. For example, if there are only four devices in a system (let us say, RAM, EPROM, and two DUARTs), we may decode only the upper two address bits. This allocates 1 gigabyte for each device—a significant overkill.

[1] See also Table 6-9.

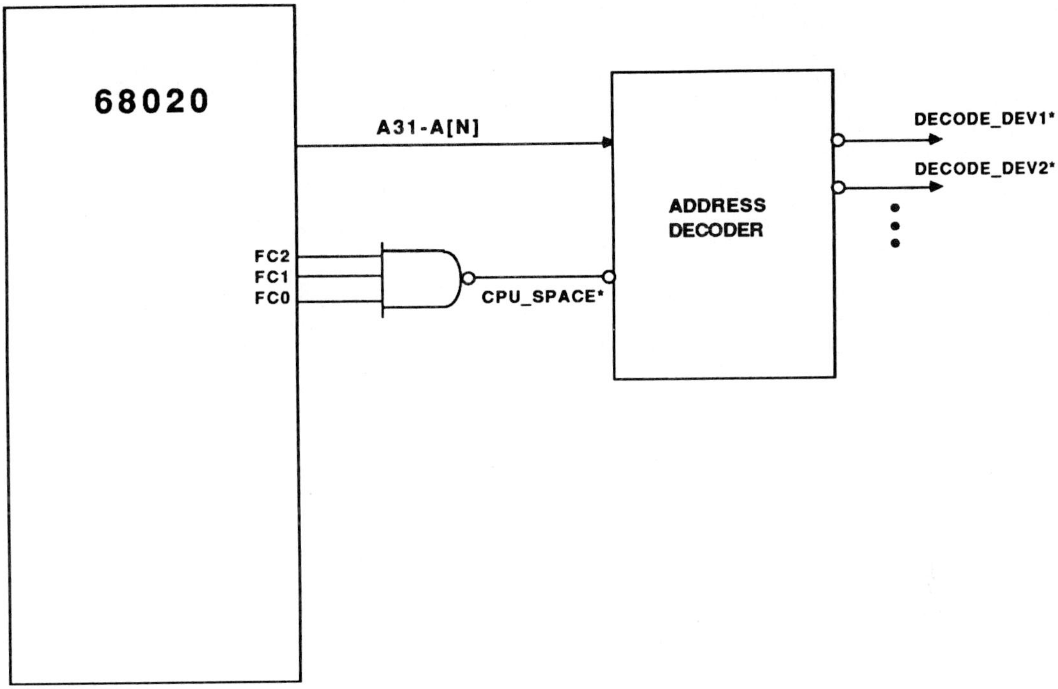

Figure 9-18 Address Decoding of Devices.

Such a partial decoding of addresses is not desirable for most but the simplest systems for several reasons. It makes system expansion very difficult. It also makes the system debug and field service more difficult since each device appears multiple times in the address space. Moreover, the incremental cost of logic for full address decoding is minimal with PLDs and other ICs available today.

The address decoder circuit may be implemented using several approaches. In any approach, the first step is preparing an address decoding table, an example of which is given in Table 9-2 using full address decoding. Three basic approaches of design are the following:

1. The address decoding logic can be implemented using a number of SSI gates such as AND, NAND, OR, NOR, and inverters. This is illustrated in Figure 9-19 for the implementation of Table 9-2.
2. Using comparators. One input of the comparator is fixed by pull-up resistors or grounded, as necessary. For example, comparator chip 74F521 may be used (see Figure 9-20). This chip can compare two 8-bit values and produces a single active-low decoded output if there is a match. The compared value is normally hardwired. To support connecting multiple decoders together, an active-low enable input is also provided. Figure 9-21 gives an implementation of Table 9-2 using this comparator chip.

TABLE 9-2 EXAMPLE ADDRESS DECODING TABLE

Device Type	Address Range	Address Lines (A31-A0) 31–28	27–24	23–20	19–16	15–12	11–8	7–4	3–0
ROM/EPROM (256 Kbytes) Expansion ROM:	00000000 – 0003FFFF 0003FFFF – 000FFFFF	LLLL	LLLL	LLLL	****	****	****	****	****
RAM (1 Mbytes)	00100000 – 001FFFFF	LLLL	LLLL	LLLH	****	****	****	****	****
DUART #1 ('68681)	00F00000 – 00F0000F	LLLL	LLLL	HHHH	LLLL	LLLL	LLLL	LLLL	****
DUART #2 ('68681)	00F10000 – 00F1000F	LLLL	LLLL	HHHH	LLLH	LLLL	LLLL	LLLL	****

Note: "*" means used by the device.

3. We may also program PLDs for the desired address decoding. This approach provides the minimum logic and maximum flexibility, an example of which is shown in Figure 9-22. Sample PLD equations are given in Figure 9-23.

9.5 DSACK GENERATION LOGIC

The DSACKn* generation involves two steps:

1. Generation of appropriate delay from the assertion of a device-select signal so that it meets the requirements for asynchronous or synchronous bus operation and the access time of a particular device. This will determine the number of wait-cycles.
2. Coding of the DSACKn* for a given port size. The port size is fixed for a given device and does not change dynamically, as we stated earlier.

This is illustrated in Figure 9-24. There are two types of peripheral devices. Most of the 68000 family peripheral chips provide a DTACK* output that can readily be used to generate the DSACKn* inputs. For example, the peripheral chips such as the '68681 DUART or the '68230 PI/T that have a 8-bit port size and provide a DTACK* output that can be connected directly to DSACK0* input of the 68020. Such peripheral chips interface asynchronously to the 68020, and has open-drain[2] DTACK* output that can be wire-ORed with other inputs and has to be pulled-up externally.

Other devices, such as RAM or ROM memory, require appropriate delay before asserting the DSACKn* inputs such that the device's access time require-

[2] Open-drain output is the CMOS equivalent of the bipolar open collector.

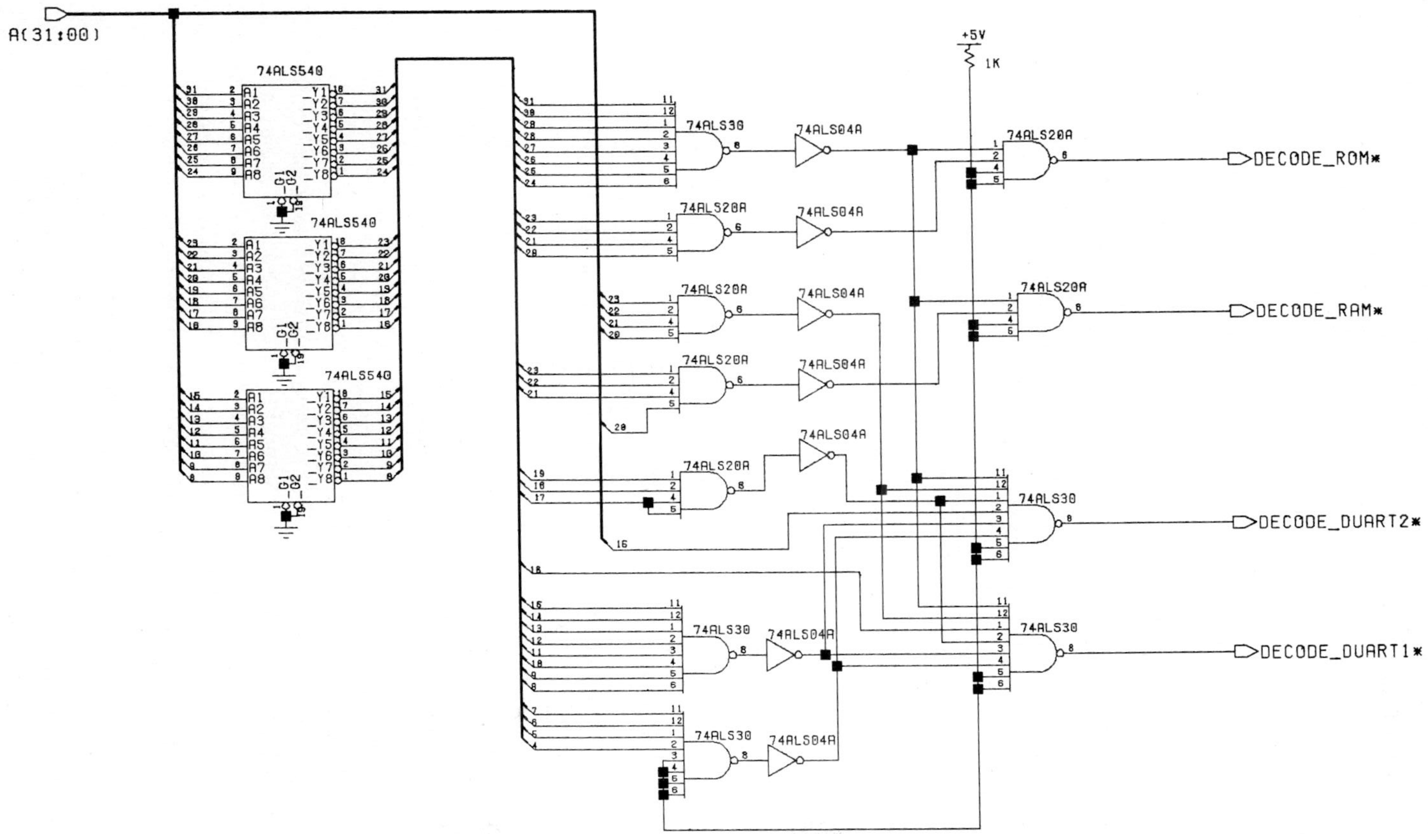

Figure 9-19 Address Decoding of Table 9-2 Using SSI-Gates.

LOGIC DIAGRAM

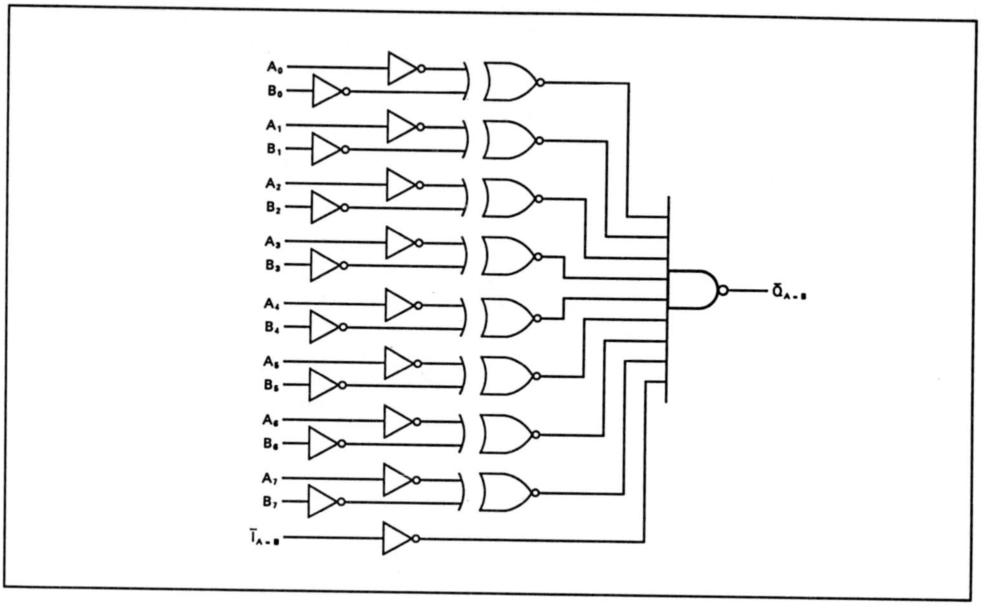

TRUTH TABLE

Inputs		Output
$\bar{I}_{A=B}$	A, B	$\bar{Q}_{A=B}$
L	A = B*	L
L	A ≠ B	H
H	A = B*	H
H	A ≠ B	H

H = High voltage level
L = Low voltage level
* $A_0 = B_0$, $A_1 = B_1$, $A_2 = B_2$, etc.

Figure 9-20 Summary of 'F521 Data Sheet. (Courtesy of Signetics.)

ment can be met under worst-case conditions. We saw earlier that the access times necessary are about the same for read and write cycles and will usually require the same number of wait-cycles. So, the address strobe AS* can be used in initiating the necessary delay times. The data strobe DS* could also be used, but it would make the write bus cycle to have one more wait-cycle since it is asserted one cycle later for write bus cycle.

The DSACKn* delay circuit is similar to the ones we discussed for the 68000. However, there is one important difference in the synchronous operation. In the 68000, the address strobe AS* is asserted after the positive-going edge of state

APPLICATION DIAGRAMS

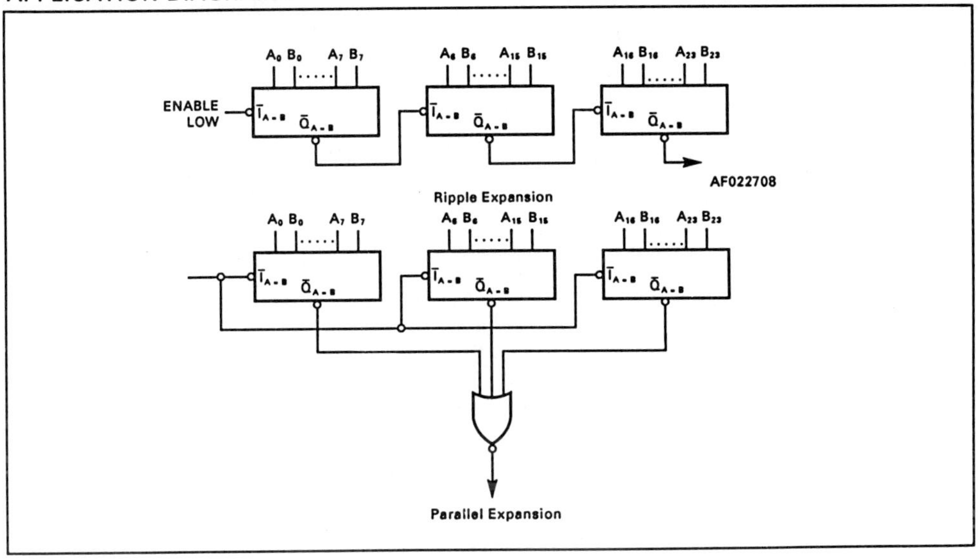

Figure 9-20 (cont.)

S1, and DTACK∗ is expected before the negative-going edge of S4 for zero wait-cycles. For the 68020, however, the AS∗ is asserted after the negative-going edge of S0, and the DSACKn∗ is expected before the negative-going edge of S2. In the worst case, this does not leave enough time to reliably latch the AS∗ at the positive-going edge of S1. Thus, a circuit like that shown in Figure 9-25 will not work efficiently. Instead, we can use the inverted sense of the 68020 clock as shown in Figure 9-26. For zero wait-cycles, the AS∗ is passed directly.

Example 9-1

Let us verify that the circuit of Figure 9-26 meets the asynchronous setup time t47a for the DSACKn∗ inputs of a 16 MHz 68020. We have the following data for zero wait-cycles from the datasheets[3]:

t9 (AS∗ assertion delay)	=	30 nsec. max.
'F04 Inverter delay	=	6.0 nsec. max.
'F38 OC AND-gate delay	=	5.5 nsec. max.
$t_{S1\text{-to-ACK}}$	=	Delay after negative-edge of S1.
	=	41.5 nsec. max.

$$t1 - t_{S1\text{-to-ACK}} = 17.8 \text{ nsec.} > t47a = 5 \text{ nsec.}$$

[3] From Signetics Fast Data Manual.

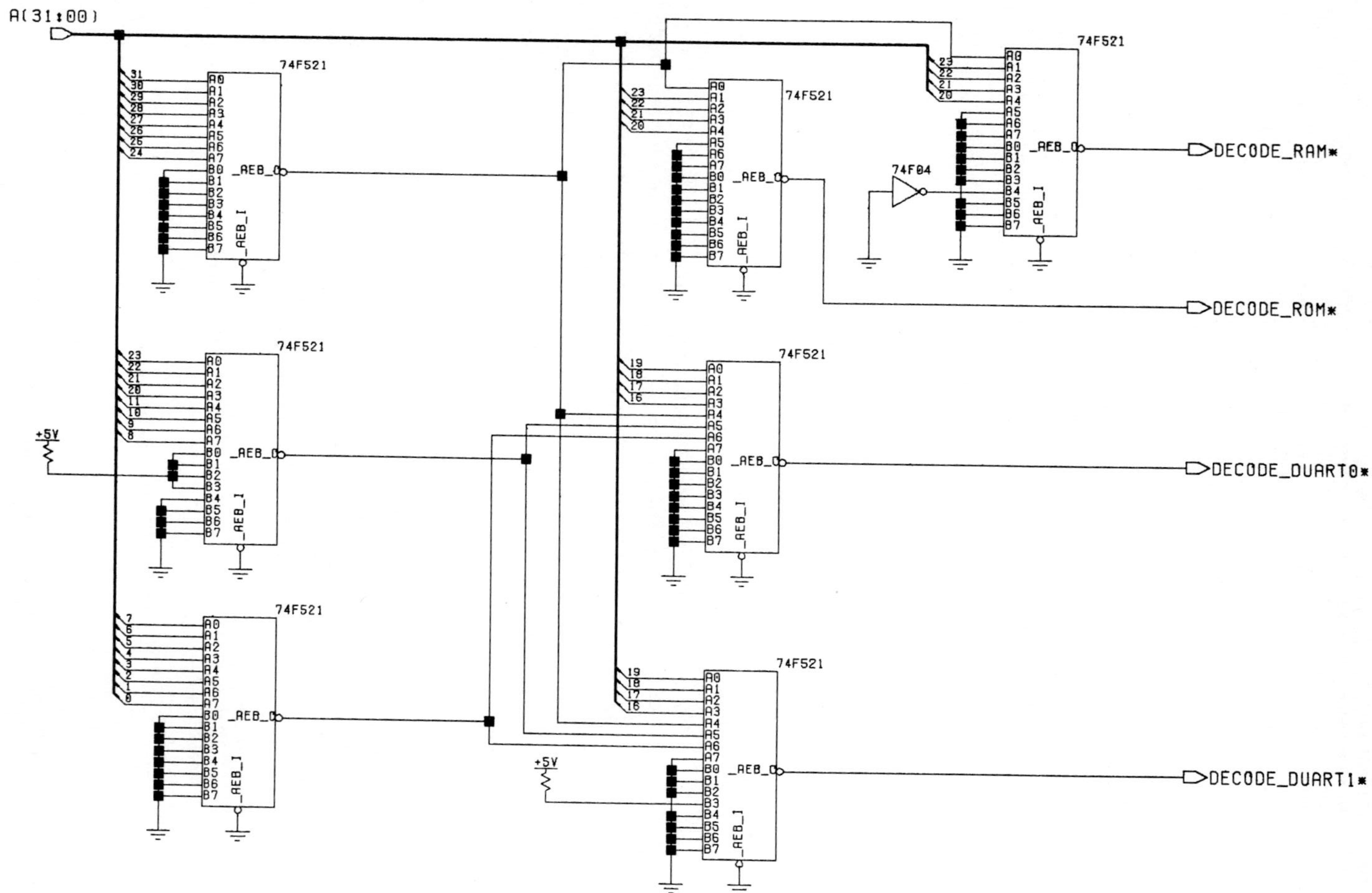

Figure 9-21 Address Decoding of Table 9-2 Using Comparators.

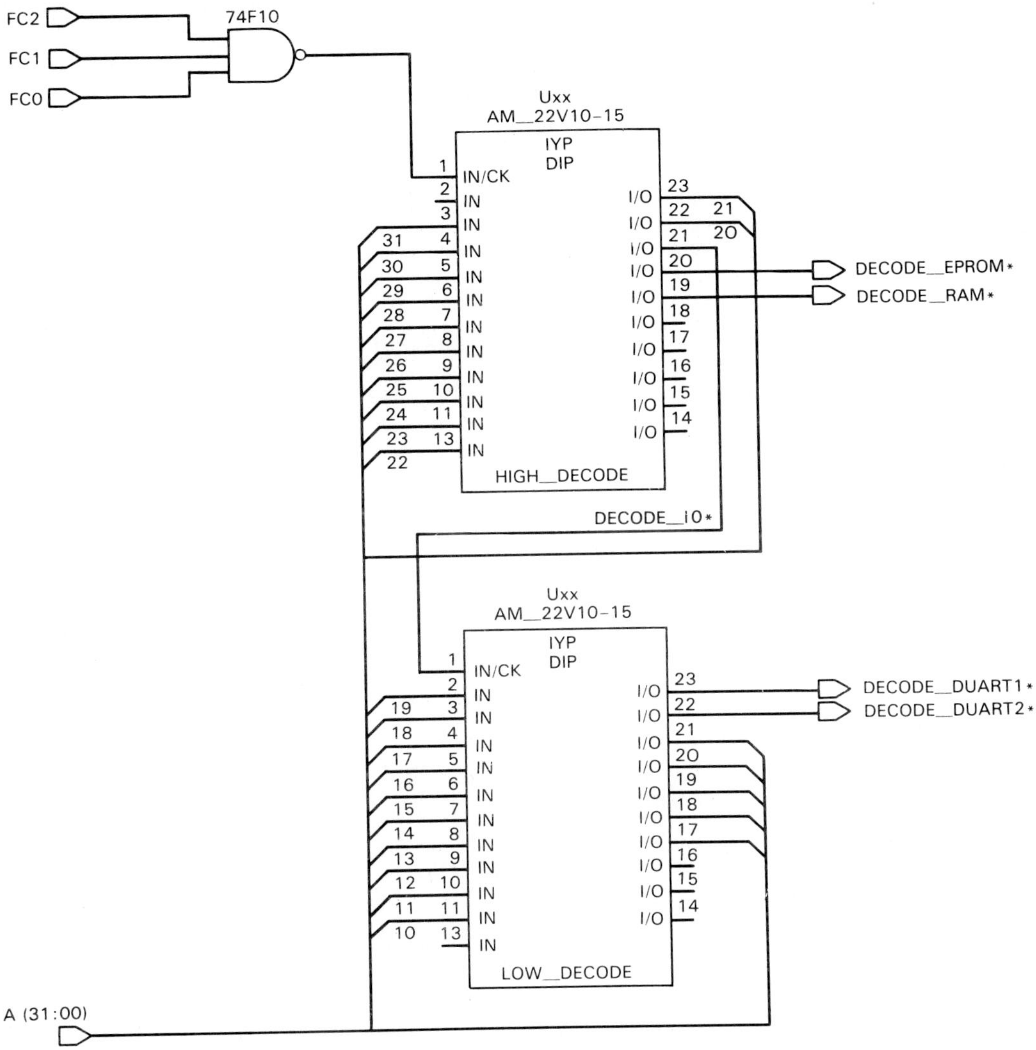

Figure 9-22 Address Decoding of Table 9-2 Using the '22V10 PLD.

For wait-cycles other than zero, we have the following critical path:

'F164 Clock-to-Qn Delay	=	11 nsec. max.
'F38 OC AND-gate delay	=	5.5 nsec. max.
$t_{SW\text{-to-ACK}}$	=	Delay after falling-edge of SW.
	=	16.6 nsec. max.

$$t1 - t_{SW\text{-to-ACK}} = 43.4 \text{ nsec.} \gg t47a = 5 \text{ nsec.}$$

```
PLD #1:
   Pin Definitions:

      Pin  1 = !CPU_SPACE           ;
      Pin  [3..13] = [A31..22]      ;
      Pin 23 = A21                  ;
      Pin 22 = A20                  ;

      Pin 21 = !DECODE_IO           ;
      Pin 20 = !DECODE_ROM          ;
      Pin 19 = !DECODE_RAM          ;

   Logical Equations:

      DECODE_IO  =   !A31 & !A30 & !A29 & !A28 & !A27 & !A26 & !A25 & !A24 &
                      A23 &  A22 &  A21 &  A20 & !CPU_SPACE  ;

      DECODE_ROM =   !A31 & !A30 & !A29 & !A28 & !A27 & !A26 & !A25 & !A24 &
                     !A23 & !A22 & !A21 & !A20 & !CPU_SPACE  ;

      DECODE_RAM =   !A31 & !A30 & !A29 & !A28 & !A27 & !A26 & !A25 & !A24 &
                     !A23 & !A22 & !A21 &  A20 & !CPU_SPACE  ;
```

```
PLD #2:

   Pin Definitions:

      Pin  1 = !DECODE_IO              ;
      Pin  [2..11] = [A19..10]         ;
      Pin [21..16] = [A9..4]           ;

      Pin 23 = !DECODE_DUART1          ;
      Pin 22 = !DECODE_DUART2          ;

   Logical Equations:

      DECODE_DUART1 = DECODE_IO & !A19 & !A18 & !A17 & !A16 &
                                  !A15 & !A14 & !A13 & !A12 &
                                  !A11 & !A10 & !A9  & !A8  &
                                  !A7  & !A6  & !A5  & !A4   ;

      DECODE_DUART2 = DECODE_IO & !A19 & !A18 & !A17 &  A16 &
                                  !A15 & !A14 & !A13 & !A12 &
                                  !A11 & !A10 & !A9  & !A8  &
                                  !A7  & !A6  & !A5  & !A4   ;
```

Figure 9-23 Sample PLD Definitions For Figure 9-20.

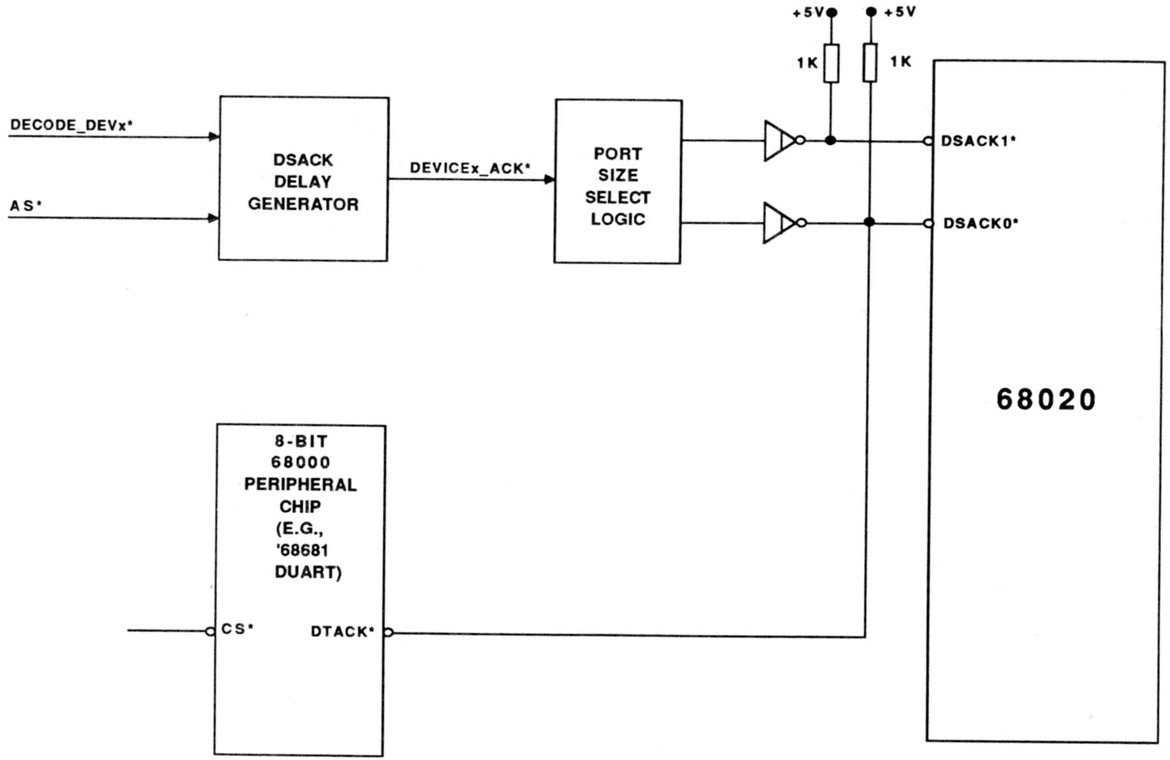

Coding of DSACKn*:

DSACK1*	DSACK0*	Result
H	H	Insert Wait-cycles.
H	L	Terminate Bus Cycle: 8-bit Port.
L	H	Terminate Bus Cycle: 16-bit Port.
L	L	Terminate Bus Cycle: 32-bit Port.

Figure 9-24 Illustration of DSACK Generation.

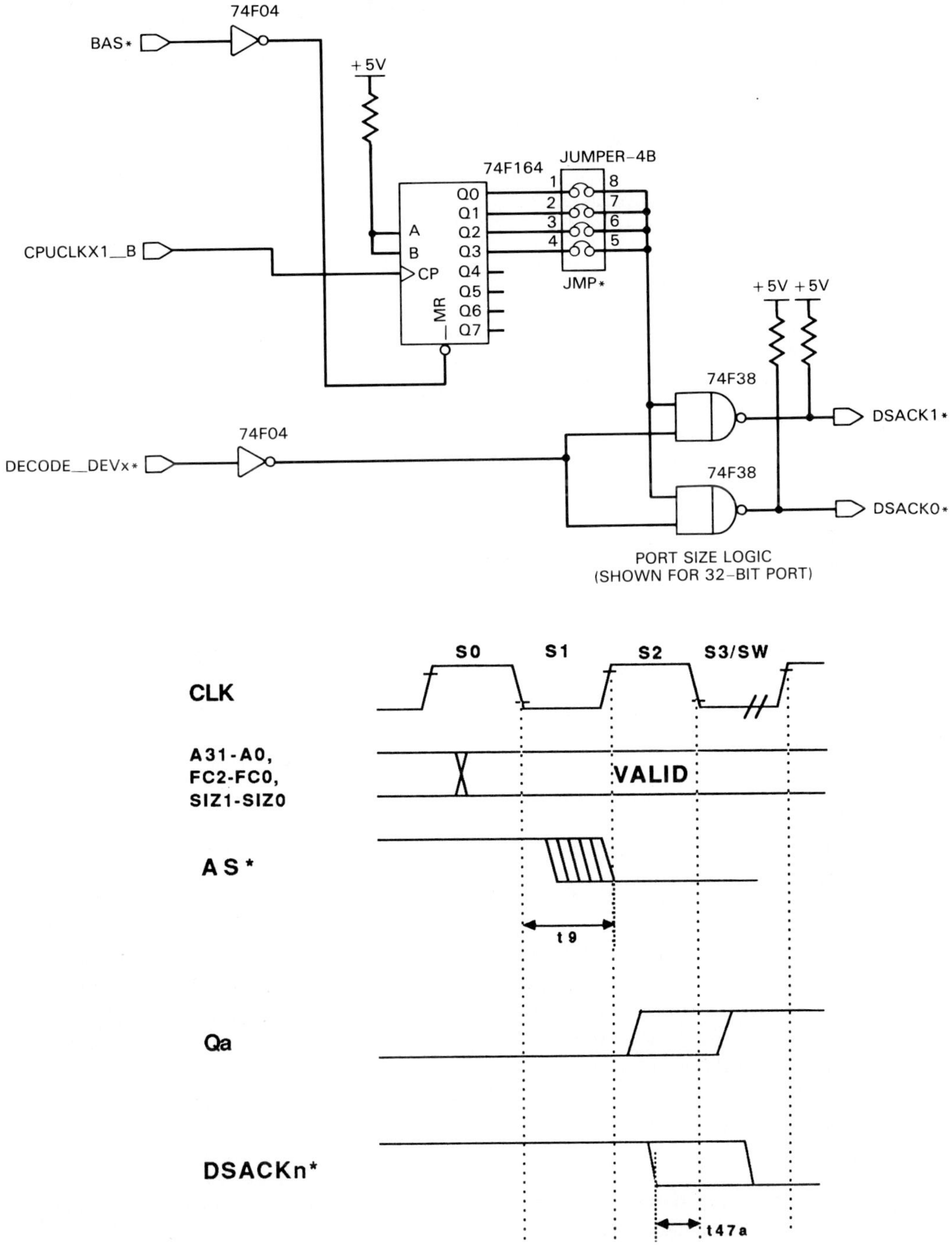

Figure 9-25 Not efficient DSACK Delay Generation.

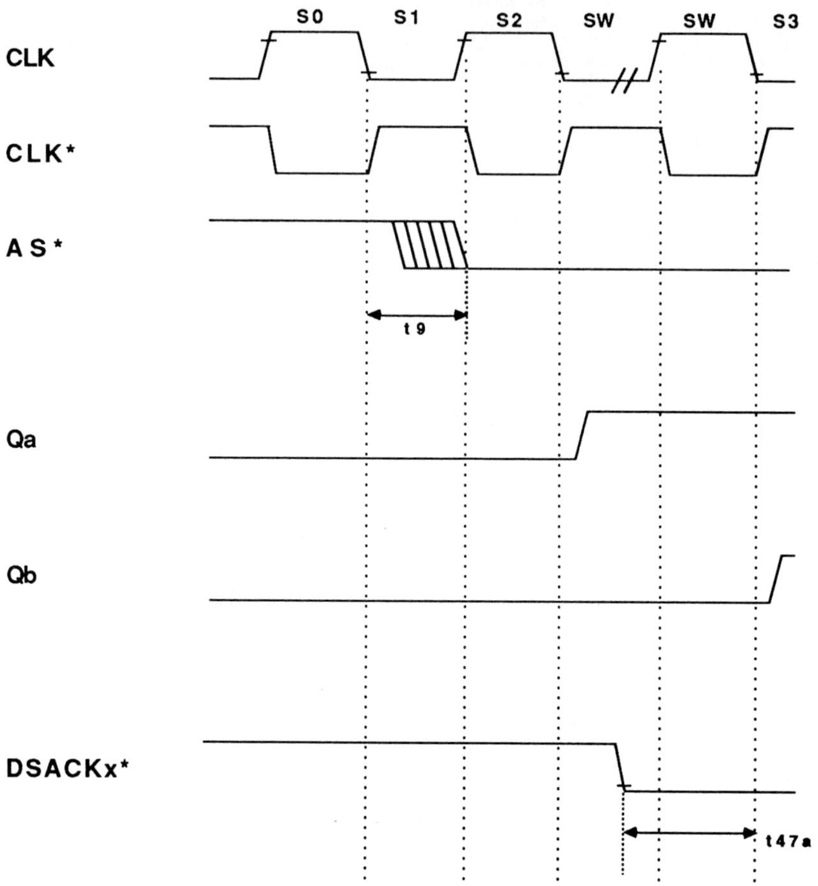

Figure 9-26 Correct DSACK Interface Circuit.

Instead of repeating the DSACK circuit of Figure 9-26 for multiple devices, we may combine them into one circuit by selecting the proper output delay for a given device. This is shown in Figure 9-27 for two devices. Normally, either selectable jumpers or permanent connections are used to select the number of wait-cycles of a particular device. The jumpers provide flexibility so that different speed versions of a device may be used. The port-size, on the other hand, is always "hard" connected for a given device.

PLDs may also be used to implement most of the DSACK circuit as the next example will illustrate.

Example 9-2

The circuit shown in Figure 9-28 replaces the logic of circuit shown in Figure 9-27. Let us assume the following:

Device #1: 0 Wait-cycles.

Device #2: 2 Wait-cycles.

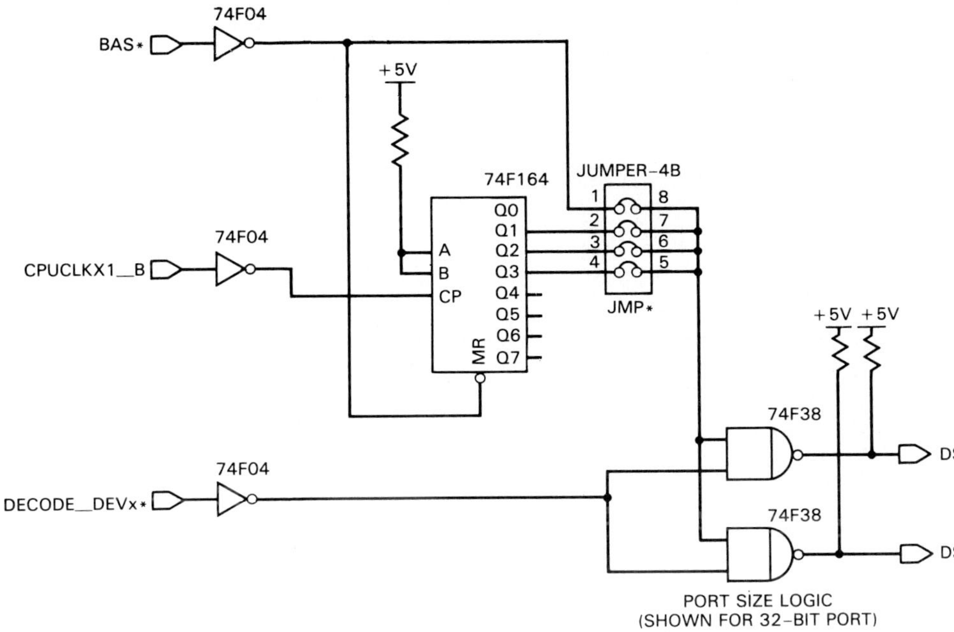

Figure 9-26 (cont.)

In order to meet the t47a setup requirement consistently, the PLD is connected to the inverted CPU clock. Assuming that the various DSACKn* inputs of the 68020 are wire-ORed, the DSACKn* output of the '22V10 must be normally disabled. We choose to enable DSACKn* outputs at the beginning of a bus cycle, if the '22V10 is to assert the DSACKn*. This relaxes the timing since output enable from a Hi-Z state usually takes longer. In the case of 22V10, the output enable time is 5 to 10 nanseconds longer than the clock to output delay, depending on the speed rating of the 22V10 (Refer to Appendix G that shows the 22V10 spec. sheet summary).

Figure 9-29 provides sample equations for this PLD. The timing is

$$t1 - (T_{cf} + T_{pd}) = t47a$$

This means that for 16 MHz 68020 we must have

$$T_{cf} + T_{pd} \leq 55 \text{ nsec.}$$

which requires us to use the "–35" version of 22V10.

9.6 DYNAMIC BUS SIZING AND BYTE-SELECT LOGIC

Consider the case that we have a 32-bit wide RAM memory and we are trying to write a single byte to it. This is illustrated in Figure 9-30. Since the 68020 always drives the entire 32-bit data bus during a write operation, external logic is nec-

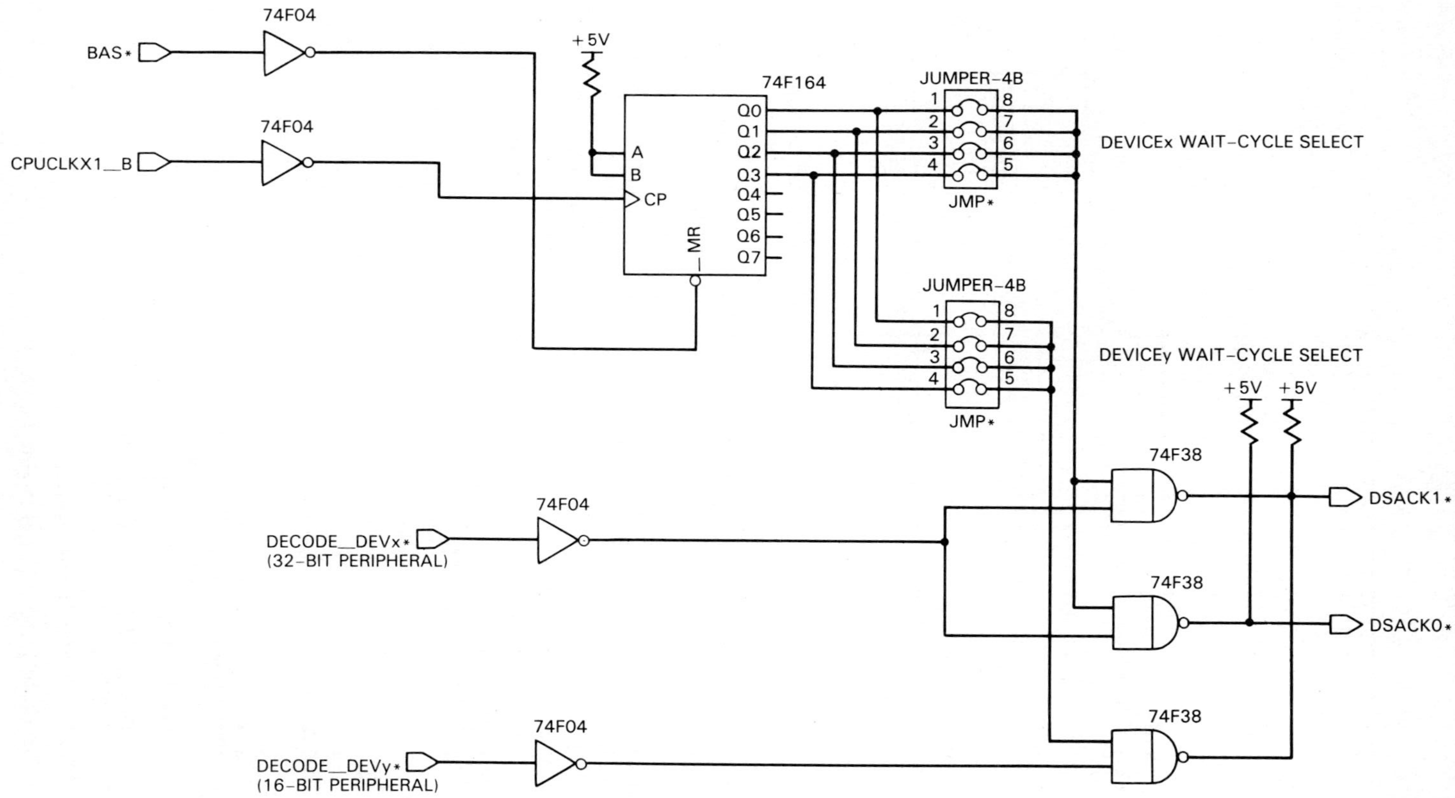

Figure 9-27 Generating DSACK for Multiple Devices.

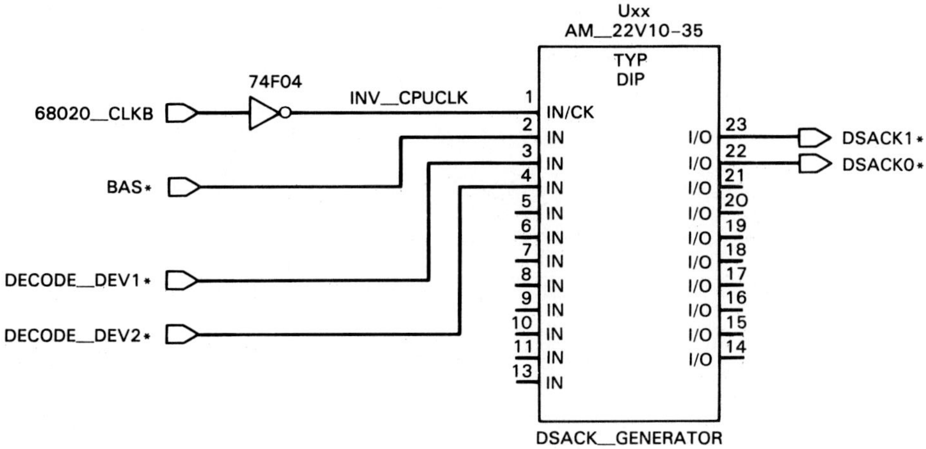

Figure 9-28 A PLD Implementation of the DSACK Interface Circuit.

```
Name      DSACK.PLD;
Partno    XXXX;
Date      XX/XX/XX;
Revision  XX;
Designer  XXXXX;
Company   XXXXX;
Assembly  XXXXX;
Location  XXXXX;

/**********************************************************************/
/* Purpose: This device generates DSACK1* and DSACK0* for two        */
/*          devices, as follows:                                      */
/*                                                                    */
/*               Device           WAIT_CYCLES      PORT SIZE          */
/*                DEV1                 0           Long-Word          */
/*                DEV2                 2             8-bits           */
/**********************************************************************/
/*  Allowable Target Device Types: 22V10*****************************/

/**  Inputs  **/

Pin   1  = INV_CPUCLK    ;      /* Inverted CPU Clock.               */
Pin   2  = !AS           ;      /* Address Strobe.                   */
Pin   3  = !DECODE_DEV1  ;      /* Device #1 Decode Signal.          */
Pin   4  = !DECODE_DEV2  ;      /* Device #2 Decode Signal.          */
```

Figure 9-29 Sample PLD File For the DSACK Circuit.

```
/**  Outputs  **/

Pin  23  = !DSACK1      ;     /* DSACK1* Three-State Output.    */
Pin  22  = !DSACK0      ;     /* DSACK0* Three-State Output.    */
Pin  21  = !DAS         ;     /* An intermediate output.        */
Pin  20  = !Qa          ;     /* An intermediate output.        */
Pin  19  = !OUTPUT_EN   ;     /* An intermediate output.        */

/**  Logic Equations  **/

DAS.D = AS        ;

QA.D  = DAS       ;

DSACK0 = DECODE_DEV1 & AS # DECODE_DEV2 & Qa & AS ;

DSACK1 = DECODE_DEV1 & AS ;

DSACK0.OE = OUTPUT_EN  ;
DSACK1.OE = OUTPUT_EN  ;

OUTPUT_EN =  (DECODE_DEV1 # DECODE_DEV2) & AS ;

QA.AR = !AS      ;
DAS.AR = !AS     ;

QA.SP = 'b'0     ;
DAS.SP ='b'0     ;
```

Figure 9-29 (cont.)

Instruction: `MOVE.B #$F5,(A0)`

Register A0 → (points to bit 24/23 boundary)

Bit # :	31 — 24	23 — 16	15 — 8	7 — 0
	NA	F5	NA	NA

NA: Not Affected.

68020 Signal Lines:
A0 = H
A1 = L
SIZ1 = L
SIZ0 = H

Byte Select Signals:
UUBYTE* = H
UMBYTE* = L
LMBYTE* = H
LLBYTE* = H

Figure 9-30 Example Byte-write to a 32-bit Memory.

essary so that only the affected bytes are selected. Thus, in general, we need a select or enable signal for each of the four bytes. Let us call these signals as follows:

UUBYTE*: Upper Upper Byte Select (Bits 31:24).
UMBYTE*: Upper Middle Byte Select (Bits 23:16).
LMBYTE*: Lower Middle Byte Select (Bits 15:8).
LLBYTE*: Lower Lower Byte Select (Bits 7:0).

During a write operation, only the selected bytes will be written; other bytes remain unchanged. During a read operation, all bytes could always be enabled because the input data multiplexer of the 68020 will only choose the bytes required by the operation.

The byte select signals are also necessary to support the dynamic bus sizing and misaligned operands. For example, in executing the instruction, `MOVE.L D0,$A001` with a 16-bit port, only the affected bytes must be selected (refer to Example 6-1, case 2). In general, the byte select signals are a function of the {A0, A1, SIZ1, SIZ0, R/W*} and the logical equations for them can be written by examining all possible byte-offsets with respect to a long-word boundary and operand sizes. This will be illustrated by the next example.

Example 9-3

Figure 9-31 shows the implementation of byte-select signals using a PLD such as '22V10. The A1-A0 defines the offset with respect to the long-word boundary. The signals UBYTE* and LBYTE* are specified to be used with a 16-bit port. Note that A1 is not required for a 16-bit port size.

In interfacing the 68020, it is important to remember that the 68020 makes certain assumptions in locating the data (refer to Figure 6-8) as follows:

1. All devices with 8-bit port size must be connected to the data bus signal lines D31-D24.
2. All devices with 8-bit port size may use the DS* as the byte select signal.
3. All devices with the 16-bit port size must be connected to data bus signal lines D31-D16.
4. All devices with the 16-bit port size must use the corresponding byte-select signals (i.e., UBYTE* and LBYTE*).

9.7 AVOIDING BUS CONTENTION

In any bus-oriented system a possible hazard is that two or more devices may simultaneously try to drive opposite logic levels on the same data bus. This is called *bus contention*. Most commonly, it occurs for brief time periods when one

```
Partno      BYTESEL ;
Date        XX/XX/XX;
Revision    XX;
Designer    XXXXX;
Company     XXXXX;
Assembly    XXXXX;
Location    XXXXX;

/*******************************************************************/
/*  Purpose: This PLD generates the byte select signals.           */
/*******************************************************************/
/*  Allowable Target Device Types: PAL 22V10                       */
/*******************************************************************/

/**  Inputs  **/

Pin   1 = SIZ1       ;        /* SIZ1-0: Remaining Operand Size.*/
Pin   2 = SIZ0       ;
Pin   3 = A1         ;        /* A1 and A0 Address Lines.       */
Pin   4 = A0         ;
pin   5 = !WRITE     ;        /* Same as R/W* signal of 68020.  */

/**  Outputs  **/

Pin  23 = !UUBYTE    ;        /* Upper Upper Byte Select.       */
Pin  22 = !UMBYTE    ;        /* Upper Middle Byte Select.      */
Pin  21 = !LMBYTE    ;        /* Lower Middle Byte Select.      */
Pin  20 = !LLBYTE    ;        /* Lower Lower Byte Select.       */
Pin  19 = !UBYTE     ;        /* 16-Bit Port Upper Byte Select. */
Pin  18 = !LBYTE     ;        /* 16-Bit Port Lower Byte Select. */
```

Figure 9-31 An Implementation of Byte Select Logic.

device is not completely turned-off before another device is turned on. Such an overlap in driving the bus causes large current spikes which increases the system noise, and furthermore, it may affect the long-term reliability of involved devices.[4] Good design practice is to avoid or minimize bus contention in a system.

One type of bus contention occurs between a buffer chip and a peripheral as illustrated in Figure 9-32. If the CPU_WRITE* changes its state when device-select, DEVICE_SEL* (connected to CS*) is still asserted, this may cause bus contention between drivers of the buffer and the peripheral. This possible timing overlap is due to the difference in turn-off and turn-on delays between the peripheral and the buffer chip. For example, if we use 'HCT245 as the data buffer to a peripheral, it is possible to have the data direction of the peripheral change before the 'HCT245, which has an output turn-off time of about 40 nanoseconds.

[4] See Reference 18 for further details.

```
/**  Logic Equations   **/

UUBYTE = !WRITE              #      /* Read Cycle- Enable all.            */
         !A1 & !A0           ;      /* Offset = 0 & Any size operand.     */

UMBYTE = !WRITE              #      /* Read Cycle - Enable all.           */
         !SIZ0 & !A1         #      /* Size = 2/4 & Offset = 0/1.         */
         !A1 & A0            #      /* Offset = 1 & Any size.             */
         SIZ1 & !A1          ;      /* Offset =0/1 & Size = 2/3.          */

LMBYTE = !WRITE              #      /* Read Cycle - Enable all.           */
         A1 & !A0            #      /* Offset = 2 & Any size.             */
         !SIZ1 & !SIZ0 & !A1 #      /* Offset = 0/1 & Size = 4.           */
          SIZ1 &  SIZ0 &  A0 #      /* Offset = 0/1 & Size = 3.           */
         !SIZ0 & !A1 & A0    ;      /* Offset = 1 & Size = 2/4.           */

LLBYTE = !WRITE              #      /* Read Cycle - Enable all.           */
         A1 & A0             #      /* Offset = 3 & Any size.             */
         !SIZ1 & !SIZ0       #      /* Any offset & Size = 4.             */
          SIZ1 &  SIZ0 & A0  #      /* Offset = 1 & Size = 3.             */
          SIZ1 & A1          ;      /* Offset = 2/3 & Size = 2/3.         */

UBYTE  = !WRITE              #      /* Read Cycle - Enable all.           */
         !A0                 ;      /* Not odd address.                   */
LBYTE  = !(!SIZ1 & !SIZ0 ) #        /* Size # 0.                          */
         A0                  ;      /* Offset = 1.                        */
```

Figure 9-31 (cont.)

In general, to avoid the bus contention, it is necessary that the chip-select or enable control signals of all connected devices be "enveloped" by the R/W* signal. This ensures that the drivers of all devices on the bus are turned-off *before* the data-flow direction is changed.

Another type of bus contention may occur between consecutive bus cycles. For example, if a peripheral device from which an operand was read does not turn off its bus drivers before the 68020 places an operand to be written on the bus in the next bus cycle, a bus contention as shown in Figure 9-33 will result.

The 68020 puts out the valid R/W* early in a bus cycle before we can decode a chip-select signal. Therefore, unless we delay the R/W* to the peripheral, it is not possible to have a bus contention at the beginning of the bus cycle. Bus contention is more likely to happen at the end of the bus cycle. To avoid any such bus contention, the 68020 timing specification requires that peripheral output drivers be turned off t29a after the AS* is negated. The maximum allowed value of t29a is 60 nanoseconds for the 16 MHz 68020. This is equivalent to requiring that data from the previous cycle must be turned off by the end of state S1 of next bus cycle. If the next bus cycle is a write operation, the data is placed on

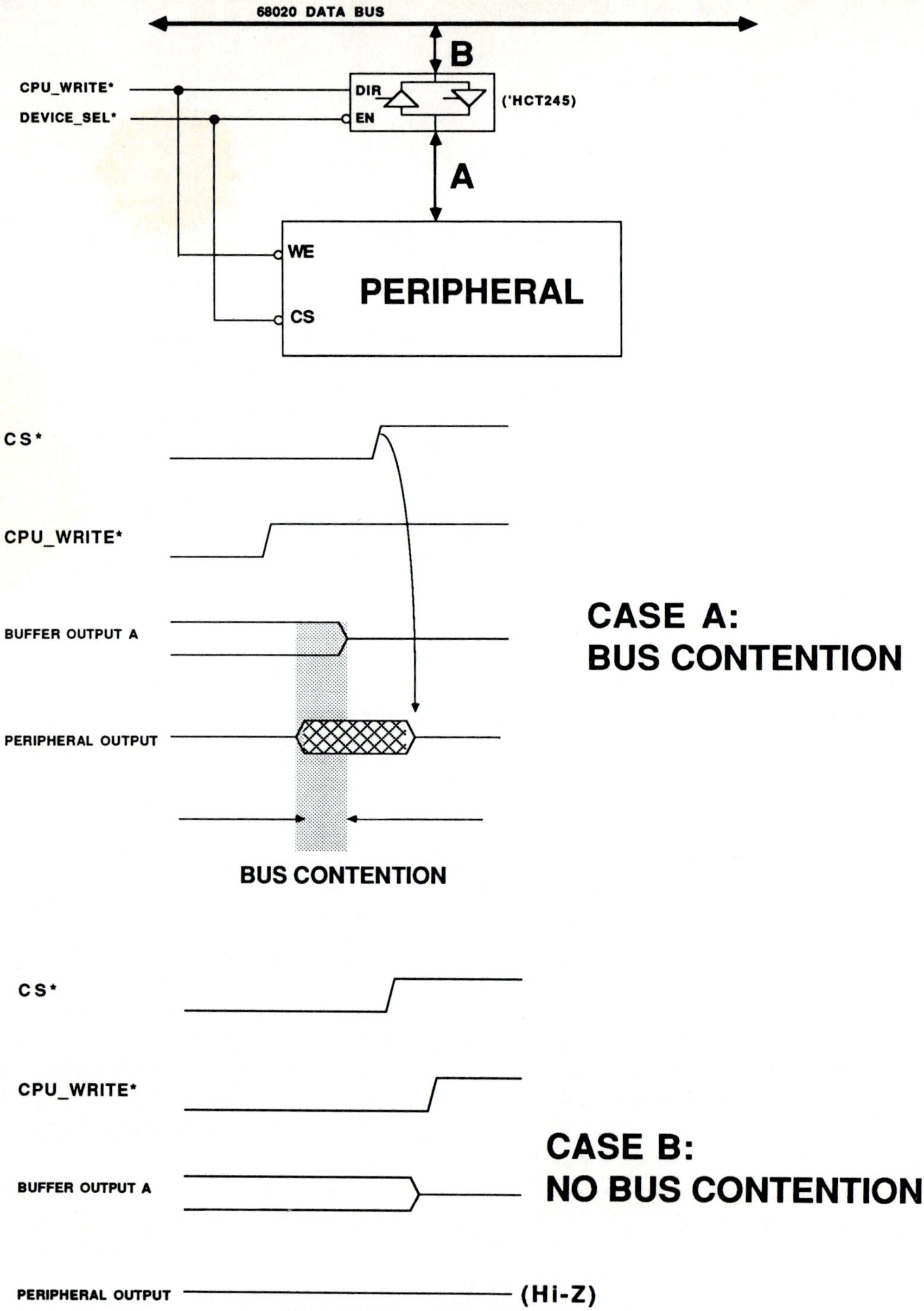

Figure 9-32 Example of Bus Contention Between a Buffer and Peripheral.

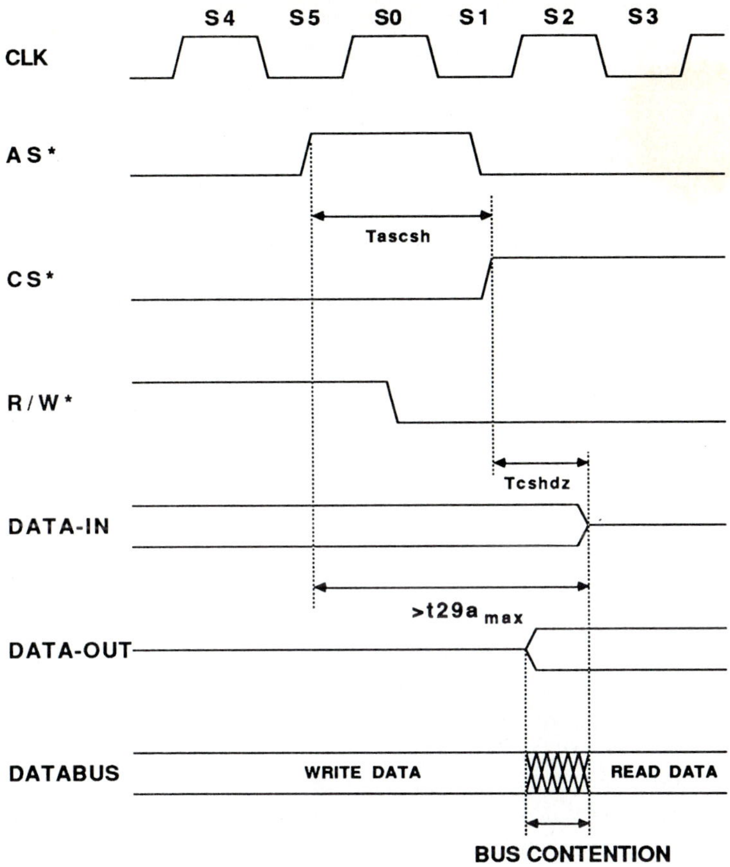

Parameter	Characteristic	Min	Max	Units
t29a	DS* Negated to Data-in in Hi-Z.	—	60	nsec.

Figure 9-33 Bus Contention Between the 68020 and a Peripheral.

the bus during the state S2 and, thus, meeting the t29a guarantees that there will be no bus contention between consecutive bus cycles. Let us look at what we need to do to meet this parameter.

The timing parameter t29a is the sum of two independent values as follows:

$$t29a = T_{ascsh} + T_{cshdz} \qquad \text{(Eq. 9-4)}$$

where

T_{ascsh}: Is the delay between the negation of AS* and CS*

T_{cshdz}: Is the time when drivers are disabled after CS* is negated.

We can minimize the first parameter based on our address decoder design and interface logic. The second parameter depends on the peripheral. However, we may still affect the value of second parameter by using data buffers at the peripheral site. A data buffer isolating the data I/O of a peripheral, in addition to providing a increased drive capability, also significantly reduce the data-in turn-off delay as seen by the 68020. For example, the '68681 DUART has a read-cycle worst-case turn-off delay of 100 nanoseconds, thereby necessitating the use of local buffer device.

We are going to see further examples of how we can avoid the data bus contention in memory and other peripheral designs during the rest of this chapter.

9.8 INTERFACING TO MEMORY DEVICES

9.8.1 Static Read/Write (SRAM) Memory Design

For high performance, that is, when the 68020 is running at a high-clock frequency and without any wait-cycles, it is necessary that we use the *static RAMs* (SRAMs) because of their fast access times. Another reason to use SRAMs is in applications that require only a small amount of read/write memory. For example, in a control module using the 68020 that requires only 64 Kbytes of local read/write memory, it would be an overkill to have one megabyte using DRAM devices.

A typical example of a SRAM memory bank and its interface to the 68020 is shown in Figure 9-34. We have organized the 128 Kbyte memory in this example as 32 Kbytes by 32 bits, because 8- or 16-bit wide organizations would have reduced the access throughput significantly. A '22V10 PLD is used for the address decoding. The byte select and enable logic is also implemented using a '22V10 PLD (as we discussed in section 9-6) except the byte-enable signals are qualified with the address-decode signal DECODE_RAM* (i.e., are mapped). The logic equations of this PLD are shown in Figure 9-35.

Assuming our design specification is zero-wait-cycle accesses, NEC's '43256 that we discussed in Chapter 8 would not meet our speed requirements. This is because we have an access window of 85 nanoseconds from Table 9-1 that includes delays of other control signals as well as any buffering for address and data buses. The access time for NEC chip, however, is in the range of 85-150 nanoseconds. Therefore, we will use another SRAM device here, the CY7C199 manufactured by Cypress Semiconductor with a 32k × 8 organization and access times in the range of 25-55 nanoseconds. We will adopt manufacturer's timing parameters for this device, as shown in Appendix F, which will be different from the parameter names of the NEC's '43256 given in Chapter 8.

The output-enable (OE*) of all RAMs are connected to digital ground. The write-enable (WE*) is connected to CPU_WRITE*, which is the buffered R/W* signal of the 68020. Note that addresses A2 through A16 are connected to the address pins of the RAMs. The order by which the address and data pins of RAMs

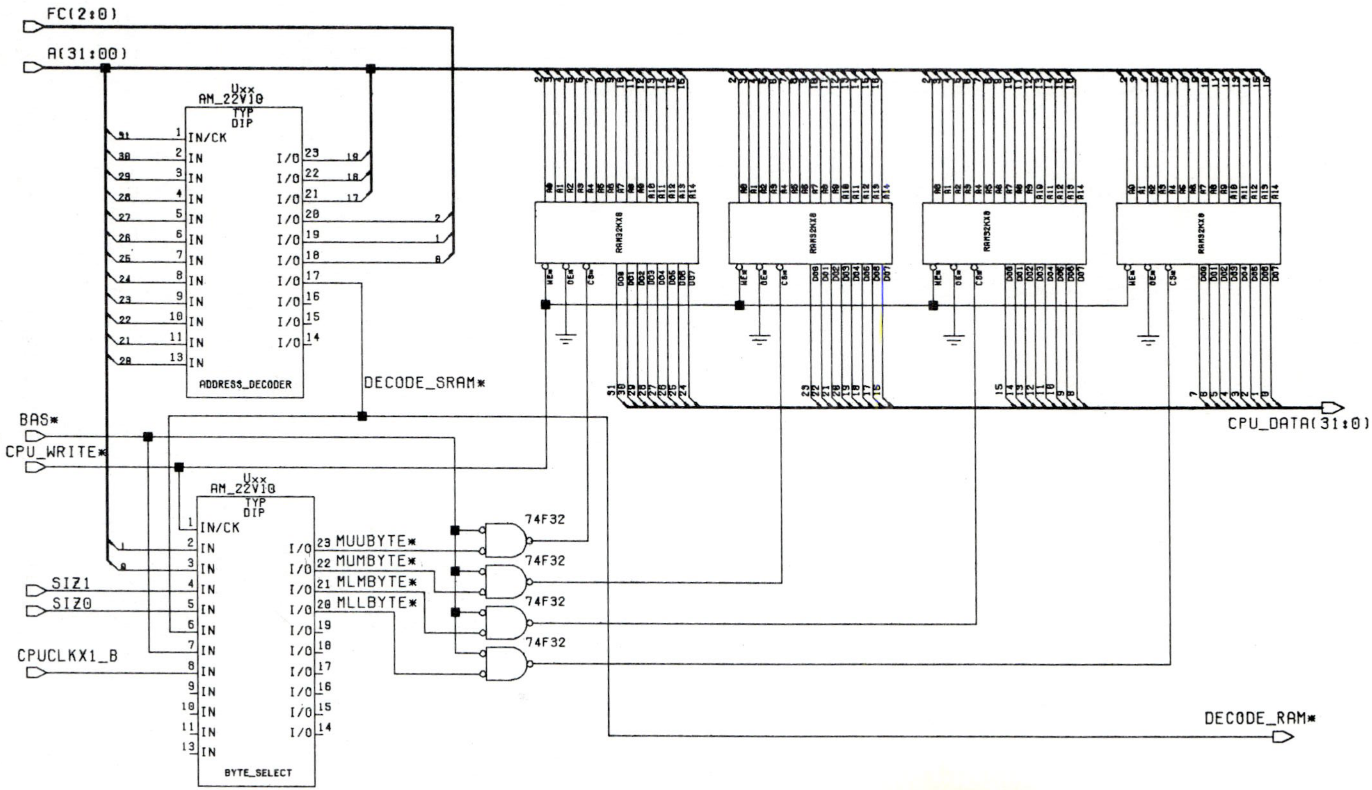

Figure 9-34 Example 128 Kbyte SRAM Memory Design.

```
Partno      BYTESELM ;
Date        XX/XX/XX;
Revision    XX;
Designer    XXXXX;
Company     XXXXX;
Assembly    XXXXX;
Location    XXXXX;

/*****************************************************************
/*  Purpose: This PLD generates the byte select signals that are
/*           memory mapped, i.e., qualified with address decoding
/*****************************************************************
/*  Allowable Target Device Types: PAL 22V10
/*****************************************************************

/**  Inputs  **/

pin   1 = !WRITE          ;      /* Same as R/W* signal of 68020.   *
Pin   2 = A1              ;
Pin   3 = A0              ;      /* A1 and A0 Address Lines.        *
Pin   4 = SIZ1            ;      /* SIZ1-0: Remaining Operand Size.*
Pin   5 = SIZ0            ;
Pin   6 = !DECODE_SRAM    ;      /* Address Decode of RAM.          *
Pin   7 = !BAS            ;      /* Buffered AS*.                   *
Pin   8 = CPUCLKX1_B      ;      /* Buffered CPU clock.             *

/**  Outputs  **/

Pin  23 = !MUUBYTE        ;      /* Upper Upper Byte Select.        *
Pin  22 = !MUMBYTE        ;      /* Upper Middle Byte Select.       *
Pin  21 = !MLMBYTE        ;      /* Lower Middle Byte Select.       *
Pin  20 = !MLLBYTE        ;      /* Lower Lower Byte Select.        *

/**  Logic Equations  **/

MUUBYTE = DECODE_SRAM & BAS & CPUCLKX1_B & (
          !WRITE           #      /* Read Cycle- Enable all.
          !A1 & !A0 )      #      /* Offset = 0 & Any size operand.
          MUUBYTE & BAS    ;      /* This term maintains MUUBYTE
                                  /* until the end of cycle.

MUMBYTE = DECODE_SRAM & BAS & CPUCLKX1_B & (
          !WRITE           #      /* Read Cycle - Enable all.
          !SIZ0 & !A1      #      /* Size = 2/4 & Offset = 0/1.
          !A1 & A0         #      /* Offset = 1 & Any size.
          SIZ1 & !A1 )     #      /* Offset =0/1 & Size = 2/3.
          MUMBYTE & BAS    ;
```

Figure 9-35 Logic Equations of '22V10 in Figure 9-34.

```
MLMBYTE = DECODE_SRAM & BAS & CPUCLKX1_B & (
          !WRITE            #     /* Read Cycle - Enable all.       */
           A1 & !A0         #     /* Offset = 2 & Any size.         */
          !SIZ1 & !SIZ0 & !A1 #   /* Offset = 0/1 & Size = 4.       */
           SIZ1 &  SIZ0 &  A0 #   /* Offset = 0/1 & Size = 3.       */
          !SIZ0 & !A1 & A0 )  #   /* Offset = 1 & Size = 2/4.       */
          MLMBYTE & BAS    ;

MLLBYTE = DECODE_SRAM & BAS & CPUCLKX1_B & (
          !WRITE            #     /* Read Cycle - Enable all.       */
           A1 & A0          #     /* Offset = 3 & Any size.         */
          !SIZ1 & !SIZ0     #     /* Any offset & Size = 4.         */
           SIZ1 &  SIZ0 & A0 #    /* Offset = 1 & Size = 3.         */
           SIZ1 & A1   )    #     /* Offset = 2/3 & Size = 2/3.     */
          MLLBYTE & BAS    ;
```

Figure 9-35 (cont.)

are connected does not matter because whatever we write, we will read at the same address and in the same bit format.

The ’F32 gates are used to qualify the byte-enable signals with the address strobe, BAS*. A cursory look may suggest that we can include this logic in the ’22V10 PLD and eliminate these four gates. However, this is not so for the following reasons:

1. This is necessary to meet the write data hold-time requirement of SRAM devices. That is, CS* has to be negated before the data becomes invalid. If we connected BAS* to an input of ’22V10 and eliminated the ’F32, the negation of CS* would be delayed by the input-to-output delay of the ’22V10, and such late “flushing-out” of CS* would violate the T_{hd} of SRAMs. If we eliminated the ’F32, we would have

$$t25 - (T_{F244} + T_{pd(22V10)}) \geq T_{hd} \qquad \text{(Eq. 9-5)}$$

   where $T_{hd} = 0$ from Appendix F and for 16.67 MHz 68020 the $t25 = 15$ (min.) We would then have

$$T_{F244} + T_{pd(22V10)} \leq 15 \text{ nsec}$$

   which is very difficult to meet in the worst-case. Therefore, we used ’F32s.
2. Our approach also prevents the possibility of any bus contention, because CS* is negated as fast as possible, meeting the t29A timing requirement of the 68020.

There are two critical paths in this design. These are:

Path A: Address → DECODE_SRAM* → MxxBYTE* → CSn*
Path B: AS* → CSn*

We have the issue of glitching of CSn* if path B timing is less than Path A (due to Eq. 8-2). As long as the address is stable, a glitch during CS* assertion would not cause circuit malfunction. However, it is still good practice to avoid such glitching. Therefore, we will use the beginning of state S2 to qualify the Mxx-BYTE*. In other words, we will use the condition (BAS & CPUCLKX1_B) to qualify the byte select and address decode. This will reduce the critical paths to one.

The read and write bus cycle timing diagrams are given in Figures 9-36 and 9-37, respectively.

Let us define the timing parameter T_{csl}, which indicates the delay in asserting a chip-select signal from the beginning of a bus cycle.

$$T_{csl} = t1 + T_{pd(22V10)} + T_{F32} \qquad \text{(Eq. 9-6)}$$

where T_{F32} is the propagation delay through the 'F32 gate.

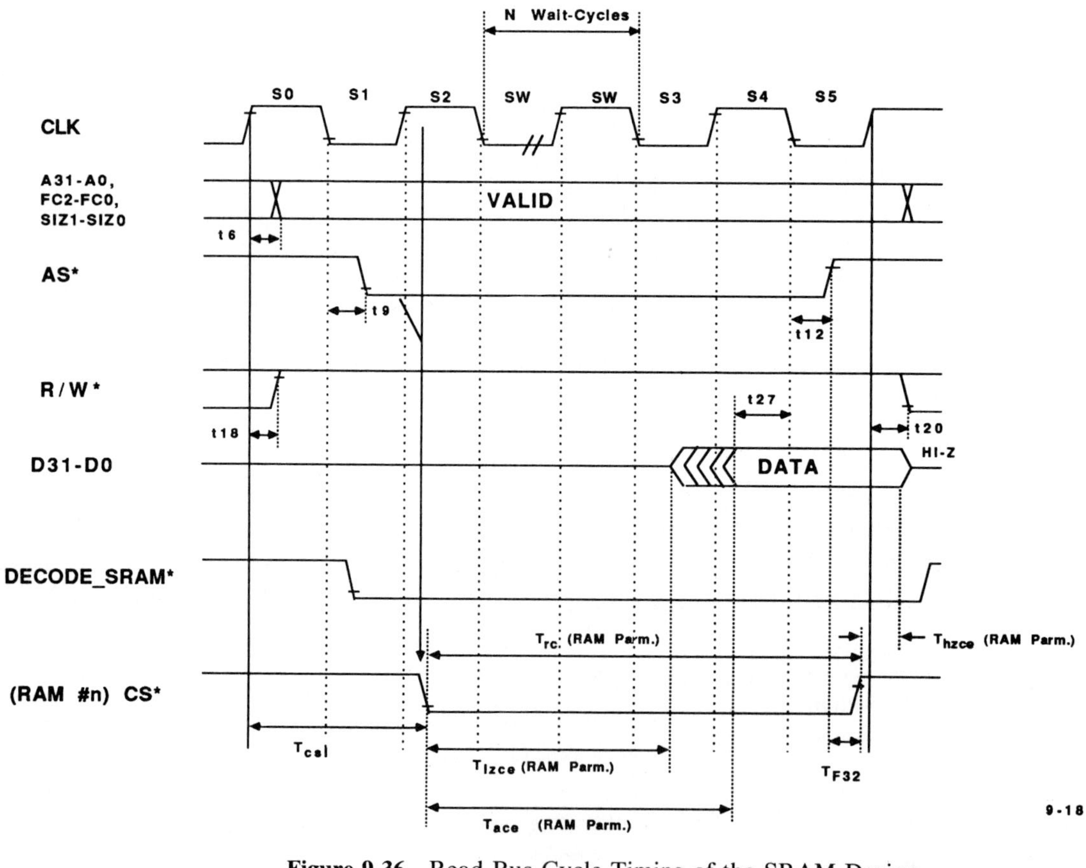

Figure 9-36 Read Bus Cycle Timing of the SRAM Design.

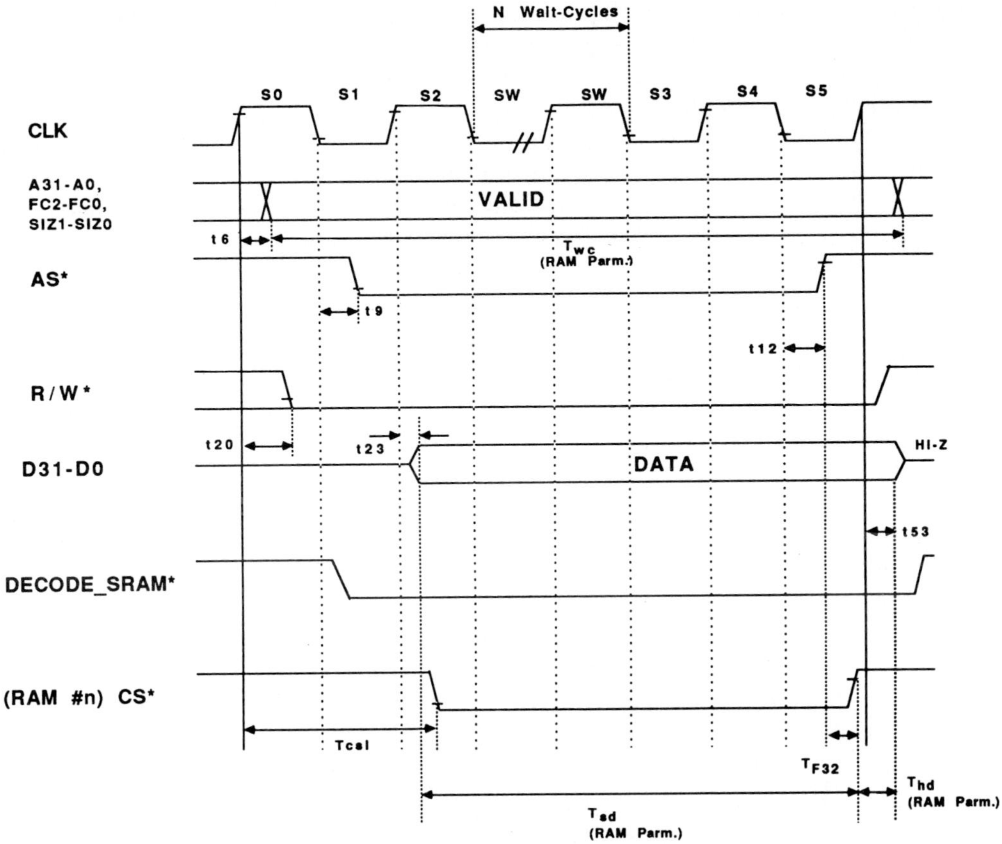

Figure 9-37 Write Bus Cycle Timing of SRAM Design.

For a read bus cycle, we have

$$T_{csl} + T_{ace} + t27 + t2 + t4 = (3 + N) * t1 \qquad \text{(Eq. 9-7)}$$

where T_{ace} is the RAM parameter that specifies CS* low to data-out-valid access time. Parameter N specifies the number of wait-cycles. Thus, the required worst-case access time for the SRAMs are

$$T_{ace(max)} = (3 + N) * t1 - T_{csl(max)} - t27 - t2 - t4 \qquad \text{(Eq. 9-8)}$$

The two critical parameters that must be met for a write cycle are the data setup and the hold times (T_{sd} and T_{hd}) of the SRAMs. The hold time is met because the chip-select signal of each SRAM will be negated before the data becomes invalid. The data setup time is given by

$$T_{sd} = t3 - t23 + t5 + (N + 1) * t1 + t12 + T_{F32} \qquad \text{(Eq. 9-9)}$$

or, for worst case we have

$$T_{sd(min)} = t3 - t23_{max} + t5 + (N + 1) * t1 + t12_{min} + T_{F32(min)} \quad \text{(Eq. 9-10)}$$

Note that T_{sd} is not a function of address decoding or interface logic. Of course, in this case we assume no data buffers are used in the data path. Otherwise, they have to be accounted in the above equations.

We have assumed here that the address decoding is completed by the end of state S1, i.e., DECODE_SRAM* asserted before state S2. This requires that we satisfy

$$t6 + T_{pd(22V10)} \leq t1 \quad \text{(Eq. 9-11)}$$

or

$$T_{pd(22V10)(max)} \leq t1 - t6_{max} \quad \text{(Eq. 9-12)}$$

or

$$T_{pd(22V10))} \leq 30 \text{ nsec for the 16.67 MHz 68020.}$$

Therefore, we have to use a 25 nanosecond or faster '22V10.

Example 9-4

In this example we will evaluate the above equations and determine the speed of SRAM and PLDs to run without any wait-cycles. Let us assume that we are using the 16 MHz version of the 68020, and have the following data:

$T_{F32(min)} = 3.0$ nsec. (See Figure 9-38.)

$T_{F32(max)} = 6.6$ nsec.

$T_{pd(22V10)} = 15$ nsec. to 45 nsec. depending on speed rating (See Appendix G).

$T_{ace(max)} = 25$ nsec. to 55 nsec. depending on speed rating (See Appendix F).

The penalty for using higher speed parts is usually higher power consumption and higher cost. As determined above, we have to use a 25 nanosecond version of the '22V10. For the byte-select PLD, let us first calculate for the −25 version.

$$\text{Eq. 9-6: } T_{csl} = 60 + 25 + 6.6 = 91.6 \text{ nsec.}$$

Before we finalize our selection of PLD speed ratings, let us look at the RAM access time requirements. Assuming we made the above selection of PLDs, we have

$$\text{Eq. 9-8: } T_{ace(max)} = 3 * 60 - 91.6 - 5 - 24 - 5 = 55 \text{ nsec.}$$

and

$$\text{Eq. 9-9: } T_{sd(min)} = 24 - 30 + 5 + 60 + 0 + 3 = 62 \text{ nsec.}$$

The above requirements can be met using the -55 version of the SRAMs.

One question the reader may raise here is that we did not use the data-strobe signal, DS*, at all in the above interface. Why? The answer is simply that it would

AC ELECTRICAL CHARACTERISTICS

SYMBOL	PARAMETER	TEST CONDITIONS	74F32					UNIT
			$T_A = +25°C$, $V_{CC} = +5.0$ V, $C_L = 50pF$, $R_L = 500\Omega$			$T_A = 0°C$ to $+70°C$, $V_{CC} = +5.0$ V ± 10%, $C_L = 50pF$, $R_L = 500\Omega$		
			Min	Typ	Max	Min	Max	
t_{PLH} t_{PLH}	Propagation delay A, B to Y	Waveform 1	3.0 3.0	4.2 4.0	5.6 5.3	3.0 3.0	6.6 6.3	ns

AC WAVEFORM

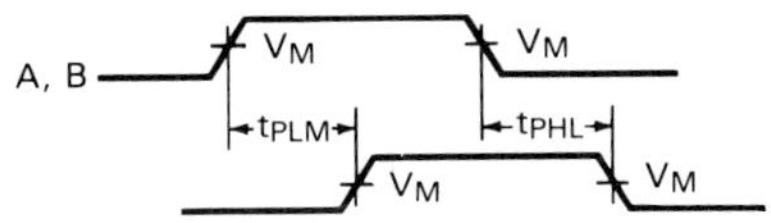

NOTE: For all waveforms, $V_M = 1.5$ V.
WAVEFORM 1. For Non-inverting Outputs

Figure 9-38 Part of 74F32 Data Sheet. (Courtesy of Signetics.)

increase the T_{csl} significantly. This would necessitate either using faster components to maintain zero wait-cycles in the above example, or one or more wait-cycles. The use of data strobe is only necessary when data has to be valid before the chip-select of a device is asserted (see Exercise 41). In a SRAM, it is important to remember that we can assert the CS* before the data-to-be-written becomes valid as long as T_{sd} and T_{hd} are met with respect to the negation of the chip-select signal.

9.8.2 EPROM Memory Design

The non-volatile EPROM memory is usually used to store power-up diagnostics, bootstrap program, and possibly the operating system kernel. As with SRAM, we may organize EPROM memory 8-, 16-, or 32-bits wide depending on the system design consideration. The disadvantage of the 32-bit organization is that it requires, at minimum, four 8-bit wide EPROM devices. This may provide more memory than we need, and thus we may choose 8-, or 16-bit wide configurations. In other words, access time or throughput is not always an important consideration with the EPROM memory, because we can, at the beginning, copy the program into the SRAM memory and execute from it.

As an example design here, we choose the 16-bit wide organization, as shown in the Figure 9-39. Each'27512 EPROM device stores 64 Kbytes, or 512 Kbits total. There are two banks of EPROM memory devices. The advantage of this configuration is that a base system may require only one bank and providing sockets for the second bank allow program size expandability.

The data outputs are connected to the data bus lines D16 through D31 of the 68020. In contrast with the SRAM memory design, we have to be more careful

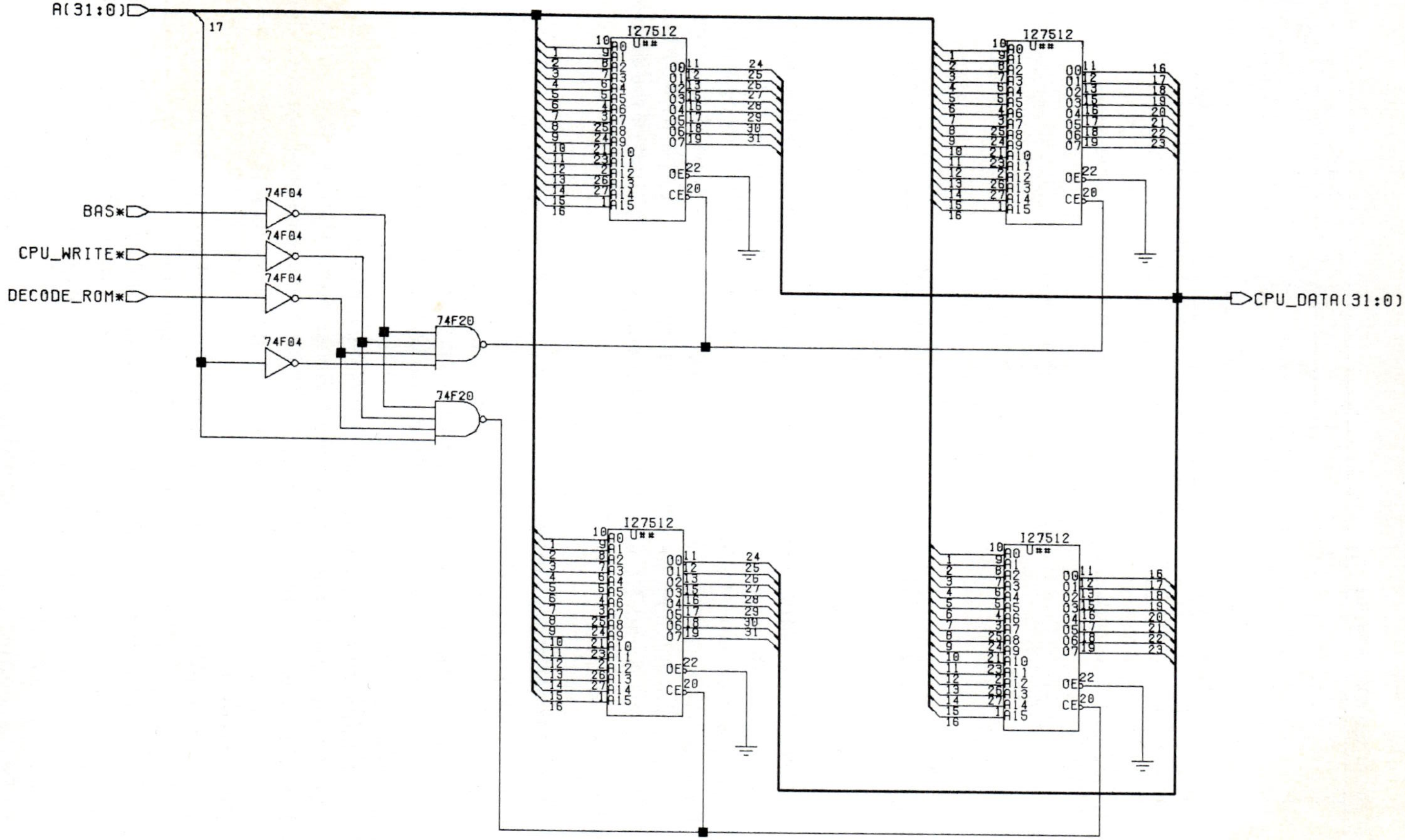

Figure 9-39 Example EPROM Memory Design.

about how we connect the address and data lines of an EPROM device. The order of the address and the data lines are important, because, otherwise we can not read the data in the format or sequence as we preprogrammed it. The address bit A0 of the 68020 is not used because we enable both bytes during any read access. The CPU_WRITE* insures that only read accesses are allowed because we connected all output-enables (OE*) to digital ground. This avoids any bus contention. Alternatively, we could have connected the inverted CPU_WRITE* to all output-enable inputs. Another option is to enable all EPROMs all the time by connecting CE* inputs to digital ground, and control outputs by connecting the 'F20 outputs to OE* inputs instead. This will cut down the access time by approximately one-half, but will increase power consumption (see exercise 28).

9.8.3 Memory Design with Dynamic RAMS

How does dynamic RAMS work? The dynamic RAM memory, or DRAM for short, employs a single transistor storage cell as shown in Figure 9-40. One megabit DRAM chip has 1,048,576 of these cells in its memory array that are internally organized in matrix form, typically as 512 rows and 2,048 columns. The capacitor that is between the drain of Q*n* and the chip substrate can hold a small amount of charge on the order of 35-125 femto-Farads (fF).[5] A single bit of information, binary one or zero, depends on whether the capacitor is charged or discharged. The transistor Q*n* acts as a switch, controlling access to the stored single bit of information. To access a memory cell, the word and the bit line corresponding to that cell are simultaneously pulled to a high voltage. This causes the transistor Q*n* to be turned on and the charge is transferred into the storage capacitor requiring relatively little charge if it were fully charged initially.

The amount of charge that the bit line must supply to a cell's capacitor is measured by the sensing circuitry. This information is used to assess whether a zero or one had been stored in that cell. Since a read access to a memory cell with no initial charge is destructive of the information, the sense circuit restores the information by writing it back at the end of access. This restoration of charge is transparent to the user.

A memory cell of DRAM memory requires about one-fourth of the area used by a four-transistor memory cell in a SRAM device. Because the memory cell of DRAM is much simpler than the SRAM, the DRAM memory provides significantly greater memory density per chip as well as reduced power consumption per stored data bit. At the time of this writing, one megabit DRAM chips are common and the four megabit ones are being sampled.

Another advantage of DRAM devices is that they are smaller in package size than the SRAMs that has significantly less storage. This is due to the multiplexing of DRAM address lines as row and column addresses, thus halving the

[5] 1 fF = 1×10^{-15} Farads.

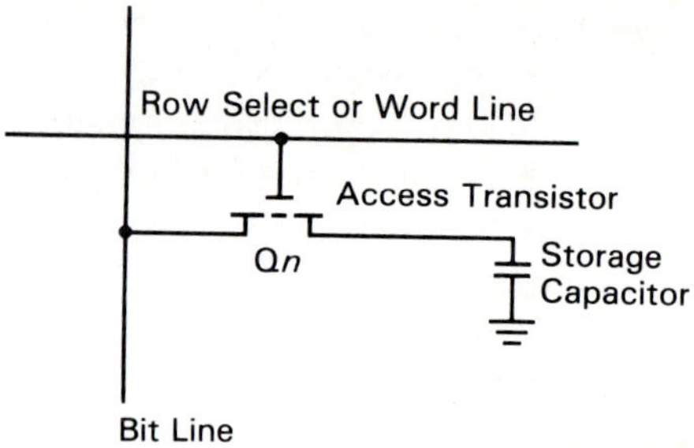

Figure 9-40 A Memory Cell of DRAM Memory Chip.

number of required address pins on the device. Otherwise, a 1M × 1 DRAM device would require 20 address pins.

The block diagram of a DRAM device is shown in Figure 9-41. The row and column address strobes that are used to latch the multiplexed addresses into the DRAM are commonly called *Row-Address-Strobe (RAS) and Column-Address-Strobe* (CAS). The write-enable (WE∗) determines whether the access is for a read or write cycle. The output-enable (OE∗) controls enabling the data-output buffers in a read access cycle.

A major drawback inherent with the DRAM storage cell is that the charge of capacitor decays with time due to the junction and dielectric leakage currents. Without any recharging, this will eventually cause the sensing circuitry to be unable to accurately interrogate its contents. ''Refreshing'' refers to the reading of all the cells contents and re-writing them back. The design and operation of DRAM devices allow an entire row of memory cells to be refreshed in one refresh cycle. Typically, 512 of these special refresh cycles are necessary to refresh a 1-megabyte DRAM device every 8 milliseconds. We will discuss the details of refresh operation later in this section.

DRAM data access and timing parameters. A DRAM device has nearly as many timing parameters as the 68020 itself. A look at the timing diagrams and tables on a DRAM datasheet may make it seem hopelessly complex to design with the DRAMs and one may be tempted to use SRAMs instead. In reality, the design of a DRAM memory and its interface to the 68020 is not even near as difficult as it seems to be. Once the underlying concepts of DRAM operation is understood, it will be a simple matter to make the appropriate design trade-offs and to sort through the tons of information provided in DRAM datasheets.

We will tackle this seemingly complex device by dividing our coverage into the basic and manageable pieces. In our examples we will use the NEC's DRAM chip with 256K by 4 bits configuration. The cover page of manufacturer's data sheet is shown in Figure 9-42. Some of the features shown on this cover page may not be understood now, but will become clear during the rest of discussion on DRAMs. The complete data sheet of this device is included in Appendix E. The abbreviations for timing parameters of DRAMs are pretty much standard across different manufacturers. We will adapt these abbreviations here.

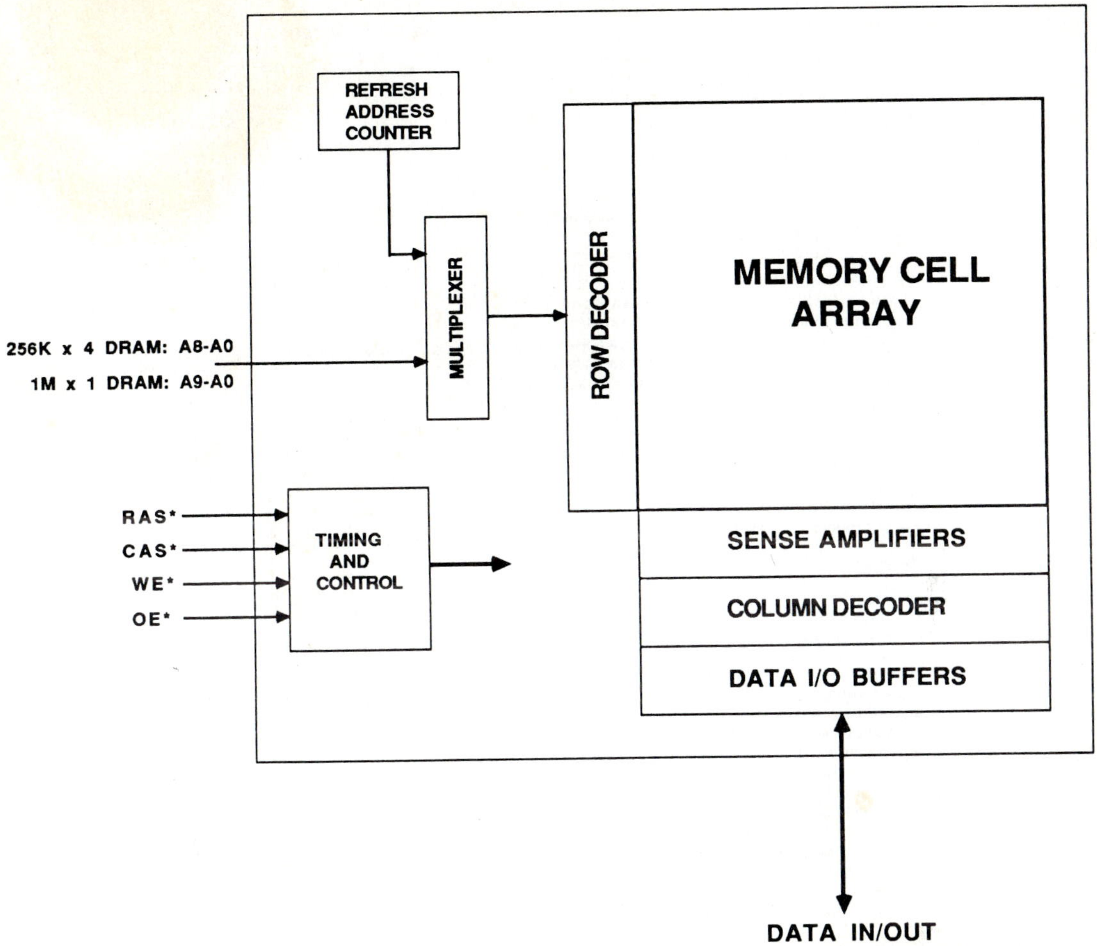

Figure 9-41 Simplified Block Diagram of DRAM Memory.

Address Timing

Both read and write accesses require two steps as shown in Figure 9-43. First, the row address is presented and RAS∗ is asserted. This latches the row address into the DRAM device and initiates access to the specified row of memory array. The required setup and hold times for row-address is specified by {T_{asr}, T_{rah}}, respectively. Second, the column address is presented and CAS∗ is asserted. The column address setup and hold times are specified by the parameters {T_{asc}, T_{cah}}, respectively. After the column address is latched into the DRAM by the CAS∗, it is no longer necessary to maintain a valid address during the rest of the cycle.

Description

The μPD424256 is a fast-page, 262,144-word by 4-bit dynamic CMOS RAM designed to operate from a single +5-volt power supply. The device is fabricated with advanced polycide technology using trench capacitors to minimize silicon area and provide high storage cell capacity, high performance, and high reliability. The μPD424256 also uses a single-transistor dynamic storage cell and advanced CMOS circuitry throughout, ensuring minimum power dissipation. The negative-voltage substrate bias is automatically generated internally.

The three-state I/O pins are controlled by $\overline{CAS}$ independent of $\overline{RAS}$. After a valid read or read-modify-write cycle, data is held on the outputs by maintaining a low $\overline{CAS}$. The data outputs are returned to a state of high impedance by returning $\overline{CAS}$ to a high logic level. The device is also capable of performing fast-page read and write cycles by cycling $\overline{CAS}$.

Refreshing may be accomplished by means of a $\overline{CAS}$ before $\overline{RAS}$ cycle, enabling the internal generation of a refresh address. Refreshing may also be accomplished by means of $\overline{RAS}$-only refresh cycles or by normal read or write cycles on the 512 address combinations of A_0-A_8 during an 8-ms refresh period.

Features

- ☐ 262,144-word by 4-bit organization
- ☐ Single +5-volt ±10% power supply
- ☐ Fast-page operation
- ☐ Low power dissipation
  - — 70 mA max (active), 80 ns version
  - — 1 mA max (standby)
- ☐ $\overline{CAS}$ before $\overline{RAS}$ internal refreshing capability
- ☐ Multiplexed address inputs
- ☐ On-chip substrate bias generator
- ☐ Nonlatched, TTL-compatible, three-state I/O
- ☐ Low input capacitance
- ☐ TTL-compatible inputs
- ☐ 512 refresh cycles during an 8-ms period
- ☐ High-density 20-pin plastic DIP, 26/20-pin plastic SOJ, or 20-pin plastic ZIP packaging

Pin Configurations

20-Pin Plastic DIP

26/20-Pin Plastic SOJ

20-Pin Plastic ZIP

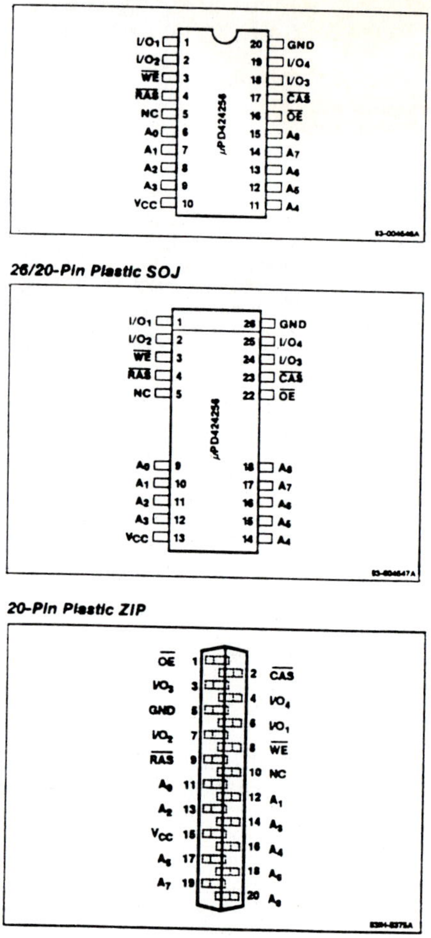

Figure 9-42 NEC's 256K × 4 DRAM Cover Page.

RAS and CAS Timing

The RAS* and CAS* input timing requirements are shown in Figure 9-44. The parameters T_{ras} and T_{cas} specify the minimum pulse width necessary for RAS* and CAS*, respectively. This is necessary to allow sufficient time for the sense amplifier operation.

The parameter T_{rcd} specifies the time delay between the assertion of RAS* and CAS* signals. The minimum allowed value of T_{rcd} is equal or greater than the sum of T_{rah} and T_{asc}. The maximum limit on the T_{rcd}, if specified, is a pseudo one. That is, we may exceed the maximum limit, but this will only slow down the access time. Actually, when CAS* is asserted within the time specified for

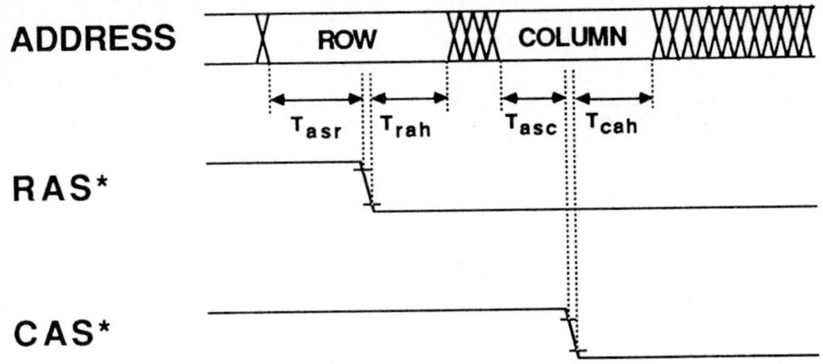

Parameter	Function	Min	Max	Units
T_{asr}	Row Address Setup Time	0	—	nsec.
T_{rah}	Row Address Hold Time	12	—	nsec.
T_{asc}	Column Address Setup Time	0	20[1]	nsec.
T_{cah}	Column Address Hold Time	20	—	nsec.

NOTE: MIN and MAX values are given for NEC's '424256, 80 nsec. version.
[1] MAX time important for page mode of operation.

Figure 9-43 Address Timing of DRAM.

maximum T_{rcd}, the setup time for column addresses is more difficult to guarantee than when T_{rcd} exceeds the maximum limit. This is due to the propagation delay variation of interface logic and also due to the increased delay times on the address lines of DRAMs that is difficult to calculate. The reason for this is that usually one address driver has to drive many DRAM devices in a memory array, and this causes timing skew between the address and control lines of DRAM.[6] The parameters T_{rp} and T_{cpn} specifies the minimum inactive time periods necessary for RAS* and CAS*, respectively. During the RAS* precharge time T_{rp}, all the capacitors of the accessed row are refreshed (i.e., are written back).

A related fundamental parameter for a DRAM device is the cycle time, T_{rc}. This is probably the number two important parameter of DRAM, right after the access time. Although the access time is the one that is most talked about, the cycle time carries more significance for consecutive bus cycles, because it is the one that determines the effective throughput.

It is important to note that meeting the minimum requirements for T_{ras} and T_{rp} does not mean that we automatically meet T_{rc}, because we need to also consider the transition times for CAS*, i.e.,

$$T_{rc(min)} = T_{ras(min)} + T_{rp(min)} + 2 * TT \qquad \text{(Eq. 9-13)}$$

where TT is typically 5 nanoseconds.

[6] See Reference 17 for a detailed discussion of this subject.

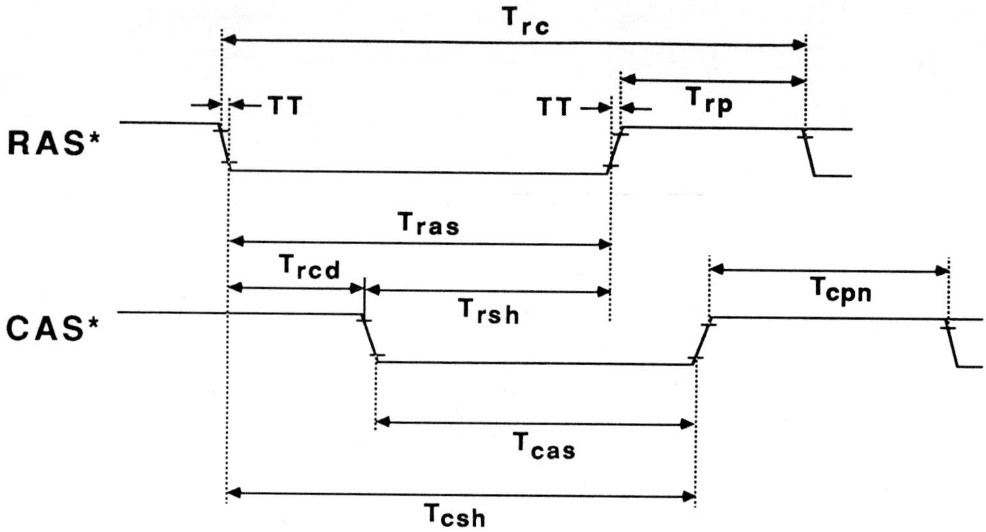

Parameter	Function	Min	Max	Units
T_{ras}	RAS* Pulse Width	80	10000	nsec.
T_{cas}	CAS* Pulse Width	20	10000	nsec.
T_{rcd}	RAS* to CAS* Delay Time	25	60	nsec.
T_{rp}	RAS* Precharge Time	70	—	nsec.
T_{cpn}	CAS* Precharge Time	10	—	nsec.
T_{rc}	Random Access Cycle Time	160	—	nsec.
T_{rsh}	RAS* Hold Time	20	—	nsec.
T_{csh}	CAS* Hold Time	80	—	nsec.

NOTE: MIN and MAX values are given for NEC's '424256, 80 nsec. version.

Figure 9-44 RAS* and CAS* Timing.

The timing parameters T_{rsh} and T_{csh} specify the earliest times that respectively RAS* and CAS* may be negated. We have

$$T_{csh(min)} > T_{rcd(min)} + T_{cas(min)}$$

and so we have to verify that a design meets T_{csh} separately.

Read Cycle Timing

The read cycle timing and parameters are shown in Figure 9-45. The write-enable signal (WE*) must be high T_{rcs} before the CAS* is asserted, and must be held high until T_{rch} after the CAS* is negated. The other two important read cycle parameters are the data access times with respect to the assertion of RAS* and CAS, given by T_{rac} and T_{cac}, respectively. The T_{rac} is commonly referred to as the access time. If we operate within the maximum value of the T_{rcd}, then this

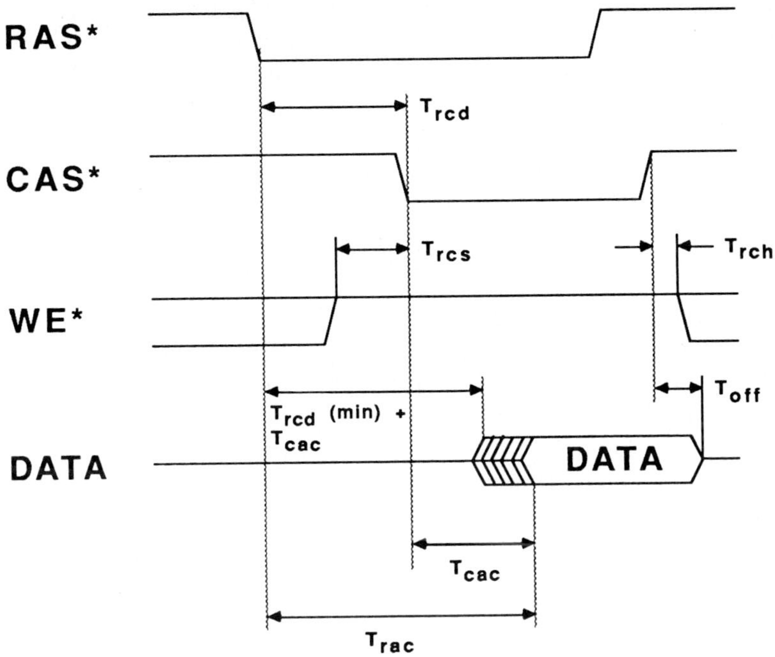

Parameter	Function	Min	Max	Units
T_{rac}	Access Time From RAS*	—	80	nsec.
T_{cac}	Access Time From CAS*	—	20	nsec.
T_{rcs}	Read Command Setup Time	0	—	nsec.
T_{rch}	Read Command Hold Time	0	—	nsec.
T_{off}	Output Buffer Turnoff Delay	0	20	nsec.

NOTE: MIN and MAX values are given for NEC's '424256, 80 nsec. version.

Figure 9-45 DRAM Read Cycle Timing.

guarantees that the data output will be valid T_{rac} after the RAS* is asserted, or T_{cac} after the CAS* is asserted. Otherwise, the access time is controlled exclusively by the T_{cac} parameter. The relation between the $T_{rcd(max)}$, T_{rac}, and T_{cac} is

$$T_{rcd(max)} = T_{rac} - T_{cac} \qquad \text{(Eq. 9-14)}$$

A typical oversight in control logic is when the minimum requirements for T_{cac} and T_{rcd} are met, but T_{rac} is not. For example, for the '424256, we have a minimum time of 25 nanoseconds for the T_{rcd}, and specifies T_{cac} as 20 nanoseconds. Therefore, if we met T_{rcd} and T_{cac}, even though data appears at the output 45 nanoseconds after the RAS* signal is asserted, it is not valid until 80 nanoseconds after its assertion, an additional 35 nanoseconds.

The only instance the DRAM data output buffer is enabled is after a RAS* followed by a CAS* sequence, and when OE* is low and WE* is high. In other words, applying RAS* or CAS* alone with OE* low and WE* high will *not* turn-on the output buffers. This information will later be used in address decoding of multiple banks of DRAM memory.

The valid data output is held by the DRAM as long as the state of CAS*, WE*, and OE* are maintained. When CAS* is negated, the output buffers are turned off with a delay of T_{off}. Thus, once a read cycle control sequence is initiated, RAS* does not play any role in maintaining the data output.

Write Cycle Timing

The write cycle timing is shown in Figure 9-46. The write cycle is indicated by asserting the WE* prior to CAS* with a setup time of T_{wcs}. The data to be written is latched by the DRAM on the falling edge of the CAS*. The two significant parameters for a write cycle are the setup and hold times of data with respect to the assertion of CAS*, given by T_{ds} and T_{dh}, respectively. Note that, in contrast with the read cycle, the state of WE* does not have to be maintained until the end of access cycle. The WE* can be negated before the CAS* is negated after it meets the WE*-low pulse width requirement specified by T_{wp}.

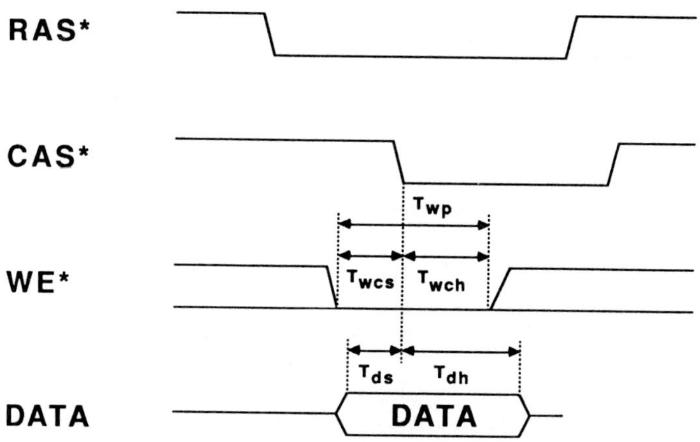

Parameter	Function	Min	Max	Units
T_{wcs}	Write Command Setup Time	0	—	nsec.
T_{wch}	Write Command Hold Time	15	—	nsec.
T_{wp}	Write Command Pulse Width	15	—	nsec.
T_{ds}	Data-in Setup Time	0	—	nsec.
T_{dh}	Data-in Hold Time	20	—	nsec.

NOTE: MIN and MAX values are given for NEC's '424256, 80 nsec. version.

Figure 9-46 DRAM Early Write Cycle Timing.

Actually, the write data is latched by the falling edge of CAS* or WE*, whichever occurs later. If WE* is low before the CAS* is asserted, the data is then latched by the CAS* as we discussed in the previous paragraph. This type of write cycle is referred to as *early write cycle* and is the one that is most commonly used. Conversely, if WE* is asserted after the CAS* is asserted, this initiates a late write cycle, whereby the data is latched by the falling edge of WE*. However, there is a disadvantage to this type of write cycle. This is because when initially CAS* is asserted and WE* is high, DRAM first initiates a read access cycle, so we cannot guarantee that the data-output buffers will not be turned on while the data pins are driven externally by the data to be written, a case of possible bus contention. Therefore we have to use OE* to ensure that the output buffers are turned-off until after WE* is asserted. So, this type of write cycle is called *OE*-Controlled Write Cycle* as shown in Figure 9-47. Alternatively, we can use external buffers that can be turned off to avoid any bus conflicts. In either case, the advantage of OE*-controlled write cycle is that it may provide faster

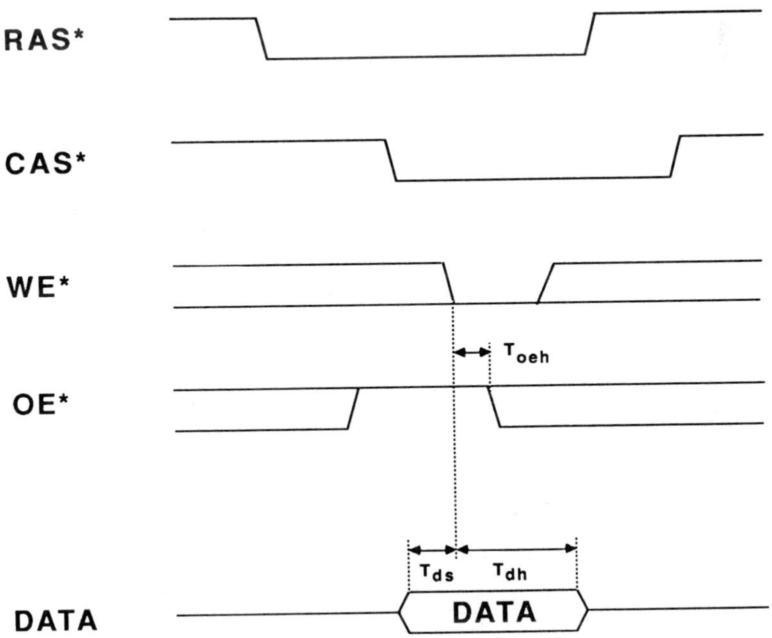

Parameter	Function	Min	Max	Units
T_{oeh}	OE* Command Hold Time	0	—	nsec.

NOTE: MIN and MAX values are given for NEC's '424256, 80 nsec. version.

Figure 9-47 OE*-Controlled Write Cycle Timing.

write cycle times. This is because the controller does not have to wait for data to stabilize before asserting the CAS* signal.

Refresh methods. Anytime a row of DRAM is accessed for a read or write operation, all the memory cells of that row are first read by the sense amplifiers and are written back at the end of the cycle. Therefore, all the cells will be refreshed on the row that is accessed. DRAM requires that *all* rows be refreshed periodically. The specified refresh period for one megabit DRAMs is 8 milliseconds or often more to maintain data integrity. Since we cannot normally guarantee that all rows will be accessed by instruction fetches or operand accesses within the required refresh period, it is necessary to perform special cycles for the purpose of refresh only. One possible approach would be to perform "dummy" read cycles on consecutive rows of DRAM for refresh purposes. This can be accomplished by periodically interrupting the 68020 to perform such read cycles. The disadvantage of this approach is twofold. First it burdens the performance of the CPU with the refreshing overhead. Second, and more importantly, it may be difficult to guarantee that refresh requirements can always be met under worst-case conditions. What happens if there is higher priority interrupt during a MOVEM instruction, or if a DMA device is the bus master preventing CPU from performing the refresh cycles?

Most commonly the DRAM memory designs incorporate hardware refreshing techniques. These memory designs do not depend on "dummy" read cycles but by special refresh cycles provided by the DRAMs. These refresh-only special cycles are much easier to perform than a read cycle. The two commonly used such refresh cycles are *RAS*-Only Refresh Cycle* and *CAS*-Before-RAS* Refresh Cycle*.

In RAS*-Only refresh cycle, external logic presents the row address and then asserts the RAS* as shown in Figure 9-48. The RAS* timing is the same as a normal read or write access cycle. The CAS* must stay inactive to distinguish this as a RAS*-Only refresh cycle whereas OE*, data signals, and WE* are "don't

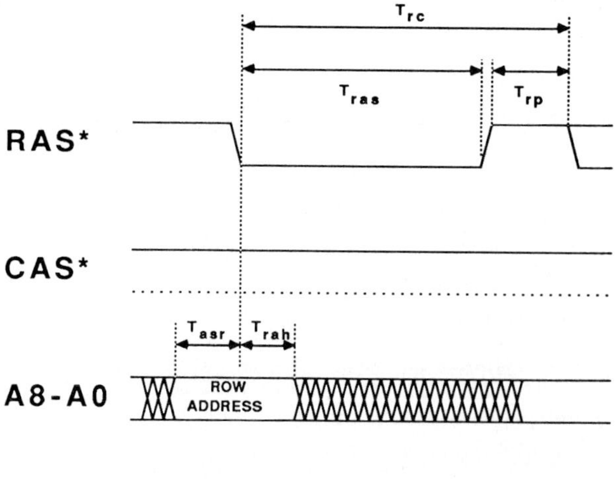

Figure 9-48 RAS*-Only Refresh Cycle.

cares" during this cycle. In order to refresh all rows, an external counter typically provides the row address, and is incremented after each refresh cycle.

In the CAS*-Before-RAS* refresh cycle, as the name implies, CAS* is asserted before the RAS* as shown in Figure 9-49. This reversal of normal RAS* followed by CAS* order activates an internal row refresh address counter on the DRAM device thereby eliminating the need for the external counter and additional multiplexing of row addresses with the refresh counter output.

The memory refresh requirement can be met in either the burst mode or the distributed mode of refresh cycles over a refresh period. In the burst mode, all refresh cycles are performed consecutively until all rows are refreshed. In the distributed mode, the refresh cycles are approximately even spaced in time intervals of one refresh every 8/512 milliseconds or 15.6 microseconds for 1-megabit DRAMs. The choice between the two approaches depends on a given system design considerations. For a system in which the CPU's memory access patterns or frequency is quite random or cannot be predicted, the distributed mode of refresh produces a better system performance. This is because in the burst-mode approach, the memory is not accessible for a relatively long time during a refresh operation causing long idle or wait-cycle times. On the other hand, the burst mode is more appropriate when continuous data transfers cannot be interrupted for certain intervals of time. For example, we may perform burst refresh just before a DMA operation. This also prevents refresh cycles in the middle of time critical data transfers. In general, we may also use a combination of the two approaches.

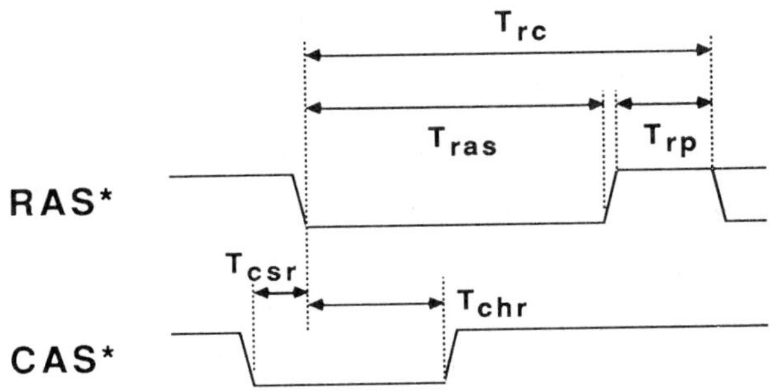

NOTE: All other signals are "don't care" and data outputs are in HI-Z state.

Parameter	Function	Min	Max	Units
T_{csr}	CAS* Setup Time	10	—	nsec.
T_{chr}	CAS* Hold Time	15	—	nsec.

NOTE: MIN and MAX values are given for NEC's '424256, 80 nsec. version.

Figure 9-49 CAS*-Before-RAS* Refresh Cycle.

For example, an intelligent controller may wait for a break in CPU accesses and then do multiple refresh cycles.

Interfacing the 68020 to DRAM memory

Memory Configuration

Let us first look at how we may organize the DRAM memory. The DRAM memory for the 68020 is typically 32-bits wide for throughput considerations although, as we saw earlier, the 68020 also allows 8- and 16-bit wide configurations due to its dynamic bus sizing feature. The 1-megabit DRAM devices are currently available in two different configurations as 1M × 1 bit and 256K × 4 bits. If we use the 1M × 1 devices, we will get four megabytes per bank of 32-bit wide memory using 32 chips and we can increment the memory size by adding additional banks at increments of 4 megabytes. Similarly, one bank of memory using eight 256 K × 4-bit DRAM devices will provide 1 megabyte and we can increment memory size in 1-megabyte increments as shown in Figure 9-50 for 4 banks. The signal lines are shown as "feed-through" in this figure and are supported by some CAE systems to draw compact schematic drawings. This means, for example, that the DRAM_RAS0* signal is connected to the RAS* input of all DRAM devices in bank zero. Similarly, the respective data outputs of memory banks are connected together.

Further study of Figure 9-50 will show that all output-enables are tied to the digital ground (i.e., always enabled) and all write-enable (WE*) signal inputs are connected together as the DRAM_WRITE* signal. Note that RAS* and CAS* signals of DRAM devices are connected to do two-dimensional device selection. There is one RAS* input per bank, DRAM_RAS3-0*. Similarly, there is one CAS* input, DRAM_CASxx*, to enable the affected bytes of 32-bit wide memory. In other words, RAS* inputs are used to enable a bank of DRAM memory and CAS* inputs enable one or more bytes of the 4-byte wide memory. For example, in accessing a aligned long-word operand at a location of bank 1, DRAM_RAS1* and all DRAM_CASxx* signals will be active. Such two-dimensional device selection is advantageous because it saves additional decoding logic that would otherwise be necessary. We use the fact that applying RAS* or CAS* alone to a DRAM device will not turn on its data-output buffers. This allows us to configure the memory as shown without the possibility of any databus contention between the multiple banks.

It may be appropriate at this time to question whether we may configure the memory where RAS* is used in enabling bytes and where CAS* is used for the bank selection. The answer is yes. The preferred method is to use RAS* for the bank selection because of the substantial power savings over a system design that employs CAS* for the bank selection. This is because a DRAM device dissipates relatively significant power when RAS* is applied since it starts reading a row of memory cells. Other other hand, applying CAS* alone has no affect.

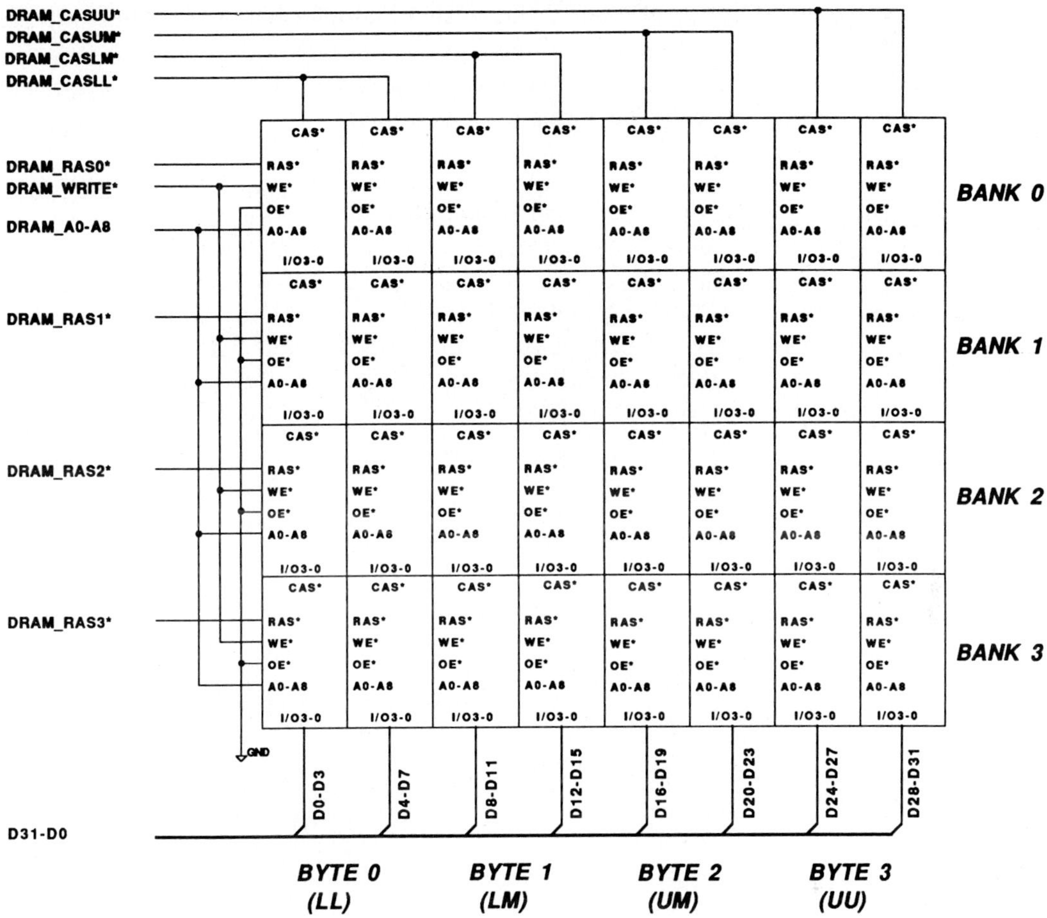

Figure 9-50 Memory Configuration using the 256K × 4-bit DRAMs.

DRAM CONTROLLER

In interfacing DRAM memory devices to the 68020 or any CPU, we need special circuitry in the address and control signal lines. This interface circuit is commonly called the *DRAM controller* and performs the following functions:

1. Multiplexes the CPU addresses as row and column addresses of DRAM devices.
2. Provides CPU-access timing signals (i.e., the generation of RAS*, CAS*, and other control signal timing during read or write bus cycles).
3. Generates refresh cycle requests and timing.
4. Arbitrates between the refresh and CPU access cycle requests.

5. Provides buffering of control signals and multiplexed address lines to drive the inputs of multiple DRAM devices.
6. Decodes multiple banks of DRAM memories and also provides byte-select logic to enable only the affected bytes of memory.

Figure 9-51 illustrates the functionality of a DRAM controller interfacing the memory of Figure 9-50 to the 68020. The low-order address bits, A1 and A0, are used in conjunction with SIZ1 and SIZ0 to enable the affected bytes of memory array. The high-order address bits, A20 and A21, are used to select one of the four banks of memory. The RAS∗ and CAS∗ generated by the timing and control unit is used to qualify the decoding of multiple RAS∗ and CAS∗ outputs. Even though it depends on the specific implementation, we effectively have the following relationship using the active-high logical equations in CUPL format:

```
DRAM_RAS0 =  RAS & !A21 & !A20 ;
DRAM_RAS1 =  RAS & !A21 &  A20 ;
DRAM_RAS2 =  RAS &  A21 & !A20 ;
DRAM_RAS3 =  RAS &  A21 &  A20 ;

DRAM_CASUU = CAS & (!A1 & !A0) ;
DRAM_CASUM = CAS & (!SIZ0 & !A1   #
                    !A1  &  A0    #
                     SIZ1 & !A1   );
DRAM_CASLM = CAS & ( A1 & !A0#
                    !SIZ1 & !SIZ0 & !A1 #
                     SIZ1 &  SIZ0 &  A0 #
                    !SIZ0 &   !A1 &  A0 ) ;
DRAM_CASLL = CAS & ( A1 & A0 #
                    !SIZ1 # !SIZ0 #
                     SIZ1 #  SIZ0 & A0 #
                     SIZ1 & A1 ) ;
```

The equations for DRAM_CASxx are the same as the byte-select equations we derived in section 9.6, except we chose not to enable all the bytes during a read operation for reduced power consumption. The above equations apply only to a CPU-access cycle, and does not take into account any refresh-cycle timing. The refresh timing depends on the type of refresh cycle we choose (i.e., RAS∗-only, CAS∗-before-RAS∗, and so on). In a design, we have to incorporate the refresh cycle logic into the above equations such that *all* banks are simultaneously refreshed.

The address lines A2 through A19 are divided into two groups to be multiplexed as row and column addresses. Although the choice is arbitrary, we may choose to connect the lower addresses such that they will become the row addresses for DRAM devices. The advantage of this is that it provides additional

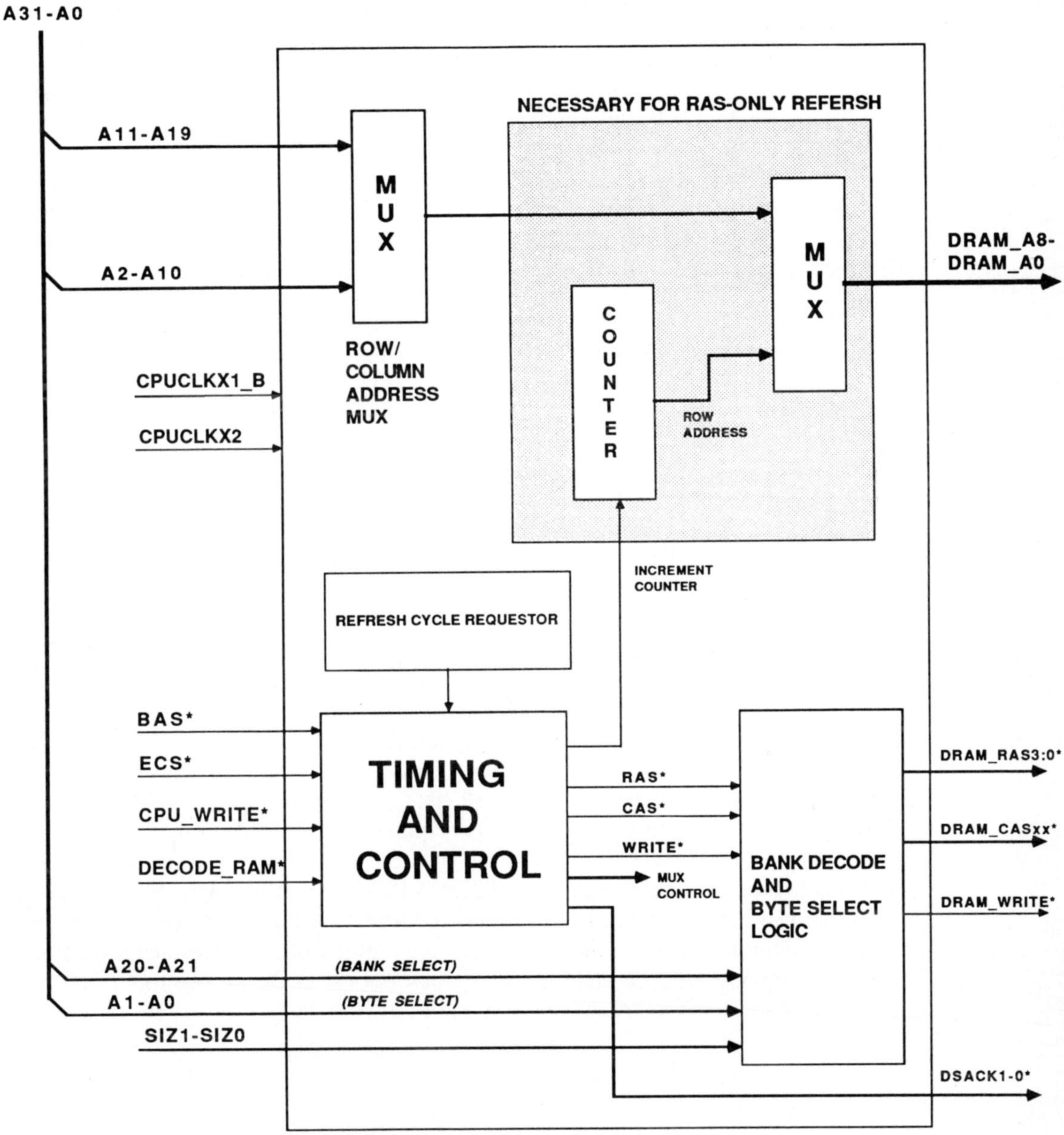

Figure 9-51 Block Diagram of DRAM Controller.

refreshing over refresh-only cycles because most CPU accesses will exercise the low-order address bits.

In addition to generating the RAS*, CAS*, and WE* timing, the timing and control unit also arbitrates between CPU-access and refresh-only cycle requests. The arbitration is done such that the highest priority is given to the currently active cycle thus allowing it to finish, it then moves next to the refresh request, and finally to the CPU-access request. This order of priorities allow support for both the distributed and the burst modes of refresh.

The 68020 requests an access cycle when DECODE_RAM* and BAS* are both asserted. If this coincides with an active refresh cycle or a refresh request, then the DSACKn* to the 68020 is delayed by the timing and control unit until the access is granted and the DSACKn* timing requirements are met.

Example DRAM memory design. As an example, let us look at the design of a 1-megabyte DRAM memory organized as 256K long-word locations. Using the 256K × 4-bit DRAM devices such as NEC's μPD424256 will require eight DRAM chips as shown in Figure 9-52. This is a single bank of memory that is a subset of the memory organization shown in Figure 9-50. Bidirectional data buffers are used because the drive capability of a DRAM is low (typically with an I_{ol} of 4 mA). These buffers may not be necessary in a small system.

The DRAM control circuit is shown in Figure 9-53. It basically consists of three '22V10 control PLDs, two 'F157 multiplexers, one 'F244 buffer, and two resistor packs.

The PLD with reference designator U1 controls the refresh cycle requests. Using the distributed refresh scheme, we need to refresh all 512 rows at least every 8 milliseconds. This requires a minimum refresh of a row every 15.6 microseconds as we saw earlier. The U1 PLD is basically an up-counter that periodically asserts the refresh request signal, REFCYC_REQ*, to the timing and arbitration PLD designated as U2. The refresh counter of U1 counts up to a fixed number and then asserts the refresh request, after which it clears itself and starts counting again. Once a refresh cycle is requested, it is held until a refresh cycle is granted by the arbiter of U2. During the refresh cycle, U2 asserts REFCYC* and this negates the refresh request REFCYC_REQ*. We will arbitrarily choose a refresh rate somewhat more frequent than the 15.6 microseconds. Let us pick 14 microseconds per row. This translates to a count value of 233 since the counter of U1 is running with a 60 nanosecond clock period as illustrated in Figure 9-54. In general, we need to satisfy the equation [20]

$$\text{REFCNT} \le \text{RC} - \text{RD} - \text{RW} \qquad \text{(Eq. 9-15)}$$

where

REFCNT: The number of clock cycles to generate the REFCYC_REQ* signal.

RC: The refresh count to satisfy the DRAM refresh specification. This is equal to Frequency/(512/8 msec) for this DRAM device.

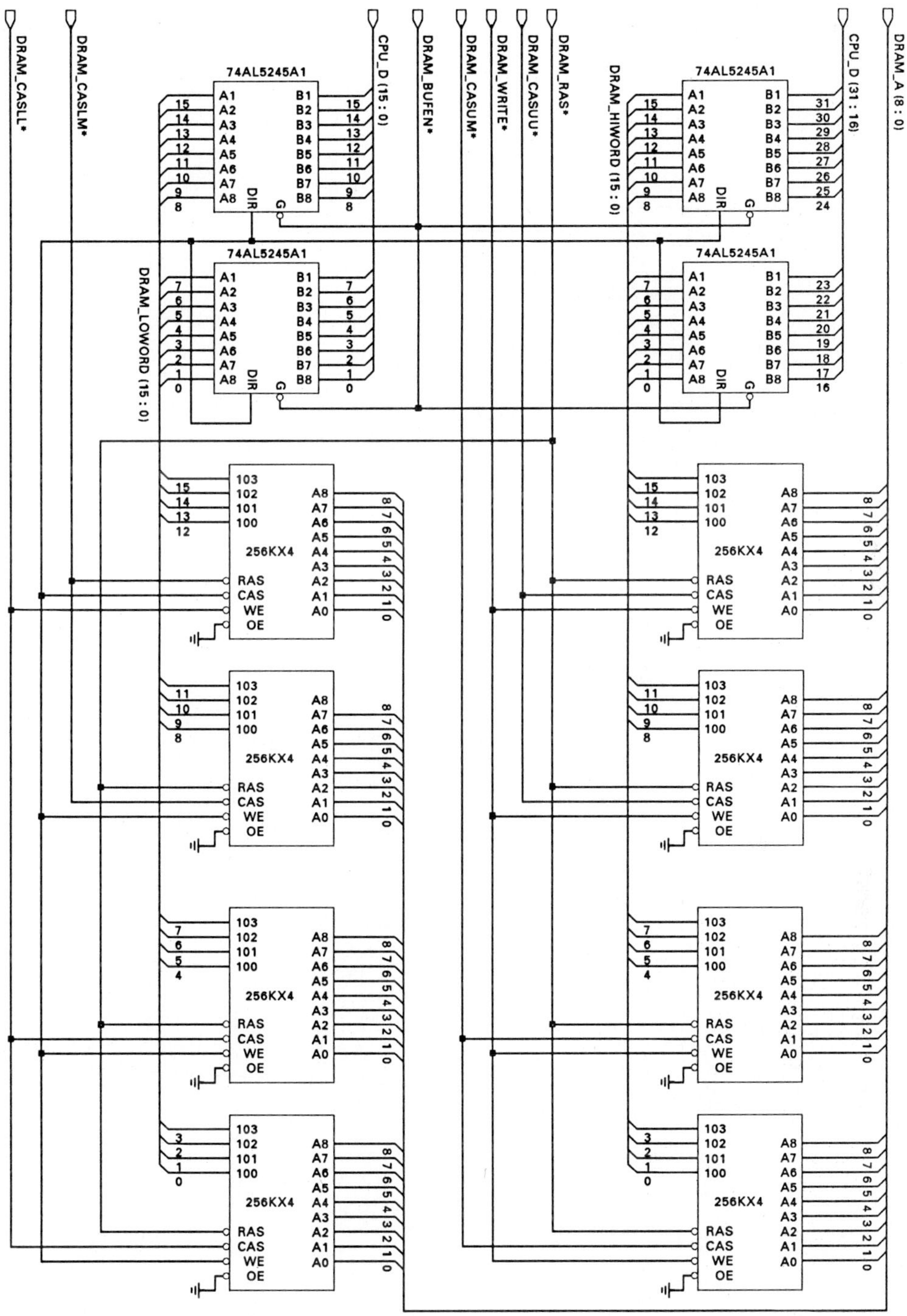

Figure 9-52 Example DRAM Memory.

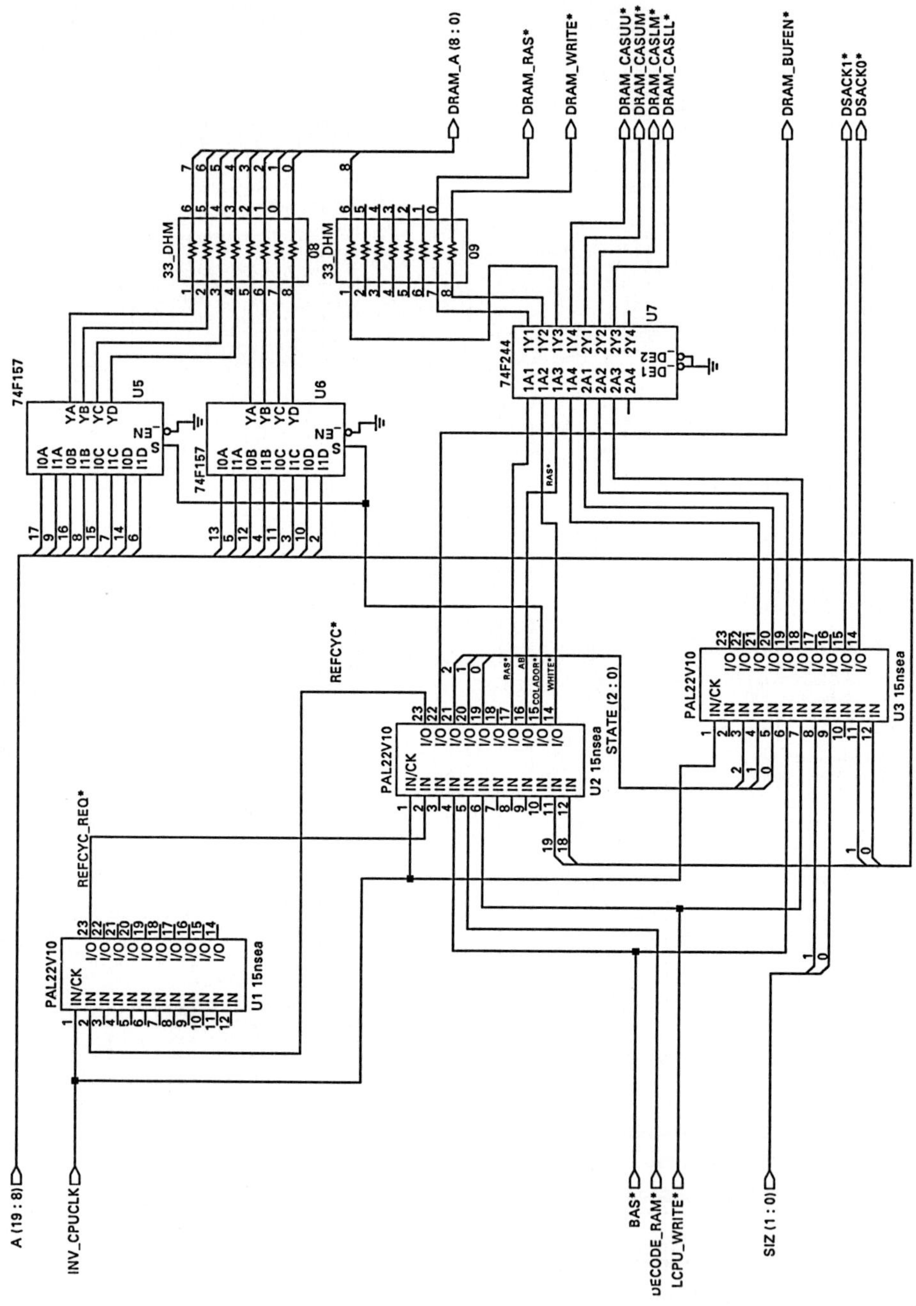
A (19 : 8)
INV_CPUCLK
BAS*
ECODE_RAM*
LCPU_WRITE*
SIZ (1 : 0)
PAL22V10
U1 15nsea
U2 15nsea
U3 15nsea
REFCYC_REQ*
REFCYC*
STATE (2 : 0)
74F157
U5
U6
74F244
U7
33_DHM
08
09
DRAM_A (8 : 0)
DRAM_RAS*
DRAM_WRITE*
DRAM_CASUU*
DRAM_CASUM*
DRAM_CASLM*
DRAM_CASLL*
DRAM_BUFEN*
DSACK1*
DSACK0*

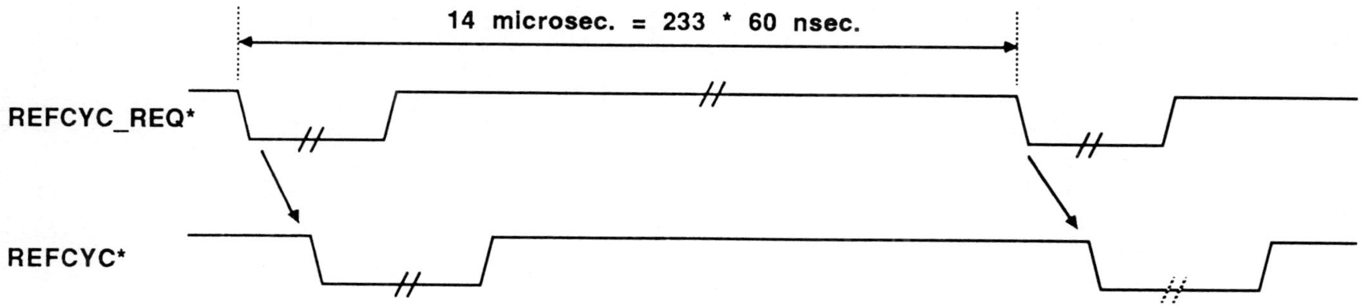

Figure 9-54 DRAM Memory Refresh Timing.

RD: The maximum number of clock cycles that refresh operation may be delayed.

RW: The length of refresh cycle.

For this example, RC = 260, and RW = 5. Let us assume that the longest bus-cycle for accessing other devices has 10 wait cycles. Therefore, RD is 13, and we have

$$\text{REFCNT} = 233 < 242.$$

Actually, in this example implementation, the value of RD is not important due to the way the U1 PLD's equations were specified (refer to Figure 8-33). This is because if one refresh cycle is delayed, then the next one will occur sooner, thus meeting the overall 8 millisecond refresh requirement.

The U2 PLD arbitrates requests for access by the 68020 and the refresh-only cycles. If both requests are detected at the same time, then the refresh request is given priority. The timing generation for all DRAM control signals (RAS*, CAS*, and so on) are handled by this PLD that is programmed as a synchronous Mealy-type state machine. The inputs to this state machine are the following:

BAS*	Buffered AS*.
DECODE_RAM*	When qualified with BAS*, this signal indicates a 68020 access request.
REFCYC_REQ*	This signal indicates a refresh cycle request.

The outputs of the state machine are the following

REFCYC*	This signal, when asserted, indicates a refresh cycle is in progress.
DRAM_BUFEN*	This signal enables the local data buffers of DRAM memory during an access.
STATE(2:0)	These three signals indicate the current state (0-7).
COLADDR*	This signal controls the selection of row or column addresses by the address multiplexer. When asserted, the multiplexer chooses the column addresses as the output of the multiplexer.
WRITE*	This is the WE* control signal of DRAMs before it is buffered.
A8	This is the multiplexed A8 address bit of DRAMs. We used part of the U2 to multiplex instead of using one more 'F157.

The control signals, CAS* and DSACKn*, are generated by the U3 PLD based on the state output, STATE(2:0), from the U2 as well as other control inputs.

The first step in the design of any state machine is to define the timing waveforms for all the functions required. The CPU-access timing for our example is shown in Figure 9-55 and we will leave the refresh cycle timing as an exercise (see Exercise 39).

To obtain the optimal access time of DRAMs, we need to generate the control signals RAS*, COLADDR*, and CAS* with a fine resolution in the order of 20 to 30 nanoseconds. One way we could accomplish this is to run the state machine at twice the clock speed of the 68020. This would provide a resolution of 30 nanoseconds between the critical control signal, while still being synchronous using the CPUCLKX2. However, there are two problems with such an approach.

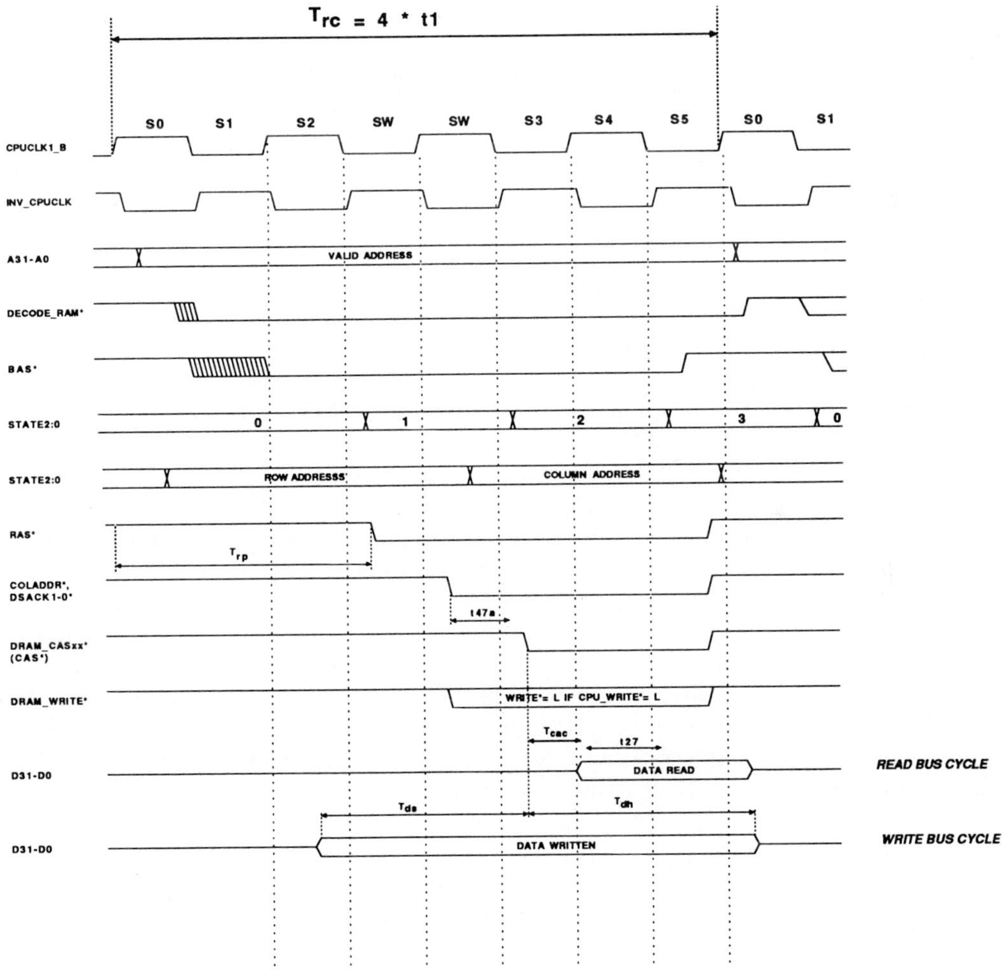

Figure 9-55 DRAM Memory Access Timing.

First, it makes the detection of 68020 access by the state machine difficult because (DECODE_RAM & BAS) may coincide with the clock edge. This could cause a metastable state which may not be resolved in 30 nanoseconds. Therefore, to prevent any circuit malfunction, this requires either a *gray-coded*[1] state machine, or double registration before the state machine. Second, any upgrades or designs running at higher clock frequencies (such as a 25 MHz 68020) would not be feasible.

Instead, we will use the 68020 clock signal to the state machine. Any synchronization we have to do for the BAS* causes loss of precious access time. Therefore, we will use the inverted version of the 68020 clock signal so that we can use the falling edge of state S2 to examine the BAS*. This allows for the BAS* to be treated as a synchronous input.

To generate signals with a finer resolution than the 60 nanosecond clock signal, we will use the following trick. We will use the clock signals' high and low periods to generate signals at twice the frequency. For example, to assert the SIGNALX* about 30 nanoseconds after the state 1, we can use the equation given by

```
SIGNALX = !CLK & STATE:1 & BAS # SIGNALX & BAS;
```

where CLK is the INV_CPUCLK. The first product term is the "turn-on" term i.e., this is true during the second half of state 1. Once the SIGNALX is asserted, the second term maintains it until the RAS* is negated.

The state flow diagram is shown in Figure 9-56. We used the states 1-2 for the 68020 access cycles and 4-7 to generate the refresh-cycle timing. The term (DECODE_RAM & BAS) indicates a 68020 access-cycle request.

One way we could implement the state machine is to wait until state 1 (i.e., STATE(2:0) = 1) before we assert RAS* signal. However, since address is already stable and the AS* is asserted before the beginning of S2, this would cause an unnecessary 30 nanosecond delay before the DRAM access is started. Instead, we will assert RAS* at the beginning of S2, before the state machine enters its state 1. This will result in one wait-cycle access time, instead of otherwise 2 if we had waited for state 1, as the reader can verify.

If there is a refresh request, then it takes priority over a concurrent 68020 access request, and the state machine makes a transition to state 4. The question that may be raised here is how we would assert RAS* immediately, if we do not know whether a refresh request is about to happen. Can we have a critical race condition between the 68020 access and the refresh cycle? The answer is that we do know if there is a refresh request before we can assert RAS*, because REFCYC_REQ* is generated synchronously by the previous clock edge of U1 PLD. The only problem that can occur is if INV_CPUCLK is delayed significantly (i.e.,

[1] Gray-coded state machine has the useful property as a *unit-distant code*. This property means only one output flip-flop change in transitioning from one state to another.

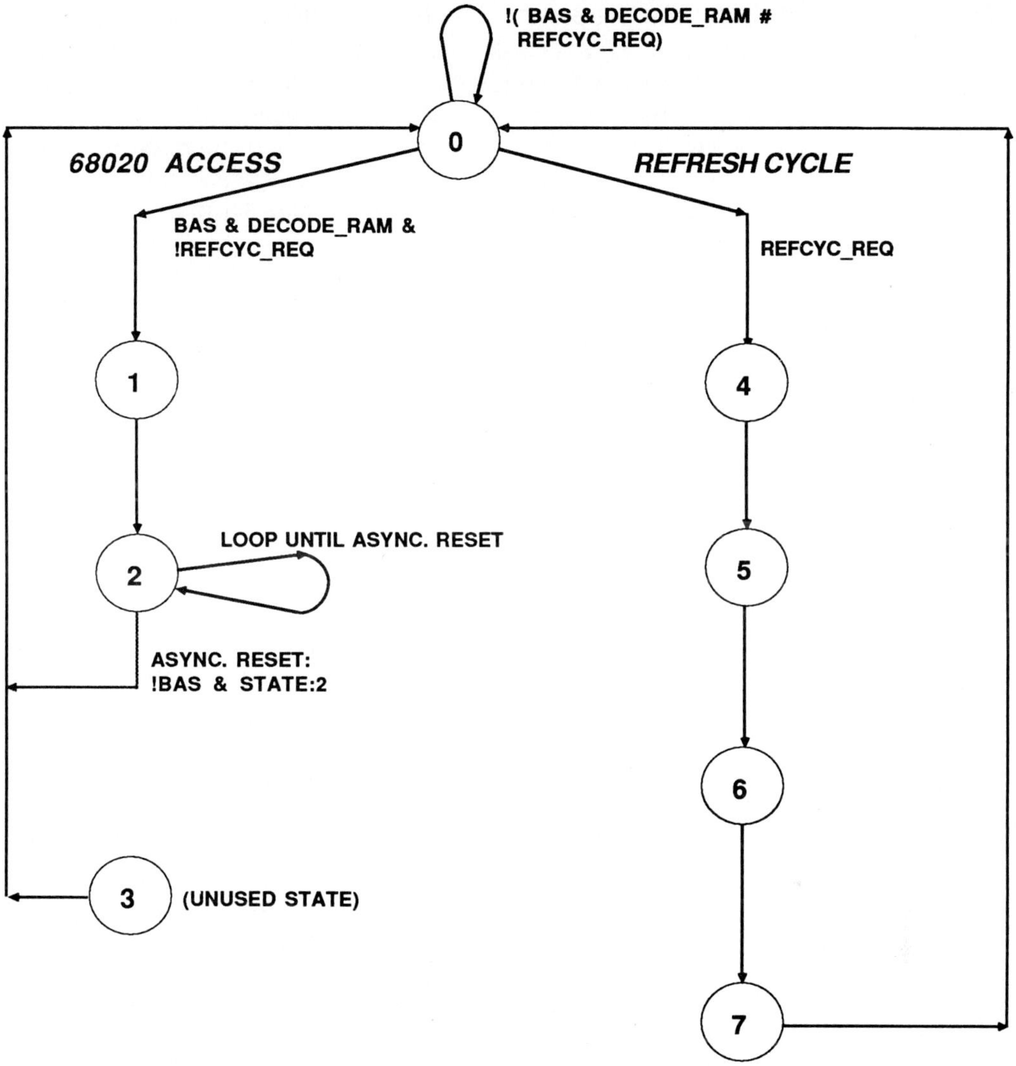

Figure 9-56 State-flow Diagram of DRAM Controller.

>10 nsec) with respect to the CPUCLKX1_B, and BAS* is asserted very early when

CPUCLKX1_B = L
INV_CPUCLK = L

and

DECODE_RAM* = L.

This would be problem, because it coincides with the clock edge when a REFREQ_CYC* may be generated. Because, during the T_{co} delay from U1, we do not yet know that a refresh request is about to happen. Preventing such an unlikely but possible situation is not difficult. We can delay CPUCLKX1_B with respect to INV_CPUCLK (as shown in Figure 9-3), and delay of AS* due to buffering also helps.

An important critical path in this design is the data setup time (t27) during a read cycle. We have

$$T_{pd} + T_{F244} + T_{rac} + 2 * T_{buf} + t27 \leq (N + 1) * t1 + t3$$

where T_{pd}: '22V10 Input-to-Output Relay

T_{F244}: 'F244 Maximum Delay

T_{rac}: RAS* to Data-Valid Delay during a read cycle of DRAM

T_{buf}: Dates Buffer Relay such as due to 'ALS245

N: Number of Wait-cycles.

For -80 version of DRAMs we have

$$15 + 6.5 + 80 + 20 + 5 = 126.5 < 2 * 60 + 24 = 144$$

which means -100 version of DRAMs would not meet the worst-case requirements.

The CAS*-Before-RAS* refresh method is used and so only one level of address multiplexing is necessary. The row and column addresses are multiplexed by the two 'F157s. However, these two are not sufficient to do 9 bits of address multiplexing. Instead of using a third 'F157, the U2 PLD is used to multiplex the addresses A18 and A19. This PLD has the multiplexer control output COLADDR* that is internally used to generate DRAM_A(8). Series resistor type termination resistors, U8 and U9, are used to avoid any "ringing" in the DRAM address lines, RAS*, and WE*, due to reflections.[7]

The PLD files are included in Appendix D for further details.

9.9 SYSTEM CONTROL SIGNAL LINES AND OPERATION

The system control signal lines of the 68020 are functionally similar to the earlier members of the family. As shown in Figure 9-57, RESET* and HALT* are bi-directional signals and BERR* is input only.

9.9.1 RESET* Signal and Interface

As an input, this signal is used to initialize the internal state of the 68020. Upon power-up, this signal must be asserted by the external logic for at least 100 milliseconds after the +5V supply is stabilized and within operating range. This is

[7] See reference 17 for further details on this topic.

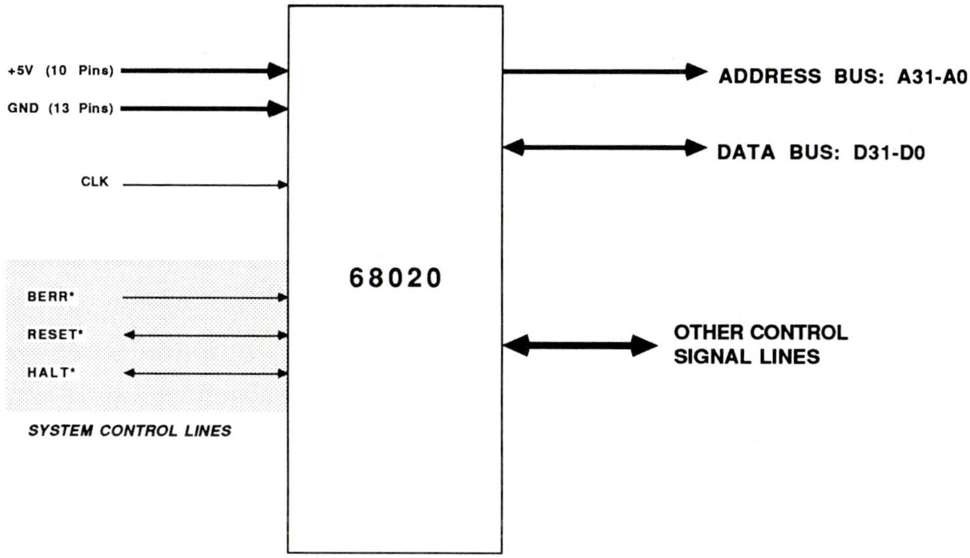

Figure 9-57 System Control Signal Lines.

illustrated in Figure 9-58. This also requires the clock signal to be stable before this reset period. However, it is safer to provide a reset time larger than this figure in order to allow for power and other circuits to stabilize before the 68020 starts executing. Typically, the reset time is set to a minimum of 200 milliseconds for reliable operation. When the RESET* signal is negated, reset exception is initiated by the 68020. Four clocks later, the 68020 starts fetching ISP and PC.

As an open-drain output, the 68020 asserts the RESET* line when executing the RESET instruction for a duration of 512 clock cycles. The RESET instruction

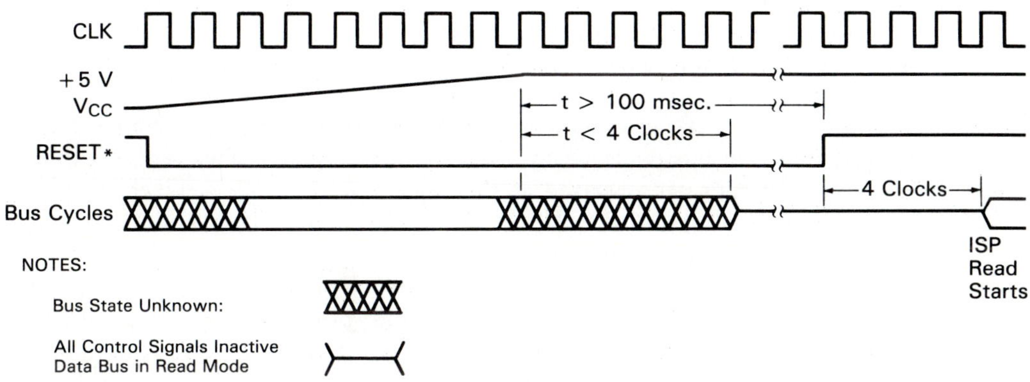

Figure 9-58 Reset Timing of the 68020.

does not affect the internal state of the 68020 and is only intended to initialize all connecting peripherals under the software control. During normal operation, we have to assert the RESET* for a minimum of 520 clock cycles for reset operation. This is to ensure that the 68020 recognizes external reset input in the worst-case, i.e., if external reset coincides with the execution of RESET instruction. Otherwise, 10 clock cycle long assertion of RESET* would be sufficient to restart the 68020. Typically, the same reset assertion time is used for power-up and system restart.

An example 68020 reset circuit is shown in Figure 9-59. This is very similar to the reset circuit we discussed for the 68000, but the 68020 does *not* require that the HALT* be asserted during a reset operation.

9.9.2 Bus Error (BERR*) and HALT* Signal Lines and Operation

The BERR* signal is generated by external logic to indicate an error condition with a bus cycle. It may be asserted in conjunction with, or instead of, the DSACKn* signals to terminate a bus cycle as illustrated in Figure 9-60. In the absence of DSACKn*, the BERR* is detected as an asynchronous input signal sampled at the negative-going edge of S2 or SW. If the BERR* is asserted at the same time, before, or within one clock cycle after the DSACKn*, it is also recognized as a bus-error termination.

The open-drain HALT* output is asserted by the 68020 when it detects a double-bus-fault condition. Otherwise, the HALT* is an input to the 68020. If asserted in conjunction with the DSACKn*, then it causes the 68020 to suspend all bus activity after the completion of current bus cycle until the HALT* is negated. However, the internal operation or the bus arbitration remains unaffected. For example, the 68020 may continue executing from the internal cache until it needs the use of the external bus. The halt mode differs from previous members in that the address lines and {R/W*, SIZ1-SIZ0, FC2-FC0} are driven with the last bus cycle information. Other control signals are driven inactive or in high-impedance state during the halt mode. The halt timing is shown in Figure 9-61.

Asserting HALT* in conjunction with the BERR* causes termination, and retry of the current bus cycle when the HALT* is negated. This requires that the HALT* and BERR* are asserted at the same time (i.e., recognized during the same sample window) and the BERR* is negated before or at the same time as the HALT* as shown in Figure 9-62.

The designer may choose to use the inputs {HALT*, BERR*} in a synchronous or asychronous manner similar to the handling of the DSACKn* input. However, the relation between the signals {DSACKn*, HALT*, BERR*} are important because when at least two of these signals are asserted approximately at the same

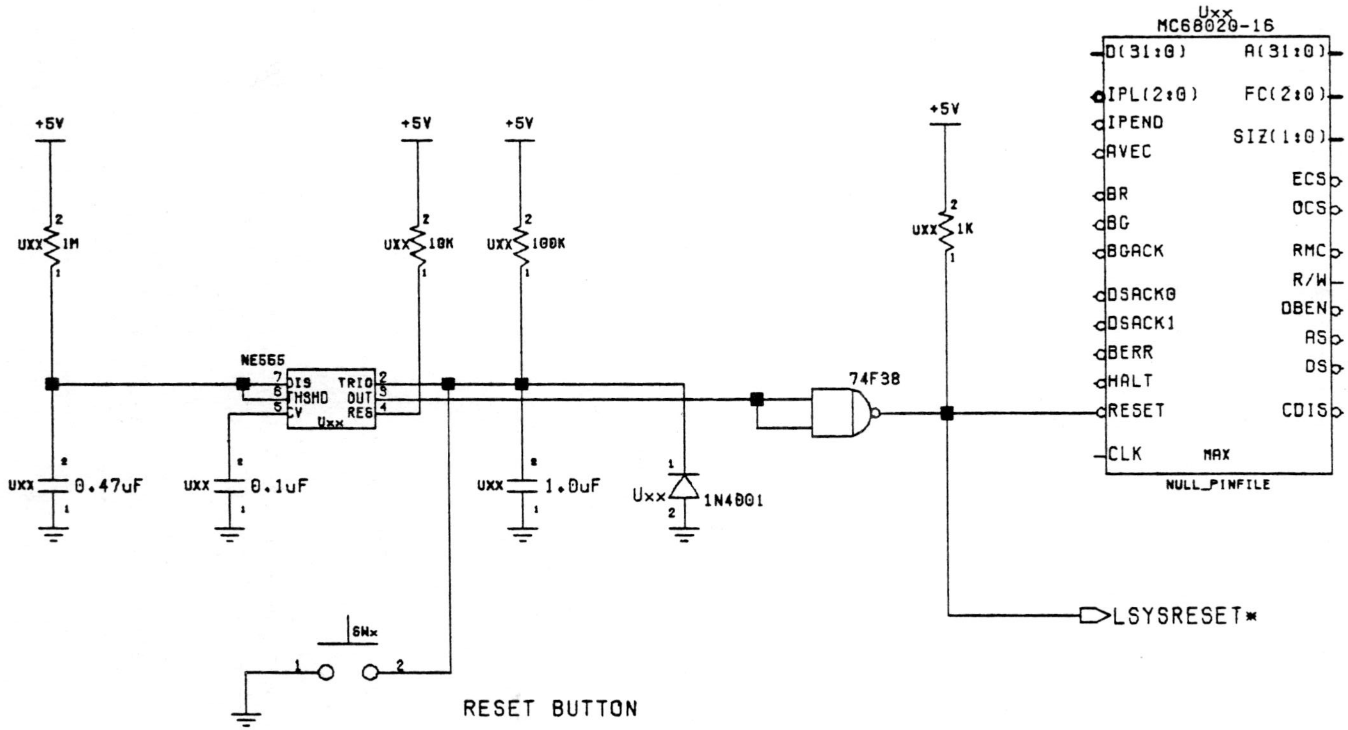

Figure 9-59 Example 68020 Reset Circuit.

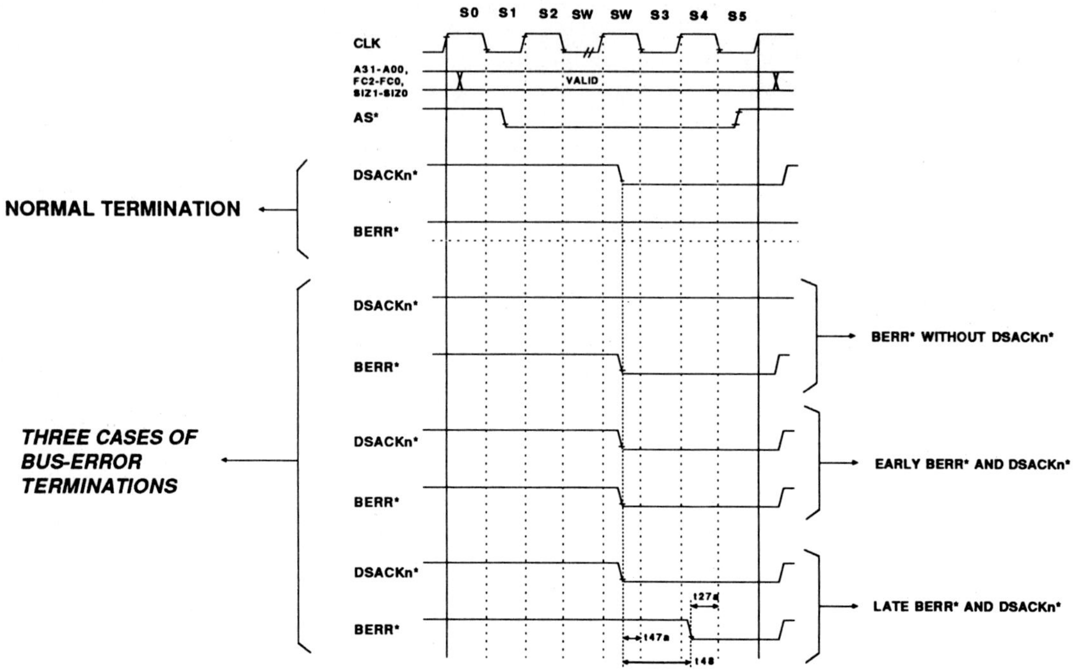

Parameter	Characteristic	Min	Max	Units
t27a	Late BERR*/HALT* Assorted to clock low.	20	—	nsec.
t48	DSACKn* asserted to BERR*, HALT* asserted[1]	—	30	nsec.

Note 1. Measured from the first DSACKn* that is asserted.

Figure 9-60 Normal and Bus-error Termination of a Bus Cycle.

time, then we must ensure that they are recognized during the same sample window of the 68020. One way of handling this is to synchronize these three signals to the positive-edge of the 68020's clock signal. This will guarantee that the asynchronous setup times of t47a will be met. Assuming that the t47a setup time during the sample window of state N will always be met, we can summarize the interaction of signal lines {DSACKn*, HALT*, BERR*} as shown in Table 9-3.

9.10 INTERRUPT CONTROL SIGNALS AND OPERATION

We studied the interrupt handling and operation of the 68020 in Chapter 6. In this section, we are going to focus on the required hardware interface for the interrupt request and acknowledge. Figure 9-63 shows the interrupt control signals of the

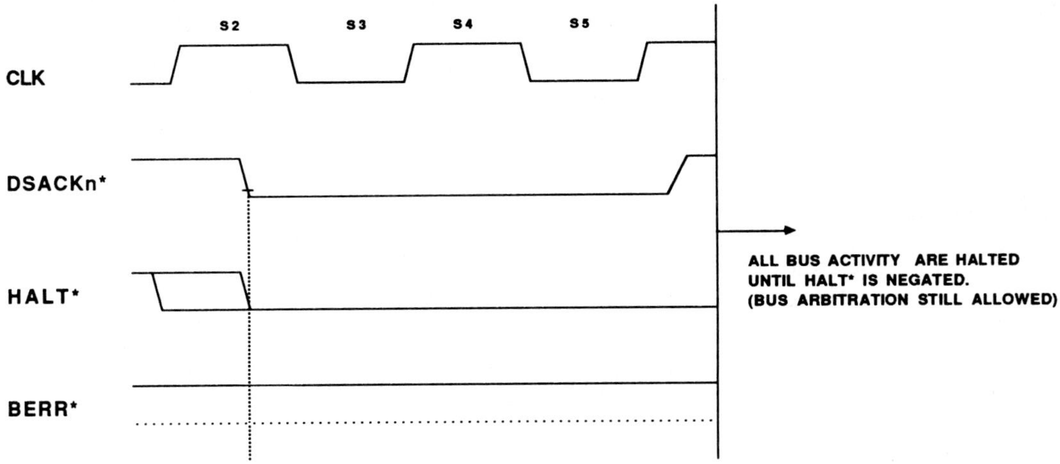

Figure 9-61 Halt Operation Timing.

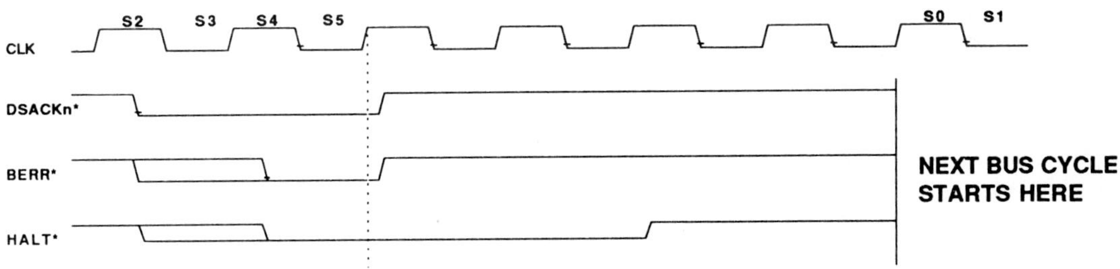

Figure 9-62 Bus-cycle Retry Timing.

68020. The interrupt request lines IPL(2:0)* function the same as the previous processors of the family (see section 4.4.3). The IPL(2:0)* are sampled on the negative-going edges of the processor clock and must remain at the same request level for two consecutive clock cycles to be considered valid. In other words, the 68020 samples and deskews the asynchronous request line before comparing the interrupt request level to the mask level (I2-I0) of the status register SR as illustrated in Figure 9-64.

If the interrupt request level is higher than the mask value or if there is a transition to level seven interrupt priority, the 68020 makes the request pending and asserts IPEND*. The IPEND* signal indicates to other peripherals that the processor has a pending request that will be serviced at the next instruction boundary. The IPEND* will be asserted even if the 68020 is not the current bus master. Its main purpose is to decrease the interrupt latency by signaling other DMA-type devices that an interrupt is pending.

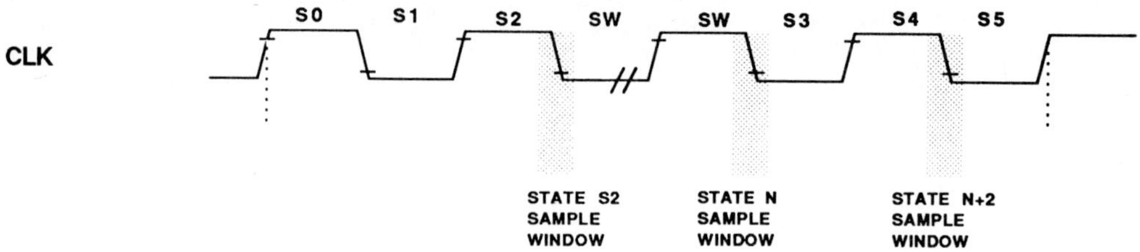

TABLE 9-3 SUMMARY OF BUS-CYCLE TERMINATIONS

Signal Line	Detected State During Sample Window #: *N*	*N* + 2	Termination Type
DSACKn* HALT* BERR*	L H H	L X H	Normal Cycle Termination.
DSACKn* HALT* BERR*	L L/S H	L L H	Halt Termination.
DSACKn* HALT* BERR*	H/L H L	X H L	Early Bus-error Termination.
DSACKn* HALT* BERR*	L H H	X H L	Late Bus-error Termination.
DSACKn* HALT* BERR*	H/L S/L L	X L L	Retry Termination.
DSACKn* HALT* BERR*	L H H	X L L	

S: Signal was asserted before and stays asserted.

As we have seen earlier, as part of the exception processing for interrupts, the 68020 performs an interrupt acknowledge bus cycle. This bus operation is a type of a CPU-space cycle and is distinguished from all other bus cycles by

$$FC(2:0) = \{HHH\}$$

and

$$A(19:16) = \{HHHH\}.$$

The external logic uses the interrupt level indicated by the address bits A(3:1) to enable the corresponding interrupting device.

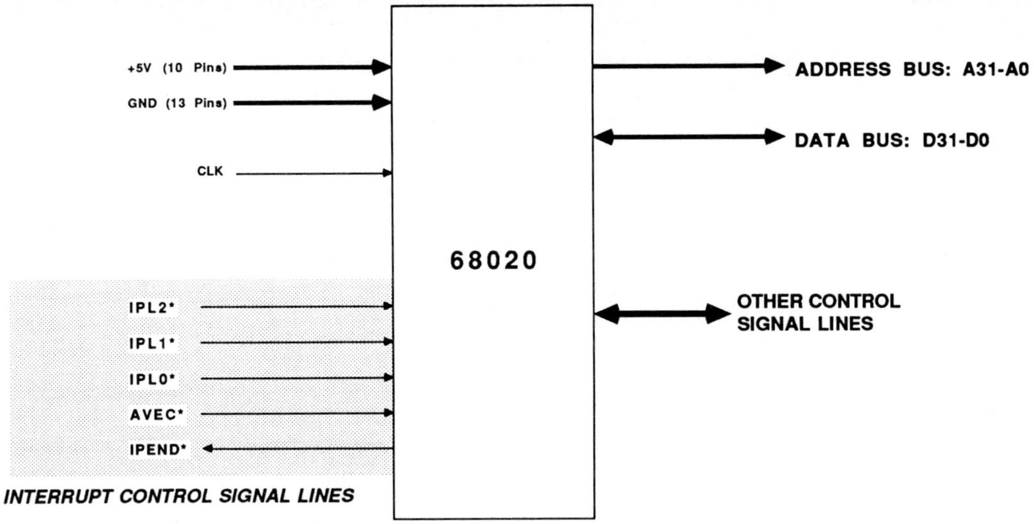

Figure 9-63 Interrupt Control Signals.

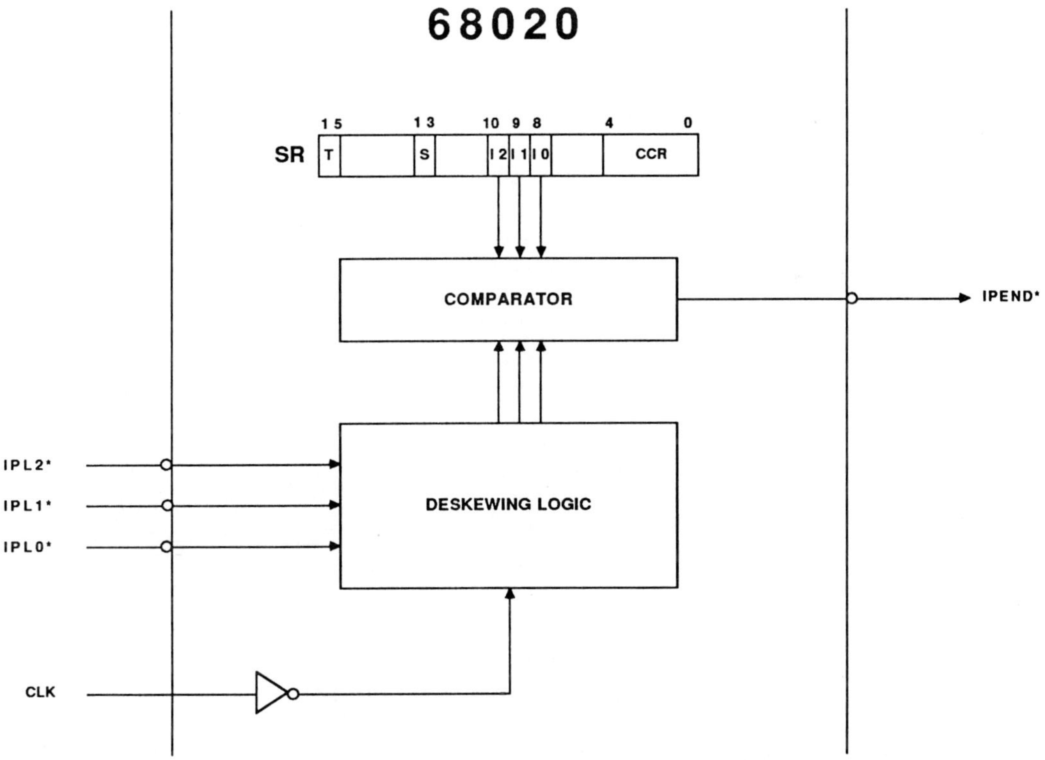

Figure 9-64 Interrupt Recognition Logic.

In the user-vectored case, the interrupting device returns an 8-bit vector number and asserts DSACK1∗ and/or DSACK0∗. The bus timing, in this case, is identical to a read bus cycle. A peripheral which does not have the capability to provide a vector number asserts AVEC∗ to request auto-vectoring. The AVEC∗ replaces interrupt functionality of the VPA∗ signal of earlier members since the 6800-interface signals are no longer supported. In the auto-vectored case, the 68020 internally generates the exception vector number as a function of the priority level (see Table 6-20). The timing of the AVEC∗ is shown in Figure 9-65. To signal auto-vectoring, it must be asserted in lieu of the DSACKn∗ signals with the same timing, in synchronous or asynchronous manner. The 68020 also recognizes the auto-vectoring if AVEC∗ is asserted before or at the same time as the DSACKn∗ signal lines.

An example of interrupt handling interface circuit is shown in Figure 9-66. This circuit supports three interrupters with the following assignments:

Interrupter #1: User-vectored.
Priority Level = 6.
Port Size = 32 Bits.
Interrupter #2: Auto-vectored.
Priority Level = 4.
Interrupter #3: User-vectored.
Priority Level = 3.
Port Size = 8 Bits.

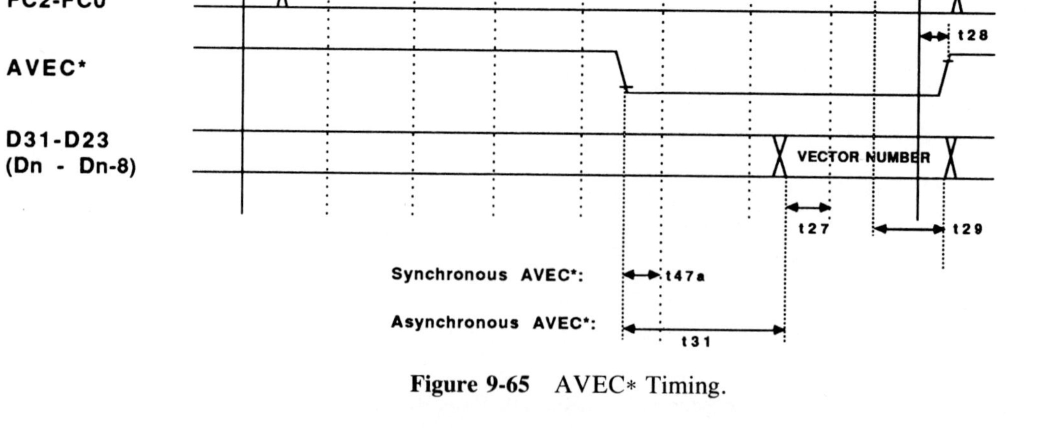

Figure 9-65 AVEC∗ Timing.

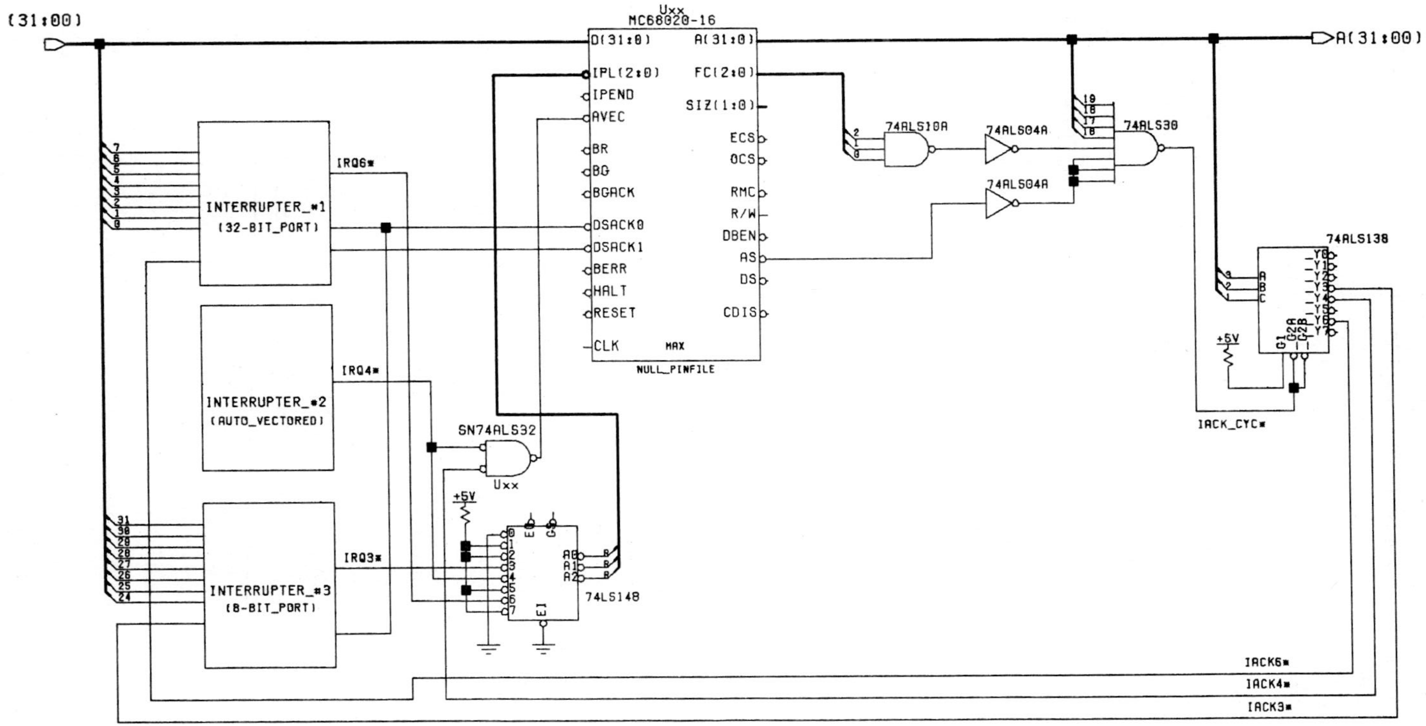

Figure 9-66 Example Interrupt Interface Circuit.

The priority encoder 'LS148 encodes the highest priority level onto the request lines IPL(2:0)*. During an interrupt acknowledge cycle, the decoder 'LS138 enables the device with matching priority level. A PLD implementation of the same circuit with reduction in parts count is given in Figure 9-67.

9.10.1 Summary of Interrupt Operation

The following are new features of the 68020's interrupt operation that are different from the earlier members of the 68000 family:

1. The IPEND* signal indicates to external devices that an interrupt request is pending.
2. The AVEC* signal is used to request auto-vectoring. It has the same timing requirements as the DSACKn*, and is typically used in lieu of the DSACKn*.
3. An 8-bit peripheral port that supports user-vectored interrupts has to be connected to the data lines D31-D24. Similarly, the vector number is transferred on the data lines D23-D16 and D7-D0 for word and long-word size ports, respectively.
4. The decode of an interrupt acknowledge bus cycle also requires that address lines A19-A16 be all H's.

The following interrupt handling features are the same as the previous members:

1. The interrupt request lines are internally synchronized and deskewed by the 68020.
2. The interrupt level seven is non-maskable (NMI). The only difference between level six and seven is that any *transition* to level seven causes an interrupt.
3. The deskewed interrupt request inputs, IPL(2:0)* are examined only once during the execution of any instruction. The timing of this is instruction dependent.
4. An interrupt request must be held until it is recognized by the 68020. Otherwise, the external logic cannot guarantee that an interrupt request will be serviced.
5. The 68020 does not perform any range checking on the provided user-vector numbers. Thus, all exception vectors could be accessed via the user-vectored interrupts.
6. If the number of interrupters exceed seven, then any number of these interrupters may be daisy-chained within a given priority level. This, effectively, creates subpriority within a priority level by daisy-chaining the IACK* line of that level.

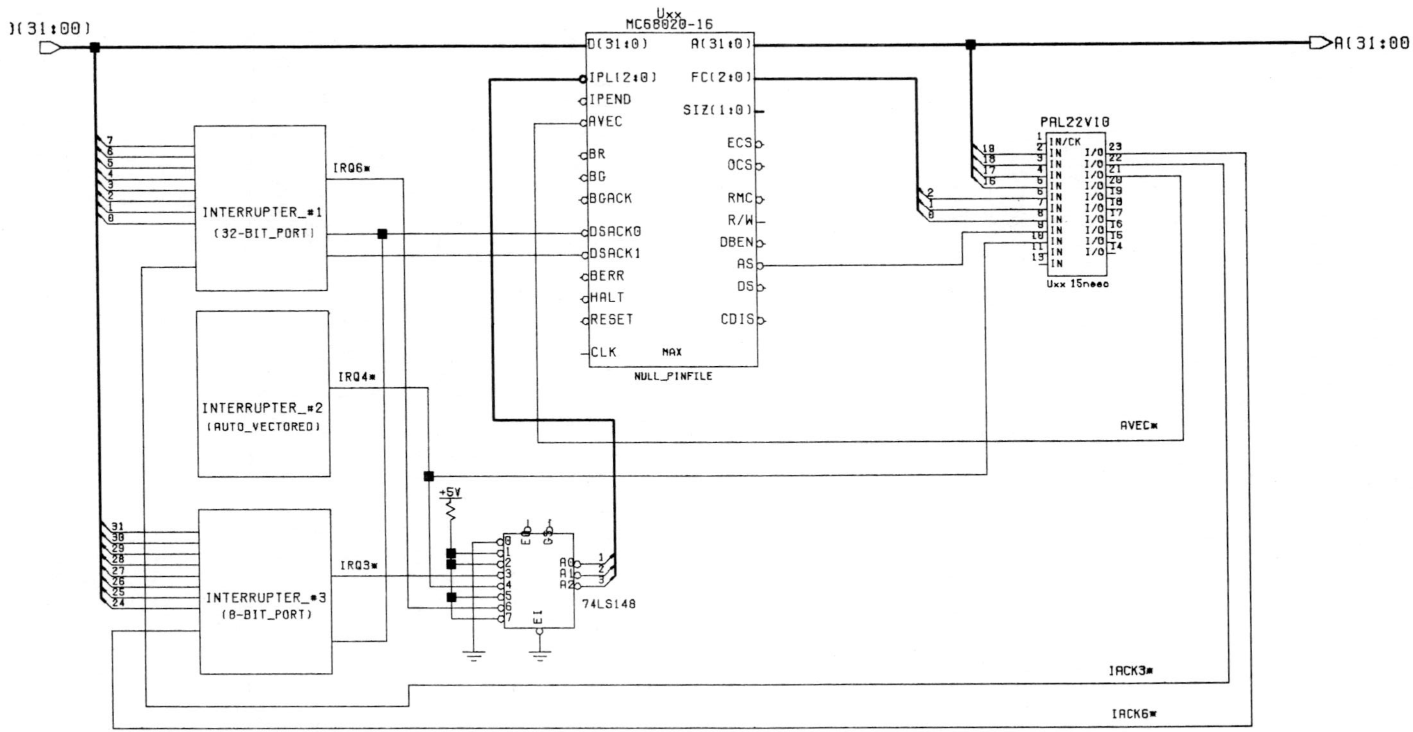

Figure 9-67 PLD Implementation of the circuit shown in Figure 9-66.

7. Asserting the BERR* input during an interrupt acknowledge bus cycle causes a spurious interrupt exception. Thus, an interrupt acknowledge bus cycle may be terminated by one of the {DSACKn*, AVEC*, BERR*} signals.

9.10.2 Example Interface to a DUART Peripheral

Figure 9-68 shows the interface of DUART '68681 to the 68020. The '68681 provides two full-duplex serial channels that are used to interface with a terminal and with a host computer via RS-232C communication links. The '68681[8] also has an 8-bit parallel output port (OP0-7), a 6-bit parallel input port (IP0-5), and a 16-bit counter/timer.

Both channels of the '68681 DUART can operate in four different modes: normal, automatic echo, local loopback, and remote loopback. A channel operating in the normal mode allows full-duplex communication. The automatic echo mode operates the same as the normal mode except DUART automatically retransmits any received data. The local and remote loopback modes are for diagnostic purposes that can be used to verify the correct operation of a channel.

The parallel ports of the '68681 can be used as general purpose inputs and outputs or for alternate programmable functions. For example, in our design we used the signals IP0-1 and OP0-1 that are used to control the handshake signals RTS and CTS of both serial channels. The handshake of these signals are handled automatically by the '68681. The status signals DTR and DSR, on the other hand, are connected to OP2-3 and IP2-3 that are programmed as general purpose I/O signals.

The data bus of DUART is connected via a bidirectional buffer ('ALS245) to prevent any bus contention and to meet the data-turn-off specification (t29a) of the 68020. Note that this buffer is enabled when DUART is accessed or during the interrupt acknowledge to read the interrupt vector number from the DUART. The DTACK* signal generated by the DUART is connected directly to DSACK0* line of the 68020. The DTACK* output of DUART is of open-drain type, so we assume that DSACK0* is pulled-up using a resistor (not shown here).

The DUART is connected to interrupt level three of the 68020 and user-vectored interrupts are used. During an interrupt acknowledge cycle, IACK3* is asserted, causing the data buffers to be turned on and DTACK* output of DUART* to be asserted. The interrupt condition must be cleared, in software, by accessing the proper registers of the DUART as part of the interrupt service routine.

A 3.6864 MHz crystal is connected between the X1/CLK and X2 pins. This crystal is required for the built-in baud-rate[9] generator. Each channel can be

[8] See *68000 Family Reference Manual* for datasheet summary of the '68681.

[9] In a serial channel, the baud rate defines the number of times the channel changes states (i.e., one baud is equivalent to one bit per second).

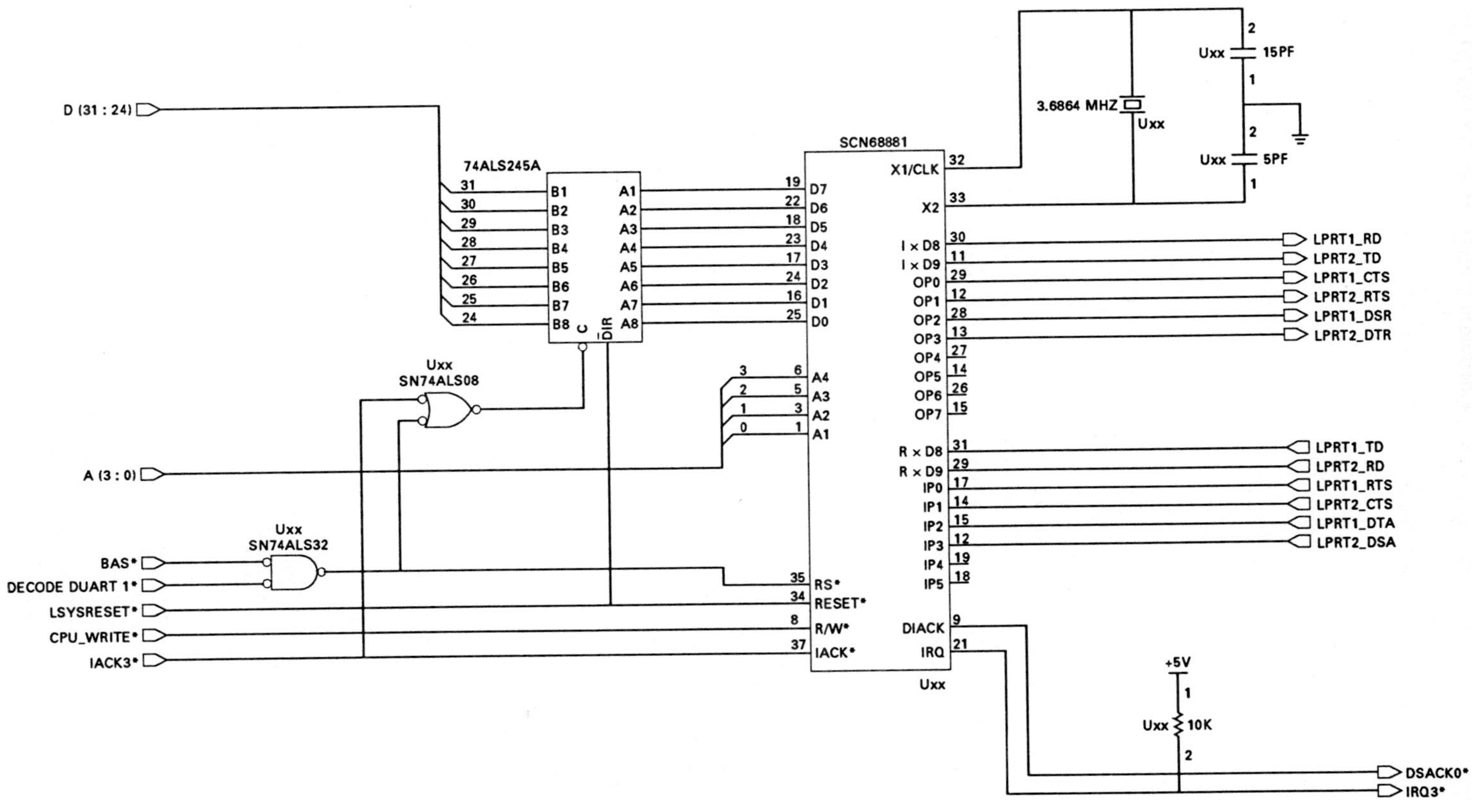

Figure 9-68 Example DUART '68681 Interface.

programmed independently for one of the 18 fixed rates, 50 to 38.4 Kbaud. The two shunt capacitors are recommended by the manufacturer to insure the proper operation of the baud rate generator.

Although the RS-232C standard is currently a very popular standard for serial binary interchange, it is still not fully understood by many working engineers. The following brief synopsis of the RS-232C is intended to clarify some of the important characteristics of this standard.

RS-232C Interface Standard. The RS-232C standard was developed by the Electrical Industry Association (EIA) in corporation with the Bell system. This standard specifies the mechanical and electrical requirements of an interface that is between a *Data Communication Equipment* (DCE) and a *Data Terminal Equipment* (DTE). The DCE is usually a modem or a computer and the DTE is usually a terminal or remote data processor. The RS-232C has an operating range of 0 to 20,000 bits per second (bps or baud) in bit-serial operation, synchronous or asynchronous.

The mechanical specifications include a 25-pin connector, referred to as DB-25, and its pin assignments as shown in Table 9-4. The DCE side of the cable is female and the DTE side is male type. This is usually indicated as DB-25S or DB-25P (socket or pins) in the specification of a serial port. One typical confusion is the direction of data between the DCE and DTE. For example, pin 2 of the connector is called *Transmitted Data*. The actual signal direction is from the DTE to DCE and, thus, the transmit-data pin of the DCE is actually an input. The best way to avoid this confusion is to remember that all naming of this signals are with

TABLE 9-4 RS-232C CONNECTOR SIGNAL ASSIGNMENTS

Mnemonic	Description	Pin No.	Direction
	Protective Ground	1	—
	Signal Ground/Common Return	7	—
TD or TxD	Transmitted Data	2	To DCE
RD or RxD	Received Data	3	From DCE
RTS	Request-to-send	4	To DCE
CTS	Clear-to-send	5	From DCE
DSR	Data Set Ready (DCE ready status.)	6	From DCE
DTR	Data Terminal Ready	20	To DCE
DCD	Data Carrier Detect (detected by Modem)	8	From DCE
	Transmitter Timing (DTE source)[1]	24	To DCE
	Transmitter Timing (DCE source)[1]	15	From DCE
	Receiver Signal Timing[1]	17	From DCE
	Ring Indicator (when connected to Modem)	22	From DCE

[1] The timing signals are used in synchronous mode.

[2] Connectors: DCE: DB-25P; DTE: DB-25S.

Table 9-5 Condensed EIA RS-232C Specifications [16]

Driver Output Voltage with Open-circuit		$-25 < V_o < +25V$
Driver Output Impedance With Power Off		$R_o > 300$ ohms
Driver Output Short Circuit Current		$I_o < 0.5$ A
Driver Slew Rate		dv/dt < 30 V/microsec.
Receiver Voltage Input Range:	+5 to +15 V	: Logic "0" = Space = Control ON
	−5 to −15 V	: Logic "1" = Mark = Control OFF
	+3 to +5 V	: Noise Margin.
	−3 to −5 V	: Noise Margin.
	−3 to +3 V	: Transition Region.

respect to the DTE, and the same signal names are used on both DTE and DCE sides. This will clarify our connections of two ports of Figure 9-68 where channel A is configured as DCE and channel B as DTE.

The condensed electrical specifications of the RS-232C are shown in Table 9-5. Except for protective and signal grounds, all signals of the RS-232C interface carry binary signals. The logic zero is called *space* and also corresponds to an active control signal. The logic one is called *mark* and corresponds to a non-active control signal. Furthermore, to provide fail-safe operation, it is specified that a receiver with an open-circuit input generates a mark condition. For example, when power is lost at the transmitter, the receiver interprets the signal condition as off or non-active. The RS-232C buffer circuit is shown in Figure 9-69. Note that the DCD is always active when power is on. The 400 pF capacitors at the data outputs are to reduce the slew rate to the specification level. These are sometimes omitted based on the load capacitances. The 100 pF capacitors at the inputs are to eliminate any line noise.

9.11 SUMMARY OF 68020 SIGNAL LINE CHARACTERISTICS AND TIMING

Table 9-6 gives a summary of DC electrical characteristics of the signal lines. Note that the output drive capability for HALT* and RESET* lines are increased to 10 mA, but the drive of other signal lines remain unchanged with respect to the 68000. The pin assignments are shown in Figure 9-70. As shown, the power and ground signal lines are separated into different groups to provide individual supply connections. Therefore, it is important to connect all supply connections, and including at least two decoupling capacitors.

The summary of AC electrical characteristics are given in Appendix A.

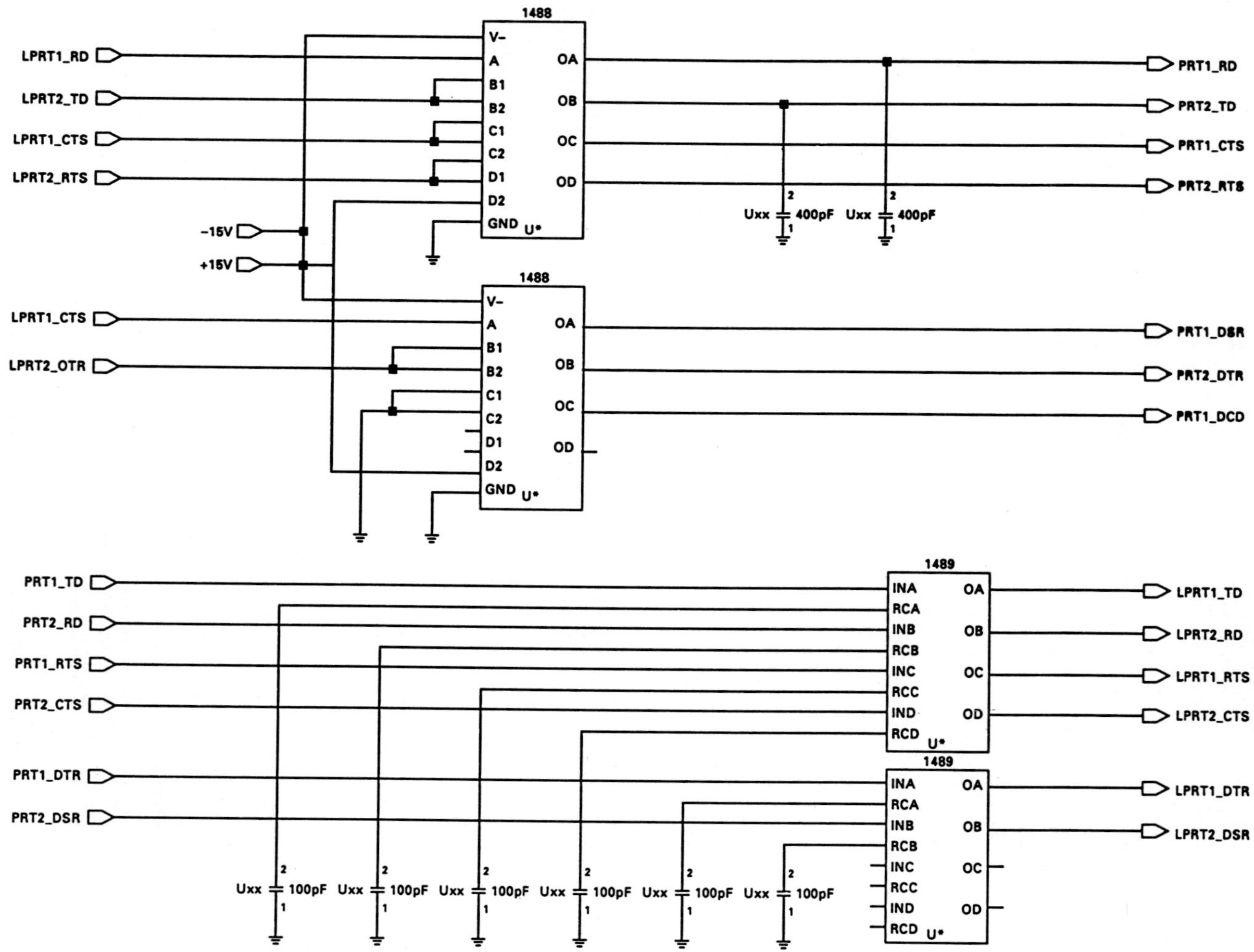

Figure 9-69 RS-232C Buffers for the Circuit of Figure 9-68.

PIN ASSIGNMENT

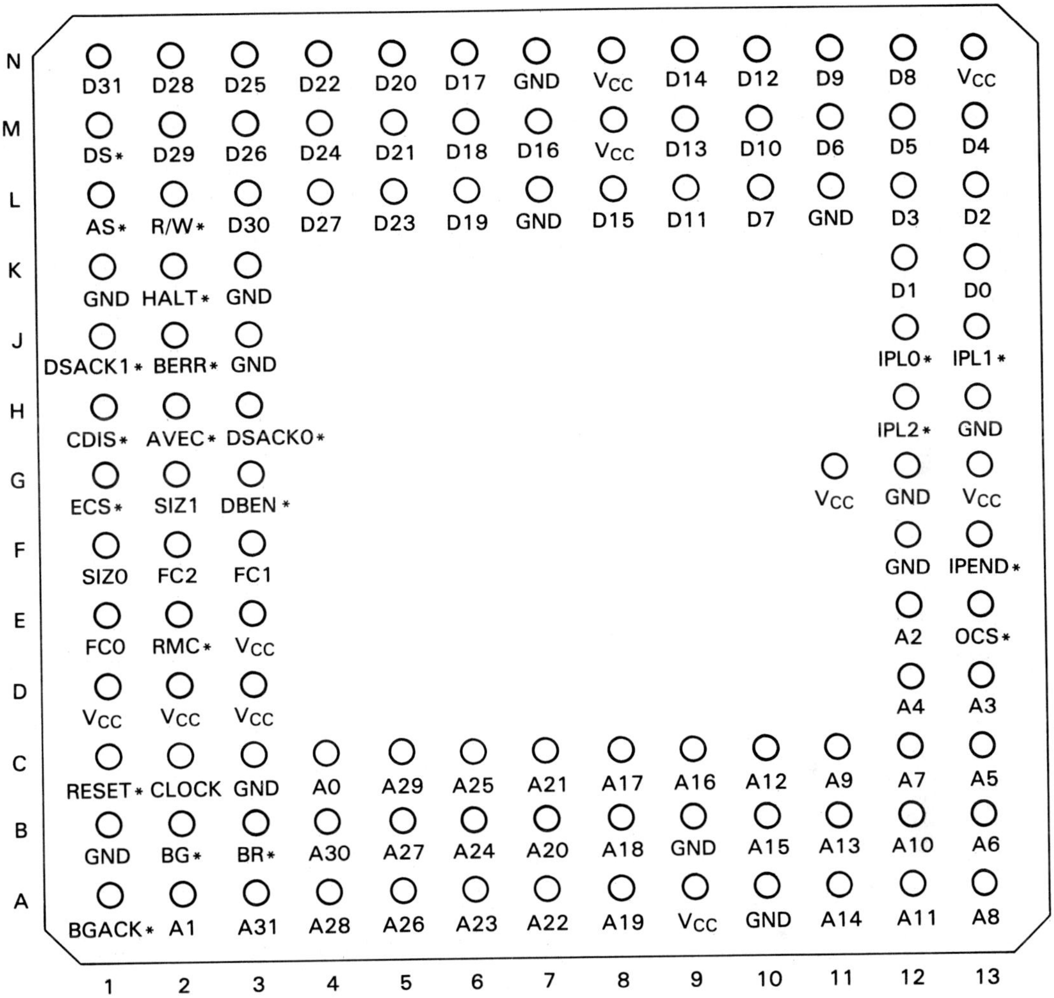

Group	+5V	Digital GND
Clock	—	B1
Address Bus Buffers	A9, D3	A10, B9, C3, F12
Data Bus Buffers	M8, N8, N13	L7, L11, N7, K3
Internal Logic	D1, D2, E3, G11, G13	G12, H13, J3, K1

Figure 9-70 68020 Pin Assignments and Grouping of the Supply Pins.

TABLE 9-6 DC Electrical Characteristics of the Signal Lines of the 68020.

Characteristic		Symbol	Min	Max	Unit
Input High Voltage		V_{IH}	2.0	V_{CC}	V
Input Low Voltage		V_{IL}	GND −0.5	0.8	V
Input Leakage Current GND ≤ V_{in} ≤ V_{CC}	BERR*, BR*, BGACK*, CLK, IPL0*-IPL2*, AVEC*, CDIS*, DSACK0, DSACK1	I_{in}	−1.0	1.0	μA
	HALT, RESET		−20	20	
Hi-Z (Off-State) Leakage Current @ 2.4 V/0.5 V	A0-A31, AS, DBEN, DS, D0-D31, FC0-FC2, R/W, RMC, SIZ0-SIZ1	I_{TSI}	−20	20	μA
Output High Voltage I_{OH} = 400 μA	A0-A31, AS, BG, D0-D31, DBEN, DS, ECS, R/W, IPEND, OCS, RMC, SIZ0-SIZ1, FC0-FC2	V_{OH}	2.4	—	V
Output Low Voltage		V_{OL}			V
I_{OL} = 3.2 mA	A0-A31, FC0-FC2, SIZ0-SIZ1, BG*, D0-D31		—	0.5	
I_{OL} = 5.3 mA	AS*, DS*, R/W*, RMC*,		—	0.5	
I_{OL} = 2.0 mA	DBEN*, IPEND* ECS*, OCS*		—	0.5	
I_{OL} = 10.7 mA	HALT*, RESET*		—	0.5	
Power Dissipation (T_A = 0°C)	f = 25 MHz f = 33.33 MHz	P_D	—	2.0	W
Capacitance (see Note 1) V_{in} = 0 V, T_A = 25°C, f = 1 MHz		C_{in}	—	20	pF

NOTE 1. Capacitance is periodically sampled rather than 100% tested.

FURTHER READING

1. Beims, Bob. (Motorola). "The MC68020 32-Bit MPU: Opening New Application Doors," *Motorola Application Note AR232*, May 1986.
2. Beims, Bob. (Motorola). "Multiprocessing Capabilities of MC68020 32-bit Microprocessor," *Motorola Application Note AR220*, May 1986.
3. MacGregor, Doug, Mothersole, Dave, and Moyer, Bill. (Motorola). "The Motorola MC68020." *IEEE Micro*, August, 1984, pp. 101–118. Also available as *Motorola Application Note AR217*.
4. "Using the MC68020 as a Dedicated DMA Controller," A Motorola Design Concept Document, DC003/D, September 1987.
5. Reddy, Al. "Dynamic Memory Refresh Considerations," *Motorola Application Note AN-887*, 1983.

6. "DRAM Refresh Modes," *Motorola Application Note AN987/D*, 1987.
7. "Considerations for System Design Using Redundant MC68020/MC68881 Pairs for High System Integrity," A Motorola Engineering Bulletin, EB115/D, 1987.
8. Reinhart, James T. "Product Development for the MC68020," *Motorola Application Note AR227*, 1984.
9. "Avoiding Data Errors with Fast Static RAMs," *Motorola Application Note AN973*, 1987.
10. "MC68020 Microprocessor to Versabus/VMEbus Interconnection Techniques," *Motorola Engineering Bulletin EB114*, 1985.
11. *M68000 Family Reference*, Motorola, FR68K/D, 1988. This databook contains datasheets on all 68000 family processor and support chips manufactured by Motorola.
12. *Dynamic Memory Control State Sequencer, Application Note Reprints, Applied Micro Devices (AMD) PAL Device Handbook*, pp. 2-224 through 2-228, 1988. This book contains collection of application notes for various PLDs.
13. *VLSI Technology*, Edited by S.M. Sze, Bell Laboratories, Inc., McGraw-Hill Book Company, 1983. See pages 473–475 for the operation of DRAMs.
14. "Metastability, A Study of Anomalous Behavior of Synchronizer Circuits," *AMD/MMI PAL Device Data Book*, pp. 3-164 to 3-169, 1988. This is an excellent article on the Metastability.
15. Del Corso, D. and et al., *Microcomputer Buses and Links*, Academic Press, 1986. See p. 25 for metastability and p. 330–340 for RS-232 interfaces. This book also provides an excellent discussion of system buses.
16. McNamara, John W. *Technical Aspects of Data Communication, Third Edition*, Digital Press. This is a popular book on data communications, covering RS-232C and other communication standards.
17. "Improving Your Memory with 'S700-family MOS Drivers," *Application Note AN-117*, Monolithic Memories (MMI), 1983. This paper is a slightly modified version of the paper by the same name in the Conference Proceedings of the 8th West Computer Fair, 18-20 March 1983.
18. "Avoiding Bus Contention in Fast Access RAM Designs," *Motorola Application Note AN971* (Rev. 1), pp. 11-8 to 11-11 in *Motorola Memory Databook* (DL113, Rev. 4), 1988.
19. "Page, Nibble, and Static Column Modes: High-Speed Serial Access Options on 1M-Bit DRAMs," *Motorola Application Note AN986*, pp. 11-4 to 11-7 in *Motorola Memory Databook* (DL113, Rev. 4), 1988.
20. "Burst-Mode DRAM Controller for the MC68030," *Motorola Application Note AN999/D*, 1988.
21. Gumm, Steve and Dreber, Carl T. (Texas Instruments). "Unraveling the intricacies of dynamic RAMs," Part 1 of 4 part designer's guide, EDN, pp. 155–166, March 30, 1989.
22. Wawrzynek, Ronald. "Tailor memory-system architecture for your chosen DRAM" (Texas Instruments), Designer's guide, part 2, EDN, pp. 157–164, April 13, 1989.
23. Adams, Robert and Seavone, Gregory, "Design a DRAM from the top down" (Texas Instruments), Designer's guide, part 3, EDN, pp. 183–188, April 27, 1989.

24. Tabaian, Fred and Toomer, Marlene M. "Attention to layout detail facilitates DRAM-board design" (Texas Instruments), Designer's guide, part 4, EDN, pp. 179–186, May 11, 1989.

EXERCISES

Signal Lines and Bus Operation

1. Explain the function of the following signal lines:
   a) CDIS*
   b) DBEN*
   c) ECS*
   d) RMC*
2. What is the difference between the ECS* and the OCS*?
3. Draw a clock signal showing the 68020 states (S0-S5) during a bus cycle with no wait states, and answer the following:
   a) Where is the sample window for an asynchronous input signal to the 68020? What happens if the input signal does not meet the setup time required?
   b) Where is the sample window where the input data is latched during a read bus cycle?
4. Repeat exercise 3 for one wait-cycle.
5. Does the DBEN* have any function during a read bus cycle? Why?
6. What do we mean by the statement "The designer may choose to interface synchronously or asynchronously with the 68020"? What is the decision criteria. Is this any different than the earlier members of the 68000 family?
7. Indicate the best and worst case timing values of parameters shown for a 16.67 MHz 68020 in the Figure 9-71.
8. What is the on/off duty cycle of LED shown in Figure 9-9 for consecutive bus cycles with no wait-cycles? What is the average current of the LED in this case? What would prevent the LED from continuously showing a "run" condition if a device does not return DSACKn*.
9. a) What are the timing parameters that we must meet for asychronous interface? How do we determine the number of wait-cycles in an asynchronous bus operation?
   b) What are the timing parameters that we must meet for synchronous bus operation?
10. In example clock interface logic of Figure 9-3, why did we use an inverting buffer ('F240)? Would a non-inverting buffer generate the same clock timing signals? Explain using a timing diagram. (Hint. Assume we want to match the positive-going edge of X1 and X2 clock outputs.)
11. Calculate the parameters t_{AVDV} and t_{SADV} for a 25 MHz 68020 (Refer to Appendix A) operating with zero and one wait-cycles.
12. What is a CPU-space cycle? How is it indicated to peripheral devices? What is the coding of address bus during an interrupt acknowledge?

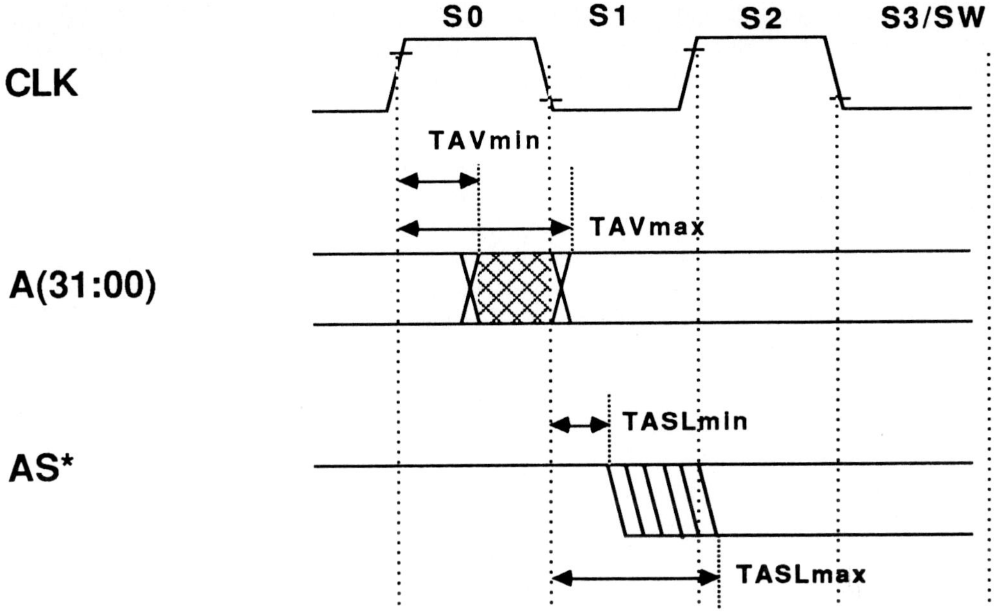

Figure 9-71

Address Decoding

13. **a)** Why is the address decoding done before the address buffers?

b) What is the use of LCPU_WRITE* and DS* as inputs to the decoder?

c) Draw the circuit diagram for the following memory map using 'F521's.

```
DECODE_DEV1* :0-7FFF (Not qualified with AS* or DS*)
DECODE_DEV2* :100000-3FFFFF (Not qualified with AS* or
DS*)
SEL_DEV3*    :F00000 (Read-Only and qualified with DS*)
SEL_DEV4*    :F00000 (Write-Only and qualified with DS*)
```

14. Modify the address decoding of circuit shown given in Figure 9-22 for the following address map:

```
ROM/EPROM   0-7FFFF           (512 Kbytes)
RAM         100000-3FFFFF     (4 Mbytes)
DUART #1    1000000-100000F   ('68681)
DUART #2    1000010-100001F   ('68681)
```

15. Modify the circuit of Figure 8-46 for the 68020 so that during fetching of the reset vector EPROM is enabled. In other words, the memory map is changed to the following after the initial PC and SP are fetched:

```
RAM:    0-FFFFF
EPROM: 100000-13FFFF (100000: Initial PC,
                      100003: Initial SP)
```

Assume EPROM memory is 16-bits wide. (Hint. Use an 'ALS164 to count the bus cycles for fetching the reset vector. The memory map is to be changed to read reset vector *only* after power-up or manual reset, and not to be affected by RESET instruction.)

DSACK Generation Logic

16. Does the circuit given in Figure 9-25 cause any problems in data transfer when the DSACKn* is recognized one clock cycle late? Or, is it just that this causes performance degradation? Please explain.

17. Verify that the circuit of Figure 9-26 meets the asynchronous setup and hold parameters t47a and t47b of the DSACK inputs.

18. Change the PLD equations of Figure 9-29 for the following:

Device 1: 0 wait-cycles, Port size = 16-bits
Device 2: 3 wait-cycles, Port size = 8-bits

Dynamic Bus Sizing and Byte-Select Support Logic

19. Why do we need byte-select logic?

20. Change the equations of PLD given in Figure 9-31 so that only the affected bytes are enabled on both read and write operations? What is the advantage of this?

SRAM Memory Design

The exercises 21 through 26 are regarding the SRAM design discussed in section 9.8.1. Assume the following speed rating of devices shown in Figure 9-34: '22V10-25, 68020RC16, and 55 nanosecond SRAMs unless otherwise specified.

21. Is the SRAM interface shown CS* or WE* controlled?

22. What is the actual data hold time (T_{hd}) as seen by the SRAMs during a write bus cycle?

23. Calculate T_{rc} and T_{wc}.

24. Modify the design to double the SRAM memory to 256 Kbytes. Specify the logical equations and pin definitions of all affected PLDs.

25. Re-evaluate the Example 9-4 for a 25 MHz 68020. What is the PLD and SRAM speed ratings necessary for zero wait-cycles.

26. Modify the example design to a non-volatile memory using a memory backup circuit.

EPROM Memory Design

The exercises 27 through 31 are regarding the example design shown in Figure 9-39.

27. If we use the 250 nsec version of the EPROMs, what is the number of wait-cycles. The access time of EPROMs are given by

$$T_{acc} = \text{Address-to-Output Delay} = 250 \text{ nsec.}$$

and

$$T_{ce} = \text{Chip-enable-to-output Delay} = 250 \text{ nsec.}$$

28. Change the circuit such that CE* is always enabled and EPROM accesses are controlled by OE*, where we have the access time given by

$$T_{oe} = \text{Output-Enable-to-Output Delay} = 150 \text{ nsec.}$$

What is the resultant number of wait-cycles?

29. Change the design to 32-bit wide configuration. What are the advantages and disadvantages of this configuration?

30. Incorporate the EPROM interface logic of Figure 3-39 in a PLD specifying the pin definitions and logical equations in CUPL format.

31. Change the design to a memory configured as 256K × 16 bits using the '27C010 EPROMs (128K × 8 bits per device), where the accesses are controlled by CE*. What EPROM access time is required for two wait-cycle read accesses with a 16.67 MHZ 68020. What would be the increase in power consumption if we enabled the EPROMs all the time and used OE* to control accesses?

DRAM Memory Design

32. Explain the following operational modes of DRAM devices:

a) Read Cycle—Draw timing diagram.

b) (Early) Write Cycle—Draw timing diagram.

c) OE*-Controlled Write Cycle (late write cycle).

d) Page Mode (see note).

e) Nibble Mode (see note).

f) Static Column Mode (see note).

g) RAS-Only Refresh Mode.

h) CAS-Before-RAS Refresh Mode.

Note: Refer to DRAM manufacturer data books or reference [21].

33. Explain how we may use the page mode to speed up instruction prefetches.

The exercises 34 through 40 are regarding the example DRAM design given in Section 9.8.3.

34. Fill in the table shown below verifying that the example design satisfies the DRAM and the 68020 parameters that are listed. Assume a 16 MHz version of the 68020, and 80 nanosecond version of the '424256 DRAMs. Are there any parameters that are violated? Based on this table, can we use a slower DRAM version (−100 or −120 nsec.)?

Device	Parameter	Actual Min.	Actual Max.	Required Min.	Required Max.	Units
'424256-80	T_{asr}					
	T_{rah}					
	T_{asc}					
	T_{cah}					
	T_{ras}					
	T_{cas}					
	T_{rcd}					
	T_{cpn}					
	T_{rsh}					
	T_{csh}					
	T_{rac}					
	T_{cac}					
	T_{rcs}					
	T_{rch}					
	T_{wcs}					
	T_{wch}					
	T_{wp}					
	T_{ds}					
	T_{dh}					
68020RC16	t27					
	t28					
	t29					
	47a					

NOTE: Fill in min. and/or max. values as applicable.

35. The three critical timing parameters for the '22V10 are:

$$T_{pd} = \text{Input-to-Output Propagation Relay (combinatorial)}$$

$$F_{max1} = \text{External Maximum Frequency} = 1/(T_{co} + T_s)$$

$$F_{max3} = \text{Internal Feedback Maximum Frequency} = 1/(T_{cf} + T_s)$$

following the notation given in Appendix G, where T_{co} is the clock-to-output delay and T_{cf} represents the clock-to-feedback delay. The T_{cf} is less than T_{co} because the signal does not have to go through the output select mux and driver. Verify that these operational limits of the state machine PLDs are met.

36. Re-design for 2 Mbytes of memory, using two banks of 256K × 4 DRAM memories. Specify the pin definitions and logical equations of all affected PLDs.

37. A. Does the example design provides support for read-modify-write cycles, or is the use of RMC* necessary? Please explain.

B. What kind of problem would occur if we made the following changes to state machine equations:

1) STATE2-0.ar = !BAS; /* STATE:2 term omitted */

2) PRESENT 'd'3 NEXT 'd'0; /* This line omitted. */

3. Omitted !(STATE:[4..7]) from the RAS equation.

4. Omitted !(STATE:[4..7]) from the DRAM-CASxx equations.

38. How would the use of 120 nanosecond '424256 DRAMs affect the design in terms of the following:

a) Number of wait-cycles.

b) State machine flow diagram.

(Note: refer to Appendix E for DRAM parameters at 120 nsec.)

39. A. Draw the timing diagram for the refresh cycle, showing all relevant signals. Use the case when refresh request occurs in the middle of a 68020 access cycle.

B. Draw the timing diagram for the case when a 68020 access begins during a refresh cycle. Show that t47a and t27 or t31 requirements are always met in such a case.

40. Modify the DRAM controller circuit for use with a 33 MHz 68020.

a) What has to be changed?

b) Re-draw the state flow chart, if affected.

c) Re-draw the control circuit, if affected.

d) Give PLD file equations, if affected.

e) What is the resultant number of wait-cycles if the DRAM speed rating is the same.

Interface to Other Peripherals

41. Figure 9-72 shows a control register that can be read back by the 68020. Design the logic to generate the read and write control signals and draw a timing diagram.

42. Draw the timing diagram for read and write cycles of the '68681 interface given in Figure 9-68. Refer to '68681 data sheet.

43. Draw the circuit diagram to interface 68020 to a PI/T ('68230). Show the connection of interrupt logic assuming it uses a level 3 user-vectors interrupt.

Miscellaneous

44. What signal lines does the 68020 use for the following functions:

a) To lock out bus arbitration during a CAS2 instruction.

b) To give the earliest indication of a possible bus cycle.

c) To learn the port size of a peripheral.

d) To indicate a double bus fault condition.

e) To indicate the remaining number of bytes to be transferred for an operand transfer.

f) To indicate the actual number of bytes to be transferred during a bus cycle.

g) When a RESET instruction is executed.

h) To signal auto-vectoring request to the 68020.

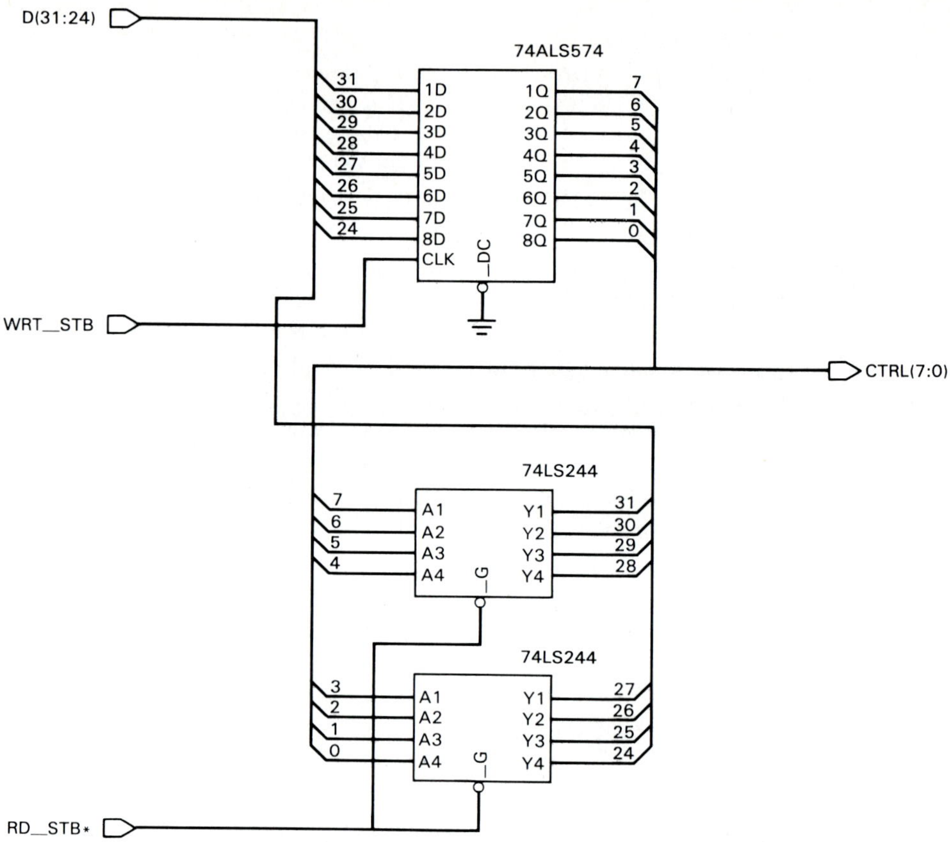

Figure 9-72

i) To signal another current bus master that an interrupt is pending.

k) To indicate a coprocessor access bus cycle.

l) To indicate an interrupt acknowledge bus cycle.

45. Answer as True or False to the following statements. If false, please indicate why.

a) The best timing for a read or write cycle of the 68020 is three clock cycles. ____

b) The 68020 continues to support the special 6800 interface signal lines. ____

c) The bus arbitration of the 68020 is the same as the 68000. ____

d) The address decoding of a device select signal is only a function of A31-A0 and AS*. ____

Appendix A

Summary of 68000 and 68020 AC Electrical Characteristics (Courtesy of Motorola)

AC ELECTRICAL SPECIFICATIONS — READ AND WRITE CYCLES (V_{CC} = 5.0 Vdc ±5%; GND = 0 Vdc; T_A = 0 to 70°C; see Figures 12, 13, and 14)

Num.	Characteristic	12.5 MHz		16.67 MHz		20 MHz		25 MHz*		33.33 MHz		Unit
		Min	Max	Min	Max	Min	Max	Min	Max	Min	Max	
6	Clock High to Address, FC, Size, $\overline{\mathrm{RMC}}$ Valid	0	40	0	30	0	25	0	25	0	21	ns
6A	Clock High to $\overline{\mathrm{ECS}}$, $\overline{\mathrm{OCS}}$ Asserted	0	30	0	20	0	15	0	12	0	10	ns
7	Clock High to Address, Data, FC, Size, $\overline{\mathrm{RMC}}$, High Impedance	0	80	0	60	0	50	0	40	0	30	ns
8	Clock High to Address, FC, Size, $\overline{\mathrm{RMC}}$ Invalid	0	—	0	—	0	—	0	—	0	—	ns
9	Clock Low to $\overline{\mathrm{AS}}$, $\overline{\mathrm{DS}}$ Asserted	3	40	3	30	3	25	3	18	3	15	ns
9A[1]	$\overline{\mathrm{AS}}$ to $\overline{\mathrm{DS}}$ Assertion (Read) (Skew)	−20	20	−15	15	−10	10	−10	10	−10	10	ns
9B[11]	$\overline{\mathrm{AS}}$ Asserted to $\overline{\mathrm{DS}}$ Asserted (Write)	47	—	37	—	32	—	27	—	22	—	ns
10	$\overline{\mathrm{ECS}}$ Width Asserted	25	—	20	—	15	—	15	—	10	—	ns
10A	$\overline{\mathrm{OCS}}$ Width Asserted	25	—	20	—	15	—	15	—	10	—	ns
10B[7]	$\overline{\mathrm{ECS}}$, $\overline{\mathrm{OCS}}$ Width Negated	20	—	15	—	10	—	5	—	5	—	ns
11	Address, FC, Size, $\overline{\mathrm{RMC}}$ Valid to $\overline{\mathrm{AS}}$ (and $\overline{\mathrm{DS}}$ Asserted Read)	20	—	15	—	10	—	6	—	5	—	ns
12	Clock Low to $\overline{\mathrm{AS}}$, $\overline{\mathrm{DS}}$ Negated	0	40	0	30	0	25	0	15	0	15	ns
12A	Clock Low to $\overline{\mathrm{ECS}}$, $\overline{\mathrm{OCS}}$ Negated	0	40	0	30	0	25	0	15	0	15	ns
13	$\overline{\mathrm{AS}}$, $\overline{\mathrm{DS}}$ Negated to Address, FC, Size, $\overline{\mathrm{RMC}}$ Invalid	20	—	15	—	10	—	10	—	5	—	ns
14	$\overline{\mathrm{AS}}$ (and $\overline{\mathrm{DS}}$ Read) Width Asserted	120	—	100	—	85	—	70	—	50	—	ns
14A	$\overline{\mathrm{DS}}$ Width Asserted Write	50	—	40	—	38	—	30	—	25	—	ns
15	$\overline{\mathrm{AS}}$, $\overline{\mathrm{DS}}$ Width Negated	50	—	40	—	38	—	30	—	23	—	ns
15A[8]	$\overline{\mathrm{DS}}$ Negated to $\overline{\mathrm{AS}}$ Asserted	45	—	35	—	30	—	25	—	18	—	ns
16	Clock High to $\overline{\mathrm{AS}}$, $\overline{\mathrm{DS}}$, R/$\overline{\mathrm{W}}$, $\overline{\mathrm{DBEN}}$ High Impedance	—	80	—	60	—	50	—	40	—	30	ns
17	$\overline{\mathrm{AS}}$, $\overline{\mathrm{DS}}$ Negated to R/$\overline{\mathrm{W}}$ Invalid	20	—	15	—	10	—	10	—	5	—	ns
18	Clock High to R/$\overline{\mathrm{W}}$ High	0	40	0	30	0	25	0	20	0	15	ns
20	Clock High to R/$\overline{\mathrm{W}}$ Low	0	40	0	30	0	25	0	20	0	15	ns
21	R/$\overline{\mathrm{W}}$ High to $\overline{\mathrm{AS}}$ Asserted	20	—	15	—	10	—	5	—	5	—	ns
22	R/$\overline{\mathrm{W}}$ Low to $\overline{\mathrm{DS}}$ Asserted (Write)	90	—	75	—	60	—	50	—	35	—	ns
23	Clock High to Data Out Valid	—	40	—	30	—	25	—	25	—	18	ns
25	$\overline{\mathrm{DS}}$ Negated to Data Out Invalid	20	—	15	—	10	—	5	—	5	—	ns
25A[9]	$\overline{\mathrm{DS}}$ Negated to $\overline{\mathrm{DBEN}}$ Negated (Write)	20	—	15	—	10	—	5	—	5	—	ns
26	Data Out Valid to $\overline{\mathrm{DS}}$ Asserted (Write)	20	—	15	—	10	—	5	—	5	—	ns
27	Data-In Valid to Clock Low (Data Setup)	10	—	5	—	5	—	5	—	5	—	ns
27A	Late $\overline{\mathrm{BERR}}$/$\overline{\mathrm{HALT}}$ Asserted to Clock Low Setup Time	25	—	20	—	15	—	10	—	5	—	ns
28	$\overline{\mathrm{AS}}$, $\overline{\mathrm{DS}}$ Negated to $\overline{\mathrm{DSACKx}}$, $\overline{\mathrm{BERR}}$, $\overline{\mathrm{HALT}}$, $\overline{\mathrm{AVEC}}$ Negated	0	110	0	80	0	65	0	50	0	40	ns
29	$\overline{\mathrm{DS}}$ Negated to Data-In Invalid (Data-In Hold Time)	0	—	0	—	0	—	0	—	0	—	ns
29A	$\overline{\mathrm{DS}}$ Negated to Data-In (High Impedance)	—	80	—	60	—	50	—	40	—	30	ns
31[2]	$\overline{\mathrm{DSACKx}}$ Asserted to Data-In Valid	—	60	—	50	—	43	—	32	—	17	ns
31A[3]	$\overline{\mathrm{DSACKx}}$ Asserted to $\overline{\mathrm{DSACKx}}$ Valid ($\overline{\mathrm{DSACK}}$ Asserted Skew)	—	20	—	15	—	10	—	10	—	10	ns

AC ELECTRICAL SPECIFICATIONS — READ AND WRITE CYCLES (Continued)

Num.	Characteristic	12.5 MHz		16.67 MHz		20 MHz		25 MHz*		33.33 MHz		Unit
		Min	Max	Min	Max	Min	Max	Min	Max	Min	Max	
32	RESET Input Transition Time	—	1.5	—	1.5	—	1.5	—	1.5	—	1.5	Clks
33	Clock Low to BG Asserted	0	40	0	30	0	25	0	20	0	20	ns
34	Clock Low to BG Negated	0	40	0	30	0	25	0	20	0	20	ns
35	BR Asserted to BG Asserted (RMC Not Asserted)	1.5	3.5	1.5	3.5	1.5	3.5	1.5	3.5	1.5	3.5	Clks
37	BGACK Asserted to BG Negated	1.5	3.5	1.5	3.5	1.5	3.5	1.5	3.5	1.5	3.5	Clks
37A[6]	BGACK Asserted to BR Negated	0	1.5	0	1.5	0	1.5	0	1.5	0	1.5	Clks
39	BG Width Negated	120	—	90	—	75	—	60	—	50	—	ns
39A	BG Width Asserted	120	—	90	—	75	—	60	—	50	—	ns
40	Clock High to DBEN Asserted (Read)	0	40	0	30	0	25	0	20	0	15	ns
41	Clock Low to DBEN Negated (Read)	0	40	0	30	0	25	0	20	0	15	ns
42	Clock Low to DBEN Asserted (Write)	0	40	0	30	0	25	0	20	0	15	ns
43	Clock High to DBEN Negated (Write)	0	40	0	30	0	25	0	20	0	15	ns
44	R/W Low to DBEN Asserted (Write)	20	—	15	—	10	—	10	—	5	—	ns
45[5]	DBEN Width Asserted Read Write	80 160	— —	60 120	— —	50 100	— —	40 80	— —	30 60	— —	ns
46	R/W Width Valid (Write or Read)	180	—	150	—	125	—	100	—	75	—	ns
47A	Asynchronous Input Setup Time	10	—	5	—	5	—	5	—	5	—	ns
47B	Asynchronous Input Hold Time	20	—	15	—	15	—	10	—	10	—	ns
48[4]	DSACKx Asserted to BERR, HALT Asserted	—	35	—	30	—	20	—	18	—	15	ns
53	Data Out Hold from Clock High	0	—	0	—	0	—	0	—	0	—	ns
55	R/W Valid to Data Bus Impedance Change	40	—	30	—	25	—	20	—	20	—	ns
56	RESET Pulse Width (Reset Instruction)	512	—	512	—	512	—	512	—	512	—	Clks
57	BERR Negated to HALT Negated (Rerun)	0	—	0	—	0	—	0	—	0	—	ns
58[10]	BGACK Negated to Bus Driven	1	—	1	—	1	—	1	—	1	—	Clks
59[10]	BG Negated to Bus Driven	1	—	1	—	1	—	1	—	1	—	Clks

*These specifications represent an improvement over previously published specifications for the 25 MHz MC68020 and are valid only for product bearing date codes of 8827 and later.

NOTES:

1. This number can be reduced to 5 nanoseconds if strobes have equal loads.
2. If the asynchronous setup time (#47A) requirements are satisfied, the DSACKx low to data setup time (#31) and DSACKx low to BERR low setup time (#48) can be ignored. The data must only satisfy the data-in to clock low setup time (#27) for the following clock cycle and BERR must only satisfy the late BERR low to clock low setup time (#27A) for the following clock cycle.
3. This parameter specifies the maximum allowable skew between DSACK0 to DSACK1 asserted or DSACK1 to DSACK0 asserted; specification #47A must be met by DSACK0 or DSACK1.
4. This specification applies to the first (DSACK0 or DSACK1) DSACKx signal asserted. In the absence of DSACKx, BERR is an asynchronous input using the asynchronous input setup time (#47A).
5. DBEN may stay asserted on consecutive write cycles.
6. The minimum values must be met to guarantee proper operation. If this maximum value is exceeded, BG may be reasserted.
7. This specification indicates the minimum high time for ECS and OCS in the event of an internal cache hit followed immediately by a cache miss or operand cycle.
8. This specification guarantees operation with the MC68881/MC68882, which specifies a minimum time for DS negated to AS asserted (specification #13A in the *MC68881/MC68882 User's Manual*). Without this specification, incorrect interpretation of specifications #9A and #15 would indicate that the MC68020 does not meet the MC68881/MC68882 requirements.
9. This specification allows a system designer to guarantee data hold times on the output side of data buffers that have output enable signals generated with DBEN.
10. These specifications allow system designers to guarantee that an alternate bus master has stopped driving the bus when the MC68020 regains control of the bus after an arbitration sequence.
11. This specification allows system designers to qualify the CS signal of an MC68881/MC68882 with AS (allowing 7ns for a gate delay and still meet the CS to DS setup time requirement (specification 8B) of the MC68881/MC68882.

AC ELECTRICAL SPECIFICATIONS — READ AND WRITE CYCLES (V_{CC} = 5.0 Vdc ± 5%; GND = 0 Vdc; $T_A = T_L$ to T_H; see Figures 7 and 8)

Num.	Characteristic	Symbol	8 MHz*		10 MHz*		12.5 MHz*		16.67 MHz '12F'		Unit
			Min	Max	Min	Max	Min	Max	Min	Max	
6	Clock Low to Address Valid	t_{CLAV}	—	62	—	50	—	50	—	50	ns
6A	Clock High to FC Valid	t_{CHFCV}	—	62	—	50	—	45	—	45	ns
7	Clock High to Address, Data Bus High Impedance (Maximum)	t_{CHADZ}	—	80	—	70	—	60	—	50	ns
8	Clock High to Address, FC Invalid (Minimum)	t_{CHAFI}	0	—	0	—	0	—	0	—	ns
9[1]	Clock High to $\overline{AS}$, $\overline{DS}$ Asserted	t_{CHSL}	3	60	3	50	3	40	3	40	ns
11[2]	Address Valid to $\overline{AS}$, $\overline{DS}$ Asserted (Read)/$\overline{AS}$ Asserted (Write)	t_{AVSL}	30	—	20	—	15	—	15	—	ns
11A[2]	FC Valid to $\overline{AS}$, $\overline{DS}$ Asserted (Read)/$\overline{AS}$ Asserted (Write)	t_{FCVSL}	90	—	70	—	60	—	30	—	ns
12[1]	Clock Low to $\overline{AS}$, $\overline{DS}$ Negated	t_{CLSH}	—	62	—	50	—	40	—	40	ns
13[2]	$\overline{AS}$, $\overline{DS}$ Negated to Address, FC Invalid	t_{SHAFI}	40	—	30	—	20	—	10	—	ns
14[2]	$\overline{AS}$ (and $\overline{DS}$ Read) Width Asserted	t_{SL}	270	—	195	—	160	—	120	—	ns
14A	$\overline{DS}$ Width Asserted (Write)	t_{DSL}	140	—	95	—	80	—	60	—	ns
15[2]	$\overline{AS}$, $\overline{DS}$ Width Negated	t_{SH}	150	—	105	—	65	—	60	—	ns
16	Clock High to Control Bus High Impedance	t_{CHCZ}	—	80	—	70	—	60	—	50	ns
17[2]	$\overline{AS}$, $\overline{DS}$ Negated to R/$\overline{W}$ Invalid	t_{SHRH}	40	—	30	—	20	—	10	—	ns
18[1]	Clock High to R/$\overline{W}$ High (Read)	t_{CHRH}	0	55	0	45	0	40	0	40	ns
20[1]	Clock High to R/$\overline{W}$ Low (Write)	t_{CHRL}	0	55	0	45	0	40	0	40	ns
20A[2,6]	$\overline{AS}$ Asserted to R/$\overline{W}$ Valid (Write)	t_{ASRV}	—	10	—	10	—	10	—	10	ns
21[2]	Address Valid to R/$\overline{W}$ Low (Write)	t_{AVRL}	20	—	0	—	0	—	0	—	ns
21A[2]	FC Valid to R/$\overline{W}$ Low (Write)	t_{FCVRL}	60	—	50	—	30	—	20	—	ns
22[2]	R/$\overline{W}$ Low to $\overline{DS}$ Asserted (Write)	t_{RLSL}	80	—	50	—	30	—	20	—	ns
23	Clock Low to Data-Out Valid (Write)	t_{CLDO}	—	62	—	50	—	50	—	50	ns
25[2]	$\overline{AS}$, $\overline{DS}$ Negated to Data-Out Invalid (Write)	t_{SHDOI}	40	—	30	—	20	—	15	—	ns
26[2]	Data-Out Valid to $\overline{DS}$ Asserted (Write)	t_{DOSL}	40	—	30	—	20	—	15	—	ns
27[5]	Data-In Valid to Clock Low (Setup Time on Read)	t_{DICL}	10	—	10	—	10	—	7	—	ns
28[2]	$\overline{AS}$, $\overline{DS}$ Negated to $\overline{DTACK}$ Negated (Asynchronous Hold)	t_{SHDAH}	0	240	0	190	0	150	0	110	ns
29	$\overline{AS}$, $\overline{DS}$ Negated to Data-In Invalid (Hold Time on Read)	t_{SHDII}	0	—	0	—	0	—	0	—	ns
29A	$\overline{AS}$, $\overline{DS}$ Negated to Data-In High Impedance	t_{SHDZ}	—	187	—	150	—	120	—	90	ns
30	$\overline{AS}$, $\overline{DS}$ Negated to $\overline{BERR}$ Negated	t_{SHBEH}	0	—	0	—	0	—	0	—	ns
31[2,5]	$\overline{DTACK}$ Asserted to Data-In Valid (Setup Time)	t_{DALDI}	—	90	—	65	—	50	—	40	ns
32	$\overline{HALT}$ and $\overline{RESET}$ Input Transition Time	$t_{RHr,f}$	0	200	0	200	0	200	0	150	ns
33	Clock High to $\overline{BG}$ Asserted	t_{CHGL}	—	62	—	50	—	40	—	40	ns
34	Clock High to $\overline{BG}$ Negated	t_{CHGH}	—	62	—	50	—	40	—	40	ns
35	$\overline{BR}$ Asserted to $\overline{BG}$ Asserted	t_{BRLGL}	1.5	3.5	1.5	3.5	1.5	3.5	1.5	3.5	Clks
36[7]	$\overline{BR}$ Negated to $\overline{BG}$ Negated	t_{BRHGH}	1.5	3.5	1.5	3.5	1.5	3.5	1.5	3.5	Clks
37	$\overline{BGACK}$ Asserted to $\overline{BG}$ Negated	t_{GALGH}	1.5	3.5	1.5	3.5	1.5	3.5	1.5	3.5	Clks
37A[8]	$\overline{BGACK}$ Asserted to $\overline{BR}$ Negated	t_{GALBRH}	20	1.5 Clks	20	1.5 Clks	20	1.5 Clks	10	1.5 Clks	ns
38	$\overline{BG}$ Asserted to Control, Address, Data Bus High Impedance ($\overline{AS}$ Negated)	t_{GLZ}	—	80	—	70	—	60	—	50	ns

AC ELECTRICAL SPECIFICATIONS — READ AND WRITE CYCLES (Continued)

Num.	Characteristic	Symbol	8 MHz*		10 MHz*		12.5 MHz*		16.67 MHz '12F'		Unit
			Min	Max	Min	Max	Min	Max	Min	Max	
39	$\overline{BG}$ Width Negated	t_{GH}	1.5	—	1.5	—	1.5	—	1.5	—	Clks
40	Clock Low to $\overline{VMA}$ Asserted	t_{CLVML}	—	70	—	70	—	70	—	50	ns
41	Clock Low to E Transition	t_{CLET}	—	55	—	45	—	35	—	35	ns
42	E Output Rise and Fall Time	$t_{Er,f}$	—	15	—	15	—	15	—	15	ns
43	$\overline{VMA}$ Asserted to E High	t_{VMLEH}	200	—	150	—	90	—	80	—	ns
44	$\overline{AS}$, $\overline{DS}$ Negated to $\overline{VPA}$ Negated	t_{SHVPH}	0	120	0	90	0	70	0	50	ns
45	E Low to Control, Address Bus Invalid (Address Hold Time)	t_{ELCAI}	30	—	10	—	10	—	10	—	ns
46	$\overline{BGACK}$ Width Low	t_{GAL}	1.5	—	1.5	—	1.5	—	1.5	—	Clks
47[5]	Asynchronous Input Setup Time	t_{ASI}	10	—	10	—	10	—	10	—	ns
48[2,3]	$\overline{BERR}$ Asserted to $\overline{DTACK}$ Asserted	t_{BELDAL}	20	—	20	—	20	—	10	—	ns
49[9]	$\overline{AS}$, $\overline{DS}$, Negated to E Low	t_{SHEL}	−70	70	−55	55	−45	45	−35	35	ns
50	E Width High	t_{EH}	450	—	350	—	280	—	220	—	ns
51	E Width Low	t_{EL}	700	—	550	—	440	—	340	—	ns
53	Data-Out Hold from Clock High	t_{CHDOI}	0	—	0	—	0	—	0	—	ns
54	E Low to Data-Out Invalid	t_{ELDOI}	30	—	20	—	15	—	10	—	ns
55	R/$\overline{W}$ Asserted to Data Bus Impedance Change	t_{RLDBD}	30	—	20	—	10	—	0	—	ns
56[4]	$\overline{HALT}$/$\overline{RESET}$ Pulse Width	t_{HRPW}	10	—	10	—	10	—	10	—	Clks
57	$\overline{BGACK}$ Negated to $\overline{AS}$, $\overline{DS}$, R/$\overline{W}$ Driven	t_{GASD}	1.5	—	1.5	—	1.5	—	1.5	—	Clks
57A	$\overline{BGACK}$ Negated to FC, $\overline{VMA}$ Driven	t_{GAFD}	1	—	1	—	1	—	1	—	Clks
58[7]	$\overline{BR}$ Negated to $\overline{AS}$, $\overline{DS}$, R/$\overline{W}$ Driven	t_{RHSD}	1.5	—	1.5	—	1.5	—	1.5	—	Clks
58A[7]	$\overline{BR}$ Negated to FC, $\overline{VMA}$ Driven	t_{RHFD}	1	—	1	—	1	—	1	—	Clks

*These specifications represent an improvement over previously published specifications for the 8-, 10-, and 12.5-MHz MC68HC000 and are valid only for product bearing date codes of 8827 and later.

NOTES:

1. For a loading capacitance of less than or equal to 50 picofarads, subtract 5 nanoseconds from the value given in the maximum columns.
2. Actual value depends on clock period.
3. If #47 is satisfied for both $\overline{DTACK}$ and $\overline{BERR}$, #48 may be ignored. In the absence of $\overline{DTACK}$, $\overline{BERR}$ is an asynchronous input using the asynchronous input setup time (#47).
4. For power-up, the MC68000 must be held in the reset state for 100 milliseconds to allow stabilization of on-chip circuitry. After the system is powered up, #56 refers to the minimum pulse width required to reset the processor.
5. If the asynchronous input setup time (#47) requirement is satisfied for $\overline{DTACK}$, the $\overline{DTACK}$-asserted to data setup time (#31) requirement can be ignored. The data must only satisfy the data-in to clock low setup time (#27) for the following clock cycle.
6. When $\overline{AS}$ and R/$\overline{W}$ are equally loaded (±20%), subtract 5 nanoseconds from the values given in these columns.
7. The processor will negate $\overline{BG}$ and begin driving the bus again if external arbitration logic negates $\overline{BR}$ before asserting $\overline{BGACK}$.
8. The minimum value must be met to guarantee proper operation. If the maximum value is exceeded, $\overline{BG}$ may be re-asserted.
9. The falling edge of S6 triggers both the negation of the strobes ($\overline{AS}$ and x$\overline{DS}$) and the falling edge of E. Either of these events can occur first, depending upon the loading on each signal. Specification #49 indicates the absolute maximum skew that will occur between the rising edge of the strobes and the falling edge of the E clock.

AC ELECTRICAL SPECIFICATIONS — BUS ARBITRATION (V_{CC} = 5.0 Vdc ± 5%; GND = 0 Vdc; $T_A = T_L$ to T_H; see Figure 11)

Num.	Characteristic	Symbol	8 MHz*		10 MHz*		12.5 MHz*		16.67 MHz '12F'		Unit
			Min	Max	Min	Max	Min	Max	Min	Max	
7	Clock High to Address, Data Bus High Impedance (Maximum)	t_{CHADZ}	—	80	—	70	—	60	—	50	ns
16	Clock High to Control Bus High Impedance	t_{CHCZ}	—	80	—	70	—	60	—	50	ns
33	Clock High to $\overline{BG}$ Asserted	t_{CHGL}	—	62	—	50	—	40	—	40	ns
34	Clock High to $\overline{BG}$ Negated	t_{CHGH}	—	62	—	50	—	40	—	40	ns
35	$\overline{BR}$ Asserted to $\overline{BG}$ Asserted	t_{BRLGL}	1.5	3.5	1.5	3.5	1.5	3.5	1.5	3.5	Clks
36[1]	$\overline{BR}$ Negated to $\overline{BG}$ Negated	t_{BRHGH}	1.5	3.5	1.5	3.5	1.5	3.5	1.5	3.5	Clks
37	$\overline{BGACK}$ Asserted to $\overline{BG}$ Negated	t_{GALGH}	1.5	3.5	1.5	3.5	1.5	3.5	1.5	3.5	Clks
37A[2]	$\overline{BGACK}$ Asserted to $\overline{BR}$ Negated	t_{GALBRH}	20	1.5 Clks	20	1.5 Clks	20	1.5 Clks	10	1.5 Clks	ns
38	$\overline{BG}$ Asserted to Control, Address, Data Bus High Impedance ($\overline{AS}$ Negated)	t_{GLZ}	—	80	—	70	—	60	—	50	ns
39	$\overline{BG}$ Width Negated	t_{GH}	1.5	—	1.5	—	1.5	—	1.5	—	Clks
46	$\overline{BGACK}$ Width Low	t_{GAL}	1.5	—	1.5	—	1.5	—	1.5	—	Clks
47	Asynchronous Input Setup Time	t_{ASI}	10	—	10	—	10	—	10	—	ns
57	$\overline{BGACK}$ Negated to $\overline{AS}$, $\overline{DS}$, R/$\overline{W}$ Driven	t_{GASD}	1.5	—	1.5	—	1.5	—	1.5	—	Clks
57A	$\overline{BGACK}$ Negated to FC, $\overline{VMA}$ Driven	t_{GAFD}	1	—	1	—	1	—	1	—	Clks
58[1]	$\overline{BR}$ Negated to $\overline{AS}$, $\overline{DS}$, R/$\overline{W}$ Driven	t_{RHSD}	1.5	—	1.5	—	1.5	—	1.5	—	Clks
58A[1]	$\overline{BR}$ Negated to FC, $\overline{VMA}$ Driven	t_{RHFD}	1	—	1	—	1	—	1	—	Clks

*These specifications represent an improvement over previously published specifications for the 8-, 10-, and 12.5-MHz MC68HC000 and are valid only for product bearing date codes of 8827 and later.

NOTES:
1. The processor will negate $\overline{BG}$ and begin driving the bus again if external arbitration logic negates $\overline{BR}$ before asserting $\overline{BGACK}$.
2. The minimum value must be met to guarantee proper operation. If the maximum value is exceeded, $\overline{BG}$ may be re-asserted.

These waveforms should only be referenced in regard to the edge-to-edge measurement of the timing specifications. They are not intended as a functional description of the input and output signals. Refer to other functional descriptions and their related diagrams for device operation.

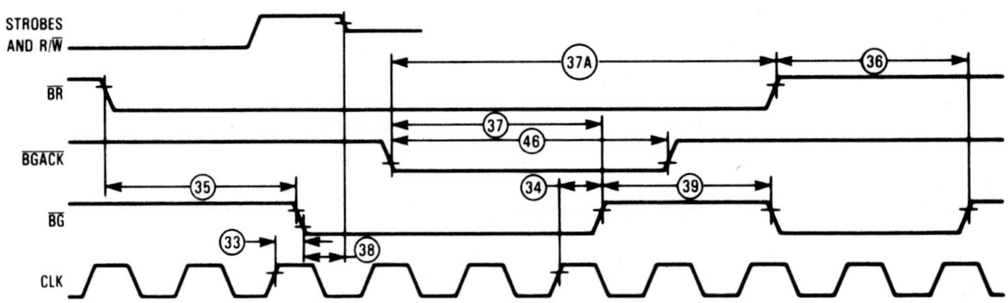

NOTE: Setup time to the clock (#47) for the asynchronous inputs $\overline{BERR}$, $\overline{BGACK}$, $\overline{BR}$, $\overline{DTACK}$, $\overline{IPL0}$-$\overline{IPL2}$ and $\overline{VPA}$ guarantees their recognition at the next falling edge of the clock.

Figure 11. MC68HC000 Bus Arbitration Timing Diagram

Appendix B

Digital Design and Layout Tips

ADDITIONAL HIGH-SPEED DIGITAL DESIGN GUIDELINES

1. Terminations

At high frequencies the traces on a printed circuit board act as transmission lines, in which impedance mismatches can cause distortions of signals. This is especially true when CMOS ICs are used in conjunction with other TTL logic, because CMOS ICs have very high impedance inputs, and to drive capacitive load and to achieve TTL compatibility, low output impedances. Terminating the lines provide the means to match impedance and significantly reduce overshoot, undershoot, and ringing of a signal line.

A wire or signal trace has to be considered as a transmission line when the time it takes the signal to travel from one end of the line to the other end (i.e., the one way signal propagation delay) amounts to one-half or more of the signal's edge rate or transition time. In other words, we have to consider reflections when

$$T_{pd} > (1/2) * T_{edge}$$

where T_{pd} : Is the signal propagation time,
T_{edge} : Is the signal rise or fall time.

Present high-speed logic families such as Fast TTL have typical rise times of 2 nanoseconds, while the propagation delay of a common PCB is about 1.77 ns per foot. Applying the above relationship, a transmission line will require termination if longer than 7 inches.

The three most commonly used terminations are the following (see Figure 1):

Series Damping and Series Termination: This type of termination eliminates reflections at

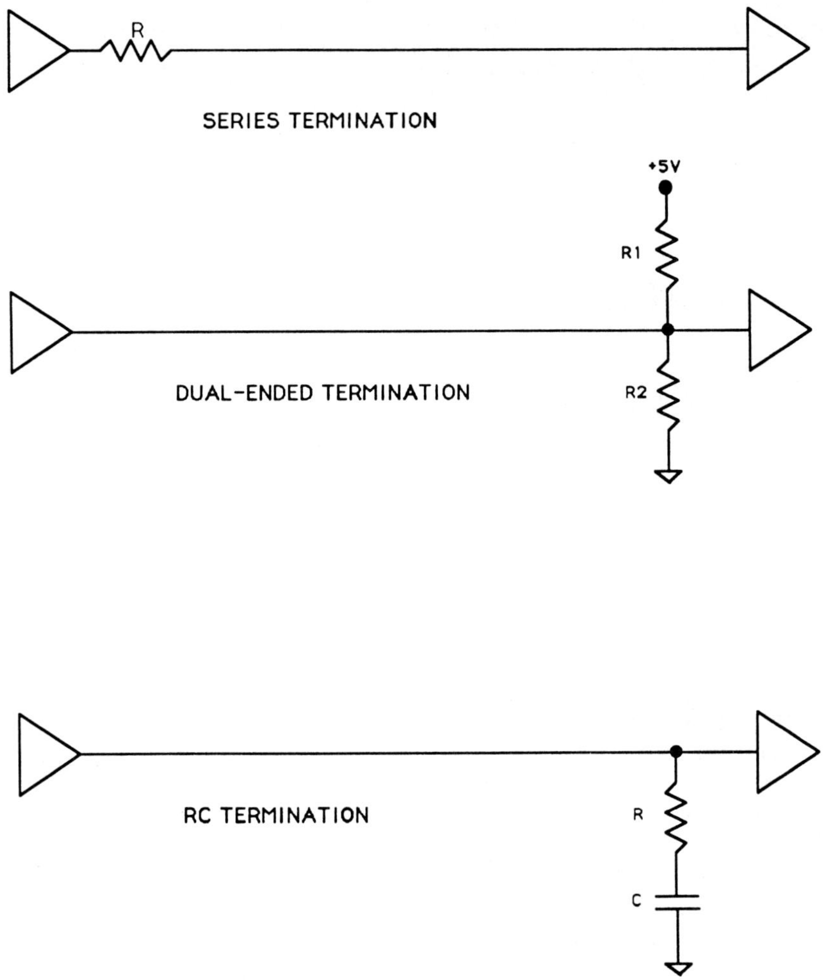

FIGURE 1. TYPES OF TERMINATIONS

the sending end of the line. It is typically used with memory type devices. The advantage of this termination is that a very rough match between the driver's impedance and the impedance of the line will still be acceptable. Its disadvantage, however, is that distributed loading along the line cannot be used because of the half-voltage waveform travelling down this line. It is okay, though, to "lump" together a number of loads at the end of the line, as is done with memory type devices. Also it is important to note that these devices are left in the signal threshold level for 2T during transitions. Typical values used for the resistor are 22-33 ohms.

<u>Dual-Ended Parallel Termination:</u> This type of termination requires that the Thevenin equivalent of the resistor network equal to the characteristic impedance of the line

(Z0).Typical values used are {R1=220, R2=330} or {R1=330, R2=470}. Its characteristics are:

* The ratio of resistor values is about 2 to 3 to provide a Thevenin voltage around three volts. As such, it helps transitions from to high level.

* Offers very high performance when used with high-speed, high-drive, open collector drivers like the 74F3038.

* For standard TTL-type devices, it is usually not possible to properly terminate a signal line. This is due to:

    1. High-DC power consumption.
    2. Too much DC-loading of drivers, and therefore low-noise margins.

* When the Thevenin equivalent impedance is much higher than Z0, such a resistor network can be used as a pull-up.

<u>RC-Type Termination:</u> This type of termination offers the following advantages:

* Limits or eliminates undershoot.
* Good Noise characteristics.
* Low DC power dissipation.
* Large Noise Margins
* Acts as a low-pass filter for short pulses due to crosstalk or glitches.

It is primarily used for incident wave switched lines. This could be a important disadvantage if the driver does not have enough output drive capability to immediately switch the signal level without depending upon reflections.

Typical values are 50 to 100 ohms for the resistor and 50 to 300 pF for the capacitor. Multiple RCs with a common point are available in Single-Inline-Packages (SIP).

2. Crosstalk

Crosstalk is the undesired coupling of a signal on one wire (active line) to a nearby wire (inactive line) or other signal trace. Since a coupled pulse in the direction of undershoot results in a reduction of noise immunity, or in the worst-case spurious pulses in adjacent signal lines, precautions must be taken for limiting the crosstalk. The following steps can be taken to reduce the effects of crosstalk:

A. Maximize distance between the parallel traces, and minimize the distance that traces are parallel to each other. How much distance between parallel traces is adequate? For a board with power and ground planes, a distance larger than 40 mils is typically adequate for the critical signal lines.

B. Use a dual-ended termination on a signal line to reduce crosstalk amplitude by about 50 percent.

It is not always possible or important to reduce or eliminate crosstalk. For example, let us consider the following scenario. First, the address lines, A31-A0, are driven with a valid address. The address strobe is specified to be asserted T_{as} nanoseconds later. In such a case, it is perfectly acceptable if there is any crosstalk between the address lines during their transitions to a valid address, as long as all transitions settle down T_{as} nanoseconds before the address strobe is asserted. It is not necessary to terminate the address lines if we allow time for any ringing to settle down while still meeting the T_{as}. However, we cannot allow any other signal lines to cross-couple to the address strobe, or any ringing on it due to reflections. Therefore, the physical layout of the address strobe is critical, and its trace has to be terminated if it is longer than 7 inches.

3. Unused Inputs

Proper design rules require that all unused inputs on all TTL devices be tied to either High or Low logic levels. This is especially required for the FAST family and CMOS-type logic inputs. As a pull-up, a resistor not less than 1000 ohms connected to +5V supply can be used. Resistor packs with up to 10 resistors with side connected to a common point on a SIP package can be used to save board space.

To connect to a logic low, we can either directly ground point to the input, or we can connect to the output of an inverter whose input is pulled up. The latter approach provides support for the Automatic Test Equipment (ATE).

4. PCB Layout Requirements

A. Critical Signal Lines

Some of the signal lines are especially critical to the operation of a given circuit. For example, the AS* of the 68000 family indicates a valid bus cycle. Special care must be exercised in both the design and the PCB layout phases to ensure signal integrity on such critical signal lines. The following guidelines are recommended for critical signal lines:

1. Using proper design techniques, any static or dynamic circuit glitches must be prevented.

2. The so called "T" connections should be avoided if at all possible. The length of any trace stubs should be limited in 2 inches or less.

3. Overall trace length should be minimized. One way this can be accomplished is by using a distribution network of parallel signal drivers. This will reduce the trace length and the loading of the driver chip. Using multiple drivers such as the 74AS1000 that are in the same package will minimize the skews between the buffered signals, especially if the load on each of the buffered lines is approximately the same.

4. Trace width should be in the range of 8 to 15 mils.

5. Any artificial loops of signal traces should be avoided. This is because any signal loops act as inductors. A signal without a loop has two unique ends.

6. Avoid sharp bends of signal traces. Sharp corners changes the impedance locally, and therefore can cause reflections.

7. Use as few Vias as possible.

8. Keep critical signal traces at least 40 mils away from other parallel signal lines, with the exception of pin crossings.

9. All critical signal lines must be driven from one end of the signal trace. This reduces the loading as seen by the driver device.

B. Clock Lines

Handle all clock lines as critical signal lines.

C. Arrangement of Multiple Layers

1. Arrange multiple layers of a PCB so that the signals on adjacent layers run perpendicular to each other. The purpose of this is to avoid layer-to-layer crosstalk. For example, for a board with six signal layers we can use the following configuration:

Layer 1	:	Signal Layer (Horizontal traces)
Layer 2	:	Signal Layer (Vertical traces)
Layer 3	:	Power (+5V)
Layer 4	:	Signal Layer (Horizontal traces)
Layer 5	:	Signal Layer (Vertical traces)
Layer 6	:	Ground
Layer 7	:	Signal Layer (Horizontal traces)
Layer 8	:	Signal Layer (Vertical traces)

2. Minimize the number of layers since this will lower the production costs. This will also make it more difficult to layout signal traces.

3. Design the trace width and trace-to-trace distances such that the impedance of signal traces are approximately the same for all signal layers.

Appendix C

The DS1210 Datasheet (Courtesy of Dallas Semiconductors)

Dallas Semiconductor Nonvolatile Controller

DS1210—8-Pin DIP
DS1210S—16-Pin SOIC

FEATURES

- Converts CMOS RAMs into nonvolatile memories
- Unconditionally write protects when V_{CC} is out of tolerance
- Automatically switches to battery when power fail occurs
- Space saving 8-pin DIP
- Consumes less than 100 nA of battery current
- Tests battery condition on power up
- Provides for redundant batteries
- Optional 5% or 10% power fail detection
- Low forward voltage drop on the V_{CC} Switch
- Optional 16-pin SOIC surface mount package

PIN CONNECTIONS

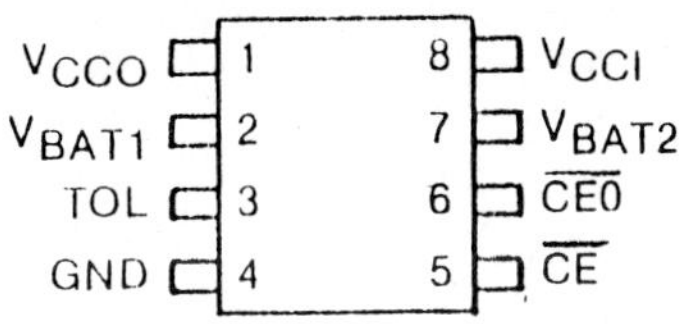

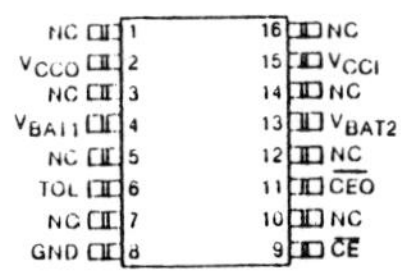

PIN NAMES

V_{CCO}	- RAM Supply
V_{BAT1}	- + Battery 1
TOL	- Power Supply Tolerance
GND	- Ground
$\overline{CE}$	- Chip Enable Input
$\overline{CEO}$	- Chip Enable Output
V_{BAT2}	- + Battery 2
V_{CCI}	- + Supply
NC	- No Connect

DESCRIPTION

The DS1210 is a CMOS circuit which solves the application problem of converting CMOS RAM into nonvolatile memory. Incoming power is monitored for an out of tolerance condition. When such a condition is detected, chip enable is inhibited to accomplish write protection and the battery is switched on to supply RAM with uninterrupted power. Special circuitry uses a low-leakage CMOS process which affords precise voltage detection at extremely low battery consumption. The 8-pin DIP package keeps PC bóard real estate requirements to a minimum. By combining the DS1210 nonvolatile controller chip with a CMOS memory and batteries, nonvolatile RAM operation can be achieved.

OPERATION

The DS1210 nonvolatile controller performs five circuit functions required to battery back up a RAM. First, a switch is provided to direct power from the battery or the incoming supply (V_{CCI}) depending on which is greater. This switch has a voltage drop of less than 0.3V. The second function which the nonvolatile controller provides is power fail detection. The DS1210 constantly monitors the incoming supply. When the supply goes out of tolerance a precision comparator detects power fail and inhibits chip enable ($\overline{CEO}$). The third function of write protection is accomplished by holding the $\overline{CEO}$ output signal to within 0.2 volts of the V_{CCI} or battery supply. If $\overline{CE}$ input is low at the time power fail detection occurs, the $\overline{CEO}$ output is kept in its present state until $\overline{CE}$ is returned high. The delay of write protection until the current memory cycle is completed prevents the corruption of data. Power fail detection occurs in the range of 4.75 volts to 4.5 volts with the tolerance Pin 3 grounded. If Pin 3 is connected to V_{CCO}, then power fail detection occurs in the range of 4.5 volts to 4.25 volts. During nominal supply conditions $\overline{CEO}$ will follow $\overline{CE}$ with a maximum propagation delay of 20ns. The fourth function the DS1210 performs is a battery status warning so that potential data loss is avoided. Each time that the circuit is powered up the battery voltage is checked with a precision comparator. If the battery voltage is less than 2.0 volts, the second memory cycle is inhibited. Battery status can, therefore, be determined by performing a read cycle after power up to any location in memory, verifying that memory location content. A subsequent write cycle can then be executed to the same memory location altering the data. If the next read cycle fails to verify the written data, then the batteries are less than 2.0V and data is in danger of being corrupted. The fifth function of the nonvolatile controller provides for battery redundancy. In many applications, data integrity is paramount. In these applications it is often desirable to use two batteries to insure reliability. The DS1210 controller provides an internal isolation switch which allows the connection of two batteries. During battery backup operation the battery with the highest voltage is selected for use. If one battery should fail, the other will take over the load. The switch to a redundant battery is transparent to circuit operation and the user. A battery status warning will only occur if both batteries are less than 2.0 volts. In applications where battery reliability is not a concern only one battery need be connected to BAT_1 or BAT_2 pin, with the other battery pin grounded.

NOTE: When batteries are first attached to one or both of the V_{BAT} pins, V_{CCO} will not show the battery potential until V_{CCI} is applied and removed for the first time.

Figure 1 shows a typical application incorporating the DS1210 in a microprocessor based system. Section A shows the connections necessary to write protect the RAM when V_{CC} is less than 4.75 volts and to back up the supply with batteries. Section B shows the use of the DS1210 to halt the processor when V_{CC} is less than 4.75 volts and to delay its restart on power up to prevent spurious writes.

FIGURE 1

SECTION A — BATTERY BACKUP

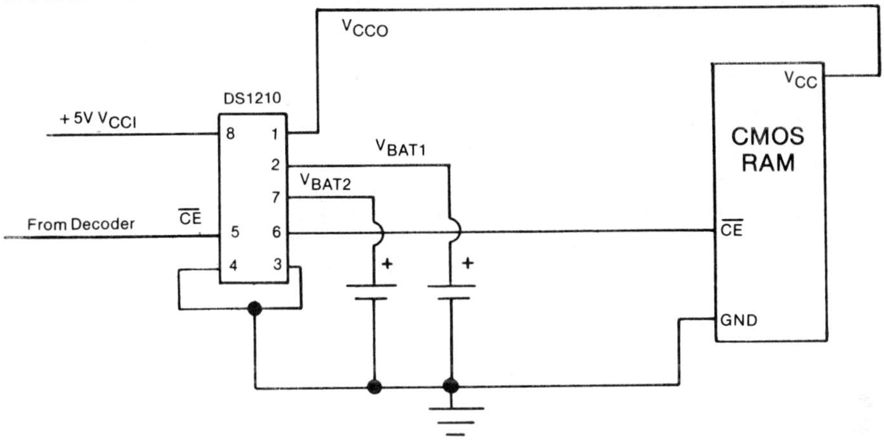

BATTERY BACKUP CURRENT DRAIN EXAMPLE

CONSUMPTION

DS1210 I_{BAT}	- 100 nA
RAM I_{CC02}	- 10 uA
Total Drain	- 10.1uA

SECTION B — PROCESSOR RESET

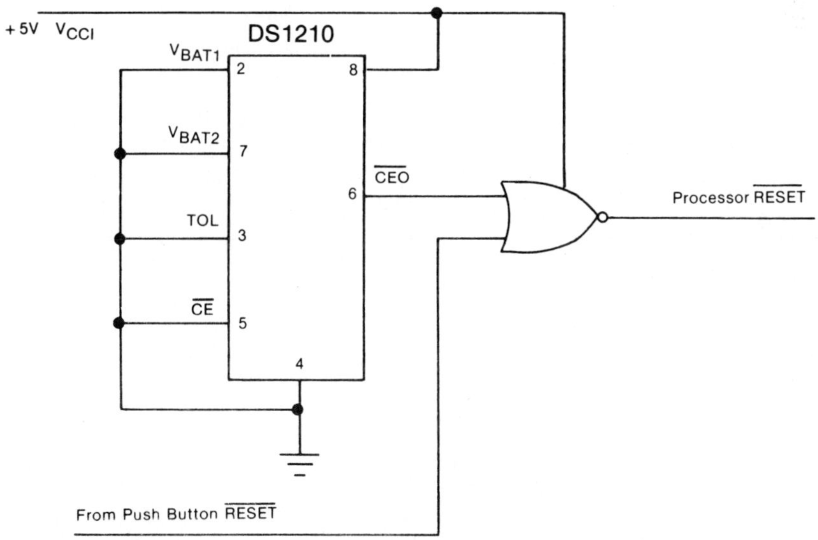

ABSOLUTE MAXIMUM RATINGS*

Voltage on Any Pin Relative to Ground − 0.3V to + 7V
Operating Temperature 0 °C to 70 °C
Storage Temperature − 55°C to 125 °C
Soldering Temperature 260 °C for 10 Sec

*This is a stress rating only and functional operation of the device at these or any other conditions above those indicated in the operation sections of this specification is not implied. Exposure to absolute maximum rating conditions for extended periods of time may affect reliability.

RECOMMENDED D.C. OPERATING CONDITIONS (0 °C to 70 °C)

PARAMETER	SYMBOL	MIN	TYP	MAX	UNITS	NOTES
PIN 3 = GND Supply Voltage	V_{CCI}	4.75	5.0	5.5	V	1
PIN 3 = V_{CCO} Supply Voltage	V_{CCI}	4.5	5.0	5.5	V	1
Logic 1 Input	V_{IH}	2.2		V_{CC} + 0.3	V	1
Logic 0 Input	V_{IL}	− 0.3		+ 0.8	V	1
Battery Input	V_{BAT1} V_{BAT2}	2.0		4.0	V	1,2

D.C. ELECTRICAL CHARACTERISTICS (0 °C to 70 °C, V_{CCI} = 4.75V to 5.5V, PIN 3 = GND) (V_{CCI} = 4.5 to 5.5V, PIN 3 = V_{CCO})

Supply Current	I_{CCI}			5	mA	3
Supply Voltage	V_{CCO}	V_{CC} − 0.2			V	1
Supply Current	I_{CCO1}			80	mA	4
Input Leakage	I_{IL}	− 1.0		+ 1.0	uA	
Output Leakage	I_{LO}	− 1.0		+ 1.0	uA	
$\overline{CE0}$ Output @2.4V	I_{OH}	− 1.0			mA	5
$\overline{CE0}$ Output @ 0.4V	I_{OL}			4.0	mA	5
V_{CC} Trip Point (TOL = GND)	V_{CCTP}	4.50	4.62	4.74	V	1
V_{CC} Trip Point (TOL = V_{CC})	V_{CCTP}	4.25	4.37	4.49	V	1

(0 °C to 70 °C, $V_{CCI} < V_{BAT}$)

$\overline{CE0}$ Output	V_{OHL}	$V_{BAT} - 0.2$		V	
V_{BAT1} or V_{BAT2} Battery Current	I_{BAT}		100	nA	2,3
Battery Backup Curent @$V_{CCO} = V_{BAT} - 0.3V$	I_{CC02}		50	uA	6,7

CAPACITANCE (t_A = 25 °C)

PARAMETER	**SYMBOL**	**MAX**	**UNITS**	**NOTES**
Input Capacitance	C_{IN}	5	pF	
Output Capacitance	C_{OUT}	7	pF	

A.C. ELECTRICAL CHARACTERISTICS

(0 °C - 70 °C, V_{CCI} = 4.75 - 5.5V, PIN 3 = GND)
(V_{CCI} = 4.5 to 5.5V, PIN 3 = V_{CCO})

PARAMETER	**SYMBOL**	**MIN**	**TYP**	**MAX**	**UNITS**	**NOTES**
$\overline{CE}$ Propagation Delay	t_{PD}	5	10	20	ns	5
$\overline{CE}$ High to Power Fail	t_{PF}			0	ns	

(0 °C to 70 °C, $V_{CCI} < 4.75V$, PIN 3 = GND)
($V_{CCI} < 4.5V$, PIN 3 = V_{CCO})

Recovery at Power Up	t_{REC}	2	80	125	ms	
V_{CC} Slew Rate Power Down	t_F	300			us	
V_{CC} Slew Rate Power Down	t_{FB}	10			us	
V_{CC} Slew Rate Power Up	t_R	0			us	
$\overline{CE}$ Pulse Width	t_{CE}			1.5	us	7,8

TIMING DIAGRAM — POWER UP

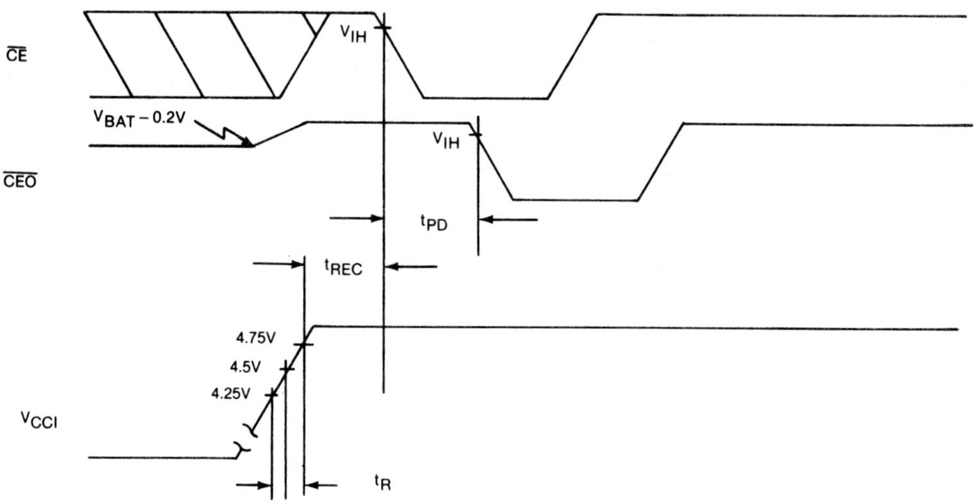

TIMING DIAGRAM — POWER DOWN

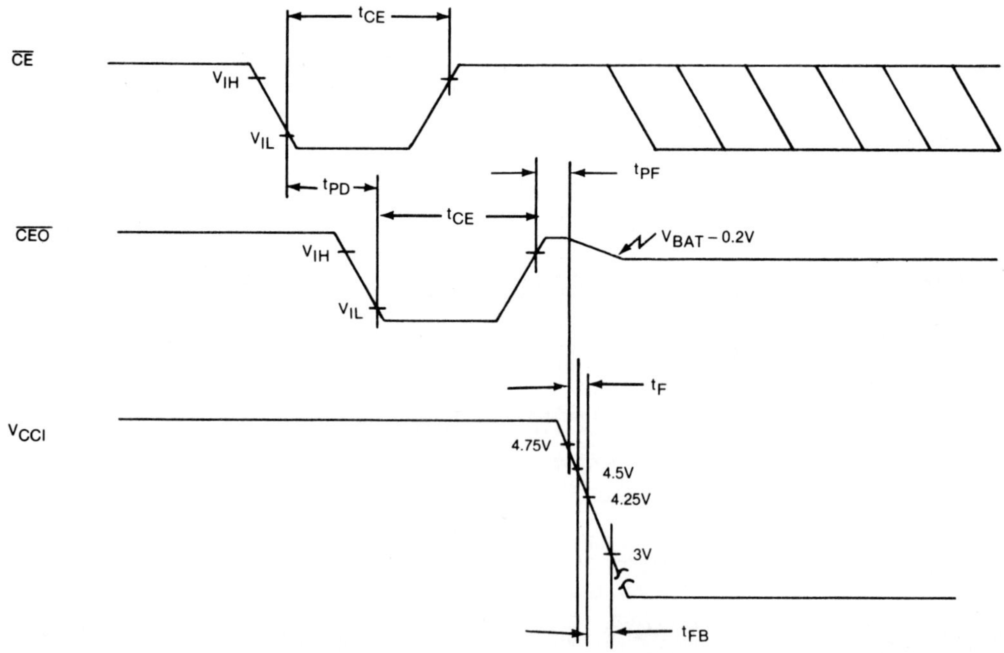

NOTES:

1. All voltages are referenced to ground.
2. Only one battery input is required.
3. Measured with V_{CCO} and $\overline{CE0}$ open.
4. I_{CC01} is the maximum average load which the DS1210 can supply to the memories.
5. Measured with a load as shown in Figure 2.
6. I_{CC02} is the maximum average load current which the DS1210 can supply to the memories in the battery backup mode.
7. t_{CE} max must be met to insure data integrity on power loss.
8. Chip Enable Output $\overline{CEO}$ can only sustain leakage current in the battery backup mode.

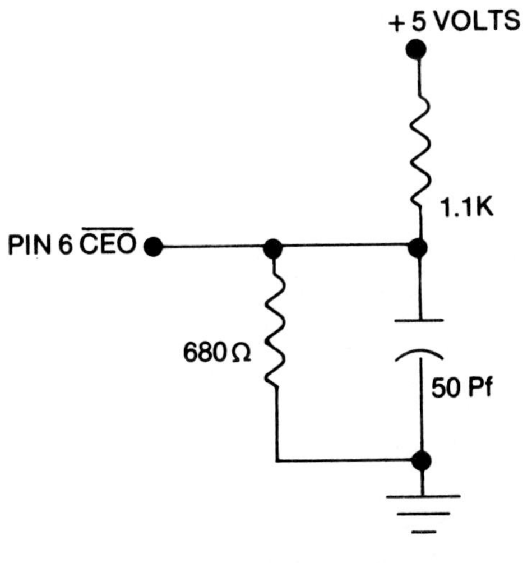

OUTPUT LOAD
Figure 2

Appendix D

PLD File Examples

```
/u/tibet/tmp/dramctl2.pld          Sun May 13 07:00:08 1990          1

Name       DRAMCTL2.PLD;
Partno     XXXX;
Date       5/28/90;
Revision   XX;
Designer   Tibet Mimar;
Company    XXX;
Assembly   XXX;
Location   XXX;

/****************************************************************/
/* Purpose: This device generates DSACK and CAS* signals for the */
/*          DRAM memory. The four CAS* signals, DRAM_CASxx* are  */
/*          generated in order to support the possible operand   */
/*          sizes and its alignment relative to a long-word      */
/*          boundary. The DSACKn* signal is generated for 32-bit */
/*          port size, when the data transfer is completed.      */
/*          The DSACKn* output is in HI-Z state when it is not   */
/*          asserted.                                            */
/****************************************************************/
/* Allowable Target Device Types: 22V10                          */
/****************************************************************/

/** Inputs **/

Pin  1   = INV_CPUCLK   ;     /* Inverted  CPU Clock.             */

Pin  [3..5] = [STATE2..0] ;   /* STATE2:0 inputs from the U2 PLD. */
Pin   6  = !BAS          ;    /* Buffered address strobe AS*.     */
Pin   7  = !LCPU_WRITE   ;    /* Indicates the local 68020 write. */
Pin  [8,9] = [SIZ1..0]   ;    /* 68020 SIZ1:0 signals.            */
Pin [11,13]= [A1,A0]     ;    /* 68020 address signal A1 and A0.  */

/** Outputs **/

Pin 21  = !DRAM_CASUU   ;     /* Upper-upper byte CAS.            */
Pin 20  = !DRAM_CASUM   ;     /* Upper-middle byte CAS.           */
Pin 19  = !DRAM_CASLM   ;     /* Lower-middle byte CAS.           */
Pin 18  = !DRAM_CASLL   ;     /* Lower-lower byte CAS.            */

Pin 16  = DSACK_OE      ;     /* Enables DSACKx* Output Buffers.*/
Pin 15  = !DSACK1       ;     /* DSACK1* return to the 68020.   */
Pin 14  = !DSACK0       ;     /* DSACK0* return to the 68020.   */

/* Declarations */

FIELD STATE = [STATE2..0]    ;

/** Logic Equations **/

DRAM_CASUU = (!A1 & !A0) & (STATE:1 & !INV_CPUCLK #
            !(STATE:[4..7]) & DRAM_CASUU) & BAS #
              STATE:[4..5];

DRAM_CASUM = (!SIZ0 & !A1 #
               !A1 & A0 #
               SIZ1 & !A1 ) & (STATE:1 & !INV_CPUCLK #
            !(STATE:[4..7]) & DRAM_CASUM) & BAS #
              STATE:[4..5];

DRAM_CASLM = (A1 & !A0 #
               !SIZ1 & !SIZ0 & !A1 #
                SIZ1 &  SIZ0 & !A1 #
               !SIZ0 & !A1 & A0 ) & (STATE:1 & !INV_CPUCLK #
            !(STATE:[4..7]) & DRAM_CASLM) & BAS #
              STATE:[4..5];

DRAM_CASLL = (A1 & A0 #
               !SIZ1 & !SIZ0 #
                SIZ1 &  SIZ0 & A0 #
                SIZ1 &  A1 ) & (STATE:1 & !INV_CPUCLK #
            !(STATE:[4..7]) & DRAM_CASLL) & BAS #
              STATE:[4..5];

DSACK_OE = STATE:[1..2] ;

DSACK1 = BAS & STATE:[1..2] ;
DSACK1.OE= DSACK_OE ;

DSACK0 = BAS & STATE:[1..2] ;
DSACK0.OE= DSACK_OE ;
```

/u/tibet/tmp/dramctl1.pld **Tue Jun 12 15:59:08 1990** **2**

```
PRESENT 'd'1
        IF (DECODE_RAM & BAS) NEXT 'd'2
        OUT  COLADDR;

        IF !(DECODE_RAM & BAS) NEXT 'd'0;

PRESENT 'd'2
        NEXT 'd'2 ;

/* REFRESH CYCLES */

PRESENT 'd'4
        NEXT 'd'5
        OUT  REFCYC ;

PRESENT 'd'5
        NEXT 'd'6
        OUT  REFCYC ;

PRESENT 'd'6
        NEXT 'd'7
        OUT  REFCYC ;

PRESENT 'd'7
        NEXT 'd'0;

/* UNUSED STATES */

PRESENT 'd'3
        NEXT 'd'0;

}

/*** Other Logical Equations ***/

A8 = COLADDR & A18 # !COLADDR & A19 ;

RAS = DECODE_RAM & BAS & !(STATE:[4..7]) &
      (STATE:0 & !REFCYC_REQ & !INV_CPUCLK # RAS) #
       STATE:[5..6] ;

WRITE  = RAS & STATE:[1..2] & BAS & LCPU_WRITE ;

BUFEN = DECODE_RAM & BAS & (STATE:0 & !REFCYC_REQ & !INV_CPUCLK # BUFEN) ;

STATE2.ar = !BAS & STATE:2 ;
STATE1.ar = !BAS & STATE:2 ;
STATE0.ar = !BAS & STATE:2 ;
```

/u/tibet/tmp/dramctl1.pld Tue Jun 12 15:59:08 1990 1

```
Name        DRAMCTL1.PLD;
Partno      XXXX;
Date        2/13/90;
Revision    XX;
Designer    Tibet Mimar;
Company     CLI;
Assembly    XXXX;
Location    XXXX;

/******************************************************************/
/* Purpose: This device is the main state machine for the control */
/*          of the DRAM memory module. There is total of 8        */
/*          states, The state assignment is as follows:           */
/*                                                                */
/*              State 0 : Waiting for refresh or 68020 access     */
/*                        request. If both requests are detected  */
/*                        at the same time, then refresh is       */
/*                        given priority.                         */
/*                                                                */
/*                        RAS* is asserted in this cycle, when    */
/*                        CPU clock is high, if an access is      */
/*                        detected.                               */
/*                                                                */
/*              States 1-2: Used for 68020 access cycles.         */
/*              State  3  : Unused.                               */
/*              States 4-7: Used for refresh cycles.              */
/*                                                                */
/*              State 1: Assert COLADDR* and DSACKn*.             */
/*              State 2: BUFEN*.                                  */
/*                       Stay in state 2 and assert CAS*, BUFEN*, */
/*                       and DSACKn* as long as BAS* is asserted. */
/*                                                                */
/*                                                                */
/*              State 4: RAS* = H, CAS* = L, REFCYC* = L.         */
/*              State 5: RAS* = L, CAS* = L, REFCYC* = L.         */
/*              State 6: RAS* = L, CAS* = H, REFCYC* = L.         */
/*              State 7: Precharge Time:                          */
/*                       RAS* = H, CAS* = H, REFCYC* = L          */
/*                                                                */
/*              The state machine is run synchronously with the   */
/*              inverted 68020 clock, and clock-low and clock-high*/
/*              are used to generate some transitions at twice the*/
/*              clock rate.                                       */
/******************************************************************/
/*  Allowable Target Device Types: 22V10                          */
/******************************************************************/

/**  Inputs  **/

Pin   1  = INV_CPUCLK    ;      /* Inverted CPU Clock.           */
Pin   2  = !REFCYC_REQ   ;      /* Refresh cycle request.        */

Pin   4  = !BAS          ;      /* Buffered address strobe.      */
Pin   5  = !DECODE_RAM   ;      /* Indicates address decode of DRAM.*/
Pin   6  = !LCPU_WRITE   ;      /* Indicates a 68020 write.      */

Pin  11  = A19           ;      /* 68020 address A19.            */
Pin  13  = A18           ;      /* 68020 address A18.            */

/**  Outputs  **/

Pin  23  = !REFCYC       ;      /* Indicates refresh cycle.      */
Pin  22  = !BUFEN        ;      /* Enables local data buffers of DRAMs. */
Pin  [21..19] = [STATE2..0] ;   /* State outputs STATE2:0.       */

Pin  17  = !RAS          ;      /* RAS* to All DRAM Devices.     */
Pin  16  = A8            ;      /* Multiplexed DRAM address A8.  */
Pin  15  = !COLADDR      ;      /* Controls muxing of addresses. */
Pin  14  = !WRITE        ;      /* Indicates a write operation.  */

/* Declarations and Intermediate Equations */

FIELD STATE = [STATE2..0]  ;

/**  State Equations  **/

SEQUENCE STATE {

/* 68020 ACCESS */

PRESENT 'd'0
        IF (DECODE_RAM & BAS & !REFCYC_REQ) NEXT 'd'1
        OUT COLADDR;

        IF (REFCYC_REQ) NEXT 'd'4;

        IF !(DECODE_RAM & BAS # REFCYC_REQ) NEXT 'd'0;
```

/u/tibet/tmp/dpram_ct.pld Sat Oct 20 16:35:35 1990 1

```
Name       DPRAM_CT.PLD;
Partno     XXXX;
Date       2/13/90;
Revision   XX;
Designer   Tibet Mimar;
Company    XX;
Assembly   XXXX;
Location   XXXX;

/*****************************************************************/
/* Purpose: This PLD arbitrates and controls accesses to a SRAM.  */
/*          Implemented as a state machine with seven states,     */
/*          where the requests from both sides (A and B) are      */
/*          treated as asynchronous signals. The request signals, */
/*          SEL_A_DPRAM and SEL_B_DPRAM, are synchronized,        */
/*          before they are used for any transitions from state 0.*/
/*                                                                */
/*              States 1-3: Used for A side access cycles.        */
/*              State  4-7: Used for B side access cycles.        */
/*                                                                */
/*          The idle priority is to prioritize A side requests.   */
/*          The busy priority is to handle requests in Round-     */
/*          Robin fashion. This will prevent one side from        */
/*          causing a bus-error to the other side.                */
/*                                                                */
/*          The CS* and x_DTACK* are generated outside the        */
/*          state machine so that we can easily meet the data     */
/*          requirement of the SRAM as well as the t28 and t29a.  */
/*          Otherwise, we would have two clock cycle, worst-case  */
/*          delay in negating the CS* and the x_DTACK*.           */
/*                                                                */
/*****************************************************************/
/*  Allowable Target Device Types: 22V10                          */
/*****************************************************************/

/**  Inputs  **/

Pin   1  = 16MHZ_CLK     ;      /* Independent 16 MHz Clock.      */
Pin   2  = !SEL_A_DPRAM  ;      /* A side access request.         */
Pin   3  = !SEL_B_DPRAM  ;      /* B side access request.         */
Pin   4  = !A_AS         ;      /* A side address strobe.         */
Pin   5  = !B_AS         ;      /* B side address strobe.         */
Pin   6  = !A_WRITE      ;      /* A side R/W* signal.            */
Pin   7  = !B_WRITE      ;      /* B side R/W* signal.            */

/**  Outputs  **/

Pin  23  = !S2           ;      /* B side select and enable signal. */
                                /* Also used as the state bi S2.    */
Pin  22  = !INT_CS       ;      /* Used to delay CS* to SRAM.       */
Pin  21  = !CS           ;      /* SRAM CS* input.                  */
Pin  20  = !SEL_A        ;      /* A side select and enable signal. */
Pin  19  = !A_DTACK      ;      /* A side DTACK* signal.            */
Pin  18  = !B_DTACK      ;      /* B side DTACK* signal.            */
Pin  17  = S1            ;      /* State output S1.                 */
Pin  16  = S0          . ;      /* State output S0.                 */
Pin  15  = !B_REQ        ;      /* Registered B side request.       */
Pin  14  = !A_REQ        ;      /* Registered A side request.       */

/* Declarations and Intermediate Equations */

FIELD STATE = [S2..0]  ;

/**  State Equations  **/

SEQUENCE STATE {

PRESENT 'd'0
        IF (B_REQ & !A_REQ) NEXT 'd'4 ;

        IF (A_REQ) NEXT 'd'1 ;

        IF !(A_REQ # B_REQ) NEXT 'd'0;

/* PROCESSOR B ACCESS */

PRESENT 'd'4
        NEXT 'd'5 ;

PRESENT 'd'5
        NEXT 'd'6 ;

PRESENT 'd'6
        IF (B_REQ ) NEXT 'd'6 ;

        IF (!B_REQ & !A_REQ) NEXT 'd'0 ;

        IF (!B_REQ &  A_REQ) NEXT 'd'1 ;
```

```
/u/tibet/tmp/dpram_ct.pld          Sat Oct 20 16:35:35 1990          2

/* PROCESSOR A ACCESS */

PRESENT 'd'1
        NEXT 'd'2 ;

PRESENT 'd'2
        NEXT 'd'3 ;

PRESENT 'd'3
        IF (A_REQ) NEXT 'd'3 ;

        IF (!A_REQ & !B_REQ) NEXT 'd'0 ;

        IF (!A_REQ &  B_REQ) NEXT 'd'4 ;

/* UNUSED STATES */

PRESENT 'd'7
        NEXT 'd'0 ;
}

/*** Other Logical Equations ***/

INT_CS = (STATE:1 # INT_CS) & A_AS # (STATE:4 # INT_CS) & B_AS ;

A_DTACK = STATE:3 & A_AS ;

A_DTACK.OE = INT_CS & A_AS ;

B_DTACK = STATE:6 & B_AS ;

B_DTACK.OE = INT_CS & B_AS ;

CS = INT_CS ;

A_REQ.D = SEL_A_DPRAM & A_AS ;

B_REQ.D = SEL_B_DPRAM & B_AS ;
```

Appendix E

NEC '424256 Electrical Characteristics Summary 1 Mbyte Dram Device (Courtesy of NEC Electronics, Inc.)

DC Characteristics

$T_A = 0$ to $+70°C$; $V_{CC} = 5.0\ V \pm 10\%$

Parameter	Symbol	Limits Min	Typ	Max	Unit	Test Conditions
Input voltage, high	V_{IH}	2.4		V_{CC} +1.0	V	Referenced to GND
Input voltage, low	V_{IL}	−1.0		0.8	V	Referenced to GND
Standby current	I_{CC2}			2.0	mA	$\overline{RAS} = \overline{CAS} = V_{IH}$
				1.0	mA	$\overline{RAS} = \overline{CAS} = V_{CC} - 0.2$
Input leakage current	$I_{I(L)}$	−10		10	μA	V_{IN} = 0 to 5.5 V; all other pins not under test = 0 V
Output leakage current	$I_{O(L)}$	−10		10	μA	D_{OUT} disabled; V_{OUT} = 0 to 5.5 V
Output voltage, low	V_{OL}			0.4	V	I_{OL} = 4.2 mA
Output voltage, high	V_{OH}	2.4			V	I_{OH} = −5 mA

Capacitance

$T_A = 25°C$; f = 1 MHz

Parameter	Symbol	Max	Unit	Pins Under Test
Input capacitance	C_{I1}	5	pF	Address
	C_{I2}	7	pF	$\overline{RAS}$, $\overline{CAS}$, $\overline{WE}$, $\overline{OE}$
Input/output capacitance	C_D	7	pF	I/O

AC Characteristics

$T_A = 0$ to $+70°C$; $V_{CC} = 5.0\ V \pm 10\%$

Parameter	Symbol	μPD424256-80 Min	μPD424256-80 Max	μPD424256-10 Min	μPD424256-10 Max	μPD424256-12 Min	μPD424256-12 Max	Unit	Test Conditions
Operating current, average	I_{CC1}		70		60		50	mA	$\overline{RAS}$, $\overline{CAS}$ cycling; $t_{RC} = t_{RC}$ min (Note 5)
Operating current, $\overline{RAS}$-only refreshing, average	I_{CC3}		70		60		50	mA	$\overline{RAS}$ cycling; $\overline{CAS} = V_{IH}$; $t_{RC} = t_{RC}$ min (Note 5)
Fast-page operating current, average	I_{CC4}		60		50		40	mA	$\overline{RAS} = V_{IL}$; $\overline{CAS}$ cycling; $t_{PC} = t_{PC}$ min (Note 5)
Operating current, $\overline{CAS}$ before $\overline{RAS}$ refreshing, average	I_{CC5}		70		60		50	mA	$\overline{RAS}$ cycling; $\overline{CAS} = V_{IL}$; $t_{RC} = t_{RC}$ min (Note 5)
Random read or write cycle time	t_{RC}	160		190		220		ns	(Note 6)
Read-write cycle time	t_{RWC}	215		255		295		ns	(Note 6)
Fast-page cycle time	t_{PC}	50		60		70		ns	(Note 6)
Access time from $\overline{RAS}$	t_{RAC}		80		100		120	ns	(Notes 7, 8)
Access time from $\overline{CAS}$ (falling edge)	t_{CAC}		20		25		30	ns	(Notes 7, 9, 10, 11)
Access time from column address	t_{AA}		45		50		60	ns	(Notes 7, 10, 11)
Access time from $\overline{CAS}$ precharge (rising edge)	t_{ACP}		45		55		65	ns	(Notes 7, 11)
Output buffer turnoff delay	t_{OFF}	0	20	0	25	0	30	ns	(Note 12)
Transition time (rise and fall)	t_T	3	50	3	50	3	50	ns	(Note 4)
$\overline{RAS}$ precharge time	t_{RP}	70		80		90		ns	
$\overline{RAS}$ pulse width	t_{RAS}	80	10000	100	10000	120	10000	ns	

AC Characteristics (cont)

T_A = 0 to +70°C; V_{CC} = 5.0 V ±10%

Parameter	Symbol	μPD424256-80 Min	μPD424256-80 Max	μPD424256-10 Min	μPD424256-10 Max	μPD424256-12 Min	μPD424256-12 Max	Unit	Test Conditions
$\overline{RAS}$ pulse width (page mode)	t_{RASP}	80	100000	100	100000	120	100000	ns	
$\overline{RAS}$ hold time	t_{RSH}	20		25		30		ns	
$\overline{CAS}$ pulse width	t_{CAS}	20	10000	25	10000	30	10000	ns	
$\overline{CAS}$ hold time	t_{CSH}	80		100		120		ns	
$\overline{RAS}$ to $\overline{CAS}$ delay time	t_{RCD}	25	60	25	75	25	90	ns	(Note 13)
$\overline{CAS}$ to $\overline{RAS}$ precharge time	t_{CRP}	10		10		10		ns	(Note 14)
$\overline{CAS}$ precharge time, non-page cycle	t_{CPN}	10		10		15		ns	
$\overline{CAS}$ precharge time, page cycle	t_{CP}	10	20	10	25	15	30	ns	(Note 11)
$\overline{RAS}$ precharge $\overline{CAS}$ hold time	t_{RPC}	0		0		0		ns	
Row address setup time	t_{ASR}	0		0		0		ns	
Row address hold time	t_{RAH}	12		12		15		ns	
$\overline{RAS}$ to column address delay time	t_{RAD}	17	35	17	50	20	60	ns	(Note 10)
Column address setup time	t_{ASC}	0	20	0	20	0	25	ns	(Note 11)
Column address hold time	t_{CAH}	20		20		25		ns	
Column address lead time referenced to $\overline{RAS}$ (rising edge)	t_{RAL}	45		50		60		ns	
Read command setup time	t_{RCS}	0		0		0		ns	
Read command hold time referenced to $\overline{RAS}$	t_{RRH}	10		10		10		ns	(Note 15)
Read command hold time referenced to $\overline{CAS}$	t_{RCH}	0		0		0		ns	(Note 15)
Write command hold time	t_{WCH}	15		20		25		ns	
Write command hold time referenced to $\overline{RAS}$	t_{WCR}	55		70		85		ns	
Write command pulse width	t_{WP}	15		20		25		ns	(Note 16)
Write command to $\overline{RAS}$ lead time	t_{RWL}	25		30		35		ns	
Write command to $\overline{CAS}$ lead time	t_{CWL}	20		20		25		ns	
Data-in setup time	t_{DS}	0		0		0		ns	(Note 17)
Data-in hold time	t_{DH}	20		20		25		ns	(Note 17)
Data-in hold time referenced to $\overline{RAS}$	t_{DHR}	60		70		85		ns	
Write command setup time	t_{WCS}	0		0		0		ns	(Note 18)
$\overline{RAS}$ to $\overline{WE}$ delay	t_{RWD}	105		130		155		ns	(Note 18)
$\overline{CAS}$ to $\overline{WE}$ delay	t_{CWD}	45		55		65		ns	(Note 18)
Column address to $\overline{WE}$ delay time	t_{AWD}	70		80		95		ns	(Note 18)

AC Characteristics (cont)

$T_A = 0$ to $+70°C$; $V_{CC} = 5.0\ V \pm 10\%$

Parameter	Symbol	Limits						Unit	Test Conditions
		μPD424256-80		μPD424256-10		μPD424256-12			
		Min	Max	Min	Max	Min	Max		
Column address hold time referenced to $\overline{RAS}$	t_{AR}	60		70		85		ns	
$\overline{CAS}$ setup time for $\overline{CAS}$ before $\overline{RAS}$ refresh	t_{CSR}	10		10		10		ns	
$\overline{CAS}$ hold time for $\overline{CAS}$ before $\overline{RAS}$ refresh	t_{CHR}	15		20		25		ns	
Refresh period	t_{REF}		8		8		8	ms	Addresses A_0-A_8
Access time from $\overline{OE}$	t_{OEA}		20		25		30	ns	
$\overline{OE}$ data delay time	t_{OED}	20		25		30		ns	
$\overline{OE}$ command hold time	t_{OEH}	0		0		0		ns	
Output turnoff delay from $\overline{OE}$	t_{OEZ}	0	20	0	25	0	30	ns	(Note 12)
$\overline{OE}$ to $\overline{RAS}$ inactive setup time	t_{OES}	0		0		0		ns	

Notes:

(1) All voltages are referenced to GND.

(2) An initial pause of 100 μs is required after power-up, followed by any 8 $\overline{RAS}$ cycles before proper device operation is achieved.

(3) Ac measurements assume $t_T = 5$ ns.

(4) V_{IH} (min) and V_{IL} (max) are reference levels for measuring timing of input signals. Transition times are measured between V_{IH} and V_{IL}.

(5) I_{CC1}, I_{CC3}, I_{CC4}, and I_{CC5} depend on output loading and cycle rates. Specified values are obtained with the output open. I_{CC3} is measured by assuming that all column address inputs are held at either a high level or a low level during $\overline{RAS}$-only refresh cycles. I_{CC4} is measured by assuming that all column address inputs are switched only once each fast-page cycle.

(6) The minimum specifications are used only to indicate the cycle time at which proper operation over the full temperature range ($T_A = 0$ to $+70°C$) is assured.

(7) Load = 2 TTL (−1 mA, +4 mA) loads and 100 pF ($V_{OH} = 2.0$ V, $V_{OL} = 0.8$ V).

(8) Assumes that $t_{RCD} \leq t_{RCD}$ (max) and $t_{RAD} \leq t_{RAD}$ (max). If t_{RCD} or t_{RAD} is greater than the maximum recommended value in this table, t_{RAC} increases by the amount that t_{RCD} or t_{RAD} exceeds the value shown.

(9) Assumes that $t_{RCD} \geq t_{RCD}$ (max) and $t_{RAD} \leq t_{RAD}$ (max).

(10) If $t_{RAD} \geq t_{RAD}$ (max), then the access time is defined by t_{AA}.

(11) For fast-page read operation, the definition of access time is as follows.

$\overline{CAS}$ and Column Address Input Conditions	Access Time Definition
$t_{CP} \leq t_{CP}$ (max), $t_{ASC} \geq t_{CP}$	t_{ACP}
$t_{CP} \leq t_{CP}$ (max), $t_{ASC} \leq t_{CP}$	t_{AA}
$t_{CP} \geq t_{CP}$ (max), $t_{ASC} \leq t_{ASC}$ (max)	t_{AA}
$t_{CP} \geq t_{CP}$ (max), $t_{ASC} \geq t_{ASC}$ (max)	t_{CAC}

(12) t_{OFF} (max) and t_{OEZ} (max) define the time at which the outputs achieve the open-circuit condition and are not referenced to V_{OH} or V_{OL}.

(13) Operation within the t_{RCD} (max) limit assures that t_{RAC} (max) can be met. t_{RCD} (max) is specified as a reference point only; if t_{RCD} is greater than t_{RCD} (max), access time is controlled exclusively by t_{CAC}.

(14) The t_{CRP} requirement should be applicable for $\overline{RAS}/\overline{CAS}$ cycles preceded by any cycle.

(15) Either t_{RRH} or t_{RCH} must be satisfied for a read cycle.

(16) Parameter t_{WP} is applicable for a delayed write cycle such as a read-write/read-modify-write cycle. For early write operation, both t_{WCS} and t_{WCH} must be met.

(17) These parameters are referenced to the falling edge of $\overline{CAS}$ for early write cycles and to the falling edge of $\overline{WE}$ for delayed write or read-modify-write cycles.

(18) t_{WCS}, t_{RWD}, t_{CWD}, and t_{AWD} are restrictive operating parameters in read-write/read-modify-write cycles only. If $t_{WCS} \geq t_{WCS}$ (min), the cycle is an early write cycle and the data I/O pins will remain open circuit throughout the entire cycle. If $t_{CWD} \geq t_{CWD}$ (min), $t_{RWD} \geq t_{RWD}$ (min), and $t_{AWD} \geq t_{AWD}$ (min), the cycle is a read-write cycle and the data I/O pins will contain data read from the selected cells. If neither of the above conditions is met, the condition of the data I/O pins (at access time and until $\overline{CAS}$ returns to V_{IH}) is indeterminate.

Appendix F

CY7C199 32K × 8 SRAM (25–55 nsec) Data Sheet Summary (Courtesy of Cypress Semiconductor Corporation)

CY7C198
CY7C199

CYPRESS SEMICONDUCTOR

32,768 x 8 Static R/W RAM

Features

- Automatic power-down when deselected
- CMOS for optimum speed/power
- High speed
  - 25 ns
- Low active power
  - 825 mW
- Low standby power
  - 193 mW
- TTL-compatible inputs and outputs
- Capable of withstanding greater than 2001V electrostatic discharge

Functional Description

The CY7C198 and CY7C199 are high-performance CMOS static RAMs organized as 32,768 words by 8 bits. Easy memory expansion is provided by an active LOW chip enable ($\overline{CE}$) and active LOW output enable ($\overline{OE}$) and three-state drivers. Both devices have an automatic power-down feature, reducing the power consumption by 77% when deselected. The CY7C199 is in the space-saving 300-mil-wide DIP package and leadless chip carrier. The CY7C198 is in the standard 600-mil-wide package.

An active LOW write enable signal ($\overline{WE}$) controls the writing/reading operation of the memory. When $\overline{CE}$ and $\overline{WE}$ inputs are both LOW, data on the eight data input/output pins (I/O_0 through I/O_7) is written into the memory location addressed by the address present on the address pins (A_0 through A_{14}). Reading the device is accomplished by selecting the device and enabling the outputs, $\overline{CE}$ and $\overline{OE}$ active LOW, while $\overline{WE}$ remains inactive or HIGH. Under these conditions, the contents of the location addressed by the information on address pins is present on the eight data input/output pins.

The input/output pins remain in a high-impedance state unless the chip is selected, outputs are enabled, and write enable ($\overline{WE}$) is HIGH. A die coat is used to ensure alpha immunity.

Logic Block Diagram

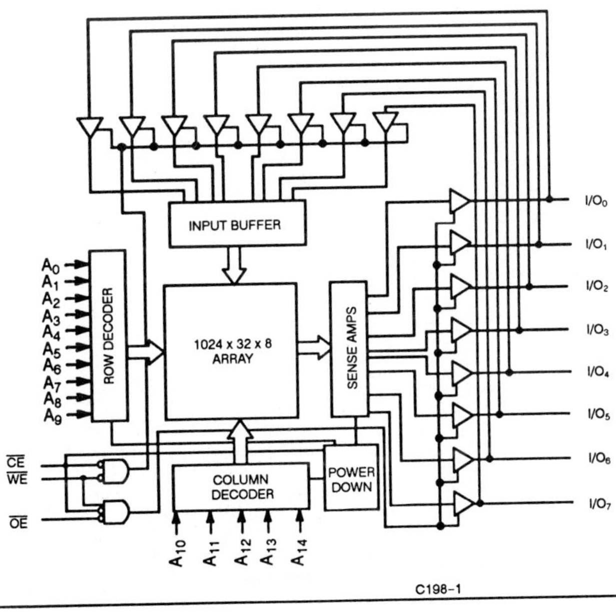

C198–1

Pin Configurations

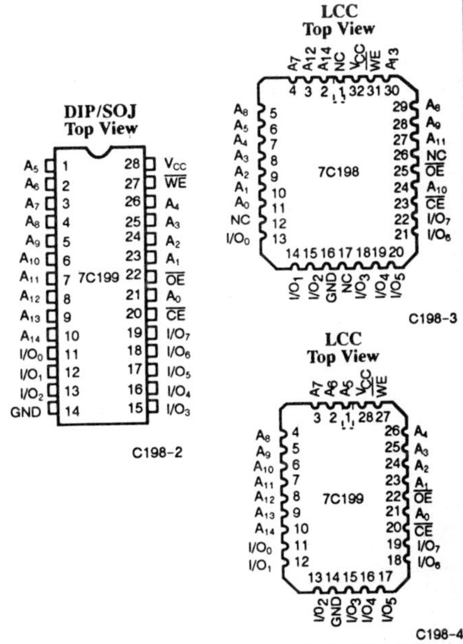

Selection Guide

		7C198-25 7C199-25	7C198-35 7C199-35	7C198-45 7C199-45	7C198-55 7C199-55
Maximum Access Time (ns)		25	35	45	55
Maximum Operating Current (mA)	Commercial	170	150	150	150
	Military		160	160	160
Maximum Standby Current (mA)		35	35	35	35

CYPRESS SEMICONDUCTOR

CY7C198
CY7C199

Maximum Ratings

(Above which the useful life may be impaired. For user guidelines, not tested.)

Storage Temperature .... −65°C to +150°C

Ambient Temperature with Power Applied .... −55°C to +125°C

Supply Voltage to Ground Potential (Pin 28 to Pin 14) .... −0.5V to +7.0V

DC Voltage Applied to Outputs in High Z State .... −0.5V to +7.0V

DC Input Voltage .... −3.0V to +7.0V

Output Current into Outputs (Low) .... 20 mA

Static Discharge Voltage .... >2001V (per MIL-STD-883, Method 3015)

Latch-Up Current .... >200 mA

Operating Range

Range	Ambient Temperature	V_{CC}
Commercial	0°C to +70°C	5V ± 10%
Military[1]	−55°C to +125°C	5V ± 10%

Electrical Characteristics Over the Operating Range[2]

Parameters	Description	Test Conditions		7C198–25 7C199–25 Min.	Max.	7C198–35, 45, 55 7C199–35, 45, 55 Min.	Max.	Units
V_{OH}	Output HIGH Voltage	V_{CC} = Min., I_{OH} = −4.0 mA		2.4		2.4		V
V_{OL}	Output LOW Voltage	V_{CC} = Min., I_{OL} = 8.0 mA			0.4		0.4	V
V_{IH}	Input HIGH Voltage			2.2	V_{CC}	2.2	V_{CC}	V
V_{IL}	Input LOW Voltage			−3.0	0.8	−3.0	0.8	V
I_{IX}	Input Load Current	GND ≤ V_I ≤ V_{CC}		−10	+10	−10	+10	μA
I_{OZ}	Output Leakage Current	GND ≤ V_I ≤ V_{CC}, Output Disabled		−10	+10	−10	+10	μA
I_{OS}	Output Short Circuit Current[3]	V_{CC} = Max., V_{OUT} = GND			−300		−300	mA
I_{CC}	Automatic $\overline{CE}$ Power-Down Current	V_{CC} = Max. I_{OUT} = 0 mA	Com'l		170		150	mA
			Mil				160	
I_{SB1}	Automatic $\overline{CE}$ Power-Down Current	Max. V_{CC}, $\overline{CE}$ ≥ V_{IH}, Min. Duty Cycle = 100%			35		35	mA
I_{SB2}	Automatic $\overline{CE}$ Power-Down Current	Max. V_{CC}, $\overline{CE}$ ≥ V_{CC} − 0.3V, V_{IN} ≥ V_{CC} − 0.3V or V_{IN} ≤ 0.3V			20		20	mA

Capacitance[4]

Parameters	Description	Test Conditions	Max.	Units
C_{IN}	Input Capacitance	T_A = 25°C, f = 1 MHz, V_{CC} = 5.0V	5	pF
C_{OUT}	Output Capacitance		7	pF

Notes:

1. T_A is the "instant on" case temperature.
2. See the last page of this specification for Group A subgroup testing information.
3. Not more than 1 output should be shorted at one time. Duration of the short circuit should not exceed 30 seconds.
4. Tested initially and after any design or process changes that may affect these parameters.

CY7C198
CY7C199

CYPRESS SEMICONDUCTOR

AC Test Loads and Waveforms

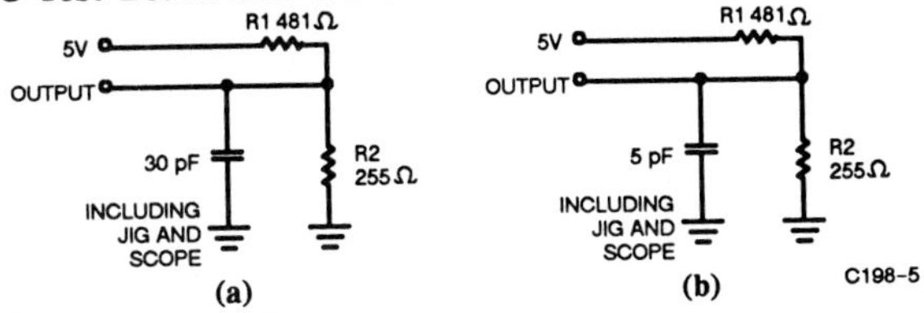

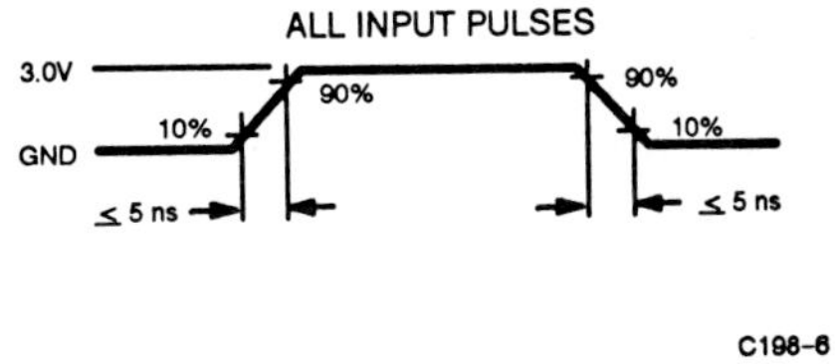

Equivalent to:

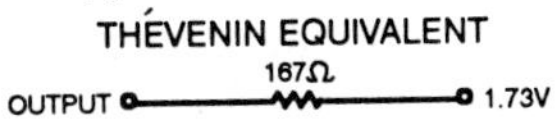

Switching Characteristics Over the Operating Range[2,5]

Parameters	Description	7C198-25 7C199-25		7C198-35 7C199-35		7C198-45 7C199-45		7C198-55 7C199-55		Units
		Min.	Max.	Min.	Max.	Min.	Max.	Min.	Max.	
READ CYCLE										
t_{RC}	Read Cycle Time	25		35		45		55		ns
t_{AA}	Address to Data Valid		25		35		45		55	ns
t_{OHA}	Data Hold from Address Change	3		3		3		3		ns
t_{ACE}	$\overline{CE}$ LOW to Data Valid		25		35		45		55	ns
t_{DOE}	$\overline{OE}$ LOW to Data Valid		15		20		20		20	ns
t_{LZOE}	$\overline{OE}$ LOW to Low Z	3		3		3		3		ns
t_{HZOE}	$\overline{OE}$ HIGH to High Z[6]		13		15		20		25	ns
t_{LZCE}	$\overline{CE}$ LOW to Low Z[7]	3		3		3		3		ns
t_{HZCE}	$\overline{CE}$ HIGH to High Z[6,7]		13		15		20		25	ns
t_{PU}	$\overline{CE}$ LOW to Power-Up	0		0		0		0		ns
t_{PD}	$\overline{CE}$ HIGH to Power-Down		20		20		25		25	ns
WRITE CYCLE[8]										
t_{WC}	Write Cycle Time	25		35		45		50		ns
t_{SCE}	$\overline{CE}$ LOW to Write End	20		30		40		50		ns
t_{AW}	Address Set-Up to Write End	20		30		40		50		ns
t_{HA}	Address Hold from Write End	0		0		0		0		ns
t_{SA}	Address Set-Up to Write Start	0		0		0		0		ns
t_{PWE}	$\overline{WE}$ Pulse Width	20		25		30		40		ns
t_{SD}	Data Set-Up to Write End	15		17		20		25		ns
t_{HD}	Data Hold from Write End	0		0		0		0		ns
t_{HZWE}	$\overline{WE}$ LOW to High Z[6]		13		15		20		25	ns
t_{LZWE}	$\overline{WE}$ HIGH to Low Z	3		3		3		3		ns

Notes:

5. Test conditions assume signal transition time of 5 ns or less, timing reference levels of 1.5V, input pulse levels of 0 to 3.0V, and output loading of the specified I_{OL}/I_{OH} and 30-pF load capacitance.
6. t_{HZOE}, t_{HZCE}, and t_{HZWE} are specified with C_L = 5 pF as in part (b) of AC Test Loads. Transition is measured ± 500 mV from steady state voltage.
7. At any given temperature and voltage condition, t_{HZCE} is less than t_{LZCE} for any given device.
8. The internal write time of the memory is defined by the overlap of $\overline{CE}$ LOW and $\overline{WE}$ LOW. Both signals must be LOW to initiate a write and either signal can terminate a write by going HIGH. The data input set-up and hold timing should be referenced to the rising edge of the signal that terminates the write.

Switching Waveforms

Read Cycle No. 1[9,10]

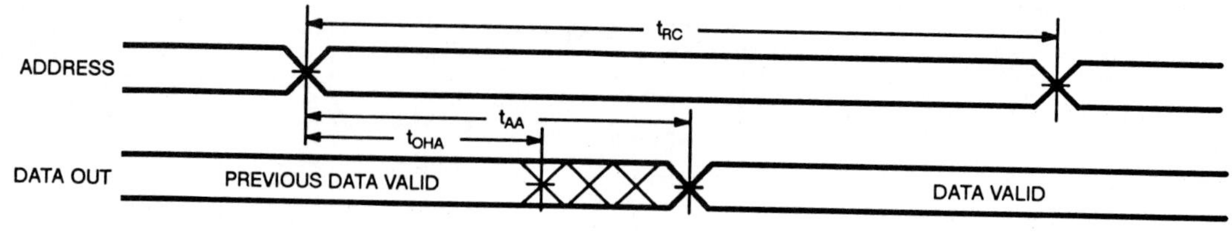

C198-7

Read Cycle No. 2[10, 11]

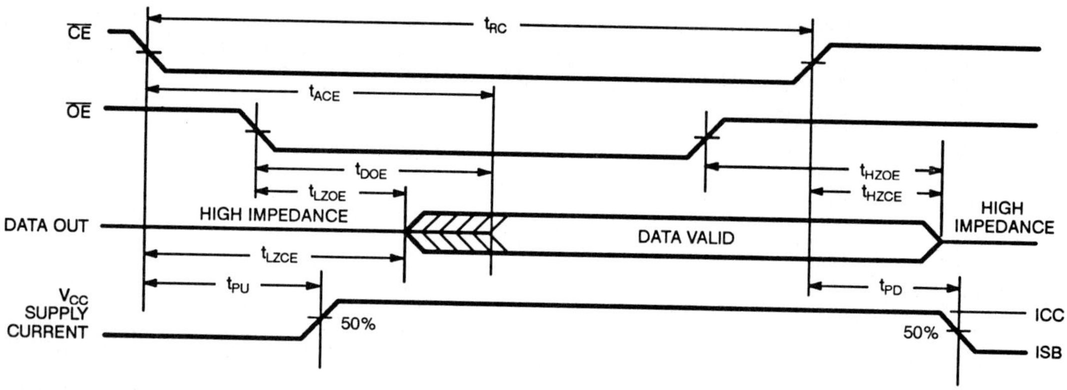

C198-8

Write Cycle No. 1 ($\overline{WE}$ Controlled)[8, 12]

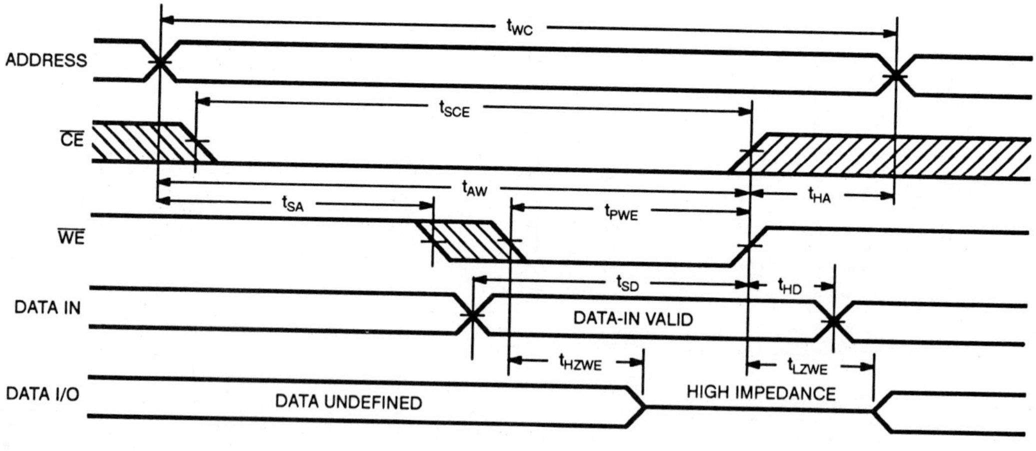

C198-9

Notes:

9. Device is continuously selected. $\overline{OE}$, $\overline{CE}$ = V_{IL}.
10. Address valid prior to or coincident with $\overline{CE}$ transition low.
11. $\overline{WE}$ is HIGH for read cycle.
12. Data I/O is high impedance if $\overline{OE}$ = V_{IH}.
13. If $\overline{CE}$ goes HIGH simultaneously with $\overline{WE}$ HIGH, the output remains in a high-impedance state.

Switching Waveforms (continued)

Write Cycle No. 2 ($\overline{CE}$ Controlled)[8, 12, 13]

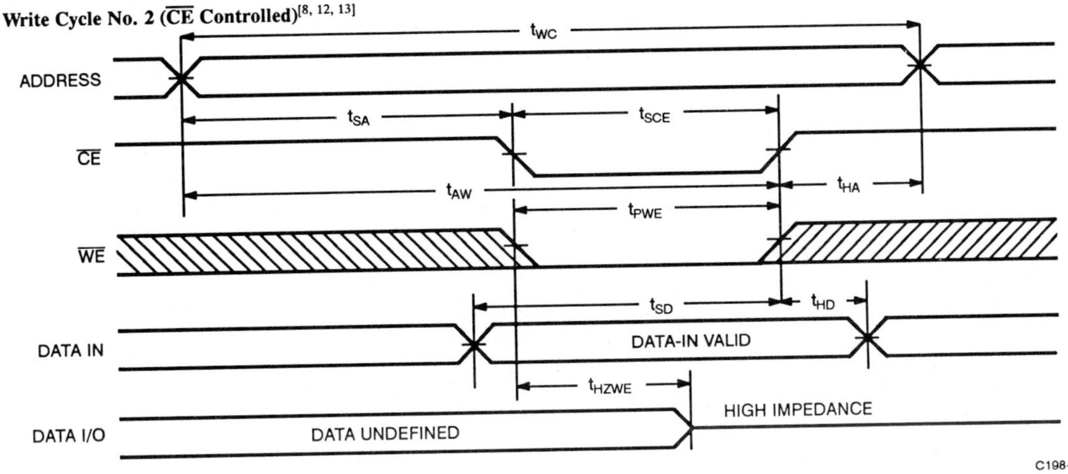

C198–10

Typical DC and AC Characteristics

NORMALIZED SUPPLY CURRENT vs. SUPPLY VOLTAGE

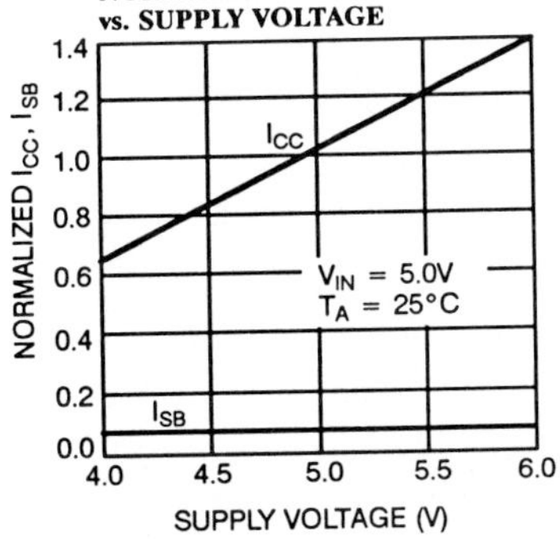

NORMALIZED SUPPLY CURRENT vs. AMBIENT TEMPERATURE

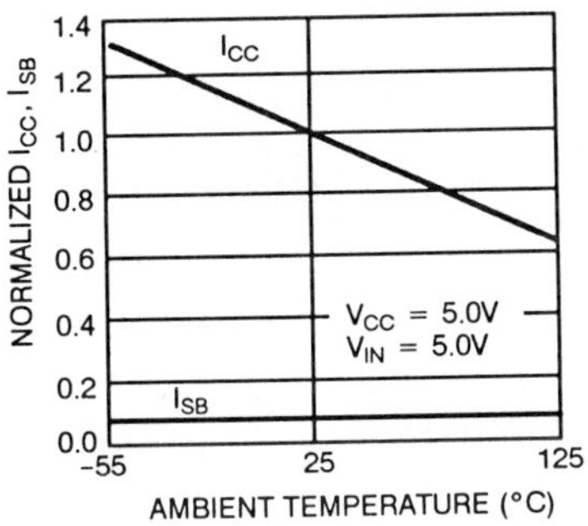

OUTPUT SOURCE CURRENT vs. OUTPUT VOLTAGE

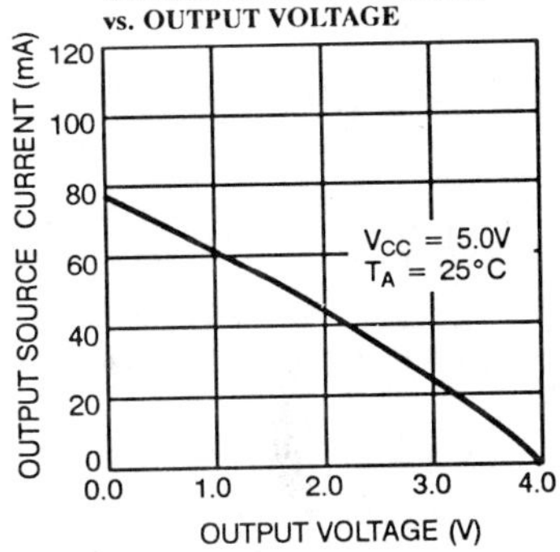

NORMALIZED ACCESS TIME vs. SUPPLY VOLTAGE

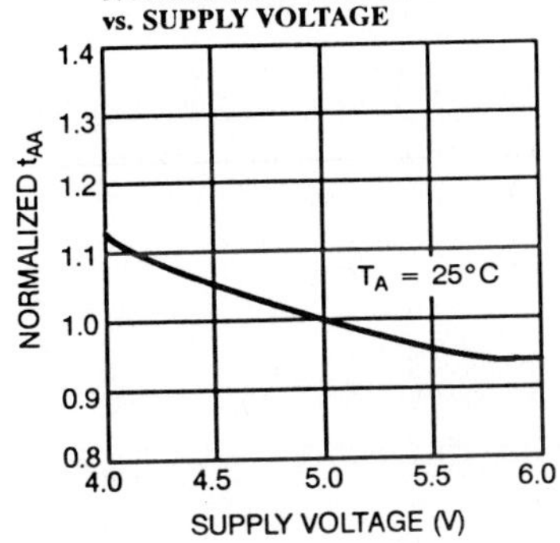

NORMALIZED ACCESS TIME vs. AMBIENT TEMPERATURE

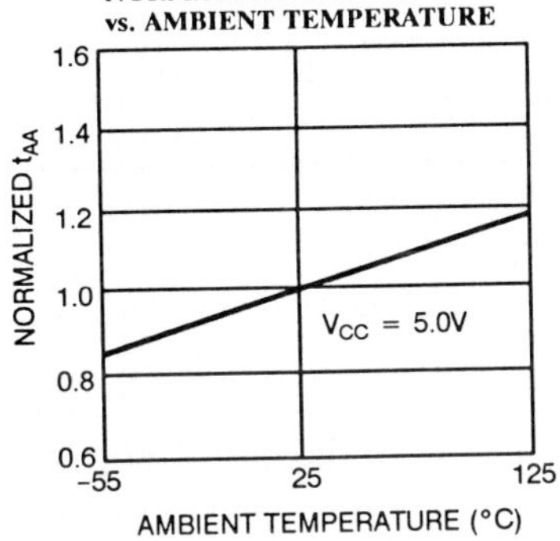

OUTPUT SINK CURRENT vs. OUTPUT VOLTAGE

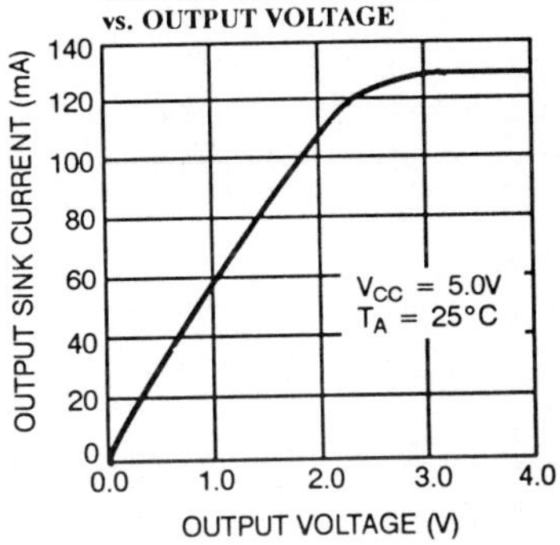

Typical DC and AC Characteristics (continued)

TYPICAL POWER-ON CURRENT vs. SUPPLY VOLTAGE

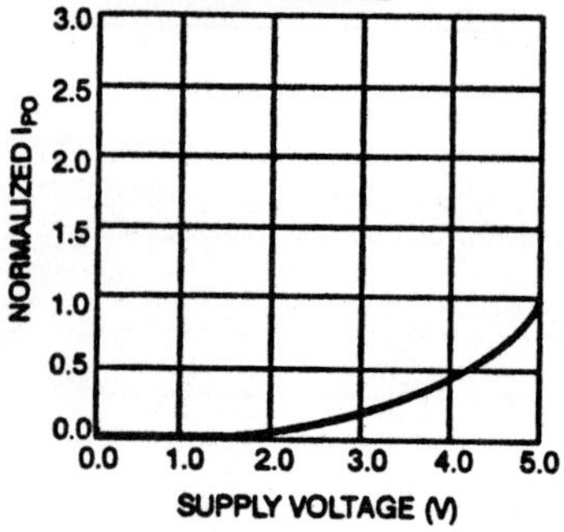

TYPICAL ACCESS TIME CHANGE vs. OUTPUT LOADING

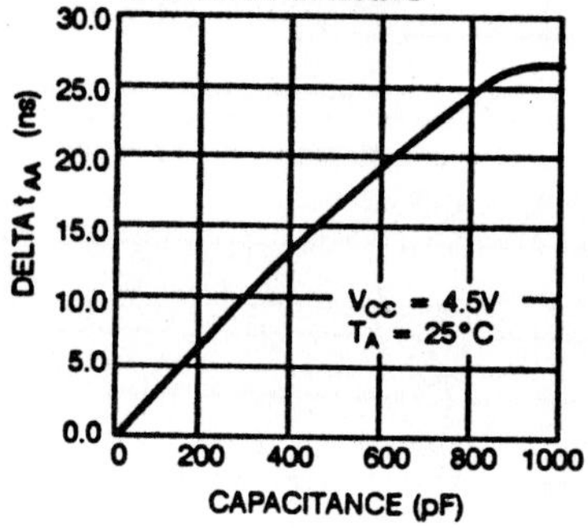

NORMALIZED I_{CC} vs. CYCLE TIME

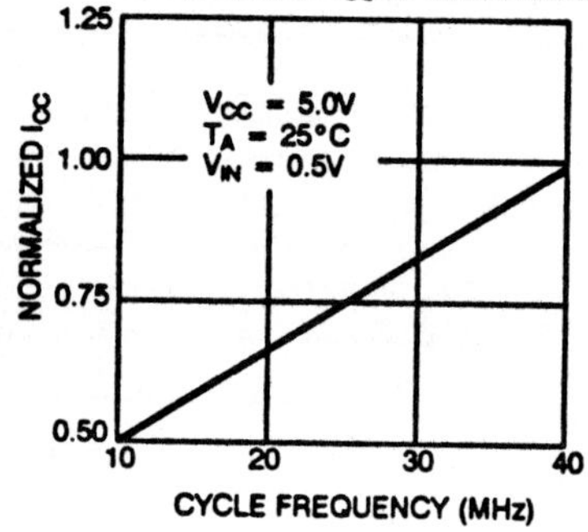

Truth Table

$\overline{CE}$	$\overline{WE}$	$\overline{OE}$	Inputs/Outputs	Mode
H	X	X	High Z	Deselect/Power-Down
L	H	L	Data Out	Read
L	L	X	Data In	Write
L	H	H	High Z	Deselect

Appendix G

22V10 PLD Device Data Sheet Summary (Courtesy of Cypress Semiconductor Corporation)

CYPRESS SEMICONDUCTOR

PAL C 22V10B/PAL C 22V10

Capacitance[3]

Parameters	Description	Test Conditions	Min.	Max.	Units
C_{IN}	Input Capacitance	$V_{IN} = 2.0V$ @ f = 1 MHz		5	pF
C_{OUT}	Output Capacitance	$V_{OUT} = 2.0V$ @ f = 1 MHz		8	pF

Switching Characteristics PAL C 22V10[4, 5]

Parameters	Description	Commercial & Industrial								Military								Units
		B-15		-20		-25		-35		B-20		-25		-30		-40		
		Min.	Max.	Min.	Max.	Min.	Max.	Min.	Max.	Min.	Max.	Min.	Max.	Min.	Max.	Min.	Max.	
t_{PD}	Input to Output Propagation Delay[13]		15		20		25		35		20		25		30		40	ns
t_{EA}	Input to Output Enable Delay		15		20		25		35		20		25		25		40	ns
t_{ER}	Input to Output Disable Delay[8]		15		20		25		35		20		25		25		40	ns
t_{CO}	Clock to Output Delay[14]		10		12		15		25		15		15		20		25	ns
t_S	Input or Feedback Setup Time	10		12		15		30		17		18		20		30		ns
t_H	Input Hold Time	0		0		0		0		0		0		0		0		ns
t_P	External Clock Period ($t_{CO} + t_S$)	20		24		30		55		32		33		40		55		ns
t_{WH}	Clock Width HIGH[3]	6		10		12		17		12		14		16		22		ns
t_{WL}	Clock Width LOW[3]	6		10		12		17		12		14		16		22		ns
f_{MAX1}	External Maximum Frequency ($1/(t_{CO} + t_S)$)[9]	50.0		41.6		33.3		18.1		31.2		30.3		25.0		18.1		MHz
f_{MAX2}	Data Path Maximum Frequency ($1/(t_{WH} + t_{WL})$)[3, 10]	83.3		50.0		41.6		29.4		41.6		35.7		31.2		22.7		MHz
f_{MAX3}	Internal Feedback Maximum Frequency ($1/(t_{CF} + t_S)$)[11]	80.0		45.4		35.7		20.8		33.3		32.2		28.5		20.0		MHz
t_{CF}	Register Clock to Feedback Input [12]		2.5		10		13		18		13		13		15		20	ns
t_{AW}	Asynchronous Reset Width	15		20		25		35		20		25		30		40		ns
t_{AR}	Asynchronous Reset Recovery Time	10		20		25		35		20		25		30		40		ns
t_{AP}	Asynchronous Reset to Registered Output Delay		20		25		25		35		25		25		30		40	ns
t_{SPR}	Synchronous Preset Recovery Time	10		20		25		35		20		25		30		40		ns
t_{PR}	Power Up Reset Time[15]	1.0		1.0		1.0		1.0		1.0		1.0		1.0		1.0		μs

Notes:

7. This parameter is sample tested periodically with the device clocked at f_{MAX} external (f_{MAX1}) with all registers cycling on each cycle and outputs disabled (in high Z state).
8. This parameter is measured as the time after output disable input that the previous output data state remains stable on the output. This delay is measured to the point at which a previous high level has fallen to 0.5 volts below V_{OH} Min. or a previous low level has risen to 0.5 volts above V_{OL} Max. Please see *Figure 4* for enable and disable test waveforms and measurement reference levels.
9. This specification indicates the guaranteed maximum frequency at which a state machine configuration with external feed back can operate.
10. This specification indicates the guaranteed maximum frequency at which an individual output register can be cycled.
11. This specification indicates the guaranteed maximum frequency at which a state machine configuration with internal only feed back can operate. This parameter is tested periodically by sampling production product.
12. This parameter is calculated from the clock period at f_{MAX} internal ($1/f_{MAX3}$) as measured (see note 11 above) minus t_S.
13. This specification is guaranteed for all device outputs changing state in a given access cycle. See *Figure 3* for the minimum guaranteed negative correction which may be subtracted from t_{PD} for cases in which fewer outputs are changing state per access cycle.
14. This specification is guaranteed for all device outputs changing state in a given access cycle. See *Figure 3* for the minimum guaranteed negative correction which may be subtracted from t_{CO} for cases in which fewer outputs are changing state per access cycle.
15. The registers in the PAL C 22V10 have been designed with the capability to reset during system power-up. Following power-up, all registers will be reset to a logic LOW state. The output state will depend on the polarity of the output buffer. This feature is useful in establishing state machine initialization. To insure proper operation, the rise in V_{CC} must be monotonic and the timing constraints depicted in *Figure 5* must be satisfied.
16. The clock signal input must be in a valid LOW state (V_{IN} less than 0.8V) or a valid HIGH state (V_{IN} greater than 2.4V) prior to occurrence of the 10% level on the monotonically rising power supply voltage as shown in *Figure 5*. In addition, the clock input signal must remain stable in that valid state as indicated until the 90% level on the power supply voltage has been reached. The clock signal may transition LOW to HIGH to clock in new data or to execute a synchronous preset after the indicated delay ($t_{PR} + t_S$) has been observed.

AC Test Loads and Waveforms (Commercial)

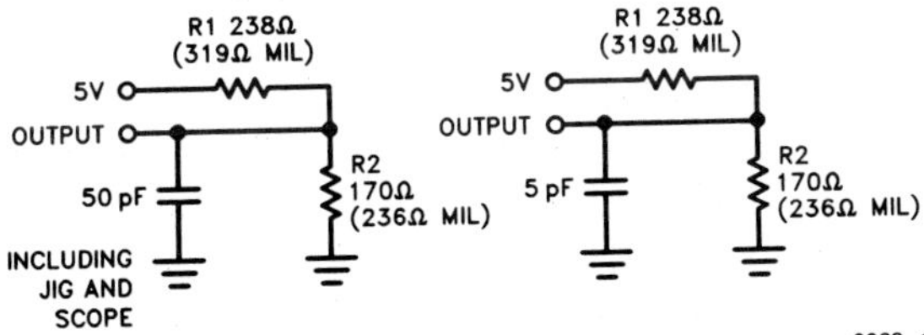

0023-11

Figure 1a **Figure 1b**

INPUT PULSES

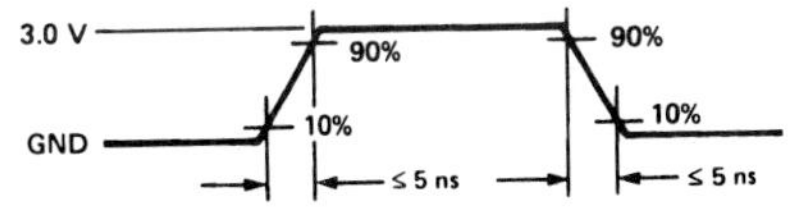

0023-12

Figure 2

Equivalent to: THÉVENIN EQUIVALENT (Commercial)

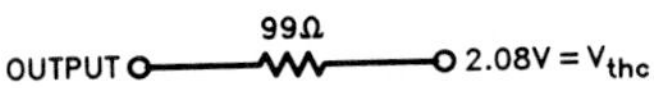

0023-13

Equivalent to: THÉVENIN EQUIVALENT (Military)

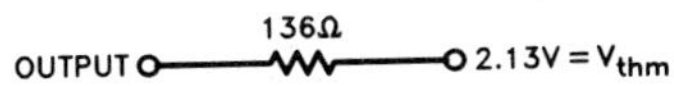

0023-14

Minimum Negative Correction to t_{PD} and t_{CO} vs. Number of Outputs Switching

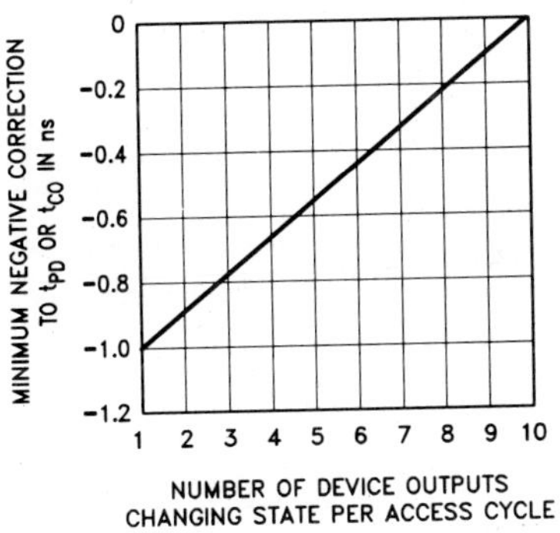

0023-20

Figure 3

Parameter	V_X	Output Waveform—Measurement Level
$t_{ER(-)}$	1.5V	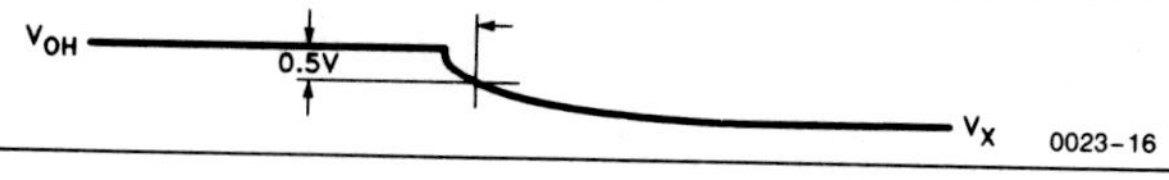
$t_{ER(+)}$	2.6V	
$t_{EA(+)}$	V_{thc}	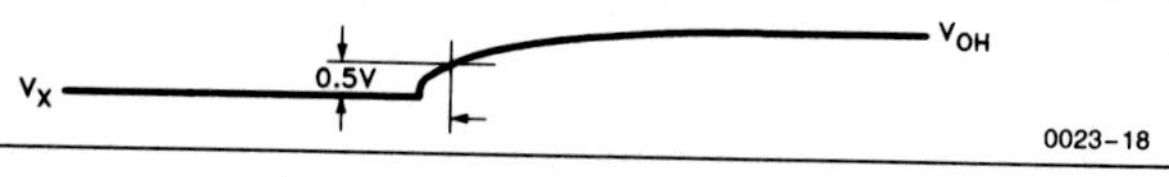
$t_{EA(-)}$	V_{thc}	

Figure 4. Test Waveforms

Switching Waveform

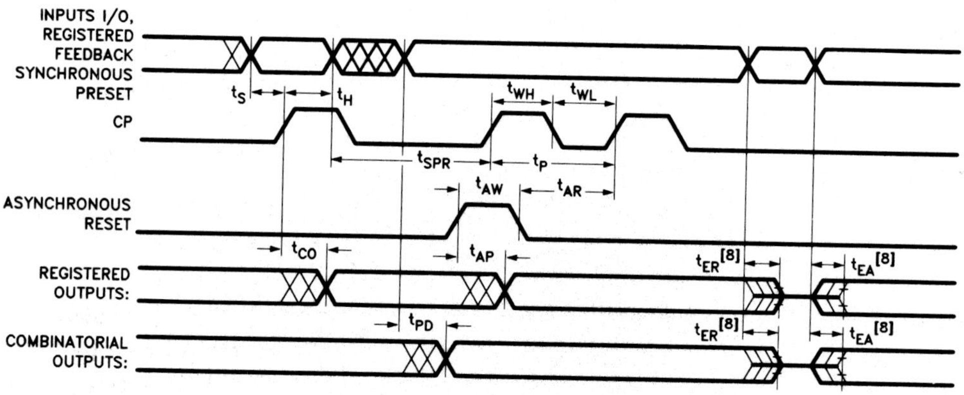

Power-Up Reset Waveform[15, 16]

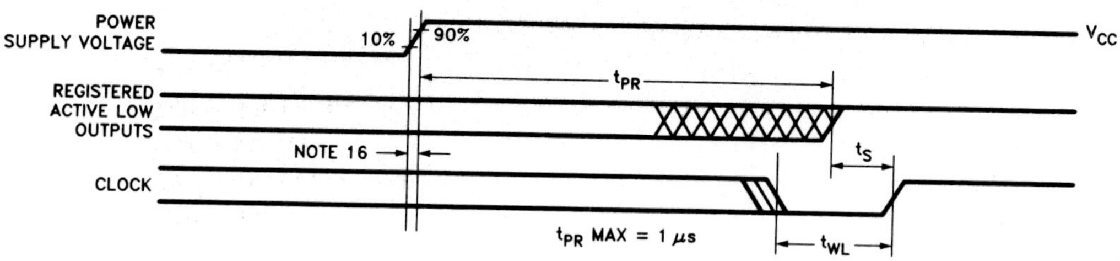

Figure 5

Appendix H

NEC 43256 32K × 8 SRAM Datasheet (85–150 nsec) (Courtesy of NEC Electronics, Inc.)

NEC

NEC Electronics Inc.

µPD43256A 32,768 x 8-BIT STATIC CMOS RAM

Description

The µPD43256A is a 32,768-word by 8-bit static RAM fabricated with advanced silicon-gate technology. Its unique circuitry, using CMOS peripheral circuits and N-channel memory cells with polysilicon resistors, makes the µPD43256A a high-speed device that requires very low power and no clock or refreshing to operate.

Minimum standby power is drawn when $\overline{CS}$ is at a high level, independent of the other inputs' levels. Data retention is guaranteed at a power supply voltage as low as 2 V. The µPD43256A is available in standard 28-pin plastic DIP or 28-pin plastic miniflat packaging.

Features

- ☐ Single +5-volt power supply
- ☐ Fully static operation—no clock or refreshing required
- ☐ TTL-compatible inputs and outputs
- ☐ Common I/O using three-state outputs
- ☐ One $\overline{CS}$ pin and one $\overline{OE}$ pin for easy application
- ☐ Data retention voltage: 2 V minimum
- ☐ Standard 28-pin plastic DIP or miniflat packaging

Ordering Information

Part Number	Access Time (max)	Data Retention Current (max) $T_A = 0$ - $70°C$	Package
µPD43256AC-85L	85 ns	50 µA	28-pin plastic DIP (600 mil)
C-10L	100 ns		
C-12L	120 ns		
C-15L	150 ns		
µPD43256AC-85LL	85 ns	20 µA	28-pin plastic DIP (600 mil)
C-10LL	100 ns		
C-12LL	120 ns		
C-15LL	150 ns		
µPD43256AGU-85L	85 ns	50 µA	28-pin plastic miniflat
GU-10L	100 ns		
GU-12L	120 ns		
GU-15L	150 ns		
µPD43256AGU-85LL	85 ns	20 µA	28-pin plastic miniflat
GU-10LL	100 ns		
GU-12LL	120 ns		
GU-15LL	150 ns		

Pin Configuration

28-Pin Plastic DIP or Miniflat

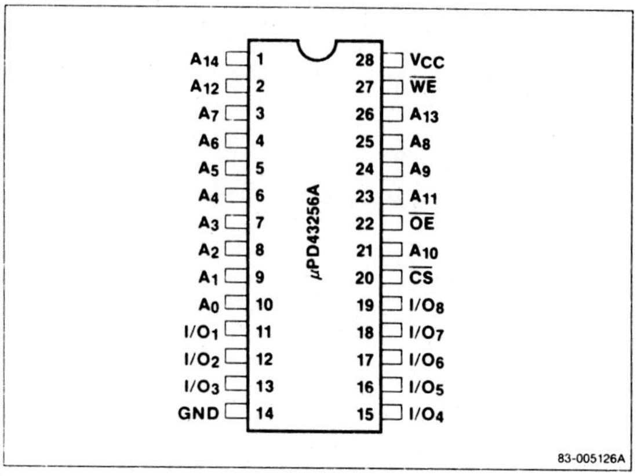

Pin Identification

Symbol	Function
A_0-A_{14}	Address inputs
I/O_1-I/O_8	Data inputs/outputs
$\overline{CS}$	Chip select
$\overline{OE}$	Output enable
$\overline{WE}$	Write enable
GND	Ground
V_{CC}	+5-volt power supply

Truth Table

$\overline{CS}$	$\overline{OE}$	$\overline{WE}$	Mode	I/O	I_{CC}
H	X	X	Not selected	High-Z	Standby
L	H	H	Not selected	High-Z	Active
L	L	H	Read	D_{OUT}	Active
L	X	L	Write	D_{IN}	Active

Notes:

(1) X = don't care.

μPD43256A

NEC

Block Diagram

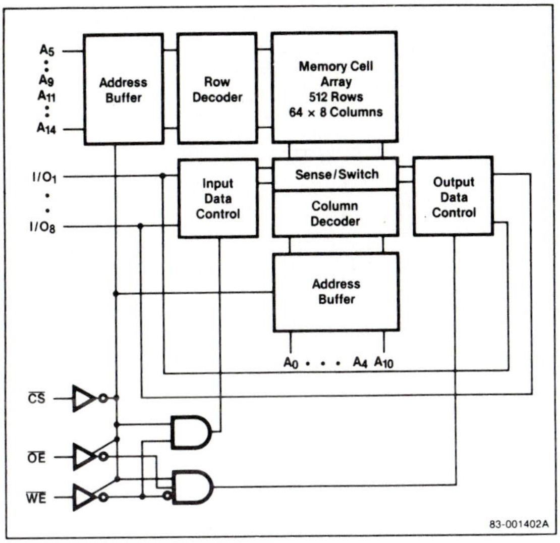

Absolute Maximum Ratings

Supply voltage, V_{CC} (Note 1)	−0.5 to +7.0 V
Input voltage, V_{IN} (Note 1)	−0.5 to V_{CC} + 0.5 V
Output voltage, $V_{I/O}$ (Note 1)	−0.5 to V_{CC} + 0.5 V
Operating temperature, T_{OPR}	0 to 70°C
Storage temperature, T_{STG}	−55 to 125°C
Power dissipation, P_D	1.0 W

Notes:

(1) −3.0 V minimum (pulse width 50 ns)

Comment: Exposure to Absolute Maximum Ratings for extended periods may affect device reliability; exceeding the ratings could cause permanent damage. The device should be operated within the limits specified under DC and AC Characteristics.

Capacitance

T_A = 25°C; f = 1 MHz

Parameter	Symbol	Limits Min	Limits Typ	Limits Max	Unit	Test Conditions
Input capacitance	C_{IN}			5	pF	V_{IN} = 0 V
Input/output capacitance	$C_{I/O}$			8	pF	$V_{I/O}$ = 0 V

Recommended Operating Conditions

Parameter	Symbol	Limits Min	Limits Typ	Limits Max	Unit
Supply voltage	V_{CC}	4.5	5.0	5.5	V
Input voltage, low (Note 1)	V_{IL}	−0.3		0.8	V
Input voltage, high	V_{IH}	2.2		V_{CC} + 0.5	V
Ambient temperature	T_A	0		70	°C

Notes:

(1) −3.0 V minimum (pulse width 50 ns)

DC Characteristics

T_A = 0 to 70°C; V_{CC} = +5.0 V ±10%

Parameter	Symbol	Limits Min	Limits Typ	Limits Max	Unit	Test Conditions
Input leakage current	I_{LI}	−1		1	μA	V_{IN} = 0 to V_{CC}
I/O leakage current	I_{LO}	−1		1	μA	$V_{I/O}$ = 0 to V_{CC}; $\overline{CS} \geq V_{IH}$ or $\overline{OE} \geq V_{IH}$ or $\overline{WE} \leq V_{IL}$
Operating supply current	I_{CCA1}			45	mA	$\overline{CS} \leq V_{IL}$ (min cycle); $I_{I/O}$ = 0 (Note 1)
	I_{CCA2}			10	mA	$\overline{CS} = V_{IL}$; $I_{I/O}$ = 0
	I_{CCA3}			10	mA	$\overline{CS} \leq 0.2$ V; f = 1 MHz; $I_{I/O}$ = 0; $V_{IL} \leq 0.2$ V; $V_{IH} \geq V_{CC} - 0.2$ V
Standby supply current	I_{SB}			3	mA	$\overline{CS} \geq V_{IH}$
	I_{SB1}		0.002	0.1	mA	$\overline{CS} \geq V_{CC} - 0.2$ V
Output voltage, low	V_{OL}			0.4	V	I_{OL} = 2.1 mA
Output voltage, high	V_{OH1}	2.4			V	I_{OH} = −1.0 mA
	V_{OH2}	V_{CC} − 0.5			V	I_{OH} = −0.1 mA

Notes:

(1) μPD43256A-10L/-10LL/-12L/-12LL: 40 mA (max)
μPD43256A-15L/-15LL: 35 mA (max)

NEC

μPD43256A

AC Characteristics

T_A = 0 to 70°C; V_{CC} = +5.0 V ±10%

		Limits									
		μPD43256A-85L/-85LL		μPD43256A-10L/-10LL		μPD43256A-12L/-12LL		μPD43256A-15L/-15LL			
Parameter	**Symbol**	**Min**	**Max**	**Min**	**Max**	**Min**	**Max**	**Min**	**Max**	**Unit**	**Test Conditions**
Read Cycle											
Read cycle time	t_{RC}	85		100		120		150		ns	
Address access time	t_{AA}		85		100		120		150	ns	(Note 2)
Chip select access time	t_{ACS}		85		100		120		150	ns	(Note 2)
Output enable to output valid	t_{OE}		40		50		60		70	ns	(Note 2)
Output hold from address change	t_{OH}	10		10		10		10		ns	
Chip select to output in low-Z	t_{CLZ}	10		10		10		10		ns	(Note 3)
Output enable to output in low-Z	t_{OLZ}	5		5		5		5		ns	(Note 3)
Chip select to output in high-Z	t_{CHZ}		30		35		40		50	ns	(Note 3)
Output enable to output in high-Z	t_{OHZ}		30		35		40		50	ns	(Note 3)
Write Cycle											
Write cycle time	t_{WC}	85		100		120		150		ns	
Chip select to end of write	t_{CW}	70		80		85		100		ns	
Address valid to endof write	t_{AW}	70		80		85		100		ns	
Address setup time	t_{AS}	0		0		0		0		ns	
Write pulse width	t_{WP}	65		70		70		90		ns	
Write recovery time	t_{WR}	5		5		5		5		ns	
Data valid to end of write	t_{DW}	35		40		50		60		ns	
Data hold time	t_{DH}	0		0		0		0		ns	
Write enable to output in high-Z	t_{WHZ}		30		35		40		50	ns	(Note 3)
Output active from end of write	t_{OW}	10		10		10		10		ns	(Note 3)

Notes:

(1) Input pulse levels = 0.8 to 2.2 V; input pulse rise and fall times = 5 ns; timing reference levels = 1.5 V.

(2) See figure 1 for output loading.

(3) See figure 2 for output loading.

Figure 1. Output Load

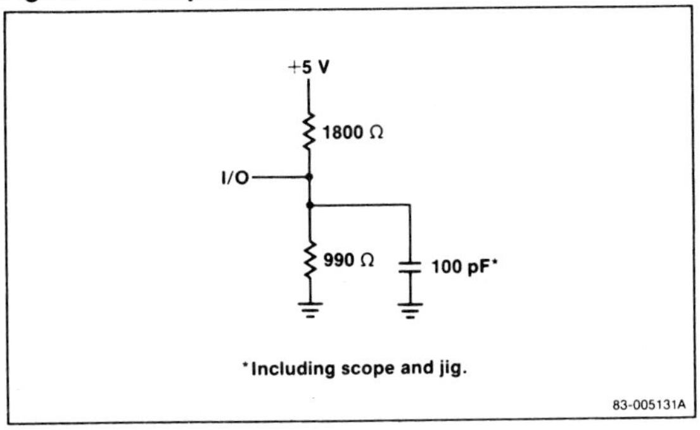

Figure 2. Output Load for t_{CLZ}, t_{OLZ}, t_{CHZ}, t_{OHZ}, t_{WHZ}, and t_{OW}

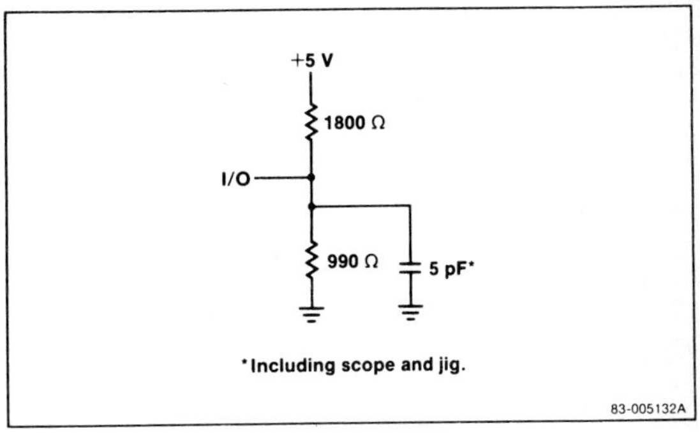

Timing Waveforms

Read Cycle No. 1 (Address Access)

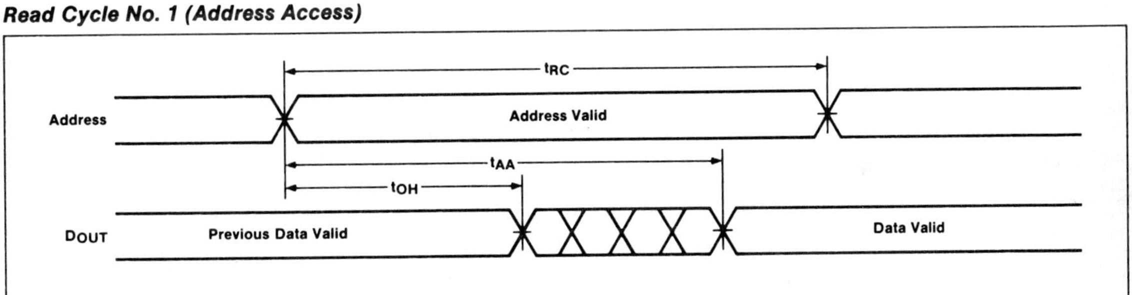

Notes:

[1] $\overline{WE}$ is high for a read cycle.

[2] The device is continuously selected; $\overline{CS} = \overline{OE} = V_{IL}$.

Timing Waveforms (cont)

Read Cycle No. 2 (Chip Select Access)

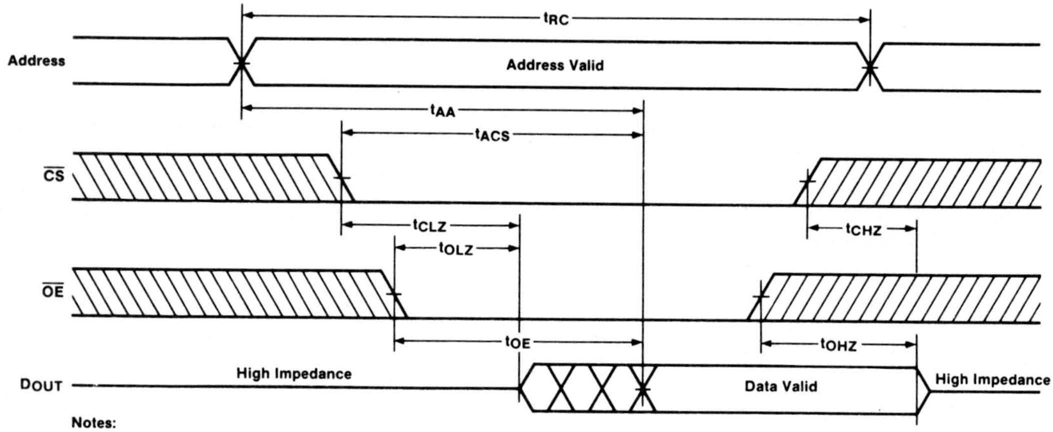

Notes:

[1] $\overline{WE}$ is high for a read cycle.

[2] Address valid prior to or coincident with $\overline{CS}$ transition low.

83-005134B

Write Cycle No. 1 ($\overline{WE}$-Controlled)

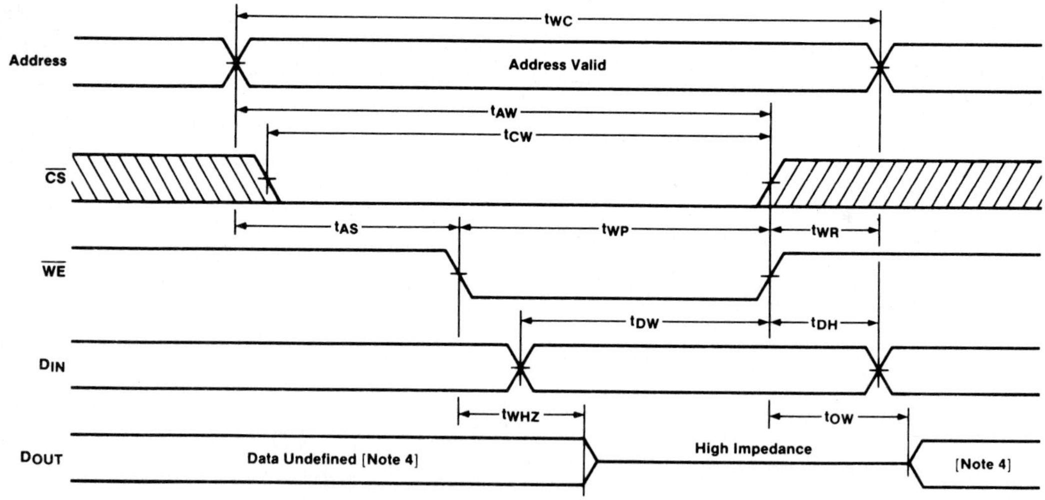

Notes:

[1] A write occurs during the overlap of a low $\overline{CS}$ and a low $\overline{WE}$.

[2] $\overline{CS}$ or $\overline{WE}$ must be high during address transition.

[3] If $\overline{OE}$ is high, the I/O pins remain in a high-impedance state.

[4] During this period, the I/O pins may be in the output state; therefore, input signals of opposite phase to the outputs must not be applied.

83-005135B

Timing Waveforms (cont)

Write Cycle No. 2 ($\overline{CS}$-Controlled)

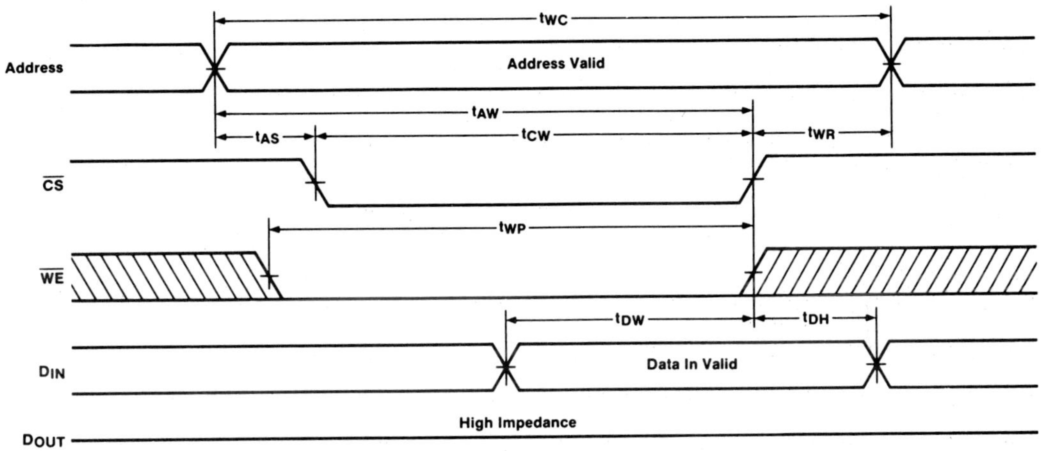

Notes:

[1] A write occurs during the overlap of a low $\overline{CS}$ and a low $\overline{WE}$.

[2] $\overline{CS}$ or $\overline{WE}$ must be high during address transition.

[3] If $\overline{OE}$ is high, the I/O pins remain in a high-impedance state.

83-005136B

Low V_{CC} Data Retention Characteristics

$T_A = 0$ to 70°C

Parameter	Symbol	Limits Min	Limits Typ	Limits Max	Unit	Test Conditions
Data retention supply voltage	V_{CCDR}	2.0		5.5	V	$CS \geq V_{CC} - 0.2$ V
Data retention supply current	I_{CCDR}		1	50	μA	$V_{CC} = 3.0$ V; $CS \geq V_{CC} - 0.2$ V (Notes 1, 2)
Chip deselection to data retention	t_{CDR}	0			ns	
Operation recovery time	t_R	t_{RC}			ns	

Notes:

(1) For μPD43256A-LL, $I_{CCDR} = 20$ μA (max) for $T_A = 0$ to 70°C and 3 μA (max) for $T_A = 0$ to 40°C.

(2) For μPD43256A-L, $I_{CCDR} = 15$ μA (max) for $T_A = 0$ to 40°C.

Data Retention Timing Chart

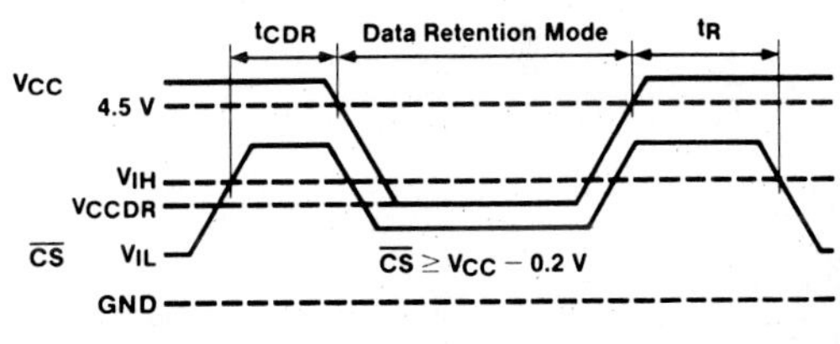

Note:

[1] The other inputs [Addresses, $\overline{OE}$, $\overline{WE}$, I/Os] can be in a high-impedance state.

83-005137A

Index

A

B

C

J

K

L

M

Q

R

S

T

U

V

W

X

Z